Lecture Notes in Business Information Processing 574

Series Editors

LNBIP reports state-of-the-art results in areas related to business information systems and industrial application software development – timely, at a high level, and in both printed and electronic form.

The type of material published includes

- Proceedings (published in time for the respective event)
- Postproceedings (consisting of thoroughly revised and/or extended final papers)
- Other edited monographs (such as, for example, project reports or invited volumes)
- Tutorials (coherently integrated collections of lectures given at advanced courses, seminars, schools, etc.)
- Award-winning or exceptional theses

LNBIP is abstracted/indexed in DBLP, EI and Scopus. LNBIP volumes are also submitted for the inclusion in ISI Proceedings.

Georg Herzwurm · Dimitri Petrik · Gero Strobel ·
Thomas Kude · Lukas Block
Editors

Software Business

16th International Conference, ICSOB 2025
Stuttgart, Germany, November 24–26, 2025
Proceedings

Springer

Editors
Georg Herzwurm
University of Stuttgart
Stuttgart, Germany

Dimitri Petrik
University of Stuttgart
Stuttgart, Germany

Gero Strobel
University of Stuttgart
Stuttgart, Germany

Thomas Kude
University of Bamberg
Bamberg, Germany

Lukas Block
Fraunhofer Institute for Industrial Engineering IAO
Stuttgart, Germany

ISSN 1865-1348 ISSN 1865-1356 (electronic)
Lecture Notes in Business Information Processing
ISBN 978-3-032-14517-8 ISBN 978-3-032-14518-5 (eBook)
https://doi.org/10.1007/978-3-032-14518-5

This Springer imprint is published by the registered company Springer Nature Switzerland AG
The registered company address is: Gewerbestrasse 11, 6330 Cham, Switzerland

Preface

It is our great pleasure to introduce the proceedings of the 16th International Conference on Software Business (ICSOB 2025). This volume presents a diverse and stimulating collection of works that reflect the state-of-the-art in software business research and practice. The ICSOB community continues to expand and evolve, bringing together scholars, practitioners, and students who share a deep interest in understanding how software drives innovation, value creation, and societal transformation in digital economies.

This year's conference was hosted by the University of Stuttgart, located in the heart of one of Europe's leading industrial and innovation regions. Stuttgart provided an ideal environment for ICSOB 2025, bridging academic excellence, industrial collaboration, and a rich tradition of engineering and technological advancement. Participants enjoyed an inspiring atmosphere fostering both intellectual exchange and interdisciplinary dialogue in the historic building of the "House of Commerce" in the center of the city of Stuttgart.

The theme of ICSOB 2025, "Software Business in Digital Societies," emphasizes the pivotal role of software in shaping economic and societal well-being. As software increasingly permeates all aspects of modern life, software businesses—both established enterprises and new ventures—face opportunities and responsibilities in driving digital progress. The conference invited contributions addressing topics such as digital ubiquity, AI-driven innovation, ethical and responsible digital transformation, as well as sustainable and human-centered software design.

ICSOB 2025 received 65 submissions from authors representing ten countries, highlighting the international reach and diversity of the community. In total, the contributions came from Egypt, Belgium, Brazil, Canada, Denmark, Germany, Finland, Italy, Netherlands, Sweden, with a few co-authors also coming from other countries. Furthermore, we are proud to have received multiple papers from industry, highlighting the practical relevance of ICSOB and the associated research endeavors. This widespread participation reflects ICSOB's strong tradition of inclusivity and collaboration across borders.

All submitted papers underwent a rigorous double-blind peer review process, with at least three reviewers contributing to the final acceptance decision. Overall, 29 submissions from the following contries were accepted: Finland (12), Germany (8), the Netherlands (3), Denmark (2), Sweden (2), Italy (1), and Brazil (1). The submissions include 18 full and 11 short papers. The conference program encompassed a wide range of topics pertinent to the evolving role of software in digital societies. Discussions addressed the growing ubiquity of software and the emergence of socially responsible business models that foster inclusion, equity, and sustainability. Contributions explored how digital platforms and ecosystems can support underserved communities, and how ethical considerations can guide software business in platform economies. Other papers examined how incumbent organizations are transforming into software-driven enterprises, focusing on the use of AI and data governance in the manufacturing, automotive, and service sectors, as well as on how standards and digital ecosystems can enable small- and medium-sized enterprises to participate in this transformation.

Innovation and deep technology also played a central role in this year's program. Several contributions investigated a wide range of technologies as enablers of new forms of software business, while others examined how emerging technologies such as generative AI and blockchain can support ethical and responsible digital transformation. Moreover, the role of software in critical infrastructures such as education, defense, and transportation was a recurring theme, drawing attention to the intersection between technological progress, geopolitical dynamics, and societal resilience.

Ethics, security, and digital rights were equally prominent, with research addressing algorithmic accountability, AI transparency and fairness, privacy-preserving technologies, and digital sovereignty. Human-centered perspectives emphasized trust, transparency, and user empowerment through responsible software design, as well as the evolving practices of post-agile software development in dynamic environments. Further contributions explored the rise of citizen development through AI and AI-platforms, reflecting on the ethical implications of democratizing software creation and on initiatives that promote accessibility and digital literacy. Finally, sustainability and responsibility emerged as cross-cutting concerns, spanning from green software engineering and energy-efficient algorithms to fairness-aware machine learning and regulatory compliance in AI-driven services.

ICSOB 2025 continued the tradition of rigorous peer review and academic excellence. Each submission was evaluated by domain experts and reviewed by a program chair if the evaluations differed, ensuring that the accepted papers reflect the highest standards of research quality and relevance. The proceedings include both full and short papers, offering theoretical insights, empirical studies, and practical experiences that advance the understanding of software business in digital societies.

As the software business domain continues to evolve rapidly, ICSOB remains a unique venue where academia and industry meet to discuss the challenges and opportunities ahead. This year's program also featured two inspiring keynote presentations that exemplified the interdisciplinary and practice-oriented spirit of ICSOB. Daniel Trabucchi from Politecnico di Milano delivered an engaging talk titled "Future-Proof Your Business: Embracing Platform Thinking for Sustainable Growth," in which he explored how platform-based strategies can drive sustainable innovation and organizational resilience in a rapidly changing digital landscape. Rose Sturm from Mercedes-Benz offered an industry perspective in her keynote on Software-Defined Vehicles, highlighting the transformation of the automotive industry through software, data, and connectivity, and discussing the implications for business models, value creation, and innovation ecosystems.

In addition, ICSOB 2025 hosted the PhD Retreat, which received three applications from doctoral researchers working on topics closely aligned with the conference theme. The retreat provided a unique setting for emerging scholars to discuss their research ideas, receive mentorship from senior academics, and engage with the broader ICSOB community. We are confident that the contributions in this volume, together with the keynotes and the PhD Retreat, will inspire further research and collaboration, and we hope that the discussions initiated at ICSOB 2025 will continue to shape the discourse on the role of software in our increasingly digital world.

The evening program complemented the academic prgram with inspiring excursions to IBM Quantum Computing, ARENA2036, and the Computermuseum at the Department of Computer Science of the University of Stuttgart, offering participants a unique blend of innovation and heritage.

We thank all authors, reviewers, and participants for their dedication an d contributions, as well as the local organizing committee at the University of Stuttgart for their outstanding work in hosting this year's conference. We look forward to meeting the community again at ICSOB 2026, building on the strong foundations and vibrant discussions of this year's event.

November 2025

Gero Strobel
Thomas Kude
Lukas Block
Georg Herzwurm
Dimitri Petrik

Organization

General Chairs

Georg Herzwurm	University of Stuttgart, Germany
Dimitri Petrik	University of Stuttgart, Germany

Program Chairs

Gero Strobel	University of Stuttgart, Germany
Thomas Kude	University of Bamberg, Germany
Lukas Block	Fraunhofer IAO, Germany

Proceedings Chair

Andrey Saltan	LUT University, Finland

PhD Retreat Chairs

Helena Holmström Olsson	Malmö University, Sweden
Jan Bosch	Chalmers University of Technology, Sweden
Edona Elshan	Vrije Universiteit Amsterdam, The Netherlands
Rodrigo Pereira dos Santos	UNIRIO, Brazil

Poster Chairs

Nirnaya Tripathi	University of Oulu, Finland
Usman Rafiq	Free University of Bozen-Bolzano, Italy

Companion Proceedings Chair

Damian Kedziora	LUT University, Finland

Communication Chair

Nadine Bisswang	University of Stuttgart, Germany

Sponsorship Chair

Andreas Helferich	International School of Management, Germany

Website Chair

Kim Stuber	University of Stuttgart, Germany

Program Committee

Pekka Abrahamsson	Tampere University, Finland
Matthew Ajimati	National University of Ireland, Galway, Ireland
Abdullah Aldaeej	Imam Abdulrahman Bin Faisal University, Saudi Arabia
Jesper Andersson	Linnaeus University, Sweden
Pablo Oliveira Antonino	Fraunhofer IESE, Germany
Kousar Aslam	Vrije University, Amsterdam, Netherlands
Alexander Bakhtin	University of Oulu, Finland
Nadine Bisswang	University of Stuttgart, Germany
Lukas Block	Fraunhofer Institute for Industrial Engineering IAO, Germany
Yevgen Bogodistov	Management Center Innsbruck, Austria
Regina Braga	UFJF, Brazil
Marc Brechtel	University of Potsdam, Germany
David Callele	University of Saskatchewan, Canada
Stanislav Chren	Aalto University, Finland
Maya Daneva	University of Twente, Netherlands
José Maria David	Federal University of Juiz de Fora, Brazil
Andreas Drechsler	Victoria University of Wellington, New Zealand
Anh Nguyen Duc	University of South-Eastern Norway, Norway
Henry Edison	Blekinge Institute of Technology, Sweden
Fabian Fagerholm	Aalto University, Finland
João M. Fernandes	Universidade do Minho, Portugal
Awdren Fontao	Federal University of Mato Grosso do Sul, Brazil
Heerko Groefsema	University of Groningen, Netherlands

Eduardo Guerra	Free University of Bolzen-Bolzano, Italy
Jurriaan Hage	Heriot-Watt University, UK
Florian Härer	Klingele Paper & Packaging, Germany
Sajid Ibrahim Hashmi	University of Oulu, Finland
Andreas Helferich	International School of Management (ISM), Germany
Georg Herzwurm	University of Stuttgart, Germany
Katharina Hölzle	Fraunhofer IAO, Germany
Sami Hyrynsalmi	LUT University, Finland
Sonja Hyrynsalmi	LUT University, Finland
Slinger Jansen	Utrecht University, Netherlands
Mohamad Kassab	Boston University, USA
Kai-Kristian Kemell	University of Helsinki, Finland
Hans-Bernd Kittlaus	Innotivium, Germany
Eriks Klotins	Blekinge Institute of Technology, Sweden
Jens Knodel	Caruso, Germany
Antti Knutas	LUT University, Finland
Thomas Kude	University of Bamberg, Germany
Katsiaryna Labunets	Utrecht University, Netherlands
Jens Lachenmaier	Ferdinand Steinbeis Institute, Germany
Casper Lassenius	Aalto University, Finland
Ulrike Lechner	University of the Bundeswehr, München, Germany
Hongxiu Li	Tampere University, Finland
Johan Linaker	RISE Research Institutes of Sweden, Sweden
Francesca Lonetti	CNR-ISTI, Italy
Andrey Maglyas	LUT University, Finland
Niko Mäkitalo	University of Jyväskylä, Finland
Gerardo Matturro	Universidad ORT Uruguay, Uruguay
Jorge Melegati	Free University of Bolzen-Bolzano, Italy
Tommi Mikkonen	University of Jyväskylä, Finland
Michael Möhring	University of Reutlingen, Germany
Frederik Möller	TU Braunschweig, Germany
Juergen Muench	Reutlingen University, Germany
Matti Muhos	University of Oulu, Finland
Valdemar Vicente Graciano Neto	Universidade Federal de Goiás (UFG), Brazil
Helena Holmström Olsson	Malmö University, Sweden
Ana-Maria Oprescu	University of Amsterdam, Netherlands
Michiel Overeem	AFAS Software, Netherlands
Efi Papatheocharous	RISE, Sweden
Dimitri Petrik	University of Stuttgart, Germany
Wolfram Pietsch	Aachen University of Applied Sciences, Germany

Luís Ferreira Pires	University of Twente, Netherlands
Dimitris Polychronopoulos	University of South-Eastern Norway, Norway
Jari Porras	LUT University, Finland
Narayan Ramasubbu	University of Pittsburgh, USA
Andrey Saltan	LUT University, Finland
Luiz Olavo Bonino Da Silva Santos	University of Twente, Netherlands
Dipti K. Sarmah	University of Twente, Netherlands
Thorsten Schoormann	Roskilde University, Denmark
Marko Seppänen	Tampere University, Finland
Dominik Siemon	LUT University, Finland
Simone Vasconcelos Silva	IFFluminense, Brazil
Kari Smolander	Lappeenranta University of Technology, Finland
Rini van Solingen	Delft University of Technology, Netherlands
Viktoria Stray	University of Oslo, Norway
Gero Strobel	University Stuttgart, Germany
Kim Stuber	Universität Stuttgart, Germany
Richard Berntsson Svensson	University of Gothenburg, Sweden
Kari Systä	Tampere University of Technology, Finland
Pasi Tyrväinen	University of Jyväskylä, Finland
Ville Vakkuri	University of Vaasa, Finland
George Valença	Universidade Federal Rural de Pernambuco (UFRPE), Brazil
Erno Vanhala	LUT University, Finland
Davi Viana	Federal University of Maranhão, Brazil
Joost Visser	Leiden University, Netherlands
Xiaofeng Wang	Free University of Bolzano, Italy
Maximilian Werling	Ferdinand Steinbeis Institute, Germany
Krzystof Wnuk	Blekinge Technikska, Sweden
Ehsan Zabardast	Blekinge Institute of Technology, Sweden
Luciana Zaina	Federal University of São Carlos, Brazil

External Reviewers

Stephan Altmann	Mannheim University of Applied Sciences, Germany
Woubshet Behutiye	University of Oulu, Finland
Zeeshan Hameed	Free University of Bozen-Bolzano, Italy
Frédéric Pattyn	Ghent University, Belgium
Diaeddin Rimawi	Free University of Bozen-Bolzano, Italy
David Rochholz	Universität Bamberg, Germany

Zlatko Stapic	University of Zagreb, Croatia
Paul Wan	Aalborg University, Denmark
Oliver Werth	OFFIS (Institute for Information Technology), Germany
Rodrigo Oliveira Zacarias	UNIRIO, Brazil
Zheying Zhang	Tampere University, Finland

Contents

Human-Centered and Socially Responsible Software Business

Keynote

Future Proof Your Business: Embracing Platform Thinking for Sustainable Growth

Daniel Trabucchi(✉) and Tommaso Buganza

School of Management, Politecnico Di Milano, Milano, Italy
{daniel.trabucchi,tommaso.buganza}@polimi.it

Abstract. Platforms have become a dominant model for value creation, enabling interactions among multiple customer sides and generating indirect cross-side network externalities. While examples such as Airbnb and Uber illustrate their disruptive potential, recent research demonstrates that legacy firms can also leverage platform mechanisms for sustainable growth by activating existing assets, relationships, and data. Building on prior work, we distinguish three archetypes—transactional, innovation, and orthogonal platforms—and show how Platform Thinking can address five recurrent business problems in established organizations, including missing transactions and innovation bottlenecks. The Digital Phoenix Effect describes how incumbents ignite dormant potential rather than disrupt their core. Cases such as Siemens, AXA, and Eni illustrate this phenomenon. Looking ahead, Generative AI acts as a catalyst for internal platforms, accelerating knowledge exchange and co-creation, as exemplified by the Fujitsu case. Together, platforms and GenAI offer a strategic pathway for legacy firms to remain competitive, resilient, and future-proof.

Keywords: Platform thinking · Innovation · Value creation · GenAI · Legacy firms

1 Introduction

Platforms have rapidly evolved from niche digital mechanisms to a foundational logic for organizing value creation across industries. Their capacity to orchestrate interactions, unlock dormant assets, and foster innovation at scale is now central to competitive advantage. Invited as keynote speaker at ICSOB 2025, Daniel presented "Future Proof Your Business: Embracing Platform Thinking for Sustainable Growth," sharing insights from our joint research. This article summarizes our latest findings, illustrating how legacy firms can leverage platform models, and how GenAI further accelerates this transformation.

2 What is a Platform?

From a management perspective, a platform is a business model that enables interactions between two or more distinct sides of customers, triggering indirect cross-side network externalities: the more users join one side, the more valuable the platform becomes for

G. Herzwurm et al. (Eds.): ICSOB 2025, LNBIP 574, pp. 3–6, 2026.
https://doi.org/10.1007/978-3-032-14518-5_1

the other (Parker & Van Alstyne, 2005; Gawer & Cusumano, 2014). Airbnb and Uber are classical examples, connecting demand and supply while orchestrating complementary activities. Building on previous research, we identify three archetypes (Trabucchi & Buganza, 2022; Gawer, 2021; Filistrucchi et al., 2014). Transactional platforms match two sides through efficient intermediation (e.g., Airbnb). Innovation platforms provide a technological foundation fostering complementary innovation (e.g., iOS). Orthogonal platforms activate interactions between sides not originally connected by the focal offering, enabling new value spaces (e.g., Advertising models or Strava Metro). Understanding these archetypes helps managers move beyond superficial imitation, and instead recognize how platforms reconfigure ecosystems, orchestrate assets, and unlock networked innovation within both digital-native and legacy contexts.

3 How Legacy Firms Can Use Platforms for Sustainable Growth

Legacy firms often consider platforms as a prerogative of digital startups. Instead, our research demonstrates how established companies can leverage platform mechanisms to achieve sustainable growth—growth enabled by already-existing assets, competencies, and relationships, rather than starting from scratch. This phenomenon, which we call *The Digital Phoenix Effect* (Trabucchi & Buganza, 2025b), emerges when incumbents ignite dormant potential within their ecosystems without burning down the legacy structures that made them successful.

The book presents three emblematic cases—AXA, Siemens, and Eni—illustrating different trajectories. Here we briefly focus on the Siemens case. Facing increasing service complexity and accelerating digitalization, Siemens recognized that customers required not only products, but dynamic access to a network of solutions, partners, and data. Siemens Xcelerator provides an open platform that integrates hardware, software, and services while activating an ecosystem of certified partners. Rather than developing every capability internally, Siemens orchestrates complementary innovation through shared standards and interoperable components. This approach enhances agility and scalability without abandoning core engineering excellence.

Platformization supports legacy firms across five business problems identified through our research (Trabucchi & Buganza, 2025b): missing or inefficient transactions, evolving customer demands, innovation bottlenecks, underutilized data, and lack of data for strategic insights. For example, platforms can address missing or inefficient transactions by enabling new interactions among actors previously unable to exchange value due to informational frictions. By orchestrating a marketplace of complementary offerings, legacy firms unlock efficiencies, reduce search costs, and create visibility across silos.

Academic research increasingly recognizes platforms as tools for innovation in established firms. Springer et al. (2025) underline that platforms offer structural openness while preserving governance; Schreieck et al. (2024; 2025) show how platformization improves modularity and resource recombination in incumbents; Teece et al. (2022) emphasize go-to-market advantages in multi-sided contexts; Dell'Era et al. (2021) highlight platform-enabled co-creation across innovation ecosystems. Taken together, these works validate that platforms are not merely marketplaces but innovation accelerators.

A critical managerial insight concerns idle assets (Trabucchi et al., 2020). Legacy organizations often accumulate dormant resources: underused data, niche capabilities, fragmented knowledge, or partner relationships. Platforms reveal, recombine, and monetize these assets through scalable interactions. This perspective reinforces the sustainable growth aspect highlighted in the keynote: growth emerges not from building more, but from activating what already exists. In a world of resource constraints and sustainability pressures, this approach aligns economic, environmental, and organizational objectives—allowing legacy firms to evolve responsibly, without discarding their history, identity, or expertise.

4 Looking Ahead: The GenAI Revolution

Looking forward, Generative AI introduces a new frontier for Platform Thinking. Internally, GenAI can act as a catalyst for the emergence of organizational platforms, enabling employees to create, adapt, and share knowledge artifacts. The Fujitsu case exemplifies this dynamic (Trabucchi & Buganza, 2025a): rather than imposing centralized AI solutions, Fujitsu cultivated a marketplace of custom GPTs developed by employees. This bottom-up approach transformed GenAI from a tool into an internal platform, connecting knowledge creators and consumers. The result was a two-sided mechanism: employees gained productivity and personalization, while corporate units benefited from distributed feedback, engagement analytics, and continuously evolving content.

This evolution loops back to *The Digital Phoenix Effect* and specifically to the first business problem—missing or inefficient transactions. GenAI-augmented internal platforms can dramatically reduce knowledge frictions, resolving micro-transactions of expertise, documentation, and explanations that previously remained trapped across organizational silos. The ability to tap into internal assets—skills, documents, tacit know-how—creates exponential returns on existing capabilities, rather than pursuing costly external developments.

For researchers, a promising direction emerges: studying how GenAI reshapes governance, participation incentives, and scaling dynamics within internal platforms. For practitioners, the message is clear: platforms and GenAI together can accelerate sustainable growth by activating latent assets, orchestrating collaborative ecosystems, and enabling continuous learning. The phoenix rises not by burning the past, but by illuminating the unrealized value already within.

References

Dell'Era, C., Trabucchi, D., Magistretti, S.: Exploiting incumbents' potentialities: from linear value chains to multisided platforms. Creat. Innov. Manag. **30**(1), 31–46 (2021)

Filistrucchi, L., Geradin, D., Van Damme, E., Affeldt, P.: Market definition in two-sided markets: theory and practice. J. Compet. Law Econ. **10**(2), 293–339 (2014)

Gawer, A.: Digital platforms' boundaries: the interplay of firm scope, platform sides, and digital interfaces. Long Range Plan. **54**(5), 102045 (2021)

Gawer, A., Cusumano, M.A.: Industry platforms and ecosystem innovation. J. Prod. Innov. Manag. **31**(3), 417–433 (2014)

Parker, G.G., Van Alstyne, M.W.: Two-sided network effects: a theory of information product design. Manage. Sci. **51**(10), 1494–1504 (2005)

Schreieck, M., Ondrus, J., Wiesche, M., Krcmar, H.: A typology of multi-platform integration strategies. Inf. Syst. J. **34**(3), 828–853 (2024)

Schreieck, M., Ondrus, J., Wiesche, M., Krcmar, H.: Platform governance for established companies. Calif. Manage. Rev. **67**(4), 48–74 (2025)

Springer, V., Randhawa, K., Jovanović, M., Ritala, P., Piller, F.T.: Platform design and governance in industrial markets: charting the meta-organizational logic. Res. Policy **54**(6), 105236 (2025)

Teece, D., Pundziene, I., Heaton, S., Vadi, M.: Managing multi-sided platforms: platform origins and go-to-market strategy. Calif. Manage. Rev. **64**(4), 5–19 (2022)

Trabucchi, D., Buganza, T.: Landlords with no lands: a systematic literature review on hybrid multi-sided platforms and Platform Thinking. Eur. J. Innov. Manag. **25**(6), 64–96 (2022)

Trabucchi, D., & Buganza, T.: GenAI adoption through platform thinking: the case of Fujitsu. California Management Review Insights (2025a)

Trabucchi, D., & Buganza, T.: The digital phoenix effect. Platform Thinking Publishing (2025b)

Trabucchi, D., Sanasi, S., Ghezzi, A., Buganza, T.: Idle asset hunters—The secret of multi-sided platforms. Res. Technol. Manag. **64**(1), 33–42 (2020)

Data Economy: Data Practices, Spaces, and Architectures

The Beauty and the Beast: Patterns and Anti-patterns in Use of Data

Helena Holmström Olsson[1(✉)] and Jan Bosch[2,3]

[1] Department of Computer Science and Media Technology, Malmö University, Nordenskiöldsgatan 1, Malmö 205 06, Sweden
helena.holmstrom.olsson@mau.se

[2] Department of Computer Science and Engineering, Chalmers University of Technology, Gothenburg, Sweden
jan.bosch@chalmers.se

[3] Department of Mathematics and Computer Science, Eindhoven University of Technology, Eindhoven, The Netherlands

Abstract. Companies in the software-intensive systems industry collect vast amounts of data from their products on a continuous basis. While many companies have more data than what they will ever use, the volumes keep growing and the frequency at which data is collected is only increasing. Still, there is little guidance for how to effectively manage and make use of this data and companies struggle with how to turn raw data into customer and business value. In this paper, we study data practices in software-intensive systems companies and we identify beneficial patterns that lead to successful use of data. Also, we identify detrimental anti-patterns that companies should avoid when working with data.

Keywords: data practices · software-intensive systems · patterns · anti-patterns

1 Introduction

Despite decades of data collection from products in the field, companies in the software-intensive systems domain keep facing challenges in relation to data management and use. Although experience and expertise is maturing, the rapidly growing volumes of data, the increasing frequency at which data is collected, and the costs and complexities involved in e.g., data storage and analysis add challenges to this already difficult task. For years, researchers have studied the adoption and use of data-driven development and decision-making practices [1–5]. In industry, effective use of data is critical and companies across industry domains keep investing heavily in infrastructures and competencies for managing the rapidly growing amounts of data [6]. In our previous research, we studied e.g., the transition towards data-driven development [2, 7], the collection

H.H. Olsson and J. Bosch—These authors contributed equally to this work.

G. Herzwurm et al. (Eds.): ICSOB 2025, LNBIP 574, pp. 9–23, 2026.
https://doi.org/10.1007/978-3-032-14518-5_2

and increasing use of data [8], experimentation practices [6,9], and how data is the key driver for digital transformation [10,11]. In a recent paper, Olsson and Bosch explored data collection strategies [12], the use of data in digital product management [13], and the steps companies evolve through when maturing their data practices [14].

However, while there is prominent research on the adoption and use of data in the software-intensive industry [2,8–10,12,13,15–17], we see little guidance for what constitutes best practices when working with data, i.e., beneficial use patterns, and what companies should really try to avoid, i.e., anti-patterns that do more harm than good.

To address this gap, we study the use of data in software-intensive systems companies and we identify beneficial patterns and how these evolve over time. Also, we identify detrimental anti-patterns that companies should avoid. Our research builds on multi-case study research in eight companies that have collected data from their products for decades. However, if compared to the software development practices in these companies, their data practices are not as well-established and still maturing.

In our previous research [18], we identified the key dimensions that help companies reason about cost versus value of collecting data. As the key contribution, we present a data framework in which the dimensions that companies need to consider when working with data are outlined. In this paper, the data framework as presented in our previous work [18] provides the foundation for identifying patterns and anti-patterns that we see in the case companies we studied.

The contribution of this paper is two-fold. First, we identify beneficial patterns and their evolution over time. Second, we identify detrimental anti-patterns that companies should avoid.

The remainder of this paper is structured as follows. In Sect. 2, we present the background for the study. In Sect. 3, we describe the research method we employed during our research. In Sect. 4, we report on our empirical findings. In Sect. 5, we identify the patterns and anti-patterns. In Sect. 6, we discuss threats to validity and in Sect. 7 we conclude the paper and outline future research.

2 Background

2.1 Data Practices in the Software-Intensive Systems Domain

Continuous delivery of customer value is a key priority for companies in the software-intensive systems domain [6,19]. As recognized in [20], the ability to deploy software on a continuous basis provides a unique opportunity to learn how systems perform in the field and how they are used by customers. To achieve this, companies adopt data-driven development practices where data is used as the basis for decisions on what to develop, what features to prioritize and how to improve and optimize existing products. For successful adoption and use of data-driven practices, several factors are recognized as important.

First, companies need to short feedback cycles [7,21,22]. In practice, this means adopting DevOps practices to ensure rapid and reliable deployment of new functionality [23,24]. Second, companies need metrics to monitor feature usage, user behaviors and overall system performance. Finally, companies need to adopt techniques such as A/B testing as the basis for evaluating hypotheses and validate what adds value to customers [6]. In literature, companies like Google, Facebook, Amazon, Netflix, Microsoft and Booking.com are often referred to as companies that run extensive A/B tests in their products. However, recent years have shown an increasing uptake of these practices also in the software-intensive systems domain. Several previous studies explored how data-driven practices and experimentation are increasingly adopted and how they provide teams with tools and techniques to help improve decision-making, prioritization efforts and develop software functionality that better meets the needs of customers, e.g., [17,25,26] [2,7,11,27–29].

Although data collection is far from a new phenomenon in the software-intensive systems domain we see that the role and the implications of data are changing. While it was used primarily for diagnostics and trouble shooting, and as an effective mechanism for quality assurance, we see that data is increasingly used as the basis for product innovations, new business models and digital services. Previous research reports on some of the changes we see in how data is used and the increasing importance of data as an asset [6,9,25,29]. Also, it is recognized how data is the backbone for machine- and deep learning technologies [5] as well as for federated and reinforcement learning [30,31].

2.2 Data Framework

In our previous research [18], we developed a data framework with the intention to capture the multiple dimensions that are involved in collection, processing, storing and use of data. The framework, as shown in Fig. 1, provides a holistic understanding of these dimensions and helps companies when reasoning about business value versus cost of data. In this paper, the data framework as presented in [18] lays the basis for studying and identifying beneficial patterns that we see companies use and how these evolve over time. Also, we use the framework to identify detrimental anti-patterns that companies should avoid when working with data.

The framework consists of an *offering part* and a *data part*. The offering part consists of a business case and a use case. The business case describes the nature of the offering and can have different levels of maturity, ranging from a hypothesis to a validated business case. The use case describes an instance of realizing the business case. The separation between business and use case is important as a business case can often be realized in different use cases. The use case has two dimensions, i.e. the scope and the lifecycle. The scope is concerned with the beneficiaries of the use case ranging from an individual team to the entire business ecosystem. The lifecycle of a use case typically has a strong relationship with the maturity of the business case and ranges from exploration to operation [18]. The data part of the framework includes three dimensions, i.e. compute, communication and storage (CCS), data quality and access [18]. The CCS is concerned with where data is processed, stored and communicated. The data

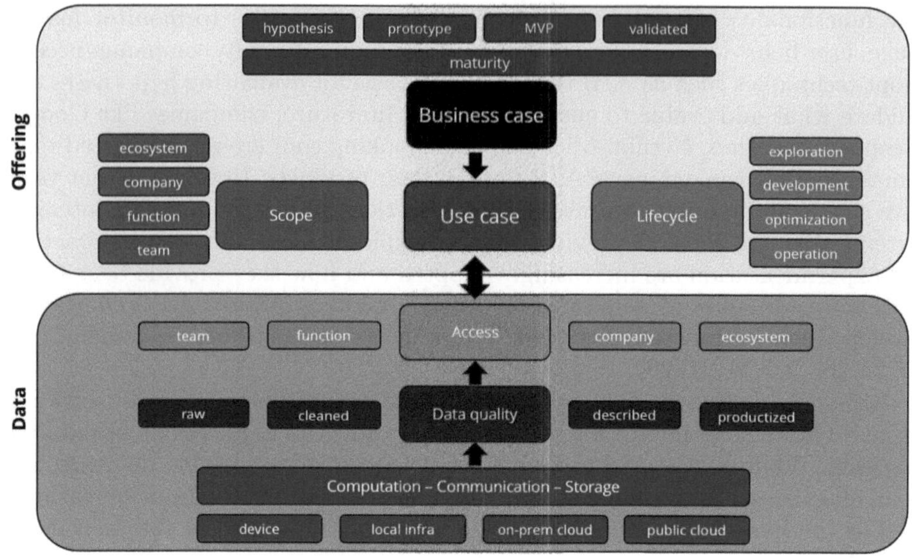

Fig. 1. Data framework as presented in [18].

quality tends to evolve with the maturity of the use case and the scope of use of the data. As outlined in the data quality dimension, data can be raw, cleaned, described or productized. Productized data is data sets or streams that can be treated (and monetized) as a product. This means the data is guaranteed to be available, cleaned and clearly described and can be used to build commercial data-driven services on top of. There are dependencies between the dimensions we identify and our assessment is that most challenges that companies experience are caused by misalignment between these dimensions.

3 Research Method

3.1 Case Study Research

The objective of this paper is to identify beneficial use patterns when working with data, and to identify detrimental anti-patterns that do more harm than good and that companies should avoid. To study this, we used the data framework as presented in [18] as the basis when exploring how companies work with data.

We employed a case study research approach when studying eight companies in the software-intensive systems domain. Case study research has become a well-established and appreciated method in software engineering research as it allows for exploring complex phenomena in real-life settings where the boundaries between the phenomenon itself and its surrounding context are unclear [32,33].

3.2 Case Companies

Below, we provide a short description of the case companies. The case companies are members of Software Center (www.software-center.se) and they are all operating in the software-intensive systems domain.

- ***Case company A*** is a company manufacturing trucks, buses and construction equipment as well as a supplier of marine systems.
- ***Case company B*** is a food packaging and processing company.
- ***Case company C*** is a company manufacturing network cameras, access control, and network audio devices for the security and surveillance industries.
- ***Case company D*** is a company developing automation and digitalization solutions for process and manufacturing industries.
- ***Case company E*** is a networking and telecommunications company.
- ***Case company F*** is a company developing advanced driver assistance systems and autonomous drive technology.
- ***Case company G*** is a company manufacturing pumps.
- ***Case company H*** is a vehicle manufacturer.

3.3 Data Collection and Analysis

In this paper, we report on research conducted between September 2023–March 2025. Throughout this period, data collection was conducted using company workshops and interviews. We engaged in 2–4 h workshop sessions at company A, B, C and H and in parallel we conducted an interview study with key stakeholders in all eight case companies.

In *company A*, we organized four workshops with the first exploratory workshop on September 12th, 2023, and the last workshop where we summarized discussions on October 11th, 2024. In between, we met on November 14th, 2023 and February 27th, 2024 to discuss data infrastructures, data management and the ways-of-working with regards to collection, analysis and use of data as the basis for new services. Our workshops involved 6–15 people representing IT, data and simulation platforms, data science, electro mobility, and architecture. In *company B*, we organized one workshop on March 20th, 2024. At this workshop, we discussed challenges and opportunities associated with data collection and use. This workshop involved a group of 10 people representing e.g., data management, connectivity, architecture, decision science, and automation. In *company C*, we organized one workshop on December 5th, 2024 and the second workshop on May 8th, 2025. In the first workshop we met with people representing architecture, platform development and engineering management and learned about the ways in which data is being used for new services. In the second workshop, we met with a data science team to discuss the efforts required in data labeling, access and governance. In *company H*, we organized one workshop on January 22nd, 2025. At this workshop, we met with three people in manager roles to discuss data management practices and the potential of data products.

In addition to these workshops, we organized one *cross-company workshop* to which we invited all case companies. The workshop was organized on November 15th, 2024. During this workshop, companies shared experiences, discussed challenges and explored best practices. In total, we organized eight workshops and we met with more than 60 people.

In parallel with the workshops, we conducted an *interview study* that involved key representatives from the case companies. The interview study was initiated on October 31st, 2024 and completed on March 7th, 2025. All interviews were conducted online (except one which was conducted in-person) using Microsoft Teams. In total, we interviewed 17 people (6 people from company A, 5 people from company B, 2 people from company C, 1 person from company D, E, F, and G). All interviews lasted for one hour and followed an interview guideline of a semi-structured format. During the interviews, both researchers shared the responsibility of asking questions and encouraging the interviewee to elaborate on the answers by asking follow-up questions.

During data analysis, we adopted an interpretive approach [34]. Following this approach, we revisited the documentation from all workshop discussions to carefully reflect on our insights from these and what implications could be drawn from the empirical material. For the interviews, one of the researchers went through all transcriptions, summarized these and based on the summaries, both researchers discussed the content to identify common themes and patterns among the interviewees.

4 Empirical Findings

Below, we present a summary of how data is collected and used within the case companies. Second, we outline some of the challenges the company representatives experience.

4.1 Collection and Use of Large Volumes of Data

All case companies collect data from their products to monitor operational performance such as e.g., downtime, efficiency, utilization, and to avoid breakdown of parts. Company A collects data from test vehicles, from production vehicles, logged data, fleet management data and field test data. In addition, road condition data, weather data and data that reflects the different variants of trucks is collected. In company B, data is collected from the filling machines to help identify stops, the reason for these stops and for analyzing equipment performance. This is reflected upon by one of the interviewees when saying: *"Data is low intensity data e.g., events, status, counters, stop reasons and whatever is needed for monitoring operational performance."* Similarly, another interviewee in company B shared that: *"There are a lot of sensors in the machines that provide us with information about the quality in the machine and the testing patterns that we are doing."* In addition, data is collected for purposes such as simulations, inventory optimization and for understanding the price elasticity of products. One of the interviewees recognized the fact that their data volumes will only grow: *"In the future, we are going to need more capacity for dealing with big data and we will need some kind of model to manage a continuous stream of data."* Similarly, another interviewee from the company noted: *"In the pipeline is the new technology where we make use of more intense data sets connected to the usage of AI- embedded applications, e.g., usage of vision, images, streaming of video to understand crashes, creation of digital twins."*

Company C collects video and sensor data to enable diagnostics and optimization of configurations. The data is compressed and is processed only in aggregated and anonymized form. The two interviewees from company C shared how the company is experiencing a transition in which customers are increasingly opening up and allowing for data to be collected from the products. According to the interviewees, this is mainly due to the many device management services they offer and that customers are starting to realize the many benefits of sharing data.

In company D, tracking data, monitoring data, image data and logistics data is collected from thousands of devices to optimize performance of factories. Typically, the company doesn't store data at its own premises but instead lets its customer own and store the data. In some cases however, data from customer sites is transferred via connectors to allow for identification issues at customer sites. In such cases however, the interviewee report on several challenges related to e.g., transferring costs and data privacy.

Company E and F collect large amounts of data and in the interview with a person in company F we learnt that people are very reluctant to getting rid of data. Although the company has limited data storage capabilities the decision on what to keep and what to not keep is a difficult one that people tend to avoid. This is something we noted also in other companies when people often referred to "just-in-case" collection of data i.e., collect everything you can in case there will be a use case for it in the future. In company G, data is collected to monitor performance of products and to allow remote maintenance. In the interview with a person from this company, it became clear that data is only increasing in value and that the products are increasingly viewed as data collection devices.

All case companies store data both in the public cloud and on-premise. This is reflected upon by one of the interviewees when saying: *"The ideal is to have a hybrid concept where we develop services with our on-prem capacity, then scale out to public cloud for computation needs."* Our workshop discussions revealed that compute costs are expensive and in particular, the costs of downloading data. In company B, the interviewees shared that: *"We see a tendency that more and more data ends up in a cloud application."* For now however, the majority of data is kept on the machines at customer sites. One of the interviewees reflects on this when sharing that: *"We have limited storage and limited processing on the machine itself. But there's been a strategy decision taken that we want to move data as soon as possible to other systems on-prem."* With regards to costs, this interviewee concludes that: *"It's basically down to the fact of whether or not we are willing to pay the price for storing everything "just in case" we need it. It's a matter of strategy and how we foresee the future."*

4.2 Challenges When Working with Data

The primary challenge that people report on is data quality. All case company representatives shared concerns with regard to quality of the data that is used as the basis for development, decisions, innovation initiatives and new services. In company F, the interviewee shared that: *"We collect and keep data without checking quality. We know that if, for example, all camera sensors are not activated the data that is collected will be useless. You need complete sensor data to be able to use it and if one sensor is not activated the entire data set is useless."* Similarly, discussions in some of the workshops in company A revealed that there are data-driven services deployed and in use at customers, but where the data that provides the foundation for the service is not productized. This challenge is touched upon also in the interview with company G in which the interviewee discussed that clean, described, and productized data is always use-case specific: *"There is no such thing as just "cleaned data" as cleaning depends on what you want to use it for."* Related to this, and with the cost perspective in mind, one of the interviewees in company A raised the risk of having low quality data, or lack of competence for analysis, as the basis for decision-making: *"It is also the cost of incorrect conclusions because of wrong analysis, or analytics on incorrect data, or simply misinterpreted data because of unclear semantics of the data."*

A second challenge is the efforts that are spent on accessing data. This is reflected in the following quote from company A: *"Many of the use cases require pulling data from a variety of different sources, and from a variety of different platforms. In general, 30% of our time is spent on getting access to the data we need. After this, another 15–30% of the time is spent on cleaning up the data so that we can actually use it."* In company B, one of the interviewees describes a situation in which even more time is spent on this when saying: *"In many cases, 80% of the job is spent on getting access to the data."* Also, several people describe a situation in which lots of efforts are spent on making data available for others. As soon as data is shared across teams, the interviewees report on a situation in which the team that originally collected the data suddenly becomes a "data provider" to other teams using that data. This implies maintaining quality of the data, ensuring the trustworthiness of the data and providing clear semantics to avoid misinterpretations by people who were not involved in the context in which the data was initially generated. As mentioned by the interviewee in company G, problems arise when teams access data but lack domain knowledge. *"Some teams only look at data as data, but have no domain knowledge of the underlying data generator. Therefore, they lack the ability to see if there is a problem in the data."*

During our study we noted that there is an on-going discussion in all companies on how to manage data access. One of the interviewees in company A reflects on the risk of having people access what is irrelevant for them when saying: *"Data on deep analytics on energy efficiency and driver behavior, is that something that everyone in the company should have access to? Would they even be able to use it? No."* However, there are also situations in which accessibility across teams and groups is critical. As the most common example, the company representatives mention development of new services as these often involve functions from different parts of the organization as well as data collected by different groups.

Third, we see several problems in relation to storage costs. Especially, companies experience challenges with cloud storage and how to reason about when and what data to store in the cloud. A common pattern is that data is kept in the cloud and on-premise depending on the data type and the purpose for which it is stored. Typically, data is processed on-premise using local infrastructures as these are more attractive from a cost perspective. In one of the interviews, the interviewee reflected on the challenges related to the balance of on-device storage and cloud storage and identified the cost of transferring data and data privacy as the two major ones: *"Compute and data download are expensive tasks and these are the major costs. When you want to crunch the data, that's when the money you pay starts to ramp up."*

5 Data Practices: Patterns and Anti-patterns

5.1 Patterns

Our study revealed several beneficial patterns that lead to successful use of data. Below, we present three patterns that we identified in the case companies.

Exploration of New Data-Driven Services
Description: The companies in our study are collecting vast amounts of data, but that does not automatically convert in new data-driven services. So, business developers and data scientists often work together to explore ideas that may result in new data driven services.
Considerations: As many of the ideas that are explored are likely not successful and will not result in new services, the focus should be at exploring as many ideas as possible at the lowest possible cost per idea. One aspect of this is that often large amounts of data are explored and when conducting this in a public cloud context, the cost can easily become prohibitively high. In our experience, exploration is often best conducted on internal compute infrastructure.
Variants: In addition to internal exploration of data-driven services, companies often have partners that are interested in joint innovation efforts around data. This can concern subsystems delivered by suppliers or partners seeking to combine their own data and the companies data to generate new insights.

Operational Data-Driven Service
Description: A second pattern, at the other end of the lifecycle, are data-services that have been confirmed to deliver value to customers and that are in operation. These services are typically monetized and need to be provided in a reliable and accurate fashion.
Considerations: This is where companies spend significant resources on ensuring data quality as this forms the basis for service quality. Also, in this case,

companies tend to operate on top of a public cloud infrastructure to assure reliability.
Variants: Especially in embedded systems companies, some data-driven services can be provided directly by the device used by the customer, e.g. a truck. In this case, no centralized deployment is required, but data quality and other concerns need to be managed in the device itself in that case.

Collaborative Data-Driven Service
Description: Many of the companies in our study closely collaborate with a set of partners and suppliers. In addition to working on the functionality in the resultant product, there is a natural extension towards collaboration around data as well.
Considerations: As the companies in our study often own the end-customer relationship, this collaboration is often driven by the partners and suppliers having to offer something of value in order to gain access to data concerning the subsystems or solutions that they provide and the context in which these operate.
Variants: In some cases, the companies in our study have even agreed to providing data to suppliers that they themselves do not even have access to, e.g. through encryption. Also, there are cases where a third party collects data directly from devices on customer premises without the companies in our study being involved at all in the data collection nor the associated data-driven services. In this case, many companies are looking for control points to avoid this.

5.2 Anti-patterns

Although the data framework as presented in [18] is helpful when modeling the intended ways of working with data, we have found that the framework is as helpful for identifying anti-patterns. Below, we share three of the most common ones. We number them 1, 2 and 3 and visualize them in Fig. 2. All anti-patterns reflect one or several misalignments in the data dimensions we identified in our previous work [18], i.e., data quality, data access, computation – communication – storage, scope and lifecycle.

Raw Data for Productized Services (1)
Description: Many services are initially developed with one or a few customers in a prototype fashion. At that stage, the quality of the data and the resultant service is not prioritized. When the service proves to be successful, it is rapidly scaled and commercially deployed and ensuring data quality may easily become deprioritized.
Consequences: As a commercial, customer-facing service is based on raw data that is not cleaned nor described, the service may easily present data that is entirely inconsistent and irrelevant. This easily decreases the value that customers associate with the service.

Mitigation: The mitigation of this anti-pattern is obvious: the quality of the data needs to be improved by putting it through a data pipeline that removes incorrect records, completes incomplete records and provides consistency checking over a window of data in order to ensure that the service always provides relevant and complete information.

Ungoverned Data Access (2)
Description: Several interviewees described cases where data access was ungoverned, meaning that data collected by and intended for a specific team was used at a company-level and by teams and functions for which it was never intended.
Consequences: Teams that collect data for their own purposes can easily stop collecting data when they don't need it anymore or to change the semantics or structure of the data as their needs change. If others are dependent on that data and the original team is not aware of this, it causes failures and downtime. If the team is aware of it, it may not be interested in becoming a service provider for others in the company as this requires significant effort.
Mitigation: In general, we see companies move towards a binary solution. Either data is provided as a data product and its quality, semantics and availability are guaranteed. Alternatively, data is only available by the party that initiated its collection and any deviations to the rule are only operationalized in mutual agreement.

Excessive Cloud Cost (3)
Description: We were exposed to a number of cases where the company received excessive cloud computing bills that took them by surprise. For instance, when conducting exploratory analysis of large amounts of data in a public cloud setting, the cost for computation can easily become quite large quite quickly.
Consequences: The first, obvious consequence is high cost that outweigh the potential value of use cases that are explored or under development. The indirect consequence is that engineers and data scientists become reluctant to explore services and use cases due to the high associated cost. This is obviously not desirable as all of our case study companies prioritized developing and monetizing data-driven services.
Mitigation: The primary mitigation strategy is to ensure access to two compute environments. An internal cloud that is purchased outright by the company and where there are no usage-based cost. Here engineers and data scientists can run any exploratory use case that they want without worrying about cost. Secondly, a public cloud where commercially deployed services are hosted and where uptime and response times are critical and can be guaranteed by cloud providers.

6 Threats to Validity

The validity of a study implies the trustworthiness of the results, which is divided into construct, internal, external, and reliability [33]. To address construct valid-

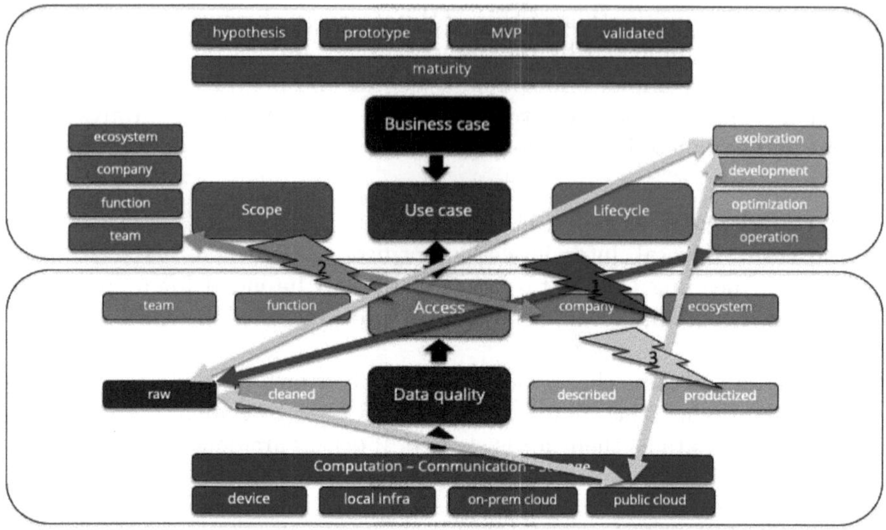

Fig. 2. Anti-patterns identified in the case companies: (1) Raw data for productized services, (2) Ungoverned data access and (3) Excessive cloud cost.

ity, we made sure to define key concepts and terminology in all our interactions with company representatives. In this way, we mitigated potential misunderstandings and we invited for a discussion around the topic and terminology of the study. To address internal validity, we engaged with key stakeholders and experts who were able to provide an understanding of the complexity of the phenomenon we studied, i.e., people with responsibility for data collection, data processing and analysis, data storage and service development. To address external validity, we used our empirical cases to inductively derive our findings with the intention to provide value for companies that have common characteristics as the companies we studied. Finally, to address reliability, we applied established methods and practices for data collection and analysis and we made sure our results were frequently reviewed and approved by company representatives.

7 Conclusions and Future Work

Effective use of data is key for companies in the software-intensive systems domain. For these companies, data from products in the field lays the basis for diagnostics, product improvements, optimization efforts, innovation initiatives and new data and AI -driven services. However, while there is prominent research on the adoption and use of data in the software-intensive industry, we see little guidance for what constitutes best practices when working with data.

In this paper, we study data practices in software-intensive systems companies and we identify beneficial patterns that lead to successful use of data. Also, we identify detrimental anti-patterns that companies should avoid when working with data. Our research builds on multi-case study research and shows that despite years of data collection, data practices are still maturing. In future research, we aim to further explore and validate the patterns and anti-patterns we identified. In addition, we seek to broaden our research to involve companies in other domains.

Acknowledgements. We would like to thank the Software Center company representatives that participated in this study.

References

1. Svensson, R.B., Feldt, R., Torkar, R.: The unfulfilled potential of data-driven decision making in agile software development. In: Kruchten, P., Fraser, S., Coallier, F. (eds.) Agile Processes in Software Engineering and Extreme Programming: 20th International Conference, XP 2019, Montréal, QC, Canada, 21–25 May 2019, Proceedings 20, pp. 69–85. Springer, Cham (2019). https://doi.org/10.1007/978-3-030-19034-7_5
2. Olsson, H.H., Bosch, J.: The HYPEX model: from opinions to data-driven software development. In: Continuous Software Engineering, pp. 155–164. Springer, Cham (2014). https://doi.org/10.1007/978-3-319-11283-1_13
3. Maalej, W., Nayebi, M., Johann, T., Ruhe, G.: Toward data-driven requirements engineering. IEEE Softw. **33**(1), 48–54 (2015)
4. Munappy, A.R., Mattos, D.I., Bosch, J., Olsson, H.H., Dakkak, A.: From Ad-Hoc data analytics to DataOps. In: Proceedings of the International Conference on Software and System Processes, pp. 165–174 (2020)
5. Munappy, A.R., Bosch, J., Olsson, H.H., Arpteg, A., Brinne, B.: Data management for production quality deep learning models: challenges and solutions. J. Syst. Softw. **191**, 111359 (2022)
6. Fabijan, A., Dmitriev, P., Olsson, H.H., Bosch, J.: The evolution of continuous experimentation in software product development: from data to a data-driven organization at scale. In: 2017 IEEE/ACM 39th International Conference on Software Engineering (ICSE), pp. 770–780. IEEE (2017)
7. Olsson, H.H., Alahyari, H., Bosch, J.: Climbing the "stairway to heaven"–a mulitiple-case study exploring barriers in the transition from agile development towards continuous deployment of software. In: 2012 38th Euromicro Conference on Software Engineering and Advanced Applications, pp. 392–399. IEEE (2012)
8. Olsson, H.H., Bosch, J.: Towards continuous validation of customer value. In: Scientific Workshop Proceedings of the XP2015, pp. 1–4 (2015)
9. Fabijan, A., Dmitriev, P., McFarland, C., Vermeer, L., Holmström Olsson, H., Bosch, J.: Experimentation growth: evolving trustworthy a/b testing capabilities in online software companies. J. Softw. Evol. Process **30**(12), 2113 (2018)
10. Bosch, J., Olsson, H.H.: Digital for real: a multicase study on the digital transformation of companies in the embedded systems domain. J. Softw. Evol. Process **33**(5), 2333 (2021)
11. Olsson, H.H., Bosch, J.: Living in a pink cloud or fighting a whack-a-mole? On the creation of recurring revenue streams in the embedded systems domain. In: 2022 48th Euromicro Conference on Software Engineering and Advanced Applications (SEAA), pp. 161–168. IEEE (2022)

12. Olsson, H.H., Bosch, J.: All data is equal or is some data more equal? on strategic data collection and use in the embedded systems domain. In: 2023 49th Euromicro Conference on Software Engineering and Advanced Applications (SEAA), pp. 319–327. IEEE (2023)
13. Olsson, H.H., Bosch, J.: Strategic digital product management in the age of AI. In: International Conference on Software Business, pp. 344–359. Springer (2023)
14. Olsson, H.H., Bosch, J.: How to get good at data: 5 steps. In: 7th International Workshop on Software-intensive Business. ACM (2024)
15. Berndtsson, M., Forsberg, D., Stein, D., Svahn, T.: Becoming a data-driven organisation. In: 26th European Conference on Information Systems (ECIS2018), Portsmouth, United Kingdom, 23–28 June 2018 (2018)
16. Kiron, D.: Lessons from becoming a data-driven organization. MIT Sloan Manage. Rev. **58**(2) (2017)
17. Mattos, D.I., Dakkak, A., Bosch, J., Olsson, H.H.: Experimentation for business-to-business mission-critical systems: a case study. In: Proceedings of the International Conference on Software and System Processes, pp. 95–104 (2020)
18. Olsson, H.H., Bosch, J.: Dealing with data: bringing order to chaos. In: 2024 50th Euromicro Conference on Software Engineering and Advanced Applications (SEAA), pp. 350–355. IEEE (2024)
19. Fagerholm, F., Guinea, A.S., Mäenpää, H., Münch, J.: The right model for continuous experimentation. J. Syst. Softw. **123**, 292–305 (2017)
20. Dakkak, A., Mattos, D.I., Bosch, J.: Success factors when transitioning to continuous deployment in software-intensive embedded systems. In: 2021 47th Euromicro Conference on Software Engineering and Advanced Applications (SEAA), pp. 1–9. IEEE (2021)
21. Bosch, J.: Speed, data, and ecosystems: the future of software engineering. IEEE Softw. **33**(1), 82–88 (2015)
22. Dakkak, A., Bosch, J., Olsson, H.H., Mattos, D.I.: Continuous deployment in software-intensive system-of-systems. Inf. Softw. Technol. **159**, 107200 (2023)
23. Zhu, L., Bass, L., Champlin-Scharff, G.: DevOps and its practices. IEEE Softw. **33**(3), 32–34 (2016)
24. Amaro, R., Pereira, R., Silva, M.M.: Capabilities and practices in DevOps: a multivocal literature review. IEEE Trans. Softw. Eng. **49**(2), 883–901 (2022)
25. Liu, Y., Mattos, D.I., Bosch, J., Olsson, H.H., Lantz, J.: Size matters? or not: A/b testing with limited sample in automotive embedded software. In: 2021 47th Euromicro Conference on Software Engineering and Advanced Applications (SEAA), pp. 300–307. IEEE (2021)
26. Mattos, D.I., Bosch, J., Olsson, H.H.: Your system gets better every day you use it: towards automated continuous experimentation. In: 2017 43rd Euromicro Conference on Software Engineering and Advanced Applications (SEAA), pp. 256–265. IEEE (2017)
27. Fabijan, A., Olsson, H.H., Bosch, J.: Data-Driven Decision-Making in product R&D. Springer (2015)
28. Fabijan, A., Olsson, H.H., Bosch, J.: Early value argumentation and prediction: an iterative approach to quantifying feature value. In: Abrahamsson, P., Corral, L., Oivo, M., Russo, B. (eds.) PROFES 2015. LNCS, vol. 9459, pp. 16–23. Springer, Cham (2015). https://doi.org/10.1007/978-3-319-26844-6_2
29. Olsson, H.H., Bosch, J.: Going digital: disruption and transformation in software intensive embedded systems ecosystems. J. Softw. Evol. Process **32**(6), 2249 (2020)

30. Zhang, H., et al.: 5G network on wings: a deep reinforcement learning approach to UAV-based integrated access and backhaul. arXiv preprint arXiv:2202.02006 (2022)
31. Zhang, H., Bosch, J., Olsson, H.H., Koppisetty, A.C.: AF-DNDF: asynchronous federated learning of deep neural decision forests. In: 2021 47th Euromicro Conference on Software Engineering and Advanced Applications (SEAA), pp. 308–315. IEEE (2021)
32. Verner, J.M., Sampson, J., Tosic, V., Bakar, N.A., Kitchenham, B.A.: Guidelines for industrially-based multiple case studies in software engineering. In: 2009 Third International Conference on Research Challenges in Information Science, pp. 313–324. IEEE (2009)
33. Runeson, P., Höst, M.: Guidelines for conducting and reporting case study research in software engineering. Empir. Softw. Eng. **14**(2), 131–164 (2009)
34. Walsham, G.: Interpretive case studies in is research: nature and method. Eur. J. Inf. Syst. **4**(2), 74–81 (1995)

What Characterizes Data Spaces in Industry 4.0? Towards a Better Understanding

Oliver Werth[1] (✉), Christian Koldewey[2], Mathias Uslar[1], and Julian Zerbin[2]

[1] OFFIS—Institute for Information Technology, Escherweg 2, 26121, Oldenburg, Germany
{oliver.werth,mathias.uslar}@offis.de

[2] Advanced Systems Engineering, Heinz Nixdorf Institute, Paderborn University, Paderborn, Germany
{christian.koldewey,julian.zerbin}@hni.uni-paderborn.de

Abstract. Data spaces are receiving an emerging interest in Information Systems Research and industry practice. They are central to many European research initiatives and shape the data economy in Industry 4.0. Generally, they aim to create secure environments for cross-organizational data management and sharing. Currently, there is considerable interest in developing new data spaces in Industry 4.0, also accelerated through regulatory changes. However, key questions about what precisely characterizes a data space in Industry 4.0 remain unresolved. Against this backdrop, we build a taxonomy of data spaces in the Industry 4.0 context. We identified nine distinctive dimensions and 40 corresponding characteristics among the 19 data spaces analyzed. The taxonomy enables clearer classification and nomenclature of data spaces in this context. This short paper will ignite planned further research on data spaces in Industry 4.0 and contribute to a conceptualization of a taxonomic theory for interested researchers.

Keywords: Industry 4.0 · Taxonomy · Data spaces · Characterization

1 Introduction and Problem Statement

In today's interconnected world, data and data ecosystems are essential enablers of digital innovation. This is particularly true for the industrial sector, where the concept of Industry 4.0 has emerged. Industry 4.0 is defined by the real-time synchronization of information flows and the ability to produce more personalized, smart products [1]. Effective data handling and exchange across organizational boundaries are central to this development, yet they present considerable challenges. Transparency, monitoring of indirect suppliers, regulations, and enhanced collaboration are all key requirements that organizations increasingly face [2, 3].

To address these challenges, industrial data ecosystems are emerging. Within them, data spaces facilitate secure, cross-organizational data sharing while preserving data sovereignty. According to Möller et al. [3], data spaces are inter-organizational information systems that implement both technical and organizational mechanisms to support

G. Herzwurm et al. (Eds.): ICSOB 2025, LNBIP 574, pp. 24–31, 2026.
https://doi.org/10.1007/978-3-032-14518-5_3

trusted data exchange. They also play an intermediary role, helping companies collaborate without losing control of proprietary information. From a technical standpoint, data spaces are decentralized, do not rely on a shared database, are nested and overlapping, and support data redundancy. These characteristics align well with the distributed and even more data-driven nature of Industry 4.0. Furthermore, data spaces promote interoperability and standardization, allowing systems across organizations to integrate efficiently and operate seamlessly [4, 5]. Moreover, data spaces enable open innovation by allowing businesses to co-develop products, optimize processes, and respond quickly to market demands from an economic standpoint. Access to real-time, high-quality data allows for better strategic decision-making, enabling companies to refine production workflows, improve product quality, and gain a competitive advantage [6]. Despite their potential, data spaces also raise concerns, particularly around data security and privacy. These concerns can hinder trust among participating entities. Therefore, strong governance frameworks, technical standards, and access controls are critical to ensuring secure and ethical data sharing [4].

While the concept of data spaces has been increasingly studied in information systems (IS) research, the literature remains fragmented, and a comprehensive taxonomy specific to Industry 4.0 is lacking [3]. Prior studies by Gieß et al. [7, 8] have developed taxonomies for general data spaces and connectors, identifying relevant dimensions and characteristics. However, they do not focus explicitly on the Industry 4.0 context. On the other hand, existing taxonomies in Industry 4.0, such as those by Weking et al. [9] and Azkan et al. [10], focus on business models or data-driven services, but do not address data spaces. In addition, small to medium enterprises in Industry 4.0 refrain from participating in data spaces based on restricted knowledge capabilities and personnel resources despite the chances that data spaces deliver [11–13]. As a result, a clear, structured view of potential data space configurations and characterizations in Industry 4.0 remains missing but could be of interest for practitioners and researchers of data spaces in Industry 4.0. To date, such an overview is not present by previous literature. A taxonomy will reduce the complexity of the market, structure knowledge, and support both theoretical development and practical applications within a particular business sector [14, 15]. We pose the following research question (RQ): *What are common characteristics and dimensions among data spaces in an Industry 4.0 context?*

2 Methodology and Data Collection for This Short Paper

For this short paper, we make use of the structured approach to taxonomy development originally introduced by Nickerson et al. [14]. The procedure is suitable for sorting a specific field and carving out characterizations and similarities. As a first step, we determine the meta-characteristic of our taxonomy [15]. We define the meta-characteristic of our objects as "documented data spaces designed for an Industry 4.0 context from the perspective of its intended stakeholders." In the second part, we define to follow six objective and all subjective ending conditions as proposed by Nickerson et al. [14]. We make use of three iterations, one conceptual-to-empirical (C2E) approach, and two empirical-to-conceptual (E2C) approaches. And started with a C2E approach to receive a preliminary taxonomic structure that served as a suitable ignition for orientation. For this, we make use of specific literature on data spaces and the Industry 4.0 context [7, 10]. Our first taxonomy contained data space generic and Industry 4.0 specific dimensions and characteristics, like "Underlying Framework" or "Application Area", without sorting any objects. To receive a meaningful list of data spaces in the Industry 4.0 context for the E2C iterations, we make use of two main data sources: (1) a publicly available dataset on use cases and data spaces in Industry 4.0, which was published within a third-party-funded project context in the Gaia-X universe [16] and (2) the Data Spaces Radar Version 4 from March 2024 [17]. We searched both data sources for data spaces with a clear context and purpose for Industry 4.0. As a result, we collected and received a set of 19 objects to classify. Within two consecutive E2C iterations, we sorted the identified data space into the taxonomic structure that we received from our first C2E iteration and refined it. We selected three data spaces (n = 3) for the first E2C iteration to check the robustness of the preliminary structure derived from the first iteration. We continued the taxonomic process since it violates several ending conditions. Then, in the second E2C iteration, we sorted the remaining 16 (n = 16) data spaces into the taxonomy. The E2C iterations were conducted in a manner that more dimensions and characteristics could be identified, merged, or added after screening more and more data spaces that were investigated. To receive meaningful information about the dimensions and characteristics, we read white papers, scientific papers, project homepages, and/or case study reports about the respective data spaces, and constantly discussed the results for appropriateness. After these three iterations, we identified that the taxonomy met all objective and subjective ending conditions as chosen before. Figure 1 depicted our research process described.

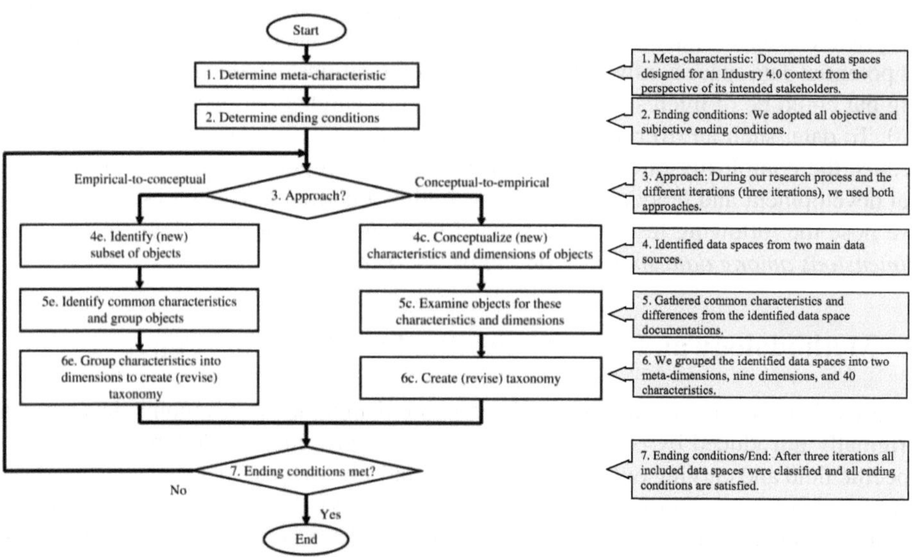

Fig. 1. Research Process

We developed an online appendix, where the taxonomy, a check of the subjective and objective ending conditions, definitions for each dimension, and data spaces are documented. It can be found here[1] to provide transparency for the reader since the iterations were briefly documented within this short paper, based on page restrictions. The final taxonomy is presented in Fig. 2. Numbers in brackets indicate the number of occurrences identified in the 19 data spaces in the Industry 4.0 context. Bold characteristics represent the most observed occurrence among a dimension.

3 Results Observed from the Taxonomy and Discussions

To answer our RQ in this short paper, "What are common characteristics and dimensions among data spaces in an Industry 4.0 context?" we can make several observations from our taxonomy: First, we identified nine **dimensions** among 40 distinct *characteristics*. We sorted the nine dimensions into two meta-dimensions, namely, an economic and technical one. This delimitation allows interpreting the data spaces in different directions through their characteristics as identified.

Economic aspects. Generally, we identified five economic dimensions that characterize the analyzed data spaces in Industry 4.0. We found a clear tendency in *publicly-funded* Industry 4.0 data spaces, e.g., Manufacturing-X (n = 18). Also, most of them have a mainly *economic* **value proposition**, e.g., CollMi (n = 13). The **key purposes** of the data spaces are quite diverse, including *predictive maintenance, manufacturing optimization*, and *supply chain optimization*; however, we found a small tendency (n = 5) for *multiple* key purposes, e.g., Boost 4.0. Only six data spaces (n = 6) explicitly mention that they are currently *operational* in the real world (dimension: **real-world operation**) based on our observations, e.g., FLEX4RES, while some are purely *conceptual*, e.g., CoLoDaS (n = 6) or have an *unknown* status, e.g., Pressious Data Space (n = 7).

Various **delivery channels**, i.e., *software solutions*, of the data spaces are used. Here, we observe different solutions like *applications*, i.e., Metal Domain Data Space (n = 1), *portals*, i.e., Sm4rtenance (n = 1), and *platforms*, e.g., DV4CUL (6), while the majority do *not explicitly mention* their delivery channel, e.g., Manuspace (n = 7). We refrain here from the term "data space connector" (for an overview of definitions see Gieß et al. [7]) since we interpreted the documentation more like a delivery channel "only" on how to carry the data space service, e.g., through a software frontend, to the participants without explaining technical details and backend functionalities. *Economic* benefits are the most frequently cited, e.g., UCIMU (n = 13), but combinations like *economic + environmental value*, e.g., e-CMR Hub (n = 2) are also present. Our observed **value propositions** are somewhat in line with the already discussed one by Möller et al. [3].

Technical aspects. We found four technical dimensions in our corpus of data spaces in Industry 4.0 that are of particular interest. Data space access is mainly based on *membership/project participation* within the dimension of **data space access**, e.g., GlobShare (18). In contrast to Gieß et al. [8], we did not find any *fee access model* (n = 0) showing a "structural hole" in our taxonomy. Also, we did not observe any pricing models. This is somewhat in line with difficulties of data value assessment or the distinction between

[1] https://osf.io/ruzg4/overview?view_only=8c50397946a042219d3ee0616bd9a2c9.

		Dimension	Characteristics			
Meta Dimension	Economic	Funding	**Public (18)**	Public + Private (1)		
		Key Purpose	(Predictive) Maintenance (4)	Optimized Manufacturing (2)	E-Signature (1)	Optimization (Supply Chain) (1)
			Data Sharing / Data Exchange (3)	Monitoring (3)	**Multiple (5)**	
		Real-World Operation	Yes (6)	No, Conceptual (6)	**Unknown (7)**	
		Delivery Channel	Application(s) (1)	Portal (1)	Platform (6)	
			Online Marketplace (1)	Multiple (3)	**Not Explicitly Mentioned (7)**	
		Value Proposition	Environmental (2)	**Economic (13)**	Economic + Environmental (2)	
			Economic + Environmental + New Business Model (1)	Unclear (1)		
	Technical	Data Space Access	**Membership / Project Participation (18)**	Fee (0)	Unknown (1)	
		Underlying Model	**IDS Reference Architecture Model (18)**	Not Explicitly Mentioned (1)		
		Data Type Shared	Repository Data (2)	Resilience Data (1)	Process Control Data (3)	
			Historical Data (1)	**Not Specified (12)**		
		Technical Enabler	Artificial Intelligence (4)	Blockchain (1)	Digital Twin (2)	Big Data Analytics (1)
			Data Space (1)	Multiple (2)	**Not Explicitly Mentioned (8)**	

Fig. 2. Taxonomy of Data Spaces in Industry 4.0 (n = 19)

data spaces and so-called data marketplaces, which are intended to help companies trade data and data assets, as identified by previous literature [18, 19]. As a result, we see this issue as suggestion for further research in terms of data spaces in Industry 4.0. The *IDS Reference Architecture Model* is the predominant **underlying model**, e.g., within the data space Underpin (mentioned 18 times). This observation is not surprising since the majority of investigated data spaces in Industry 4.0 are dedicated to the standards provided by the International Data Space Organization.

Various **data types** that are shared and processed in the corresponding data spaces were found. Here, we observed data types such as *historical data*, i.e., Pressious Data Space (n = 1) and *process control data*, e.g., UCIMU (n = 3), though "*Not Specified*" appears most frequently, e.g., OSME (12 times), indicating no further information on the processed data. This fuzziness is somewhat surprising since data space participants should be aware of what data types can be shared in a data space. However, our taxonomy shows a smaller step towards clarity on data types than the two characteristics for the same dimension examined by Gieß et al. [8]. Data spaces investigated articulated (further) **technical enablers** that are used within the space. Commonly cited technologies include *artificial intelligence*, e.g., Underpin (n = 4), *blockchain*, i.e., CollMi (n = 1), and *big data analytics*, i.e., Boost 4.0 (n = 1). "*Not Explicitly Mentioned*" appears most frequently, e.g., CoLoDaS (8 times). Also, we found one data space that named the *data space itself* as an enabler, i.e., the Metal Domain Data Space (n = 1). As a result, we identified a diverse mix of technological enablers without any explicit tendency.

Discussions and first contributions. As a theoretical contribution from this short paper, currently, data space or data ecosystem researchers in general and Industry 4.0 researchers in particular, interested in the dimensions and characterizations, can use the taxonomy to receive an initial look at this phenomenon. An overview of data spaces in Industry 4.0 remains missing with this short paper we close the call for further investigations on the fragmentation of the data space market in this particular sector [3].

In this short paper, we make use of the process of taxonomy development by Nickerson et al. [14]. As an implication for research, we can conclude that the process was suitable to some extent to provide meaningful dimensions and characteristics in the context of data spaces and Industry 4.0. However, most problems came up with the diverse quality and depth of information provided by the data spaces, resulting in characteristics like "Not Explicitly Mentioned" or "Unclear" which are sometimes the most common ones inside the dimensions provided. We were able to achieve mutually exclusiveness within the dimensions and characteristics provided by adding a "multiple" characteristic to some dimensions. For example, the value proposition provided by the usage of the data pace was mentioned in a fuzzy way by the data spaces and within the documents. Economic values were proposed with no concrete measurement. Therefore, no further refinement through more explicit characteristics was possible. As a limitation, validity of the taxonomy is somewhat restricted based on the information found and further interpreted.

Also, it was surprisingly difficult to verify if a data space was productive in an industry environment or not, by the documentation of the data space provided. Here, as an implication for data space providers, we argue that a clearer and more standardized communication of use cases and values, e.g., economic ones are necessary for outreach and external communication.

Taxonomies order the complexity and serve as a foundation that can lead to future research and serve as a nomenclature on a specific phenomenon [14]. Therefore, IS researchers can use the taxonomy provided as inspiration for their research inquiries and clearer classification of data spaces in Industry 4.0. Practitioners, like small and medium enterprises in Industry 4.0, can use this taxonomy as a general and initial background for discussing patterns and similarities of data spaces to participate in them (or not) with data space providers or other sector representatives.

4 Next Steps and Conclusions

We plan to conduct the following next research steps towards ICSOB and for the ultimate goal of a journal article: First, our objects were chosen from two databases, and the data space market is constantly changing. For some data spaces mentioned in the two databases, no information was available anymore. An update of possibly more data spaces that will emerge is necessary. As the topic of data spaces is a vital research field, we will first revise the taxonomy based on completeness and potential new knowledge for dimensions and characteristics from recent literature [20] after the conference in November 2025, since the taxonomy provided in this short paper was developed in July 2025.

Second, as Design Science Research artefacts [14], taxonomies should be further evaluated in terms of their completeness and appropriateness for their intended purposes as solution-building instruments [15]. Examined classifications, e.g., through clustering techniques, can lead to higher theorizing, and will allow us to provide a more unified view of the data space context in Industry 4.0 [3, 21]. We expect that classifications and provided clusters would carve out interrelations and connections between services bundles within data space. This will show a more nuanced overview on the data spaces market and what is currently offered to interested participants in Industry 4.0. Here, we will recent developments on adequate clustering methods designed for taxonomy data [22] and suggestions for taxonomy evaluation, e.g., through interviews with data space providers [15].

Third, with this more comprehensive overview and clusters of other data space researchers will have a foundation for stronger theoretical contributions to the conceptualization of data spaces toward a taxonomic theory. This theory is useful in developing testable propositions and relationships between dimensions and characteristics provided, researching the phenomenon towards a theory for analysis. It will equip IS researchers to describe novel Information Technology-related phenomena with eloquent knowledge [21, 23]. To the best of our knowledge, such an investigation and proposition of a taxonomic theory has not been conducted so far for data spaces. Our package of planned research outputs will be contributed to a subsequent journal article.

Acknowledgments and Use of Generative AI. This research was conducted within the project URANOS-X. It was funded by the Federal Ministry of Education and Research of Germany under the subsidy indicator 02J21D001. The authors would like to thank all people involved who provided feedback on the manuscript in subsequent discussions. We used Generative AI for proofreading some parts of the manuscript.

References

1. Lasi, H., Fettke, P., Kemper, H.-G., Feld, T., Hoffmann, M.: Industry 4.0. Bus. Inf. Syst. Eng. **6**, 239–242 (2014)
2. Leckel, A., Linnartz, M.: Towards the internet of production—How to increase data sharing for successful supply chain collaboration. J. Prod. Syst. Logist. (2023)
3. Möller, F., Jussen, I., Springer, V., Gieß, A., Schweihoff, J.C., Gelhaar, J., Guggenberger, T., Otto, B.: Industrial data ecosystems and data spaces. Electron Mark. **34** (2024)
4. Otto, B., ten Hompel, M., Wrobel, S.: Designing data spaces. Springer International Publishing, Cham (2022)
5. Contreras, J.D., Garcia, J.I., Diaz, J.D.: Developing of Industry 4.0 applications. Int. J. Onl. Eng. **13**, 30–47 (2017)
6. Czvetkó, T., Abonyi, J.: Data sharing in industry 4.0–AutomationML, B2MML and international data spaces-based solutions. J. Ind. Inf. Integr. **33**, 100438 (2023)
7. Gieß, A., Hupperz, M., Schoormann, T., Möller, F.: What does it take to connect? Unveiling characteristics of data space connectors proceedings of the 57th Hawaii international conference on system sciences (2024)
8. Gieß, A., Möller, F., Schoormann, T., Otto, B.: Design options for data spaces proceedings of the 31st European conference on information systems (2023)
9. Weking, J., Hein, A., Böhm, M., Krcmar, H.: A hierarchical taxonomy of business model patterns. Electron Markets **30**, 447–468 (2020)
10. Azkan, C., Iggena, L., Gür, I., Möller, F., Otto, B.: A taxonomy for data-driven services in manufacturing industries proceedings of the 24th Pacific Asia conference on information systems (2020)

11. Dumitrescu, R., Riedel, O., Henke, M., Metternich, J., Ihlenfeldt, S., Koldewey, C.: Gaia-X in industriellen Wertschöpfungsnetzwerken—Erkenntnisse aus der Förderlinie InGAIA-X. VDI Verlag (2025)
12. Dorkaev, E., Werth, O., Uslar, M.: MAMOGI–A maturity model towards Gaia-X conformity in industry 4.0 proceedings of the 31st Americas conference on information systems (2025)
13. Lick, J., Lamarz, J., Dohmann, F., Kulkarni, J.P., Zerbin, J., Koldewey, C.: Guidance on dataspaces: development of a learning environment for industrial SMEs. In: Proceedings of the 6th international conference on control and robotics (ICCR), pp. 348–354. IEEE (2024)
14. Nickerson, R.C., Varshney, U., Muntermann, J.: A method for taxonomy development and its application in information systems. Eur. J. Inf. Syst. **22**, 336–359 (2013)
15. Kundisch, D., et al.: An update for taxonomy designers. Bus. Inf. Syst. Eng. **64**, 421–439 (2022)
16. Hilger, T., Schütz, J.: Data preparation on state-of-the-art and progress of European Gaia-X and data space initiatives with a focus on Industry 4.0 use cases (v1.0.0). Zenodo (2024)
17. International data space association: the data spaces radar version 4–Data spaces support centre edition (2024), https://internationaldataspaces.org/wp-content/uploads/dlm_uploads/The-Data-Spaces-Radar-Version-4.pdf
18. Werling, M., Stuber, K., Petrik, D., Lachenmaier, J., Herzwurm, G.: Enabling Inter-organizational data sharing: towards a method for assessing data assets. In: Papatheocharous, E., Farshidi, S., Jansen, S., Hyrynsalmi, S. (eds.) Software business. Lecture Notes in business information processing, vol. 539, pp. 89–96. Springer Nature Switzerland, Cham (2025)
19. Jussen, I., Möller, F., Schweihoff, J., Gieß, A., Giussani, G., Otto, B.: Issues in inter-organizational data sharing: Findings from practice and research challenges. Data Knowl. Eng. **150**, 102280 (2024)
20. Brechtel, M.: From hesitation to participation in industrial data ecosystems: analysis of motives and incentives in the automotive industry. Electron Mark. **35** (2025)
21. Gregor.: The nature of theory in information systems. MIS Q. **30**, 611–642 (2006)
22. Heumann, M., Kraschewski, T., Werth, O., Breitner, M.H.: Reassessing taxonomy-based data clustering: unveiling insights and guidelines for application. Decis. Support. Syst. **187**, 114344 (2024)
23. Baier, M.-S., Berger, S., Kreuzer, T., Oberländer, A.M., Röglinger, M.: What makes digital technology? A categorization based on purpose. CAIS. 52, 332–384 (2023)

What Are Digital Identities in Practice? Initial Insight from Finnish B2B Software Companies

Eerika Peltonen(✉), Sonja M. Hyrynsalmi, and Kari Smolander

LUT University, Lappeenranta, Finland
{eerika.peltonen,sonja.hyrynsalmi,kari.smolander}@lut.fi

Abstract. Digital identities are implemented and used in software products increasingly. They allow businesses to perform a variety of tasks, including managing customer relationships or performing financial management activities. Software companies that offer software-as-a-service products must take growing amount of stakeholder needs and regulatory developments into consideration when implementing or using digital identities in their products. This research paper presents the initial findings of a qualitative interview study conducted in two software companies in Finland. Both companies offer business-to-business products with a strong role of digital identities. The research goal was to understand the identity provider and software product company perspective on digital identities. This goal was achieved by presenting initial results on the use of the term of digital identity in practice, identify relevant stakeholder priorities, and present both disruptors and accelerators to match these priorities. Some identified stakeholder priorities include security, communication and user experience. Accelerators for matching these include company strategies and communication while disruptors include security concerns and unknown regulative requirements. Research data was collected during Summer 2025 followed by thematic analysis.

Keywords: Digital Identity · Software Product Company · Identity Provider · B2B

1 Introduction

People all around the world have different identities in different scopes. One can have different identity when they are at work, and different identity, or multiple, when they are at home with their family [1]. Due to the rapidly digitalizing world, there simultaneously exists a digital identity, more or less connected to our real world identity [1]. The use of these digital identities extends both on individual level as well as business level. Individuals can use them for healthcare, traveling and e-government. In business context, digital identities can be used for various activities, such as maintaining customer relations or recording working hours.

This worldwide change to digital has caused concerns for the digital identity and its management, such as security, privacy, usability and trust [1]. New technologies to keep digital identities safe are developed while new regulations and laws are set to help

G. Herzwurm et al. (Eds.): ICSOB 2025, LNBIP 574, pp. 32–40, 2026.
https://doi.org/10.1007/978-3-032-14518-5_4

address digital identity concerns. Among other entities, identity providers and software companies share the responsibility of fair and legitimate use of digital identities, while also navigating through the concerns, stakeholder needs and upcoming changes in the identity field.

The aim of this paper is to understand digital identity from the identity provider and software product company perspective. The main research question of this paper is "*How does digital identity appear in a software company setting?*" while the sub questions of this paper include "*How is digital identity as a term understood inside software companies?*" as well as "*From company perspective, what are the priorities of each stakeholder for digital identities?*" and "*What are the current disruptors and accelerators for digital identity related activities in software companies?*". The study in this paper was made in collaboration with two Finnish software companies that offer business-to-business software solutions. Research data was collected through qualitative interviews with people who work in product management, security or as advisors. Collected data was thematically analyzed. Initial findings include understanding the use of term "digital identity" in company setting, identifying digital identity related priorities for stakeholders, and identifying disruptors and accelerators that either slow down or speed up the company's ability to match these digital identity related priorities.

The remainder of this paper is structured as follows: Sect. 2 provides background on the related concepts while Sect. 3 outlines the methodology used in this research. Section 4 presents the initial findings, followed by related discussion in Sect. 5. Finally, Sect. 6 concludes the paper.

2 Background

Digital identity attributes and credentials can include things such as name, age, an identity number, ID cards, certificates and number sequences [2]. This information can then be used in digital identification process, which consists of three stages to identify, authenticate and authorize a person. Identification refers to the process of establishing digital identifier, which can be alphanumeric string or biometric information [3]. Authentication refers to the process of determining if the user is who they have identified themselves as, while authorization is the mapping of different user identities to organizational policies so that user's access to is regulated [3].

On the regulatory side, one of the biggest current changes for digital identities on European Union (EU) level is the newest instalment of the regulation on electronic identification and trust services. This regulation proposes the concept of European Digital Wallet [4]. The purpose of this wallet is to offer EU-wide access to for citizens and businesses of EU Member States to their national identity as well as proof of other personal attributes, such as diplomas or driving licenses [4].

Stakeholders related to digital identities from the company perspective are presented in Fig. 1. These include customer, software product company, identity provider (IdP), and external stakeholders and regulators. If moving outward from the center of the circle, the first stakeholder is the customer. This refers to the party who buys the product or service from the software company.

The next stakeholder, a software product company, is responsible for offering products for other businesses to improve or accelerate their operations. This research will be

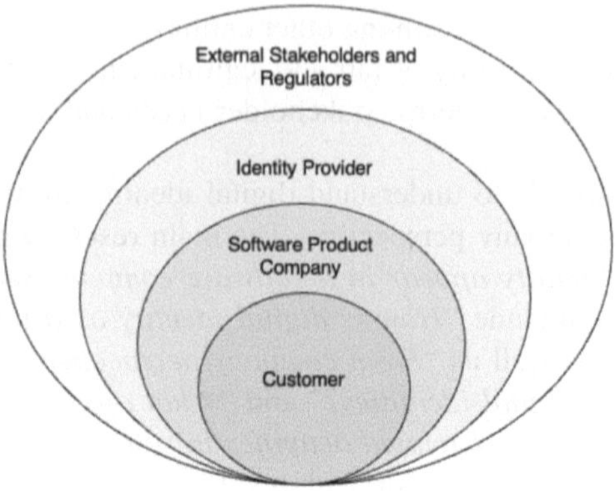

Fig. 1. Stakeholders related to digital identity in business-to-business software context

focusing on business-to-business (B2B) software product company offering software-as-a-service financial management product. The third stakeholder, an identity provider, supplies identities to subjects and have four essential responsibilities of generating, assigning, binding and arranging identity attributes [2]. Lastly, regulators can include national regulators that make sure that the product is compliant with the current regulations and laws while external stakeholders can refer to different institutions or unions that overlook related activities.

3 Methodology

3.1 Data Collection

Research data for this paper was collected through semi-structured interviews. Semi-structured interview refers to a type of an interview where questions are planned beforehand but are not necessarily asked in the same order [5]. Interviews, with a conversation approach [6], were chosen as an approach as it allows to explore personal experiences and collect rich data. In the conversation interview approach, the interview is viewed as a conversation and is seen as to construct meaning rather than confirmation of facts [6]. All interviews were held in Finnish and both recorded and transcribed. After each interview, a Finnish transcript was generated and anonymized. Then, the transcript was translated to English and language match was checked. English translation was created since the research findings will be reported in English. Therefore, analysis and reporting will be easier with English transcripts. Location-wise, two of the interviews were held on premise, four remotely. Interviews lasted 60 to 90 min. In Table 1, background information about interviewees can be observed, including their roles and location between the two companies. Interviewees were recruited through an external contact, who passed on the email information of the interviewees to be contacted after inquiring them of their interest.

As can be observed from Table 1, the interviewees have varying roles. Some work more on the product side while some emphasize more security or business. Five of the interviewees work in the software product company (Company 1) and one interviewee

Table 1. Roles and companies of interviewees

Company	ID	Role
1	1	Senior advisor
1	2	Product manager
1	3	Information security and data privacy director
1	4	Product manager and portfolio lead
1	5	Business specialist
2	6	Product manager

work on the external identity provider side (Company 2). All interviewees were informed of anonymity of the data and consent at the beginning of interviews, and they were given a detailed description of the research project and its purposes before the interview.

3.2 Analysis

We followed the practical guide of thematic analysis created by Braun and Clarke [7]. The thematic analysis includes six major phases: (1) Familiarizing yourself with data, (2) Coding, (3) Generating Initial themes, (4) Developing and reviewing themes, (5) Refining, defining and naming themes, and (6) Writing up [7]. The first phase consisted of immersing oneself with the data through listening and (re-) reading the recordings and transcripts of interviews. In this phase, for each interview, general notes on analytic ideas and insight were written. The second step, coding, done only by the researcher herself, included inductive approach to go through the dataset and identify segments that could be interesting and labeling them. Next, the initial themes were generated by outlining of the end results through a mind map, including themes such as the "difficulty of the term", "challenges", "opportunities". These initial themes were then developed further in the fourth step. Fifth step included returning to the dataset and making further developments and adjustments while also collecting suitable quotes to be included as part of the results. The sixth phase of writing concludes in this research paper.

4 Digital Identities in a Software Company Setting

4.1 Use of the Term

When a user of a work-related software product logs in, they are often identified through their identity as an employee. The information for the identification and authentication activities can include things such as work credentials, an employee number, and even biometrics. As Interviewee 4 expressed on the use of digital identity:

> "Digital identities, are they based on things that can be cracked with raw computing power, or does it have to be something that I also own?"

To answer the first sub research question of the research "*How is digital identity as a term understood inside software companies?*", inside software companies, people often refer to more specific activities related digital identities instead of using the term "digital identity" itself. As highlighted by Interviewee 6 on the matter:

> "We haven't really talked about digital identities. It goes to the level of concreteness quite often. We talk about authentication, login, user roles, rights and more."

These all are components connected to digital identity. This way of using digital identity in the company setting makes it appear very much like a practical concept.

4.2 Stakeholder Priorities

Different stakeholders related to digital identities from the software company perspective were presented in Fig. 1. To answer the second sub research question of this research "*From company perspective, what are the priorities of each stakeholder for digital identities?*" key stakeholder priorities for each digital identity related stakeholder are presented in Fig. 2.

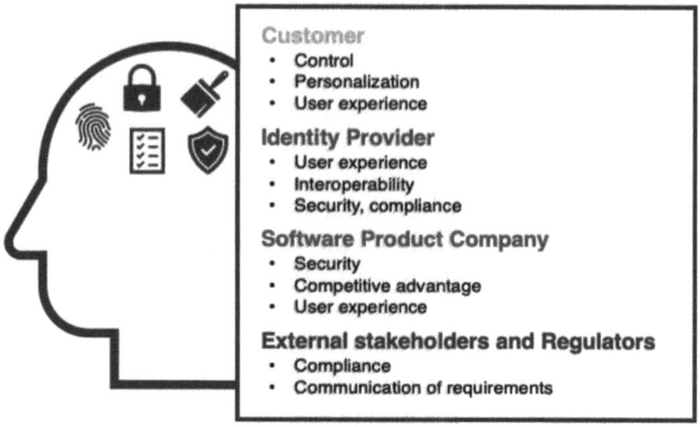

Fig. 2. Stakeholder priorities related to digital identities

Customer priorities include the control over their own identity, meaning that the user can choose what information they want to share. Another customer priority is personalization. This can refer to using certain digital identity type to log into the system or choosing background color or the theme for the system. As said by Interviewee 6:

> "I'm thinking that the trend is personalization. You want the product to feel like your own."

The third and the last priority for the customers is the user experience. For customers, it is important that they have good experience when using the system. One of the priorities for **Identity Provider** is also user experience. As highlighted by Interviewee 6 on the user experience:

> "We want to make it as easy as possible for the user to log in or create an account. It actually starts from the user's need."

Closely related to the use of different identity types is interoperability, which refers to the ability to use one digital identity type across different systems. Lastly, security and compliance are important priorities for identity providers. As Interviewee 6 stated:

> "Starting to support a standard is a matter of examining quite carefully what you are going to support in the first place. It can't be just anything."

To ensure interoperability, security and compliance, technological standards related to different identity types must be examined carefully and any regulative requirements must be followed. **Software Product Company** follows similar priorities with the identity provider. In a software product company, there is constant seeking for balance between the security measures and the user experience. As described by Interviewee 3 on the balance of security, regulations and user experience:

> "Often, it alone poses challenges to understand what the right requirements are, which ones come from legislation, which ones come from customers, which ones are internal requirements, and to ensure that all those requirements are met in a way that is not too difficult for the user."

On top of security and user experience, competitive advantage is one of the priorities. However, as expressed by Interviewee 2 in relation to competitive advantage:

> "Competitive advantage must not be sought from taking a shortcut in the requirements of information security or by shortening some process."

This highlights the importance between the security and competitive advantage. Lastly, for **External Stakeholders and Regulators**, compliance and communication are the key priorities. Regulators and other external stakeholders have the responsibility to oversee the regulative aspects and other requirements. Both parties are also responsible for communicating them to all relevant parties.

4.3 Disruptors and Accelerators for Matching the Priorities

To answer the third and last sub research question of this paper "*What are the current disruptors and accelerators for digital identity related activities in software companies?*", identified disruptors and accelerators are presented in Fig. 3. Disruptors refer to aspects that slow down the ability to match the priorities of stakeholders. Identified disruptors include security concerns, interoperability issues, unknown regulative requirements and lack of standardization.

Accelerators speed up the ability or processes to match the priorities. Identified accelerators for matching digital identity related priorities include emphasis on user experience and ease of use, company strategies for security and use of identities, and collaboration with stakeholders.

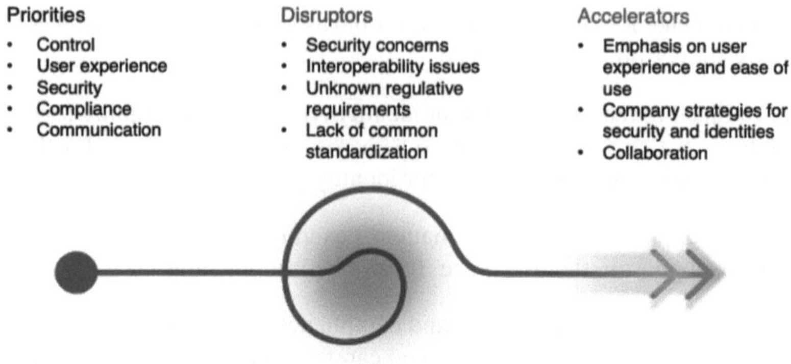

Fig. 3. Disruptors and accelerators for matching stakeholder priorities

5 Discussion

5.1 Interpretation of Results

As was identified in this research, the use of the term "digital identity" is not common in the software company setting. Instead, more practical terms related to digital identity are used, such as authentication or logging in. As identified in [8], digital identity is used as a proxy for single sign-on, also known as SSO. Therefore, confusion can be detected when using the terms "digital identity" or "identity" itself. As what to comes to the multifaceted aspect of identity in this research, people in general have multiple identities, some lasting throughout person's life and some just for limited time [1]. Every identity a person has, there are corresponding identifiers for each [1].

Next, user experience was identified spawning over multiple stakeholders as one of their priorities (Fig. 2), including customer, identity provider and software product company. This user-centricity of systems has been at the center of previous research. For example, when co-creating user requirements for digital identity enabled platforms users identify aspects such as efficiency of the identification process, usability and interoperability as important [9].

Lastly, security and privacy are one of the overarching themes in the initial findings. Previous research shows strong social contract between the supplier and buyer, and that data breaches cause negative effects on trust and dissatisfaction of customers [10]. Identified also in [9], security is one of the concerns of the users towards the identity management platforms. The previous research further emphasizes the importance of security.

5.2 Implications

This research draws attention towards software companies and presents initial findings. Different stakeholders and their priorities around the digital identity field and priorities for each are identified. Furthermore, disruptors and accelerators are for matching these priorities are identified. Future research will include governmental actors and other relevant entities in the digital identity field.

5.3 Limitations

The limitations include the number of interviewees, which in this case includes six individuals. Despite that, we believe that the current results already provide important insight to those that integrate digital identities into software products. Research in that area is rare and therefore new insights are needed.

6 Conclusions

This research sheds initial light on the software company perspective on digital identities through interviews with two Finnish software companies. Thematic analysis was utilized to understand the use of "digital identity" in software companies and identifying relevant stakeholders and their key priorities. These include compliance, user experience, security and communication. To understand the company's ability to match these priorities, disruptors and accelerators were identified. Some of the disruptors include interoperability issues and security concerns while accelerators include company strategies and collaboration. Future research aims to expand on these initial findings, by including more stakeholders in the identity field in Finland, such as governmental actors.

Acknowledgments. This work has been supported by FAST, the Finnish Software Engineering Doctoral Research Network, funded by the Ministry of Education and Culture, Finland. We also thank all interviewees for making this research possible.

References

1. Alpár, G., Hoepman, J.-H., Siljee, J.: The identity crisis security, privacy and usability issues in identity management. J. Inf. Syst. Secur. **9**(1), 23–53 (2013). https://doi.org/10.48550/arXiv.1101.0427
2. Natarajan, H., Appaya, M.S., Balasubramanian, S.: Digital Identity Onboarding (2018)
3. Mueller, M.L., Park, Y., Lee, J., Kim, T.-Y.: Digital identity: how users value the attributes of online identifiers. Inf. Econ. Policy **18**(4), 405–422 (2006). https://doi.org/10.1016/j.infoecopol.2006.04.002
4. European Commission: European Digital Identity (EUDI) Regulation. https://digital-strategy.ec.europa.eu/en/policies/eudi-regulation. Last accessed 19 July 2024
5. Runeson, P., Höst, M.: Guidelines for conducting and reporting case study research in software engineering. Empir. Softw. Eng. **14**(2), 131–164 (2009). https://doi.org/10.1007/s10664-008-9102-8
6. Schultze, U., Avital, M.: Designing interviews to generate rich data for information systems research. Inf. Organ. **21**(1), 1–16 (2011). https://doi.org/10.1016/j.infoandorg.2010.11.001
7. Braun, V., Clarke, V.: Thematic Analysis: A Practical Guide. SAGE Publications, London (2022)
8. Grayson, T.R.D.: Philosophy of Identity. https://timothygrayson.com/PDFs/PhilosophyOfIdentity.pdf. Last accessed 18 Nov 2024

9. Bakhaev, S., Naqvi, B., Wolff, A., Smolander, K.: Co-creating requirements for the emerging electronic identity management platform. In: 14th Scandinavian Conference on Information Systems, pp. 1–15. AIS, Porvoo, Finland (2023). https://aisel.aisnet.org/scis2023/1
10. Swani, K., Labrecque, L., Markos, E.: Are B2B data breaches concerning? Consequences of buyer's or firm's data loss on buyer and supplier related outcomes. Ind. Mark. Manage. **119**, 43–61 (2024). https://doi.org/10.1016/j.indmarman.2024.03.007

Engineering Data Architectures for AI/ML Integration in Regulated Manufacturing

Viktoriia Shubina[1](✉), Tuomas Ranti[1], Anne Juppo[2], and Tuomas Mäkilä[1]

[1] Department of Computing, University of Turku, 20014 Turku, Finland
{viktoriia.shubina,tuomas.ranti,tuomas.makila}@utu.fi
[2] Division of Pharmaceutical Chemistry and Technology, University of Helsinki, 00014 Helsinki, Finland
anne.juppo@helsinki.fi

Abstract. Life science, i.e. pharmaceutical and medical device, manufacturers are increasingly exploring artificial intelligence (AI) and Machine Learning (ML) to enhance production quality and regulatory compliance. However, current data handling practices result in data fragmentation, and complex regulatory requirements present barriers to wide implementation. In this study, we conducted 20 qualitative interviews with data architects, AI specialists, and regulatory compliance officers. Our aim was to get a better understanding of the current state of the field, challenges and future outlook in regulated manufacturing, employing the Gioia methodology. Our findings highlight data silos and legacy infrastructures as primary technical barriers, while evolving regulatory frameworks and uncertainties in AI validation create significant compliance challenges. Interviewees emphasized the necessity of unified data architectures and platforms, embedded governance mechanisms, enhanced security, and proactive regulatory operations (RegOps) to enable both innovation and compliance. Based on the interview results, we propose a conceptual framework to guide the design of AI-driven data architectures that bridge fragmented systems and support compliant AI/ML lifecycle management. This study is the first phase of research efforts aiming to implement and validate AI/ML solutions grounded in industry needs.

Keywords: AI adoption · data architecture · regulated manufacturing · Gioia method

1 Introduction

Artificial Intelligence (AI) and Machine Learning (ML) are increasingly recognized as transformative technologies in regulated manufacturing sectors, including pharmaceuticals and medical devices manufacturing [1]. However, their adoption introduces a dual imperative for the life science manufacturing industry. While AI/ML enable strategic advancements in automation, prediction, and

G. Herzwurm et al. (Eds.): ICSOB 2025, LNBIP 574, pp. 41–57, 2026.
https://doi.org/10.1007/978-3-032-14518-5_5

decision support, they also impose significant challenges related to regulatory compliance, particularly concerning system integration, validation, and traceability [2].

The life-science sector is undergoing a profound transformation, as advances in automation and AI/ML reshape research, development, and manufacturing practices across biological domains [3]. Real-world implementation of AI/ML in these settings requires data architectures capable of supporting end-to-end traceability, robust validation, and secure data flow across fragmented and often legacy infrastructures. These environments are typically characterized by data silos, manual processes, and limited interoperability. All conditions that constrain scalable and compliant AI/ML deployment. Designing such architectures requires harmonization of real-time data processing with regulatory demands for auditability, involving careful orchestration of metadata management, interface design, and validation workflows in alignment with Good Practice (GxP) standards.

GxP standards is an umbrella term encompassing regulatory guidelines such as Good Manufacturing Practice (GMP), Good Laboratory Practice (GLP), and Good Clinical Practice (GCP), among others [4]. These frameworks define the principles and procedures necessary to ensure that products in life science sectors are consistently produced, tested, and monitored to the required quality, safety, and efficacy. In the context of data-driven systems, GxP compliance extends beyond physical manufacturing to include rigorous controls over data integrity, traceability, and reproducibility. This necessitates that AI/ML-enabled architectures embed compliance considerations into every stage of the data lifecycle, from acquisition and preprocessing to model deployment and monitoring, ensuring that digital processes meet the same evidentiary and auditability standards as traditional operations.

While the theoretical dimensions of AI explainability, fairness, and validation have received substantial scholarly attention [5], understanding of how these issues are addressed in regulated manufacturing practice remains scarce. In particular, the design and operationalization of compliant data architectures to enable trustworthy and auditable AI/ML systems are underexplored. Recent advances, such as the use of Large Language Models (LLMs) to enhance explainability, offer promising technical pathways [6], yet their applicability in highly regulated domains remains to be systematically investigated. Bridging this gap is essential for advancing AI/ML capabilities in software-intensive systems subject to stringent regulatory oversight.

To investigate these challenges, we conducted a qualitative interview study involving 20 professionals from the pharmaceutical and medical device manufacturing companies, operating in Finland and internationally. Participants were selected based on their expertise in one of three focal domains: data architecture (6 experts), AI/ML applications (6 experts), and regulatory compliance (8 experts). Using the Gioia methodology [7], we systematically analyzed the interview transcripts to construct a grounded theoretical understanding of current practices, obstacles, and emerging trajectories within regulated manufacturing environments.

We organize our study around the following research questions (RQs):

- **RQ1:** What are the current practices and system designs used for data architecture, AI integration, and regulatory compliance in regulated manufacturing?
- **RQ2:** What technical, organizational, and regulatory challenges do regulated manufacturers face in managing data, implementing AI, and maintaining compliance?
- **RQ3:** How do regulated industry professionals envision the future development of data architectures, AI applications, and regulatory practices in their organizations?

This paper makes the three contributions. First, it provides evidence on the technical and regulatory barriers to AI/ML adoption in regulated manufacturing, grounded in 20 expert interviews. Second, it offers overview of the current industry practices. Third, it introduces a conceptual framework for designing AI-driven data architectures that enable compliant AI/ML lifecycle management in regulated industrial contexts.

The remainder of this paper is structured as follows: Sect. 2 reviews related work on AI and data architecture strategies, especially in regulated domains. Section 3 describes our research design and the Gioia coding process. Section 4 presents the results, including the data structure and conceptual framework. Section 5 discusses implications for system design and regulatory innovation. Section 6 concludes with directions for future research.

2 Related Work

The deployment of AI systems within regulated life-science manufacturing environments necessitates the existence of high-quality and well-governed data infrastructures. Fragmented, siloed, or weakly contextualized data continues to represent a major impediment to the large-scale adoption of AI in GxP-regulated domains. Recent industry frameworks underscore the need for unified data platforms that combine technical robustness with conformance to regulatory and validation requirements [8].

A comprehensive analysis of reference architectures for smart manufacturing demonstrates their critical role in establishing interoperability, modularity, and scalability across heterogeneous production systems [9]. The reviewed frameworks formalize layered architectural structures that specify the interactions among physical assets, data acquisition and integration layers, and analytical components within a unified environment. These abstractions underpin the design of GxP-compliant data fabrics, as articulated by NTT DATA, that focus on the consolidation of distributed data sources while ensuring end-to-end traceability, regulatory compliance, and validation integrity across the manufacturing data lifecycle [8].

In parallel, industry bodies such as the International Society for Pharmaceutical Engineering (ISPE) have proposed governance models for AI/ML in GxP environments [10]. They emphasize the connection between AI lifecycle management and regulatory expectations, including risk-based access control, MLOps integration, and documentation readiness.

While algorithmic auditing frameworks offer structured mechanisms for assessing accountability and transparency in AI systems [11], the practical realization of responsible AI governance within regulated industrial environments remains in its early stages. Recent conceptual advances extend these ideas beyond algorithm-level audits toward organization-wide governance structures that integrate ethical, technical, and compliance perspectives [12]. This emerging research emphasizes the need for multidimensional frameworks that align AI lifecycle management with established governance principles and regulatory expectations. Such connection is particularly critical in life-science manufacturing, where AI-driven decision-making directly intersects with product quality, patient safety, and GxP compliance.

Validation is a particularly complex aspect of AI system deployment in life sciences. Traditional validation approaches are often ill-suited to the dynamic and non-deterministic nature of AI models. Emerging strategies, including those from the ISPE AI Maturity Model [13], propose risk-based model based on the control design tailored to AI. Scholars have also begun to distinguish between narrow AI validation (focused on specific tasks) and platform-level validation (covering ML pipelines and tooling) [14]. These strategies are increasingly aligned with recent regulatory initiatives, such as the EU AI Act [15], which introduces tiered risk categories and compliance obligations for AI systems in high-stakes domains.

From a methodological point of view, prior research provides a basis for qualitative research on technological transformation in manufacturing. A study based on 33 semi-structured interviews in incumbent industrial firms developed a dual-mode digital transformation framework that balances exploration and exploitation [16]. Another meta-analysis of 22 manufacturing companies identified a four-dimensional capability model, highlighting strategic, organizational, technical, and process competencies as key determinants of digital maturity [17].

Thus, prior research provides methodological precedents for interview-based studies in complex industrial environments and highlights the value of thematic and comparative analysis in understanding industrial transformation processes. However, empirical understanding on how data architectures are designed and implemented to enable compliant and trustworthy AI in regulated manufacturing remains limited. And this study addresses that gap through a qualitative exploration. The literature review was conducted to establish a conceptual and regulatory foundation, rather than to provide a systematic synthesis, ensuring coherence between the theoretical framework and the empirical focus of the study.

3 Methodology and Research Design

This study adopts a qualitative, exploratory design based on expert interviews to examine the intersection of data architecture, AI and ML integration, and regulatory practices in pharmaceutical and medical device manufacturing. The methodological approach was structured to ensure rigor, transparency, and analytical depth in line with established standards for qualitative research in complex and regulated environments.

Empirical data were collected through semi-structured interviews with 20 experts representing diverse roles and organizational contexts within the life-science manufacturing ecosystem. The sample comprised 6 data architects responsible for digital infrastructure and enterprise data platforms, 6 AI and automation specialists engaged in the design and deployment of ML-based systems, and 8 professionals specializing in regulatory compliance, validation, and quality assurance. Participants were drawn from 6 organizations operating in Finland and internationally, all compliant with related regulatory standards. Their professional experience ranged from 3 to 43 years, providing first-hand insights into both technical and regulatory challenges across varying levels of digital maturity.

Interviews were conducted online between April and June 2025. The protocol was designed to capture detailed accounts of data architecture design, AI/ML integration, and regulatory practices in manufacturing operations. Each session lasted 30–70 min and was recorded with participant consent. The interview guide was developed based on insights from the literature and the practical objectives of the LifeFactFuture research project, financed by Business Finland, ensuring relevance to ongoing initiatives in data-driven transformation and AI adoption within regulated manufacturing. It was subsequently refined through pilot testing to enhance clarity, validity, and alignment with the study's research objectives.

All interviews were transcribed verbatim, anonymized, and stored securely in accordance with ethical and data-protection requirements. The resulting dataset was analyzed systematically using NVivo 15 to identify themes and relationships relevant to data management, validation, and regulatory compliance.

The study employed the Gioia methodology [7], a rigorous inductive approach widely recognized in organizational and technology studies for enabling structured, theory-building research from qualitative data. An illustrative example of the coding process and resulting Gioia structure for RQ1 is provided in Table 1.

First-order codes were generated by adhering to participant language and terminology, capturing grounded concepts and practitioner-centric perspectives. These codes were then systematically organized into second-order themes, reflecting higher-level patterns, processes, and challenges articulated across interviews. Finally, the themes were synthesized into aggregate dimensions, aligning with the study's core research questions regarding data architectural strategies, AI integration, and regulatory compliance mechanisms.

Coding and interpretation were conducted collaboratively by the two researchers from our team to ensure reliability and minimize individual bias.

Table 1. Illustrative Gioia data structure for RQ1: Current practices and system designs in regulated manufacturing.

1st-Order Concepts	2nd-Order Themes	Aggregate Dimensions
Everything must be documented	(Fragmented) data collection practices	**Fragmented digital ecosystem in regulated manufacturing**
Local data storage and in-place analysis	Localized processing and limited data integration	
Building centralized cloud data platform	Emergence of centralized repositories for select data	
Ongoing AI proof-of-concept projects	Early and isolated AI/ML experiments	**Limited and cautious experimentation with new technologies**
Use of ML models in product development	Application of ML for design optimization	

Discrepancies were resolved through discussions, and a codebook was maintained to document analytical decisions and facilitate transparency. Reflexivity was maintained throughout, with regular memoing to capture emerging insights, uncertainties, and researcher positioning.

All participants received written information about the study objectives, data handling procedures, and their rights, and provided informed consent prior to participation. Identifying details were removed during transcription, and findings are reported in aggregate to preserve confidentiality.

4 Results

This section presents the findings of our qualitative study, structured according to the three research questions. The analysis follows a Gioia-informed coding approach, grouping first-order concepts into second-order themes and aggregate dimensions. Each thematic area is supported by illustrative quotations from participants to highlight contextual insights and lived practices within regulated manufacturing environments.

4.1 RQ1: Current Practices and System Designs

Participants described the current state of data architectures and AI usage in regulated manufacturing as fragmented but slowly evolving. Legacy systems and siloed practices dominate, yet early attempts at integration and selective modernization suggest a gradual shift toward more connected infrastructures. Overall, current practices remain compliance-driven and reactive, with limited strategic planning for long-term digital transformation.

Aggregate dimension: Fragmented Digital Ecosystem in Regulated Manufacturing

This dimension illustrates how historical system choices continue to shape digital infrastructures, resulting in parallel data environments with limited interoperability. Participants consistently highlighted fragmentation as a structural rather than temporary issue.

2nd-Order Theme: (Fragmented) Data Collection Practices. Participants described in general their companies' data practices, alongside with challenges as highly fragmented data storage practices, with isolated systems for production, quality, and analytics. Data acquisition remains compartmentalized across Manufacturing Execution System (MES), Laboratory Management System (LIMS), Enterprise Resource Planning (ERP), and equipment-specific systems, resulting in silos that hinder data accessibility and transparency. Moreover, participants emphasized that every step in data handling must be documented, further increasing the complexity of managing dispersed systems. As one Data Architect reported, "*Data siloing, especially in document management, stems from old organizational structures. That's exactly why there's a push to rethink and redesign how things are done*".

2nd-Order Theme: Localized Processing and Limited Data Integration. Many organizations continue to rely on localized, on-premise data processing, with minimal cross-functional integration. Integration efforts are often reactive and project-specific, rather than systematic. One Data Architect Expert explained, "*We have a MES at the core of our production environment–it's essentially the heart of manufacturing operations. In parallel, our laboratories operate with a LIMS, while environmental monitoring systems continuously collect data, such as temperature to ensure that manufacturing conditions remain within acceptable thresholds. Each of these systems stores and processes data locally, primarily for operational monitoring and compliance*".

2nd-Order Theme: Emergence of Centralized Repositories for Select Data. Notably, there is a trend towards the development of centralized repositories–often in the form of data lakes or hybrid cloud platforms: for select, high-priority data streams. However, these are frequently constrained to specific use cases (such as regulatory reporting or AI initiatives), rather than being organization-wide solutions. One interviewee observed, "*The core task of our product management is to build the product structure into our ERP system–this includes the materials needed for manufacturing, the required process operations, and also the production masters compiled from customer-provided documentation*".

Aggregate Dimension: Limited, Cautious Experimentation with New Technologies

Alongside fragmented infrastructures, organizations are beginning to explore AI/ML. However, experimentation tends to remain narrowly scoped and pilot-driven, with projects serving as both technical trials and organizational learning exercises rather than large-scale deployments.

2nd-Order Theme: Early and Isolated AI/ML Experiments. While regulatory frameworks are still evolving, many companies have already initiated pilot projects to explore the potential of AI technologies in regulated manufacturing settings. Reported use cases ranged from predictive maintenance, inventory optimization, and documentation support to regulatory chatbots and coding assistants. Several firms also experimented with AI in product development and testing, molecule screening, and non-GMP applications, while stressing that deployment into GMP-critical processes is not yet a top priority. As one participant noted, these efforts are often tied to preparing underlying data platforms and MLOps practices, laying the groundwork for future integration. Another interviewee observed, "*Earlier this year, we launched an AI proof-of-concept to validate a specific use case and assess whether the expected outcomes can be achieved with AI. At the same time, it's also about maturing the organization towards an AI culture: understanding data quality, risk management, and the potential benefits like cost savings or new services*".

However, one large global company reported initiating a project to implement a digital twin, highlighting the increasing relevance of such technologies in regulated manufacturing. As one Data Architect noted, digital twins offer a valuable opportunity to design data and system architectures from scratch, free from legacy and other constraints. Beyond process simulation, digital twins provide a structured environment for continuous data collection, model validation, and scenario testing, thereby creating a robust foundation for AI integration and lifecycle management. This dual role, as both a mirror of production processes and a controlled space for validating AI-driven insights, positions digital twins as an enabler for compliant and scalable AI adoption in the regulated industries [18].

4.2 RQ2: Challenges in Data Management, AI Implementation, and Compliance

The barriers identified by participants reveal how technical, regulatory, and organizational factors are tightly interwoven. Challenges extend beyond technology to encompass validation practices, compliance demands, and cultural resistance, illustrating the systemic nature of transformation obstacles.

Aggregate Dimension: Systemic Barriers to Digital and AI Transformation

This dimension highlights the intertwined obstacles that collectively slow down the adoption of integrated data architectures and AI. Beyond isolated technical limitations, participants emphasized that regulatory complexity and organizational culture form a reinforcing cycle that constrains innovation.

2nd-Order Theme: Need for Data Standards and Poor Interoperability. Disparate data formats, lack of harmonized taxonomies, and proprietary vendor solutions persist as major obstacles to integrated analytics and AI deployment. Participants pointed out that metadata is often used to address these issues by adding contextual information and supporting integration across systems. Yet, metadata practices are inconsistent and not standardized, which limits their impact. Alongside these technical challenges, interviewees highlighted explainability as a critical concern: many AI models still operate as "black boxes", producing outcomes without sufficient transparency. For regulated industries, this is particularly problematic, as understanding and justifying model decisions is essential for compliance, trust, and acceptance. As one interviewee reflected, "*Machine learning systems are not explainable. They might give you really good results, but you might not be able to understand*". These findings align with broader initiatives in the scientific community that emphasize the need for standardized metadata and data governance frameworks, most notably the FAIR data principles (Findable, Accessible, Interoperable, and Reusable) [19]. Adherence to these principles facilitates data traceability, reuse, and semantic interoperability across organizational and regulatory boundaries. In parallel, the integration of *explainable AI* (XAI) techniques (such as SHAP, LIME, and counterfactual reasoning) has been increasingly recognized as essential for ensuring model transparency, interpretability, and accountability in regulated environments [20]. Together, these approaches establish a foundation for technically robust and governance-aware AI systems that support regulatory compliance and stakeholder trust.

2nd-Order Theme: Burden of Documentation and Validation. Participants cited the weight of documentation and validation processes as a limiting factor in system evolution and AI adoption. Regulatory requirements for comprehensive audit trails, validation protocols, and versioning impose significant overhead. As one AI professional stated, "*Regulations are constantly evolving, and with the new AI Act already being implemented, it's crucial to integrate it into the development process for machine learning systems–something that's still largely missing today*".

Another limiting factor identified by participants is the manual workload associated with regulatory compliance and documentation. In particular, the need to generate, maintain, and verify logs in accordance with strict regulatory standards imposes a significant burden on personnel, often diverting resources away from innovation and system optimization efforts.

2nd-Order Theme: Organizational Resistance and Skills Gaps. Technical transformation is further constrained by cultural resistance and insufficient in-house expertise for regulated environments, particularly in advanced analytics and digital validation. One interviewee noted, "*People aren't using AI at work as much as they should–or could–and the reason might simply be resistance to anything new*".

4.3 RQ3: Future Visions for Data Architecture, AI, and Compliance

Looking ahead, participants described strategic directions that emphasize unification, scalability, and regulatory readiness. Future visions reflect a shift from reactive compliance and isolated pilots toward proactive, systemic planning of data and AI infrastructures.

Aggregate Dimension: Strategic Digital Transformation for Intelligent Manufacturing

This dimension reflects the ambition to transition from fragmented systems to unified, real-time, and intelligent data architectures that can simultaneously deliver operational efficiency and regulatory trustworthiness.

2nd-Order Theme: Aspirations for Unified and Real-Time Data Architectures. There is broad consensus on the value of unified data architectures capable of supporting both real-time and historical analytics. Envisioned systems emphasize modularity, interoperability, and seamless data lineage across all manufacturing functions. One interviewee noted, "*We need some common data architecture, including data definitions. I would even call it common data model*".

2nd-Order Theme: Cloud and Edge Computing as Platforms for Future Growth. Respondents see hybrid cloud and edge architectures as foundational for scalable, secure, and regulatory-compliant operations. This includes deploying AI models at the edge for local inferencing and leveraging cloud services for centralized analytics and model management. As one expert noted, "*Our architecture should evolve in this direction: whatever makes sense to run at the edge, should be at the edge*".

Aggregate Dimension: Building Organizational Readiness for AI-Driven Compliance

Finally, participants emphasized the importance of preparing organizations for continuous regulatory adaptation and AI integration. Beyond technology, this requires evolving compliance strategies, workforce skills, and governance structures.

2nd-Order Theme: Proactive Adaptation to Emerging Regulatory Guidance. Organizations increasingly anticipate regulatory shifts related to digital and AI technologies, highlighting the importance of proactive, forward-looking compliance strategies. Rather than waiting for finalized regulatory texts, several participants described efforts to interpret draft guidance, engage in early dialogue with authorities, and integrate continuous validation into development pipelines. As one professional reflected, "*The requirements keep getting stricter, or at least it feels that way.*" This sentiment reflects a broader shift from reacting to new rules after they appear toward staying ahead of them by monitoring changes and updating validation practices as part of everyday work.

5 Discussion

This study shows that while pharmaceutical and medical device manufacturers increasingly explore AI and ML to improve production and compliance, progress is constrained by two interconnected factors: fragmented data infrastructures and regulatory uncertainty. Our analysis highlights how legacy system silos limit data accessibility, and how evolving validation requirements create friction for AI adoption. At the same time, interviewees identified pathways forward, emphasizing the need for unified data architectures, embedded governance mechanisms, and compliance-by-design approaches such as RegOps. These findings suggest that advancing AI in regulated manufacturing requires not only technical innovation but also systematic integration of RegOps into digital architectures.

5.1 Regulation as a Structuring Force in AI-Driven Systems

Our findings show that regulation is not only a constraint but also shapes system design and governance, aligning with studies highlighting how regulatory expectations influence AI-enabled healthcare solutions [21]. Regulatory frameworks such as GxP/GMP, GAMP 5, and ISO 13485 influence architectural decisions, validation workflows, and organizational governance structures. Interviewees described how system modularity, auditability, and data lineage are often tailored explicitly to meet regulatory requirements.

Some participants viewed regulations as slowing AI development, while others saw them as enablers for digitalization. Aligning model lifecycle management with regulatory expectations was seen as essential for trustworthy, scalable AI [21]. Yet, AI integration challenges traditional validation in traceability, reproducibility, and change control, leading organizations to pilot solutions in low-risk settings before broader adoption.

5.2 Data Architecture as a Prerequisite for Compliant AI

A central theme emerging from the interviews is the foundational role of data architecture in enabling compliant AI systems. Participants highlighted the challenges posed by fragmented data landscapes, undocumented pipelines, and inconsistent metadata standards. To address these issues, several organizations are implementing enterprise-wide data platforms (such as validated data lakes or industrial data fabrics) that support data integrity, traceability, and contextualization.

These architectures form the basis for AI readiness, allowing for the integration of machine learning pipelines into GxP-compliant environments. However, the development and maintenance of such infrastructures require sustained coordination across quality, IT, data engineering, and domain-expert functions. Interviewees described the difficulty of harmonizing GxP documentation requirements with the iterative nature of machine learning, underscoring the need for architectural frameworks that bridge compliance and agility. Our results align with prior work on data fabrics and smart manufacturing architectures [22], extending them by emphasizing the need for embedded validation traceability and audit-ready provenance in regulated environments.

5.3 Toward Compliance-by-Design and RegOps

The convergence of AI adoption and digital transformation is prompting a shift toward *compliance-by-design*, which is a proactive strategy in which regulatory considerations are embedded into the design and operation of technical systems from the outset. Emerging practices observed in the field include:

- Modular system design to isolate validated components from experimental subsystems [23];
- Integration of automated documentation (e.g., model cards, data lineage trackers) [24];
- Use of version-controlled pipelines to capture training data, hyperparameters, and performance metrics [25].

These practices align with the emerging paradigm of *Regulatory Operations (RegOps)* [26], which seeks to operationalize compliance as an integrated part of system development lifecycles. Several organizations reported initial steps toward formalizing RegOps practices, often through cross-functional teams that span regulatory affairs, quality assurance, and digital engineering. Nevertheless, there is limited methodological guidance or standardized tooling in this area, representing a critical area for further development.

5.4 Proposed Layered Architecture Framework

The proposed framework in Fig. 1 illustrates a validation-aware, layered architecture for compliant AI/ML deployment in regulated manufacturing. It integrates data ingestion, storage, lifecycle management, deployment, and compliance logging within a unified structure that ensures traceability and continuous oversight. Cross-cutting traceability and compliance layers embed auditability into every stage, supporting adaptation to evolving regulations.

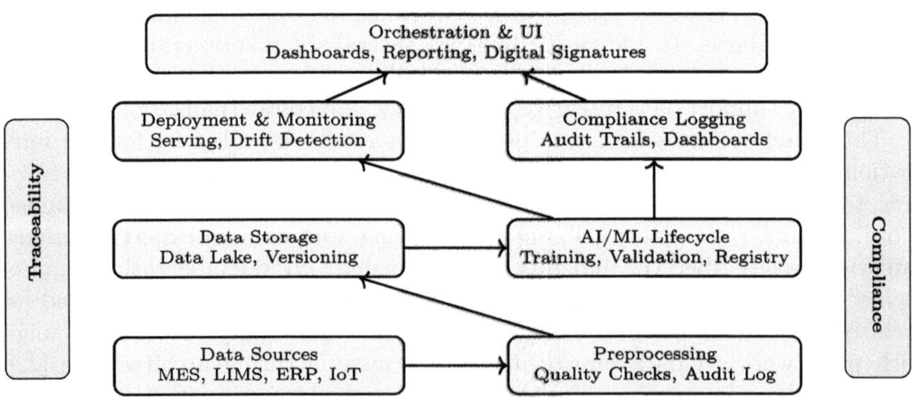

Fig. 1. Validation-aware data architecture for AI in regulated manufacturing. Cross-cutting compliance and traceability layers ensure end-to-end validation and auditability.

Table 2 complements the architectural model by comparing common data architectures used in regulated manufacturing. Figure 1 explains the internal logic of a validation-aware system, while the table shows how different architectures handle governance, validation, and scalability. Together, they outline the design space for building AI-ready infrastructures that ensure both performance and regulatory compliance. Both artefacts are based on findings from the literature and expert interviews.

Table 2. Comparison of data architecture paradigms in regulated manufacturing, focusing on their principles and implications for software business and AI governance.

Architecture Type	Core Principles/Keywords	Implications for Software Business and AI Governance	Ref.
Centralized Data Lake/Warehouse	Unified data hub, ETL pipelines, role-based access, analytics integration.	Facilitates centralized analytics capabilities and enterprise-wide AI initiatives but limits local innovation and agility across sites.	[27]
Operational Data Historian	Time-series storage, SCADA integration, contextual metadata, event traceability.	Acts as a high-integrity data backbone supporting traceable software updates and predictive maintenance services.	[28]
Medallion (Layered/Lakehouse)	Layered curation (Bronze-Silver-Gold), schema evolution, version control.	Enables modular software pipelines, transparent data refinement, and staged AI model deployment with reproducibility.	[29]
Data Mesh	Domain ownership, federated governance, APIs, data-as-product concept.	Promotes cross-organizational collaboration and scalable data product ecosystems, but increases coordination and compliance complexity.	[30]
Data Fabric	Semantic layer, active metadata, automation, orchestration.	Supports interoperability and explainability across business units; useful for AI lifecycle monitoring and governance automation.	[31]
Hybrid/Federated Architecture	Multi-cloud connectors, governance overlay, distributed nodes.	Balances global compliance control with local autonomy, enabling platform-based business models and continuous AI validation.	[14]

Both frameworks emphasize that compliant AI adoption is not solely a technical challenge but a systemic design problem. The layered model demonstrates how traceability and validation can be embedded directly into data and model workflows, while the comparative analysis shows alternative pathways for achieving this integration across organizational boundaries. Together, they provide a foundation for developing RegOps-oriented architectures that align AI innovation with the regulatory expectations of the life science industry.

Collectively, these comparisons position our study within the growing research connecting regulatory frameworks, data architecture design, and AI governance [31]. By extending these ideas into the manufacturing context, we show how RegOps principles can turn *compliance-by-design* from a conceptual goal into a practical framework for continuous validation. This highlights that trustworthy AI in regulated industries relies not only on technical accuracy but also on architectural and organizational readiness.

5.5 Limitations of the Study

This study has several limitations that should be acknowledged. First, due to the highly regulated nature of pharmaceutical and medical device manufacturing, participants were constrained in what they could share regarding internal systems, data architectures, validation workflows, and AI implementation strategies. These confidentiality requirements limited the granularity of some responses, particularly those concerning proprietary tools and processes, leading to higher-level descriptions rather than detailed technical disclosures.

Second, the participating companies represented a range of organizational sizes and geographic contexts. While this diversity offered a broad view of the sector, it also introduced variation in digital maturity, infrastructure, and regulatory environments. Smaller and regionally focused firms tended to be more reserved in discussing ongoing AI or data initiatives, whereas larger multinational organizations often operate with greater internal resources and established digital strategies.

Notably, large pharmaceutical companies such as Pfizer and Siemens, although not part of this interview study, have openly reported their adoption of AI/ML and digital technologies in manufacturing. Pfizer, for instance, applies AI/ML across its global production network, supporting use cases such as automated visual inspection, real-time anomaly detection, and AI-driven root cause analysis, all underpinned by its Manufacturing Intelligence Platform and Manufacturing Excellence (IMEx) program [32]. Siemens has also emphasized the integration of digital twins, IoT sensors, and robotics into production workflows to improve process reliability, yield, and cycle time efficiency [32]. These examples illustrate that AI/ML implementation is gaining traction in the regulated sector, with leading companies demonstrating both the technical feasibility and organizational value of digital transformation in compliance-intensive environments.

Future research may benefit from broader international sampling and, potentially, even sector-specific segmentation.

6 Conclusion

This study examined how data architectures, AI adoption, and regulatory practices co-evolve in GxP/GMP-regulated manufacturing. Drawing on interviews with industry experts, it shows that organizations are in a transitional phase: data systems remain fragmented, AI initiatives are exploratory, and compliance practices are still largely reactive. Nevertheless, there is a clear shift toward aligning digital transformation with regulatory expectations through validation-aware architectures and emerging RegOps approaches.

The study contributes by empirically linking three domains often addressed separately: data architecture design, regulatory governance, and AI lifecycle management. It positions validation-aware architectures as technical enablers and RegOps as an integration strategy for scalable and trustworthy AI within regulated environments.

From a practical perspective, the proposed framework supports organizations seeking to operationalize compliance-by-design, strengthen data governance under GxP constraints, and automate validation without compromising auditability. From a research perspective, it opens opportunities to evaluate RegOps implementation across industrial contexts, measure its effect on compliance effort, and explore how AI/ML techniques (such as explainable models, probabilistic reasoning, and hybrid approaches) can be engineered to meet lifecycle validation requirements [33]. As regulated industries advance toward data-driven automation, the ability to design AI systems that are transparent, auditable, and compliant will remain central to both industrial practice and research.

References

1. Kodumuru, R., Sarkar, S., Parepally, V., Chandarana, J.: Artificial intelligence and Internet of Things integration in pharmaceutical manufacturing: a smart synergy. Pharmaceutics **17**(3), 290 (2025)
2. Niazi, S.K.: Regulatory perspectives for AI/ML implementation in pharmaceutical GMP environments. Pharmaceuticals **18**(6), 901 (2025)
3. Cizauskas, C., DeBenedictis, E., Kelly, P.: How the past is shaping the future of life science: the influence of automation and AI on biology. New Biotechnol. **88**, 1–11 (2025)
4. Shah, M., Kakkar, A., Natarajan, V.: CMC and GxP. In: Translational Pulmonology, pp. 437–441. Academic Press (2025)
5. Abhilash, P.M., Luo, X., Liu, Q., Madarkar, R., Walker, C.: Towards next-generation smart manufacturing systems: the explainability revolution. npj Adv. Manuf. **1**(1), 8 (2024)
6. Bilal, A., Ebert, D., Lin, B.: LLMs for explainable AI: a comprehensive survey. arXiv preprint arXiv:2504.00125 (2025)
7. Gioia, D.A., Corley, K.G., Hamilton, A.L.: Seeking qualitative rigor in inductive research: notes on the Gioia methodology. Organ. Res. Meth. **16**(1), 15–31 (2013)
8. NTT DATA: A GxP data fabric: the foundation of AI in pharma manufacturing (2024). https://www.nttdata.com/global/en/insights/focus/2024/data-fabric-for-the-pharmaceutical-industry

9. Moghaddam, M., Cadavid, M.N., Kenley, C.R., Deshmukh, A.V.: Reference architectures for smart manufacturing: a critical review. J. Manuf. Syst. **49**, 215–225 (2018)
10. International Society for Pharmaceutical Engineering (ISPE): Artificial intelligence. ISPE.org (2025). https://ispe.org/topics/artificial-intelligence. Accessed 25 Jul 2025
11. Raji, I.D., Buolamwini, J., Gebru, T., Mitchell, M., Moran, T., Barocas, S.: Closing the AI accountability gap: defining an end-to-end framework for internal algorithmic auditing. In: Proceedings of the 2020 Conference on Fairness, Accountability, and Transparency (FAT*), pp. 33–44 (2020)
12. Papagiannidis, E., Mikalef, P., Conboy, K.: Responsible artificial intelligence governance: a review and research framework. J. Strat. Inf. Syst. **34**(2), 101885 (2025)
13. International Society for Pharmaceutical Engineering (ISPE): AI maturity model for GxP applications: a foundation for AI deployment. Pharm. Eng. (2022). https://ispe.org/pharmaceutical-engineering/march-april-2022/ai-maturity-model-gxp-application-foundation-ai. Accessed 25 Jul 2025
14. Higgins, D.C., Johner, C.: Validation of artificial intelligence-containing products across the regulated healthcare industries. Ther. Innov. Regul. Sci. **57**(4), 797–809 (2023)
15. European Parliament and Council: Regulation (EU) 2024/1689 of 13 June 2024 laying down harmonised rules on artificial intelligence ("EU AI Act"). Official J. European Union, L 1689 (2024)
16. Hoessler, S., Carbon, C.C.: Digital transformation in incumbent companies: a qualitative study on exploration and exploitation activities in innovation. J. Innov. Entrepreneurship **13**(1), 46 (2024)
17. Ren, X., Jing, H., Zhang, Y.: Construction of digital transformation capability of manufacturing enterprises: qualitative meta-analysis based on current research. Sustainability **15**(19), 14168 (2023)
18. Al Zami, M.B., Shaon, S., Quy, V.K., Nguyen, D.C.: Digital twin in industries: a comprehensive survey. IEEE Access **13**, 67890–67925 (2025)
19. Wilkinson, S.R., et al.: Applying the FAIR principles to computational workflows. Sci. Data **12**(1), 328 (2025)
20. Presciuttini, A., Cantini, A., Portioli-Staudacher, A.: From explanations to actions: leveraging SHAP, LIME, and counterfactual analysis for operational excellence in maintenance decisions. In: Proceedings of the 4th International Conference on Electrical, Computer, Communications and Mechatronics Engineering (ICECCME), pp. 1–6. IEEE (2024)
21. Ajmal, C.S., et al.: Innovative approaches in regulatory affairs: leveraging artificial intelligence and machine learning for efficient compliance and decision-making. AAPS J **27**(1), 22 (2025)
22. Armbrust, M., Ghodsi, A., Xin, R., Zaharia, M.: Lakehouse: a new generation of open platforms that unify data warehousing and advanced analytics. In: Proceedings of CIDR, vol. 8, p. 28 (2021)
23. Dubey, A., Yang, Z., Anžel, A., Hattab, G.: Protocol for implementing the nested model for AI design and validation in compliance with AI regulations. STAR Protoc. **6**(2), 103771 (2025)
24. Kalokyri, V., et al.: AI model passport: data and system traceability framework for transparent AI in health. arXiv preprint arXiv:2506.22358 (2025)
25. Schlegel, M., Sattler, K.U.: Capturing end-to-end provenance for machine learning pipelines. Inf. Syst. **132**, 102495 (2025)

26. Toivakka, H., Granlund, T., Poranen, T., Zhang, Z.: Towards RegOps: a DevOps pipeline for medical device software. In: Product-Focused Software Process Improvement Conference, pp. 290–306 (2021)
27. Zhao, X., Zhang, C., Guan, S.: A data lake-based security transmission and storage scheme for streaming Big Data. Clust. Comput. **27**(4), 4741–4755 (2024)
28. Huang, S., et al.: The next-generation operational data historian for IoT based on Informix. In: Proceedings of the ACM SIGMOD International Conference on Management of Data, pp. 169–176 (2014)
29. Strengholt, P.: Building Medallion Architectures: Designing with Delta Lake and Spark. O'Reilly Media, Sebastopol, CA (2025)
30. Machado, I.A., Costa, C., Santos, M.Y.: Data Mesh: concepts and principles of a paradigm shift in data architectures. Procedia Comput. Sci. **196**, 263–271 (2022)
31. Blohm, I., Wortmann, F., Legner, C., Köbler, F.: Data products, data mesh, and data fabric: new paradigm(s) for data and analytics? Bus. Inf. Syst. Eng. **66**(5), 643–652 (2024)
32. The Pharmaceutical Post: AI and data in pharmaceutical manufacturing. Pharm. Post Issue **18**, 10–13 (2024)
33. Bhat, V.N., Bharati, S., Bothiraja, C., Sangshetti, J., Gaikwad, V.: A review on intervention of AI in the pharmaceutical sector: revolutionizing drug discovery and manufacturing. Intell. Pharm. (2025)

Security, Trust, and Ethical Practices in Software Business

Trust in Practice: Evaluating Third-Party Software in Large Organisational Procurement

Hannah Lear[1], Majdouline Hamdi[1], Kim van Leussen[1], Aminul Didar Islam[1,2](✉), and Slinger Jansen[1,2]

[1] Utrecht University, Heidelberglaan 8, 3584 CS Utrecht, The Netherlands
[2] LUT University, Yliopistonkatu 34, 53850 Lappeenranta, Finland
aminul.islam@lut.fi

Abstract. As large organisations increasingly rely on third-party software to support core operations, trust has emerged as a critical factor. This study reports how trust-related considerations influence the procurement and evaluation of third-party software in large enterprises. Drawing from the literature and nine semi-structured interviews, this study identified specific trust factors, such as certifications, regulatory obligations, and vendor transparency. The findings offer practical insights for improving procurement and evaluation strategies, contribute novel understanding of the trust dimensions specific to software procurement and risk assessment, and provide software vendors with insights on how to make their software more trustworthy.

Keywords: Trust · Third-party software · Procurement · Compliance management · Organisational cybersecurity

1 Introduction

Software procurement is the structured process through which organizations select, evaluate, acquire, and maintain third-party software tools and services that support their operations. It has become a strategic activity in modern software ecosystems, where interdependencies between vendors, platforms, and users shape both economic and security outcomes [14]. Procurement decisions increasingly determine not only cost efficiency but also the resilience, compliance, and long-term viability of digital infrastructures.

In practice, software procurement combines formal procedures and informal decision-making. While structured frameworks and tender processes are well documented in procurement research [15,22], studies consistently show that organizations often adapt or even bypass formal models to align with internal culture, urgency, and perceived risks [2,3]. This tension between prescriptive procurement models and situated practices highlights a persistent gap between how organizations are advised to procure and how they actually make software decisions.

The growing complexity of software and business ecosystems amplifies the stakes of these choices. Interconnected systems, multi-layered dependencies, and

G. Herzwurm et al. (Eds.): ICSOB 2025, LNBIP 574, pp. 61–76, 2026.
https://doi.org/10.1007/978-3-032-14518-5_6

cloud-based architectures mean that a single compromised vendor may trigger cascading failures across an organization. High-profile supply chain incidents such as SolarWinds have demonstrated how vulnerabilities in trusted suppliers can escalate into systemic risks [8,23]. Moreover, compliance with regulatory frameworks such as the GDPR and the NIS2 Directive now forms a central determinant in vendor selection, alongside concerns about data sovereignty and geopolitical exposure [5,20].

In this landscape, trust becomes a central decision determinant. Trust in software procurement refers to the willingness of organizational actors to accept risk based on confidence in a vendor's reliability, competence, and integrity [12]. However, empirical evidence about how such trust is evaluated and maintained across the procurement lifecycle remains limited. While multiple trust models exist in the broader software ecosystem literature [11,16], little is known about how large organizations operationalize these models when assessing third-party software suppliers or how they re-evaluate trust after procurement.

This study focuses on trust in third-party software procurement across product software, SaaS, and infrastructure contexts. It examines which trust mechanisms organizations apply, how these interact with formal procurement procedures, and how trust evolves over time. While prior studies on outsourcing and supplier relationship management provide valuable insights [6,9], software procurement differs by its technical opacity, frequent updates, and layered dependencies. Addressing this gap, we explore how procurement teams integrate trust factors such as certifications, compliance audits, and transparency into their decision-making, leading to the following research question: *"What is the process of identifying and evaluating trust factors in procurement processes for third-party software products within large organizations?"*

The paper contributes by (1) mapping how trust considerations are embedded in real-world procurement processes, (2) proposing a conceptual model of trust mechanisms across procurement phases, and (3) extending theoretical understanding of trust beyond outsourcing to the domain of digital software acquisition. The remainder of this paper is structured as follows. Section 2 provides background on trust in software ecosystems and procurement, highlighting the limitations of existing frameworks and introducing the concept of trust factors, such as certifications, performance, and transparency. Section 3 describes the research method, including the selection criteria for participants, the interview protocol, and the thematic coding approach used to analyse the data. Section 4 presents the results of the study, organised into key dimensions of procurement practice: the structure and flexibility of procurement processes, the roles and interactions of stakeholders, the trust mechanisms used across procurement phases, and the evaluation of risk categories. This section also includes a model that synthesizes how trust is operationalised in procurement organizations (see Fig. 2). Section 5 discusses the implications of these findings, comparing them to existing procurement models, and reflecting on challenges such as shadow IT and procurement under legal uncertainty. It also offers practical recommendations for improving procurement strategies. Section 6 concludes by summarising the main findings on trust in software procurement.

2 Background

Procurement research traditionally conceptualizes software acquisition as a multi-stage decision process involving need identification, vendor evaluation, negotiation, and post-contract management [15,22]. In public and private sectors alike, structured approaches such as the six-stage ERP model [22] provide governance and accountability but are frequently adapted to accommodate contextual pressures such as innovation speed or departmental autonomy [3]. Recent studies have emphasized hybrid or agile procurement strategies that balance compliance with flexibility [5,20].

Within this process, trust serves as a mechanism to mitigate uncertainty about vendor reliability, data protection, and long-term performance. Trust factors include technical indicators (e.g., security certifications), institutional assurances (e.g., regulatory compliance), and relational dimensions such as transparency and prior collaboration. In complex software ecosystems, these factors collectively shape procurement outcomes by influencing perceived vendor credibility and risk tolerance [6,11].

Security and compliance certifications, such as ISO/IEC 27001 or SOC 2, often function as baseline trust signals, ensuring that vendors meet minimum legal and technical standards [13]. However, scholars caution against equating certification with genuine trustworthiness, since certificates reflect only a momentary compliance status [12]. Empirical work shows that high-reliability organizations complement formal audits with continuous monitoring, reputation assessments, and transparent reporting mechanisms [19].

From a relational perspective, procurement success depends on interpersonal and organizational trust. Factors such as responsiveness, prior experience, and openness in communication help sustain trust beyond the initial contract [6]. Moreover, evidence from outsourcing and supplier management literature suggests that trust and control coexist rather than substitute each other, jointly shaping risk perception and collaboration quality [18].

Despite the existence of mature procurement models, there remains limited empirical understanding of how large organizations operationalize trust in the acquisition of third-party software. Most existing studies focus on either technical evaluation or contractual governance, while the integration of trust as an evolving construct across the procurement lifecycle remains underexplored. This study addresses that gap by examining how organizations combine formal mechanisms (certifications, contracts, SLAs) and relational mechanisms (transparency, reputation, responsiveness) to manage risk and sustain trust over time.

3 Research Method

A qualitative research method was applied in this study to enable an in-depth investigation of organisational perspectives on software procurement and trust. Third-party software tools are often embedded within complex IT environments, requiring procurement teams to carefully evaluate trust-related factors.

To explore these practices, multiple interviews were conducted with members of such teams to gain practical insights into how trust is assessed and managed. Participants were recruited through desk research, using publicly available contact information, and through outreach on platforms such as LinkedIn. To ensure consistency across respondents, the researchers applied the following selection criteria:

1. The company needs to be large and have a minimum of 250 employees[1].
2. The company has to make use of one or multiple third-party software.
3. The company needs to have both procurement departments and internal risk assessment teams.

After approaching 47 large organizations, nine participants were gathered. To achieve diversity, the roles included professions such as IT managers, risk assessors, and professors. With the nine participants, semi-structured interviews were conducted that lasted between 30 and 60 min, with the option of either in person or online, based on the participant's preference. To minimise interviewer bias, two researchers were present during these interviews. Beforehand, permission was requested to record the interview so that all relevant information could be analysed afterwards. The questions that were asked during the interviews were predetermined and put in an interview guide so that consistency among the different researchers was ensured, of which a preview is given in Table 1.

Table 1. A sample of the questions asked during the interviews. The full interview protocol is posted here: Interview Protocol.

Theme	Key Question
Trust Requirements	What trust-related requirements are typically checked before approving a third-party software vendor (e.g., certifications, audit results, reputation)?
Regulatory Compliance	Are there standard compliance checks or regulatory obligations that third-party vendors must meet (e.g., GDPR, ISO, etc.)?
Ongoing Evaluation	Do you re-evaluate the trustworthiness of third-party vendors periodically? If yes, how often and through which mechanisms?
Risk vs. Functionality	How do you balance risk and functionality when a tool is highly useful but has questionable trust signals?

The interview guide was divided into three sections: opening questions, which addressed the participants' role and involvement in procurement; main questions, which focused on trust-related evaluation practices; and concluding prompts,

[1] A threshold of 250 employees is commonly used in the literature to classify an organisation as *large* [7].

which invited participants to share any additional insights. The main section drew on themes identified in the literature review, including certifications, compliance, and risk assessment, to ensure alignment between theoretical frameworks and real-world practices. Primarily, the study of Hou et al. [11] was used to deductively inspire the interview protocol.

Data Analysis Process. To analyse the interview data, the researchers first transcribed the recordings. The coding process followed a pragmatic, theory-informed approach. Trust-related guidelines identified in prior literature [11] served as a deductive framework for initial code construction, ensuring conceptual alignment with existing models of trust in software ecosystems. During analysis, semi-open coding was applied to capture additional factors that emerged inductively from the interviews, following the adaptive logic of thematic analysis [4]. This combination of deductive and inductive coding reflects a pragmatic stance toward qualitative inquiry [17], ensuring that both established and context-specific trust mechanisms were systematically represented in the findings. Additional codes were included if they were mentioned by more than three respondents. Two examples of the coding process are provided in Table 2.

Table 2. Examples of the semi-open coding process.

Guideline	Nvivo code	Interview segment
Security & compliance certifications	Certification	Respondent 5: *"Um, right now I think we work with, um, ISO 27001, ISO 27001, and also, um, another one, which I don't know from my head, but um, we work with two certificates, if that helps"*
Performance & reliability	Past performance	Respondent 9: *"And the CISO knows when some suppliers don't have a good reputation about the security if there have been security incidents in the past. She will know that. And then she will say such as, okay, this is not just an application we have to go for"*

To ensure coding consistency and intercoder reliability, the researchers reviewed each other's work. Moreover, the program, NVivo, was used as it easily views the overall coverage of the nodes that were set up. In the end, this resulted in multiple codes surrounding trust factors mentioned by different participants and their perspective towards the selection process and the associated requirements. By analysing these codes, the following themes were found: 1) Software procurement process, 2) Trust mechanisms, 3) Monitoring trust, and 4) Risk perception and evaluation. This enabled conclusions about the role of trust factors during the procurement of third-party software products.

Reliability, Validity, and Limitations. Participant selection may vary across different researchers due to the availability of respondents. However, this limitation was reduced by applying clear selection criteria, which helped maintain consistency if another researcher were to replicate the study. To ensure internal validity, the study used a consistent interview protocol[2] and conducted thematic coding using NVivo software. While the trust factors found in the literature were used as a guideline, other factors could also emerge. To address this, the study applied a semi-open coding process to capture additional relevant factors identified by participants, enhancing the validity of the findings. It is, however, acknowledged that the results may not be generalisable to countries with different legal frameworks, market conditions, or cultural attitudes toward risk, thereby limiting external validity.

Ethical issues were carefully considered throughout both the data collection and analysis processes. Participants were explicitly asked for permission to record their interviews, with clear assurances that their responses would remain anonymised and used only for educational purposes related to Utrecht University. Recordings were permanently deleted after the analysis phase, ensuring that participants' privacy was fully protected.

Finally, this study is limited in scope and generalisability. All participants were based in Dutch organisations, which may not fully represent procurement practices elsewhere. While organisations from multiple sectors were included, their internal processes vary. Moreover, three interviews originated from a single organisation, albeit from individuals holding different roles.

4 Results: Software Procurement Process Dimensions

This section presents the findings from nine semi-structured interviews, structured around three key dimensions of procurement practice observed across the participating organisations. First, it examines the varying configurations of procurement processes, including differences in procedural structure, decision-making logic, and stakeholder engagement. Second, it analyses the trust-related requirements embedded within procurement activities, encompassing regulatory compliance, technical standards, and institutional risk classifications. Third, it investigates the mechanisms through which trust is monitored and reassessed over time, with attention to performance tracking, contractual enforcement, and supplier accountability, each of which contributes to sustaining reliable vendor relationships.

Software Procurement Process: Formal and Flexible. A formal procurement process was common among our respondents. Typically, the companies initially had a request for a particular software or identified a need for software. They would then hold a structured tender or structured intake, followed by the risk and privacy checks, before signing a contract or tender agreement. This layout is visualised in Table 3.

R.9 described the process beginning with an "*assignment to attract a new kind of software*", typically due to dissatisfaction with the existing solution (Stage 1 of Table 3). This initiates the formation of a multidisciplinary team (Stage 2), composed of representatives from various departments depending on the software

[2] A link to the protocol is found here: https://zenodo.org/records/17338732.

needs. The team proceeds to define specific requirements and formulate a request for proposal (RFP), incorporating legal, functional, and security-related questions (Stages 3 and 4). Vendors responding to the RFP are evaluated based on multiple criteria such as security, privacy, architecture, corporate social responsibility (CSR), and references (Stage 5). Shortlisted vendors are invited to a demonstration session (Stage 7), in which they will also be scored based on their performance, after which, the final selection would be made and a contract signed (Stages 8–9).

Table 3. Stages in the Procurement Process Observed in Practice. Please note that the rows in which formal trust dominates are blue, whereas the rows in which relational trust dominates are light green. These colors are similar to the ones in Fig. 1, as are the four phases.

No.	Stage	Description
		Pre-contracting phase
1	Need Identified	Triggered by user demand, dissatisfaction, or contract expiration
2	Team Formed	Multidisciplinary team including procurement, IT, privacy, and business users
3	Define Requirements	Legal (GDPR), security (ISO), data hosting, and data processing agreements
4	Send RFP	Use of templates with audit rights, certification checks, and functional needs
5	Vendor Response & Scoring	Evaluation of answers, certifications, documentation, and references
6	Shortlist Vendors	Selection of top candidates based on predefined scoring criteria
7	Demo & Deep Dive	Vendor presentations and detailed Q&A with domain experts and CISOs
8	Final Evaluation	Risk, legal, trust, and compliance assessment before approval
		Contracting phase
9	Contract Signed	Contractual agreement including (Data Processing Agreement) DPA, (Service-level Agreement) SLA, and legal clauses
		Monitoring phase
10	Implementation	Technical deployment and internal onboarding
11	Monitoring	Periodic review of certifications, SLAs, and performance incidents
		Evaluation phase
12	Re-evaluation or Renewal	Triggered at contract end or due to performance/risk concerns

Some organisations applied a more flexible procurement approach depending on the scope of product use. *R.5*, for example, noted that if a tool was intended for a single department, the process was relatively simple. In contrast, broader or more costly requests involving multiple departments trigger a more formal procedure: "*If it's a big request for something that is for more [departments] and more users, and maybe also a bit expensive, then I will discuss it [with a procurement officer]... and we will see several things - technical specifics, procurement measures.*"

Similarly, there were variations in the procurement process based on the sensitivity of the software and the data it would process. For example, *R.3* explained that "*if the classification [of risk] is very high, [they] need to take a lot of measures, and the supplier needs to take a lot of measures,*" and *R.6* mentioned, "*if they don't [have ISO], we make [sic] a risk assessment if it's necessary, and we can still do business with them.*" This necessity to continue business was a common theme among respondents, with many noting that a lack of alternatives often meant they had to compromise on certain aspects of their procurement checklist (see Appendix B for more). A preference often mentioned was that servers should be European Union-based, but due to the lack of alternatives, many companies had to continue working with large companies such as Microsoft or Google, whose servers are located in the United States. Had an alternative solution with EU-based servers and the necessary security measures been available, it would have been the preferred option, particularly given that several respondents cited increasing political uncertainty as a concern.

Key Stakeholders and Roles. Software procurement involves multiple stakeholders with varying roles and interpretations, often leading to coordination challenges. *R.9* described aligning strategic and maintenance IT, contract managers, and business users, with the strategic IT department advising the board when needed: *"Maybe we should reconsider this supplier..."*. While no major conflicts between procurement and risk teams were reported, differences in language, templates, and structural setups were common. For instance, *R.7* noted departmental variation in interpreting risk documentation.

Across all organisations, the Chief Information Security Officer (CISO) played a central role in defining trust policies, reviewing certifications, and escalating risks. Procurement teams tracked vendor performance and enforced contract terms; legal departments ensured compliance through managing DPAs and SLAs; and IT teams handled technical assessments such as encryption and access control. Procurement structures varied: some followed decentralised but coordinated models, others maintained central oversight with distributed execution. Overall, trust maintenance was a shared responsibility, shaped by institutional structure and the clarity of interdepartmental collaboration.

Trust Mechanisms in Procurement. Organisations use a layered trust strategy, combining formal mechanisms (classification model based on confidentiality, integrity, and availability (CIA) model, certifications, legal documents) and relational mechanisms (for example past experience, transparency, risk dialogue). These mechanisms are applied at different stages of the procurement lifecycle. Figure 1 shows a timeline in which it is seen how trust mechanisms evolve during a vendor relationship. This timeline demonstrates that while formal mechanisms dominate early stages, relational and experience-based mechanisms also play a role during ongoing collaboration and contract renewal. The following section will dive deeper into each of these mechanisms.

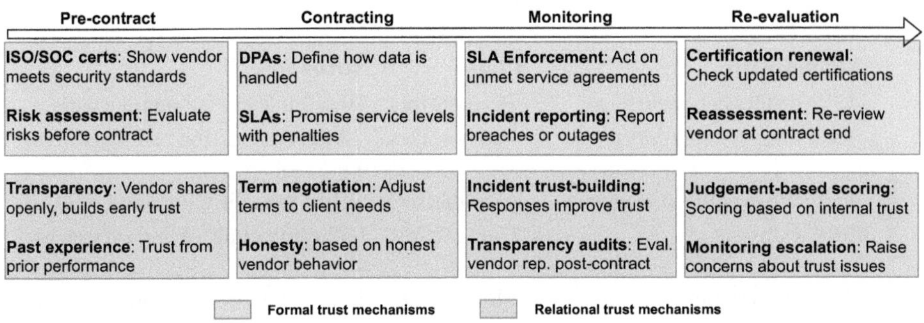

Fig. 1. Trust mechanisms across procurement phases.

Formal Mechanisms. Most respondents, including *R.6*, explained that ISO 27001 certification is required for vendors whose services touch the organisation's IT infrastructure. Other organisations also mentioned ISO 27002 certification and SOC 2 & 3. If a vendor does not have this certification, often the case with small, innovative startups, a risk assessment is performed to decide whether collaboration is still possible. All respondents required GDPR compliance, supplemented by sector-specific frameworks such as SURF agreements in academia, BIO for government, and NEN 7510 for healthcare; sub-processors were explicitly checked for compliance and data residency.

Few organizations check whether the certification is in fact valid. As *R.3* noted: *"You still need to look into it to see, 'Okay, what did you test? When was the certification? Because if it's ten years old, 'yeah, thanks', but we need something that's a little bit newer."* Some organisations implemented internal frameworks that go beyond certification requirements, highlighting recognition that formal trust mechanisms alone do not guarantee reliability. In such cases, certifications function more as entry criteria than full assessments. Respondents also highlighted the need for formal legal instruments such as DPAs, especially when personal data is involved and SLAs that hold post-contract obligations such as incident reporting.

Relational Mechanisms. A recurring theme was transparency; vendors who fail to clearly explain their processes or avoid answering detailed questions raise red flags early in the procurement process. *R.3* explained: *"If they're not transparent about how they work... more questions pop up."* Trust was also shaped by transparency about past performance, with *R.8* even increasing trust in a vendor after a ransomware attack, interpreting their improved protocols as a sign of maturity. *R.9* implemented a quantified trust score, based on responses to structured questionnaires, while *R.8* rejected such models in favour of case-by-case judgment. This variation illustrates the coexistence of formalised and subjective approaches, depending on the organisation's culture and capacity. Table 4 summarises all the different trust mechanisms.

Table 4. Expanded list of trust mechanisms across procurement phases.

	Mechanism	Phase	Notes
Formal	ISO / SOC certifications	Pre-contract	Baseline security qualification
	Risk assessment reports	Pre-contract	Alternative for small/startup vendors
	Data Processing Agreement	Contracting	When handling personal data
	SLA clauses	Contracting	Includes penalties and service levels
	SLA enforcement	Monitoring	Used when SLA breaches occur
	Incident reporting	Monitoring	Obligatory in case of breaches
	Certification renewal check	Re-evaluation	Ensures certifications stay current
	Formal reassessment	Re-evaluation	Periodic review before contract renewal
Relational	Transparency in communication	All phases	Lack of openness is a red flag
	Past experience with vendor	All phases	Especially relevant for renewals
	Term negotiation flexibility	Contracting	Adjusting terms to organisational needs
	Honesty / trust signals	Pre-contract	First impressions
	Incident trust-building	Monitoring	Vendor response builds trust
	Transparency audits	Monitoring	Reviewing vendor openness
	Judgement-based trust scoring	Selection	Subjective scoring in absence of metrics
	Monitoring escalation	Re-evaluation	Internal escalation when trust drops

Monitoring Trust. Organisations do not rely on a single, static assessment of trust but instead monitor it throughout the vendor relationship. Most respondents mentioned a periodic re-evaluation of industry certifications, especially when certificates expire and need to be renewed. *R.6* explained that certifications are reassessed as part of a broader technical and legal verification process. In other cases, such as with *R.3*, vendors who initially lacked the required certifications were allowed to proceed under the condition that improvements would be made within a set time frame.

R.7 described monitoring through contractual obligations, including SLAs and incident reporting duties. Vendors were required to share system logs and relevant information when incidents occurred, so the organisation could inform authorities and evaluate the impact. If expectations were not met or incidents were poorly handled, the issue escalated internally. *R.2* acknowledged that communication was sometimes lacking because IT and procurement were not always informed about software acquisitions. As they admitted, *"I have no idea what everyone is purchasing"*, and often only learnt about tools after the fact.

Risk Perception and Evaluation. The interviews revealed several categories of trust-related risks in third-party software procurement, which can be broadly grouped into technical, relational, and legal/compliance concerns. While these categories often overlap, distinguishing them provides a clearer view of how organisations assess and respond to risk.

Technical Trust Concerns. The most frequently mentioned technical risk was the threat of data breaches. *R.9* identified hacking as the most concerning issue due to its potential to compromise sensitive client information. Although most respondents had not personally experienced breaches, *R.8* described a case where a third-party vendor failed to delete data after the contract end date. The data remained on an outdated server, which was later hacked, leading to the theft of alumni information. This experience led the respondent to place greater emphasis on secure data deletion.

Relational and Operational Concerns. Several respondents described trust issues stemming from supplier behaviour and internal organisational limitations. *R.7* reported that some vendors impose unusual conditions, such as requiring non-disclosure agreements (NDAs) to access essential security documentation such as SOC 2 reports. *R.2* noted instances where suppliers promised one thing but delivered another, though they clarified that these discrepancies had not yet led to concrete security issues. These tensions highlight the challenge of maintaining clear expectations and oversight in supplier relationships.

Trust issues also arose from internal decentralisation. *R.2* explained that individual departments sometimes procured software without involving IT or procurement, which meant the organisation lacked visibility and contractual control over these tools. To address this, they advocated for centralising procurement oversight. Similarly, *R.7* stated that due to the organisation's size, it was difficult to conduct risk assessments for every supplier, which sometimes led to ambiguity about when a certification or formal evaluation was necessary.

Legal and Compliance Concerns. A third major category of risk is related to compliance and jurisdictional uncertainty, especially around U.S.-based cloud providers. All educational institutions interviewed expressed concern over reliance on dominant suppliers such as Microsoft and Google due to the implications of the U.S. CLOUD Act[3]. *Respondents 4* and *6* stressed the importance of knowing where data is stored and whether customers retain control. While these vendors were sometimes approved, the process involved penetration testing and a case-by-case risk evaluation.

R.8 described the legal complexities of cross-border data transfers, stating: *"We ask the supplier who will be transporting the data for us to the third country*

[3] The CLOUD Act amends the 1986 Stored Communications Act (SCA) to allow U.S. federal law enforcement to compel U.S.-based technology companies, via warrant or subpoena, to provide data, even if it is stored on servers outside the United States [1].

to tell us how the legal protection mechanism in that other country is organised. Yeah, that is very complicated." As the GDPR does not apply outside the EU, working with U.S. suppliers increases legal uncertainty. *R.4* echoed this concern, stating: *"The US has been proven to be not such a reliable partner as it used to be. So there is [a] big uncertainty, but we are very much depending on you know, stuff such as Microsoft, Google, Amazon, and they store their data wherever they want to."* These accounts reflect how legal and political factors can limit procurement choices, even when risks are well understood.

Managing Risk Through Evaluation and Monitoring. Given the range of risks, respondents emphasised the importance of ongoing evaluation and monitoring. *R.3* described a tiered approach where high-risk vendors were reviewed more frequently-monthly, quarterly, or annually, depending on risk level. In contrast, *respondents 3 and 8* said that some suppliers were only re-evaluated at contract renewal, typically every three to four years. Other organisations reported more regular reviews, often every three months, to assess performance. In addition to supplier dialogue, *R.2* used customer satisfaction surveys as part of their monitoring strategy. These findings suggest that organisations must tailor their trust assessments based on the type of risk involved. Technical, relational, and legal risks each require distinct mitigation strategies, and often necessitate layered governance and monitoring mechanisms.

Conceptual Procurement Trust Model. We present our findings in the form of a conceptual procurement trust model, with entities and transitions between those entities. The conceptual model of trust in third-party software procurement begins with **Trust Factors**, such as certifications, transparency, and prior performance data. These factors are *used by* various **Procurement Actors**, including procurement teams, risk officers, CISOs, and vendors, who *conduct* key **Procurement Processes** such as evaluation, contracting, and monitoring. These processes *produce* measurable **Outputs**, such as procurement decisions, trust scores, and risk mitigation plans. The outcomes of these outputs *inform* future activities and, through a feedback Loop, can *shape* policies and trigger reassessments of trustworthiness over time. This means that what happens after the contract, such as new risks or incidents, can lead to changes in how trust is measured or how future decisions are made. For example, the organisation might update its policies or reassess how much it trusts a vendor.

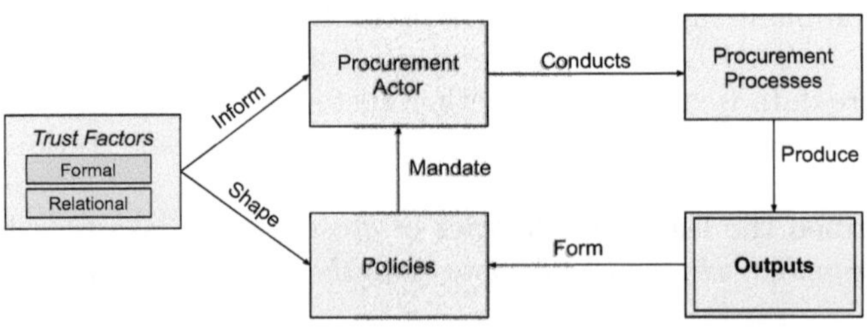

Fig. 2. The conceptual models shows how trust factors shape procurement decisions and actions through an extensive feedback loop.

The conceptual model echos the interviews: trust is not just something that happens at the start, but something that can change over time based on what the vendor does and how the situation develops. The model also shows that trust is built using both formal steps, such as certificates and contracts, and informal factors, such as transparency and past experience. These elements often work together during different stages of procurement.

5 Discussion

The procurement process observed in this study builds on the six-stage model [22], but extends it with a more iterative structure. In addition to standard phases, organisations include steps such as team formation, vendor demonstrations, trust scoring, ongoing monitoring, and reassessment. This reflects the practical complexity of managing procurement risks and trust factors over time, and demonstrates that procurement should be understood as a cyclical process rather than a linear one.

Shadow IT and Bypassing Formal Processes. The interviews revealed cases of shadow IT, where employees acquire software without involving central procurement or IT. This typically happens when formal processes are too slow or rigid. While sometimes justified by urgency, such practices introduce risks related to compliance, integration, and security. A more flexible procurement track for low-risk cases may help organisations maintain oversight while avoiding bottlenecks [21].

Proposed Improvements to Procurement Practices. The interviews suggest several actionable improvements. Flexible tracks for low-risk software could coexist with stricter controls for high-risk tools. Trust scoring mechanisms, vendor demos, and deep-dive sessions support clearer comparisons. Strengthening monitoring routines, especially around certification expiry and incident response, can help maintain trust over time. Internal consistency could be improved with shared templates and training, and vendor transparency should be incentivised by requiring disclosure of sub-processors, hosting locations, and prior incidents.

Consequences for Software Vendors. Vendors entering formal procurement need to demonstrate that their products are mature or strategically important enough to warrant evaluation. They must meet baseline requirements, including certifications and legal documentation, or present a clear and credible rationale for missing elements. In the latter case, trust may still be established through transparency, performance history, or risk assessments.

Future Research. Certification alone is rarely sufficient. Instead, organisations adapt evaluation practices based on internal risk tolerances and operational realities. To support this, publishing trust-relevant documents such as certifications in centralised procurement dashboards could improve oversight [10].

Legal and geopolitical concerns are becoming more prominent. Organisations expressed unease about U.S.-based cloud services due to data sovereignty issues. Trust frameworks must adapt to address extraterritorial data access and jurisdictional complexity.

For researchers, the findings call for new models that reflect trust as a dynamic, ongoing process. Future studies could explore trust trajectories over time, differences across sectors, and the integration of automated trust scoring tools. There is also room to investigate how cross-border procurement alliances shape trust and market balance. Finally, analysing real-world procurement documents may yield deeper insights into how trust, risk, and compliance are formalised in practice.

6 Conclusion

This study examined how large organisations assess and maintain trust throughout the lifecycle of third-party software procurement. Rather than relying solely on static indicators like certifications or compliance checklists, organisations apply a layered approach that evolves with shifting risks, vendor performance, and institutional priorities. Trust emerges not at a single decision point but through ongoing processes: structured evaluations, lived experiences, and negotiated compromises. It is shaped as much by legal frameworks and security standards as by transparency, responsiveness, and organisational context.

By mapping formal and relational trust mechanisms to procurement stages, this study clarifies how trust is operationalised in practice and how it is monitored over time. The findings challenge simplistic models of procurement and highlight the need for more flexible, risk-aware strategies; especially as legal uncertainty and supply chain complexity grow.

Statement of AI Usage. AI was used during the writing process to improve the English clarity and conciseness. None of the content was generated, however, without the author reviewing and editing. AI was also used to translate documents from Dutch to English; however, the translations were checked before being included.

References

1. Alston and Bird LLP: The cloud act and its impact on cross-border access to contents of communications. https://www.alstonprivacy.com/cloud-act-impact-cross-border-access-contents-communications/. Accessed 10 Jun 2024
2. Ayala, C., Hauge, Ø., Conradi, R., Franch, X., Li, J.: Selection of third party software in off-the-shelf-based software development–an interview study with industrial practitioners. J. Syst. Softw. **84**(4), 620–637 (2011)
3. Bjarnason, E., Åberg, P., Ali, N.B.: Software selection in large-scale software engineering: a model and criteria based on interactive rapid reviews. Empir. Softw. Eng. **28**, 51 (2023)
4. Braun, V., Clarke, V.: Using thematic analysis in psychology. Qual. Res. Psychol. **3**(2), 77–101 (2006)
5. Bromberg, D., Manoharan, A.: E-procurement implementation in the united states: understanding progress in local government. Public Adm. Q. **39**(3), 360–392 (2015)
6. Cheng, X., Fu, S., de Vreede, G.J.: Determinants of trust in computer-mediated offshore software-outsourcing collaboration. Int. J. Inf. Manage. **57**, 102301 (2021)

7. Crowther, D., Aras, G.: Corporate social responsibility in medium to large enterprises. In: Aras, G., Crowther, D., Vettori, S. (eds.) Corporate Social Responsibility in SMEs. Social Responsibility Research Network (2009)
8. DeFranco, J.F., Kshetri, N.: Software supply chains. Computer **55**(10), 16–17 (2022)
9. Grover, V., Cheon, M.J., Teng, J.T.C.: The effect of service quality and partnership on the outsourcing of information systems functions. J. Manag. Inf. Syst. **12**(4), 89–116 (1996)
10. Hou, F., Farshidi, S., Jansen, S.: TrustSECO: a distributed infrastructure for providing trust in the software ecosystem. In: Polyvyanyy, A., Rinderle-Ma, S. (eds.) CAiSE 2021. LNBIP, vol. 423, pp. 121–133. Springer, Cham (2021). https://doi.org/10.1007/978-3-030-79022-6_11
11. Hou, F., Jansen, S.: A systematic literature review on trust in the software ecosystem. Empirical Softw. Eng. **28** (2022)
12. Hou, F., Jansen, S.: A survey of the state-of-the-art approaches for evaluating trust in software ecosystems. J. Softw. Evol. Process **36** (2024)
13. Ilori, O., Nwosu, N., Naiho, H.: Third-party vendor risks in it security: a comprehensive audit review and mitigation strategies. World J. Adv. Res. Rev. **22**(3), 213–224 (2024)
14. Jansen, S., Cusumano, M.A., Brinkkemper, S.: Software Ecosystems: Analyzing and Managing Business Networks in the Software Industry. EE Publishing (2013)
15. Lonsdale, C.: The effect of the market on is/it outsourcing decisions: a review of the literature and a research agenda. J. Strat. Inf. Syst. **10**(3), 241–268 (2001)
16. McKnight, D.H., Choudhury, V., Kacmar, C.: Developing and validating trust measures for e-commerce: an integrative typology. Inf. Syst. Res. **13**(3), 334–359 (2002)
17. Morgan, D.L.: Pragmatism as a paradigm for social research. Qual. Inq. **20**(8), 1045–1053 (2014)
18. Poppo, L., Zenger, T.: Do formal contracts and relational governance function as substitutes or complements? Strateg. Manag. J. **23**(8), 707–725 (2002)
19. Siddiqui, S., Thapa, C., Holland, R., Shao, W., Camtepe, S.A.: Elevating software trust: unveiling and quantifying the risk landscape. arXiv preprint arXiv:2408.02876 (2024)
20. Vaidya, K., Sajeev, A.S.M., Callender, G.: Critical factors that influence e-procurement implementation success in the public sector. J. Pub. Procurement **6**(1/2), 70–99 (2006)
21. Van Acken, J.P., Jansen, F., Jansen, S., Labunets, K.: Who is the it department anyway: an evaluative case study of shadow it mindsets among corporate employees. In: 20th Symposium on Usable Privacy and Security, SOUPS 2024, pp. 527–545 (2024)
22. Verville, J., Halingten, A.: A six-stage model of the buying process for ERP software. Ind. Mark. Manage. **32**(7), 585–594 (2003)
23. Williams, L., et al.: Research directions in software supply chain security. ACM Trans. Softw. Eng. Methodol. **34**(5) (2025)

Simulating ERP Cyber Incidents: A Serious Game for Awareness and Incident Management

Judith Strussenberg(✉), Alexander Henkel, Steffi Rudel, and Ulrike Lechner

University of the Bundeswehr Munich, Neubiberg, Germany
{judith.strussenberg,alexander.henkel,steffi.rudel, ulrike.lechner}@unibw.de

Abstract. ERP systems are fundamental to enterprise operations. As a result, they are increasingly targeted by sophisticated cyberattacks. This paper presents the design, implementation and evaluation of a serious game scenario titled *ERP-Systems in Need*, developed to raise awareness of cybersecurity specifically within ERP contexts. Building on the existing game *A Question of Security*, this work applies a Design Science Research approach to simulate realistic ERP security incidents. The serious game emphasizes experiential learning through multirole scenarios and was evaluated in academic settings. The findings suggest that the game is effective in increasing knowledge, participation, and preparedness for ERP-related cyber threats.

Keywords: Serious games · ERP · IT security · Cybersecurity · Awareness

1 Introduction

Enterprise Resource Planning (ERP) systems are critical to the operational backbone of many organizations, supporting essential processes such as procurement, logistics, finance, and human resource management. As these systems become increasingly interconnected and exposed to external networks, their vulnerability to cyberattacks has increased substantially. A successful cyberattack on an ERP system can paralyze entire supply chains, disrupt production, and cause significant financial and reputational damage. An actual survey shows that ERP systems are in the focus of ransomware attackers. 62 % of the attacked companies faced a downtime of at least 24 h. Experts see one reason for the lack of knowledge about ERP-specific security [22].

Although cybersecurity training and awareness programs are a common mitigation strategy, traditional approaches such as classroom lectures, slide-based tutorials, or compliance checklists often fail to engage users or produce lasting behavioral change. Recent research suggests that serious games, interactive simulations with educational objectives, offer a promising alternative. By immersing

G. Herzwurm et al. (Eds.): ICSOB 2025, LNBIP 574, pp. 77–91, 2026.
https://doi.org/10.1007/978-3-032-14518-5_7

users in realistic scenarios and enabling experiential learning, serious games can foster understanding and long-term awareness of cybersecurity risks.

This paper addresses the lack of gamified training tools specifically aimed at ERP security. Building on the existing serious game *A Question of Security* [26], which focuses on ransomware attacks on mobile devices, we present the design, implementation, and evaluation of a new scenario titled *ERP-Systems in Need.* The game simulates a multi-phase cyberattack on an ERP system and places participants in dual roles: as individual employees and as decision-makers in management. The objective is to improve participants' awareness of ERP system vulnerabilities, incident response strategies, and business continuity.

The development followed the Design Science Research (DSR) methodology according to Hevner and incorporated iterative design evaluation through two playtest sessions. Feedback from these sessions informed improvements to the game structure, content and user interaction elements [12].

This paper is structured as follows. Section 2 reviews the relevant background on ERP systems, cybersecurity training, and serious games. Section 3 outlines the applied research methodology. Section 4 details the game scenario and game development. Section 5 presents the implementation and playtesting process. Section 6 discusses the evaluation results, followed by a critical reflection and future work in Sect. 7.

2 Theoretical Background and Related Work

The following section deals with theories and topics for this serious game. After a look at the challenges related to the security of ERP systems, we consider the background of serious games and discuss the question of which serious games related to ERP are known for research.

2.1 ERP Systems and Cybersecurity

Enterprise Resource Planning (ERP) systems are integrated software platforms that support and automate core business functions such as finance, supply chain management, procurement, and human resources. Their centrality in business operations and their role as comprehensive data and process hubs make them high-value targets for cyberattacks. In recent years, attackers have increasingly exploited ERP-specific vulnerabilities, particularly in widely used platforms such as SAP and Oracle ERP [8]. In the basic protection module APP.4.2, the German Federal Office for Information Security (BSI) lists four key reasons for the current vulnerability of ERP systems: failure to take into account SAP security recommendations, failure to apply patches and SAP security notices promptly or at all, lack of planning, implementation and documentation of an SAP authorization concept, and lack of documentation and emergency concept. The measures to be implemented are derived from this, such as secure configuration and rights management, network security, and securing the ERP database and the associated interfaces and servers [3]. SAP itself also provides documents on this topic, such as the SAP Security Baseline Template, which has also been included in the implementation notes for the module APP.4.2 SAP ERP system. The five main topics of the baseline template are infrastructure security, secure code, installation and operational security, and security guidelines [4].

A notable example of a ERP-related security risk occurred in early 2025 with the discovery and active exploitation of the vulnerability CVE-2025-31324. This vulnerability, rated with a maximum CVSS score of 10.0, allowed attackers to gain full administrative control over affected SAP systems. As reported by SAP and Onapsis, exploitation allowed access to sensitive business processes and data, and opened pathways for the deployment of ransomware and lateral movement across enterprise networks [14,19]. Particularly impacted were organizations classified as critical infrastructure providers.

According to Onapsis' mid-year threat report, the first half of 2025 alone revealed an unusually high number of critical vulnerabilities in SAP systems. These weaknesses were found to expose companies to risks such as espionage, sabotage, fraud, and service disruption through malware or ransomware [14]. Numbers like this are also an issue for SAP itself and its relationship with its customers because it leaves some of their most critical processes vulnerable. This causes trust issues and a SAP 2012 awareness campaign shows that they are well aware of the fact that trust is the ultimate currency in their business [17]. The figures mentioned above on vulnerabilities seem somewhat abstract until you look at specific cases, such as the Conapi case study, which shows how human decisions combined with a lack of technical security measures led to a data leak from a medium-sized company's ERP system that ended up costing it around 1.8 million euros and led to the publication of company secrets, a GPDR fine, the loss of customers, and orders [6]. In the case of Stoli Group USA, an SAP security breach was at least partly responsible for the company's insolvency in 2024 [23].

In addition, there are other digital attacks that do not directly target ERP systems but use them as a vehicle, such as deep fake scams. The case of a Hong Kong financial employee has become widely known. He transferred around 25.6 million dollars to cyber criminals after a video call with his 'chief financial officer' and other board members that were all deep faked [11]. Increasing employee awareness of cases like these is essential. Although there were still some sensational cases in 2024, Sam Altman, CEO of OpenAI, the company behind ChatGPT, warned of a global 'fraud crisis' in the summer of 2025. He claimed that AI has now fully defeated most of the ways people currently authenticate, other than passwords [5].

Despite the increasing risk profile of ERP platforms, cybersecurity awareness initiatives in many organizations continue to focus on endpoints, office software, or generic IT systems. ERP platforms are often excluded from such training programs or treated as black-box systems managed solely by IT departments. This creates a dangerous gap, especially as attacks increasingly target ERP users via phishing, misconfigurations, and compromised credentials. To train ERP security tailored to the needs of an organization is crucial because even the smallest affected parts of a critical supply chain can cause massive alterations. We showed this in the example of an infected label printer that was used to print labels to store and ship goods or labels for traceability. Without this small piece of hardware attached to an ERP system, a company's activity can come to a complete stop [9].

2.2 Serious Games

Serious games integrate educational objectives with game-based elements, creating interactive learning experiences that go beyond mere entertainment [7,10,16]. They have proven to be effective in various domains, such as education, healthcare care and corporate training, by enhancing the motivation, engagement, and retention of the learner's knowledge [13,15,25]. Research suggests that features such as progressive difficulty, real-time feedback, and structured reflection phases significantly improve learning outcomes [24]. Immersive and scenario-based game environments contribute to deeper emotional engagement and knowledge retention. In addition, serious games have shown the potential to foster awareness, empathy, and even behavior change in areas such as response to crisis, ethics, and social responsibility [20].

Collaborative gameplay mechanics have also been shown to strengthen communication, negotiation, and coordination skills, especially in multi-role training contexts [1]. These elements are particularly relevant for fields like cybersecurity and incident response, where teamwork is essential.

To be effective, serious games must integrate learning content and game mechanics in a way that is not only educationally sound, but also intuitive and motivating [16]. Designs that support usability, clarity, and low cognitive overhead ensure that learners can focus on content rather than interface. Layered complexity and increasing challenges help maintain motivation, while timely feedback and space for reflection reinforce skill acquisition [15,25].

In sum, serious games offer a powerful approach for conveying complex real-world competencies in a structured yet engaging manner. When applied to domains such as ERP cybersecurity and incident management, they can simulate realistic stress scenarios, encourage active problem solving, and build practical skills that can be transferred to workplace settings.

2.3 ERP-Systems in Serious Games

Several gamified approaches have been developed to support ERP learning, primarily in educational settings. One of the most widely used is the ERP Simulation Game (ERPSim), which allows students to experience the integration of business processes and the transaction flow using SAP software in a competitive environment [2]. Similarly, Legner et al. propose a role-based simulation game to teach ERP architecture and process logic in academic curricula [18].

These games have shown benefits in fostering understanding of business concepts and improving soft skills such as problemsolving, teamwork, communication, and time management [21]. However, they primarily focus on process efficiency, system usage, and business decision making under normal operating conditions.

Unlike ERPSim, which emphasizes transactional accuracy and integrated process learning, the game presented in this document prioritizes incident response, role-specific decision making under uncertainty, and cross-functional communication during cybersecurity crises. Changes the learning focus from operational optimization to organizational resilience and situational awareness.

Although there are limited examples of security-focused ERP games, one notable exception is the multiplayer game by Tritscher et al., which explores the misuse of ERP systems for financial fraud scenarios [27]. Although thematically relevant, this game does not emphasize defense mechanisms or awareness training for ERP users.

This indicates a gap in the existing landscape: while simulation-based ERP games are well-established in business education, few address ERP-specific cybersecurity threats. This paper contributes to closing this gap by presenting a serious game adapted to the compromise of the ERP system, enabling players to experience and manage the organizational consequences of a security breach.

3 Research Design

This study follows the principles of Design Science Research (DSR) to develop, evaluate and iteratively refine a serious game aimed at increasing cybersecurity awareness in ERP system contexts. DSR provides a structured approach to creating artifacts that are both practically relevant and theoretically grounded [12].

The research process incorporated the following elements:

Relevance Cycle: The problem was identified through a gap in existing cybersecurity training, which rarely addresses ERP-specific risks. ERP systems were recognized as critical and highly vulnerable, and users lack contextual awareness and structured response training.

Design Cycle: The scenario for the game was developed iteratively, with five structured rounds that simulate a cyber attack on an ERP system. Roles, materials, and mechanics were refined based on user feedback, game testing, and alignment with real-world threat patterns (e.g. ransomware, lateral movement). The core design decisions were informed by the gamification principles and the educational design literature.

Rigor Cycle: The artifact is grounded in established knowledge bases, including cybersecurity standards (e.g. BSI, NIST), serious game design research, and ERP threat models. Reviews of the literature and empirical studies on gamified learning shaped the mechanics, role structure, and evaluation metrics of the game.

The game was test played in two academic sessions with groups of technical and non-technical students. Mixed method evaluation was used, combining Likert scale questionnaires, facilitator observations, and open feedback to assess usability, engagement, and perceived learning impact. Revisions were made between sessions to address the complexity of the quiz, the fairness of scoring, and the clarity of the role.

In general, the DSR methodology allowed the development of a validated, context-sensitive learning tool that addresses a concrete organizational need.

4 Scenario Design and Game Development

The serious game *ERP-Systems in Need* was developed as a scenario-driven role-based training tool designed to simulate cybersecurity incidents in enterprise environments. It builds on the foundational mechanics of the previously established game *A Question of Security* [26], which focused on the compromise of mobile devices. In contrast, the new scenario shifts focus to the compromise of the entire organization's ERP system, requiring a more complex design to reflect enterprise-level decision-making and coordination.

4.1 Scenario Concept and Objectives

The primary objective of the game is to increase awareness of ERP-specific cybersecurity threats and improve players' ability to assess and respond to incidents from both technical and organizational perspectives. The scenario models a progressive cyberattack targeting an ERP environment, involving indicators such as data corruption, access anomalies, and system unavailability. Learning goals include recognizing indicators of compromise within ERP processes, practicing decision making under uncertainty in different organizational roles, understanding interdependencies within supply chain and HR modules, and applying knowledge of best practices for security from standards such as BSI and NIST.

4.2 Structure and Gameplay Flow

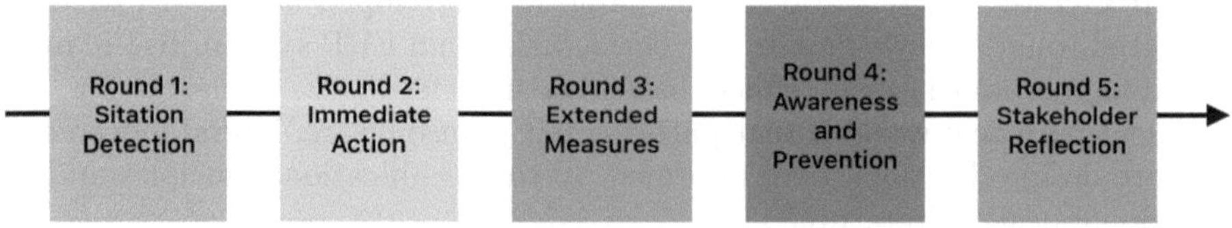

Fig. 1. Round scheme of *ERP-Systems in Need.*

The game consists of five rounds, each representing a phase in the incident lifecycle (Fig. 1):

1. **Situation Detection:** Players analyze symptoms and system behavior to identify a possible breach.

2. **Immediate Action:** Groups develop short-term containment and communication strategies.
3. **Extended Measures:** Participants propose strategic and technical follow-up actions to limit impact and resume operations.
4. **Awareness and Prevention:** A technical quiz challenges players to reflect on real-world attack vectors and mitigation measures.
5. **Stakeholder Reflection:** Teams assume the roles of affected departments (e.g., HR, Finance, Management) and evaluate the scenario from their perspective.

Each round builds on the results of the previous phase, encouraging cumulative learning. The design incorporates both cooperative and competitive elements through point-based scoring and structured group roles.

4.3 Role Design and Group Dynamics

The game is designed for groups of 6–10 participants, divided into mixed teams consisting of two primary roles: operational employees and management representatives. This dual-role system enables perspective taking across functional hierarchies and reflects real-world ERP use cases.

Operational players focus on technical implications, such as failed transactions or missing purchase orders, while management roles address business continuity, stakeholder communication, and regulatory concerns. Throughout the game, players are encouraged to coordinate actions and justify decisions based on role responsibilities.

4.4 Game Materials and Facilitation

Physical implementation includes the following.

- A printed game board visualizing the round progression (see Fig. 2).
- Scenario and role description cards.
- Event and response cards, some introducing disruptive "surprise" scenarios.
- Quiz sheets based on the BSI guidelines and attack typologies.
- A point tracking mechanism for feedback and gamification.

A trained facilitator moderates the session, introduces round content, provides optional hints, and awards points based on correctness, creativity, and collaboration. Additional tools such as mind maps and help cards assist less experienced players in identifying threats and appropriate responses.

4.5 Iterative Refinement and Adaptability

Between version 1 and version 2 of the game, there was one key improvement made based on participant feedback: the point distribution system was adjusted to reward early rounds more evenly and to encourage consistent engagement.

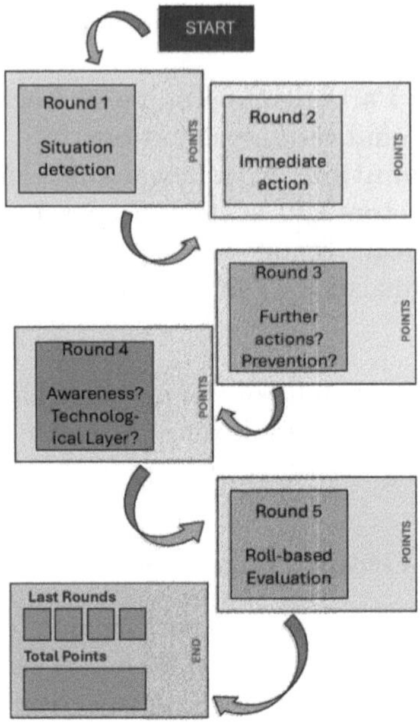

Fig. 2. The board of *ERP-Systems in need.*

During the second iteration, there was some feedback, that will lead to some major changes in the next iteration to follow: the quiz questions in round four will be simplified and supplemented with support cards to accommodate nontechnical participants. Lastly, the visual design of the materials will be enhanced by color-coded laminated cards for improved usability.

The modular structure of the game allows future expansions and the training of other ERP related topics like cloud compromise or third-party access breaches. The game is easily adaptable for both in-person and potential digital formats as described for the digital version of *A Question of Security* [26].

4.6 Pedagogical Considerations

The design decisions were guided by the principles of experiential learning and gamification. By simulating a time-sensitive multirole incident, the game promotes participation, decision-making, and knowledge transfer. Reflection phases at the end of each round encourage metacognitive processing and reinforce key concepts.

Through tentative action and structured facilitation, *ERP-Systems in Need* provides a low-risk, yet realistic environment to explore complex challenges in cybersecurity and organizational resilience.

5 Implementation and Playtesting

The serious game *ERP-Systems in Need* was implemented and evaluated through two playtesting sessions with students from the University of the Bundeswehr München. The goal was to assess the usability, relevance and impact of the game on cybersecurity awareness among participants of varying backgrounds.

5.1 Participants and Setup

The first group consisted of nine students from the Information Systems. Most had prior experience with ERP systems and basic cybersecurity knowledge. The second group included eight participants from social and political sciences with limited technical experience but a strong interest in digital security issues. This cross-disciplinary mix allowed for a comparative assessment of how diverse users interact with and benefit from the game.

The sessions were held in a classroom setting with printed game boards, cards, pens, and a time keeping tool. The participants were split into teams, each assuming one of two primary roles: operational employee or strategic manager. The facilitator (game master) explained the rules, introduced the scenarios, moderated the game play, and encouraged reflection throughout the session.

Each session followed the full five-round structure:

1. Identification of a security incident
2. Immediate containment strategies
3. Strategic and technical response measures
4. Awareness through quiz-based learning
5. Role-based stakeholder evaluation

The first group demonstrated fast adoption of technical concepts, but initially underappreciated the strategic decisions required at the management level. The facilitator's guidance helped bridge this gap. The second group needed more time to engage with the technical vocabulary and threat models but showed a high degree of collaboration and creativity once the core mechanics were understood.

5.2 Observations

Playtesting led to multiple refinements. Participants in both groups provided feedback via structured Likert scale questionnaires and open-ended comments. Based on this, improvements were implemented like a weighted point system to balance early and late game influence. Color-coded and laminated cards were introduced to improve clarity and usability, as well as optional support cards for players unfamiliar with cybersecurity terminology. Regarding the quiz, difficulty adjustments were made to adapt to the group experience.

The duration of the game was averaged 90 to 100 min, including feedback sessions. The sessions confirmed that the game successfully promoted cross-role understanding, encouraged realistic incident thinking, and highlighted the complexity of ERP security incidents. Participants reported a greater confidence in identifying and responding to cyberattacks within critical business systems.

These findings validate the potential of the game as a flexible and engaging tool for cybersecurity training in both academic and professional contexts.

6 Evaluation Results

Table 1. Survey results of *ERP-Systems in need* on a 5-point Likert scale (means).

Question	It. 1 (N = 9)	It. 2 (N = 8)
How did you like the game?	4.78	4.75
Did the game meet your expectations?	4.44	4.63
Were you satisfied with the transported information?	4.78	4.88
Did you enjoy the game design?	4.11	4.75
Were you satisfied with the Game Master?	4.89	4.88
Did you enjoy the technological focus?	4.44	4.00
Would you like to see further serious games like the given one?	3.89	4.88

Two play testing sessions were conducted with students from the University of the Bundeswehr Munich to evaluate the game. Quantitative feedback was collected using a 5-point Likert scale from –2 (very negative) to +2 (very positive). The results were transformed using a 5-point Likert scale from 1 to 5 to make them comparable to the results of the serious game *A Question of Security* that will be discussed in this section. The results showed high satisfaction: 7 of 9 participants rated the overall experience of the game as 'very good' and all agreed that the scenario improved their awareness of cybersecurity. Some confusion arose in the first round with respect to player roles, but this was resolved through facilitator guidance. Although game design received slightly mixed feedback - attributed to early-stage prototyping - facilitation and content clarity were highly rated (Tables 1 and 2).

The second group included eight students with limited technical knowledge. Their interest in ERP systems was strong and they welcomed the serious game format as a new learning experience. Most of the participants rated the game positively, although the technical quiz in round four proved challenging. Feedback suggested that the technological focus should be simplified or more gradually introduced for non-technical audiences. Despite this, the group found the game engaging and valuable. Both groups expressed interest in seeing the further development of serious games for cybersecurity training. The session durations were 82 and 101 min, respectively, exceeding the planned time of 60 min due to active discussions and clarifications.

Table 2. Selected results of the questionnaires from *A Question of Security*

Question	N	Min.	Max.	Mean
How would you rate your knowledge of IT security?	85	1	5	3.78
How much fun did you have with this serious game?	85	3	5	4.50
The serious game has increased my awareness of IT security.	84	1	5	3.58
The serious game taught me something new about the correct behavior during a ransomware incident.	85	1	5	3.67
I believe that by participating in the serious game, I will be able to behave appropriately in the event of a ransomware attack in the future.	83	3	5	4.30
How suitable do you think the serious game is for learning more about how to deal with ransomware incidents? (personally)	84	2	5	4.40
How suitable do you think the serious game is for learning more about how to deal with ransomware incidents? (your organization)	83	2	5	4.24

As explained, *ERP-Systems in Need* is based on the serious game *A Question of Security.* It has largely adopted the mechanics of the game and developed a new scenario for it. Although there are differences in terms of sample size (ERP n = 17, Security n = 85), it is worth taking a brief comparative look at the two serious games, because although different, the scenarios have the fact in common that the user cannot do a lot on their own in case of an incident but needs help from experts. Although an attack on an ERP system has a more probable bigger impact on a business than a single compromised mobile device, the things users can do in both cases are basically the same: they can coordinate, organize, and communicate. As the surveys were based on different questionnaires, the results were clustered thematically. Both games scored highly on player experience (ERP: 4.76; Security: 4.50), which makes it a good tool for awareness campaigns and a promising base for more scenarios to be developed. The most noticeable difference appeared in the perceived learning content, where the ERP game reached 4.83 compared to 3.67 for the security game. There may be several reasons for this result. Firstly, ERP security has already been shown to be an issue that is still underestimated in terms of importance. There may be several reasons for this result. Firstly, ERP security has already been shown to be an issue that is still underestimated in terms of importance. In other words, even regular users can still learn a lot of new things here, while IT security awareness is already widely discussed, whether at work or in emails from your own bank or other service providers, for example. Secondly, it is important to consider the target group of players when interpreting the results. The results of the security game have shown a relatively high overall knowledge of IT security. Observations during the games showed that the experts gain less new factual knowledge but are able to rethink their own processes or engage more with the user's perspective when the serious game is played in mixed groups. The question "Would you like to see more serious games like the given one?" from the ERP game is comparable to the question from the security game questionnaire as to whether players would recommend the game to others in terms of a positive overall assessment and acceptance. In the second iteration of the ERP game, all 8 players agreed very strongly or strongly, in iteration 1, only one player disagreed. 82 of 85 respondents to the security game would also recommend the serious game to others.

7 Discussion

The evaluation results of the serious game *ERP-Systems in Need* show its potential as an effective training tool for ERP-specific cybersecurity awareness. The dual-role setup (employee and management) appears valuable for promoting perspective taking and fostering discussion across organizational levels. Both technical and non-technical participants showed increased confidence in identifying threats and responding to incidents, indicating the accessibility and relevance of the game.

However, some limitations must be acknowledged. The game was tested exclusively in an academic environment, which may not fully reflect the pressure, complexity, or accountability present in corporate settings. The sessions were also facilitated by a knowledgeable moderator, which may not always be feasible in practical deployments. Furthermore, the game requires group and time coordination, which may be a barrier in fast-paced enterprise contexts.

The participants noted that the structure of the game encouraged collaboration, strategic thinking, and communication. In particular, the scenario-based progression and the stakeholder reflection of round five were praised for deepening the understanding. However, some players, especially those with less technical background, found the quiz in round four challenging, suggesting the need for more flexible and adaptive content delivery.

These findings highlight two key design considerations for future iterations: first, balancing technical depth with clarity, and second, enabling scalable facilitation through modular, digital, or self-guided formats. Furthermore, integration of resource constraints, time pressure, or branching narratives could more realistically simulate crisis dynamics and decision fatigue, enhancing transferability to workplace scenarios.

In general, the game successfully translates abstract risks into actionable learning, supports role-based participation, and stimulates critical reflection - the key ingredients for meaningful awareness training in ERP cybersecurity.

8 Conclusion and Future Work

This paper presented the design, implementation and evaluation of the serious game *ERP-Systems in Need*, which aims to raise awareness of cybersecurity in ERP environments through a role-based scenario-driven serious game. Building on the established game framework of *A Question of Security*, the extended version introduced a scenario that allowed participants to explore the security challenges of the ERP from both the operational and managerial perspectives.

The game was evaluated in two academic playtesting sessions that included participants with technical and non-technical backgrounds. The results indicate that the format is well suited to engage learners, foster collaboration, and support knowledge retention. The combination of progressive rounds, structured facilitation, and real-world threat scenarios proved effective in illustrating the complexity of ERP-specific incidents.

However, the findings also highlight several opportunities for further development. First, the game requires broader validation beyond academic settings. Future studies should assess its applicability and effectiveness in corporate environments, where ERP systems are mission critical and user responsibilities vary widely.

Second, the integration of an adaptive difficulty model is a promising enhancement. By adjusting the technical complexity, the pressure of decisions, and the information flow according to the level of experience of the players, the game can better support heterogeneous learning groups. This could include time-sensitive decision-making elements, resource constraints (e.g. limited staff or IT capacity), and dynamic scenario branches based on player actions.

Third, the role system can be extended to reflect more nuanced organizational structures. Additional roles, such as IT forensics, data protection officers, C-level executives, or legal advisors, could enrich the game and promote deeper reflection on real-world interdependencies and decision trade-offs.

Together, these future directions aim to increase the realism, scalability, and educational impact of the game. A digital implementation may further support hybrid delivery formats and facilitate automated feedback. Ultimately, *ERP-Systems in Need* seek to serve as a flexible training platform that empowers organizations to strengthen their security culture through collaborative, experiential learning.

Acknowledgments and Disclosure of Funding. This work originates from CONTAIN and the LIONS research projects. We acknowledge funding for CONTAIN by the Bundesministerium für Forschung, Technologie und Raumfahrt (BMFTR) (grant number 13N16581-13N16587) as part of the SIFO program. LIONS is funded by dtec.bw—Digitalization and Technology Research Center of the Bundeswehr, which we gratefully acknowledge. dtec.bw is funded by the European Union—NextGenerationEU.

References

1. Almås, H., Giæver, F.: The emergence of collaboration in serious games. an exploratory study. Int. J. Serious Games **11**(3), 89–108 (2024)
2. Beranič, T., Heričko, M.: The impact of serious games in economic and business education: a case of erp business simulation. Sustainability **14**(2), 683 (2022)

3. Bundesamt für Sicherheit in der Informationstechnik: APP.4.2 SAP-ERP-System (2023). https://www.bsi.bund.de/SharedDocs/Downloads/DE/BSI/Grundschutz/IT-GS-Kompendium_Einzel_PDFs_2023/06_APP_Anwendungen/APP_4_2_SAP_ERP_System_Edition_2023.pdf
4. Bundesamt für Sicherheit in der Informationstechnik: Umsetzungshinweise zum Baustein APP.4.2 SAP-ERP-System (2023). https://www.bsi.bund.de/SharedDocs/Downloads/DE/BSI/Grundschutz/Umsetzungshinweise/Umsetzungshinweise_2022/Umsetzungshinweis_zum_Baustein_APP_4_2_SAP_ERP_System.pdf
5. Clare Duffy: OpenAI CEO Sam Altman warns of an AI 'fraud crisis' (2025). https://edition.cnn.com/2025/07/22/tech/openai-sam-altman-fraud-crisis
6. Conapi GmbH: Case Study: ERP API Security Breach Costs Distributor €1.8M (2025). https://conapi.at/erp-api-security-breach-case-study/
7. Djaouti, D., Alvarez, J., Jessel, J.P.: Classifying serious games: the g/p/s model. In: Handbook of Research on Improving Learning and Motivation through Educational Games: Multidisciplinary Approaches, pp. 118–136. IGI global (2011)
8. Gangapatnam, K.: Securing the digital core: cybersecurity challenges and strategies in sap erp systems. J. Comput. Sci. Technol. Stud. **7**(3), 270–276 (2025)
9. Greiner, M., et al.: Scared? prepared? toward a ransomware incident response scenario. In: International Conference on Innovations for Community Services, pp. 289–320. Springer (2024)
10. Hamari, J., Shernoff, D.J., Rowe, E., Coller, B., Asbell-Clarke, J., Edwards, T.: Challenging games help students learn: an empirical study on engagement, flow and immersion in game-based learning. Comput. Hum. Behav. **54**, 170–179 (2016)
11. Chen, H., Magramo, K.: Finance worker pays out $25 million after video call with deepfake 'chief financial officer' (2024). https://edition.cnn.com/2024/02/04/asia/deepfake-cfo-scam-hong-kong-intl-hnk
12. Hevner, A.R., March, S.T., Park, J., Ram, S.: Design science in information systems research. MIS Quart. 75–105 (2004)
13. Hofstede, G.J., De Caluwé, L., Peters, V.: Why simulation games work-in search of the active substance: a synthesis. Simul. Gaming **41**(6), 824–843 (2010)
14. JP Perez-Etchegoyen: SAP Security Notes & CVEs 2025: Analysis & Threats (2025). https://onapsis.com/blog/critical-sap-security-notes-cves-2025/
15. Kerres, M., Bormann, M., Vervenne, M.: Didaktische Konzeption von Serious Games: Zur Verknüpfung von Spiel- und Lernangeboten. MedienPädagogik: Zeitschrift für Theorie und Praxis der Medienbildung, pp. 1–16 (2009)
16. Lameras, P., Arnab, S., Dunwell, I., Stewart, C., Clarke, S., Petridis, P.: Essential features of serious games design in higher education: linking learning attributes to game mechanics. Br. J. Edu. Technol. **48**(4), 972–994 (2017)
17. Lechner, U., Dännart, S., Rieb, A., Rudel, S.: Case Kritis-Fallstudien zur IT-Sicherheit in Kritischen Infrastrukturen. Logos Verlag Berlin (2018)
18. Legner, C., Estier, T., Avdiji, H., Boillat, T.: Designing capstone courses in management education: Knowledge activation and integration using an erp-based simulation game. In: Proceedings of the International Conference on Information Systems 2013 (ICIS 2013) (2013)
19. NIST: CVE-2025-31324 Detail (2025). https://nvd.nist.gov/vuln/detail/CVE-2025-31324
20. Ntoa, S., et al.: Serious games beyond entertainment and learning: an evaluation methodology for assessing awareness raising, empathy, and social change. In: International Conference on Human-Computer Interaction, pp. 141–164. Springer (2024)

21. Octavio, M.F.R., et al.: New learning method with erp business simulation games: what can we learn? user perception. J. Contemp. Account. (2024)
22. Onapsis: 46% of Enterprises Experience Four or More Ransomware Attacks in a Single Year, Affecting ERP Applications and Systems 89% of the Time (2024). https://onapsis.com/press-releases/new-onapsis-ransomware-research/
23. Laudanski, P.: SAP security breach cited as a major factor in company's bankruptcy (2025). https://onapsis.com/blog/sap-security-breach-cited-in-companys-bankruptcy/
24. Ravyse, W.S., Seugnet Blignaut, A., Leendertz, V.E.A.: Success factors for serious games to enhance learning: a systematic review. Virt. Real. **21**, 31–58 (2017)
25. Serrano-Laguna, Á., Martínez-Ortiz, I., Haag, J., Regan, D., Johnson, A., Fernández-Manjón, B.: Applying standards to systematize learning analytics in serious games. Comput. Stand. Interfaces **50**, 116–123 (2017)
26. Strussenberg, J., Seidenfad, K., Greiner, M.: From paper to pixel: the digitalization. In: Innovations for Community Services: 25th International Conference, I4CS 2025, Munich, Germany, 11–13 June 2025, Proceedings, vol. 2513, p. 307. Springer (2025)
27. Tritscher, J., Krause, A., Schlör, D., Gwinner, F., Von Mammen, S., Hotho, A.: A financial game with opportunities for fraud. In: 2021 IEEE Conference on Games (CoG), pp. 1–5. IEEE (2021)

The Ethical Requirements Stack: Operationalizing Adaptive Ethical Requirements with Human-AI Collaboration and GPT-Based LLMs

Mamia Agbese[1(✉)], Rebekah Rousi[2], and Pekka Abrahamsson[3]

[1] University of Jyväskylä, Seminaarinkatu, 40014 Jyväskylä, Finland
mamia.o.agbese@student.jyu.fi
[2] University of Vaasa, Wolffintie 32, 65200 Vaasa, Finland
rebekah.rousi@uwasa.fi
[3] Tampere University, Kalevantie 4, 33100 Tampere, Finland
pekka.abrahamsson@tuni.fi

Abstract. The ongoing evolution and societal impact of AI systems demand systematic methods to embed ethics into AI development. Existing approaches often struggle to translate high-level ethical principles into concrete, adaptable software requirements, resulting in "ethical debt" that risks reputational harm, regulatory issues, and diminished stakeholder trust. This paper introduces the Ethical Requirements Stack (ERS), a structured, multi-layered artifact designed to elicit, decompose, and manage ethical requirements (ERs) from abstract themes to actionable development tasks. The ERS is operationalized through a human–AI collaborative workflow that leverages GPT-based Large Language Models (LLMs) for scalable ideation, complemented by human oversight to ensure contextual and ethical alignment. Using a design science research methodology, we demonstrate how the ERS supports the translation of stakeholder-elicited ethical values—aligned with frameworks such as IEEE 7000™-2021—into traceable software specifications. Our findings show that the ERS enables structured ethical reasoning and highlights the complementary strengths of AI-generated breadth and human critical judgment. This work contributes a practical approach for integrating ethics into the AI development lifecycle, supporting responsible innovation and reducing ethical debt through a combination of human-centered design and LLM-assisted requirements engineering.

Keywords: Ethical Requirements Stack · Human-AI Collaboration · Large Language Models (LLMs)

1 Introduction

The ongoing evolution of Artificial Intelligence (AI) continues to drive innovation in Software Engineering (SE). Modern AI-powered systems automate tasks, process vast datasets, generate content, act autonomously, and support

G. Herzwurm et al. (Eds.): ICSOB 2025, LNBIP 574, pp. 92–107, 2026.
https://doi.org/10.1007/978-3-032-14518-5_8

real-time interaction [1], transforming domains such as healthcare, finance, and autonomous systems [2–4]. While these advancements offer substantial benefits, they also introduce significant and evolving ethical challenges. Longstanding concerns, including bias, privacy, and accountability, are compounded by new risks such as AI-driven disinformation and unpredictable model behaviors [5]. Addressing these issues requires proactive integration of ethics across the AI development lifecycle to ensure sustainable and responsible software systems.

A central challenge lies in Requirements Engineering (RE): identifying, articulating, and managing ethical requirements (ERs)—explicit representations of values like fairness and transparency [6]. ERs are often abstract, interdisciplinary, and dynamic, evolving with rapid development cycles. Although Ethics by Design (EbD) approaches stress the importance of ERs, most frameworks lack adaptability for iterative environments, struggling to translate high-level principles into actionable and continuously evolving ERs [7,8]. These shortcomings contribute to what can be described as *ethical debt*—a growing misalignment between high-level ethical principles and their concrete implementation in software systems. Similar to technical debt (the future cost of taking shortcuts), ethical debt accumulates when ethical considerations are deferred, only partially addressed, or inconsistently managed, creating risks that compound over time [9,10]. Managing this debt requires mechanisms that make ERs explicit, traceable, and adaptable across the lifecycle, especially in iterative development contexts.

The IEEE Standard 7000™-2021 addresses this challenge by providing a process model for integrating ethical considerations into system design. The standard guides the elicitation of stakeholder values, their translation into ethical value requirements, and the traceability of these requirements from high-level principles to implementable specifications. It also emphasizes early integration, stakeholder engagement, and continuous alignment between ethical values and system functionality throughout the lifecycle [11]. Although the IEEE 7000 establishes a high-level process, practical instantiations that translate these principles into actionable methods, particularly in dynamic environments like Agile, remain limited.

To address this gap and extend the Ethical Requirements Stack (ERS) [12], this paper presents its design and operationalization within the Design and Demonstration phases of the Design Science Research Methodology (DSRM) [13]. The ERS provides a multi-layered structure that operationalizes ethical principles by translating them into context-sensitive and adaptable system requirements, aligning with standards such as IEEE 7000™–2021 and contributing to the mitigation of ethical debt. Designed for iterative methodologies like Agile, it provides a structured approach to integrating ethics into dynamic development processes. Our Demonstration validates the ERS's core mechanisms—its multi-layered structure using human–AI collaboration—as a proof of concept. Central to this is the use of GPT-based large language models (LLMs), specifically ChatGPT, to enhance efficiency, while human oversight ensures contextual sensitivity and stakeholder awareness. This study examines how combining human and AI strengths can support the elicitation and refinement of ERs. Accordingly, we address the following research questions:

- **RQ1:** How can the ERS be operationalized to elicit, structure, and manage ethical requirements within an Agile environment?
- **RQ2:** What are the benefits and challenges of integrating Human–AI collaboration in the ERS workflow for generating and refining ethical requirements?

This study focuses on the design and demonstration of the ERS in early RE phases, situated within a broader Ethics by Design (EbD) for AI context. The primary contributions are threefold: (1) the design of the ERS as a structured, multi-layered artifact for managing adaptive ERs in RE; (2) The demonstration of Human–AI collaboration within the ERS workflow, showcasing the integration of GPT-based AI into requirements elicitation, refinement, and structuring; and (3) an empirical evaluation of the ERS in practice, assessing how Human–AI collaboration affects the comprehensiveness, clarity, and adaptability of ERs. The remainder of the paper is structured as follows: Sect. 2 reviews related work, Sect. 3 outlines the methodology, Sect. 4 presents the ERS artifact, the workflow, and findings, Sect. 5 discusses the evaluation, and concludes with limitations and future work.

2 Background and Related Work

Software Engineering (SE) faces new challenges as Artificial Intelligence (AI) systems continue to evolve and become integral to modern applications across various domains, including healthcare, finance, and autonomous systems [2–4]. AI, defined as computational systems capable of perceiving, learning, and making decisions with minimal human intervention [14], differs from traditional software that follows explicitly programmed rules, relying instead on data-driven models that introduce uncertainty, opacity, and adaptability [15]. These characteristics enable powerful capabilities in content generation, decision-making, and human–AI interaction [16,17], but they also complicate established SE practices, particularly Requirements Engineering (RE). Traditional RE assumes that requirements can be elicited, specified, and validated, yet AI systems are adaptive, data-driven, and often opaque. This makes it difficult to translate stakeholder values into precise, testable requirements and to ensure traceability between requirements and system behavior [10].

The field of AI ethics addresses the moral, societal, and human-centered implications of AI technologies, emphasizing principles such as transparency, accountability, fairness, and privacy [18,19]. However, rapid AI progress has introduced dynamic ethical challenges—disinformation, privacy breaches, and manipulative technologies like deepfakes and surveillance systems [3,5]. Embedding ethics throughout the system lifecycle is essential. Yet, conventional AI ethics principles often remain abstract and difficult to operationalize, leading to implementation gaps and ethical blind spots [18]. These unresolved concerns accumulate as *ethical debt*: deferred or inconsistently managed ethical issues that, like technical debt, compound risks over time [9]. RE—the discipline of identifying, analyzing, and managing requirements—is a natural avenue for managing this debt. Ethical Requirements (ERs) translate abstract principles into actionable system specifications [20], yet existing RE practices often struggle to capture and adapt ERs in fast-moving Agile contexts [10].

Several frameworks and methods have been developed to bridge this gap. IEEE Std 7000™-2021 provides a structured process for Value-Based Engineering (VbE), guiding stakeholder value elicitation, ethical value requirements (EVRs), and traceability from concept exploration to design [11]. While comprehensive, its phased, linear orientation can be misaligned with iterative Agile practices [7,21]. ECCOLA offers a more Agile-oriented tool, organizing ethical themes into card-based prompts and practical recommendations [22]. It raises awareness but lacks mechanisms for systematically connecting high-level values to granular development tasks across iterations. Ethical User Stories (EUSs) adapt the user story format to embed ethical concerns (e.g., "As a user, I want my data anonymized so that my privacy is protected") [23]. They are effective for capturing specific ethical needs but lack a hierarchical or evolving structure for managing ERs across project lifecycles.

These approaches have advanced the field but share common limitations: they are often static, difficult to adapt in dynamic AI contexts, and may overlook context-specific ethical risks [24]. As a result, ethical debt continues to accumulate, widening the gap between high-level principles and their actionable implementation. This creates space for frameworks that combine the rigor of standards like IEEE 7000 with the iterative flexibility of Agile methods. Human–AI (H-AI) collaboration provides a promising direction. Large Language Models (LLMs), such as GPT-based ChatGPT, can generate, organize, and refine ERs at scale, complementing human expertise in contextual understanding, moral reasoning, and oversight [25,26]. While current research highlights the potential of H-AI collaboration in RE [27], there remains a lack of structured methodologies for systematically embedding it into the continuous elicitation and management of ERs.

The Ethical Requirements Stack (ERS) was first proposed in [12] as a multilayered framework for translating abstract ethical values into Epics, Features, User Stories, and Tasks. Its conceptual strength lies in combining hierarchical structuring with iterative adaptability, aligning ethical requirements with Agile portfolio management principles. By explicitly linking ethical principles to evolving system requirements, the ERS offers a pathway for systematically managing and reducing ethical debt. This paper advances the ERS by presenting its detailed design and operationalization, focusing on how H-AI collaboration can enhance its workflow and address the limitations of existing frameworks.

3 Methodology

This study adopts an exploratory approach following the *Design Science Research (DSR)* paradigm to address the challenge of integrating ethical requirements (ERs) into AI development [28]. The Design Science Research Methodology (DSRM) by [13] is appropriate because the study involves both the creation of an artifact—the *Ethical Requirements Stack (ERS)*—and the demonstration of its utility in a relevant setting. Accordingly, the research followed three phases: (1) designing the ERS as the core artifact, (2) demonstrating it through collaborative workshops with human–AI teams in an Agile-inspired environment, and (3) conducting a mixed-methods evaluation of its utility. Rather than testing hypotheses, the methodology emphasizes building and demonstrating a practical solution to a real-world problem [13,28].

To complement DSR, we used the ECCOLA method [22,29] and Ethical User Stories (EUSs) [23]. ECCOLA consists of 22 cards across nine AI ethics themes—analyze, transparency, data, agency and oversight, safety and security, fairness, wellbeing, accountability, and governance—each posing questions to prompt ethical reflection. EUSs adapt Agile user stories ("As a [user], I want [goal] so that [reason]") to embed ethical reflections to help elicit ERs in AI development [23], where the "goal" states the ethical outcome and the "reason" its motivation. For example: "As a user, I want my data anonymized so that my privacy is protected." This makes abstract ethical principles actionable, promoting ethically informed AI design [23].

3.1 ERS Design and Development (DSRM: Design)

The Ethical Requirements Stack (ERS), first introduced by [12], is a multi-layered framework for embedding ethical requirements (ERs) into AI development (see Fig. 1). The ERS operationalizes high-level ethical principles by systematically decomposing them into context-sensitive, actionable system requirements, maintaining traceability and alignment with standards and regulations, while supporting continuous feedback to adapt to evolving contexts. Inspired by Agile portfolio management and requirements stacks [30,31], it organizes ERs hierarchically: *Themes* represent broad ethical principles; *Epics* define strategic objectives; *Features* describe necessary system functionalities; and *User Stories/Tasks* specify actionable development steps [32]. ERs are drawn from ethical guidelines, societal values, or AI ethics standards (e.g., IEEE 7000–2021), ranging from general mandates like "prevent discrimination" to specific ones such as "obtain informed consent before data collection." This structure translates abstract principles into actionable requirements, promoting ethical alignment in practice. A core strength of the ERS is its adaptability, supporting ongoing refinement as new concerns or regulations arise. For this study, the ERS was refined through: (1) Conceptual adaptation of Agile principles; (2) Integration of ethical AI literature and tools like ECCOLA and Ethical User Stories (EUSs); and (3) Iterative structuring of abstract principles into practical, context-sensitive ERs [12].

3.2 ERS Operationalization: Workshops (DSRM: Demonstration)

The ERS was demonstrated through two scenario-based workshops (each approximately three hours), serving as exploratory case illustrations of its practical use. The workshops served as exploratory demonstrations of the ERS in practice

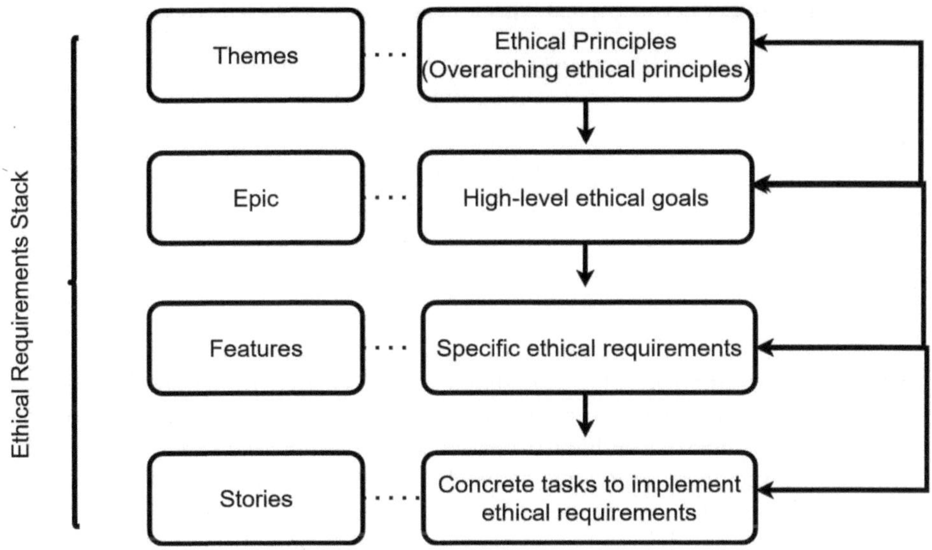

Fig. 1. Hierarchical organization of the ERS.

rather than as formal empirical validation. The outcomes of these workshops are reported in Sect. 4, where we illustrate how the ERS was operationalized in practice and what it yielded.

3.3 Participants and Data Collection

Ten researchers (Table 1) and ChatGPT collaborated in the study. Participants were purposively recruited from an international software engineering conference and a university research lab, with expertise in *Software Engineering, Information Systems, and Cybersecurity*—chosen for relevance to Agile methods, requirements engineering, sociotechnical insights, and security/privacy perspectives [33]. Their analytical skills and detailed feedback supported the exploration of the ERS's practical use. All participants provided informed consent (redacted for anonymity Consent Form), which outlined anonymization measures, rights, voluntary participation, confidentiality, and potential risks. Workshop artifacts included human- and AI-generated EUSs and ERs, notes from ERS usability discussions, and Flinga exports of collaborative work.

Table 1. Participant Roles and Expertise

Participant Role	Area of Expertise
R1–R2, R7–R9	Software Engineering
R3	Cyber Security
R4–R6, R10	Information Systems

Table 2. Central Ethical Themes and Selected ECCOLA Cards

ECCOLA Ethical Theme [18,22,29]	ECCOLA Ethical (Sub-theme) [22,29]
Well-being	Societal Effect (#17)
Transparency	Communication (#3), Documenting Trade-offs (#4)
Data	Privacy and Data (#7)
Analyse	Stakeholder Analysis (#0)
Governance	Retention and Disposition (#21)
Agency/Oversight	Human Oversight (#11)

Agile-Inspired Setup. The workshops adopted Agile principles [34], structuring activities like sprints to enable iterative refinement. Cross-functional collaboration was simulated by having participants role-play managers, developers, and other stakeholders. Frequent feedback loops allowed continuous refinement of ERs for clarity, ethical alignment, and actionability [35].
Scenario and Activities. The workshops focused on a fitness tracking app, chosen for its accessibility and relevant ethical challenges, such as privacy. The app enables users to monitor health data via smart devices (e.g., smartwatches, fitness bands, smartphones), requiring explicit permission for biometric data collection while also allowing manual input. A full use case description is provided in the supplementary materials at Zenodo Repository. This scenario highlighted ethical concerns like privacy and transparency. Participants used seven ECCOLA cards spanning six ethical themes (Table 2) to develop Ethical User Stories (EUSs) and Ethical Requirements (ERs). Using the Flinga online whiteboard, they followed a four-stage process: (i) identifying ethical concerns via ECCOLA prompts, (ii) drafting EUSs, (iii) translating EUSs into system-level ERs, and (iv) refining ERs for clarity and alignment. For example, from the EUS "As a user, I want my fitness data to remain private...", the ER "The system must enable users to delete their fitness data at any time" was derived by reframing the core ethical concern as a concrete, ECCOLA-aligned requirement. These ERs were then refined to enhance clarity, ethical fit, and actionability, enabling a collaborative, iterative approach to ethical design.

Human-AI Collaboration. ChatGPT was integrated to complement human input by generating ERs from three sources: the fitness app use case, ECCOLA cards (e.g., #7—Privacy and Data), and human-authored EUSs. For some themes (e.g., Stakeholder Analysis, Documenting Trade-offs), ERs were generated directly from the use case and ECCOLA prompts due to missing human-authored EUSs. Outputs were iteratively refined through prompt adjustments guiding ChatGPT toward ethical alignment and actionable formulation. Table 3 illustrates this process, showing how refinement shifted responses from vague user stories to operational requirements.

Table 3. Iterative Prompt Refinement During Human–AI Collaboration

Prompt Version	Description/Outcome
Initial Prompt	Example: "Using ECCOLA card #7—Privacy and Data, and this EUS, generate ERs." **Outcome:** Responses included user stories and vague suggestions.
Refinement #1	Prompt: "Ensure ERs align with the ethical theme." **Outcome:** Stronger alignment with ECCOLA themes.
Refinement #2	Prompt: "ERs should be actionable requirements, not user stories." **Outcome:** Clarity improved; ERs became operationalizable

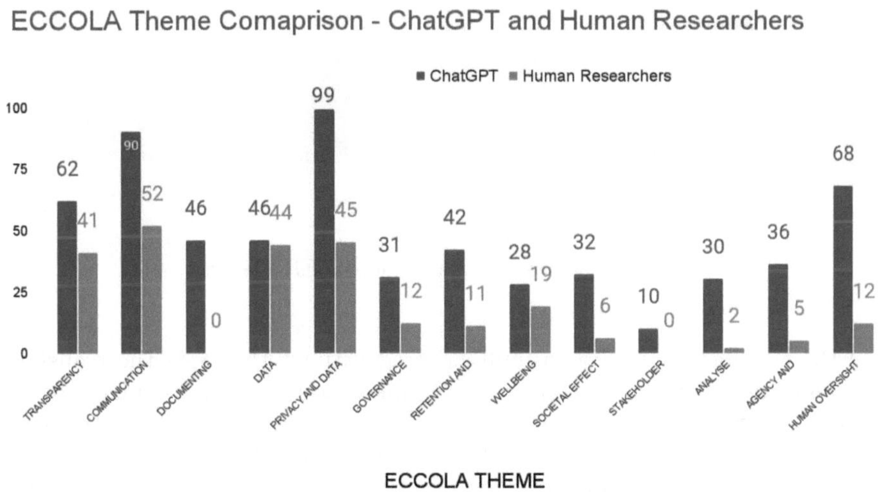

Fig. 2. Human vs AI ERs by ECCOLA theme.

3.4 Data Analysis

We employed a mixed-methods approach combining qualitative and quantitative analysis [36]. The ERS was managed in Microsoft Excel to structure ERs hierarchically (Theme → Epic → Feature → Story), remove duplicates and irrelevant items, and refine inconsistent phrasing. For **qualitative analysis**, Framework Analysis [37] was used to deductively code ERs against ECCOLA themes and map them into ERS layers by abstraction, with consensus checks ensuring reliability. For **quantitative analysis**, frequency counts of 869 ERs (620 from ChatGPT, 249 from humans) measured theme coverage and abstraction levels, highlighting differences in focus between human- and AI-generated ERs (Figs. 2, 3).

4 ERS as a Design Artifact

This section presents (i) the ERS as a design artifact, and (ii) outcomes from its operationalization in workshops.

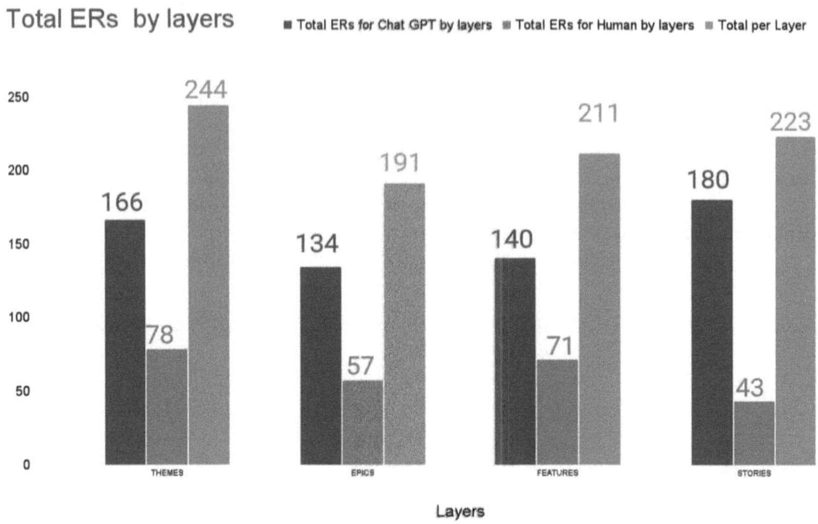

Fig. 3. Distribution of ERs across ERS layers.

The ERS was instantiated as a multi-layered artifact that aids the translation and management of abstract ethical principles to actionable requirements. Its hierarchy - (Themes, Epics, Features, Stories; Fig. 1) enables systematic decomposition of values elicited via tools like ECCOLA and EUSs. The design emphasizes three key value propositions for practitioners: *Traceability*, through hierarchical links from the Theme layer down to individual Stories,; *Adaptability*, achieved through the granular, loosely coupled layers that allow requirement changes without system-wide refactoring; and *Scalability*, which supports the decomposition of broad ethical values across large, complex systems. By providing a formalized structure, the framework offers a means to address ethical debt as development contexts change. Table 4 shows how the privacy theme was decomposed during workshops, refining high-level principles (e.g., GDPR compliance) into implementable requirements.

Table 4. Illustrative ERS decomposition for Privacy

Layer	Example Requirement
Theme	Ensure GDPR compliance, including consent and deletion mechanisms
Epic	Users must be able to revoke data collection consent at any time
Feature	Provide user-friendly consent screens with permission controls
Story	Allow users to view, modify, or delete their data at any time

4.1 Results — What Operationalization Yielded

The workshops resulted in two instantiations of the ERS (available at Zenodo Repository). The first was a *human-only ERS*, derived entirely from participant-authored EUSs and ERs. The second was a *ChatGPT-assisted ERS*, where the AI generated ERs directly from human-authored EUSs based on ECCOLA prompts and the use case, with guided prompts to ensure contextual and ethical alignment. This hybrid instantiation broadened thematic coverage while preserving precision through human oversight. Together, these versions illustrate the ERS's adaptability to different collaboration modes.

4.2 Findings

We present our findings aligned with the two research questions (RQs).

Answering RQ1: Design and Decomposition of the ERS. RQ1 examined how the ERS supports systematic decomposition and adaptive management of ethical requirements in Agile AI development. We assess its role across core Requirements Engineering (RE) stages: elicitation, analysis, specification, prioritization, validation, and management.

Elicitation drew on seven ECCOLA cards across six ethical themes, embedding ethics early in the process. *Analysis* involved clarifying ambiguities and checking feasibility against the fitness app scenario. *Specification* translated EUSs into preliminary ERs, refined into Themes, Epics, Features, and Stories (Table 3). *Prioritization* structured ERs into ERS layers by granularity and abstraction, ensuring traceability and prioritization [30]. *Validation and verification* were achieved through collaborative refinement for clarity and ethical alignment, though without deployment. *Management* positions the ERS as a dynamic backlog, enabling continuous adaptation across iterations. Table 4 illustrates the decomposition for Privacy-related requirements. Overall, the ERS operationalizes RE phases iteratively rather than sequentially, consistent with Agile principles.

Answering RQ2: Insights from Human-AI Collaboration. Our analysis of human- and AI-generated ERs produced five Preliminary Insights (PIs) on the benefits and challenges of Human–AI collaboration. The first three address quantitative traits; the last two focus on qualitative dynamics.

Quantitative Findings.

> *PI1: Coverage and Focus Divergence* — ChatGPT generated a much higher volume of ERs with broad thematic coverage, while human researchers contributed fewer but more concentrated ERs.

A total of 869 ERs were produced (620 ChatGPT, 249 human). ChatGPT's outputs spanned all ECCOLA themes, with a peak in *Privacy & Data*. In contrast, humans emphasized *Communication* while omitting others such as *Stake-*

holder Analysis. This divergence reflects the trade-off between AI's breadth and humans' selective depth.

PI2: Alignment with Core Themes — Both groups emphasized *Privacy & Data* and *Communication*, but *Stakeholder Analysis* was consistently underrepresented (Figure 2).

PI3: Layered Focus Divergence — ChatGPT concentrated on granular Story-level ERs, while humans focused on higher-level Themes and Epics, reflecting complementary strengths (Figure 3).

Qualitative Findings

PI4: Agile's Iterative Refinement — Both ChatGPT and human researchers improved ERs through iterative cycles: prompt tuning for ChatGPT and group discussion for humans, enhancing clarity, alignment, and actionability.

Agile-inspired feedback loops supported continuous refinement. For ChatGPT, this involved adjusting prompts to yield clearer, more actionable ERs (Table 3), while for humans, collaborative discussion refined ERs for depth and contextual alignment. This iterative process produced structured requirements across ERS layers (Theme–Epic–Feature–Story), as illustrated in Table 4.

PI5: Synergistic Refinement — ChatGPT ensured breadth and scalability, while humans added contextual nuance and ethical precision, together producing layered, actionable ERs.

For instance, ChatGPT's broad ERs (e.g., "protect user privacy") became actionable only after refined prompting (Table 3). Human researchers further resolved ambiguities, grounding requirements in context and stakeholder needs. This synergy highlights a complementary model: AI accelerates ideation at scale, while human input ensures ethical clarity and implementation relevance.

5 Discussion and Conclusion

We synthesize key benefits and challenges, organizing the discussion thematically while explicitly referencing each Preliminary Insight (PI) to ensure empirical traceability.

5.1 The Benefits of Human-AI Synergy in ERS Development

The collaboration between human researchers and AI in the ERS process leverages their complementary strengths, enhancing scalability, actionability, and adaptability—without replacing human expertise.

Enhanced Comprehensiveness and Scalability (PI1): As identified in PI1, ChatGPT's high-volume, cross-theme generation offers substantial scalability in early ethical analysis. In our study, ChatGPT generated 620 ERs compared to 249 from human researchers, ensuring broad initial coverage across ECCOLA themes. This reduces the risk of overlooking important ethical considerations, particularly in complex AI systems, and accelerates brainstorming in Agile environments [38]. By rapidly simulating stakeholder perspectives and mapping potential impacts, AI can enable teams to devote more human resources to refining and contextualizing ERs rather than starting from scratch [39].

Complementary Strengths and Actionability (PI3): PI3 highlighted a layered focus divergence that creates productive synergy. ChatGPT concentrated on story-level ERs—concrete, actionable items aligned with Agile's specificity—while human researchers contributed more theme-level ERs, focusing on strategic and value-driven considerations. This combination bridges the gap between abstract ethical principles and operational system requirements. AI accelerates the production of actionable items, while human oversight ensures alignment with overarching ethical intent [40].

Dynamic and Adaptive Refinement (PI4, PI5): The iterative nature of Agile cycles, emphasized in PI4 and PI5, proved critical for adapting ethical frameworks in real time. Through successive feedback loops and iterative prompt adjustments, both AI- and human-generated ERs were refined for greater adaptability, precision, and contextual relevance. This continuous refinement transforms static frameworks into dynamic, evolving tools. AI's speed enables quick updates in response to feedback, while human oversight ensures these adjustments remain ethically sound and contextually appropriate [41].

5.2 The Challenges of Human-AI Collaboration in ERS Development

Despite its benefits, our analysis uncovered persistent challenges that must be addressed to fully harness Human–AI synergy in RE.

Struggles with Contextual Nuance (PI2, PI5): As observed in PI2 and PI5, ChatGPT often lacked the contextual nuance needed for subtle ethical distinctions. For example, in PI2, the *Stakeholder Analysis* theme was underrepresented and occasionally misinterpreted, with the ECCOLA card treated as a principle rather than a contextual analysis tool [22]. This gap underscores AI's limitations in translating framework guidance into real-world applications without targeted human intervention.

Risk of Blind Spots and Oversimplification (PI2, PI4): PI2 revealed a shared blind spot: both human and AI outputs underemphasized stakeholder inclusivity. Additionally, PI4 noted that iterative refinement—while beneficial—can lead to overfitting to a specific use case, risking oversimplification of broader ethical concepts and the erosion of nuance. Robust human oversight is therefore essential to prevent ethical debt and ensure generalizability [42].

Resource Strain from Oversight (PI1, PI5): While AI accelerates ER generation (PI1), the large volume of outputs requires careful human review to filter irrelevant or "hallucinated" requirements (PI5). This oversight involves active re-prompting, detailed contextual analysis, and strategic refinement, which can strain resources in development teams. Balancing AI-driven efficiency with the necessary depth of human oversight remains a practical challenge.

Implications for Agile Requirements Engineering: Our findings show a dynamic approach to embedding ethics in Agile RE by combining the *ERS framework* with *Human–AI collaboration*. The ERS decomposes high-level ethical requirements into actionable Stories linked to Epics, while human–AI workflows enable rapid ideation and nuanced refinement. This process translates abstract ethical values into concrete, adaptable requirements that evolve with technical development cycles [41].

Limitations: This study offers initial insights but has limitations. Internal validity is influenced by reliance on predefined themes and frequency analysis, which may miss nuance; qualitative coding and consensus discussions helped mitigate this. Researcher subjectivity and AI bias introduced variability, though transparency was supported by documenting researcher backgrounds. The single-use case limited diversity but allowed in-depth exploration, with findings aligned against established frameworks. External validity is constrained by the scope and use of a single ChatGPT version, though the interaction method is transferable. Limited Agile iterations restricted longitudinal observation, and the use of ECCOLA and prompting strategies shaped the results. Future work will explore multiple use cases, longitudinal settings, varied domains, and analysis of the ERs in the ERS [43–45].

5.3 Conclusion

This study applied a DSRM approach and Human–AI collaboration to generate the ERS for embedding ethics into Agile RE using a fitness app use case. Five key insights emerged: (1) AI generated broader, higher-volume ERs, while humans focused more deeply; (2) both emphasized *Privacy & Data* and *Communication*, but underrepresented *Stakeholder Analysis*; (3) AI leaned toward concrete Story-level ERs, humans toward abstract Themes; (4) Agile iterations supported ongoing refinement; and (5) combining AI scalability with human judgment improved clarity and nuance. Together, these findings show how the ERS dynamically operationalizes ethics—AI brings breadth, while humans provide ethical depth. This work sets the foundation for adapting the ERS across domains and Agile AI contexts.

Acknowledgments. I would like to acknowledge The Foundation for Economic Education (LSR) in Finland for its invaluable support.

References

1. OpenAI, R.: Gpt-4 technical report. arxiv 2303.08774. View in Article **2**(5) (2023)
2. Bhuyan, S.S., et al.: Generative artificial intelligence use in healthcare: opportunities for clinical excellence and administrative efficiency. J. Med. Syst. **49** (2025) Article 10
3. Reddy, S.: Generative ai in healthcare: an implementation science informed translational path on application, integration and governance. Implementation Sci. **19** (2024) Article 27
4. Jabbour, J., Reddi, V.J.: Generative ai agents in autonomous machines: a safety perspective. arXiv preprint arXiv:2410.15489 (2024)
5. Alanazi, S., Asif, S.: Exploring deepfake technology: creation, consequences and countermeasures. Hum.-Intell. Syst. Integr. 1–12 (2024)
6. Habiba, U., Haug, M., Bogner, J., Wagner, S.: How mature is requirements engineering for ai-based systems? a systematic mapping study on practices, challenges, and future research directions. Requirements Eng. **29**, 567–600 (2024)
7. Cabrero-Daniel, B., Herda, T., Pichler, V., Eder, M.: Exploring human-ai collaboration in agile: customised llm meeting assistants. In: International Conference on Agile Software Development, Springer Nature Switzerland, Cham, pp. 163–178 (2024)
8. Fragiadakis, G., Diou, C., Kousiouris, G., Nikolaidou, M.: Evaluating human-ai collaboration: a review and methodological framework. arXiv preprint arXiv:2407.19098 (2024)
9. Spiekermann, S., Winkler, T.: Ethical it innovation: a value-based system design approach. Sci. Eng. Ethics **21**(3), 527–545 (2015)
10. Vogel, C., Petersen, K.: Ethics in software engineering: a systematic literature review. J. Syst. Softw. **176**, 110925 (2021)
11. IEEE standards association: the standard model process for addressing ethical concerns during system design. Technical report (2021)
12. Agbese, M., Mohanani, R., Khan, A., Abrahamsson, P.: Implementing ai ethics: making sense of the ethical requirements. In: Proceedings of the 27th International Conference on Evaluation and Assessment in Software Engineering, pp. 62–71 (2023)
13. Peffers, K., Rothenberger, M.A., Tuunanen, T., Chatterjee, S.: A design science research methodology for information systems research. In: Proceedings of the 40th Annual Hawaii International Conference on System Sciences (HICSS), p. 219. IEEE (2007)
14. Leijnen, S., Aldewereld, H., van Belkom, R., Bijvank, R., Ossewaarde, R.: An agile framework for trustworthy ai. In: NeHuAI@ ECAI, pp. 75–78 (2020)
15. Alenezi, M., Akour, M.: Ai-driven innovations in software engineering: a review of current practices and future directions. Appl. Sci. **15**(3), 1344 (2025)
16. Müller, V.C.: Ethics of artificial intelligence and robotics. Stanford Encyclopedia of Philosophy (2020)
17. OpenAI: Chatgpt: optimizing language models for dialogue. https://openai.com/chatgpt (2023). Accessed 18 Feb 2024
18. Jobin, A., Ienca, M., Vayena, E.: The global landscape of ai ethics guidelines. Nat. Mach. Intell. **1**(9), 389–399 (2019)
19. Floridi, L.: The Ethics of Artificial Intelligence: Principles, Challenges, and Opportunities. Oxford University Press (2023)

20. Liywalii, E.: Requirements engineering (re) in artificial intelligence (ai) systems implementation: the need to emphasize non-functional requirements (nfrs) for ethical ai. In Gerber, A., et al., eds.: SACAIR 2024, CCIS 2326, Springer, pp. 423–439 (2025)
21. Turk, D., France, R.: Assumptions underlying agile software development processes. J. Softw. Syst. Model. **17**, 19–25 (2003)
22. Vakkuri, V., Kemell, K.K., Jantunen, M., Halme, E., Abrahamsson, P.: Eccola–a method for implementing ethically aligned ai systems. J. Syst. Softw. **182**, 111067 (2021)
23. Halme, E., Jantunen, M., Vakkuri, V., Kemell, K.K., Abrahamsson, P.: Making ethics practical: User stories as a way of implementing ethical consideration in software engineering. Inf. Softw. Technol. **167**, 107379 (2024)
24. Lin, Z.: Beyond principlism: practical strategies for ethical ai use in research practices. AI and Ethics, pp. 1–12 (2024)
25. Song, B., Zhu, Q., Luo, J.: Human-ai collaboration by design. Proc. Des. Soc. **4**, 2247–2256 (2024)
26. Hasan, M.M., et al.: Human-ai collaboration in software design: a framework for efficient co-creation. AIJMR-Adv. Int. J. Multidisciplinary Res. **3**(1) (2025)
27. Gomez, C., Cho, S.M., Ke, S., Huang, C.M., Unberath, M.: Human-ai collaboration is not very collaborative yet: a taxonomy of interaction patterns in ai-assisted decision making from a systematic review. Front. Comput. Sci. **6**, 1521066 (2025)
28. Hevner, A.R., March, S.T., Park, J., Ram, S.: Design science in information systems research. MIS Quart. 75–105 (2004)
29. Agbese, M., et al.: Governance in ethical and trustworthy ai systems: extension of the eccola method for ai ethics governance using garp. e-Inf. Softw. Eng. J. **17**(1) (2023)
30. Cockburn, A., Highsmith, J.: Agile software development, the people factor. Computer **34**(11), 131–133 (2001)
31. Franch, X., Palomares, C., Quer, C., Chatzipetrou, P., Gorschek, T.: The state-of-practice in requirements specification: an extended interview study at 12 companies. Requirements Eng. **28**(3), 377–409 (2023)
32. Cohn, M.: User stories applied: for agile software development (2004)
33. Teddlie, C., Yu, F.: Mixed methods sampling: a typology with examples. J. Mixed Methods Res. **1**(1), 77–100 (2007)
34. Dingsøyr, T., Nerur, S., Balijepally, V., Moe, N.B.: A decade of agile methodologies: towards explaining agile software development (2012)
35. Thoring, K., Mueller, R., Badke-Schaub, P.: Workshops as a research method: guidelines for designing and evaluating artifacts through workshops. Des. Sci. **6** (2020)
36. Creswell, J.W., Clark, V.L.P.: Designing and Conducting Mixed Methods Research, 3rd edn. SAGE Publications, Thousand Oaks, CA (2018)
37. Ritchie, J., Lewis, J.: Qualitative Research Practice: A Guide for Social Science Students and Researchers. SAGE Publications, London, UK (2003)
38. Resnik, D.B., Hosseini, M.: The ethics of using artificial intelligence in scientific research: new guidance needed for a new tool. AI Ethics 1–23 (2024)
39. Conti, C.J., Varde, A.S., Wang, W.: Human-robot collaboration with commonsense reasoning in smart manufacturing contexts. IEEE Trans. Autom. Sci. Eng. **19**(3), 1784–1797 (2022)
40. Morley, J., Kinsey, L., Elhalal, A., Garcia, F., Ziosi, M., Floridi, L.: Operationalising ai ethics: barriers, enablers and next steps. AI Soc. 1–13 (2023)

41. Pflanzer, M., Traylor, Z., Lyons, J.B., Dubljević, V., Nam, C.S.: Ethics in human-ai teaming: principles and perspectives. AI Ethics **3**(3), 917–935 (2023)
42. Binns, R.: Fairness in machine learning: Lessons from political philosophy. In: Conference on Fairness, Accountability and Transparency, pp. 149–159. PMLR (2018)
43. Eswaran, U., Eswaran, V., Murali, K., Eswaran, V.: Human-centric ai balancing innovation with ethical considerations in the age of soft computing. In: Soft Computing in Industry 5.0 for Sustainability. Springer, Cham, pp. 87–116 (2024)
44. Odong, L.A., Perini, A., Susi, A.: Requirements engineering for collaborative artificial intelligence systems: a literature survey. In: Research Challenges in Information Science, Springer, Cham, pp. 409–425 (2022)
45. Taylor, C.S. In: External Threats to Validity. Oxford University Press, pp. 55–64 (2013)

Addictive UX: Heuristic Evidence from Online Gambling UX and the Need for Ethical Guidelines

Gessé Evangelista(✉)

Federal University of São Carlos (UFSCar), São Carlos, SP, Brazil
gesse.pereira@estudante.ufscar.br

Abstract. With the rise of online gambling platforms, concerns have emerged regarding the intensive use of UX Design strategies that foster compulsive engagement. This article critically examines how these platforms apply usability, playability, and behavioral persuasion heuristics to keep users active, often by exploiting cognitive vulnerabilities. Through an adapted heuristic evaluation, five platforms were assessed for the presence of patterns such as sensory reinforcement, variable rewards, artificial scarcity, and the absence of protective barriers. The results indicate a standardization of UX practices oriented toward user retention, raising significant ethical concerns. As a contribution, the article proposes the beginning of a broader discussion on the need for more ethical and conscious design practices in high-risk digital environments.

Keywords: Addictive UX · Online Gambling · Ethical Design · Heuristic Evaluation

1 Introduction

In recent years, increased internet access and the widespread adoption of mobile devices have driven the growth of online gambling platforms [6]. Digital roulette and slot machine games have become especially popular among younger, connected audiences, often propelled by influencers and aggressive marketing campaigns [7]. This sociotechnological phenomenon is largely sustained by the sophisticated application of User Experience (UX) Design strategies aimed at maximizing user retention [8].

These platforms employ design elements that go beyond usability or esthetic pleasure [9]. They use techniques such as sensory reinforcement, intermittent reward loops, artificial scarcity, and manipulated social proof—among other persuasive mechanisms—that have been associated with compulsive behavior patterns and the potential development of addiction [12]. While some of these strategies are based on legitimate engagement principles, the lack of transparency and the exploitation of users' cognitive and emotional vulnerabilities raise critical ethical and social responsibility issues in digital product design [2].

G. Herzwurm et al. (Eds.): ICSOB 2025, LNBIP 574, pp. 108–114, 2026.
https://doi.org/10.1007/978-3-032-14518-5_9

Based on the problem described above, a research question (RQ) was formulated: *How are UX Design heuristics applied to online gambling platforms to encourage compulsive engagement, and what are the ethical implications of these practices?* To answer this question, this article proposes a critical heuristic analysis of five of the most widely used online gambling platforms today, based on a set of adapted heuristics [1–3,5]. The analysis is complemented by a systematization of recurring experience manipulation practices, identified as common across the platforms.

As its main contribution, the article aims to initiate a broader discussion on the need for a more ethical and conscious use of UX Design, and potentially, on the regulation of its application in high-risk digital environments. The structure of the article includes: Related Work (Sect. 2), Research Design (Sect. 3), Results and Discussion (Sect. 4), and Final Considerations (Sect. 5).

2 Related Work

The use of persuasive design in digital products has been widely studied by Fogg [4], who proposed the Behavior Design model to explain and influence users' attitudes and behaviors. Subsequent studies have deepened this perspective by focusing on users' decision-making processes [10]. In this context, the concept of digital nudging emerges as an extension of behavioral economics principles to the digital environment [10]. A nudge represents a subtle push in the user's choice architecture—altering behavior in predictable ways without restricting available options or changing economic incentives—while digital nudging adapts this logic to interface design [2].

Kollmer and Eckhardt [11] show that although nudges and dark patterns rely on the same underlying psychological mechanisms—namely, non-rational influence—they differ fundamentally in intent. Nudging aims to promote user well-being or socially desirable outcomes, whereas dark patterns exploit cognitive vulnerabilities to serve corporate interests. Witte *et al.* [12] go further, demonstrating that manipulative interface practices can lead to negative psychological consequences such as reduced perceived control and increased compulsive behaviors, precisely by crossing the ethical boundary between persuasion and manipulation. The challenge, therefore, lies in identifying heuristic criteria capable of detecting interface elements that, while functionally sound, can be used persuasively or even manipulatively—particularly in environments such as online gambling platforms [2].

3 Research Design

This qualitative and exploratory study applies a critical heuristic analysis to identify UX design elements that foster compulsive engagement in online gambling platforms. Guided by heuristics adapted from classical and modern models, the analysis emphasizes ethical, emotional, and behavioral aspects, following three steps: (1) Platform Selection; (2) Heuristic Construction; and (3) Execution.

3.1 Platform Selection

To select the platforms, a search was conducted on Google Trends[1] using a search *string* ("*online gambling*" OR "*casino games*" OR "*betting*"). For the definition of the *string* a relevance-based selection strategy grounded in semantic clarity, user familiarity, and prior use in academic and grey literature on digital gambling. The terms were chosen because they are widely searched by the general public, conceptually cover key segments of the gambling ecosystem (general betting, gamified casino experiences, and sports betting), and are semantically distinct enough to allow comparative analysis without significant overlap.

The five platforms with the highest and most consistent search interest in the last twelve months were chosen as the relevant and accessible services to users. To ensure neutrality and avoid legal issues, they were anonymized using coded identifiers, as detailed in Table 1.

Table 1. Description of the analyzed online gambling platforms (anonymized)

Code	Neutral Game Description
J01	Game with a simplified visual interface, based on a single-attempt betting mechanic. It presents a playful environment with an animated mascot and immediate visual rewards
J02	Real-time sports betting platform focused on popular sports. Structured and minimalist interface with advanced betting options and features such as "early cash-out"
J03	Platform with a dark, modern interface aimed at crypto users. Offers fast and simplified games with high unpredictability and animated feedback
J04	Friendly and intuitive platform for sports betting and daily promotions. Features smooth navigation and vibrant colors
J05	Local platform targeting a national audience, with strong integration to instant payment systems. Simplified interface with direct appeal and low-complexity games

3.2 Heuristic Construction

The set of heuristics used in this analysis was developed by integrating four main sources. These include Nielsen's ten usability heuristics [5], which are widely recognized for their applicability across various interface domains; the playability heuristics proposed by Desurvire et al. [1], designed for evaluating interactive and game-based experiences; the taxonomy of addictive elements in games, as described by King, Delfabbro, and Griffiths [3]; and the conceptual framework on dark patterns and manipulative design practices, as systematized by Gray et al. [2]. Based on these foundations, ten adapted heuristics were defined and are presented in Sect. 4 in Table 2.

3.3 Execution

The study adopted a document analysis approach [13] to systematically review and interpret each of the five platforms, as well as to observe their interfaces and the interactive features available. For each heuristic, the presence or absence of corresponding elements was assessed using objective descriptors and observable examples. To illustrate the analytical process, one example can be drawn from

---

[1] Google Trends is a public analytics tool by Google that displays the relative popularity of search terms over time. Available at: https://trends.google.com/trends/.

Platform J01. During the observation, animations and sound effects triggered after each spin or win were identified as evidence of *H1 Immediate Feedback and Sensory Reinforcement*, since they provide immediate gratification and reinforce continuous user engagement.

The collected evidence was organized into a heuristic matrix, enabling cross-comparison between platforms and heuristics. All the documentation is available **at this Link**. Subsequently, both quantitative synthesis (occurrence frequency) and qualitative interpretation (critical reading of patterns) were carried out, with emphasis on identifying points of convergence among addictive UX practices.

3.4 Threats to Validity

It is important to acknowledge that this analysis is based exclusively on external observation of the platforms' interfaces and publicly available materials. The study does not include access to source code, backend systems, or internal algorithms. Moreover, although no user testing was conducted, the findings are grounded in a robust body of literature on behavioral design and digital ethics, which supports the interpretation of the identified patterns. This methodological choice ensures analytical rigor while recognizing the inherent limitations of interface-level assessments.

4 Results and Discussion

The heuristic analysis across all platforms revealed a consistent use of UX design strategies focused on maximizing user retention, often displaying persuasive and occasionally manipulative patterns. All ten heuristics were fully present on every platform, indicating a 100% convergence and a shared design logic that favors behavioral engagement over ethical transparency. Full results are in Table 2.

Regarding **Heuristic 1**, all platforms were observed to use sounds, flashing lights, and animations to reinforce actions such as wins, near misses, or simple clicks—establishing immediate sensory reinforcement with strong emotional appeal.For **Heuristic 3**, the use of intermittent rewards, surprise bonuses, and unpredictable elements—such as mystery boxes—fosters engagement loops that encourage compulsive user behavior.

Heuristic 6 was also widely evident: all analyzed interfaces included countdown timers and phrases like "last chance," activating scarcity and urgency triggers that drive impulsive decisions.In relation to **Heuristic 7**, social proof is strategically manipulated through the constant display of messages showcasing alleged winnings from other users, distorting the perception of ease and generalized luck. As for **Heuristic 9**, a notable absence of control mechanisms was found: none of the platforms display warnings about risky behavior or offer visible configurations for betting or time limits, reflecting a lack of concern for responsible gambling practices. Finally, **Heuristic 10** reveals that the deliberate combination of the above patterns—without any moderation or user protection mechanisms—constitutes a clear ethical risk.

Table 2. Adapted Heuristics for UX Analysis in Online Gambling Platforms.

No	Heuristic Name	Adapted Description	Theoretical Basis	Evidence Observed on Platforms
1	Immediate Feedback and Sensory Reinforcement	The game provides instant visual and sound responses to every user action (win, near miss, click), generating immediate gratification.	Nielsen (1994); King et al. (2010)	Flashy animations, vibrant sound effects, and mascots celebrating wins—even minimal ones—reinforcing constant clicking
2	Illusion of Control	The player is led to believe they influence outcomes, despite the system being essentially random.	King et al. (2010); Gray et al. (2018)	Features like bet amount selection, game speed, or cash-out buttons simulate choice but do not alter randomness
3	Variable Reward (Intermittent Loop)	The unpredictability of rewards encourages continuous repetition, exploiting Skinner's reinforcement model.	King et al. (2010); Desurvire et al. (2004)	Presence of random bonuses, near misses, and intermittent prizes, keeping the player engaged without predictability
4	Emotional and Affective Design	Use of characters, colors, mascots, and cheerful environments to create emotional attachment and empathy.	Desurvire et al. (2004); King et al. (2010)	Visual interface with friendly mascots (e.g., tiger), warm colors, and festive settings that humanize the system
5	Progression and Persistence	Elements like progress bars, daily bonuses, and missions encourage habitual behavior and constant return.	Desurvire et al. (2004); King et al. (2010)	Incentives for daily logins, spin goals, cumulative rewards, and notifications reminding users to "keep playing"
6	Scarcity and Urgency	Limited-time offers and bonuses trigger impulsive decisions and fear of missing out.	Gray et al. (2018)	Countdown timers, "last chance" banners, and time-limited promotions create artificial urgency
7	Social Proof and Anchoring	Display of other users' winnings, leaderboards, and high-value bets to encourage larger bets.	Gray et al. (2018); King et al. (2010)	Panels show recent wins from other users; high bet amounts are displayed as default suggestions
8	Low Cognitive Load	Simplified, intuitive interface with continuous flow to minimize critical thinking and maximize impulsivity.	Nielsen (1994); Gray et al. (2018)	Navigation reduced to few buttons, no explanatory text, and visual emphasis on automatic and quick actions
9	Absence of Warnings and Barriers	Lack of clear messages about losses, usage time, or betting limits. Risks are hidden from the interface.	Gray et al. (2018)	Interfaces do not show excessive usage or accumulated loss warnings. No forced breaks or visible configurable limits
10	Violation of UX Ethics	Deliberate exploitation of cognitive and emotional vulnerabilities without transparency or user protection mechanisms.	Gray et al. (2018); Nielsen (1994)	Set of persuasive practices without ethical safeguards, such as alerts, voluntary exclusion, or visible limits

5 Final Considerations

This study examined how UX heuristics are systematically applied in online gambling platforms to foster compulsive engagement. Findings of this analysis directly address the research question by showing that UX Design heuristics are systematically applied in online gambling platforms to foster compulsive engagement. Specifically, the study revealed that design principles originally intended to enhance usability and enjoyment—such as feedback, progression, and emotional design—are strategically adapted to sustain behavioral loops and exploit users' cognitive and emotional vulnerabilities. This convergence of persuasive techniques demonstrates how UX heuristics can be transformed into mechanisms of manipulation when user well-being is not prioritized. Consequently, the ethical implications are significant, as these practices blur the boundary between engagement and exploitation, calling for critical reflection on the role of design ethics in digital entertainment ecosystems.

In future work, we intend to expand the scope of this study by conducting a broader comparative analysis, including additional gambling and gamified platforms, as well as complementary data sources such as advertising content and user testimonials. This will allow for a deeper understanding of how persuasive and manipulative design patterns evolve in digital ecosystems. Furthermore, we plan to develop and evaluate a heuristics-based assessment framework that can help designers and regulators identify high-risk UX practices and promote responsible design standards. Beyond its academic contribution, this research aims to inform public discussion and ethical guidelines for digital environments where user vulnerability is systematically exploited for profit.

References

1. Desurvire, H., Caplan, M., Toth, J.A.: Using heuristics to evaluate the playability of games. In CHI 2004 Extended Abstracts on Human Factors in Computing Systems (2004)
2. Gray, C.M., Kou, Y., Battles, B., Hoggatt, J., Toombs, A.L.: The dark (patterns) side of UX design. In Proceedings of the 2018 CHI Conference on Human Factors in Computing Systems (2018)
3. King, D., Delfabbro, P., Griffiths, M.: Video game structural characteristics: a new psychological taxonomy. Int. J. Ment. Heal. Addict. **8**(1), 90–106 (2010)
4. Fogg, B.J.: Persuasive Technology: Using Computers to Change What We Think and Do. Morgan Kaufmann, San Francisco (2003)
5. Nielsen, J.: Usability Engineering. Morgan Kaufmann, San Francisco (1994)
6. Wardle, H.: The lancet public health commission on gambling – industry growth is fuelled by the rise of online gambling, widespread mobile accessibility, and legal reforms. Lancet Public Health (2024)
7. Bolat, E., Panourgia, C., Yankouskaya, A., Kelly, M.: Influencer-driven gambling content and its impact on children and young people: a scoping study. Curr. Addict. Rep. **12**, 3 (2025)
8. Galmés-Cerezo, M., López-Aza, C., Martinez-Navarro, G.: Responsible marketing communication in online gambling: a systematic review of strategies targeting youth. Rev. Commun. Res. **13**, 172–191 (2025)
9. Sánchez Chamorro, L.: Ethical tensions in UX design practice: exploring the fine line between persuasion and manipulation (2023)
10. Weinmann, M., Schneider, C., vom Brocke, J.: Digital nudging. Bus. Inf. Syst. Eng. **58**(6), 433–436 (2016)
11. Kollmer, T., Eckhardt, A.: Dark patterns: conceptualization and future research directions. Bus. Inf. Syst. Eng. **65**(2), 201–208 (2023)
12. Witte, J., Kenning, P., Brock, C.: Consequences of user manipulation through dark patterns. In: Proceedings of the Forty-Fourth International Conference on Information Systems (ICIS 2023), Hyderabad, India (2023)
13. Bowen, G.A.: Document analysis as a qualitative research method. Qualitative Res. J. **9**(2), 27–40 (2009)

AI Adoption and Governance in Software Organizationss

Cost of Not Investing (CONI) in Intelligent Processes Automation

Damian Kedziora[1,2], Andrey Saltan[1(✉)], and Artur Modliński[3]

[1] LUT University, Lahti, Finland
{damian.kedziora,andrey.saltan}@lut.fi
[2] Kozminski University, Warsaw, Poland
[3] University of Łódź, Łódź, Poland
artur.modlinski@uni.lodz.pl

Abstract. As organisations navigate complex AI-driven workplace transformations through intelligent automation of business processes, traditional investment evaluation methods inadequately capture the strategic risks of its delayed adoption. Our study introduces the concept of the Cost of Not Investing (CONI), exploring how automation delays can impact organisational competitiveness and workforce dynamics. Drawing on existing theories, such as Opportunity Cost, Real Options Theory, Dynamic Capabilities, and Game Theory, we conceptualise a framework identifying three CONI dimensions: operational inefficiencies, strategic disadvantages, and human capital impacts. We operationalise CONI with a measurement-based model that maps each dimension to auditable indicators (e.g., process mining logs, service level penalties, talent attrition premiums) and test initial perceptions from a cross-sector survey of 108 professionals in the US and EU. Respondents perceive material consequences of delay: talent migration (81%), lower productivity (77%), increased training and rework costs (72%), reduced market responsiveness (7%), and loss of early mover advantages (74%). Yet evaluation practices reveal a critical implementation gap: only 16.7% systematically incorporate strategic costs, and 33.3% report no structured method. Our contribution lies in demonstrating how CONI operates as a cascading mechanism (not merely additive costs), where delayed options reduce capability-building opportunities, which amplifies competitive disadvantages. We provide a research agenda for validating objective and longitudinal CONI estimates in IPA-intensive settings.

Keywords: Intelligent Process Automation · Cost of Not Investing · Real Options · Dynamic Capabilities

1 Introduction

The nature of organisational work has been rapidly changing as intelligent systems cover a growing share of cognitive, coordinative, and transactional tasks. Intelligent Process Automation (IPA), i.e. the combination of robotic process

G. Herzwurm et al. (Eds.): ICSOB 2025, LNBIP 574, pp. 117–131, 2026.
https://doi.org/10.1007/978-3-032-14518-5_10

automation (RPA) with machine learning (ML) and agentic artificial intelligence (AI), reconfigures who does what, when, and with what data [6,7,32]. At the same time, firms confront increasingly tight labour markets, rising capability requirements, and a shift toward human-machine complementarity aligned with Industry 5.0 priorities. While the direct benefits of IPA, such as cycle-time reduction, error minimisation, and compliance-by-design, are well documented [1,29], investment appraisals rarely quantify the penalties incurred by delaying adoption [39].

Such oversight matters because IPA fundamentally differs from traditional IT investments in three ways: (1) it generates compounding learning effects where early data collection improves future model performance, (2) it creates irreversible capability gaps as competitors accumulate automation-specific knowledge, and (3) it triggers workforce dynamics where talent migrates to more automated environments, creating self-reinforcing cycles of disadvantage [17].

Organisations frequently underestimate strategic flexibility gained through timely investments, overlooking that delays may result in irreversibly lost opportunities or reduced managerial options [37]. The dynamic capabilities perspective underscores that companies failing to invest timely risk losing abilities to sense and seize market opportunities, limiting sustained competitive advantage in digital environments [12]. From a game-theoretic perspective, delayed automations risk competitive takeover, where early adopters gain strategic advantages through operational superiority [40].

Our paper aims to make two main contributions. First, it is to advance theory by sequencing Real Options, Dynamic Capabilities, Opportunity Cost, and Game Theory into a cascading CONI construct for IPA, demonstrating how option value feeds capability accumulation under competitive timing. Second, it addresses the gap between theoretical understanding and practical implementation, proposing a research agenda for further studies on objective, longitudinal CONI estimates.

Traditional investment appraisal methods prove insufficient for automation decisions involving strategic uncertainties and irreversibility, failing to account for managerial flexibility and competitive interactions [3,11]. Hence, our research addresses this gap by exploring CONI in Intelligent Process Automation, aiming to integrate strategic perspectives to understand broader implications of automation investment timing and the future of work. Therefore, we shall explore the below Research Question:

RG: How do organisations understand, measure, and act on the costs of not investing in intelligent process automation?

2 Literature Background

This section introduces the two streams of literature that provided the foundation for our study and led to its formulation. These are the reviews of works on process automation technologies, as well as cost theories related to strategic investments.

2.1 Process Automation Technology

Process automation technologies have undergone rapid transformation with intelligent solutions fundamentally changing organisational approaches to digital transformation [28]. Robotic Process Automation (RPA) enables organisations to automate repetitive, rule-based tasks by mimicking human interactions with information systems, operating at the user interface level without requiring infrastructure changes [19,35]. Successful RPA implementation requires careful governance, organisational readiness, and change management strategies [20].

AI capabilities have expanded automation scope from rule-based tasks to complex, judgment-based tasks through Intelligent Process Automation (IPA), which combines RPA's structured processing with cognitive capabilities via machine learning, natural language processing, and computer vision [18,23]. This enables organizations to address sophisticated process scenarios while improving decision-making through data-driven insights [14]. Implementing modern process automation solutions presents both opportunities and challenges, requiring process standardization, employee training, strategic alignment, and comprehensive governance frameworks to manage technological complexity [22,27]. Economic implications have become critical, with traditional cost accounting methods insufficient for evaluating automation investments' long-term strategic benefits and indirect costs [39].

Automation initiatives increasingly focus on augmenting human capabilities rather than replacement, requiring new workforce development approaches that balance technological capabilities with human factors for both operational efficiency and employee satisfaction [15,26]. However, the literature lacks frameworks for understanding how automation timing affects talent retention and competitive positioning, gaps our CONI framework addresses.

2.2 Strategic Perspectives on IT Investment Costs

We draw on four theoretical perspectives that, while previously applied separately to IT investments, have not been integrated to explain automation delay costs. We show how these theories connect in a temporal sequence: opportunity costs occur immediately, triggering option value loss, which constrains capability development, ultimately affecting competitive outcomes.

Opportunity Cost. Opportunity cost represents foregone value from choosing one alternative over another [5,16]. In IPA contexts, maintaining manual processes means forgoing efficiency gains, accuracy improvements, and cost reductions available through automation. While opportunity cost typically assumes independent choices, we argue that in IPA, today's foregone opportunities affect tomorrow's options, a connection existing literature overlooks [2,9].

Previous studies measure opportunity costs through NPV analysis [37], Real Options Analysis for technology investments with uncertain outcomes [3], and Market Share Analysis incorporating competitive dynamics [24].

In technology investment contexts, opportunity cost analysis addresses Technical Debt from delayed updates [21], Strategic Position Erosion from delayed adoption [33], and Innovation Capability Impact from outdated systems [36]. Key measurement challenges include counterfactual estimation uncertainty, dynamic technology market changes, and quantifying intangible benefits affecting organizational capabilities and employee satisfaction.

Real Options Theory. Real Options Theory extends traditional investment appraisal by recognizing managerial flexibility value in strategic decision-making under uncertainty, conceptualizing investments as 'options' granting flexibility to defer, scale, expand, or abandon investments based on evolving market conditions [4,37]. This flexibility enables proactive risk management through adaptive resource allocation as uncertainty resolves. Applied to IPA, Real Options Theory highlights strategic benefits from the solution's flexibility under technological volatility and competitive uncertainty. While IPA investments involve substantial initial outlays, they create valuable future strategic adaptation opportunities. Conversely, delaying automation investments compromises long-term strategic options, potentially locking companies into suboptimal configurations as competitive landscapes evolve [11].

From this perspective, CONI in automation would extend beyond immediate financial impacts to address strategic opportunity costs including permanently lost managerial flexibility, diminished competitive responsiveness, and reduced ability to capture market opportunities, enabling richer strategic valuation transcending traditional short-term focused appraisal methods.

Dynamic Capabilities Dynamic Capabilities theory emphasizes organizations' ability to adapt, sense opportunities, and dynamically reconfigure resources in rapidly evolving competitive environments, enabling sustained competitive advantage through ongoing adaptation [12,36]. In the Process Automation contexts, dynamic capabilities relate to rapidly integrating digital technologies, exploiting real-time analytics, enhancing operational agility, and reorganizing processes in response to market demands, being essential capabilities in digital transformation environments [30,38].

Organizations delaying automation investments risk substantial dynamic capability deterioration, significantly impacting strategic resilience, innovation potential, and competitive adaptability, thus amplifying CONI. Delayed investment consequences transcend short-term inefficiencies to encompass reduced organizational agility, slower technological response, diminished opportunity capture, and impaired market leadership maintenance [10,12].

Dynamic capabilities theory therefore underlines automation investment urgency, highlighting that delayed investments fundamentally weaken organisational adaptability and competitiveness with long-lasting strategic effects beyond conventional measures.

Game Theory. Game theory considers strategic interactions among competing companies and interdependencies in decision-making, where investments are influenced by competitor actions, market conditions, and asymmetric information creating strategic complexity [34, 40]. Investment timing and nature profoundly influence competitive positioning, as companies delaying investments risk are losing strategic advantages to proactive competitors, while early adopters achieve first-mover benefits including market dominance and network effects, creating entry barriers [34]. Underestimating competitor strategies or misinterpreting market signals leads to severe strategic miscalculations. Companies hesitating or failing to anticipate competitor moves face irreversible disadvantages, including market share loss and diminished competitive leverage, beyond immediate operational considerations [40].

Synthesis. Taken together, these lenses specify CONI as a time-indexed expected costs with four observable components: (i) operational leakage relative to an IPA-feasible baseline; (ii) decaying option value as flexibility windows close; (iii) slower dynamic capability accumulation that lengthens time-to-competence and reduces automation coverage; and (iv) competitive interaction losses as rivals move first.

3 Methodology

This exploratory study examines how organisations perceive CONI in IPA investments. Following Gregor's [13] Type II theory (analysis and explanation), we aimed to describe current understanding and practices to build theory about CONI awareness and evaluation gaps.

For this purpose, we developed our survey following guidelines by DeVellis [8], adapting validated scales where available. Specifically, we took operational efficiency items from van der Aalst et al. [1], strategic flexibility measures from Trigeorgis and Reuer [37], capability assessment items from Teece et al. [36], and competitive positioning scales from Lieberman and Montgomery [24]. For CONI-specific dimensions not covered by existing scales, we developed new items based on our literature study. The preliminary survey questions were reviewed by all three authors to improve content validity. We conducted pilot testing with five automation practitioners, leading to refinement of ambiguous items.

The final survey consisted of four sections addressing the following constructs: Organisational Context, Current Automation Status, CONI Perception, and CONI Awareness. Responses were collected through open-ended questions, as well as single and multiple-choice questions, and a 5-point Likert scale ranging from 1 = "Strongly Disagree" to 5 = "Strongly Agree". Example items included: "Employees' innovation potential is underutilised due to the burden of manual tasks" (Human Capital Impact) and "Competitors with higher automation levels are gaining market share" (Strategic Impact). Demographic information, including experience, role, and organisation size, was collected at the end of the survey. To minimise common method bias, we implemented procedural remedies recommended by Podsakoff et al. [31], including survey design separation and anonymity assurance.

We recruited participants from two sources: (1) the Vainu business register covering Nordic companies, and (2) authors' professional networks in automation consulting, providing access to knowledgeable respondents across diverse industries. The survey was available online between February and May 2025 via MS Forms. We sent 723 email invitations in two iterations, receiving 108 complete responses from professionals at companies based in Europe and the US, achieving a 15% response rate typical for organisational surveys.

4 Results and Discussion

4.1 Descriptive Statistics on Respondents

The most represented sectors were Financial Services and Retail (each 20.4%), followed by Technology (18.5%) and Healthcare (14.8%). This sector distribution provides a diverse industry perspective on automation challenges.

Regarding organisation size, respondents predominantly represented companies with 251–1000 employees (40.7%), followed by companies with 51–250 employees (23.1%), companies with 1001–5000 employees (19.4%), smaller companies with 1–50 employees (13.0%), and larger enterprises with over 5000 employees (3.7%). This heterogeneity captures CONI perspectives across different organisational scales.

Respondents mostly held Senior Management roles (35.2%), followed by Technical Specialists (24.1%), Middle Management (22.2%), and C-level Executives (14.8%), ensuring strategic and technical perspectives were represented. In terms of automation knowledge, 45.4% rated themselves as experts, 34.3% reported basic awareness, and 20.4% claimed working knowledge, providing varied viewpoints on automation impacts.

Regarding automation maturity, 37.0% reported extensive automation in multiple areas, 31.5% had full automation including AI/ML, 17.6% had partially automated complex processes, and 12.0% had only basic automations. This variation from basic to advanced automation provides insights across the full automation journey spectrum.

4.2 CONI Perception

We start this section by summarising our key findings on CONI dimensions in Table 1.

Operational impacts were aligned with Opportunity Cost theory. The most frequently selected evaluation criteria were competitive analysis (46.3%), strategic necessity evaluation (43.5%), and cost-benefit analysis (42.6%). Interestingly, only 35.2% use ROI analysis and 34.3% conduct risk assessment, suggesting evaluation frameworks are evolving beyond traditional financial metrics. Total Cost of Ownership (TCO) was noted by 42.6%. Only 6.5% reported uncertainty about their organisation's evaluation methods.

When asked about factors considered in calculating the cost of not automating, the most frequently cited were customer satisfaction (45.4%), error rates

Table 1. Key findings across CONI dimensions

CONI Dimension/Finding	%	Theory
Operational		
Manual processes costs	75	Opportunity Cost
Strategic		
Competitors gain share	71	Game Theory
Human Capital		
Talent migration	81	Dynamic Capabilities
Evaluation		
Systematic consideration	16.7	Implementation Gap

(43.5%), and labour costs (41.7%), reflecting concerns about customer experience, operational precision, and workforce efficiency. Market share loss was identified by 39.8%, and employee satisfaction by 37.0%, demonstrating recognition of both competitive and internal cultural impacts. Operational inefficiencies (26.9%) and competitive disadvantage (25.9%) were selected less frequently, while 11.1% selected "I do not know."

Regarding measurement methods for costs of not automating, internal systems and reporting data were most frequently mentioned (46.3%), followed by ROI estimation tools (38.0%), business case forecasting (35.2%), and cost-benefit analysis (33.3%). Project cost estimations and strategic prioritisation processes were mentioned by 29.6%, while risk evaluation appeared in 27.8% of responses. Notably, 23.1% use unstructured or intuition-based methods, whilst 13.9% report not measuring these costs at all, revealing varying levels of measurement sophistication across organisations.

Barriers to automation implementation revealed an important paradox: while initial investment costs scored lowest (3.78), implementation complexity (4.21) and expertise gaps (4.13) scored highest. Security concerns (4.18), uncertain ROI (4.10), regulatory compliance (4.07), organisational culture (4.03), and resource constraints (4.00) also scored highly. Employee resistance (3.99) and legacy system integration (3.87) were rated lower. This suggests organisations now recognise capability-building challenges over financial constraints, supporting our Dynamic Capabilities argument that delayed adoption creates cumulative skill gaps.

Operational Impact. Approximately 67% agreed that postponing automation investments increases operational costs, and 64% perceived that delays exacerbate efficiency gaps with competitors. Manual processes are viewed as increasingly expensive to maintain (75% agreement), with slower process execution contributing to lost market opportunities (65% agreement). Insufficient automation undermines service quality (70% agreement) and organisational agility, with 75% agreeing that delayed automation hampers swift market response. Additionally, 70.4% highlighted that delays result in increased downtime and business process disruptions. These operational perceptions strongly support our opportunity cost component.

Strategic Impact. The majority (71%) agreed that competitors with higher automation levels are gaining market share. This perception aligns with our Game Theory component. Over half (52%) agreed their organisation misses data-driven decision-making opportunities, whilst 40% remained neutral, indicating varying strategic awareness levels. Manual processes limit innovation capability (73% agreement), negatively impact customer satisfaction (61% agreement), and create operational scaling difficulties (71% agreement). Delayed automation investments reduce strategic flexibility and hinder competitive response capabilities (75% agreement). Moreover, 74% perceive lost first-mover advantages, confirming the strategic dimensions of CONI.

Human Capital Impact. The strongest consensus emerged around workforce issues: 67% agreed that outdated processes hinder recruitment of skilled personnel, 68% believed manual and repetitive tasks affect employee satisfaction. Staff turnover is higher in low-automation areas (70% agreement), and training costs are increasing due to complex manual processes (72% agreement). Workforce productivity is limited by lack of automation (77% agreement), with repetitive manual tasks hindering employees' innovation potential (74% agreement). Most strikingly, 81% believe valuable employees leave for competitors with better automated processes, our highest agreement rate, establishing talent migration as the most visible CONI manifestation.

4.3 CONI Awareness

A critical implementation gap emerged: Among 108 respondents, only 16.7% reported always systematically considering strategic costs, whilst 42.6% indicated often considering them. 23.1% noted such considerations occur sometimes, whilst 13.0% rarely and 4.6% never consider them. This reveals a significant gap between theoretical importance and practical application.

Regarding formal evaluation methods, 33.3% have partial methods or are developing them, 31.5% reported fully established methods, whilst 29.6% have no formal method, and 5.6% have no consideration at all. These findings highlight the nascent state of CONI evaluation practices.

Organisations identified clear priorities for improving CONI evaluation: ROI calculators (70.4%), case studies (69.4%) and industry benchmarks (64.8%). Better measurement tools were identified by 58.3%, whilst external consulting (45.4%) and specialised training (39.8%) were less commonly selected. The strong demand for ROI calculators and case studies indicates practitioners seek practical tools for CONI quantification.

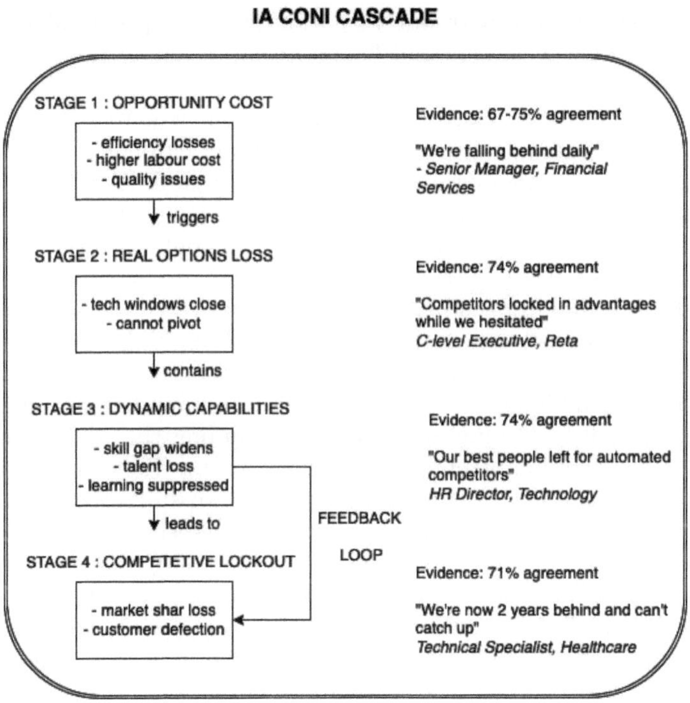

Fig. 1. The CONI Cascade Model: Sequence From Independent Costs to Compounding Consequences.

4.4 Theoretical Implications and Managerial Insights

Our findings provide support for the CONI cascade framework. Figure 1 illustrates how survey findings map to our model, demonstrating the sequential nature of automation delay costs.

The pattern emerged across three dimensions. First, operational costs (67–75% agreement) confirm the opportunity cost foundation. The respondents recognise immediate efficiency losses from maintaining manual processes. This aligns with van der Aalst et al. [1] who found 60–80% efficiency gains from RPA implementation, suggesting our respondents accurately perceive foregone benefits. However, unlike Ylä-Kujala et al. [39] who focus on quantifiable ROI metrics, our respondents emphasise qualitative costs like service quality degradation (70% agreement), indicating practitioners consider broader impacts than traditional frameworks capture.

Second, lost flexibility concerns (74% perceive lost first-mover advantages) support the real options component. This extends Trigeorgis and Reuer's [37] real options framework by revealing automation-specific option expiry patterns. Whilst they emphasise uncertainty reduction over time, our findings suggest automation options expire more rapidly due to talent migration and competitive lock-in. Benaroch's [3] finding that only 20% of the firms use real options analysis contrasts sharply with our 74% awareness of option value, suggesting practitioners intuitively understand flexibility loss even without formal frameworks.

Third, the 81% agreement on talent migration validates the human capital dimension of dynamic capabilities. This finding extends Teece et al.'s [36] dynamic capabilities framework, which focuses on organisational routines rather than human capital flight. Our results align with Manyika and Miremadi [25] who identify workforce transformation as critical, but go further by showing talent migration as a cascade trigger rather than isolated consequence. Interestingly, whilst Qureshi and Syed [32] found employees resist automation, our data suggest they actively seek automated environments, a reversal possibly reflecting generational shifts in automation attitudes.

The gap between high CONI awareness (67–81%) and low systematic consideration (16.7%) reflect Osmundsen et al.'s [29] finding that despite recognising digital transformation importance, only 23% of organisations have formal digital strategies. However, our gap is more pronounced, possibly because CONI evaluation requires integrating multiple theoretical perspectives. The 33.3% using informal methods echoes Kedziora and Penttinen's [20] observation that even successful RPA implementations may lack systematic governance.

Our barrier analysis reveals surprising contrasts with existing literature. Whilst Hofmann et al. [14] identify cost as the primary automation barrier, our respondents rank initial investment costs lowest (3.78/5), prioritising implementation complexity (4.21) and expertise gaps (4.13) instead. This inversion suggests organisations now recognise capability-building challenges over financial constraints. Similarly, contrary to Mendling et al.'s [27] emphasis on technical integration challenges, our respondents worry more about organisational readiness, indicating a shift from technology-centric to capability-centric concerns.

The human capital findings extend beyond existing automation literature. Whilst Isaza and Cepa [15] document how automation reshapes tasks, they do not address workforce mobility. Our results reveal a new phenomenon: automation-driven talent markets where skilled workers actively select employers based on automation sophistication. This finding represents a novel automation-specific dimension of employer attractiveness.

Our findings offer practitioners three specific considerations:

1. Developing cascade metrics, as not just direct costs should be tracked, but also option expiry dates (when competitors lock in advantages), capability development timelines (skill-building requirements), and talent retention indicators (automation's role in recruitment). This extends beyond traditional metrics suggested by Dos Santos [9] by incorporating temporal dependencies.
2. Creating decision triggers. Rather than periodic reviews, thresholds should be established when talent turnover exceeds specific levels, when competitors achieve certain automation milestones, or when process costs rise beyond targets that prompt immediate CONI evaluation. This operationalises Zhu and Weyant's [40] game-theoretic timing insights for practical use.

3. Mapping interdependencies. It should be documented how operational delays affect future flexibility, how reduced flexibility constrains capability building, and how capability gaps influence competitive position. This addresses the integration gap between theories that Felsberger et al. [10] identify in Industry 4.0 contexts.

5 Conclusion

This study introduced *Cost of Not Investing* (CONI) as a cascading cost mechanism in IPA decisions, revealing a critical gap between theoretical understanding and practical application. Whilst 67–81% of respondents recognise operational, strategic, and human capital risks from delayed automation, only 16.7% systematically consider these costs in decision-making, suggesting organisations make suboptimal investments by focusing on direct costs while overlooking cascading effects. The human capital implications are particularly striking, with 81% believing talent migrates to better-automated competitors, indicating workforce dynamics may be the most visible CONI case.

Our study makes two key contributions. First, we introduce and operationalise the CONI concept, extending traditional IT investment evaluation beyond financial metrics to include strategic flexibility, dynamic capabilities, and competitive positioning dimensions. By sequencing Real Options Theory, Dynamic Capabilities perspective, and Game Theory, we provide a framework for understanding how automation investment delays cascade rather than simply accumulate. Second, our empirical investigation reveals how organisations perceive delayed automation costs across three distinct CONI dimensions (operational, strategic, and human capital), whilst identifying that 70.4% desire ROI calculators and 69.4% want case studies for evaluation improvement.

IPA CONI is a decision construct that captures these time-sensitive lenses. Specifically, it differs from traditional opportunity cost by capturing cascading interdependencies: foregone options limit future flexibility (Real Options), which constrains capability development (Dynamic Capabilities), that in turn determines competitive positioning (Game Theory). This temporal sequencing reveals why delays compound rather than simply accumulate. Opportunity Cost clarifies the foregone current value from known inefficiencies. Real Options adds the value of managerial flexibility that decays as uncertainty resolves and rivals move; unexercised options can expire or become dominated [37]. Dynamic Capabilities explains how delay erodes a firm's ability to sense, seize, and transform: data that would have trained models are not collected; process telemetry that would have informed redesign is not captured; and complementary routines are not learned [12]. Game-theoretic timing underscores that when competitors adopt earlier, payoff asymmetries widen through experience effects, switching costs, and reputation signals [40]. Our key theoretical assumption is that these mechanisms form a cascade: postponement shrinks option value, which slows capability accumulation, which magnifies competitive payoff gaps, including human-capital frictions as digitally skilled workers gravitate to environments where their productivity and learning are higher. Hence, we formally define CONI as a time-varying expected cost function that aggregates four theoretically distinct yet measurable components: (i) operational inefficiencies relative to a feasible IPA baseline; (ii) lost option value as flexibility windows close; (iii) capability erosion from deferred sensing/seizing/transforming; and (iv) strategic interaction losses driven by rival adoption and market responses.

Several limitations should be acknowledged. Our sample of 108 respondents from Europe and the US may not reflect automation challenges in Asian or other markets. The cross-sectional design captures perceptions at a single point rather than tracking how CONI evolves over time. We rely on self-reported perceptions rather than objective CONI measures, and our focus on IPA may not generalise to broader AI workplace technologies. The varying levels of automation knowledge amongst respondents (34.3% with only basic awareness) may affect response reliability. Most critically, we cannot establish causal relationships between perceived CONI and actual business outcomes, i.e. validation that requires longitudinal research with objective performance metrics.

Future research should address three priorities. First, validate the cascade mechanism through longitudinal studies tracking how initial delays compound over time. Second, develop objective CONI metrics using process mining data, talent analytics, and competitive benchmarking rather than perceptions. Third, test whether organisations using cascade-aware evaluation frameworks make better automation timing decisions than those using traditional ROI methods.

By formalising CONI and demonstrating its cascading nature, we extend IS investment evaluation beyond near-term ROI to include compounding penalties of inaction. In IPA-intensive environments where data and learning effects compound, delay can degrade option value, slow capability formation, and widen payoff gaps. Treating CONI as cascading, rather than additive, allows organisations to make timing decisions that account for trajectories, not only snapshots, and to align automation roadmaps with both productivity goals and talent strategy. As automation becomes central to competitive advantage, understanding and measuring CONI will become increasingly critical for strategic decision-making.

References

1. van der Aalst, W.M., Bichler, M., Heinzl, A.: Robotic process automation. Bus. Inf. Syst. Eng. **60**(4), 269–272 (2018)
2. Barney, J.: Firm resources and sustained competitive advantage. J. Manag. **17**(1), 99–120 (1991)
3. Benaroch, M.: Managing information technology investment risk: a real options perspective. J. Manag. Inf. Syst. **19**(2), 43–84 (2002). https://doi.org/10.1080/07421222.2002.11045726
4. Benaroch, M.: Real options models for proactive uncertainty-reducing mitigations and applications in cybersecurity investment decision making. Inf. Syst. Res. **29**(2), 315–340 (2018). https://doi.org/10.1287/isre.2017.0714
5. Buchanan, J.M.: Opportunity cost. In: Eatwell, J., Milgate, M., Newman, P. (eds.) The World of Economics, pp. 520–525. Palgrave Macmillan (1991)

6. Cheon, G., Choi, Y., Lee, D., Baek, J.: Generative ai agents in language learning: a randomized field experiment. In: Proceedings of the 58th Hawaii International Conference on System Sciences, pp. 4949–4958 (2025)
7. De Vreede, T., Cheng, X., Siemon, D.: Introduction to the ai and the future of work minitrack. In: Proceedings of the 58th Hawaii International Conference on System Sciences, pp. 101–102 (2025)
8. DeVellis, R.F.: Scale Development: Theory and Applications. Sage Publications, 4th edn. (2016)
9. Dos Santos, B.L.: Justifying investments in new information technologies. J. Manag. Inf. Syst. **7**(4), 71–90 (1991)
10. Felsberger, A., Qaiser, F.H., Choudhary, A., Reiner, G.: The impact of industry 4.0 on the reconciliation of dynamic capabilities: evidence from the European manufacturing industries. Prod. Plann. Control **33**(2-3), 277–300 (2022)
11. Freitag, B., Häfner, L., Pfeuffer, V., Übelhör, J.: Evaluating investments in flexible on-demand production capacity: a real options approach. Bus. Res. **13**(1), 133–161 (2019). https://doi.org/10.1007/s40685-019-00105-w
12. Ghosh, S., Hughes, M., Hodgkinson, I., Hughes, P.: Digital transformation of industrial businesses: a dynamic capability approach. Technovation **113**, 102414 (2022)
13. Gregor, S.: The nature of theory in information systems. MIS Q. **30**(3), 611–642 (2006)
14. Hofmann, P., Samp, C., Urbach, N.: Robotic process automation. Electron. Mark. **30**(1), 99–106 (2020)
15. Isaza, L., Cepa, K.: Automation and augmentation: a process study of how robotization shapes tasks of operational employees. Eur. Manage. J. (2021)
16. Jones, S.K., Frisch, D., Yurak, T.J., Kim, E.: Choices and opportunities: another effect of framing on decisions. J. Behav. Decis. Mak. **11**(3), 211–226 (1998)
17. Kedziora, D., Leivonen, A., Piotrowicz, W., Öörni, A.: Robotic process automation (RPA) implementation drivers: Evidence of selected Nordic companies. Issues Inf. Syst. **22**(2), 21–40 (2021). https://doi.org/10.48009/2_iis_2021_21-40
18. Kedziora, D., Hyrynsalmi, S.: Turning robotic process automation onto intelligent automation with machine learning. In: Proceedings of the 11th International Conference on Communities and Technologies, pp. 1–5. ACM (2023)
19. Kedziora, D., Kiviranta, H.M.: Digital business value creation with robotic process automation (rpa) in northern and central europe. Management **13**(2), 161–174 (2018)
20. Kedziora, D., Penttinen, E.: Governance models for robotic process automation: The case of nordea bank. J. Inf. Technol. Teach. Cases **11**(1), 20–29 (2020)
21. Kruchten, P., Nord, R.L., Ozkaya, I.: Technical debt: from metaphor to theory and practice. IEEE Softw. **29**(6), 18–21 (2012)
22. Lacity, M., Willcocks, L.: Robotic Process and Cognitive Automation: The Next Phase. SB Publishing (2018)
23. Latinovic, M., Pammer-Schindler, V.: Automation and artificial intelligence in software engineering: experiences, challenges, and opportunities. In: Proceedings of the 54th Hawaii International Conference on System Sciences, pp. 146–155 (2021)
24. Lieberman, M.B., Montgomery, D.B.: First-mover advantages. Strateg. Manag. J. **9**(S1), 41–58 (1988)
25. Manyika, J., Miremadi, M.: Where machines could replace humans—and where they can't (yet). McKinsey Quarterly (2020)
26. Manyika, J., Miremadi, M.: Where machines could replace humans—and where they can't (yet). Technical Report, McKinsey & Company (2020)

27. Mendling, J., Decker, G., Hull, R., Reijers, H.A., Weber, I.: How do machine learning, robotic process automation, and blockchains affect the human factor in business process management? Commun. Assoc. Inf. Syst. **43**(1), 19 (2020)
28. Neis, D., Pereira, G.V., Maccari, E.A.: Digital transformation in organizations: a systematic literature review and research agenda. Gov. Inf. Q. **42**(1), 101–115 (2025)
29. Osmundsen, K., Iden, J., Bygstad, B.: Digital transformation: drivers, success factors, and implications. In: Proceedings of the 12th Mediterranean Conference on Information Systems, pp. 1–15 (2019)
30. Pan, G., Pan, S.L., Lim, C.Y.: Examining how firms leverage it to achieve firm productivity: Rbv and dynamic capabilities perspectives. Inf. Manage. **52**(4), 401–412 (2015)
31. Podsakoff, P.M., MacKenzie, S.B., Lee, J.Y., Podsakoff, N.P.: Common method biases in behavioral research: a critical review of the literature and recommended remedies. J. Appl. Psychol. **88**(5), 879–903 (2003)
32. Qureshi, M.O., Syed, R.S.: The impact of robotics on employment and motivation of employees in the service sector, with special reference to health care. Saf. Health Work **5**(4), 198–202 (2014)
33. Rahmandad, H., Repenning, N.: Capability erosion dynamics. Strateg. Manag. J. **37**(4), 649–672 (2016). https://doi.org/10.1002/smj.2354
34. Smit, H.T.J., Trigeorgis, L.: Strategic NPV: real options and strategic games under different information structures. Strateg. Manag. J. **38**(13), 2555–2578 (2017). https://doi.org/10.1002/smj.2665
35. Syed, R., Suriadi, S., Adams, M., Bandara, W., Leemans, S.J., Ouyang, C., Ter Hofstede, A.H., Van De Weerd, I., Wynn, M.T., Reijers, H.A.: Robotic process automation: contemporary themes and challenges. Comput. Ind. **115**, 103162 (2020)
36. Teece, D.J., Pisano, G., Shuen, A.: Dynamic capabilities and strategic management. Strateg. Manag. J. **18**(7), 509–533 (1997). https://doi.org/10.1002/(SICI)1097-0266(199708)18:7<509::AID-SMJ882>3.0.CO;2-Z
37. Trigeorgis, L., Reuer, J.J.: Real options theory in strategic management. Strateg. Manag. J. **38**(1), 42–63 (2017). https://doi.org/10.1002/smj.2593
38. Vilkas, M., Stefanini, A., Ghobakhloo, M., Grybauskas, A.: Digital technology-enabled capability development pathways. Comput. Ind. Eng. **196**, 110473 (2024)
39. Ylä-Kujala, A., Kedziora, D., Metso, L., Kärri, T., Happonen, A., Piotrowicz, W.: Robotic process automation deployments: a step-by-step method to investment appraisal. Bus. Process. Manag. J. **29**(8), 163–187 (2023)
40. Zhu, K., Weyant, J.P.: Strategic decisions of new technology adoption under asymmetric information: a game-theoretic model*. Decis. Sci. **34**(4), 643–675 (2003). https://doi.org/10.1111/j.1540-5414.2003.02460.x

Understanding Organizational Decision to Adopt AI Technologies: A Qualitative Study

Maryam Gulzar(✉)

Department of Software Engineering, Lappeenranta, Finland
maryam.gulzar@lut.fi

Abstract. Artificial intelligence (AI) continues to transform organizational operations by introducing advanced methods that enhance efficiency and productivity. However, many organizations struggle with critical decisions about when to adopt such technologies and how to integrate them effectively into their existing IT infrastructures. To address this gap, the current study conducted a multicase study and collected data through 15 semi-structured interviews. By applying Gioia's method, it identifies the motivations, triggers, and decision-making considerations that influence the adoption of AI within organizations. This work proposed a process model that reveals AI adoption is not driven by a single factor but emerges from a complex interplay of motivations, triggers, and evaluative logic that collectively shape an organization's decision for its adoption.

Keywords: AI adoption · motivations · challenges · decision making · organizational change

1 Introduction

Artificial Intelligence (AI) has evolved from a theoretical promise into an operational reality, encouraging organizations to explore and adopt AI-based tools and technologies [1]. This rapid AI advancement has played a positive role in transforming business processes from automation to integration of generative AI and machine learning technologies. A growing number of organizations now feel pressure to integrate advanced AI technologies into their operations to maintain innovation, relevance, and competitiveness, but often lack strategic clarity [2]. Many companies rush to implement AI tools without clearly understanding how these technologies align with their broader business objectives, which results in falling short of expectations [3]. Organizations vary widely not only in whether they adopt AI, but also in why they pursue it, when they decide to explore it, and how they evaluate its fit within their unique context.

Prior research works, such as the Technology Acceptance Model (TAM) [4], the Diffusion of Innovation theory [5], or the Technology–Organization–Environment (TOE) framework [6], mostly talked about technical implementation and performance outcomes or individual user acceptance models. Though these models are useful in explaining macro-level patterns and user-level behavior, they often overlook the complex, contextual, and interpretive processes through which organizations deliberate the adoption of

G. Herzwurm et al. (Eds.): ICSOB 2025, LNBIP 574, pp. 132–138, 2026.
https://doi.org/10.1007/978-3-032-14518-5_11

emerging technologies like AI. In particular, they underrepresent the strategic thinking, internal debates, and evaluative considerations that shape AI adoption decisions at the organizational level. Recent studies acknowledge that AI adoption is not only a matter of technological readiness, but it involves deep strategic, cultural, and organizational reflection [7, 8]. Organizations must determine whether AI aligns with their business goals, operational capacities, and ethical standards.

2 Research Methodology

This study explores how organizations make decisions about adopting AI technologies by applying the Gioia method [9]. For this purpose, we conducted a qualitative multicase study, having 15 semi-structured interviews over 6 months (Nov 2024 to Apr 2025), ranging from 40–60 min. To gain a broad yet deep knowledge of AI adoption decision-making, we sampled organizations from diverse industries, and participants were chosen who were directly involved in the decision-making or implementation of AI initiatives. Table 1 presents the information about the organizations interviewed.

Table 1. Case organizations and interviewees' information.

Case ID	Organization Name	Orgn. size	Interview's Position
A	Business Consulting and Services	800,000	Senior Manager, Data & AI
			Data & AI Lead
B	IT Development, Services, Consulting	220000	Data & AI Sales Director
			Global AI Architect
			AI and Analytics Sales Executive
C	Industrial Machine Manufacturing	20,000	Director of Data & AI Projects
D		18000	Head of AI Development
			Senior Manager
E	Educational Institute	3400	Leading Senior Advisor
F		1400	Head of AI
G	IT Services and IT Consulting	1000	Innovation Lead
			AI Principal
			Lead developer
H	AI Solutions Lab	500	AI Consultants
			Lead AI Solutions Strategist

2.1 Data Analysis

We have transcribed the interviews as text and imported all transcriptions into NVivo for further qualitative analysis. This stage involved a detailed examination of texts to discover underlying patterns, themes, and dimensions. For this purpose, we have followed the three-stage coding process of the Gioia method [9] to analyze raw data. The following elaborates on each of the three-step processes.

Step 1: 1st-Order Coding. This step began with open coding, where researchers adhered strictly to the participants' terms and tried to reduce the categories into a manageable number by labeling them or using some sort of phrasal descriptors. This resulted in a set of 1st-order codes representing the terms, concerns, and mental models used as participant-centric.

Step 2: 2nd-Order Theme Development. At this stage, the emerging first-order codes were organized into second-order theoretical developments based on the interpretation of the researchers. We examined first-order codes by constant comparisons to identify patterns, similarities, and relationships, grouping them into 2nd-order themes that captured the underlying structures of organizational reasoning.

Step 3: Aggregate Dimension. Finally, we make sense of the data at this stage, aimed at developing the data structure. We clustered 2nd-order themes into three aggregate theoretical dimensions that directly aligned with the objective of the study: Strategic Motivations (*Why*), Triggering Conditions (*When*), Decision Logic and Evaluation (*How*). A complete analytical coding process in the form of emergent terms, themes, and aggregate dimensions is presented in Table 2.

Table 2. Analytical coding process.

Aggregate Dimension	2nd-Order Theme	1st-Order Coding
Strategic Motivations	Efficiency and optimization	Automation reduces time, effort, enhances work quality, improves employee operational efficiency, and productivity
	Bridging and retaining expertise	Addressing labor shortages and bridging knowledge gaps, retain & utilize the knowledge of retired employees
	Innovation-driven growth	Early adoption for learning and the emergence of new business models, enabling innovative approaches to compete
	Market and client responsiveness	Enhanced client advisory services, global trends, competitive pressure, and improved customer interactions
Preconditions & Triggers	Inter-infrastructural barriers	Insufficient, inaccurate, and mismanaged data for AI tools, inconsistent data management standards, and integration issues

(*continued*)

Table 2. *(continued)*

Aggregate Dimension	2nd-Order Theme	1st-Order Coding
	Organizational need & growth	Ensuring value alignment, addressing business growth & organizational needs
	Process improvement & business transformation	Enable people to achieve more with fewer resources, improving operational tasks to transform business, and enhancing work processes
Evaluation Criteria	Problem identification & strategic alignment	Define actual problems to solve with AI, alignment with broader strategy & goals, focus on value creation and business case, prioritize and assess user-centered needs
	Organization capability & readiness	Organizations' readiness to support AI adoption, develop a change management plan, ensure employees' training, and in-house development to match needs
	Technical fit & compatible	Ensuring the tools comply with security protocols, analyze the cost, usability & accessibility of AI tools, and scalability & align with organizational infrastructure
	Expected ROI & value justifications	Cost justification by expected gains in productivity, needs financial modelling and benefit assumptions, AI tool evaluation to perform the required tasks

3 Findings and Discussion

This study explores the reasoning processes behind organizational decisions to adopt AI technologies. It is mainly guided by three central questions: **why** organizations pursue AI, **when** challenges prompt exploration, and **how** decision-makers approach adoption. We developed a process model that demonstrates AI adoption as a multi-stage reasoning journey rather than a singular technical decision. The model reveals three interdependent dimensions: strategic motivations, preconditions and triggers, and evaluative criteria, each of which contributes to shaping the eventual adoption decision. **Strategic motivations** capture the underlying reasons why organizations initially chose to explore and pursue AI technologies. Rather than being driven solely by technological enthusiasm, AI adoption was motivated by a combination of internal strategic goals and external pressures. **Preconditions and triggers** encompass the conditions and triggers that prompted organizations to initiate active exploration of AI. These often-represented systemic limitations underscore the urgent need for and the more obvious adoption of AI. In **evaluation criteria,** once organizations are motivated to explore AI and confront practical challenges, they need to adopt a structured decision-making process to determine whether AI is worth pursuing. This dimension captures the evaluative reasoning of the "how" behind AI adoption. Building on these aggregate dimensions, we developed a process model (Fig. 1) that illustrates how organizations move through various phases of AI adoption decision-making.

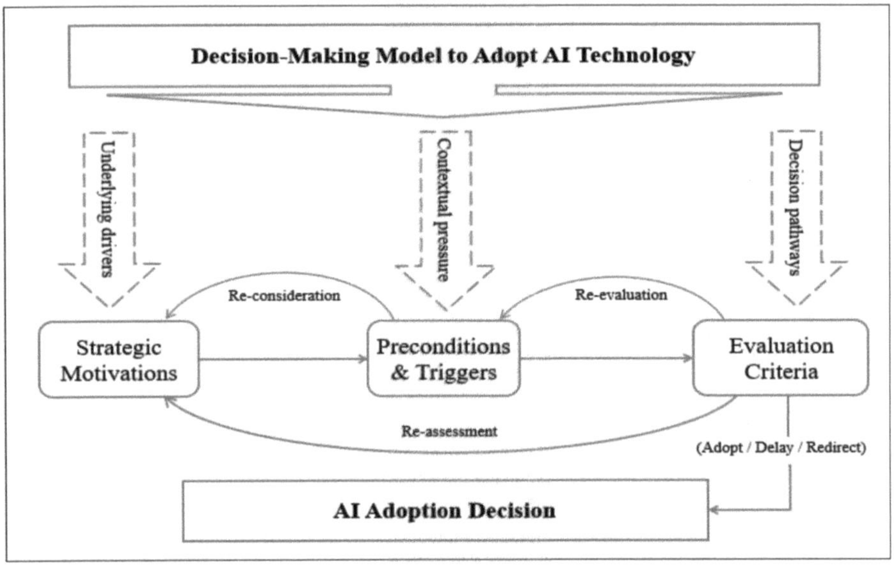

Fig. 1. Process model of organizational AI adoption decisions

These stages collectively shape the ultimate decision to adopt, delay, or redirect AI initiatives. Importantly, the model also depicts feedback loops, signifying that AI adoption is not a linear process. Organizations often revisit earlier stages as new needs emerge, technologies evolve, or implementation challenges occur. Rather than being purely technical, the adoption journey is deeply interpretive, context-dependent, and shaped by both opportunities and constraints. Prior research on the adoption of technology has often emphasized efficiency gains and cost reduction as the principal drivers [11, 15]. However, beyond these central motivations, organizations also pursued AI adoption to bridge expertise gaps, retain organizational knowledge, respond to evolving client demands, and enable innovation-driven growth. Existing literature on AI adoption often treats challenges such as poor data quality, workforce resistance, and complexity as barriers that hinder adoption [10, 12]. Our findings complicate this view. Rather than acting solely as inhibitors, these challenges and preconditions often served as catalysts that triggered the exploration of AI solutions.

The third dimension of our findings concerns how organizations approached AI adoption decisions. Traditional models often emphasize cost-benefit analyses, ROI, or technical feasibility [9]. While these factors were indeed central, our data reveals a more layered and iterative process. Organizations first emphasized problem identification and strategic alignment [13] that addressed real, high-impact business problems rather than irrelevant tasks. Second, they evaluated organizational readiness and capability [14], which included internal training, cultural acceptance, and infrastructure maturity. Third, technical fit, compatibility, and security considerations played a role, particularly concerning privacy, compliance, and enterprise-level scalability. Finally, organizations assessed ROI and outcomes but framed them not only in financial terms but also in broader organizational value creation and long-term positioning.

4 Conclusion

This study demonstrates that AI adoption is not a linear or purely technical decision, but a multi-stage reasoning process driven by motivations, preconditions & triggers, and evaluative logics. By framing adoption through the lenses of why, when, and how, we provide a process model that both advances theory and offers practical guidance. Ultimately, understanding AI adoption as organizational reasoning, rather than as a technical inevitability. This study has limitations as it draws on qualitative data from a specific set of organizations, which may limit generalizability. Future research could extend these insights across a number of industries or geographic contexts. Our study captures adoption reasoning at a particular point in time; longitudinal studies could reveal how motivations, challenges, and evaluation criteria evolve as organizations progress through implementation.

References

1. Dittmar, E.C.: AI as a catalyst for organizational learning: moving beyond tool implementation to learning transformation. Dev. Learn. Org. Int. J. (2025)
2. Al-kfairy, M.: Strategic integration of generative AI in organizational settings: Applications, challenges, and adoption requirements. IEEE Eng. Manag. Rev. (2025)
3. Boo, C.: When a customer meets AI failure: expectation discrepancy perspective. Appl. Econ. Lett. **32**(7), 1039–1043 (2025)
4. Davis, F.D.: Technology acceptance model: TAM. In: AlSuqri, M.N., Al-Aufi, A.S. (eds.) Information Seeking Behavior and Technology Adoption, vol. 205, pp. 219
5. Rogers, E.M.: Diffusion of Innovations, vol. 32, pp. 891–937. The Free Press of Glencoe (2003)
6. Tornatzky, L.G., Fleischer, M.: The Process of Technological Innovation. Lexington Books, United Kingdom (1990)
7. Shrestha, Y.R., Ben-Menahem, S.M., von Krogh, G.: Organizational decision-making structures in the age of AI. Calif. Manage. Rev. **63**(3), 46–68 (2021)
8. Somayajula, P.P.: AI-augmented strategic decision-making in business organizations. Int. J. Glob. Tech Manag. **1**(1), 63–74 (2024)
9. Gioia, D.A., Corley, K.G., Hamilton, A.L.: Seeking qualitative rigor in inductive research: notes on the Gioia methodology. Organ. Res. Methods **16**(1), 15–31 (2013)

10. Bérubé, M., Giannelia, T., Vial, G.: Barriers to the Implementation of AI in Organizations: Findings from a Delphi Study (2021)
11. Merhi, M.I., Harfouche, A.: Enablers of artificial intelligence adoption and implementation in production systems. Int. J. Prod. Res. **62**(15), 5457–5471 (2024)
12. Dwivedi, Y.K., Hughes, L., Ismagilova, E., Aarts, G., Coombs, C., Crick, T., et al.: Artificial intelligence (AI): Multidisciplinary perspectives on emerging challenges, opportunities, and agenda for research, practice, and policy. Int. J. Inf. Manag. **57**, 101994 (2021)
13. Ansari, I., Barati, M., Sadeghi Moghadam, M.R., Ghobakhloo, M.: An Industry 4.0 readiness model for new technology exploitation. Int. J. Qual. Reliab. Manag. **40**(10), 2519–2538 (2023)
14. Shea, C.M., Jacobs, S.R., Esserman, D.A., Bruce, K., Weiner, B.J.: Organizational readiness for implementing change: a psychometric assessment of a new measure. Implement. Sci. **9**(1), 7 (2014)
15. Gulzar, M., Naqvi, B., Smolander, K.: Technology change adoption in organizations: drivers, challenges, and success enablers. In: International Conference on Software Business, pp. 407–422. Springer, Berlin (2024)

Investigating Generative AI's Impact on Software Organizations' Security Practices: A Multi-case Study Using Gioia Methodology

David Kinnberg Hein(✉)

Department of Computer Science, Aalborg University, Selma Lagerlöfs Vej 300, 9220 Aalborg, Denmark
davidkh@cs.aau.dk

Abstract. The integration of generative AI in software organizations presents promising opportunities for automating and enhancing security activities; however, its practical impact on the security practices of software organizations and associated risks remains underexplored. This study investigates how generative AI can enhance software security practices through a multi-case study involving five software organizations. By conducting semi-structured interviews with developers and managers, we identified four security practices where generative AI can support threat assessment, security testing, operational management, and education & guidance. At the same time, we uncover sociotechnical risks that may impede adoption, including concerns about inadequate data management of AI, inaccurate output, and a lack of trust. Guided by the OWASP SAMM framework and rooted in the Gioia methodological approach, our findings are synthesized into a theoretical model of generative AI adoption impacting security practices. This model highlights both the perceived benefits and the risks organizations encounter. Our work provides insights for software organizations looking to adopt generative AI into security-related workflows and contributes a foundational understanding of how such tools are perceived in practice. The paper emphasizes the importance of balancing innovation with caution as software organizations increasingly incorporate generative AI within secure development.

Keywords: Security Practices · Generative AI · Multi-case study · Gioia Methodology

1 Introduction

In recent years, software organizations have seen a notable rise in security threats and vulnerabilities [11]. With the current rise of cyberattacks and data breaches, there is an increasing need for software organizations to prioritize security as part of the development process. However, manual security activities can be time-consuming, prone to errors, and expensive, making it difficult for software organizations to identify and mitigate security risks effectively [12]. In response to this challenge, generative AI has

G. Herzwurm et al. (Eds.): ICSOB 2025, LNBIP 574, pp. 139–157, 2026.
https://doi.org/10.1007/978-3-032-14518-5_12

emerged as a promising tool to enhance software development tasks and security activities [11]. Generative AI can be trained to analyze software code, vulnerability management data, and security logs to identify potential security risks and prioritize remediation efforts [8]. By automating security activities, software organizations can reduce the risk of human error, accelerate the detection and mitigation of security threats, and enhance the overall security posture of their software systems [16]. There have even been attempts to develop tailored generative AI for security purposes [1]. However, it remains largely unexplored how software practitioners themselves perceive the usefulness of using generative AI to enhance their security practices, in combination with the risks associated with using these tools.

Bridging this gap, we conducted a multi-case study with five software organizations to extend our knowledge on how generative AI can be used to improve security practices and the associated risks. Against this backdrop, we formulate our research question as follows:

How can the adoption of generative AI impact software organizations' security practices?

We conduct a multi-case study with five software organizations, using the Gioia methodology and the OWASP SAMM framework to categorize and link statements to security practices. Our study suggests that four security practices, Threat Assessment, Security Testing, Operational Management, and Education & Guidance, can be enhanced with generative AI, although sociotechnical risks pose challenges. We present a model integrating these factors to enhance security and address AI risks. The paper is organized as follows: Sect. 2 reviews related work on generative AI in security and risks; Sect. 3 details the research approach; Sect. 4 presents findings; and Sects. 5 discuss these, limitations, and future directions.

2 Related Work

2.1 Generative AI in Software Development and Security

Previous research on generative AI in software development has explored its potential to assist developers with code generation, optimization, review, automated testing, and vulnerability scanning [25, 27]. Automated code generation is well-established, with tools like GitHub Copilot evaluated for quality, though results vary. Effectiveness depends on factors such as programming language and task complexity [30]. These studies highlight the importance of human review of AI-generated code. Empirical evidence suggests that generative AI can enhance productivity by streamlining routine tasks [19]. Beyond code generation, AI assistance can improve developer knowledge, abilities, and productivity. Generative AI aims to enhance software engineering by automating routine tasks, freeing developers to focus on creative work [2]. For security activities, generative AI aids risk analysis, multilingual code auditing, and software testing. Its ability to process multiple programming languages helps detect hidden connections in architectures and source code, supporting accurate risk assessments [16]. In testing, it creates test cases from natural language and enables automation for broader coverage. In binary analysis, interactive AI gathers contextual information to better understand complex code [6].

Many studies discuss generative AI as useful for vulnerability detection and remediation [26], but it's more effective at fixing vulnerabilities than detecting them [35]. Its accuracy depends on the model and task complexity, so caution is needed in security-critical areas. Generative AI has also been found to be suitable for logging [22], penetration testing [17], and code reviews [31]. However, most research is survey-based, lacking evaluation of impact on specific security practices or analysis of security benefits versus risks.

2.2 Risks of Using Generative AI

Trust is a central theme and risk in studies of generative AI adoption. Research has explored factors influencing developer trust [22], designs for trust-enhancing interfaces [24], and the role of online communities in shaping trust perceptions [5]. Findings show that perceived risks directly influence trust [33], and some studies suggest that users attribute similar trustworthiness to AI-generated and human-generated content [18]. Transparency has been repeatedly identified as a key factor in improving trust [9]. Thus, we must investigate the risks of using generative AI, as we want to manage and address them to ease adoption for software organizations. Several studies have identified critical risks associated with generative AI in software development. Generative AI tools may leak sensitive data [3] and spread misinformation [35]. In 2024, McGraw identified ten prominent risks: recursive pollution, data debt, improper use, black box opacity, prompt manipulation, poisoned data, reproducibility economics, unclear data ownership, lack of model trustworthiness, and insufficient encoding integrity [23].

More specifically, for software developers, include the risks of generating insecure code containing backdoors and vulnerabilities, risks of data manipulation, and unintended data transfer to external entities [10]. Another concern arises from generative AI models pre-trained on external datasets, which may introduce intellectual property violations when proprietary prompts are used to further train these models. A mixed-method study has examined the factors influencing the adoption of generative AI tools in software development. The findings show that, while these tools promise clear advantages, their adoption is far from guaranteed. The study highlights *compatibility* with the software organization as the primary enabler. Thus, generative AI must integrate seamlessly into an organization's existing development workflows and align with its values to gain traction. The study also points to risks that may hinder adoption, including inaccurate outputs and embedded biases in generated results [29].

3 Research Approach and Case Selection

We adopted a multi-case study approach, investigating five cases to enhance the generalizability of our findings and facilitate data triangulation [28], as opposed to the more in-depth approach of a single case study [14]. Our findings are detailed and general, enabling the development of a theoretical model. We focus on exploring how software companies can automate security activities using generative AI. The five cases were selected for their diverse contexts and shared interest in enhancing security activities with generative AI. This range helps identify cross-case patterns, allowing greater generalization of results [13]. All companies had prior knowledge of generative AI and security. The selected companies have varying levels of knowledge and experience in generative AI and security practices, providing insights into the roles of software professionals across organizational structures. We assessed participants' familiarity with these areas through interviews and explored their current experience in their role. This helped evaluate their ability to answer our questions. Experience with generative AI was limited to using tools, not developing large language models. Their prior experience is summarized in Table 1. To ensure confidentiality, all identifiers were anonymized, sensitive details were omitted or paraphrased, and informed consent was obtained.

3.1 Data Collection and Analysis

We undertook a comprehensive data collection via semi-structured interviews with 22 respondents from five software organizations. Conducted as focus groups of 2–4 participants, lasting 25–70 min, these groups included managers and developers. Selecting both roles was strategic, recognizing their unique perspectives on generative AI's impact on security practices. Their roles provide distinct insights that enhance our study. We developed an interview guide to ensure consistency and thoroughly explore our research question. This guide structured the interviews, ensuring relevant questions were consistently asked. Throughout the interviews, note-taking helped streamline data transcription, capturing participants' responses and observations for analysis [28, 34].

Table 1. Description of participants and the five cases.

Participant	Case	Sector	Org. size	Role	Years of exp.	Exp/genAI	Exp/security
P1	The bankers	Financial sector	> 4000	Back-End Developer	1	Low	Low
P2	The bankers	Financial sector	> 4000	Back-End Developer	22	Low	Low
P3	The bankers	Financial sector	> 4000	Front-End Developer	4	Low	Low
P4	The bankers	Financial sector	> 4000	Architect	8	Low	Low
P5	The bankers	Financial sector	> 4000	Security Director	2	Medium	High
P6	The bankers	Financial sector	> 4000	IT-Operations Manager	5	Low	Medium
P7	The educators	Education	> 60	Back-End Developer	2	Low	Low

(continued)

Table 1. *(continued)*

Participant	Case	Sector	Org. size	Role	Years of exp.	Exp/genAI	Exp/security
P8	The educators	Education	> 60	DevOps	1	High	High
P9	The educators	Education	> 60	DevOps	2	High	High
P10	The educators	Education	> 60	DevOps	3	High	High
P11	The educators	Education	> 60	CEO	2	Medium	Medium
P12	The data analysts	Software vendors	> 60	DevOps	4	Medium	Medium
P13	The data analysts	Software vendors	> 60	Back-End Developer	2	Low	Low
P14	The data analysts	Software vendors	> 60	CTO	1	Low	Medium
P15	The data analysts	Software vendors	> 60	Team Lead	1	Low	Medium
P16	The software lawyers	Lawyer firms	> 40	CEO	34	Low	Medium
P17	The software lawyers	Lawyer firms	> 40	Team Lead	3	Low	Medium
P18	The software lawyers	Lawyer firms	> 40	CCO	3	Low	Low
P19	The software lawyers	Lawyer firms	> 40	Back-End Developer	2	Low	Low
P20	The software lawyers	Lawyer firms	> 40	Front-End Developer	1	Low	Low
P21	The consultants	Software vendors	> 20	CEO	10	Low	Low
P22	The consultants	Software vendors	> 20	COO	3	Low	Low

Following data transcription, our analysis focused on cross-case comparisons to identify patterns and themes [13]. We used a grounded theory approach based on the Gioia methodology to enhance rigor and structure [15]. The Gioia method offers a systematic framework, ensuring disciplined exploration of patterns and themes in qualitative data

[21]. We adopt a theory-driven approach [4] to build a solid foundation for understanding security practices in software organizations. Our thematic analysis follows six steps: 1) Deeply familiarize with the dataset. 2) Outline initial coding schemes (1st order concepts) to categorize data. 3) Derive themes (2nd order themes) from codes, identifying patterns. 4) Review and refine themes for coherence. 5) Categorize and define themes to reflect nuances. 6) Produce a report summarizing findings and data structures [15]. NVivo was used to code our qualitative data. In the Gioia methodology, the interpreter combines 1st order concepts and 2nd order themes into aggregate dimensions, which serve as data structure titles. The categorization of security practices in the OWASP SAMM framework informs these themes. The framework has five business functions: Governance, Design, Implementation, Verification, and Operations, each with three practices. Governance includes Strategy & Metrics, Policy & Compliance, Education & Guidance. Design covers Threat Assessment, Security Requirements, and Secure Architecture. Implementation includes Secure Build, Secure Deployment, and Defect Management. Verification entails Architecture Assessment, Requirements-driven Testing, and Security Testing. Operations comprise Incident Management, Environment Management, and Operational Management.

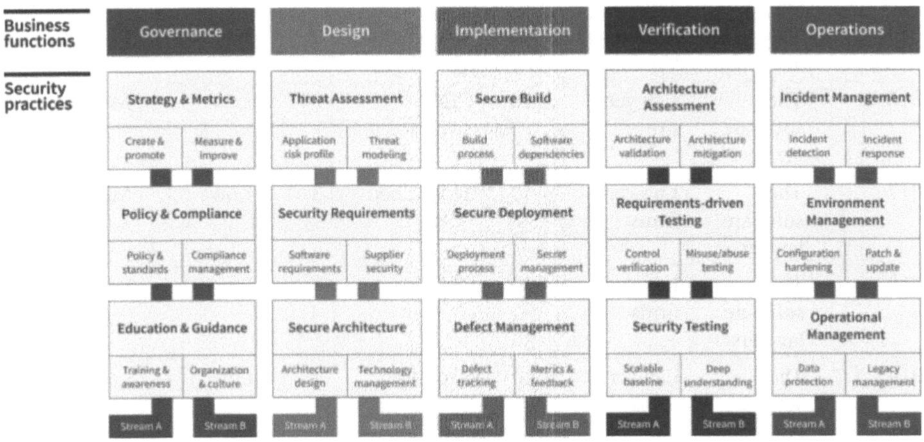

Fig. 1. The OWASP SAMM framework showing the five business functions and their three security practices.

4 Findings

We have grouped our results into six data structures, comprising six distinct aggregate dimensions based on our 1st order concepts and 2nd order themes from the data analysis, as well as the security practices from OWASP SAMM.

4.1 Security Practices Improvement with Generative AI

Table 2 shows five security activities—Vulnerability scanning, repair, assessment, phishing attack simulation, and script analysis—that could benefit from generative AI across our five cases. Threat assessment involves identifying potential threats with tools to mitigate risks. Participants identified using AI for vulnerability scanning, with both developers and managers seeing it as crucial and feasible. A manager noted: "*In relation to security scanning of code, I believe that AI-technology can be used*" (P6). This suggests AI for code scanning is viable and viewed as a key security improvement. A developer, however, expressed doubts: "*It probably can, if you need to be kept up to date, then I think there are existing tools for scanning repositories in the background, because they are passive... The concept of constantly prompting does not seem relevant*" (P7). This implies that such tools could reduce cognitive load, but human validation remains necessary.

Table 2. Data structure of the aggregate dimension: "threat assessment"

Quote	1st order concepts	2nd order themes	Coverage (%)
"Basically, getting notifications from Chat-GPT to tell us, well, you have such a system, and then you get a notification that on your system, you might be vulnerable to that. I can see that work." (P9)	Security code scan automation, increased effectiveness, reduced effort	Vulnerability scanning	55
"We became aware of a redux vulnerability…then asked ChatGPT to rewrite it without the vulnerability. That worked." (P3)	Fix vulnerability in code, security bug fixing, threat response, increased effectiveness, reduced effort	Vulnerability repair	23
"I see value in having a language model synthesizing everything on your system and then getting you a clear message on, for example, you have this vulnerability on that machine, and then you should probably do that to resolve it." (P8)	Vulnerability classification optimization, increased effectiveness	Vulnerability assessment	18
"We can have them write custom spear phishing emails… And give it access to an API, so it can send an email from our domain." (P13)	Phishing attack automation, defence hardening, reduced effort, time saving	Phishing attack simulation	9

(*continued*)

Table 2. (*continued*)

Quote	1st order concepts	2nd order themes	Coverage (%)
"Say we find a script on a machine, and we need to figure out how it works. They can deal with it quicker than a human analyst trying to comprehend the code. It would be an obvious way of using them." (P5)	Script analysis automation, reverse engineering, time saving	Script analysis	4,5

We report six security activities in operational management, including logging, data leakage prevention, access control, data flagging, flow documentation, and retrieval. Developers identified these activities, with logging being most prominent. A DevOps demonstrates using generative AI for automating log analysis: "*Let's say a log file in the cloud, saying, is there anything that is not of the ordinary in this, and it will actually be able to pass it much faster than we would be able to. So, I could see it being a good tool in the long run*" (P9). This shows a positive view of generative AI for this task, mainly improving security efficiency and freeing staff for proactive measures (Table 3).

Table 3. Data structure of the aggregate dimension: "operational management"

Quote	1st order concepts	2nd order themes	Coverage (%)
"I believe if you gave it access to log data, it could more quickly and effectively identify suspicious behavior." (P5)	Data logging automation, increased effectiveness	Logging	45
"I believe it is useful in many areas also for data leakage prevention." (P12)	Reduce data leakage, increased effectiveness, reduced effort	Data leakage prevention	23
"But I think it's obvious. Role configuration: which roles do we have, what do they have access to, and are there any holes?" (P14)	Improved role configuration, increased effectiveness, reduced effort	Access and permission control	14

(*continued*)

Table 3. (*continued*)

Quote	1st order concepts	2nd order themes	Coverage (%)
"That's what they do all day; they get a ticket with all the data, and then you need to go through the whole ticket and confirm that nothing is wrong. So, yes, it could replace those centers specifically for that, you know, flagging." (P10)	Data analysis automation, task replacement, increased effectiveness	Data flagging	14
"I believe it can help us with documenting data flows." (P2)	Documentation automation, report and flow generation, increased effectiveness	Data flow documentation	9
"I could upload the message I received to ChatGPT and it could probably give me the data in 30 s instead of writing a SQL command." (P1)	Optimized data retrieval, convert text to SQL command, reduced effort	Data retrieval	4,5

Six security activities were identified: penetration testing, integration with static analysis tools, false-positive handling, secure code suggestions, unit testing, and code reviews. Security testing involves detecting vulnerabilities through techniques like static analysis, dynamic testing, penetration testing, and fuzz testing. It helps find weaknesses that attackers could exploit. Developers mainly identified these activities, with many noting penetration testing. A DevOps team member said, "*I could see those being used here as well as a helping hand in doing penetration testing*" (P12). Participants emphasized these outputs should supplement, not replace, human testing (Table 4).

Table 4. Data structure of the aggregate dimension: "security testing"

Quote	1st order concepts	2nd order themes	Coverage (%)
"I do know of tools that utilizes ChatGPT for guided penetration tests, where you have a tool that says, I want to attack this target, give me some suggestions on how to do it." (P10)	Attack scenario generation, test generation, improved penetration testing, increased effectiveness	Penetration testing	23

(*continued*)

Table 4. (*continued*)

Quote	1st order concepts	2nd order themes	Coverage (%)
"It could make you more effective and faster, if it was integrated with static analysis tools." (P4)	Optimize static analysis tools, increased effectiveness, increased accuracy	Integration with static analysis tools	18
"So, not so skilled developers could be guided through a process of investigating false positives… Let's say he finds out that the false positive is present on the machine, then it can guide them through the process of figuring out if the issue is persistent, and how to remedy it." (P10)	Improved assessment of false positives, task replacement, increased effectiveness, increased accuracy, reduced effort	False positive handling	18
"Send it some code and ask if this is ok regarding security. I very much believe that's possible." (P1)	Improved security code assessment, code optimization, reduced effort	Secure code suggestions	14
"It dawned on me that they can help us with writing unit tests for our code." (P14)	Security test automation, test generation, increased effectiveness	Unit testing	9
"It can autogenerate code reviews." (P12)	Code review automation, reduced effort, increased effectiveness	Code reviews	4,5

Regarding the education and guidance practice, two activities were identified: acquiring knowledge of security threats and understanding security activities. These involve raising awareness and training employees, developers, and stakeholders. Participants highlighted generative AI as an educational resource, aiding staff in understanding threats and procedures, improving processes, and answering security questions. One manager noted its explanatory power: "*Some cyberattacks have funny names. It would be great at explaining them*" (P21). Others use it for reflecting on processes: "*Ask it for input on our security process and improvements. It should do that*" (P4). These accounts show that generative AI acts as a tool for automation and as an accessible knowledge partner for developers and managers (Table 5).

Table 5. Data structure of the aggregate dimension: "education & guidance"

Quote	1st order concepts	2nd order themes	Coverage (%)
"It would be a good idea to ask for advice, it would never hurt to ask for recommendations for improving our security model and approaches" (12)	Continuous knowledge generation, reduced effort, keeping up to date with cyber threats	Acquire knowledge of security threats	36
"You could ask it for input on our security process and ask for improvements. It should be able to do that." (P4)	Increased security knowledge acquisition, increased domain knowledge	Obtain understanding of security activities	27

4.2 Sociotechnical Risks of Using Generative AI

Despite optimism, participants expressed significant concerns about using generative AI for security, mainly 'sociotechnical' risks detailed in Table 6. The primary technical worry was 'Insufficient data management of AI,' cited by over half of the participants, involving uncertainty about how AI providers handle data. As an IT-operations manager said: "*How is the data stored? Is it trained to spit some of the same data out to somebody else?'* "This affects software professionals' willingness to use LLMs with sensitive data. A developer added that data could become dangerous if accessible to others. Lack of transparency into data storage raises privacy concerns and limits AI use in security tasks, given the sensitive data many organizations handle, like logs, social security numbers, and scripts. Participants also worried about AI providing inaccurate or fabricated outputs, with such issues noted in all cases. Other technical risks included data poisoning, outdated knowledge, and potential 'jailbreaking' into unsafe responses, revealing tension between AI's efficiency and its fragility as a security tool.

Table 6. Data structure of the aggregate dimension: "sociotechnical risks"

Quote	1st order concepts	2nd order themes	Coverage (%)
"I would probably not use it to send code the other way around. So, there is an aspect of trust." (P2)	Hesitant towards generative AI, privacy concerns, accuracy concerns	Lack of trust	68
"Who is behind the AI is one thing, but it remains a black box how it prioritizes and how it manages your data." (P5)	Difficult to decipher how Generative AI work, privacy concerns	Lack of transparency	64

(*continued*)

Table 6. (*continued*)

Quote	1st order concepts	2nd order themes	Coverage (%)
"The only big issue I see there is, again, how is the data stored? Is it trained to spit some of the same data out to somebody else? That's the main concern when using large language models in general." (P6)	Unsatisfactory data storage and management, privacy concerns, sensitive data	Insufficient data management of AI	59
"Generative AI pose a security risk in itself because we have no control over what they send elsewhere." (P6)	Limited power over generative AI	Lack of control	45
"I think people are nervous about using it right now, because we don't have regulations for it yet." (P2)	Legal concerns, sensitive data, insufficient policies	Lack of regulations	36
"We have all seen many examples of it fabricating convincing answers that are wrong." (P4)	Inaccurate responses, requires assessment of output. Lacking reliability	Inaccurate output of AI	32
"I am afraid of people, hackers or states systematically poisoning the well, and influencing the model's scales and responses." (P12)	Potential misuse application, potential for hackers	Data poisoning	18
"I'm missing the last two years of data when I'm using ChatGPT and that's very irritating, especially if I start asking ChatGPT questions about Terraform." (P16)	Missing the newest data, limitation of use, lacking reliability	Lack of data novelty	14
"I am afraid that within 10 years it has taken over my job." (P3)	Worried about losing job, competitor for developer	Threat to job security	14
"It's still very new to me, what can they do and what can it not do?" (P3)	Limited knowledge of use, learning curve	Lack of competencies	9

(*continued*)

Table 6. *(continued)*

Quote	1st order concepts	2nd order themes	Coverage (%)
"I remember that ChatGPT would not answer, but if it was asked to answer through a poem it would help you with suspicious things. If you can cheat ChatGPT to give you information about something it potentially becomes very dangerous." (P1)	Circumventing security protocols, possible to access prohibited information	Susceptible to jailbreaking	4,5
"If such a model turns on you instead of being a protective factor, exploiting the information you give and weaponizing it. That could be bad." (P22)	Potential of generative AI having ill intentions, reluctant to use for sensitive tasks	Malicious AI	4,5

More than half of the participants expressed concerns about 'lack of trust' and 'lack of transparency' affecting all five cases. Trust in the organization is essential for using service providers, especially as software engineers hesitate to rely on generative AI for security tasks due to mistrust. This distrust centers on privacy and the accuracy of AI, and hampers adoption. Participants also noted that models operate as a "*black box*" (P5), and additional concerns included a lack of regulations, job security fears, and skill gaps. These issues show that AI adoption involves organizational culture, governance, and perceptions, not just technology.

In summary, we highlighted the perceived benefits of using generative AI to improve security practices in software organizations. We focus on its potential to boost efficiency in areas like "Threat Assessment," "Operational Management," "Security Testing," and "Education & Guidance" through automation and increased productivity. However, our study also revealed concerns among software practitioners about "Sociotechnical Risks" linked to generative AI. Key technical risks include poor data management, inaccurate results, data poisoning, and limited data novelty. Additionally, social risks such as lack of trust, transparency, control, and regulation were identified. For practitioners, this mix of potential security improvements and risks underscores the need to carefully balance AI-driven efficiency with effective risk management and governance.

4.3 Theoretical Model and Hypotheses Formulation

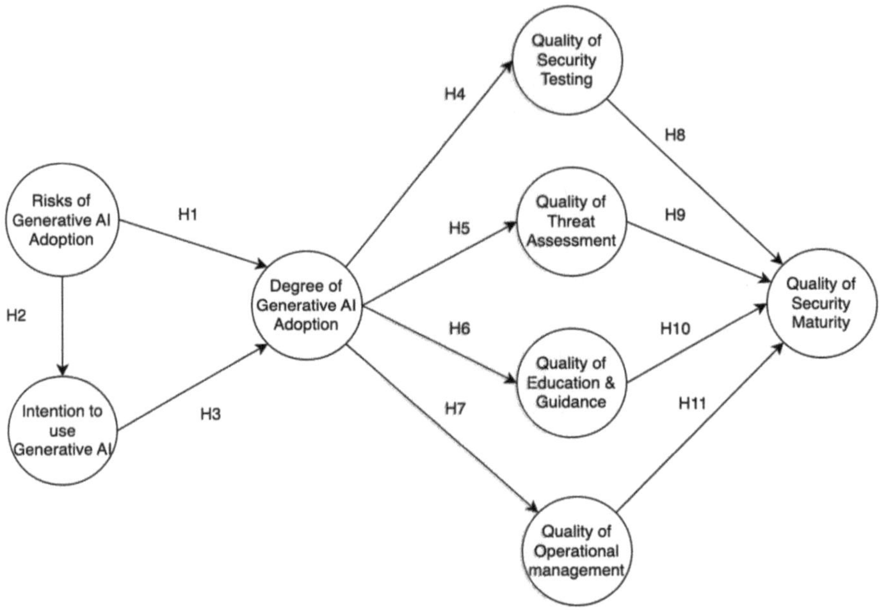

Fig. 2. Theoretical model of generative AI adoption for security practices

The findings laid the foundation for our conceptual model, depicted in Fig. 1. The data structures from the findings section constitute our constructs. Four constructs serve as indicators of perceived improvements in security practices using generative AI. These constructs include Threat and Risk Assessment, Operational Management, Security Testing, and Education & Guidance. We added "Quality" in front of the four constructs to facilitate validation with quantitative methods. The final data structure, Sociotechnical Risks, was combined into the construct "Risks of using Generative". The construct "Intention to use generative AI" was drawn from prior work [7, 29, 32]. Hence, we focus on both the positive and negative impact of generative AI on security practices, formulated as hypotheses among the six constructs (Fig. 2).

Drawing upon our qualitative results and general knowledge of software security and generative AI, we propose the following hypotheses:

Hypothesis H1: Risks of generative AI adoption negatively impact the degree of generative AI adoption in software organizations.

Technical risks of adopting generative AI in software organizations include insufficient data management, inaccurate output, malicious use of AI, lack of data novelty, susceptibility to jailbreaking, and malicious use of generative AI. These risks hinder the adoption of generative AI for security activities.

Social-related risks associated with adopting generative AI for security activities include uncertainties such as a lack of trust, transparency, control, and regulations, as well as threats to job security and competencies. Through qualitative theory generation, we observed that these risks can hinder software engineers from viewing generative AI as an appropriate tool for enhancing security practices. As a result, we formulate the following hypothesis:

Hypothesis. H2: Risks of Generative AI adoption negatively impact software organizations' intention to use generative AI.

Hypothesis H3: Intention to use positively impacts the degree of generative AI adoption in software organizations.

Hypothesis. H4: The degree of generative AI adoption has a positive impact on security testing.

The hypotheses have been formulated based on our analysis, which identified five different security activities for the security practice of security testing: logging, penetration testing, integration with static analysis tools, false positive assessment, and unit testing.

Hypothesis H5: The degree of generative AI adoption positively impacts the quality of threat assessment.

For the threat assessment security practice, we identified five distinct security activities: vulnerability scanning, vulnerability repair, vulnerability assessment, phishing attack simulation, and script analysis.

Hypothesis H6: The degree of generative AI adoption positively impacts the quality of education and guidance.

In relation to the education and guidance security practice, we identified two security activities: acquiring knowledge of security threats and obtaining knowledge of security activities.

Hypothesis H7: The degree of generative AI adoption positively impacts the quality of operational management.

Operational management identified five security activities that could be improved by adopting generative AI: data leakage prevention, access and permission control, data flagging, data flow documentation, and data retrieval. Building on these findings, we propose the following:

Hypothesis. H8: Utilizing generative AI for security testing has a positive impact on the quality of security maturity.

Hypothesis H9: Employing generative AI for threat assessment has a positive impact on the quality of security maturity.

Hypothesis H10: Adapting generative AI for education and guidance positively impacts the quality of security maturity.

Hypothesis H11: Adopting generative AI for operational management has a positive impact on the quality of security maturity.

5 Discussion

5.1 Contributions to Research

This study contributes to software engineering research at the intersection of generative AI and software security by addressing two critical and previously underexplored dimensions: the risks associated with generative AI tools and their potential for optimizing security practices. While previous work has examined generative AI in terms of productivity gains or code generation quality [2, 20, 29], our research extends this conversation to include its role in enhancing security practices and the obstacles to using these tools from a purely qualitative approach.

We build on existing research on generative AI risks [10, 23, 30] by identifying sociotechnical risks, such as a lack of trust, inadequate data management, inaccurate output, and a threat to developers. Using a qualitative multi-case study, we explore practitioners' perceptions, providing an empirical view of security risks. We also demonstrate how generative AI tools support threat assessment, operational management, security testing, and education, guided by the OWASP SAMM framework and Gioia methodology, showing where AI complements security processes. Additionally, we propose a theoretical model linking AI adoption risks and benefits, highlighting the roles of organizational enablers, perceived benefits, and risks. Based on detailed qualitative data analysis, the model offers hypotheses for future research.

5.2 Implications for Research

Our study offers practice implications, highlighting that while Generative AI shows promise in tasks like secure coding and threat modeling, organizations must use these tools carefully with a clear understanding of risks. Practitioners shouldn't assume AI output is secure; validation is necessary to ensure quality and security compliance. Organizations should assess their security maturity and governance before adopting AI tools. Based on the OWASP SAMM framework, successful integration depends on technical readiness and organizational alignment. Policies, training, and guidelines are key to managing risks like inaccurate output, accountability issues, and data exposure. By considering enablers, benefits, uncertainties, and risks, software teams can better focus efforts and engage stakeholders, supporting informed decisions and reducing resistance. Security leaders should monitor evolving regulations and ethics, since rapid AI development and weak governance require an adaptive risk approach for secure, responsible use.

5.3 Limitations and Future Research

Our study has limitations. A multi-case design offers cross-context insights but limits depth within each case. Focusing longer on fewer organizations could have yielded a richer understanding and observed changes over time. The study relies solely on qualitative data from semi-structured interviews, which captures perceptions but lacks generalizability and statistical rigor. Future research should use surveys or experiments to validate the model across broader samples. Although we included diverse industries and sizes, all companies are from Denmark, potentially biasing applicability to other regions. Lastly, participant perceptions reflect early generative AI adoption, and evolving tools and practices may reveal new risks and opportunities beyond this study. The key future research is empirically validating the theoretical model. While based on rich qualitative data, it needs quantitative testing with larger samples for generalizability and statistical robustness.

Future work involves structural equation modeling to test hypotheses and increase sample size. This validation could clarify causal links between enablers, risks, and adoption outcomes, advancing understanding of generative AI in security. Further research should examine model applicability across various organizational sizes, industries, and experience levels to better understand adoption dynamics and risks.

References

1. Aghaei, E., Niu, X., Shadid, W., Al-Shaer, E.: SecureBERT: a domain-specific language model for cybersecurity. In: Li, F., Liang, K., Lin, Z., Katsikas, S.K. (eds.) Security and Privacy in Communication Networks, pp. 39–56. Springer Nature Switzerland, Cham (2023)
2. Bird, C., et al.: Taking flight with copilot: early insights and opportunities of AI-powered pair-programming tools. Queue **20**, 35–57 (2022)
3. Carlini, N., Tramer, F., Wallace, E., Jagielski, M., Herbert-Voss, A., Lee, K., Roberts, A., Brown, T., Song, D., Erlingsson, U., Oprea, A., Raffel, C.: Extracting Training Data from Large Language Models
4. Cash, P.J.: Developing theory-driven design research. Des. Stud. **56**, 84–119 (2018)
5. Cheng, R., Wang, R., Zimmermann, T., Ford, D.: It Would Work for Me Too: How Online Communities Shape Software Developers' Trust in AI-Powered Code Generation Tools (2023)
6. Das, S.S., Dutta, A., Purohit, S., Serra, E., Halappanavar, M., Pothen, A.: Towards automatic mapping of vulnerabilities to attack patterns using large language models. In: 2022 IEEE International Symposium on Technologies for Homeland Security (HST), pp. 1–7 (2022)
7. Davis, F.D.: Perceived usefulness, perceived ease of use, and user acceptance of information technology. MIS Q. **13**, 319–340 (1989)
8. Ding, A., Li, G., Yi, X., Lin, X., Li, J., Zhang, C.: Generative artificial intelligence for software security analysis: fundamentals, applications, and challenges. IEEE Softw. 1–8 (2024)
9. Drozdal, J., Weisz, J., Wang, D., Dass, G., Yao, B., Zhao, C., Muller, M., Ju, L., Su, H.: Trust in AutoML: exploring information needs for establishing trust in automated machine learning systems. In: Proceedings of the 25th International Conference on Intelligent User Interfaces, pp. 297–307. ACM, Cagliari Italy (2020)
10. Ebert, C., Arockiasamy, J.P., Hettich, L., Weyrich, M.: Hints for generative AI software development. IEEE Softw. **41**, 24–33 (2024)
11. Ebert, C., Beck, M.: Artificial intelligence for cybersecurity. IEEE Softw. **40**, 27–34 (2023)
12. Ebert, C., Louridas, P.: Generative AI for software practitioners. IEEE Softw. **40**, 30–38 (2023)
13. Eisenhardt, K.M., Ott, T.E.: Rigor in theory building from multiple cases. In: The Routledge Companion to Qualitative Research in Organization Studies. Routledge (2017)
14. Flyvbjerg, B.: Five misunderstandings about case-study research. Qual. Inq. **12**, 219–245 (2006)
15. Gioia, D.A., Corley, K.G., Hamilton, A.L.: Seeking qualitative rigor in inductive research: notes on the Gioia methodology. Organ. Res. Methods **16**, 15–31 (2013)
16. Gupta, M., Akiri, C., Aryal, K., Parker, E., Praharaj, L.: From ChatGPT to ThreatGPT: impact of generative AI in cybersecurity and privacy. IEEE Access **11**, 80218–80245 (2023)

17. Happe, A., Cito, J.: Getting pwn'd by AI: penetration testing with large language models. In: Proceedings of the 31st ACM Joint European Software Engineering Conference and Symposium on the Foundations of Software Engineering, pp. 2082–2086. ACM, San Francisco CA USA (2023)
18. Huschens, M., Briesch, M., Sobania, D., Rothlauf, F.: Do You Trust ChatGPT? Perceived Credibility of Human and AI-Generated Content
19. Imai, S.: Is GitHub copilot a substitute for human pair-programming? an empirical study. In: Proceedings of the ACM/IEEE 44th International Conference on Software Engineering: Companion Proceedings, Association for Computing Machinery, pp. 319–321. New York, NY, USA (2022)
20. Liu, Y., Le-Cong, T., Widyasari, R., Tantithamthavorn, C., Li, L., Le, X.-B.D., Lo, D.: Refining ChatGPT-generated code: characterizing and mitigating code quality issues. ACM Trans. Softw. Eng. Methodol. **33**, 1–26 (2024)
21. Magnani, G., Gioia, D.: Using the Gioia methodology in international business and entrepreneurship research. Int. Bus. Rev. **32**, 102097 (2023)
22. Mastropaolo, A., Pascarella, L., Bavota, G.: Using deep learning to generate complete log statements. In: Proceedings of the 44th International Conference on Software Engineering, pp. 2279–2290. ACM, Pittsburgh Pennsylvania (2022)
23. McGraw, G., Bonett, R., Figueroa, H., McMahon, K.: 23 security risks in black-box large language model foundation models. Computer **57**, 160–164 (2024)
24. Mylrea, M., Robinson, N.: AI trust framework and maturity model: improving security. Ethics Trust. AI Cybersecur. Innov. Technol. J. **1**, 1–15 (2023)
25. Napier, K., Bhowmik, T., Wang, S.: An empirical study of text-based machine learning models for vulnerability detection. Empir. Softw. Eng. **28**, 38 (2023)
26. Pearce, H., Tan, B., Ahmad, B., Karri, R., Dolan-Gavitt, B.: Examining Zero-Shot Vulnerability Repair with Large Language Models (2022)
27. Ross, S.I., Martinez, F., Houde, S., Muller, M., Weisz, J.D.: The programmer's assistant: conversational interaction with a large language model for software development. In: Proceedings of the 28th International Conference on Intelligent User Interfaces, Association for Computing Machinery, pp. 491–514. New York, NY, USA (2023)
28. Runeson, P., Host, M., Rainer, A., Regnell, B.: Case Study Research in Software Engineering: Guidelines and Examples. Wiley (2012)
29. Russo, D.: Navigating the complexity of generative AI adoption in software engineering. ACM Trans. Softw. Eng. Methodol. **33**(5), 1–50 (2024)
30. Sergeyuk, A., Golubev, Y., Bryksin, T., Ahmed, I.: Using AI-based coding assistants in practice: state of affairs, perceptions, and ways forward. Inf. Softw. Technol. **178**, 107610 (2025)
31. Sghaier, O.B., Sahraoui, H.: A multi-step learning approach to assist code review. In: 2023 IEEE International Conference on Software Analysis, Evolution and Reengineering (SANER), pp. 450–460 (2023)
32. Venkatesh, V., Thong, J.Y.L., Xu, X.: Unified theory of acceptance and use of technology: a synthesis and the road ahead. J. Assoc. Inf. Syst. **17**, 328–376 (2016)
33. Wang, S., et al.: Machine/deep learning for software engineering: a systematic literature review. IEEE Trans. Softw. Eng. **49**, 1188–1231 (2023)
34. Yin, R.K.: Case Study Research and Applications: Design and Methods, 6th edn. SAGE, Los Angeles (2018)
35. Zhang, N., Li, L., Chen, X., Deng, S., Bi, Z., Tan, C., Huang, F., Chen, H.: Differentiable Prompt Makes Pre-trained Language Models Better Few-shot Learners (2022)

Sustainable and Responsible Software and Reporting

Recommended Features for Digital Reporting Systems to Support Emissions Disclosures for Small and Medium-Sized Enterprises

Tijn van Gerven, Konstantinos Tsilionis(✉), and Baris Ozkan

Eindhoven University of Technology, Eindhoven, The Netherlands
k.tsilionis@tue.nl

Abstract. Sustainability reporting has evolved from a voluntary practice into a regulatory obligation, particularly within the European Union, where the Corporate Sustainability Reporting Directive (CSRD) mandates extensive Environmental, Social, and Governance (ESG) disclosures. Among its most demanding components is greenhouse gas (GHG) emissions disclosure, which poses significant challenges, particularly for small and medium-sized enterprises (SMEs) lacking the technical infrastructure, expertise, and resources to accurately collect, measure, and report the required data. Despite the urgency of CSRD compliance, there is limited academic research on how SMEs adopt or struggle with digitally enabled solutions to meet their emissions reporting requirements. To address this gap, this study investigates key digital and workflow-related challenges SMEs face in collecting and reporting emissions data in preparation for compliance. Adopting a multi-method approach, the study begins with a document analysis of white papers, policy reports, and CSRD standards to establish normative expectations for emissions reporting. Concurrently, a qualitative case study involving semi-structured interviews with professionals from SMEs takes place to identify recurring obstacles and practices. Finally, through a gap analysis between regulatory expectations and actual SME practices, the study identifies key barriers to CSRD compliance and offers recommendations for digital reporting system features that facilitate verifiable, consistent, and machine-readable emissions reporting. In doing so, the study contributes to an emergent ESG literature by offering insights into SME emissions reporting practices. It is also intended to inform software vendors aiming to support SMEs in navigating the technology-driven CSRD compliance landscape.

Keywords: CSRD Compliance · Emissions Reporting · Digital Reporting Systems · SMEs

1 Introduction

Sustainability reporting refers to the process through which organizations measure, disclose, and take accountability for their performance related to sus-

G. Herzwurm et al. (Eds.): ICSOB 2025, LNBIP 574, pp. 161–177, 2026.
https://doi.org/10.1007/978-3-032-14518-5_13

tainable development goals, addressing the needs of both internal and external stakeholders for transparency [25]. Initially embraced by a small number of forward-thinking organizations, sustainability reporting was primarily driven by reputational concerns and stakeholder engagement rather than regulatory mandates [4]. However, in today's business environment, shaped by complex social and environmental challenges such as recurring public health crises and climate change-induced natural disasters [32,33], companies are under growing pressure to report not only their financial performance but also the broader environmental, social, and governance (ESG) impacts of their activities [24].

A key regulatory development reinforcing this increasing pressure on companies to adopt sustainability reporting practices is the European Union's Corporate Sustainability Reporting Directive (CSRD) [16]. Designed to guide and compel firms toward more transparent and standardized ESG disclosures, the CSRD mandates detailed, auditable sustainability reporting aligned with broader EU climate and social goals [16]. While initially targeting large organizations, those with more than 250 employees and an annual turnover exceeding €50 million [15], its scope is set to progressively expand, ultimately encompassing small and medium-sized enterprises (SMEs).

Even though the legal language and regulatory intricacies of the CSRD are intended to be clarified through the European Sustainability Reporting Standards (ESRS)[1], its practical implementation remains fraught with challenges. Organizations must navigate several obstacles, including the need to collect granular, disaggregated ESG data across their entire value chain [11], the limited availability and reliability of internal ESG data [18], difficulties in reconciling CSRD requirements with existing financial reporting frameworks, and the methodological complexity involved in conducting double materiality[2] assessments [8]. Among the ESG dimensions mandated by the CSRD, emissions reporting, widely regarded as the most representative indicator of an organization's environmental impact, has proven particularly challenging. Scope 3 emissions, in particular, refer to indirect greenhouse gas (GHG) emissions that occur throughout a company's value chain and often represent the largest portion of its total carbon footprint [30]. Accurately accounting for these emissions, is especially difficult, as it relies on data from upstream suppliers who often lack standardized reporting practices and transparency [8]. These difficulties are compounded by fragmented data governance structures and poor interoperability across data collection and reporting systems, which hinder traceability and undermine data quality across supply chains.

[1] The ESRS consist of 12 standards covering all ESG dimensions required by the CSRD [4,9]. The number and complexity of these standards, requiring the establishment of extensive data collection and management processes, make CSRD compliance particularly challenging for resource-constrained SMEs [8,11,18,29].

[2] Double materiality refers to the obligation to assess both a company's impact on the environment and society (inside-out perspective) and the impact of environmental and social changes on its financial performance (outside-in perspective) [6,9].

That said, large corporations are often better positioned to manage emissions data reporting challenges, drawing on institutional knowledge and support from dedicated ESG teams [7]. Contrastingly, SMEs frequently lack the resources, expertise, and technological infrastructure necessary to comply with the data-intensive demands specific to emissions reporting under the CSRD [19]. These limitations are further compounded by the absence of automated reporting systems for tracking and reporting emissions data and a continued reliance on manual data collection from diverse, decentralized sources across the value chain [19]. Additionally, the financial burden associated with compliance, including the acquisition cost of ESG-management software, external audits, and consultancy services, can be prohibitively high for SMEs, creating a substantial barrier to meeting the emissions reporting requirements mandated by the CSRD [29].

In this regard, the present study aims to gain a deeper understanding of how SMEs navigate the complex data collection and reporting challenges of CSRD implementation, particularly with respect to GHG emissions reporting. It also seeks to derive practical insights for eliciting digital reporting system features that enable consistent, reliable, and scalable sustainability disclosures. Accordingly, this study is guided by the following research questions: *"What are the key barriers SMEs encounter in aligning their emissions reporting practices with CSRD regulatory expectations?"* and *"What recommendations for digital reporting system features can be derived from these regulatory expectations and practical challenges?"*.

In the context of this study, the term *'digital reporting systems'* or, more succinctly, *'systems'*, aligns with the definition provided by Pizzi et al. [26]. This refers to configurable technological infrastructures, including software platforms, application programming interfaces (APIs), emissions calculators, and data validation tools, designed to support data integration, enhance data quality, and automate sustainability reporting in alignment with CSRD requirements. However, the aim of this study is not to prescribe exact technical specifications or architectures for such systems. Instead, it focuses on identifying features that should inform their design, drawing from both regulatory mandates and the practical challenges SMEs encounter in real-world implementation, particularly in the context of emissions reporting. Developing such systems in-house requires substantial technical expertise and resources, often beyond the reach of many SMEs [29]. Therefore, this study aims to derive a set of *feature recommendations* to guide software vendors and solution providers in designing or adapting off-the-shelf solutions that can be customized to meet SME needs. Drawing on best practices[3], the recommendations outline essential system features and their rationale, providing practical guidance for translating compliance requirements into system capabilities.

To address the research questions, this study adopts a multi-method approach [35]. First, a document analysis is conducted to extract normative requirements for emissions reporting, as prescribed in policy documents detailing CSRD

[3] The format of these recommendations follows the guidance of ISO/IEC/IEEE 29148:2018.

implementation. This serves as a desk-based method for establishing a reference baseline for regulatory expectations. Next, a qualitative case study [37] is carried out involving semi-structured interviews with professionals from a diverse set of SMEs currently preparing for CSRD compliance. The interviews explore tools, processes, and organizational constraints shaping emissions data collection and reporting. Finally, insights from both steps are integrated into a comparative gap analysis that contrasts current organizational practices with CSRD regulatory demands. This analysis informs the development of targeted feature recommendations to help bridge the gap between compliance expectations and practical implementation realities. In doing so, this study aims to contribute to the growing body of empirical research on sustainability-oriented system design by offering actionable insights tailored to key stakeholder groups such as: system designers and vendors of digital reporting solutions, policymakers involved in refining CSRD-related implementation with consideration of technological factors, and SMEs seeking to enhance their operational preparedness for emissions-related compliance.

Section 2 outlines the research methodology. Section 3 presents the key findings on the normative expectations SMEs are required to fulfill under the CSRD, outlines the challenges they face in emissions reporting, and introduces the corresponding feature recommendations. Sections 4 and 5 discuss limitations and conclude the paper.

2 Research Methodology

2.1 Research Approach

To investigate how SMEs manage the data-intensive emissions reporting obligations under the CSRD, and to identify system design implications that can support compliance, we conducted an exploratory study [2]. Given the limited normative and empirical understanding in this area, the study adopted a multi-method approach [35] to bridge regulatory expectations with the practical realities of emissions reporting in SME contexts. This approach was chosen for its ability to generate rich insights into complex, context-sensitive topics and to integrate diverse methods of knowledge acquisition and data extraction [22]. Since we were interested in integrating theoretical insights with empirical data in real-time, an abductive research approach (i.e., a combination of deduction and induction [28]) was adopted. To be specific, our study began with a document analysis of white papers, policy reports, and institutional implementation guidelines, all related to the CSRD, to deductively extract high-level, emissions reporting normative expectations. This analysis served to establish a baseline for understanding essential system-related demands for achieving CSRD compliance. Concurrently, we conducted a qualitative case study focused on multiple SMEs preparing for CSRD implementation. Drawing on semi-structured interviews with professionals involved in sustainability reporting and compliance, the case study explored how these organizations navigate emissions data challenges within their specific organizational contexts. The interviews were thematically analyzed to inductively identify key challenges, practices, and perceptions related to emissions data collection and reporting. Finally, by comparing regulatory expectations with the challenges faced by SMEs, a nuanced understanding of the implementation gap was established to inform practical recommendations for key features of digital systems that support CSRD-compliant emissions reporting. Below, we outline the research strategies employed.

2.2 Document Analysis

Given the limited peer-reviewed research on the practical implementation of the CSRD, this study primarily relies on analyzing documents such as white papers, policy briefs, consultancy reports, and official publications from European Union (EU) institutions. This analysis served two purposes: *First*, to develop an understanding of the broader CSRD framework, with particular emphasis on the ESRS[4], the standards specifying the reporting demands for companies to comply with the CSRD. Our focus was particularly on ESRS 1 and ESRS 2, which cover general ESG disclosure requirements and business conduct, as these form the core structure of the directive. In addition, ESRS E1 was considered to capture climate-related disclosures, especially GHG emissions, given its centrality to environmental reporting and its alignment with the study's focus on SME emissions reporting challenges. *Second*, we sought to identify documents deriving emissions reporting requirements and implications for SMEs. To ensure relevance, we applied a set of criteria in the document selection process. Documents were required to originate from authoritative bodies such as EU institutions, leading consultancy firms with demonstrable expertise in sustainability and regulatory compliance, and think tanks with influence on European environmental policymaking. The initial document search was conducted across publicly accessible repositories, including official EU websites and consultancy publication portals, with priority given to documents published within the last five years to capture the most current regulatory developments. Additionally, sources were required to address CSRD obligations or implications for SMEs, with a particular focus on emissions data collection and reporting practices. Although this narrowed the number of documents included, it helped us prioritize those offering actionable insights for SMEs. At this stage, we did not aim to extract system feature specifications from the documents; rather, our goal was to identify those defining regulatory expectations and operational requirements to inform potential feature development later on. This approach allowed us to build a practical, experienced-based understanding of the CSRD-along with the fundamentals of the ESRS-and their regulatory implications on SMEs. A list of all included documents, with their origin, type, and reason for inclusion in this study, is provided in Appendix A[5].

Next, narrative synthesis [20] was employed to review, integrate, and present the findings of the retrieved documents in a cohesive manner. The process began with the extraction of key requirements, guidance, and recommendations from

[4] For an overview of all ESRS standards, see: https://shorturl.at/knxDZ.

[5] The online Appendices can be found at: https://shorturl.at/aWy23.

ESRS 1, ESRS 2, and ESRS E1, which were initially grouped into broad descriptive themes such as reporting procedures, emissions data requirements, and double materiality. These contributions were then synthesized into a coherent narrative, integrating findings across documents to provide a clear overview of the CSRD, its purpose, and its obligations for SMEs. Building on this synthesis, the descriptive themes were further refined into actionable normative expectations, capturing recurring trends and translating general guidance into specific obligations, such as robust Scope 3 emissions estimation and quantification, and integrated emissions reporting data management practices, among others. Throughout the process, the narrative was cross-checked against the original documents to ensure completeness, reflecting regulatory requirements while maintaining practical relevance for SMEs. The narrative summary, together with the refined normative expectations and their corresponding sources, is presented in Sect. 3.1.

2.3 Case Study

Case studies are particularly well-suited for exploring complex, real-world phenomena where contextual factors are deeply intertwined with organizational behaviors [37]. Accordingly, we employed a case study approach centered on the IT auditing division of an international advisory firm based in the Netherlands. This division plays an increasingly important role in assessing the integrity and reliability of sustainability-related data as organizations begin aligning with the reporting expectations set by the CSRD. Through our engagement with this division, we first gained insight into the practical challenges of CSRD implementation, as observed in their advisory work. Drawing on their sectoral expertise and established client relationships, the division then facilitated access to a diverse portfolio of SME clients at various stages of preparing for CSRD compliance. Although these SMEs are not yet formally subject to the directive, they are already facing pressure to develop robust emissions reporting capabilities. Rather than focusing on individual sub-units or specific practices within the SMEs, this study considered each SME's overall approach to emissions data management. Accordingly, the unit of analysis was each individual SME operating in the European market, treated as a cohesive whole. This approach was meant to capture the broader organizational context, including structures, technologies, and regulatory interpretations, while avoiding fragmentation into departmental or team-level activities.

Data collection was conducted through semi-structured interviews with individuals from the selected SMEs. Purposive sampling [28] was used to select participants who held responsibilities in sustainability reporting, financial reporting with responsibilities relevant to sustainability disclosures, regulatory compliance, data management or at the intersection of these areas, with each participant having expertise in emissions data practices within SMEs. The sampling frame was initially defined through collaboration with the advisory firm, which facilitated identification of SME clients actively engaged in preparations for CSRD-aligned sustainability reporting. This partnership enabled targeted outreach to organizations fitting the research criteria across diverse sectors such as retail, consulting, logistics, and healthcare, ensuring a representative mix of contexts for exploring sector-specific and cross-industry challenges. From this sampling frame, key informants within each SME were identified with the firm's assistance, focusing on individuals meeting the aforementioned criteria. To enhance internal validity and reduce bias, we aimed to conduct at least two interviews per organization where possible, allowing within-case comparability and the emergence of deeper insights into emissions data collection, measurement, and reporting practices.

A total of 9 interviews were conducted across 6 distinct SMEs (see Table 1). Interviews lasted up to 1 h, and guided by a semi-structured format to facilitate in-depth discussions. This approach enabled participants to share their experiences, providing context-rich insights into operational and strategic challenges related to emissions reporting and the use of current systems. The interview questionnaire (see Appendix B) addressed key themes including data availability, technological preparedness, integration of reporting processes, verification mechanisms, and perceived barriers to achieving CSRD alignment. Section 3.2 presents the interview analysis results.

3 Findings

3.1 Normative Emissions Reporting Expectations Under the CSRD

This section presents the findings of the document analysis as an integrative narrative summary. It synthesizes SME regulatory requirements from ESRS 1 and 2 on business conduct and general disclosure stipulations, alongside emissions reporting requirements from ESRS E1. Based on this synthesis, the passage below outlines key, non-exhaustive normative expectations, highlighted in *italics*, specifying the obligations SMEs must meet under the CSRD for emissions reporting.

To begin with, the CSRD aims to improve ESG reporting by improving transparency, consistency, and accountability across EU member states and sectors. Responding to longstanding inconsistencies, the CSRD aims to ensure that ESG disclosures, particularly emissions reporting under the ESRS E1, are *structured, accurate, reliable, complete, verifiable, and auditable* [13]. One of the directive's core objectives is to enhance comparability and ensure that *sustainability information can provide the level of quality and mandatory assurance* to support its evaluation with the *same level of scrutiny as financial statements* [17,27].

A central principle embedded in the CSRD is the concept of double materiality, compelling companies to report both on how their activities impact people and the planet (impact materiality), and on how environmental and social developments affect their financial performance (financial materiality) [6,9]. Impact materiality encompasses disclosures related to issues such as GHG emissions under the ESRS E1 and contributions to biodiversity loss. Conversely, the financial materiality focuses on how environmental risks might disrupt business operations or revenues. For effective implementation of double materiality, SMEs

Table 1. Interview Participants and Their Affiliated SMEs.

Participant	Role	Responsibilities	SME	Sector
P1	ESG reporting manager	Responsible for ESG reporting	A	Retail
P2	Sustainability advisor	Leads sustainability initiatives	B	Healthcare
P3	Head of CSRD	Leads implementation of CSRD	C	Construction
P4	Sustainability manager	Oversees sustainability initiatives on climate change and waste	C	Construction
P5	Financial & sustainability manager	Leads financial/sustainability reporting and ESG strategic advisory	D	Logistics
P6	Reporting analyst	Preparing internal and external financial reports	D	Logistics
P7	Sustainability advisor	Strategic lead for sustainability	E	Healthcare
P8	Corporate group controller	Financial control, including oversight of CSRD-related processes	E	Healthcare
P9	Facility advisor	Collecting and analyzing building-related emissions data	F	Consulting

would have to *gain access to value chain data and develop methodologies to evaluate sustainability risks in a manner compatible with short-term financial reporting cycles (i.e., monthly or quarterly)* [9,21].

A critical requirement of the CSRD, as specified in ESRS E1, is the mandatory reporting of GHG emissions, classified into Scope 1, Scope 2, and Scope 3 emissions [12]. Scope 1 refers to direct emissions from company-controlled sources. Scope 2 includes indirect emissions from purchased electricity. Scope 3 encompasses all other indirect emissions across the value chain. Accurate emissions reporting relies on the use of standardized methodologies and verifiable data sources. For Scope 1 and 2 emissions, data is usually derived from direct measurements, such as fuel consumption and electricity usage records. However, Scope 3 emissions, representing the largest share of a company's carbon footprint, require complex estimation methods such as supplier surveys and lifecycle assessments [31]. SMEs face added difficulties in this area due to siloed data systems, lack of expertise, and limited access to emissions benchmarks [5]. As a result, *ensuring data accuracy and robust estimation methodologies in Scope 3 emissions disclosures* emerges as a critical requirement in regulatory compliance, particularly when SMEs depend on estimates rather than direct measurements [36]. In addition, the *quantification of Scope 3 emissions using verifiable data* can be particularly difficult for organizations that rely on external partners for such estimates [30].

One of the key difficulties SMEs face in implementing the CSRD is ESG data collection and management. Without centralized systems or dedicated sustainability teams, SMEs often collect ESG data through decentralized manual processes involving multiple departments, external consultants, and third-party actors across the broader supply chain. This approach increases the risk of errors and inconsistencies [5] and goes against an important mandate of the CSRD which is the *presentation of sustainability information in a retrievable, comparable, and machine-readable format* [14]. To address these challenges, SMEs are often compelled to invest heavily in integrated sustainability management systems or seek partnerships with larger firms to *improve data harmonization*, exposing them to further costs [1].

Finally, achieving CSRD compliance entails a substantial time commitment, which can detract from the operational focus of SMEs, particularly those with limited resources [3]. While the ESRS are designed to reflect the principle of proportionality for smaller companies, they remain legally binding for in-scope SMEs, including listed entities. These standards aim to balance regulatory expectations with practical capacities of smaller firms, yet still require the establishment of *structured and verifiable reporting processes and the allocation of dedicated resources* to achieve those [10].

3.2 Practical Challenges and Practices of SMEs in Emissions Reporting

This section presents the results of the analysis of interview data from the case study. The interviews were audio-recorded and transcribed verbatim for analysis. We employed thematic content analysis [34], a method well-suited for identifying, organizing, and interpreting patterns of meaning across qualitative datasets. Adopting a bottom-up, inductive approach, we began with an initial round of open coding, conducted manually without a predefined codebook. During this phase, segments of text conveying meaningful insights were highlighted and assigned descriptive, in vivo codes, allowing salient concepts to emerge directly from the data. Following this exploratory analysis, recurring and conceptually significant codes were identified, refined, and consolidated into a preliminary structured codebook (see Appendix C). This codebook functioned as an analytical scaffold to support consistency in the subsequent stages of analysis. Next, a second, more systematic round of coding was performed: all transcripts were revisited and recoded using the structured codebook. During this phase, code refinements were made to reduce redundancy, clarify code definitions, and ensure consistent application across the dataset. To maintain analytical parsimony, only codes mentioned by at least three interviewees ($n>33\%$) were retained for the final analysis. These retained codes were then grouped into higher-order themes, each representing a distinct category of challenges SMEs face in the collection and reporting of emissions-related data. These themes were not imposed a priori but rather inductively derived from the coded data through constant comparison and interpretive synthesis.

The full set of themes, codes, and supporting quotations is presented in Appendix D. Due to space constraints and in the interest of conciseness, a summary of the thematic findings is presented in Table 2, which is structured in accordance with the guidelines of Miles et al. [23] for the systematic presentation of qualitative data derived from interviews. Specifically, the first column identifies the emergent theme; the second lists the associated codes; the third provides representative, abbreviated quotation excerpts from interview transcripts offering a condensed yet interpretable view of the challenges SMEs encounter in emissions data reporting; the fourth column reports the participant identifiers for each excerpt. Overall, our analysis revealed four overarching themes: *(1) Fragmented and manual data acquisition*, *(2) Low quality of emissions data*, *(3) Complexity of Scope 3 data*, and *(4) Compliance overload.* Each theme consolidates a set of underlying codes and captures recurring, practice-oriented challenges that SMEs experience as they prepare to comply with the CSRD.

The first theme, fragmented and manual data acquisition, highlights that current emissions data reporting practices among SMEs are largely ad hoc, labor-intensive, and prone to error. Across multiple cases, participants described a persistent reliance on Excel spreadsheets and non-integrated tools to manage emissions data. Inputs are typically sourced from a wide range of disconnected systems, including energy invoices, HR surveys, and operational logs, and must be manually compiled. This patchwork process often requires repetitive copy-pasting and manual consolidation, which introduces inefficiencies and increases the likelihood of errors. Moreover, the absence of automation and real-time validation mechanisms leads to common mistakes, such as decimal misplacements or omitted data entries. The infrequency of updates, often limited to annual cycles, further undermines the accuracy and responsiveness of emissions reporting.

Another key theme emerging from the analysis concerns the systemic challenges SMEs face in accounting for Scope 3 emissions, a central requirement under the CSRD. Interviewees reported limited access to emissions data from suppliers, which often compels SMEs to rely on spend-based estimation methods which approximate Scope 3 emissions by multiplying expenditures by average emissions per monetary unit. While practical, these methods were widely perceived as imprecise and insufficiently representative of actual environmental impact. Compounding this issue is the lack of robust digital tools to support Scope 3 reporting, in contrast to the more structured solutions available for Scope 1 and 2 emissions. As a result, SMEs resort to manual workarounds in spreadsheets, further increasing reporting complexity. Participants also raised growing concerns about compliance fatigue, noting that the reporting burden often falls on finance departments, sidelining operational teams and reducing overall organizational engagement in sustainability efforts.

Table 2. Summary of Key Themes, Codes, Illustrative Quotes, and Contributing Participants.

Theme	Code	Illustrative Quotes (Abbreviated)	Participant
Fragmented and manual data acquisition	Reliance on Excel	*We do a lot in Excel... Still waiting for a global system...*	1,2,4,6,9
	Manual data input	*Colleagues enter data manually... We paste everything into the tool by hand...*	1,2,3,4,8
	Data from scattered sources	*Data comes from emails, invoices, surveys... We glue things together manually...*	1,2,3,5,6,9
Low quality of emissions data	Incomplete supplier data	*Few suppliers provide CO_2 data... Most have no idea about their emissions...*	1,2,3,7,9
	Human entry errors and typos	*Typos turn millions into billions... Wrong decimals, missed rows...*	1,4,6,8
	Reporting infrequency	*Annual water usage only... No month-to-month visibility...*	2,7,3,9
Complexity of Scope 3 data	Spend-based estimates	*We estimate based on spend... No unit-level CO_2 data...*	1,2,3,4,5,7,9
	Lack of tool support for Scope 3	*No Scope 3 support in our tools... Done manually in Excel...*	1,2,3,4,7,9
Compliance overload	Delegation to finance	*Finance took over sustainability... Accountants now handle reporting...*	2,5,8,9
	Compliance vs. actual impact	*Less time for real projects... Reporting eats all the time...*	2,4,7,9
	Declining motivation	*We're just reporting, not doing sustainability... Front-runners get no reward...*	2,6,7,8

3.3 Feature Recommendations

This section presents the feature recommendations (see Table 3) developed to address discrepancies between CSRD regulatory demands and the practical challenges SMEs face during implementation. Through an iterative process, the normative expectations identified in Sect. 3.1 were juxtaposed with the analyzed SME interview data presented in Sect. 3.2 to identify instances where regulatory requirements influenced, conflicted with, or were unmet by SME practices. This mapping was conducted by comparing the language and intent of these expectations with detailed accounts of SME workflows and challenges, aiming to pinpoint specific areas where SMEs struggled to comply with these requirements. This cross-referencing informed the development of system-level features aimed at supporting SMEs in achieving CSRD compliance, with a specific focus on emissions reporting. Each feature is presented in Table 3 as a structured recommendation, detailing the system's required capability, explaining its operation through specific actions, and outlining complementary capabilities that support the primary one. Presenting these features as capabilities rather than functionalities is intentional since capabilities emphasize what the system enables SMEs to achieve, without prescribing specific technical operations that would require detailed knowledge of each organization. For example, the automated data integration capability mentioned below consolidates dispersed emissions data while allowing customization to meet each SME's specific needs. Grounded in empirical evidence, each capability is therefore adaptable, scalable, and actionable, ensuring system features are both technically meaningful and flexible enough to accommodate the diverse constraints of different SMEs.

Building on these recommendations, effective systems should directly respond to the specific reporting challenges SMEs face. For instance, to meet the CSRD's emphasis on structured and verifiable data collection, SMEs would benefit from reporting systems that enable automated data integration via APIs with relevant external platforms. This directly addresses the prevalent reliance on manual data entry methods such as the use of Excel spreadsheets and fragmented email workflows and surveys, reported by participants. By eliminating repetitive data entry and enabling real-time synchronization, such systems can significantly improve efficiency and reduce input errors. Additionally, to ensure data quality, auditability, and assurance in emissions reporting, these systems should include robust data validation layers that automatically detect and flag incomplete, inconsistent, or erroneous entries. This helps mitigate common issues such as typos, unit mismatches, and formatting inconsistencies. In addition to data integration and quality assurance, several other CSRD expectations call for tailored system capabilities. One critical area is the quantification of Scope 3 emissions, which many SMEs find particularly challenging due to limited access to supplier-specific data and an over-reliance on spend-based estimation methods. A recommended system feature is a modular Scope 3 estimation engine supporting hybrid calculation methods, accommodating activity-based data, supplier inputs, and industry averages. This should be complemented by a supplier engagement portal to facilitate third-party emissions data collection and validation. To comply with

Table 3. Feature Recommendations for CSRD-Aligned SME Reporting.

Normative Expectation	SME Challenge	Feature Recommendation
Data collection process is expected to be structured and verifiable to support accurate, complete, and auditable emissions disclosures	Reliance on manual data input and fragmented sources (e.g., Excel, emails)	The system enables seamless retrieval and consolidation of emissions-related data from diverse external platforms via standardized APIs, to reduce manual effort and improve traceability
Emissions data is expected to meet standards of quality, accuracy, auditability, and assurance to support credible reporting	Introduction of human entry errors, typos, and inconsistent formatting	The system ensures high-quality emissions data by applying real-time validation rules that detect anomalies, missing values, and formatting inconsistencies
Scope 3 emissions are expected to be quantified using consistent methodologies and supported by traceable data sources	Lack of supplier chain data and reliance on spend-based estimates	The system supports flexible Scope 3 emissions estimation using supplier-specific inputs, activity-based data, and industry benchmarks, complemented by supplier engagement tools allowing the collection, integration, and validation of emissions data
Data updates are expected to occur regularly and align with the financial reporting cycle to ensure timeliness and consistency	Collection of data occurs infrequently, mostly on an annual basis, through surveys	The system allows emissions data to be captured and analyzed at monthly, quarterly, and annual intervals, enabling timely insights and alignment with financial cycles
Data management processes are expected to be consistent, standardized, and well-documented, supported by dedicated resources	Operational strain on finance staff due to the lack of dedicated ESG teams	The system facilitates distributed data management by enabling granular role assignments (e.g., data contributors, reviewers, auditors, financial controllers), promoting secure and efficient collaboration
Data reporting is expected to achieve a level of structure and verifiability comparable to financial reporting	Increasing effort on compliance with reduced perceived impact, coupled with reporting fatigue	The system provides structured reporting templates aligned with mandated disclosure areas, and interactive dashboards that visualize emissions trends and sustainability metrics
Reports are expected to be machine-readable to enable seamless data exchange across departments and organizations	Excessive reliance on manual reporting and absence of digital outputs	The system supports machine-readable exports (e.g., XBRL, XML, CSV), enabling automated processing and interoperability with external reporting platforms

the CSRD's requirements for timely and frequent data updates, systems must allow SMEs to configure the temporal granularity of data collection, enabling transitions from annual surveys to monthly or quarterly reporting intervals. Furthermore, role-based access control and collaboration functionalities are essential to prevent operational overload, particularly in finance teams, and to promote secure, cross-functional engagement in ESG data management. By integrating these capabilities, SMEs can implement reporting systems that not only streamline compliance workflows but also reduce reporting fatigue and enhance the strategic value of sustainability reporting within their organizations.

4 Limitations

This section outlines key limitations that may have influenced our results. *First*, this study focuses solely on ESRS E1 for emissions reporting. E1 was prioritized for its central role in GHG reporting, while other dimensions of the CSRD (social, governance) and other ESRS standards (e.g., biodiversity) were excluded, as they involve different metrics. As a result, challenges specific to these areas are not captured here. Future research should address these additional areas for a more comprehensive view of SME reporting under the CSRD. *Second*, the empirical data are drawn from 9 semi-structured interviews across 6 SMEs in the Netherlands. While this sample enabled a context-sensitive exploration of emissions data practices and challenges, its size remains limited. The SMEs cover a select range of industries and are primarily located in the Netherlands, which may restrict the transferability of insights to other sectors or geographic contexts. In addition, one planned follow-up interview could not be conducted due to participant scheduling constraints. We therefore stress the importance of independent evaluations and larger multi-country studies with more diverse samples to further validate and generalize these findings. *Third*, the document analysis relied predominantly on grey literature. While such sources provide timely and relevant regulatory insights, their findings should be interpreted with some caution. Moreover, the normative expectations identified from this analysis are inherently non-exhaustive, as they reflect the insights available in the publicly accessible documents retrieved for this study and may not capture the full range of regulatory interpretations. However, we applied a structured document retrieval approach, and the identified expectations serve as a basis for comparing real-world practices with the intent of formal legal and policy requirements as set forth in official implementation materials. *Fourth*, the proposed feature recommendations are presented at a high level and do not include the conditions or constraints needed to implement them. While they draw on both theory and practice to address compliance challenges and translate them into operational pathways to improve emissions reporting, they must be further refined, specified, and empirically validated before guiding the development of concrete system specifications.

5 Conclusion

At this stage, we can return to our stated research questions. The first, concerning the key challenges SMEs face in preparing for CSRD-compliant emissions reporting, was addressed through an empirical, inductive approach. We conducted a case study using semi-structured interviews with SME representatives to capture firsthand experiences, operational challenges, and organizational practices in emissions data management. Recognizing that empirical insights alone may not fully capture the demands placed on SMEs in terms of CSRD compliance, we complemented this perspective with a top-down (deductive) analysis of regulatory expectations. The integration of these two perspectives revealed recurring barriers to digitally enabled emissions reporting practices, including reliance on manual data entry, limited supplier data access, fragmented workflows, difficulties estimating Scope 3 emissions, and reporting cadence. To address the second research question, on how digital reporting systems could support SMEs, we translated the previously identified insights into a set of feature recommendations. These recommendations are intended to guide the design and adaptation of digital systems in a way that reconciles regulatory requirements and addresses gaps in SME practices. They provide practical solutions, expressed as system capabilities, to support compliant emissions reporting. It is important to note that the proposed features are tailored to the operational realities of SMEs rather than large organizations. Each capability in the feature recommendations is designed to address concrete challenges identified in the study (fragmented data sources, manual reporting workflows, limited access to supplier emissions data, etc.,) without making presuppositions regarding the presence of enterprise-level infrastructure or dedicated ESG teams. For example, automated data integration helps SMEs move beyond spreadsheets and emails by consolidating data from multiple sources automatically, while hybrid Scope 3 modeling and estimation allows SMEs to produce reliable emissions estimates even when supplier-specific data is incomplete or unavailable. Role-based access control and configurable reporting cadence enable lightweight collaboration and granular reporting cycles, best suited to SME needs. Although grounded in empirical evidence of SMEs' practices, these features remain non-prescriptive. Future research can extend the investigation to additional ESG dimensions for a more comprehensive understanding of SME reporting under the CSRD and translate the identified features into formal system requirements.

References

1. Abdul Rahman, N.H., Hamzah, N.: Climate risk assessment for small and medium enterprises: Strategies, challenges, and adaptation. In: Corporate Governance and Sustainability: Navigating Malaysia's Business Landscape, pp. 225–234. Springer (2024)
2. Benbasat, I., Goldstein, D.K., Mead, M.: The case research strategy in studies of information systems. MIS Quart. 369–386 (1987)
3. Chanal, G.B., Arun Kumar, A., Sowmyya, T., Suryadevara, R.: Climate neutrality in small and medium enterprises (smes): the role of smart eco-innovation. In: Climate Neutrality Through Smart Eco-Innovation and Environmental Sustainability. Springer (2025)
4. Christensen, H.B., Hail, L., Leuz, C.: Mandatory csr and sustainability reporting: Economic analysis and literature review. Rev. Acc. Stud. **26**(3), 1176–1248 (2021)

5. Clemente-Almendros, J.A., Vallejo García, M., Blanco-Hernández, M.: Smes and sustainable practices: identifying key factors from Spanish evidence. SAGE Open **15**(1) (2025)
6. DFGE – Institute for Energy, Ecology and Economy: Double materiality. https://bit.ly/43mNUaD (2025)
7. Dilling, P.F., et al.: Sustainability reporting in a global context: what are the characteristics of corporations that provide high quality sustainability reports an empirical analysis. Int. Bus. Econ. Res. J. (IBER) **9**(1) (2010)
8. Dragomir, V.D., Dumitru, M., Chersan, I.C., Gorgan, C., Păunescu, M.: Double materiality disclosure as an emerging practice: the assessment process, impacts, risks, and opportunities. Account. Europe **22**(1), 103–140 (2025)
9. EFRAG: ESRS E1 Climate change. https://bit.ly/44p9Bqk, pp. 2–45 (2022)
10. EFRAG: Esrs exposure drafts: overview. https://www.efrag.org/lab3 (2023)
11. Esty, D.C., Cort, T.: Values at work: sustainable investing and ESG reporting. Springer (2020)
12. European Commission: Guidelines on reporting climate-related information. https://bit.ly/4npxkzj (2019)
13. European commission: corporate sustainability reporting directive. http://bit.ly/3TnICq6 (2022)
14. European commission: frequently asked questions: corporate sustainability reporting directive. https://bit.ly/45M8X8L (2024)
15. European commission: omnibus package: simplifying sustainability reporting. https://bit.ly/4kgug5J (2025)
16. European parliament, & council of the EU: directive (eu) 2022/2464 of the european parliament and of the council. https://bit.ly/44HP15M (2022)
17. EY: How the eu's new sustainability directive is becoming a game changer. https://bit.ly/46njes8 (2022)
18. Figueiredo, P., Ciccarino, I., Joaquim, A.F., Arnaut, C., Diogo, A.: Opportunities and challenges of sustainability reports for corporate governance and transparency in portugal. Environ. Soc. Govern. Digit. Trans. Organ. (2025)
19. Kassem, E., Trenz, O.: Automated sustainability assessment system for small and medium enterprises reporting. Sustainability **12**(14), 5687 (2020)
20. Lisy, K., Porritt, K.: Narrative synthesis: considerations and challenges. JBI Evid. Implementation **14**(4), 201 (2016)
21. Manifest Climate: double materiality in csrd: why it matters and how to conduct an assessment. https://bit.ly/48q9jTQ (2025)
22. Mik-Meyer, N.: Multimethod qualitative research. Qual. Res. **5**(1), 357–374 (2020)
23. Miles, M.B., Huberman, A.M., Saldaña, J.: Qualitative Data Analysis: A Methods Sourcebook. Sage Publications (2018)
24. Moolman, A.M., Fouché, J.P., Leendertz, V.: Sustainability reporting in pandemics: theoretical development of guidelines for improved reporting. Cogent Econ. Finan. **11**(2), 2246321 (2023)
25. Nasreen, T., Baker, R., Rezania, D.: Sustainability reporting-a systematic review of various dimensions, theoretical and methodological underpinnings. J. Finan. Rep. Account. **23**(3), 1057–1088 (2025)
26. Pizzi, S., Mastroleo, G., Venturelli, A., Caputo, F.: The digitalization of sustainability reporting processes: a conceptual framework. Bus. Strateg. Environ. **33**(2), 1040–1050 (2024)
27. PwC: the promise and reality of csrd reporting. https://bit.ly/4l6Odgx (2024)
28. Saunders, M., Lewis, P., Thornhill, A.: Research Methods for Business Students. Pearson Education (2009)

29. Setyaningsih, S., Widjojo, R., Kelle, P.: Challenges and opportunities in sustainability reporting: a focus on small and medium enterprises (smes). Cogent Bus. Manage. **11**(1), 2298215 (2024)
30. Shrimali, G.: Scope 3 emissions: measurement and management. J. Impact ESG Invest. **3**(1), 31–54 (2022)
31. Teske, S., Nagrath, K.: Global sector-specific scope 1, 2, and 3 analyses for setting net-zero targets: agriculture, forestry, and processing harvested products. SN Appl. Sci. **4**(8), 221 (2022)
32. Tsilionis, K., Wautelet, Y.: A model-driven framework to support strategic agility: value-added perspective. Inf. Softw. Technol. **141**, 106734 (2022)
33. Tsilionis, K., Wautelet, Y., Tupili, D.: Digital transformation and operational agility: love story or conceptual mismatch. In: CEUR Workshop Proceedings Co-organized with the 14th Conference on the Practice of Enterprise Modelling (PoEM 2021), vol. 3031, pp. 1–14 (2021)
34. Vaismoradi, M., Jones, J., Turunen, H., Snelgrove, S.: Theme development in qualitative content analysis and thematic analysis (2016)
35. Venkatesh, V., Brown, S.A., Bala, H.: Bridging the qualitative-quantitative divide: Guidelines for conducting mixed methods research in information systems. MIS quarterly (2013)
36. Vieira, L.C., Longo, M., Mura, M.: Impact pathways: the hidden challenges of scope 3 emissions measurement and management. Int. J. Oper. Prod. Manage. **44**(13), 326–334 (2024)
37. Yin, R.K.: Case Study Research and Applications: Design and Methods. Sage (2017)

A Thematic Analysis of Environmental Sustainability in Software-Intensive Business: Understanding Practices, Barriers, and Benefits

Laura Partanen(✉), Katariina Vakkuri, Sonja Hyrynsalmi, and Jari Porras

LUT University, Lahti, Lappeenranta, Finland
{laura.partanen,katariina.vakkuri,sonja.hyrynsalmi,jari.porras}@lut.fi

Abstract. Software-intensive businesses play a dual role in environmental sustainability by enabling efficiency and resource optimization while contributing to environmental impact through energy use, software evolution, and hardware dependence. This study examines how environmental sustainability is manifested in software-intensive organizations and what factors hinder or motivate sustainable practices. Based on 22 semi-structured interviews with 38 individual participants from two Finnish Green ICT projects (2022–2025), thematic analysis identified practices across organizational, process, product, and external aspects. Key barriers include low prioritization, unclear roles, limited client influence, and lack of expertise, while benefits relate to competitiveness, reputation, and efficiency. The study emphasizes the need for shared understanding, integrated competencies, and measurable metrics to enhance sustainability in the software industry.

Keywords: Environmental Sustainability · Software-Intensive Business · Sustainable Software Development · Green ICT · Thematic Analysis

1 Introduction

Software-intensive businesses play a dual role in environmental sustainability. Advanced software systems enable efficiency gains, resource optimization, and process dematerialization, yet the energy demands of data centers, continuous software updates, and hardware dependencies contribute significantly to growing carbon footprints. As digital transformation accelerates, understanding how software-intensive business models align with environmental goals is essential for sustainable development. Awareness of the ICT sector's environmental impact has grown globally, and in Finland, both policymakers and companies have recognized its significance. Finland was the first country to publish an ICT Climate Strategy in 2021 [1], addressing environmental impacts across hardware, software, resources, and emerging technologies. Despite this progress, environmentally sustainable practices remain limited in software-intensive organizations,

G. Herzwurm et al. (Eds.): ICSOB 2025, LNBIP 574, pp. 178–185, 2026.
https://doi.org/10.1007/978-3-032-14518-5_14

revealing a persistent gap between research and practice [2,3]. To address this gap, this study examines how sustainability is manifested in software-intensive businesses, the challenges they face, and the drivers that support environmentally sustainable practices. This research is guided by the following questions:

RQ1: How is environmental sustainability manifested in software-intensive organizations?
RQ2: What factors hinder or motivate software-intensive organizations to implement environmentally sustainable practices?

2 Background

The modern concept of sustainability, introduced in the Brundtland Report, defines sustainable development as meeting present needs without compromising the ability of future generations to meet theirs [4]. It emphasizes balancing environmental, social, and economic dimensions within the limits of natural resources [5,6]. Contemporary sustainability science expands this view by recognizing the interdependence and non-linear dynamics of Earth systems [7]. The planetary boundaries framework identifies nine critical Earth system processes, six of which have already been exceeded [8,9], underscoring the urgency of embedding sustainable practices across all sectors, including technology.

Software-intensive business (SiB) refers to organizations in which software plays a central role in value creation, delivery, and operations. Schönhofen et al. [10] describe this shift as a move from product-centric innovation to cross-industry collaboration, encompassing both software producers and software-dependent industries. The research field, grounded in software engineering, information systems, and economics, was formally consolidated at the Dagstuhl Seminar 18182 [11,12], identifying four core themes: software product management, software ecosystems, Continuous X and Agile practices, and software startups. The domain focuses on sustainable value creation and delivery within and across organizations, responding dynamically to technological, economic, and environmental change [12].

In this context, environmental sustainability in SiB has emerged as both a challenge and an opportunity. ICT sector accounts for approximately 2.1-3.9% of global greenhouse gas emissions [13]. This includes not only operational energy use but also emissions from hardware manufacturing, distribution, and disposal. The software sector therefore plays a dual role: it enables "Green by IT" solutions that enhance efficiency and eco-innovation, yet it also contributes to environmental burdens through "Green IT" concerns such as energy consumption and material waste [14,15]. Despite growing awareness of ICT's dual impact [16,17], the practical implementation of sustainable software practices remains limited. Recent studies identify barriers such as the lack of standardized metrics, insufficient training and governance, and weak alignment between sustainability and corporate strategy [18,19] and indicate that the benefits of sustainable practices are largely business- and value-oriented [20].

Prior studies examine sustainability across both software processes and software products [21–23]. They have also studied the environmental impacts of software in the corporate context [24], but have also identified the differentiation of software companies from traditional industries because it produces intangible products, complicating the assessment of environmental impacts [25]. The challenge of responsibility of software emissions and energy consumption is also discovered in earlier studies [26,27]. Effective organizational change, particularly the deep integration of sustainability, requires a foundation of shared mental models and clearly communicated goals across stakeholder groups [28].

3 Methodology

3.1 Data Collection

To address our research questions, we conducted semi-structured interviews between 2022 and 2025 within two national Green ICT projects, with total number of 22 of interviews. During the first project, 31 participants from 15 organizations were interviewed during 06/2022–02/2023, all with experience in software procurement and environmental sustainability. During the second project 8 participants from seven organizations were interviewed in 03–05/2025 for this ongoing project. One organization and participant was interviewed twice (P9), once in both projects, resulting in total 21 different organizations and 38 individual participants. Table 1 presents the interviewee IDs, industry categorization of the interviews, organization headcount, and the role of the interviewee.

Table 1. Interview organizations and participants. P9 was interviewed twice, once in year 2022, once in year 2025.

ID	Industry category	Org. headcount	Sample size	Role of the participants in the company
P1	Education	250-999	2	IT Manager, Lead IT Designer
P2	Public Procurement	250-999	2	Legal Expert
P3	Public Procurement	250-999	3	Legal Expert, Lead Product Manager, Senior Management Specialist
P4	City	over 1000	3	Project Manager, ICT Project Manager, Senior ICT Specialist
P5	Education	over 1000	4	IT Service Manager (n=2), Systems Architect, Digital Architect
P6	City	over 1000	2	Project Manager, Development Manager
P7	Software Services and Consulting	50-249	1	Executive Leadership
P8	Software Consulting	250-999	1	Sustainability Manager
P9	Software Consulting	50-249	1	Executive Leadership
P10	Consulting	over 1000	5	Executive Leadership, Senior Software Expert, Service Designer, Procurement Expert, Service Architect
P11	Software Consulting	50-249	1	Account Manager
P12	Software Consulting	10-49	1	Lead Architect
P13	Consulting	10-49	2	Design lead, Software Developer
P14	Software Consulting	10-49	2	Executive Leadership, Expert
P15	Software Services	10-49	1	Senior Developer
P16	Software Consulting	1-9	1	Executive Leadership
P17	Software Consulting	over 1000	2	Business Development Manager, Senior Consultant
P18	Software Consulting	50-249	1	Sustainability and Operations Leader
P19	Software Consulting	50-249	1	Executive Leadership
P20	Software Consulting	1-9	1	Technical Team Lead
P21	Software Consulting	10-49	1	Executive Leadership
			38	

3.2 Thematic Analysis Process

After the transcription of the interviews, we reviewed the data following Braun & Clarke's thematic analysis process [29]. In the analysis phase, we did not use seed codes, but the codes were derived from the data guided by the research questions. We reviewed the transcripts, coded them, and built initial themes (see Fig. 1, upper boxes). After further analysis and review of the initial themes, we identified six final themes: *organization*, *software process*, *software product*, *external factors*, *barriers*, and *benefits*. The first four themes address RQ1, while the last two address RQ2.

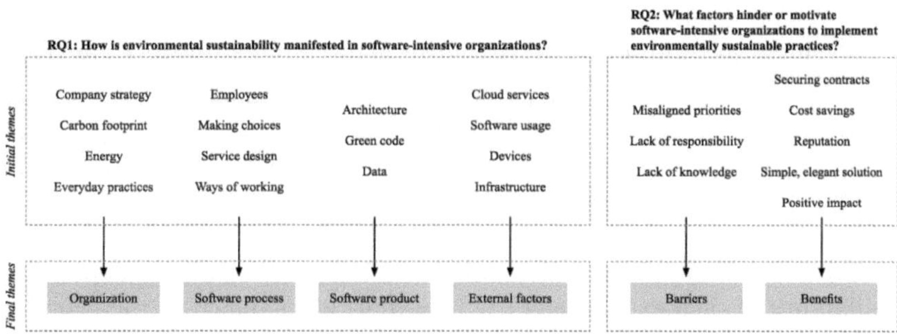

Fig. 1. Initial and final themes and the research questions.

4 Results

4.1 Environmental Sustainability in Software-Intensive Businesses

We found that the practice of environmental sustainability takes diverse forms and operates from multiple aspects within ICT organizations. Environmental sustainability is observed across four primary aspects: organization, software development process, software product, and external factors. In the organization aspect, sustainability is fundamentally a strategic concern, evidenced by organizations incorporating it into their goals (P10, P12, P15) and calculating or preparing to calculate their carbon footprint (P8, P10, P13, P12, P14). While its importance is widely acknowledged, the maturity of implementation varies. Common practices include managing business travel, event food, office energy use, and energy sourcing (P4, P8, P9, P14, P16). Efforts such as extending computer lifetimes (P18) and using digital tools to reduce travel and paper use (P4) are common, though some organizations only minimally address the topic (P7). The software process focuses on ways of working and human choices, adding a sustainability perspective to service design and early development phases (P8, P9, P10). Sustainability is linked to individual choices (P11, P16, P18), such as selecting carbon-neutral hosting (P9) or writing energy-efficient code (P7), with organizational values indirectly guiding these practices (P11). The software product aspect highlights technical attributes such as green code and architectural simplicity. Sustainability is associated with creating simple, maintainable, adaptable, and modular architectures (P9, P16). Practical measures focus on data efficiency, including minimizing transferred bytes through deferred media loading and using content delivery networks (P8), aiming for lean software with minimal waste (P9). Finally, external factors include cloud infrastructure, hardware, and the software's usage phase. The environmental impact of cloud services is a frequent discussion point (P4, P12), and hardware and infrastructure are seen as major sources of emissions, though organizations have limited influence over user device replacement cycles (P8).

4.2 Barriers and Benefits of Implementing Sustainable Practices

Our analysis revealed both clear barriers and distinct benefits in implementing environmental sustainability. Among the barriers, the most significant challenges are prioritization and unclear responsibilities (P7, P9, P11). Environmental considerations often remain secondary to cost, quality, or safety in corporate planning (P21). Implementation is further limited by a lack of knowledge, specialized skills, and a sustainability-oriented mindset (P18), with success depending on the availability of such expertise (P6). This shortage is linked to the topic's novelty (P21) and developers' limited time to acquire new competencies (P19). In contrast, the benefits of prioritizing sustainability are substantial, including commercial and reputational gains. Sustainable criteria are increasingly required for public procurement and tender eligibility (P5, P18), expanding business opportunities and client bases. Digital transformation initiatives, such as paperless operations and remote work, offer dual advantages of environmental improvements and cost savings (P4, P17, P20). Commitment to sustainability strengthens branding and reputation (P17, P11), helping attract both employees and clients (P11). Sustainability is also seen as a component of software quality, emphasizing simple and efficient solutions that minimize resource use (P9). Many organizations additionally focus on projects with measurable environmental impact, such as those achieving concrete resource savings (P11).

5 Discussion

Our first RQ examined how sustainability is manifested in software-intensive businesses. We identified four main aspects through which environmental sustainability appears: organization, software process, software product, and external factors. In practice, these aspects are deeply interconnected. For example, ways of working manifest at the software process level but are influenced by the organization and further shape the software product. Or organizational strategies and structures shape software processes that, in turn, influence the resulting products, while external conditions such as clients and market expectations affect how software is developed and used. Indirect links also exist, as organizational choices can determine product characteristics and external factors can drive process-level decisions. These interdependencies illustrate the complex and context-dependent nature of sustainability in software-intensive businesses. Despite years of discussion within software context, sustainability still lacks shared definitions, practices, and metrics. Our findings contribute by providing an empirically grounded and more holistic understanding of how environmental sustainability manifests within software-intensive businesses.

Our second RQ examined the barriers and benefits of implementing sustainable practices. The main barriers involve low prioritization and unclear roles and responsibilities. Environmental considerations often fall on individual developers or, in some cases, on customers. Consultants especially reported limited influence over sustainability when clients were unwilling to modify existing technologies. Another major barrier is the lack of knowledge and of a sustainability-oriented mindset. As the IT industry evolves rapidly, sustainability skills are rarely prioritized, and a fragmented understanding of sustainability further hinders skill development. The identified benefits of sustainable practices are mainly business- and value-driven, including cost savings, contract opportunities, enhanced reputation, and elegant solutions. These findings align with previous studies. While barriers appear across all four aspects, the benefits are primarily concentrated at the organizational and external levels. However, as some themes extend across multiple aspects, further research is needed to clarify where the benefits most strongly emerge within software processes and products.

Overall, our findings highlight the need for a stronger shared organizational commitment, integrated sustainability competencies, and measurable metrics within software-intensive businesses. The observed challenges related to prioritization and limited sustainability awareness reflect the absence of a shared mental model of environmental goals across organizations, which is essential for achieving lasting systemic change [28]. As a final analysis, we propose a three-step roadmap to address these challenges in software-intensive businesses. First, organizations should build a shared understanding of environmental sustainability and define what it means within their specific contexts. Second, this understanding should be integrated into everyday practices. Third, measurable metrics should be established and monitored. These steps should be implemented in this specific order.

6 Conclusion

We studied and identified how environmental sustainability is manifested in software-intensive organizations and how related challenges and benefits appear at different aspects. We identified four aspects (organization, software process, software product, and external stakeholders) where practices, constraints, and responsibilities differ, creating diversity in the maturity. We also identified conflicts between roles (clients vs. consultants, management vs. teams). We suggest a joint understanding of environmental sustainability within the organization at every level. This further enables shared practices together with measurable metrics.

References

1. Ojala, T., Oksanen, P.: Climate and environmental strategy for the ICT sector. Ministry of Transport and Communications, Tech. Rep. (2021)
2. Noman, H., et al.: An exploratory study of software sustainability at early stages of software development. Sustainability **14**(14), 8596 (2022)
3. Venters, C.C., Capilla, R., Nakagawa, E.Y., et al.: Sustainable software engineering: Reflections on advances in research and practice. Inf. Softw. Technol. **164** (2023)
4. Brundtland, G.: Our Common Future: Report of the World Commission on Environment and Development (1987)
5. Kuhlman, T., Farrington, J.: What is Sustainability? Sustainability **2**(11), 3436–3448 (2010)
6. Purvis, B., Mao, Y., Robinson, D.: Three pillars of sustainability: in search of conceptual origins. Sustain. Sci. **14**(3), 681–695 (2019)
7. Walker, B., Salt, D.: A crash course in the science of resilience. In: Lerch, D. (ed.) The Community Resilience Reader, pp. 163–178. Island Press/Center for Resource Economics, Washington, DC (2017)
8. Rockström, J., Steffen, W., Noone, K., et al.: A safe operating space for humanity. Nature **461**(7263), 472–475 (2009)
9. Richardson, K., Steffen, W., Lucht, W., et al.: Earth beyond six of nine planetary boundaries. Sci. Adv. **9**(37), eadh2458 (2023)
10. Schönhofen, F., Schockert, S., Herzwurm, G.: ISO 16355 in Software- Intensive Business (2018)
11. Jansen, S.: There's no business like software business: trends in software intensive business research. In: Hyrynsalmi, S., Suoranta, M., Nguyen-Duc, A., Tyrväinen, P., Abrahamsson, P. (eds.) ICSOB 2019. LNBIP, vol. 370, pp. 19–27. Springer, Cham (2019). https://doi.org/10.1007/978-3-030-33742-1_3
12. Abrahamsson, P., et al.: Software business, platforms, and ecosystems: fundamentals of software production research (Dagstuhl Seminar 18182), pp. 164–198. Tech. Rep., en, Schloss Dagstuhl – Leibniz-Zentrum für Informatik (2018)
13. Freitag, C., et al.: The climate impact of ICT: a review of estimates, trends and regulations (2021)
14. Coroama, V.C., Hilty, L.M.: Energy consumed vs. energy saved by ICT–A closer look (2009)
15. Charfeddine, L., Umlai, M.: ICT sector, digitization and environmental sustainability: a systematic review of the literature from 2000 to 2022. Renewable Sustain. Energy Rev. **184**, 113–482 (2023)
16. Berkhout, F., Hertin, J.: De-materialising and re-materialising: digital technologies and the environment. Futures **36**(8), 903–920 (2004)
17. Naumann, S., et al.: The GREENSOFT model: a reference model for green and sustainable software and its engineering. Sustain. Comput. Inform. Syst. **1**(4), 294–304 (2011)
18. Lee, S.U., et al.: A survey of energy concerns for software engineering. J. Syst. Softw. **210**, 111–944 (2024)
19. Abdullai, L., Sipilä, A., Porras, J.: Green ICT adoption and challenges: evidence from the finish ICT sector. In: Carroll, N., Nguyen-Duc, A., Wang, X., Stray, V. (eds.) Software Business, vol. 463, pp. 337–343. Springer, Cham (2022). https://doi.org/10.1007/978-3-031-20706-8_24
20. Purwandani, J.A., Michaud, G.: What are the drivers and barriers for green business practice adoption for SMEs?" Environ. Syst. Decis. **41**(4), 577–593 (2021)

21. Penzenstadler, B., Femmer, H.: A generic model for sustainability with process- and product-specific instances. In: Proceedings of the 2013 Workshop on Green in/by Software Engineering, Fukuoka Japan, pp. 3–8. ACM (2013)
22. Sarker, K.U., et al.: SQ-framework for improving sustainability and quality into software product and process. Int. J. Adv. Comput. Sci. Appl. **11**(9), 69 (2020)
23. McGuire, S., et al.: Sustainability is stratified: toward a better theory of sustainable software engineering. In: 2023 IEEE/ACM 45th International Conference on Software Engineering (ICSE), Melbourne, Australia, pp. 1996–2008. IEEE (2023)
24. Jiménez, E., et al.: Towards a software industry corporate social responsibility reference model for software sustainability. Sustain. Dev. **32**(4), 3471–3494 (2024)
25. Sipilä, A., Partanen, L., Porras, J.: Carbon footprint calculations for a software company – adapting GHG protocol scopes 1, 2 and 3 to the software industry. In: Hyrynsalmi, S., Münch, J., Smolander, K., Melegati, J., (eds.) Software Business, vol. 500, pp. 442–455. Springer, Cham (2024). https://doi.org/10.1007/978-3-031-53227-6_31
26. Partanen, L., Sipilä, A., Porras, J.: Energy consumption and CO2 emissions of a software – who is responsible?" In: ICSOB-C 2023 Software Business: PhD Retreat and Posters & Demos Track 2023 (2023)
27. Partanen, L., et al.: Mapping of the system of software-related emissions and shared responsibilities. In: 2025 IEEE/ACM 9th International Workshop on Green and Sustainable Software (GREENS), Ottawa, ON, Canada, pp. 39–46. IEEE (2025)
28. Senge, P.M.: The fifth discipline: the art and practice of the learning organization, 1st edn. Doubleday/Currency, New York (1990)
29. Braun, V., Clarke, V.: Using thematic analysis in psychology. Qual. Res. Psychol. **3**(2), 77–101 (2006)

Design Principles for IT-Driven Circular Economy Initiatives

Kay Hönemann(✉) and Manuel Wiesche

TU Dortmund University, Dortmund, Germany
{kay.hoenemann,manuel.wiesche}@tu-dortmund.de

Abstract. The concept of the circular economy (CE) has gained widespread attention in academia, practice, and policy over the past decades. However, its implementation poses significant challenges, including diverse interpretations and a lack of conceptual clarity. These challenges hinder both research and practice, making it difficult for organizations to identify IT-driven CE initiatives and for researchers to build on a consistent foundation. We propose design principles that codify actionable design knowledge for IT-driven CE initiatives. Using a mixed-methods approach, we conducted a structured literature review, a quantitative and qualitative text analysis, and a nominal group workshop to identify three design principles, offering actionable design knowledge for practitioners and a structured foundation for researchers. The proposed design principles provide guidance on identifying and implementing IT-driven CE initiatives, thereby facilitating more effective and systematic adoption.

Keywords: Circular Economy · Design Principles · CE Principles · Sustainability · Mixed-Methods

1 Introduction

Despite its widespread use [1], the circular economy (CE) concept suffers from a significant lack of conceptual clarity, stemming from a large number of scientific definitions [2]. This ambiguity is not just an academic debate; it poses great challenges for implementation [3, 4], with 50% of companies identifying the absence of a clear definition as a major obstacle to implementing IT-driven CE initiatives [5]. This uncertainty directly hinders the adoption of IT-driven CE initiatives, as 39% of organizations report difficulties in identifying suitable strategies [6]. Given that the potential of IT for advancing CE is not fully realized, it is essential to systematize existing knowledge.

Design principles address these issues by structuring prescriptive knowledge and detailing the specific goals, contexts, mechanisms, and actors involved in a phenomenon to make it actionable and applicable within sociotechnical systems [7]. This short paper aims to develop design principles to investigate the following research question: **RQ1:** *What are the design principles to identify and implement IT-driven circular economy initiatives?*

G. Herzwurm et al. (Eds.): ICSOB 2025, LNBIP 574, pp. 186–192, 2026.
https://doi.org/10.1007/978-3-032-14518-5_15

2 IT-Driven Circular Economy

The CE is a framework aimed at addressing global sustainability challenges by balancing environmental preservation with economic development [8]. At its core, CE seeks to retain the ecological and economic value of natural resources within the system for as long as possible, allowing nature sufficient time to regenerate. This is achieved by extending product lifespans, recycling materials for comparable or new applications, and encouraging reuse through retained ownership of products [9].

As an economic model, CE aims to minimize resource consumption, waste generation, and emissions by optimizing, slowing, and ultimately closing material loops [2]. Although widely considered a modern approach, CE's origins are traced back to Boulding's [10] foundational concept. Over the past six decades, discussions around waste and resource management have evolved CE into a comprehensive framework, albeit with varying interpretations.

Since its early fragmented initiatives, CE has gained widespread recognition as a holistic framework addressing actors, products, components, and material flows across all stages of product lifecycles. CE offers the potential to tackle sustainability challenges, reverse ecosystem degradation, and harmonize economic development with environmental preservation [8]. CE creates opportunities for income generation and improved working conditions, enhancing its socio-economic appeal [11].

The success of the transition to a CE relies heavily on the availability and effective use of extensive information and data, a capability significantly enhanced by technological advancements. Today, over 50 billion sensors are connected to more than 20 billion economic assets, enabling real-time monitoring and data generation [3, 12]. This unprecedented integration of material and information flows along value chains offers an opportunity to accelerate the transition to CE. Harnessing this data holds transformative potential for achieving more efficient and sustainable resource management [13].

From an IS perspective, digital technologies act as both direct and indirect facilitators in shifting from a linear economic model to a CE [4]. Advances in IS enable resource monitoring and optimization, create feedback loops between end use and recycling, and integrate material and information flows throughout the value chain [4]. These developments build trust among supply chain actors and address socio-technical challenges associated with coordinating diverse stakeholders [14].

One of the most significant challenges in implementing IT-driven CE initiatives is ensuring the effective provision and utilization of information across the entire social and material value chain. Linking material and information flows is critical to enhancing resource utilization and facilitating seamless coordination among heterogeneous actors [3, 4].

3 Methodology

Our research aimed to develop design principles for IT-driven CE initiatives. To do this, we chose to use a sequential mixed-methods approach as proposed by Venkatesh et al. [15]. In this approach, quantitative and qualitative data collection is carried out in different phases, with the results of the earlier phase theoretically or empirically underpinning the later ones to increase the overall richness of the study. Such a mixed-methods approach exploits the complementary strengths and non-overlapping weaknesses of quantitative and qualitative methods to provide a holistic perspective on the phenomenon under study and to gain deeper insights into the interrelationships [15].

Literature Search: We used the approach of vom Brocke et al. [16] to identify the relevant literature. In this phase, we first identified a real-world problem motivating the research. We began by defining the scope of the search, incorporating a combination of synonyms for IT and CE, followed by a conceptualization of the topic. At first, we conducted a search (title, abstract, keywords) with the search term ((“circular economy”) OR (“circular model”)) AND (“information system*” OR “green information system*” OR “green IT” OR “green information technolog*” OR ICT) using four databases: Scopus, ScienceDirect, EBSCOhost Business Source Premier, and AISeLibrary. This search resulted in a total of 1.777 hits. Only literature referencing IS or related concepts was considered. In addition, literature in which the CE played only a minor role was excluded. We focused on primary data only. Publications based solely on secondary analyses, such as literature-based studies, were excluded, while those including case studies on the CE were included.

At the end of this literature analysis and synthesis process, 118 publications were identified as relevant. A forward and backward search were then carried out on these publications. In this way, 75 additional relevant sources were identified. A total of 193 publications were thus identified as relevant for this study. These form the basis for the following quantitative and qualitative text analyses.

Quantitative Text Analysis: In the next phase, a quantitative text analysis was performed to extract keywords and phrases from a large corpus of documents [17]. Quantitative text analysis makes it possible to simplify the semantic complexity of the text, discover more efficient structures, and make classifications, which is important for further qualitative analysis and interpretation of the literature.

As part of the quantitative text analysis, natural language processing methods were used to identify and extract keywords and topics. These computational techniques allow for the automatic analysis and representation of the linguistic content of the text. Our approach to quantitative text analysis was based on the concepts of Grimmer & Stewart [17]. This procedure resulted in a list of 142,026 word stems with 10,551 unigrams, 93,217 bigrams, and 38,258 trigrams, which are mentioned two times or more.

Qualitative Text Analysis: The identified word stems were subjected to a detailed qualitative textual analysis carried out independently by two researchers. The sentences in which the words appeared in the publications were analyzed to capture the contextual meaning of the words for subsequent analysis. Following Grimmer and Stewart's [17] recommendations to exclude very rare word stems, we focused our analysis on the first 500 unigrams, the first 250 bigrams and the first 100 trigrams. This focus allowed for an efficient and meaningful analysis of the most common word stems. The results were then aggregated, and any discrepancies were discussed and resolved in a joint meeting.

Nominal Group Workshop: We concluded with a qualitative nominal group workshop, where ten practitioners with various professional backgrounds and company affiliations further refined the qualitative results and contextualized them in practical applications to identify the final DPs. The participants included two experts from the plastics industry, four professionals from the service sector, and four consultants specializing in digital sustainability. This iterative process ensured that the DPs were grounded in empirical evidence and aligned with real-world needs.

The nominal group workshop, a structured method for decision-making and consensus-building within a group, was based on the recommendations of Van De Ven and Delbecq [18]. In the beginning, one of the authors brought the participants up to the same level of knowledge by presenting the results from the qualitative and quantitative text analysis and the eleven identified clusters. The participants were then divided into two groups. Their task was to group the eleven clusters and assign suitable headings to the groupings that represent the final DPs. The two groups then presented their groupings to each other. In the final step of the workshop, the participants were asked to agree on an aggregated solution based on the groupings presented.

4 IT-Driven Circular Economy Design Principles

Based on the methodological approach, we identified eleven clusters for developing our DPs by extracting design-relevant information critical for identifying and implementing IT-driven CE initiatives from previous research. These clusters serve as the foundation for our meta-requirements (MRs) and our DPs, developed in collaboration with CE experts during a nominal group workshop. This approach led to the identification of seven MRs and three DPs (see Fig. 1).

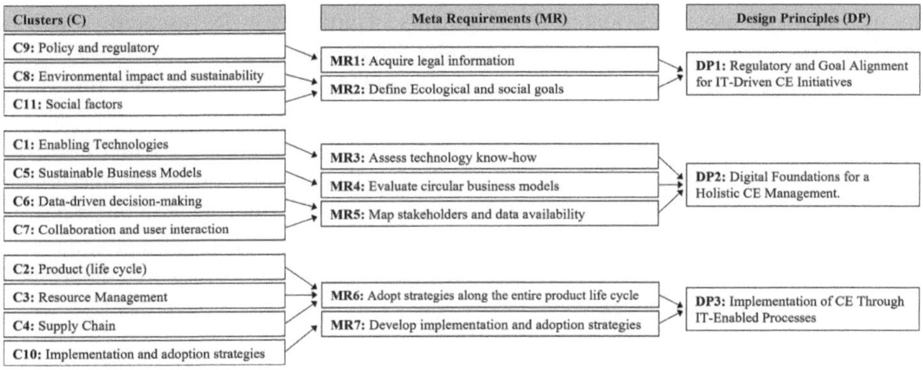

Fig. 1. Mapping from clusters to meta-requirements and design principles.

DP1: Regulatory and Goal Alignment for IT-Driven CE Initiatives. This DP addresses two topics in IT-driven CE initiatives. First, it recognizes that decision-makers often lack specialized legal knowledge, leading to compliance risks and missed policy-driven opportunities [19]. Therefore, the system must (MR1) provide access to current regulatory frameworks. Second, it counters the common tendency to prioritize economic objectives at the expense of sustainability by (MR2) prompting decision-makers to define measurable ecological and social goals, ensuring that CE initiatives are balanced, compliant, and holistically sustainable [20].

DP2: Digital Foundations for a Holistic CE Management. This DP addresses three topics in IT-driven CE initiatives. First, it counters the underutilization of existing assets by (MR3), prompting organizations to document their current IT-driven CE technologies implemented and internal expertise [3, 4]. Second, it provides (MR4) a structured framework, using criteria like the Circularity Matrix, to systematically evaluate the feasibility and value-recovery potential of CE business models, ensuring adopted initiatives are both impactful and viable [21]. Finally, it closes information and collaboration gaps by (MR5) guiding decision-makers to map their stakeholders and the data available across the value chain [21].

DP3: Implementation of CE through IT-Enabled Processes. This DP highlights two main requirements: First, it mandates (MR6) a comprehensive, closed-loop approach by guiding decision-makers to select and integrate specific strategies, such as those from the 9R framework, across the entire product life cycle to maximize resource efficiency [22]. Second, it counters the failure of generic approaches by (MR7) demanding the development of concrete implementation and adoption strategies, which are critical for overcoming specific organizational barriers and ensuring the engagement of all stakeholders.

5 Discussion

This paper contributes to the discussion on IT-driven CE initiatives in academia and practice. By providing codified design knowledge in the form of DPs for IT-driven CE initiatives, this paper forms the foundation for future design theories while promoting the mediation of practice-oriented developments of artifacts in IS research, which is necessary for a well-founded scientific discourse on the topic [23].

Through the codified domain knowledge embedded in the proposed DPs, this study helps address the uncertainties surrounding the definition of CE, which many organizations have identified as a significant barrier to their implementation [5]. Furthermore, the proposed DPs support practitioners in overcoming conceptual uncertainties that hinder the identification of suitable IT-driven CE initiatives [6]. By offering structured design knowledge, DPs clarify what actions should be taken and provide guidance on how to implement these strategies effectively, enabling organizations to identify better and realize IT-driven CE initiatives.

References

1. Lieder, M., Rashid, A.: Towards circular economy implementation: a comprehensive review in context of manufacturing industry. J. Clean. Prod. **115**, 36–51 (2016)
2. Kirchherr, J., Reike, D., Hekkert, M.: Conceptualizing the circular economy: an analysis of 114 definitions. Resour. Conserv. Recycl. **127**, 221–232 (2017)
3. Zeiss, R., Ixmeier, A., Recker, J., Kranz, J.: Mobilising information systems scholarship for a circular economy: review, synthesis, and directions for future research. Inf. Syst. J. **31**, 148–183 (2021)
4. Ixmeier, A., Kranz, J., Recker, J., Zeiss, R.: How to unlock the potential of information systems for a circular economy. In: Research Handbook on Information Systems and the Environment, pp. 74–99. Edward Elgar Publishing (2023)

5. Stumpf, L., Schöggl, J.P., Baumgartner, R.J.: Climbing up the circularity ladder?—A mixed-methods analysis of circular economy in business practice. J. Clean. Prod. **316** (2021)
6. Capgemini: Sustainable IT.: https://www.capgemini.com/wp-content/uploads/2021/07/Sustainable-IT_Report-2.pdf (2021). Last accessed 29 Oct 2024
7. Gregor, S., Jones, D.: The anatomy of a design theory. J. Assoc. Inf. Syst. **8**, 312–335 (2007)
8. van Schalkwyk, R.F., Reuter, M.A., Gutzmer, J., Stelter, M.: Challenges of digitalizing the circular economy: assessment of the state-of-the-art of metallurgical carrier metal platform for lead and its associated technology elements. J. Clean. Prod. **186**, 585–601 (2018)
9. den Hollander, M.C., Bakker, C.A., Hultink, E.J.: Product design in a circular economy: development of a typology of key concepts and terms. J. Ind. Ecol. **21**, 517–525 (2017)
10. Boulding, K.E.: The Economics of the Coming Spaceship Earth. Johns Hopkins Press (1966)
11. Robinson, S.: Social Circular Economy: Opportunities For People, Planet and Profit. https://circulareconomy.europa.eu/platform/sites/default/files/social_circular_economy_2017.pdf. (2017). Last accessed 08 Jan 2025
12. Zhang, H.: Planet of the things. Comput. Fraud. Secur. **2016**, 16–17 (2016)
13. French, A.M., Shim, J.P.: The digital revolution: internet of things, 5G and beyond. Commun. Assoc. Inf. Syst. **38**, 840–850 (2016)
14. Bauwens, T., Hekkert, M., Kirchherr, J.: Circular futures: what will they look like? Ecol. Econ. **175** (2020)
15. Venkatesh, V., Brown, S.A., Bala, H.: Bridging the qualitative-quantitative divide: guidelines for conducting mixed methods research in information systems. MIS Q. **37**, 21–54 (2013)
16. vom Brocke, J., Simons, A., Niehaves, B., Riemer, K., Plattfaut, R., Cleven, A.: Reconstructing the giant: on the importance of Rigour in documenting the literature search process. In: ECIS (2009)
17. Grimmer, J., Stewart, B.M.: Text as data: the promise and pitfalls of automatic content analysis methods for political texts. Polit. Anal. **21**, 267–297 (2013)
18. van de Ven, A.H., Delbecq, A.L.: The Effectiveness of Nominal, Delphi, and Interacting Group Decision Making Processes. Acad. Manage. J. **17** (1974)
19. Carlsson, R., Nevzorova, T., Vikingsson, K.: Long-lived sustainable products through digital innovation. Sustainability **14** (2022)
20. Hojnik, J., Ruzzier, M., Konečnik Ruzzier, M., Sučić, B., Soltwisch, B.: Challenges of demographic changes and digitalization on eco-innovation and the circular economy: Qualitative insights from companies. J. Clean. Prod. **396** (2023)
21. Atasu, A., Dumas, C., van Wassenhove, L.N.: The circular business model. Pick a strategy that fits your resources and capabilities. Harv. Bus. Rev. (2021)
22. Potting, J., Hekkert, M., Worrell, E., Hanemaaijer, A.: Circular economy: measuring innovation in the product chain. Neth. Environ. Assess. Agency (2017)
23. Dickhaut, E., Janson, A., Hevner, A.R., Leimeister, J.M.: Sharing design knowledge through codification in interdisciplinary DSR collaborations. In: HICSS (2023)

GenAI for Software Engineering and Education

Comparative Analysis of Generative AI Performance in University Programming Courses

Eero Suomalainen(✉), Erno Vanhala, and Jouni Ikonen

LUT University, Yliopistonkatu 34, 53850 Lappeenranta, Finland
{eero.suomalainen,erno.vanhala,jouni.ikonen}@lut.fi

Abstract. Generative artificial intelligence (GenAI) has had an impact on university education and also to the software industry. This can be seen in many different courses where GenAIs can complete exercises, exams, and even whole courses by themselves. This study aims to find out how effectively different GenAI tools can complete exercises in programming courses. Our objective is to find how GenAI's performance varies across courses and what differences there are in results between multiple GenAI tools. During the study, five programming courses were evaluated using five different GenAI tools. These tools were able to solve 43–90% of programming assignments and 80–100% of quizzes. In practice, the result is that any of the selected GenAIs could have been used to pass the majority of all the tested course parts. Results indicate that we have to rethink how courses' tasks are designed and that courses need to have an element where learning is verified in a controlled environment to verify that we are educating software professionals for the industry.

Keywords: Artificial Intelligence · cheating · education · programming

1 Introduction

The release of ChatGPT, chatbot built on generative pre-trained transformers (GPT) models, and the generative artificial intelligence (GenAI) boom following it has garnered significant interest, attracting a large user base to AI tools that can create texts, images and videos from user input. GenAIs can also provide answers to user queries, although their responses are not always accurate. As these tools can produce artefacts resembling human-created work, there is a chance that students could skip manual work in education by using GenAI tools.

Previous studies have demonstrated that GenAI can pass university-level programming courses, sometimes achieving the highest grades [4,9,11,15,16,22, 31,34,43,47,56]. Different types of GenAI tools and models, such as ChatGPT and GitHub Copilot, have been tested in these studies, often focusing on programming languages commonly taught in universities. In addition, research has examined how the use of GenAI affects students' learning on courses [36,42],

G. Herzwurm et al. (Eds.): ICSOB 2025, LNBIP 574, pp. 195–211, 2026.
https://doi.org/10.1007/978-3-032-14518-5_16

what role GenAI could have in course curriculum, what benefits it has for student use [9,14] and how to combat likely misuse of GenAI on courses [37].

However, previous studies on how GenAI's ability to solve coursework tend to focus only on one course per research and on a single GenAI tool. These studies often favour the most common and freely available GenAIs intended for code generation. In this study, we use multiple different GenAI tools and models to complete course exercises, aiming to explore what other GenAI's besides ChatGPT can be used for this purpose. This study also extends the findings of Suomalainen [46]. Our research addresses the following research questions: **RQ1**: What previous research has been conducted on using GenAI to complete university-level programming courses?, **RQ2**: What different GenAI tools can be used to solve exercises in programming courses? and **RQ3**: How well do the selected GenAIs perform on university programming course exercises?

Literature review addresses RQ1, while RQ2 involves inspecting and testing GenAIs. A subset of these GenAIs is then selected to complete course exercises and afterwards their results are analysed to form the artefact for RQ3. The aim is to mimic students' behaviour and see how much they could get points from the course tasks if they are just using GenAIs to try to pass the courses.

2 State of the Art of Using AI in Programming Courses

A literature review was conducted on the topic of the use of GenAI tools (often called *chatbots*) in programming courses. The literature review follows snowballing guidelines by Wohlin [51], beginning with a core set of articles gathered from academic databases and subsequently expanded through both backward and forward snowballing. Institute of Electrical and Electronics Engineers (IEEE) Xplore and Web of Science (WoS) were used as sources to gather the core set of articles. In both academic libraries following search query was used: *("University" OR "College") AND "AI" AND "Course*" AND "Programming"* and in WoS search was also limited to the topic (title, abstract and keywords). This resulted in 200 articles in IEEE and 27 articles in Web of Science. These 227 articles were filtered based on their title and abstract at first and later on by full text on how they answer at least one of the following questions: *how the use of GenAI affects students learning on courses*, *how GenAI can help in learning course topics* or *how well GenAI alone can pass programming courses*. First, a core set of 14 articles was identified. Forward snowballing added 15 articles, while backward snowballing contributed 11, culminating in a total of 40 articles. The literature review was conducted at the end of January 2024 and the beginning of February 2024. Due to time constraints, the process of gathering a core set, forward and backward snowballing was conducted only once. The literature was updated in June 2025, when the original databases were re-searched for new journal articles published in 2024 or 2025. 12 additional core articles were found.

The articles found can be divided into four distinct themes (Effects on learning, Use cases for GenAI, Performance of GenAI in courses, and Response to potential problems), with some articles fitting into multiple themes. These themes emerged by analysing the core topics of each article and grouping related insights. Three themes align with the questions used for article selection and the fourth theme was found during article analysis.

2.1 Effects of Using Generative AI on Student Learning

Numerous studies have explored the effects GenAI (such as ChatGPT and GitHub CoPilot) has on students' learning in programming courses. Findings of Sheese et al. [42] suggests that students who used CodeHelp (a GenAI with guardrails preventing it from providing straight-up solution) for help in course topics more frequently also performed better in the course, although the study states that this does not suggest or support claims that higher usage results better performance. However, when Carreira et al. [6] used a chatbot of their creation as a teaching assistant on an introductory programming course and later conducted a survey to students, the results indicate that using a chatbot as a teaching assistant can facilitate students' learning. Another study examining students' experiences with a chatbot designed to teach Structured Query Language queries found responses to be positive about its usefulness, suggesting that the chatbot is a useful tool in learning [38]. Chatbots can be used to summarize code and explain different aspects of a given code snippet, such as time complexity [29], what mistakes and errors might happen when writing it and how to avoid them [29,35], help to refactor code [17], acquire background knowledge [18] and provide simplified explanations of more complicated concepts [26]. In addition, chatbots can be used to give more personalised hints that are adjusted to the problem at hand [27] and as a brainstorming companion to support creativity [5,23]. As chatbots give the answer almost instantly to the question, their speedy assistance can help students save time and effort [26]. In addition, using chatbots during courses exposes students to emerging technologies in a structured manner [20] and, as Ji et al. [23] and Wang et al. [49] found, chatbots can ease the students' learning process by alleviating their cognitive load.

Many studies also highlight negative impacts GenAI has on learning if students solely rely on it to solve assignments [5,17,32,36,49]. Personal development may suffer [5], critical thinking might reduce [17,23,49], plagiarism may go unnoticed, and knowledge on the topics of the course can be lacking [32]. In addition, students' self-efficacy has been reported to decrease if a chatbot is used as an advanced search engine offering ready-made solutions [8]. Despite these concerns, unless instructed otherwise, students are likely to choose to use ChatGPT to do homework on courses, including both asking for help and asking to solve the exercise for them (some not even consider the latter as cheating) [3].

The overall impact of GenAI on student learning largely depends on how it is utilized. As Banić, Konecki and Konecki found out in their research [2], after students performed certain algorithmic tasks on Python with ChatGPT they felt programming to be interesting and they learned faster with ChatGPT but they also agreed more with statement "I feel that I don't need to know how to program because I can create programs using ChatGPT" than before the tasks. The study by Suh et al. [45] found that beginner-level programming students did not significantly benefit from using the chatbot and even performed worse on exams but more intermediate-level students the chatbot seemed more helpful, suggesting that using chatbots is more effective when students have some prior knowledge on the topic. Students point out the possibility for misuse when using ChatGPT in studies but also acknowledge its benefits in assisting [30]. And while chatbots can ease students' cognitive load, it is important to keep an appropriate level of cognitive challenge to promote deep learning [49]. Other concerns arise from the fact that there are inaccuracies in GenAI's responses [8,24] and it's not always clear how to apply solutions it provides to code queries [8]. In addition, students have reported the process of making an account and having to log in to use these GenAI services as a hindrance in the information-seeking process [26].

2.2 Use Cases for Generative AI in Education

One prominent use case for chatbots in university courses was to use them in a role similar to a teaching assistant (TA). Roldán-Álvarez and Mesa reported in their study [40] that the use of GenAI as a tutor has helped students to pass obstacles more quickly and learn from their mistakes more efficiently than traditional tutoring. This is because GenAI provides instant replies, coding examples and in-depth explanations to course topics. As TAs, chatbots would likely be most useful when explaining contextual applications for course's concepts and providing examples that are relevant to course topics [17,19,23,34,35,48] but they could also provide guidance and help with syntax errors students are facing [35,47], address queries about documentation and templates related to course assignments [33] or provide code reviews for student homework [9,36]. In addition, chatbots are not limited to text-only answers but can also assist students in other forms, such as images and interactive simulations [21]. As such, using chatbots in university education can facilitate the learning process and enhance critical thinking if students do not rely solely on chatbot-provided answers [17,39]. Another potential application is the use of chatbots as peers in a peer-instruction model in courses as results indicate it improved students' performance in skills and conceptual understanding when compared to traditional peer learning and students have reported higher learning, engagements and satisfaction through faster response and opportunity to learn from the GenAI [14].

To aid in learning, students could also use chatbots to create more exercises for self-practice when they wish to develop their skills further [10,21]. It has been reported that GPT-3.5's predecessor GPT-3 is able to create well-crafted exercises for beginner to intermediate programming courses that focus on flow structure, use of Application Programming Interface (API) and inheritance, while error detection was particularly bad [44]. In addition, GPT-3 could create unit tests for programming exercises [9]. In an academic context, chatbots can also be used to provide suggestions to students on appropriate literature for self-study or literature review [10]. Students could also evaluate strengths and weaknesses of the chatbot by creating the same artefacts with a chatbot that students themselves created and compare their own manually created ones to those of the chatbot [20].

Another use case is to provide personalized learning with chatbots. For example, a system was proposed by Wu et al. [54], which can generate personalized tutorials based on students' learning preferences and adjust them to their knowledge levels. Personalized learning can also adapt to students' individual needs, like providing more resources for slower learners and more advanced guidance for faster ones [49]. For learning paths, a system called SKYRAG was proposed by Setyawan Soekamto et al. [41], which addresses weaknesses of the traditional retrieval augmented generation (RAG) by providing more accurate keyword retrieval for better personalization and creating more suitable learning paths.

However, in all of these cases, it must be kept in mind that chatbots are not 100% reliable and are susceptible to occasional errors and misleading information [35]. For example, ChatGPT's accuracy on topics may vary as it depends on the information it was trained with, phrasing of the prompts and what is the context of the questions [25]. When Jalil et al. (2023) [22] questioned ChatGPT on topics of software testing courses, the GenAI was able to give a correct answer 49.4% or a partially correct answer 6.2% of the time. ChatGPT is not efficient when used as a definitive guide [25,36] or completely reliable in evaluating code quality or correctness but it can provide many suggestions on how to improve code modularity and structure [1].

2.3 Performance of Generative AI in Courses

Chatbots have been tested on a variety of tasks including object-oriented programming (OOP) in Java [9,34], Python programming [11,15,16,47], data structures and algorithms exam including true/false (TF) and multiple choice (MC) questions. They have also been used to write pseudo-code and drawing diagrams [4], written exams and essays, and programming assignments in cyber security [31], embedded systems quizzes composing of TF questions, code analysis, code completion and writing code from scratch [43] and an exam on Swift programming language and SwiftUI [56]. In all of these cases, chatbots can achieve passing grades or higher.

GenAI struggle most with complicated concepts such as self-balancing binary search trees like AVL-trees [53] and interpreting non-textual information like API documentation and Unified Modelling Language (UML) diagrams. In a study by Zhang et al. [56], most of the time GPT-3.5 and GPT-4 models got lower scores as the sections of the exam got more challenging. The structure of task descriptions can have an effect on the chatbots' performance as GPT-3 was found to struggle with simple exercises embedded in lengthy, overly descriptive, or contextually unnecessary text [47]. Additionally, task-specific restrictions, such as prohibiting certain features or requiring specific formatting, affected performance.

2.4 Response to Potential Problems

Some introductory programming instructors wanted to ban the use of GenAIs in courses, while others wanted to implement them in some way to prepare students for future work life [28]. One potential response is to design programming exercises in a way that it is not possible to solve them simply by giving inputs to the chatbot [9,34]. To do this, Chan et al. [7] created a method that uses ChatGPT to create exercises for programming courses by iteratively mutating the exercise until it cannot be solved simply using ChatGPT.

Courses could also teach students how to write correct prompts to a chatbot so that it can create accurate coding solutions [12], as a study found out many students may have problems with creating well-structured queries to the GenAI, resulting in poor responses [42]. Or teaching topics by fact-checking chatbot's solutions if it is known to perform poorly on the topic [55]. In addition, chatbots can be integrated with traditional teaching but must be done carefully, so that the chatbot remains as a supportive tool and does not become a replacement for human instructions [17,23,35].

Other responses include focusing on problem solving and mathematical reasoning over coding proficiency [13], develop students' critical thinking skills to analyse chatbots responses better [17,21,23,49], distinguish accurate, partially correct and misleading answers and encourage students to verify information from reliable sources [18], adjusting grading criteria to accommodate the use of chatbots in exercises [24] or sifting the focus of the grading more on the whole process instead of the end product.

3 Research Process

The process of evaluating GenAIs' performance followed the guidelines of an experiment. This approach involves establishing a predefined structure in which actors perform specific tasks while the researcher observes their performance [52]. Actors in this case are chosen GenAI tools and tasks course exercises. To help define the preset frame, the first course's exercises that were completed with GenAIs served as a "pilot course" to determine the appropriate steps for evaluating GenAIs' performance. Based on the literature review, a hypothesis was formed that "selected GenAIs should be able to complete exercises", meaning that they should obtain at least the minimum required score to pass the exercises.

The evaluation process also followed a simulation method, where a model is created which imitates behaviours of interest and its performance is observed [50]. The model here would be a student on these courses as the study tries to imitate how well a student could succeed by solely relying on the GenAI.

3.1 Selection of GenAI Tools and Models

Main criterion for choosing which GenAI tools was to select tools that students are potentially using. These tools were assumed to have a conversational interface, allowing users to input prompts and receive generated outputs. As most of the exercises were programming exercises, GenAIs also had to be able to write code. As ChatGPT provided both options, an initial search for potential GenAI tools was done by searching "AIs similar like ChatGPT" and "Programming AIs similar like ChatGPT". The results were used to get an understanding of what

GenAIs were available at the time. To supplement this, we surveyed students (N = 187) to see what GenAIs they use. 74% of the respondents reported using ChatGPT, 3% mentioned GitHub Copilot and 4% listed Gemini. Other GenAIs also appeared in student responses, like Claude, Microsoft Copilot and Bai Du, but they were mentioned less frequently. Some of the students reported that they did not use any GenAIs. In addition, our industry contact reported using Codeium, which was also identified during the initial search.

The identified GenAIs were evaluated based on their availability in Finland (i.e., no VPN needed), their ability to generate code and have a conversations, are they behind a paywall as free-to-use was preferred to simulate student use. The aim was to find five different GenAI tools and models to be used in the study for completing exercises. Based on this evaluation, the following tools were selected:

GPT-3.5 was developed by OpenAI and is the model that the free version of ChatGPT used until May 2024. GPT-3.5 is a language model trained to produce text and has been optimised with Reinforcement Learning with Human Feedback where human demonstration is used to guide the model to desired output[1].

GPT-4 was, before May 2024, the most advanced OpenAI's GPT model in consumer use. It is meant to be more reliable, creative and able to handle more complex tasks than GPT-3.5. It has been replaced by GPT-4o mini in free-to-use plan[2] and GPT-4o, o1 and o1-mini in paid subscriptions in November 2024.

Codeium is a GenAI programming tool designed for software developers. It features autocomplete, search and chat features, of which the last one was used in this study. Chat feature uses both Codeium's developers' own proprietary model and Open AI APIs in its operations[3]. The free version of Codeium was used in this study, which utilised GPT-3.5 model. As of December 2024, the plan with monthly cost offers GPT-4o support.

GitHub Copilot is an AI coding assistant developed by GitHub that has been trained on public natural language and code sources, including public GitHub repositories. GitHub Copilot uses Anthropic's Claude 3.5 Sonnet, Google's Gemini 1.5 Pro, and OpenAI's GPT-4o, o1-preview and o1-mini models[4], of which GPT-4o was used as it was only one with unlimited access in Finland at the time of November 2024. GitHub Copilot offers only paid subscriptions but students can use it for free through GitHub Pro.

Gemini is a GenAI model developed by Google[5]. For free, it offers Gemini 1.5 Flash model while more powerful Gemini 1.5 Pro model is included in paid Google One AI Premium subscription. 1.5 Flash model was used in this research.

ChatGPT, GitHub Copilot and Gemini were chosen as they were mentioned most in the student survey. We chose to include both at the time free (GPT-3.5) and premium (GPT-4) ChatGPT GenAIs to create a comparison between two different models from the same service provider, even though premium model

---

[1] https://help.openai.com/en/articles/6783457-what-is-chatgpt.
[2] https://openai.com/index/gpt-4o-and-more-tools-to-chatgpt-free/.
[3] https://codeium.com/faq.
[4] https://github.com/newsroom/press-releases/github-universe-2024.
[5] https://gemini.google.com/faq.

requires paid membership to use. During the data collection process free and premium ChatGPT models were updated. As such, models we used in this research can be considered legacy models at this point. Finally, we included Codeium due to recommendation and its focus on programming.

3.2 Completing Course Exercises

Table 1. List of courses, their content and types of exercises.

ID	Course	Year	Size	Content	Inspected course parts
CS1	Introduction to Programming (in Finnish)	1st year	6 ECTS	Programming basics with Python language, history and current state of programming, good programming style	- Programming exercises - T/F quizzes
OOP	Object-Oriented Pro-gramming (in Finnish)	1st year	6 ECTS	Basics of Java language, classes and inheritance, graphical UI with Android Studio	- Programming exercises - T/F quizzes
C	Principles of C-Programming (in Finnish)	1st year	3 ECTS	C programming language, pointers and dynamic memory allocation, good programming style	- Programming exercises
Web1	Introduction to Web Programming (pilot course, in English)	3rd year	3 ECTS	Web standards like HTML, CSS and JavaScript, browser environment with Document Object Model, building websites with commonly used tools	- Programming exercises - T/F quizzes
Web2	Advanced Web Applications (in English)	3rd year	6 ECTS	Use of APIs, creating interactive server and client software (Node.js and React), managing web software with MongoDB	- Programming exercises - T/F quizzes

This study focused on the selection of bachelor-level programming courses, representing the stage in the degree program where students are acquiring foundational programming skills. The objective was to evaluate how effectively GenAI tools can perform at this level of university education. Exercises from five programming courses were included as part of this study. All courses featured programming assignments and most of them also included quizzes, as seen in Table 1. Programming exercises typically consisted of five tasks per week and were either their separate tasks or part of one assignment divided into five steps. All of the quizzes were in True/False format. These quizzes can be considered quite straightforward, thus their weight in the final course grade is relatively low, around 10%. The main purpose of the quizzes is to make sure students have reviewed all the material related to the topic before they start the programming assignments. The automatic evaluation of programming exercises was done with an automated assessment system used to evaluate coding assignments. Quizzes were created and graded by tools from the learning management system and Android Studio tasks in Object-Oriented Programming were manually graded.

In all courses, exercises and larger course projects are graded automatically or manually without meeting the student or the student group, and exams are done in a monitored exam hall with restricted-access computers (no use of GenAI is possible).

Most of the courses use a 100-point system or a similar system when grading students. 50 points are required to pass the course and receive grade 1 and every 10 points increase the grade by one, resulting in the highest grade of 5 with 90 points. All exercises contribute to these points but students cannot pass courses with exercises alone as there are other mandatory parts, such as course project or exam. Usually half of maximum points available from exercises are needed to pass the course (in addition to minimum 50 points total). Exceptions here are CS1 and C courses where exercise sections have their own grades and course grade is calculated from weighted average of grades from exercises, exam and course project. Still, to pass exercises with grade 1, half of them must be solved.

The process of completing exercises with GenAIs was as follows:

1. The assignment was copied from instructions for a prompt for GenAI.
   - If the prompt needed additional instructions, (e.g. definition of programming language), they were added and irrelevant information for completion of the task was removed.
   - If instructions referred to the previous material, the code was added to the prompt as text at the end.
   - For True/False quizzes, the claim was turned to a question.
   - If the quiz task was to fill sections with given options, both sections and options were added to the prompt with the task instructions.
2. The type of exercise determines what is done with the GenAI's output
   - For programming exercises the solution was copied to the code editor, the file was zipped and submitted to the automatic assessment system.
   - For quizzes the correct solution was chosen based on the GenAI's answer.
3. If the GenAI's output was insufficient, then the task was reiterated
   - The GenAI was given a description of what was missing (the output from assesment system) and what needed to be changed.
   - With T/F quizzes, reiteration was only done if the output did not clearly say the claim was either true or false.
4. After iterations and reiterations, the results were written down.

The process of iteration and reiteration was designed to simulate how a student with no prior knowledge of the subject could complete tasks using only the GenAI. As such, when reiterating, the prompt only included the response from the automatic assessment system, a description of what was missing based on exercise instructions or a request for a more precise answer. The process did not include any other prompt engineering besides what was described in this section.

4 Results

Five GenAIs, GPT-3.5, GPT-4, Gemini, GitHub Copilot and Codeium, were tested on weekly exercises in all courses. Web1 acted as a pilot course to determine how many iterations per exercise task we needed to see if a GenAI can solve the task. Apart from GPT-4 and GitHub Copilot, all were free to use. Students can obtain GitHub Copilot for free, and all tools featured a simple sign-up process, such as using Google or GitHub accounts.

Overall, the GenAIs performed well in the exercises. To pass, they needed to solve at least half of the available tasks in exercises and in most of the weekly exercise parts, they managed to pass that limit. Only Codeium failed programming exercises in one course, OOP. It can be concluded that students are very likely to pass exercises in these courses by using GenAI alone without trying to solve them by themselves and if a student decides to do that, it is not very difficult, as most of these GenAIs are free to use and easily accessible for students.

Score-wise wise GenAIs also performed well. In most cases, they passed at least half of the exercises. In quizzes, GenAIs performed very well (Fig. 1), always getting at least 80% correct and most often getting 90% or more. Performance was weaker in CS1 and OOP courses, which were in Finnish, while in Web1 and Web2 courses, GenAIs performed better, which in turn were in English. However, while GenAIs performed well in quizzes, programming exercises are worth two or three times more in course grading. So, accomplishments in quizzes do not have the same impact as the same level of performance would have in programming exercises.

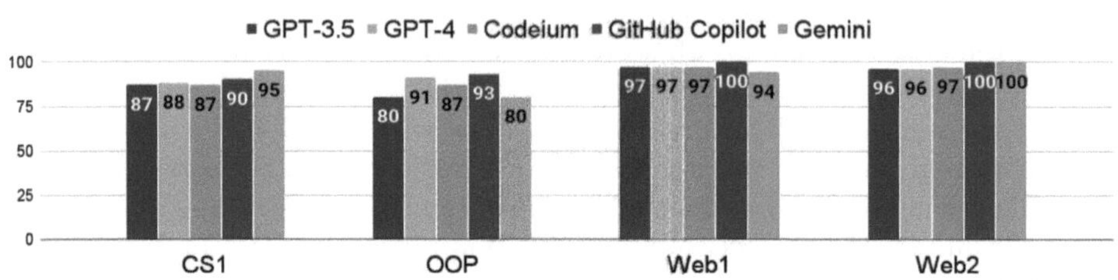

Fig. 1. Total percentage of quiz questions GenAIs managed to pass in all courses.

GenAIs managed to solve at least half of the available programming tasks and assignments in most courses, with only exception being Codeium in OOP (Fig. 2). GitHub Copilot consistently delivered the best performance, while Codeium and GPT-3.5 often performed the worst. Between courses, Web1 and Web2 had a higher average pass percentage (73.2% and 72.2% respectively) than CS1, C and OOP (69.8%, 66% and 63.2% respectively). In this sense, GenAIs performed better on courses that are designed for third-year students (Web1 and Web2) than they did on first-year courses and Web2 itself is generally considered to be the most difficult programming course during bachelor's studies. Furthermore, CS1 is a prerequisite for all of these courses and while average performance in CS1 was better than it was on C and OOP it was also worse than in Web1 and Web2. Although averages between Web2 and CS1 are not very big and the Web2 average is affected by GitHub Copilot's and Gemini's scores, which for those GenAIs were their best scores across all five courses, only GPT-4 had its worst performance in Web2. Another aspect that can affect these results is that CS1, C and OOP have strict requirements for each task's output, as it has to match exactly what is the expected output, whereas in Web1 and Web2, automatic grading only expects certain elements or API calls. OOP had the lowest average percentage due to each AI's poor performance in Android Studio programming exercises.

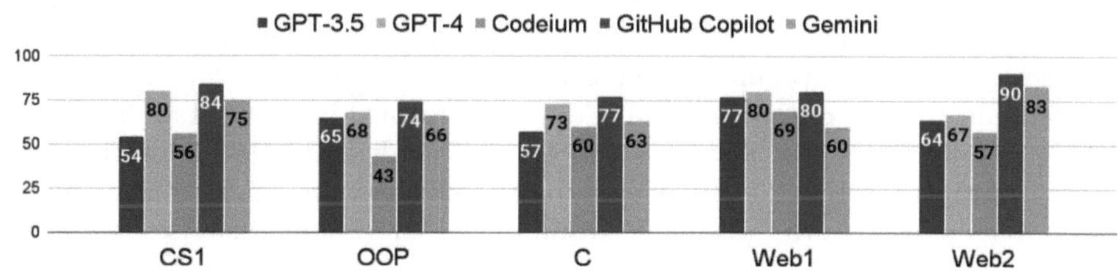

Fig. 2. Total percentage of programming exercises GenAIs managed to pass in all courses.

There were some common instances where GenAIs struggled. Reading files often caused troubles as the format of the text file was not always clear to GenAIs and it was not always easy to say if problems in the printed output originated from it. The same happened with APIs and how they were structured and how GenAI should read them. If the previous week's solution was used in the next programming exercise, it was more likely to fail, as the solution needed to be added as text to the prompt, making it more complex. Similarly, programming exercises where the entire exercise was one assignment and tasks were steps in it, failing one task could result in failing some or even all following tasks, depending on how much they rely on previous ones. Still, the most common cause for failing was the complexity of the programming task. A common trend was that exercises from the first weeks were generally completed successfully, while later weeks saw more failures. Typically, the simpler tasks at the beginning of each week were more likely to be passed.

5 Findings and Discussion

In regard to the research on using GenAI in university programming courses (RQ1), multiple studies have explored this topic. Since GenAI became a hot topic after the launch of ChatGPT with model GPT-3.5, most of the research is very recent, with the majority of studies being from 2023 and onwards. From these studies, four major themes were identified, focusing on how the use of

GenAI affects students' learning, how GenAI could be utilised in courses, how GenAIs have performed in courses and what sort of response there has been in using GenAI in courses.

Regarding which GenAI tools and models can be used to complete programming courses (RQ2) there are many options at the moment. ChatGPT still has a large monthly user base, many GenAI tools offer both free models and more powerful models for paid subscription, there are a lot of alternatives to ChatGPT and more specialised GenAI tools, such as Gemini and Codeium. Besides GenAIs used in this study, there are many more that could be used instead, like Claude3 and Microsoft Copilot, a combination of all Microsoft's previous Copilot GenAIs.

The main point of this study was to evaluate how selected GenAIs perform in university programming course exercises (RQ3). Results show that GenAIs can pass most, if not all, parts in selected courses and can often achieve a moderately high score in course grading. GitHub Copilot performed best out of all five, with GPT-4 usually coming as a second and Gemini tended to be a bit better than already outdated GPT-3.5 and Codeium in exercises. In quizzes, all GenAIs achieved very high scores and while results in programming exercises were not as good, GenAIs managed to pass at least half of them most of the time. Difficulty of the course (at least on the level of bachelor's studies) doesn't seem to affect GenAIs performance as they performed a little bit better on third-year courses (Web1 and Web2) than they did on first-year courses. The complexity of the exercise, iterating on previous tasks or week's solution, and relaying the format of the file to read or API to use caused trouble to GenAIs. These results indicate that a student with no prior knowledge on the course topics and with no personal input could pass exercises in these courses by solely relying on the GenAI. This aligns with previous research on how well GenAIs can pass courses. GenAIs' struggles identified in previous studies, such as complicated concepts [53] and API documentation [34] are also consistent with those found in this study.

It is possible that a student could pass exercises in courses discussed here using only a GenAI but by doing so might hinder their learning [36], critical thinking [17,23] and give a lacking knowledge on course topics [32]. These could be prevented by giving focus in grading to the whole process of doing exercises instead of just the end product and having students give detailed statements on their AI usage [37] or emphasising more on problem solving and mathematical reasoning over coding proficiency [13]. Critical thinking skills can be improved if students are taught to analyse chatbots' responses better [21,23] and distinguish accurate, partially correct and misleading answers and verify information from reliable sources [18]. In the end, teachers are now living in a world where students have the option to use GenAIs and it has and it will continue to form methods and ways of teaching. Our findings fortify existing research and underline that cheating is easier than ever.

There is also the option to use GenAI in a way that boosts learning. One way to do so is to use GenAI as a teaching assistant in courses [40] and GenAI can provide simplified and easy-to-understand explanations to course topics [26].

Personalised learning can also be provided more easily to students as GenAIs can quickly create tutorials and other learning resources based on individual students' preferences [49,54]. As selected GenAIs in this study could pass exercises in the courses relatively well, they could potentially assist students struggling with topics. Of course, GenAIs are not 100% reliable and, as the study by Suh et al. [45] suggests, the usefulness of GenAI to students seems to depend on how much prior knowledge they have on the course topics, as more intermediate-level students benefited from GenAI more than beginner-level students, so this should be considered when deciding how to use GenAIs in courses.

However, the results here do not paint the whole picture of how GenAIs could pass these courses. Only exercises were considered in this study and their portion of the overall course grade is less than half in all cases. Courses have at least either a course project or an exam, usually both, besides exercises. While it is possible to use GenAI in those, except in supervised exams, this study did not include them and cannot tell how GenAIs would perform in those contexts. Also we do not have any long-term data yet. It would be interesting to see how the GenAI affects to students' skill retention or critical thinking. Also, it is noteworthy to emphasise how these results are valid in the programming education context and might not be the same outside this scope.

6 Conclusions

The results obtained here show that GenAIs can pass most of the different parts of weekly exercises and obtain decent scores, often reaching around 75% of available points. Five GenAIs were selected for this experiment, and every GenAI was used in every course: GPT-3.5, GPT-4, Codeium, GitHub Copilot and Gemini. GitHub Copilot performed better than others and GPT-3.5 and Codeium most often had the worst performance. GenAIs often excelled in quizzes, while performance in programming exercises was not as good but still decent. GenAIs struggled most with complex programming tasks and using external data sources like text files and APIs.

This indicates that a student could pass exercises in these courses by solely relying on GenAI. As previous research indicates, this would likely harm students' learning. This makes teaching challenging as university degree programs are trying to educate software professionals for the industry.

References

1. Anishka, Mehta, A., Gupta, N., Balachandran, A., Kumar, D., Jalote, P.: Can ChatGPT play the role of a teaching assistant in an introductory programming course? (2023). Version Number: 2 - https://arxiv.org/abs/2312.07343
2. Banić, B., Konecki, M., Konecki, M.: Pair programming education aided by ChatGPT. In: 2023 46th MIPRO ICT and Electronics Convention (MIPRO), Opatija, Croatia, May 2023, pp. 911–915. IEEE (2023)

3. Bego, C.R.: Using ChatGPT for homework: does it feel like cheating? (WIP). In: 2023 IEEE Frontiers in Education Conference (FIE), College Station, TX, USA, October 2023, pp. 1–4. IEEE (2023)
4. Bordt, S., von Luxburg, U.: ChatGPT participates in a computer science exam (2023). Version Number: 2 - https://arxiv.org/abs/2303.09461
5. Budhiraja, R., Joshi, I., Challa, J.S., Akolekar, H.D., Kumar, D.: "It's not like Jarvis, but it's pretty close!" - examining ChatGPT's usage among undergraduate students in computer science. In: Proceedings of the 26th Australasian Computing Education Conference, Sydney NSW Australia, January 2024, pp. 124–133. ACM (2024)
6. Carreira, G., Silva, L., Mendes, A.J., Oliveira, H.G.: Pyo, a Chatbot assistant for introductory programming students. In: 2022 International Symposium on Computers in Education (SIIE), Coimbra, Portugal, November 2022, pp. 1–6. IEEE (2022)
7. Chan, W.K., Yu, Y.T., Keung, J.W., Lee, V.C.: Toward AI-assisted exercise creation for first course in programming through adversarial examples of AI models. In: 2023 IEEE 35th International Conference on Software Engineering Education and Training (CSEE&T), Tokyo, Japan, August 2023, pp. 132–136. IEEE (2023)
8. Choudhuri, R., Liu, D., Steinmacher, I., Gerosa, M., Sarma, A.: How far are we? The triumphs and trials of generative AI in learning software engineering (2023). Version Number: 1 - https://arxiv.org/abs/2312.11719
9. Cipriano, B.P., Alves, P.: GPT-3 vs object oriented programming assignments: an experience report. In: Proceedings of the 2023 Conference on Innovation and Technology in Computer Science Education, Turku Finland, June 2023, vol. 1, pp. 61–67. ACM (2023)
10. Daun, M., Brings, J.: How ChatGPT will change software engineering education. In: Proceedings of the 2023 Conference on Innovation and Technology in Computer Science Education, Turku, Finland, June 2023, vol. 1, pp. 110–116. ACM (2023)
11. Denny, P., Kumar, V., Giacaman, N.: Conversing with Copilot: exploring prompt engineering for solving CS1 problems using natural language (2022). Version Number: 1 - https://arxiv.org/abs/2210.15157
12. Denny, P., et al.: Promptly: using prompt problems to teach learners how to effectively utilize AI code generators (2023). Version Number: 1 - https://arxiv.org/abs/2307.16364
13. Dickey, E., Bejarano, A., Garg, C.: Innovating computer programming pedagogy: the AI-lab framework for generative AI adoption (2023). Version Number: 1 - https://arxiv.org/abs/2308.12258
14. Dos Santos, O.L., Cury, D.: Challenging the confirmation bias: using ChatGPT as a virtual peer for peer instruction in computer programming education. In: 2023 IEEE Frontiers in Education Conference (FIE), College Station, TX, USA, October 2023, pp. 1–7. IEEE (2023)
15. Finnie-Ansley, J., Denny, P., Becker, B.A., Luxton-Reilly, A., Prather, J.: The robots are coming: exploring the implications of OpenAI codex on introductory programming. In: Proceedings of the 24th Australasian Computing Education Conference, Virtual Event, Australia, February 2022, pp. 10–19. ACM (2022)
16. Finnie-Ansley, J., Denny, P., Luxton-Reilly, A., Santos, E.A., Prather, J., Becker, B.A.: My AI wants to know if this will be on the exam: testing OpenAI's codex on CS2 programming exercises. In: Proceedings of the 25th Australasian Computing Education Conference, Melbourne, VIC, Australia, January 2023, pp. 97–104. ACM (2023)

17. Haindl, P., Weinberger, G.: Does ChatGPT help novice programmers write better code? Results from static code analysis. IEEE Access **12**, 114146–114156 (2024)
18. Haindl, P., Weinberger, G.: Students' experiences of using ChatGPT in an undergraduate programming course. IEEE Access **12**, 43519–43529 (2024)
19. Hajj, J.A., Sah, M.: Assessing the impact of ChatGPT in a PHP programming course. In: 2023 7th International Symposium on Innovative Approaches in Smart Technologies (ISAS), Istanbul, Turkiye, November 2023, pp. 1–10. IEEE (2023)
20. Haldar, S., Pierce, M., Fernando Capretz, L.: Exploring the integration of generative AI tools in software testing education: a case study on ChatGPT and Copilot for preparatory testing artifacts in postgraduate learning. IEEE Access **13**, 46070–46090 (2025)
21. Hochmair, H.H.: Use and effectiveness of Chatbots as support tools in GIS programming course assignments. ISPRS Int. J. Geo Inf. **14**(4), 156 (2025)
22. Jalil, S., Rafi, S., LaToza, T.D., Moran, K., Lam, W.: ChatGPT and software testing education: promises & perils. In: 2023 IEEE International Conference on Software Testing, Verification and Validation Workshops (ICSTW), Dublin, Ireland, April 2023, pp. 4130–4137. IEEE (2023)
23. Ji, Y., Zhan, Z., Li, T., Zou, X., Lyu, S.: Human-machine cocreation: the effects of ChatGPT on students' learning performance, AI awareness, critical thinking, and cognitive load in a STEM course toward entrepreneurship. IEEE Trans. Learn. Technol. **18**, 402–415 (2025)
24. Johanyák, Z.C., Cserkó, J., Pásztor, A.: AI-assisted university programming education in practice. In: 2023 IEEE 35th International Conference on Software Engineering Education and Training (CSEE&T), Tokyo, Japan, August 2023, pp. 185–186. IEEE (2023)
25. Joshi, I., et al.: ChatGPT in the classroom: an analysis of its strengths and weaknesses for solving undergraduate computer science questions. In: Proceedings of the 55th ACM Technical Symposium on Computer Science Education, Portland, OR, USA, March 2024, vol. 1, pp. 625–631. ACM (2024)
26. Joshi, I., et al.: "With great power comes great responsibility!": student and instructor perspectives on the influence of LLMs on undergraduate engineering education (2023). Version Number: 2 - https://arxiv.org/abs/2309.10694
27. Kochmar, E., Vu, D.D., Belfer, R., Gupta, V., Serban, I.V., Pineau, J.: Automated personalized feedback improves learning gains in an intelligent tutoring system. In: Bittencourt, I.I., Cukurova, M., Muldner, K., Luckin, R., Millán, E. (eds.) AIED 2020. LNCS (LNAI), vol. 12164, pp. 140–146. Springer, Cham (2020). https://doi.org/10.1007/978-3-030-52240-7_26
28. Lau, S., Guo, P.: From "ban it till we understand it" to "resistance is futile": how university programming instructors plan to adapt as more students use AI code generation and explanation tools such as ChatGPT and GitHub Copilot. In: Proceedings of the 2023 ACM Conference on International Computing Education Research, Chicago, IL, USA, August 2023, vol. 1, pp. 106–121. ACM (2023)
29. MacNeil, S., Tran, A., Mogil, D., Bernstein, S., Ross, E., Huang, Z.: Generating diverse code explanations using the GPT-3 large language model. In: Proceedings of the 2022 ACM Conference on International Computing Education Research, Lugano and Virtual Event, Switzerland, August 2022, vol. 2, pp. 37–39. ACM (2022)
30. Maher, M.L., Tadimalla, S.Y., Dhamani, D.: An exploratory study on the impact of AI tools on the student experience in programming courses: an intersectional analysis approach. In: 2023 IEEE Frontiers in Education Conference (FIE), College Station, TX, USA, October 2023, pp. 1–5. IEEE (2023)

31. Malinka, K., Peresíni, M., Firc, A., Hujnák, O., Janus, F.: On the educational impact of ChatGPT: is artificial intelligence ready to obtain a university degree? In: Proceedings of the 2023 Conference on Innovation and Technology in Computer Science Education, Turku, Finland, June 2023, vol. 1, pp. 47–53. ACM (2023)
32. Memarian, B., Doleck, T.: ChatGPT in education: methods, potentials, and limitations. Comput. Hum. Behav. Artif. Hum. **1**(2), 100022 (2023)
33. Neyem, A., González, L.A., Mendoza, M., Alcocer, J.P.S., Centellas, L., Paredes, C.: Toward an AI knowledge assistant for context-aware learning experiences in software capstone project development. IEEE Trans. Learn. Technol. **17**, 1599–1614 (2024)
34. Ouh, E.L., Gan, B.K.S., Jin Shim, K., Wlodkowski, S.: ChatGPT, can you generate solutions for my coding exercises? An evaluation on its effectiveness in an undergraduate Java programming course. In: Proceedings of the 2023 Conference on Innovation and Technology in Computer Science Education, Turku, Finland, June 2023, vol. 1, pp. 54–60. ACM (2023)
35. Ouyang, F., Guo, M., Zhang, N., Bai, X., Jiao, P.: Comparing the effects of instructor manual feedback and ChatGPT intelligent feedback on collaborative programming in China's higher education. IEEE Trans. Learn. Technol. **17**, 2173–2185 (2024)
36. Popovici, M.D.: ChatGPT in the classroom. Exploring its potential and limitations in a functional programming course. Int. J. Hum. Comput. Interact., 1–12 (2023)
37. Prather, J., et al.: The robots are here: navigating the generative AI revolution in computing education. In: Proceedings of the 2023 Working Group Reports on Innovation and Technology in Computer Science Education, Turku, Finland, December 2023, pp. 108–159. ACM (2023)
38. Pérez-Mercado, R., Balderas, A., Muñoz, A., Cabrera, J.F., Palomo-Duarte, M., Dodero, J.M.: ChatbotSQL: conversational agent to support relational database query language learning. SoftwareX **22**, 101346 (2023)
39. Rathore, A.S., Sharma, A., Massoudi, M.: Personalized engineering education model based on artificial intelligence for learning programming. In: 2021 6th International Conference on Computing, Communication and Security (ICCCS), Las Vegas, NV, USA, October 2021, pp. 1–10. IEEE (2021)
40. Roldán-Álvarez, D., Mesa, F.J.: Intelligent deep-learning tutoring system to assist instructors in programming courses. IEEE Trans. Educ. **67**(1), 153–161 (2024)
41. Setyawan Soekamto, Y., Christopher Limanjaya, L., Kaleb Purwanto, Y., Kang, D.K.: From queries to courses: SKYRAG's revolution in learning path generation via keyword-based document retrieval. IEEE Access **13**, 21434–21455 (2025)
42. Sheese, B., Liffiton, M., Savelka, J., Denny, P.: Patterns of student help-seeking when using a large language model-powered programming assistant. In: Proceedings of the 26th Australasian Computing Education Conference, Sydney, NSW, Australia, January 2024, pp. 49–57. ACM (2024)
43. Shoufan, A.: Can students without prior knowledge use ChatGPT to answer test questions? An empirical study. ACM Trans. Comput. Educ. **23**(4), 1–29 (2023)
44. Speth, S., Meißner, N., Becker, S.: Investigating the use of AI-generated exercises for beginner and intermediate programming courses: a ChatGPT case study. In: 2023 IEEE 35th International Conference on Software Engineering Education and Training (CSEE&T), Tokyo, Japan, August 2023, pp. 142–146. IEEE (2023)
45. Suh, J., Lee, K., Lee, J.: Programming education with ChatGPT: outcomes for beginners and intermediate students. Educ. Inf. Technol. (2025)

46. Suomalainen, E.: Education in transition: a study on artificial intelligences' performance in university software engineering courses. Master's thesis, LUT University (2024)
47. Torres, N.: Do robots dream of passing a programming course? In: 2023 42nd IEEE International Conference of the Chilean Computer Science Society (SCCC), Concepcion, Chile, October 2023, pp. 1–8. IEEE (2023)
48. Verleger, M., Pembridge, J.: A pilot study integrating an AI-driven Chatbot in an introductory programming course. In: 2018 IEEE Frontiers in Education Conference (FIE), San Jose, CA, USA, October 2018, pp. 1–4. IEEE (2018)
49. Wang, H., Wang, C., Chen, Z., Liu, F., Bao, C., Xu, X.: Impact of AI-agent-supported collaborative learning on the learning outcomes of University programming courses. Educ. Inf. Technol. (2025)
50. White, K.P., Ingalls, R.G.: Introduction to simulation. In: 2015 Winter Simulation Conference (WSC), Huntington Beach, CA, USA, December 2015, pp. 1741–1755. IEEE (2015)
51. Wohlin, C.: Guidelines for snowballing in systematic literature studies and a replication in software engineering. In: Proceedings of the 18th International Conference on Evaluation and Assessment in Software Engineering, London, England, United Kingdom, May 2014, pp. 1–10. ACM (2014)
52. Wohlin, C., Höst, M.: Special section: controlled Experiments in Software Engineering. Inf. Softw. Technol. **43**(15), 921–924 (2001)
53. Wollowski, M.: Using ChatGPT to produce code for a typical college-level assignment. AI Mag. **44**(1), 129–130 (2023)
54. Wu, X., Wang, H., Zhang, Y., Zou, B., Hong, H.: A tutorial-generating method for autonomous online learning. IEEE Trans. Learn. Technol. **17**, 1532–1541 (2024)
55. Zastudil, C., Rogalska, M., Kapp, C., Vaughn, J., MacNeil, S.: Generative AI in computing education: perspectives of students and instructors. In: 2023 IEEE Frontiers in Education Conference (FIE), College Station, TX, USA, October 2023, pp. 1–9. IEEE (2023)
56. Zhang, Z., Wen, L., Jiang, Y., Liu, Y.: Evaluate Chat-GPT 's programming capability in swift through real university exam questions. Softw. Pract. Exp. **54**(11), 2129–2143 (2024)

Enhancing Agile Workflows with AI-Driven, Sustainability-Aware Requirements Engineering: A Design Science Approach

Oshani Weerakoon[1(✉)], Shola Oyedeji[2], Md Abdus Samad[2], Abdulkadir Abubakar[2], Ahsan Ishan[2], Muhammad Shayan[2], Tuomas Mäkilä[1], and Erkki Kaila[1]

[1] University of Turku, Turku, Finland
osweer@utu.fi
[2] LUT University, Lappeenranta, Finland

Abstract. Generative AI presents growing opportunities across various fields, including Requirements Engineering (RE). RE, which is the backbone of software projects, drives the entire product development toward respective business goals. However, sustainability is not considered a primary need during the requirement elicitation, and as a result, software engineers are usually unable to envision the sustainability impacts of the products they build. To explore this gap, we introduce Reqwire, an AI-driven, sustainability-aware multi-agent system that (i) generates user stories from software requirement documents, (ii) enriches them with sustainability attributes, and (iii) integrates with common agile project management tools, like Jira. The system consists of specialized agents, namely as root, distributor, user story generator, and Jira. We followed a Design Science Research (DSR) approach under seven iterative cycles, incorporating feedback from an industry partner and academia to design and evaluate the Reqwire workflow. Our results indicate that Reqwire reduces manual effort by generating structured user stories, estimating story points, and assigning sustainability tags across five sustainability dimensions: environmental, economic, social, individual, and technical. The multi-agent-based framework enables integration with third-party tools, supporting consistent, systematic project tracking. Reqwire shows promise for enhancing agile workflows and promoting sustainable software practices from initial test rounds with the client.

Keywords: Requirement Engineering · Agile Development · User Stories · Generative AI · AI Agents · Sustainability

1 Introduction

Effective software systems begin with a clear understanding of user needs and requirements, and aligning functionality with user expectations helps prevent

G. Herzwurm et al. (Eds.): ICSOB 2025, LNBIP 574, pp. 212–229, 2026.
https://doi.org/10.1007/978-3-032-14518-5_17

functional discrepancies [35]. Requirements Engineering (RE) is the discipline that identifies a system's real-world objectives, intended functions, and operational constraints [21]. Within agile software development, user stories are commonly used [7] to capture requirements during the elicitation of requirements. They offer a lightweight format to concisely record the who, what, and why of a functionality and are readily understood by stakeholders with diverse technical backgrounds [36]. However, manually created user stories are prone to inconsistency, incompleteness, and error [10].

Furthermore, sustainability has emerged as an important factor in RE and software development because of the sustainability impacts of software systems solutions on people, the environment, and society [8]. Sustainability within software requirements, design, and development can be viewed from these five dimensions: environmental, social, technical, economic, and individual [27]. In software development, early design choices incorporated into requirements have an impact on whether the sustainability of a software system is enabled or impeded, which may lead to *sustainability debt* [4,24]. However, software development practitioners lack the understanding of how to operationalize sustainability during early RE stages and agile software development [25]. The absence of systematic tools to identify, prioritize, and link requirements to each of the sustainability dimensions at the same level as functional and non-functional related requirements [5,8,30], further contributes to this issue.

The recent advances in generative artificial intelligence (AI) and large language models (LLMs) provide a good opportunity for addressing both the challenges that come with manual user story generation and linking requirements (user stories) to sustainability during requirement elicitation and software development. Within RE, several recent studies have leveraged LLM-based approaches to explore the state-of-the-art RE tasks [31,33], such as generating elicitation interview scripts [12], evaluating the ability to transform natural language requirements to post-conditions [11], generating specifications [37], user story generation [29], user story quality evaluation [39], and multiple AI agents handling requirement-related tasks [32]. Despite its capabilities, LLMs also exhibit notable limitations, such as generating factually incorrect information (hallucinations) [38] and potentially impeding one's cognitive or creative processes [18]. These challenges must be carefully monitored in human–AI collaborative contexts before LLMs are fully integrated into operational workflows.

The central research question guiding this study is: ***How can generative AI be leveraged to automate user story creation and incorporate sustainability considerations into agile requirements engineering workflows?***. To explore this question, we developed and evaluated *Reqwire*, a sustainability-aware, AI-driven requirements engineering (RE) workflow designed to automate the generation of structured user stories derived from product specification documents, estimate story points, and annotate them with sustainability-related tags. Reqwire also integrates seamlessly with the Jira project management environment.

Reqwire was piloted and evaluated in collaboration with a leading telecommunications and digital services enterprise in Finland, which served as the industrial partner. Within this organization, product managers had previously encountered challenges stemming from ambiguous or incomplete requirements, resulting in miscommunication, rework, prolonged sprint cycles, and misalignment with strategic objectives. Furthermore, the company demonstrated a growing interest in embedding sustainability as a first-class concern during early requirements elicitation, aligning with its broader corporate sustainability strategy. The novelty of this study lies in the automation of user story generation and the integration of sustainability considerations by automatically tagging user stories according to their corresponding sustainability dimensions: environmental (e.g., energy consumption, CO_2 emissions), social (e.g., accessibility), technical (e.g., usability, maintainability), and economic. This approach positions sustainability as a core development objective alongside traditional software engineering goals.

The rest of the paper is structured as follows: Sect. 2 reviews related work, while Sect. 3 outlines the research methodology and design of the AI-driven approach. Section 4 details the system implementation across several cycles of design iterations, while Sect. 5 discusses the findings and limitations. Finally, Sect. 6 concludes the study and suggests avenues for future research.

2 Related Work

The core aim of RE is to systematically gather, define, and document requirements from stakeholders in a clear and structured manner, establishing a foundation for reliable and user-centered software systems [14]. Inam [15] characterizes a well-specified requirement as a software feature that accurately reflects client needs, emphasizing the necessity for precision at this stage. A study examining 32 software projects conducted between 2003 and 2005 within a large enterprise development division in Tokyo investigated the relationship between requirements specification quality and project success [17], where the researchers observed that balanced and comprehensive Software Requirement Specification (SRS) descriptions are characteristic of successful projects. While improperly engineered requirements are not the only reason for project failures, proper requirements contribute substantially to the overall success of software projects [15]. Furthermore, minimal documentation and neglect of non-functional requirements undermine traceability, contribute to budget overruns, and reduce system usability, as demonstrated in a systematic literature review of 21 studies [16].

Sustainability, also as a non-functional requirement, can play an important role in incorporating broader perspectives and strategic goals to the project [30]. The Karlskrona Manifesto advocates and provides guidelines for integrating sustainability principles into software system requirements, design, and development [3]. Complementing this, Lago et al. introduced a sustainability analysis framework that can assist professionals in evaluating software qualities across environmental, social, technical, and economic dimensions, including their interdependencies [20] as well as, Penzenstadler et al. introduced a generic sustainability model that integrate both process and product-specific instances to help requirements engineers assess their work across multiple dimensions and identify areas for improvement [27]. Extending this line of research to more RE focus, requirements have been identified as the driving force behind sustainability [4] and as a crucial non-functional requirement of the 21st century [28]. The underlying rationale is that software developers can better understand and manage the sustainability impact of the systems they design through properly elicited sustainability-aware requirements. Therefore, the role of requirement elicitation with the mindset of sustainability is crucial for developing better software systems for everyone on the planet.

Early research studies also explored the application of Natural Language Processing (NLP) and Machine Learning (ML) to RE processes, including the classification of functional and non-functional requirements [6, 19], assessment of requirements quality [26], and management of requirements by identifying requirement changes [22]. However, the process was labor-intensive, language-specific, and brittle, unable to generalize across domains or capture true semantics. Since the introduction of publicly accessible generative AI models, such as ChatGPT in 2022[1], several generative AI models have enhanced language processing capabilities in software engineering [1], ranging from generating [29] and refining user stories [31] to producing structured requirement documentation [1]. More recent RE-related developments include LLM-powered agentic systems [32], and different prompt engineering techniques like, Refine and Thought (RAT) [29]. As Generative AI and RE continue to advance rapidly, we identify the need for exploring the capability of defining sustainable aspects, encompassing environmental, social, technical, individual, and economic dimensions of requirements during the elicitation stage.

3 Research Methodology

This section details the research design and methodology used to develop and evaluate Reqwire. Our approach is fundamentally rooted in the Design Science Research (DSR) paradigm, which systematically addresses real-world problems through the creation and investigation of innovative artifacts [13]. In Information Systems (IS) and Software Engineering (SE), DSR comprises two primary activities: designing the artifact and subsequently investigating it within its practical context. This context encompasses a wide array of elements, including stakeholders and their objectives, existing scientific and engineering theories, current designs and products, and the accumulated experience and common sense of researchers. Specifically, we employed Hevner's three-cycle view of DSR [13], which emphasizes the interconnected and iterative nature of DSR activities. The cycles are listed below.

- **The Relevance Cycle**grounds DSR in real-world contexts by identifying domain problems and opportunities, setting acceptance criteria, and field testing artifacts, with outcomes guiding further iterations [5]. In Reqwire,

[1] https://openai.com/index/chatgpt/.

this involved addressing inefficiencies in manual agile artifact creation and enabling sustainability tagging, validated by our industry partner. The evaluation of Reqwire considered task completion rates, number of corrections required, quality of user stories, accuracy of sustainability tagging, and the correlation of story point estimation with expert reference points.

- **The Rigor Cycle** ensures scientific validity by grounding design in established theories, methods, and artifacts, while contributing new knowledge through innovation and evaluation [5]. In our case, this involved leveraging existing knowledge in RE, AI, and sustainability frameworks to inform the design of Reqwire.
- **The Design Cycle** is the core iterative component of DSR, involving repeated construction and evaluation of artifacts until requirements are met [34]. It draws requirements from the Relevance Cycle and theories and methods from the Rigor Cycle, balancing both in iterative testing before field deployment. For Reqwire, this meant prototyping, incorporating stakeholder feedback, and refining features such as sustainability tags and Jira integration.

3.1 Participants

We engaged two main types of participants in the various cycles of our research.

- **IT Practitioners:** Our primary industry partner was a leading telecommunications and digital services provider, which contributed through the Head of Service Development and 12 Developers. They were central to the Relevance Cycle, engaging in workshops and feedback loops to identify and refine problem scope, emphasize key needs (like sustainability tagging and Jira integration), and provide continuous feedback on preliminary designs. They also played a key role in the evaluation and empirical validation, offering insights on integration depth, usability, and tagging accuracy during the Minimum Viable Product (MVP) demonstrations. Data collected included insights from collaborative workshops, feedback from bi-weekly sessions, and observations from client-focused seminars, all contributing to the iterative refinement of Reqwire.
- **Students and Academic Researchers:** From academia, 22 software engineering master's students with industry experience and 4 researchers in a Green ICT and sustainability-focused software engineering program contributed primarily during the second validation phase. They provided peer evaluation on the robustness of the AI pipeline, the novelty of integrating sustainability metadata into user stories, and the system's modularity. Data gathered from seminars and technical reviews offered qualitative feedback that informed assessments of Reqwire's scientific contribution and its potential for future research.

Two workshops, each lasting 4–5 h, were held with industry stakeholders at the client's company premises to test and provide feedback, followed by a final seminar intended for both industry and academic participants.

4 Implementation of Reqwire

Reqwire was developed using DSR to address the challenge of anticipating sustainability effects in IT products and services. This section discusses the DSR process across the relevance, rigor, and design cycles introduced in Sect. 3. Figure 1 provides an overview of all cycles. Each cycle contributed to designing the Reqwire prototype and verifying relevance in practice.

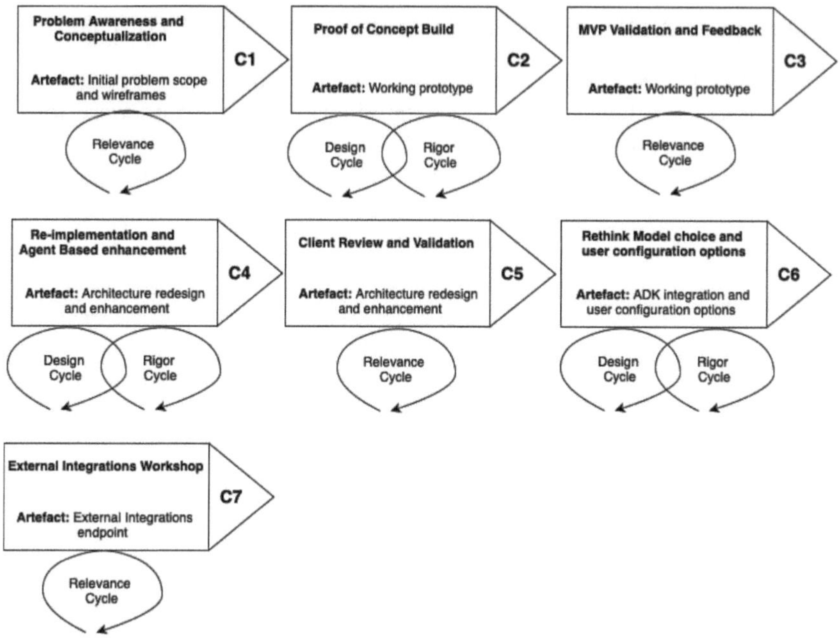

Fig. 1. Seven cycles of design and evaluation of Reqwire.

4.1 [Relevance] Cycle 1 Problem Awareness and Conceptualization

This cycle focused on the problem space. The industry partner highlighted inefficiencies in the Software Development Life Cycle (SDLC), particularly in the manual requirements elicitation process and the poor integration of AI within the SDLC. Discussion among the industry stakeholders and the project team refined the scope to a key challenge to address: the lack of useful AI tool support for automating the generation of actionable user stories in the RE phase of

agile software development. The industry stakeholders emphasized three critical requirements for adoption of such an AI tool: (i) the ability to generate user stories from varying depths of specifications, (ii) attach sustainability metadata to the user stories, and (iii) seamlessly integrate with agile project management tools.
Participants: Industry side stakeholders, academic researchers, and the project research team.
Lessons Learned: This cycle revealed that while AI tools support many SDLC phases, the RE stage, especially the formulation of clear and actionable user stories, remains underserved in practice. The industry partner emphasized this as a critical bottleneck that affects sprint velocity, project budget, developer clarity, and sustainability tracking.

4.2 [Design and Rigor] Cycle 2 Proof-of-Concept (POC) Build

Designed Artifacts: Early requirements, architecture, and an initial working prototype. Based on Cycle 1, sets of preliminary requirements were identified that covered key capabilities, and these were visualized using low-fidelity wireframes and interaction sketches that illustrated the envisioned workflow.

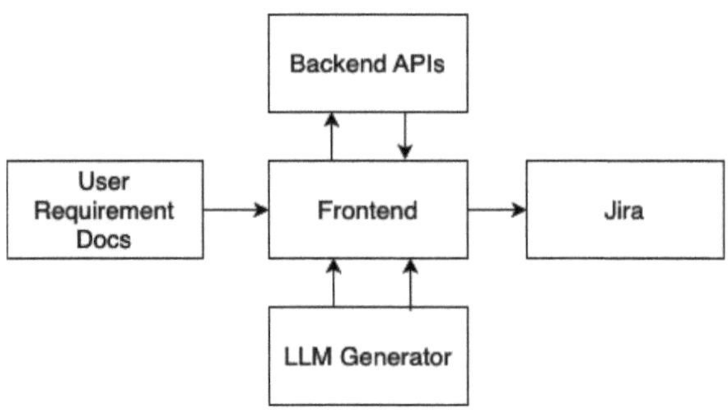

Fig. 2. First working prototype blackboard architecture with five components.

In this cycle, a preliminary architecture was designed as shown in Fig. 2; a simple blackboard architecture with five components. The Frontend serves as a central blackboard, integrating updates from Backend APIs, user inputs, and knowledge sources like the LLM Generator and Jira, enabling independent components to exchange data and coordinate effectively. The first working prototype comprised the following three functionalities:

1. **Local Project Management:** Reqwire enables users to initiate and manage projects within a local workspace. Projects are organized in a modular structure and can also be linked with Jira for centralized tracking.

2. **Intelligent User Story Generation:** The central feature of the platform is its AI-powered user story generation engine (Fig. 3). These are the details of the prompt design, the input, and output of the system.
   (a) **Prompt Structure:** The prompt defines an *Agentic Requirements Engineer* composed of cooperating sub-agents that simulate distinct stages of a human requirements process: *Planner*, *Generator*, *Sustainability Analyst*, *Reviewer*, and *Finalizer*. Each sub-agent operates under explicitly defined roles, performing specialized reasoning tasks that contribute to a coherent, traceable workflow.
      i. **Input Specification:** The input to the system is natural-language software requirements expressed as free text. Each requirement describes a desired function, constraint, or condition of a system. The model interprets this text as the source for generating structured user stories.
      ii. **Rules and Workflow:** The workflow consists of five sequential roles. The *Planner* defines internal subtasks based on the requirement, but does not output them. The *Generator* converts each subtask into candidate user stories following a strict template containing title, description, acceptance criteria, priority, and story points. The *Sustainability Analyst* evaluates each story across five predefined dimensions: environmental, economic, social, individual, and technical, based on the Sustainability Awareness Framework (SusAF) [5]. Impacts are assigned a polarity (+, -, or +/-) and accompanied by short, evidence-based justifications. The *Reviewer* enforces quality through deterministic checks on structure, testability, and completeness, allowing one regeneration attempt for any rejected story. Finally, the *Finalizer* compiles all accepted stories into a validated output array.
      iii. **Output Design:** The model produces a strictly formatted JSON array containing the generated set of user stories, which follow the widely adopted user story template popularized by Mike Cohn [9]: "As a [user], I want to [action], so that [value]." Each story is represented as an object with the following fields: *title*, *description*, *acceptance criteria*, *priority*, *story points*, and *sustainability* (consists of dimension, polarity, and reasoning). The output is required to be syntactically valid JSON, UTF-8 encoded, and free from explanatory or intermediate text.

   (b) **Measures to Minimize Hallucination:** The prompt incorporates several safeguards to reduce hallucination and maintain factual grounding. First, strict output constraints prohibit additional commentary or unsupported reasoning traces. Second, sustainability tagging is explicitly evidence-based: dimensions are omitted if cues are not clearly present in the requirement or story context. Third, the *Reviewer* role enforces concrete rejection criteria, such as detecting vague acceptance conditions or incomplete story structure. Fourth, the prompt instructs the model to prefer omission when confidence is low, preventing speculative or inconsistent content. Finally, few-shot examples are provided to anchor the model's responses to consistent patterns of style, detail, and sustainability reasoning.

3. **Sustainability Tagging**: As mentioned in the previous Subsect. 2, *Sustainability Analyst* analyzes each user story across the five sustainability dimensions using an explicit, rule-based reasoning sequence: defining context, mapping relevant dimensions, and assessing polarity (+, -, or +/-). These results are then embedded into the final user story as structured sustainability tags. For example: environmental, + (feature reduces server load), - (requires frequent heavy computation); economic, + (reduces maintenance cost), - (increases cost); technical, + (reusable APIs), - (hard-coded dependencies); social, + (improves accessibility), - (reduces accessibility); individual, + (supports privacy), - (invasive data collection). From the sample user story generated by Reqwire, shown in Fig. 4, on the real-time location tracking of the delivery partner, the user story has a positive technical impact on system's technical quality but introduces a negative environmental impact due to increased energy and resource consumption. Accordingly, Reqwire labels this story with a Technical (+) and Environmental (–) tag. This feature allows teams to gain early insight into the sustainability impacts of their requirements and enables them to make informed trade-offs and adjustments.

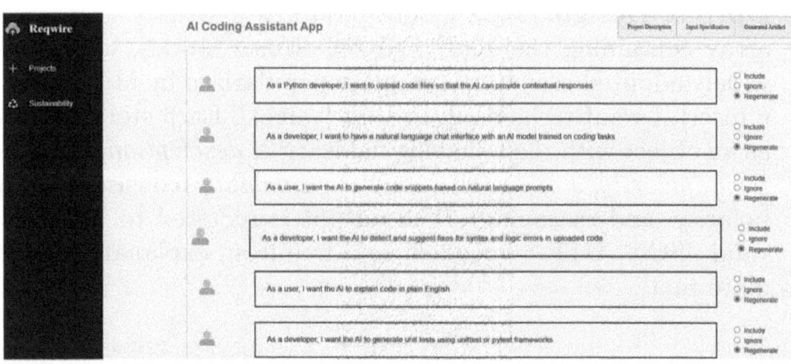

Fig. 3. Interface 2: Generated user stories page.

Participants: Industry client, academic researchers, and the project researchers team.

Fig. 4. Interface 3: A generated user story with assigned story points and sustainability label.

Lessons Learned: Building a functional vertical slice early exposes integration and accuracy issues, explainability for sustainability tags is essential for trust, and error handling is required for smooth tool adoption.

4.3 [Relevance] Cycle 3 MVP Validation and Feedback

Artifacts to Be Validated: The MVP developed in Cycle 2 was evaluated for usability, alignment with agile workflows, accuracy of generated stories and tags, and overall feasibility in addressing the identified RE gaps.
Participants: Industry-side software product development team, software engineering master's student with industry experience, and the project research team (facilitators).
Data Collected: Interaction notes from the on-site workshop and quantitative metrics such as task completion times for generating and exporting user stories, and feedback from the instructor and peer engineering students.
Evaluation: The MVP was presented and tested during an on-site seminar with the client's product teams and also tested with 22 Software engineering master's students with industry experience at the university. Hands-on interaction with the tool included uploading sample requirements, generating user stories, applying sustainability tags, and exporting to Jira. Feedback was gathered through open discussions, with key results highlighting high satisfaction with the generated stories, the potential time savings for requirements engineers provided by the solution, and the intuitive flow of the application. However, there was a concern regarding the linearity of the workflow. The industry product development

team noted that in most real-world scenarios, the flow from RE to project management (PM) tools is often non-linear, so the workflow needs to be modified to allow regeneration of artifacts.

Additional concerns were raised about tag accuracy, for example, occasional misclassifications of environmental impacts, which heavily depend on the level of detail in the specifications. Since Reqwire generates user stories from specifications of varying levels and depth, it can lack sufficient detail to accurately match features to sustainability tags. This becomes an issue when the generated tags are fully trusted without verification. Furthermore, the client expressed a desire for the user stories, sustainability tags, and estimated story points to be made available for integration with sustainability evaluation and visualization tools, to enable sustainability efforts tracking from the user story level.

Lessons Learned: To better align with real-world practices, the workflow should be redesigned to support iterative artifact regeneration and non-linear progression. Enhancing the system's ability to handle varying levels of specification detail will improve tag accuracy, potentially through more advanced natural language processing or user-guided refinements. Addressing these issues will increase the tool's practicality and trustworthiness in diverse project contexts.

4.4 [Design and Rigor] Cycle 4 Re-implementation and Agent-Based Enhancements

Designed Artifacts: Drawing from the feedback in Cycle 3, this cycle focused on re-implementation to address key limitations, particularly the need for non-linear workflows, improved tag accuracy, and greater flexibility in handling diverse specification inputs. A major redesign involved shifting from the initial blackboard architecture to a hybrid agent-based and layered architecture (Fig. 5), which introduced multi-agent coordination to enable conversational interactions, dynamic task delegation, and improved interoperability. The new architecture comprises four layers:

1. **Presentation Layer**: A web-based GUI for uploading requirements and managing projects, plus a new agent chat interface for natural language interactions (e.g., users can conversationally refine stories or issue commands like *"regenerate this story with more environmental context"*).
2. **Agent Coordination Layer**: A Root Agent serves as the central coordinator, interpreting user intents via the Agent Control Protocol (ACP) and delegates tasks. A Distributor Agent handles exports and communications with external systems using the Agent-to-Agent (A2A) protocol.
3. **Tool and Processing Layer**: Houses the User Story Generator Agent (powered by Gemini 1.5 Pro) with structured prompting for bias mitigation and context awareness, backend RESTful APIs for operations such as regeneration, and modular task tools (e.g., Create Jira Project, Export to Jira).
4. **External Integration Layer**: Connections to third-party services like Jira via authenticated REST APIs, with an External Agent placeholder for future expansions.

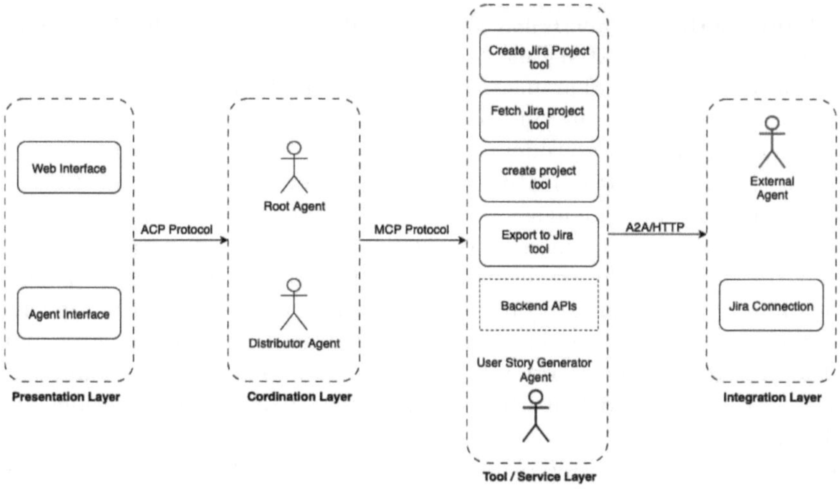

Fig. 5. Hybrid agent-oriented and layered architecture.

This agent-based design supports iterative, non-linear workflows by allowing agents to handle complex instructions adaptively, reducing hallucinations through guardrails and validation loops. Accessibility was enhanced, and human-in-the-loop controls were strengthened, enabling users to override tags or provide additional context during regeneration.
Participants: Project research team, industry side development team, and solutions architects for iterative reviews.
Evaluation: Internal testing assessed the new architecture's performance, including workflow flexibility (e.g., regeneration success rates and ease), tag accuracy, and latency. Bi-weekly feedback sessions with the industry stakeholders helped validate enhancements.
Lessons Learned: Agent-oriented designs significantly boost automation and adaptability in RE tools, but require robust protocols (e.g., ACP, A2A) to prevent coordination failures. Addressing AI biases and hallucinations demands layered safeguards like custom prompts and validation, while emission optimizations must be balanced with functionality to maintain sustainability goals.

4.5 [Relevance] Cycle 5 Client Review and Validation

Artifacts to Be Validated: The refined MVP, now incorporating the agent-based architecture, enhanced sustainability tagging, dynamic regeneration, and Jira integration, was evaluated for overall robustness, novelty, and enterprise readiness. Key focus areas included the accuracy of AI-generated artifacts, interoperability potential, and contribution to sustainable RE practices.
Participants: Academic researchers, software engineering students, industry-side team, and the project research team.

Data Collected: Seminar notes and qualitative insights from discussions on modularity and future extensibility.
Evaluation: The updated artifact was presented and tested in a technical seminar to client stakeholders and in class to the academic researchers and peer software engineering master's students with industry experience. Attendees interacted with the tool, testing features such as conversational refinements via the agent chat, multi-dimensional sustainability labeling, and Jira exports. Feedback was highly positive on the integration of sustainability metadata into user stories and the agent architecture for modularity and potential for broader tool interoperability. A key suggestion from this cycle was to address the challenge of integrating the newer AI models into the system with minimal changes. Therefore, the system should incorporate a mechanism to seamlessly adapt to and integrate the latest model of choice with minimal or no modifications to the overall architecture.
Lessons Learned: The rapid evolution of generative AI models emphasizes the need for flexible, model-agnostic designs that facilitate seamless upgrades with minimal architectural changes, ensuring long-term adaptability and relevance in the landscape of applied generative AI.

4.6 [Design and Rigor] Cycle 6 Rethink Model Choice and User Configuration Option

Artifact Designed and to Be Validated: Drawing from the feedback in Cycle 5, the agent was re-implemented using the Google Agent Development Toolkit[2], which provides out-of-the-box tools for implementing agents. Gemini 1.5 was selected as the base model, but it is swappable via the configuration interface without code or architectural modifications. The configuration allows to use of both commercial and self-hosted models through configuration fields on the application GUI. The input from this configuration is used to set the model parameter of the agent.
Participants: Project research team, industry-side development team.
Lessons Learned: Adopting a standard Agent Development Kit (ADK), such as the Google Agent Development Toolkit, enabled seamless use of the latest advancements in generative AI. It also allowed focus on the specific use case, rather than foundational implementation details, which are provided out-of-the-box. This enables some form of confidence in the future-proof nature of the solution.

4.7 [Relevance] Cycle 7 External Integrations Workshop

Artifacts to Be Validated: A workshop to test Reqwire and its endpoints for integrating with other systems that evaluate and visualize sustainability efforts across projects.

[2] https://google.github.io/adk-docs/.

Participants: Industry-side stakeholders, the project's research team, and teams working on sustainability tracking, estimation, and visualization.
Data Collected: Workshop session notes and cross-team discussion notes, participant feedback, system metrics such as API response times, and error rates during data exchanges.
Evaluation: Participants connected Reqwire's endpoints (e.g., via REST APIs and A2A protocols) to existing sustainability tools, such as internal dashboards for sustainability efforts estimation and visualization platforms (for example, custom green metrics trackers[3]). Simulated workflows included generating user stories, exporting tagged data to Jira, and pulling sustainability metadata into visualization tools for aggregate reporting across projects. Feedback indicated strong performance in data interoperability, with visualizations effectively highlighting trends like negative environmental impacts from high-energy features.
Lessons Learned: External integrations are crucial for enterprise adoption, as they extend Reqwire's value beyond isolated RE tasks to holistic sustainability management in software development workflows. Workshops expose practical scalability issues early, emphasizing the need for secure and optimized APIs with standardized data formats.

5 Discussion

The findings of this study provide evidence that generative AI can enhance agile requirements engineering by addressing two enduring challenges: the inefficiency of manual user story creation and the lack of structured sustainability integration during requirements generation in the early stage of software development. The results show that Reqwire makes sustainability trade-offs visible and actionable within agile workflows. Reqwire's automated user story generation and sustainability tagging feature (Fig. 3 and 4) to the five sustainability dimensions reduces the manual task with problems of inconsistency, incompleteness, errors in user story generation [10] and manual efforts for requirement engineers interested in sustainability during requirement gathering. By embedding these sustainability dimensions at the user story level, Reqwire operationalizes the sustainability principles proposed in earlier sustainability design frameworks [3,20,27] by bringing sustainability concerns closer to requirement elicitation.

Recent studies on generative AI in RE have primarily emphasized productivity gains and automation capabilities [1,32], our study highlights the added value of embedding sustainability tagging of requirements (in the form of user stories) during the requirement elicitation. This position requires, as an extension of prior AI-based RE tools, offering not only improved efficiency of user story generation but also advocating sustainability as a non-functional requirement in software development. Furthermore, the growing body of work on AI in RE has primarily focused on requirement generation and analysis [2,23]. However, few studies [32] have explored multi-agent architectures that are capable

[3] https://greenmetrics.co/.

of dynamic regeneration and continuous improvement of requirement artifacts. Reqwire's design, which allows integration with AI models like Gemini and open-source LLMs, contributes to this emerging paradigm by enabling adaptability and model-agnostic scalability.

The iterative development process was essential for aligning Reqwire's capabilities with real-world agile practices. Nevertheless, challenges remain that sustainability tagging accuracy depends on input detail, and LLMs carry limitations as discussed in Sect. 2. We also identify the need for wider testing of Reqwire, which will be conducted in a future client project.

6 Conclusion and Future Work

This study presents Reqwire, a generative AI–driven, sustainability-aware Requirements Engineering (RE) tool that automates user story creation and integrates sustainability tagging at the user story level, addressing a gap in recent RE and sustainability studies. Future work will include expanding the range of input modalities (diagrams, meeting transcripts, etc.), refining agent-to-agent protocols, and mitigating the model's limitations, like hallucinations (using techniques like Retrieval-augmented generation (RAG)). Most importantly, we plan to conduct wider testing in industry projects to validate Reqwire's effectiveness and adoption potential in real-world settings.

Declaration on Generative AI. During the preparation of this work, the author(s) utilized Generative AI tools to ensure grammatical correctness and improve sentence structure. Following the use of these tools, the authors thoroughly reviewed the content to the best of their knowledge.

Acknowledgment. This work has been supported by FAST, the Finnish Software Engineering Doctoral Research Network, funded by the Ministry of Education and Culture, Finland. And also, the SE4GD - Software Engineers for Green Deal program under Grant 619839 from the Erasmus Mundus Instrument of the European Union.

References

1. Arora, C., Grundy, J., Abdelrazek, M.: Advancing requirements engineering through generative AI: assessing the role of LLMs. In: Nguyen-Duc, A., Abrahamsson, P., Khomh, F. (eds.) Generative AI for Effective Software Development. Springer, Cham (2024). https://doi.org/10.1007/978-3-031-55642-5_6
2. Barzamini, H., Nazaritiji, F., Brockmann, A., Ferdowsi, H., Rahimi, M.: An AI-driven requirements engineering framework tailored for evaluating AI-based software. In: 2025 IEEE/ACM 4th International Conference on AI Engineering–Software Engineering for AI (CAIN), pp. 138–149. IEEE (2025)

3. Becker, C., et al.: Sustainability design and software: the Karlskrona Manifesto. In: 2015 IEEE/ACM 37th IEEE International Conference on Software Engineering, vol. 2, pp. 467–476. IEEE (2015)
4. Becker, C., et al.: Requirements: the key to sustainability. IEEE Softw. **33**(1), 56–65 (2016). https://doi.org/10.1109/MS.2015.158
5. Betz, S., et al.: Lessons learned from developing a sustainability awareness framework for software engineering using design science. ACM Trans. Softw. Eng. Methodol. **33**(5), 1–39 (2024)
6. Binkhonain, M., Zhao, L.: A review of machine learning algorithms for identification and classification of non-functional requirements. Exp. Syst. Appl. X **1**, 100001 (2019)
7. Brockenbrough, A., Feild, H., Salinas, D.: Exploring LLMs impact on student-created user stories and acceptance testing in software development. In: Proceedings of the 56th ACM Technical Symposium on Computer Science Education, SIGCSETS 2025, vol. 2, pp. 1401–1402. ACM, New York (2025)
8. Chitchyan, R., et al.: Sustainability design in requirements engineering: state of practice. In: Proceedings of the 38th International Conference on Software Engineering Companion, pp. 533–542 (2016)
9. Cohn, M.: User Stories Applied: For Agile Software Development. Addison-Wesley Professional (2004)
10. Dos Santos, C.A., Bouchard, K., Minetto Napoleão, B.: Automatic user story generation: a comprehensive systematic literature review. Int. J. Data Sci. Anal. **20**(1), 1–24 (2025)
11. Endres, M., Fakhoury, S., Chakraborty, S., Lahiri, S.K.: Can large language models transform natural language intent into formal method postconditions? Proc. ACM Softw. Eng. **1**(FSE) (2024). https://doi.org/10.1145/3660791
12. Gorer, B., Aydemir, F.B.: GPT-powered elicitation interview script generator for requirements engineering training. arXiv arXiv:2406.11439 [cs], June 2024. https://doi.org/10.48550/arXiv.2406.11439
13. Hevner, A.: A three cycle view of design science research. Scand. J. Inf. Syst. **19**(2), 87–92 (2007)
14. Hussain, A., Mkpojiogu, E., Kamal, F.: The role of requirements in the success or failure of software projects. Int. Rev. Manag. Mark. **6**, 306–311 (2016)
15. Inam, A.: A Study of requirements engineering practices among software developers at uum information technology. Master's thesis, Universiti Utara Malaysia, Malaysia (2015)
16. Inayat, I., Salim, S., Marczak, S., Daneva, M., Shamshirband, S.: A systematic literature review on agile requirements engineering practices and challenges. Comput. Hum. Behav. **51B**, 915–929 (2015)
17. Kamata, M., Tamai, T.: How does requirements quality relate to project success or failure? In: 15th IEEE International Requirements Engineering Conference, RE 2007, pp. 69–78 (2007)
18. Kosmyna, N., et al.: Your brain on ChatGPT: accumulation of cognitive debt when using an ai assistant for essay writing task. arXiv preprint arXiv:2506.08872 (2025)
19. Kurtanović, Z., Maalej, W.: Automatically classifying functional and non-functional requirements using supervised machine learning. In: 2017 IEEE 25th International Requirements Engineering Conference (RE), pp. 490–495. IEEE (2017)
20. Lago, P., Koçak, S., Crnkovic, I., Penzenstadler, B.: Framing sustainability as a property of software quality. Commun. ACM **58**(10), 70–78 (2015)

21. Laplante, P.A., Kassab, M.: Requirements Engineering for Software and Systems, 4th edn. Auerbach Publications (2022)
22. Lyutov, A., Uygun, Y., Hütt, M.: Managing workflow of customer requirements using machine learning. Comput. Ind. **109**, 215–225 (2019)
23. Myllynen, S., Suominen, I., Raunio, T., Karell, R., Lahtinen, J.: Developing and implementing artificial intelligence-based classifier for requirements engineering. J. Nucl. Eng. Radiat. Sci. **7**(4), 041201 (2021)
24. Oyedeji, S., Naqvi, B., Penzenstadler, B., Adisa, M.O., Abdulkareem, M., Seffah, A.: The interplay between usability, sustainability and green aspects: a design case study from a developing country. In: ICT4S (2019)
25. Oyedeji, S., Shamshiri, H., Adisa, M.O., Capilla, R., Chitchyan, R.: Integrating sustainability into scrum agile software development: an action research approach. In: Papatheocharous, E., Farshidi, S., Jansen, S., Hyrynsalmi, S. (eds) Software Business, ICSOB 2024. LNBIP, vol. 539, pp. 236–250. Springer, Cham (2024). https://doi.org/10.1007/978-3-031-85849-9_20
26. Parra, E., et al.: A methodology for the classification of quality of requirements using machine learning techniques. Inf. Softw. Technol. **67**, 180–195 (2015)
27. Penzenstadler, B., Femmer, H.: A generic model for sustainability with process- and product-specific instances. In: Proceedings of the 2013 Workshop on Green in/by Software Engineering, GIBSE '13, pp. 3–8. ACM, New York (2013)
28. Penzenstadler, B., Raturi, A., Richardson, D., Tomlinson, B.: Safety, security, now sustainability: the nonfunctional requirement for the 21st century. IEEE Softw. **31**(3), 40–47 (2014)
29. Rahman, T., Zhu, Y.: Automated user story generation with test case specification using large language model. arXiv preprint arXiv:2404.01558 (2024). https://doi.org/10.48550/arXiv.2404.01558
30. Raturi, A., Penzenstadler, B., Tomlinson, B., Richardson, D.: Developing a sustainability non-functional requirements framework. In: Proceedings of the 3rd International Workshop on Green and Sustainable Software, pp. 1–8 (2014)
31. Ronanki, K., Cabrero-Daniel, B., Berger, C.: ChatGPT as a tool for user story quality evaluation. In: Kruchten, P., Gregory, P. (eds.) Agile Processes in Software Engineering and Extreme Programming – Workshops, XP XP 2022 2023. LNBIP, vol. 489. Springer, Cham (2024). https://doi.org/10.1007/978-3-031-48550-3_17
32. Sami, M., Waseem, M., Zhang, Z., Rasheed, Z., Systä, K., Abrahamsson, P.: AI based multiagent approach for requirements elicitation and analysis. arXiv preprint arXiv:2409.00038 (2024). https://doi.org/10.48550/arXiv.2409.00038
33. dos Santos, C.: Leveraging text generation for enhanced user story quality. Ph.D. thesis, Université du Québec à Chicoutimi, Chicoutimi (2025). https://constellation.uqac.ca/id/eprint/10176/
34. Simon, H.: The Sciences of the Artificial, 3rd edn. MIT Press, Cambridge, MA (1996)
35. Swarnalatha, K., Srinivasan, G., Dravid, N., Kasera, R., Sharma, K.: A survey on software requirements engineering for real time projects based on customer requirements. Int. J. Adv. Res. Comput. Commun. Eng. **3**(1), 5045–5050 (2014)
36. Tikayat Ray, A., Cole, B.F., Pinon Fischer, O.J., Bhat, A.P., White, R.T., Mavris, D.N.: Agile methodology for the standardization of engineering requirements using large language models. Systems **11**(7), 352 (2023). https://doi.org/10.3390/systems11070352
37. Xie, D., et al.: How effective are large language models in generating software specifications? pp. 1–12 (2025). https://doi.org/10.1109/SANER64311.2025.00014

38. Xu, Z., Jain, S., Kankanhalli, M.: Hallucination is inevitable: an innate limitation of large language models. arXiv preprint arXiv:2401.11817 (2024)
39. Zhang, Z., Rayhan, M., Herda, T., Goisauf, M., Abrahamsson, P.: LLM-based agents for automating the enhancement of user story quality: an early report. In: Šmite, D., Guerra, E., Wang, X., Marchesi, M., Gregory, P. (eds.) XP 2024. LNBIP, pp. 117–126. Springer, Cham (2024). https://doi.org/10.1007/978-3-031-61154-4_8

Narrative AI Strategies for Media, Ethics and Higher Education Impulse Perspectives from Practice Based Media Education

Marcus Simon(✉) and Daniel Khafif

International School of Management, Karlstraße 35, 80333 München, Germany
marcus.simon@ism.de, Daniel.khafif@dozent.ism.de

Abstract. The transformation of narrative creation, authorship, and authenticity in the age of Generative AI is not merely a technological shift, but a cultural, epistemic, and ethical realignment. This paper argues that this transformation requires a threefold competence profile—technical proficiency, narrative design capability, and ethical reflexivity—cultivated in both higher education and corporate practice. This motive connects interdisciplinary teaching with strategic implications for communication, marketing, and oragnisational governance, bridging theory and real-world applications.

Keywords: GenAI · narrative creation · media ethics · higher education · corporate communication

1 Introduction and Motivation

The widespread adoption of Generative Artificial Intelligence (GenAI) technologies is reshaping core paradigms of narration, authorship, and authenticity in both media and academic discourse. As digital transformation accelerates, higher education institutions are not only challenged to incorporate GenAI technically, but also to reflect on its ethical, epistemic, and didactic implications. This short paper draws on practice-based teaching experiences from interdisciplinary media and business programs at International School of Management (ISM) Munich. It presents a conceptual and exploratory framework for integrating GenAI tools (e.g., GPT-5, Midjourney, ElevenLabs, Elicit, Perplexity) in educational formats that foster narrative literacy, media ethics, and innovation capability. This article pursues a multi-method conceptual approach based on media ethics, AI governance, and narrative theory. This threefold concept (see info box in Chap. 4) covers (1) conceptual foundations, (2) practical applications in academic education, and (3) narrative implications for business practice.

The aim of this paper is to stimulate discussion and initiate empirical research in the future. The text itself, however, merely aims to provide a conceptual framework for more in-depth scientific studies.

G. Herzwurm et al. (Eds.): ICSOB 2025, LNBIP 574, pp. 230–238, 2026.
https://doi.org/10.1007/978-3-032-14518-5_18

2 Conceptual Foundations

Media shape human thinking and perception. It is not the content of a medium that is decisive, but the medium itself that changes how we think and communicate [1]. This means an unconscious, gradual shaping of consciousness: media determine which of our senses become more pronounced and which become "impoverished." When a sensory ability is technologically outsourced, the corresponding sensory capacity in humans often atrophies. For example, the cognitive ability to remember declines with the cultural technique of writing, as memory is externalized as a "data set." The new "medium" GenAI is already influencing the way we think and how we perceive content.

In this article, we understand GenAI as systems that generate new content based on existing training data: text, images, videos, sound. They are characterized by pattern recognition and operate with statistical models of probability distribution. The decisive factor is that the creative act is no longer performed purely by humans, but co-productively with machines. This raises the question of the role of humans in the future creation of content. Specifically, we must ask: How does GenAI change expectations regarding authenticity, authorship, and meaning in narrative areas?

The fact that human intelligence cannot (yet) be replaced by AI is also evident in Douglas R. Hofstadter's concept of narrative cognition [2]. According to Hofstadter, human thinking and understanding are based essentially on the formation and recognition of analogies and categories—that is, our consciousness constructs meaning by understanding experiences as stories and patterns and linking them together. Hofstadter sees analogy as the foundation of human cognition: when we experience new situations, we constantly draw on previous experiences by making analogies and thus linking new concepts with familiar ones. Every term and concept is "woven" from a multitude of unconscious analogies that shape our understanding of the world. Language, concept formation, and understanding are not clearly defined, fixed processes, but dynamic, context-dependent, and narrative: words, meanings, and categories are fluid and ascend from relationships, not from static definitions. Meaning arises from a combination of thinking, remembering, and categorizing, from the "continuous formation of analogies, from patterns", and from "narratives" (structures that develop over time) [3]. Meaning and consciousness are not a rigid sum of information, but rather the work of dynamic narrative connections—the telling, recognizing, and reinterpreting of patterns is at the heart of the human mind.

GenAI is not like a human entity, but works with a predefined set of training data and defined rules that are processed. Such Information systems change how knowledge is generated, disseminated, and validated. This is where Luciano Floridi comes in with his epistemological reflections. Floridi understands information as a structural entity, not merely as a representation of facts. He describes information as "well-formed, meaningful, and truthful data" [4]. This definition allows for a clear distinction between raw data and epistemically relevant information. Floridi introduces the term "infosphere," which encompasses the totality of all information-processing entities, processes, and environments—i.e., humans, machines, and digital infrastructures.

This means that information systems are not just tools, but part of our cognitive environment. They influence how we access the world and construct knowledge. Floridi emphasizes that in modern information systems, knowledge is increasingly generated in a decentralized manner. This is evident in the phenomenon of distributed cognition, where knowledge no longer arises exclusively within the human mind, but emerges from the interaction between humans and machines. Search engines, AI systems, and recommendation algorithms, for example, play an active role in shaping what we know and how we think. At the same time, the concept of epistemic delegation highlights our growing tendency to transfer epistemic tasks—such as recognizing patterns, classifying data, or evaluating information—to technological systems. In doing so, we rely on these systems not only to provide information, but also to perform parts of the reasoning process itself, thereby reshaping the very nature of human knowledge production.

This ties in with the ideas of Ted Striphas, who describes a fundamental transformation of cultural processes through the growing influence of algorithms with his concept of algorithmic culture [5]. Whereas in the past, people (e.g., editors, PR professionals, marketers) made cultural selection decisions, algorithm-based systems are increasingly taking over this role. Accordingly, social discourse today is increasingly shaped by algorithmic systems that structure processes such as curation, selection, classification, and circulation of content. Algorithms not only act as technical tools, but also decide what is considered relevant, visible, and significant. Algorithms define trends, shape attitudes and opinions, and change cultural practices. They become carriers of meanings and norms and influence how people orient themselves in the digital world. In doing so, they operate in a non-transparent manner and as a kind of black box, which limits users' ability to critique and reflect.

Against this backdrop, the question of professional and ethical training in an academic context arises anew. What skills and abilities will university graduates need in the future when dealing with GenAI? How will they be enabled to assess the quality of AI-generated content and consider its ethical implications? We will explore these questions in the following two chapters, first by establishing links to teaching practice at universities and then by addressing the changed conditions in business practice.

3 Practical Relevance in Academic Education

Several recent studies explore the role of GenAI in higher education. Singh and Huang [6] compare human and AI-generated content in marketing storyboards: while humans bring depth, adaptability, and emotional nuance, AI delivers speed, scalability, and consistency—but struggles with contextual interpretation and transparency. Pirjan and Petroşanu [7] find that large language models in seminars can boost engagement and critical thinking if combined with human oversight to mitigate bias, inaccuracies, and privacy concerns. Stoyanova and Angelova [8] emphasize that adaptive AI learning systems improve engagement but require governance and ethical safeguards. Slepchuk and John [9], Flink et al. [10], and Sihi and Ryan [11] contribute further perspectives on AI's effective and responsible integration in teaching and career development.

Beyond these findings, our teaching experience suggests that academic programs should shift focus from if to how GenAI is used—specifically, on the skills graduates must acquire to thrive in AI-augmented professions. According to the World Economic Forum [12], GenAI can readily replace tasks such as translations, summaries, simple design, data analysis, and basic coding. More resistant to automation are capabilities like strategic thinking, situational judgement, creativity, emotional intelligence, and physical-world interactions (e.g., coaching, consulting). From this follows a competency profile for graduates in marketing and communication (see Table 1).

Table 1. Competency profile for graduates (marketing & communication)

Dimension	Description	Examples/Reference
Creativity & strategic thinking	Ability to design novel, context-aware solutions; think beyond templates	Campaign ideation, brand storytelling
Curiosity & openness to technology	Proactive exploration of AI tools and workflows	Piloting new GenAI-based content systems
Critical reflection	Assessing AI outputs for accuracy, bias, and ethical soundness	Fact-checking, bias detection
Data-sensitive mindset	Understanding and respecting data privacy, security, and governance rules	GDPR compliance, secure data handling
Media literacy	Reflecting on media, recognizing production conditions, and designing own messages	Media criticism, design projects
Prompt literacy	Crafting precise, context-sensitive prompts; managing prompt libraries	Creative briefs, multi-step task prompts
Post-processing skills	Refining AI-generated text, images, and datasets for final delivery	Editing, visual adaptation
Cybersecurity awareness	Recognizing vulnerabilities in AI workflows	Secure collaboration tools

Thus, University curricula should address four developmental dimensions:

1. Understanding—Basic knowledge of how GenAI systems function.
2. Application—Intentional control and use of GenAI in creative, collaborative processes.
3. Reflection—Critical review, post-processing, and quality assurance of AI outputs.
4. Co-creation—Building prompt libraries, adapting AI tools to specific contexts.

Integrating GenAI into education inevitably raises ethical and legal questions [13, 14]. Key teaching topics include:

- Sustainability of AI use (e.g., energy consumption).
- Accessibility and inclusion.
- Competition and market diversity.
- Privacy protection, data security, and transparency of data use.

- AI content labelling.
- Copyright and intellectual property of training data and outputs.
- Distribution of value from AI-generated content.
- Liability and risk management for AI-related legal violations.

4 Narrative Implications for Business Practice

4.1 Strategic Shift: From Production to Narrative Orchestration

GenAI is transforming marketing and corporate communication by automating a wide range of repetitive tasks—from standard copy to basic image editing and routine reports [15] The traditional paradigm, which rewarded manual production skills such as writing press releases, designing websites, or producing product imagery, is giving way to a model in which strategic value lies in story design, ethical framing, and the orchestration of coherent narrative worlds. As documented by AG CommTech [16], this shift replaces linear, content-driven workflows with adaptive, data-informed storytelling ecosystems in which human creativity and machine intelligence operate in tandem.

The conceptual foundation draws on narrative cognition [2], media philosophy [1, 3], the epistemology of information [4, 17], and algorithmic culture [5, 6], following the threefold guiding structure: Thesis → Education → Practice (see Table 2).

Table 2. The red treat – from theory to practice

Dimension	Focus & Application	Key References
Thesis [Narrative cognition & media logic explain why GenAI shifts meaning production.]	Narrative cognition and media logic explain why GenAI shifts meaning production. Cognitive and media-theoretical foundations show how AI alters meaning-making, demanding new interpretive and design frameworks	Hofstadter & Sander (2013); McLuhan (2001); Floridi (2005, 2021); Striphas (2015)
Education [Competencies in higher education]	Competencies in higher education: development of prompt literacy, reflective practice, co-creation skills, and ethical/governance awareness within academic curricula. These skills prepare graduates for AI-augmented communication environments	AG CommTech (2025); UNESCO (2025)

(*continued*)

Table 2. *(continued)*

Dimension	Focus & Application	Key References
Practice [Translation into business applications.]	Translation into business applications: narrative orchestration through worldbuilding, content operations, and role-play ethics—anchored in measurable processes (KPIs) and governance frameworks	AG CommTech (2025); Singh & Huang (2025)

4.2 Core Competencies in the AI-Augmented Era

Three interlinked capabilities are essential for thriving in AI-augmented communication:

- **Worldbuilding**: Organizations leverage GenAI to architect immersive narrative universes, ensuring thematic consistency across all touchpoints. This supports strategic brand leadership but must be grounded in authentic corporate practice to avoid "marketing myths." Participatory worldbuilding fosters engagement and authenticity, while speculative storytelling enables strategic foresight.
- **Prompt Literacy**: Crafting precise, context-aware prompts is now a foundational skill, analogous to traditional literacy. Prompt libraries and guidelines help maintain brand voice and content quality. However, over-standardization risks stifling creativity and fostering dependence on proprietary AI platforms. Educational initiatives increasingly integrate prompt engineering as a core competency [19]).
- **Ethical Framing:** Ethics-by-design is promoted via role-play and simulation, modeling diverse stakeholder perspectives before message release. Robust governance, transparency, and ethical leadership are critical for responsible AI use [17, 18] Simulations and experiential labs in higher education enhance crisis readiness and ethical awareness. Trust depends on human oversight and clear governance frameworks.

4.3 Applied Use Case: Story Lenses

Building upon the conceptual and educational foundations outlined above, the following use case illustrates how these competencies are operationalized in a software-intensive environment. The Story Lenses project exemplifies how the conceptual triad of worldbuilding, prompt literacy, and ethical framing can be operationalized within a software-intensive communication environment. Developed as part of an applied research initiative at the International School of Management (ISM Munich), the non-commercial beta platform Story Lenses (storylenses.app/de) explores narrative cognition and AI-assisted communication design. Drawing on Hofstadter's theory of analogy and recursive cognition, the system iteratively compares AI-generated and human-authored drafts. This recursive feedback fosters narrative self-reflection, turning human–machine interaction into a loop of adaptation and refinement.

The underlying architecture integrates three interlinked layers: (1) a narrative-linguistic layer capturing contextual meaning and intertextual coherence; (2) a cognitive-analytical layer modeling iteration and analogy for adaptive learning; and (3) an ethical-simulation layer providing feedback from multiple stakeholder perspectives (e.g., recruiter, peer, audience) to train judgment and reflective communication ethics.

Story Lenses follows a classical communication journey, progressing from self-definition and problem framing to dialogue, persuasive presentation and reflective integration (Table 3).

Table 3. Dimensions of the story lenses use case

Dimension	Description	Relevance to ICSOB-framework
Technology	GPT-based text & semantics engine, multimodal prompting	Demonstrates software-intensive design
Didactics	Interactive feedback for narrative reflection	Operationalizes prompt literacy
Ethics	Role-play simulation of stakeholder views	Embodies ethical framing
Metrics	Narrative coherence index, prompt efficiency score, AI-human delta	Enables empirical validation
Transfer	Career centers, universities, corporate communication	Connects theory and practice

5 Limitations and Outlook

This discussion paper remains conceptual and exploratory in nature. It outlines an applied framework rather than presenting empirical validation. Future research should take an interdisciplinary approach—at the intersection of communication science, AI ethics, media education, and management studies. Key desiderata are (1) the development of valid competence models for AI augmentation, (2) the measurement of "narrative authenticity" in the interaction between humans and machines, and (3) the establishment of empirically based governance frameworks. This can contribute to a sustainable paradigm shift: from the instrumental use of artificial intelligence to a reflective, responsible, and creative co-evolution of humans and technology.

The evolution of narrative creation in the age of generative AI demonstrates technological acceleration amplifies, rather than replaces, human meaning-making. Throughout this paper, the intersection of technical proficiency, narrative design capability, and ethical reflexivity has been identified as the competence triad connecting education, communication, and organizational strategy.

In practice, hybrid competence ecosystems are required—AI systems can support but never substitute human judgment. Future curricula must therefore integrate prompt literacy, ethical framing, and reflective governance as foundational literacies across disciplines. For organizations, sustainable value depends on aligning machine intelligence with narrative coherence, cultural awareness, and ethical transparency.

References

1. McLuhan, M.: Understanding media: the extensions of man. Routledge, London (2001 [1964])
2. Hofstadter, D.R., Sander, E.: Surfaces & Essences: Analogy as the Fuel & Fire of Thinking. Basic Books, New York (2013)
3. Hofstadter, D.R.: I Am a Strange Loop. Basic Books, New York (2008)
4. Floridi, L.: Is semantic information meaningful data? Philos. Phenomenol. Res. **70**(2), 351–370 (2005)
5. Striphas, T.: Algorithmic culture. Eur. J. Cult. Stud. **18**(4–5), 395–412 (2015)
6. Singh, P., Huang, L.: AI meets brainstorming: enhancing creativity & collaboration in marketing education. Mark. Educ. Rev. 1–9 (2025). https://doi.org/10.1080/10528008.2025.2501790
7. Pirjan, A., Petroşanu, D.-M.: Exploring large language models in the education process: with a view towards transforming personalized learning. J. Inf. Syst. Oper. Manage. **18**(2), 125–171 (2024)
8. Stoyanova, T., Angelova, M.: Good practices of using artificial intelligence in the digitalization of higher education. Entrep. Sustain. Issues **11**(4), 44–62 (2024)
9. Slepchuk, A.N., John, J.: Exploring perceptions of AI in the marketing classroom: a stimuli–organism–response framework. Mark. Educ. Rev. 1–9 (2025). https://doi.org/10.1080/10528008.2025.2478869
10. Flink, N.A., Black, H.G., Dingus, R.: Explore, identify, & align: utilizing generative AI as a career coach. Mark. Educ. Rev. **35**(2), 1–11 (2024)
11. Sihi, D., Ryan, A.: Crafting & evaluating generative AI prompts: insights from students, educators, & marketers. Mark. Educ. Rev. **35**(2), 1–7 (2024)
12. World Economic Forum [WEF]: The future of jobs report. https://www.weforum.org/publications/the-future-of-jobs-report-2025/digest/ (2025). Last Accessed 11 Aug 2025
13. Ferrell, O.C., Ferrell, L.K.: Building a better world: the role of AI ethics & social responsibility. J. Macromark. **44**(4), 928–935 (2024)
14. Hermann, E., Puntoni, S.: Generative AI in marketing & principles for ethical design & deployment. J. Public Policy Mark. **44**(3), 332–349 (2025)
15. McKinsey Global Institute: The state of AI: How organisations are rewiring to capture value. https://www.mckinsey.com/~/media/mckinsey/business%20functions/quantumblack/our%20insights/the%20state%20of%20ai/2025/the-state-of-ai-how-organizations-are-rewiring-to-capture-value_final.pdf?ref=filipeoliveira.pt. Last Accessed 11 Aug 2025
16. AG CommTech: Künftige Rollen und Kompetenzen in der Kommunikationsprofession im Wandel der Digitalisierung. https://agcommtech.de/download-bereich/#1753356764941-bc8e79ea-db1b. Last Accessed 11 Aug 2025
17. Floridi, L.: Ethics, Governance, and Policies in Artificial Intelligence. Springer, Heidelberg (2021)
18. UNESCO: Guidance for generative AI in education and research. https://www.unesco.org/en/articles/guidance-generative-ai-education-and-research. Last Accessed 11 Aug 2025

The Role of AI in Software Release Management

Muhammad Faizan Tahir, Andrey Saltan(✉), and Sami Hyrynsalmi

LUT University, Lahti, Finland
{andrey.saltan,sami.hyrynsalmi}@lut.fi

Abstract. Software release management coordinates planning, gating, deployment and monitoring in CI/CD-intensive environments where rapid iteration compresses decision windows and increases risk. This paper examines how *Analytical AI* and *Generative AI* support those decisions. Based on qualitative interviews with industry experts, we identify key benefits of AI integration, such as increased automation of repetitive tasks, more efficient resource allocation, enhanced risk forecasting, and improved over-all decision-making. These advances support faster, more reliable software deployments by streamlining processes and enabling data-driven insights. However, the study also highlights significant hurdles to effective AI/ML adoption, including integration complexity, the opacity of AI models, and organizational resistance. Addressing these challenges proves essential for realizing the full potential of AI in software release management. By examining both the practical advantages and limitations, this research offers actionable guidance for industry practitioners and contributes to broader discussions on the responsible application of AI in contemporary software product management.

Keywords: Release Management · Analytical AI · Generative AI

1 Introduction

Software release management links product intent with operational reality: it plans scope and cadence, stabilizes changes, governs deployment, and monitors outcomes so that evolving requirements are delivered reliably and on time [8,9]. In Agile/DevOps settings, releases are smaller and more frequent, supported by CI/CD pipelines and extensive automation [4–6]. Shorter lead times enrich feedback but also push more choices toward production, intensifying coordination across engineering, operations, security, and product [3]. Under tight decision windows, release gates must integrate heterogeneous signals—quality, reliability, interoperability, security, compliance, and market timing—while remaining auditable and aligned with organizational risk tolerances.

Recent advances in Artificial Intelligence offer new instruments for these decisions. To avoid terminological ambiguity, we use *AI* as an umbrella and distinguish two classes relevant to release work. *Analytical AI* denotes predictive and diagnostic models—often labeled "ML"—that learn from historical and

G. Herzwurm et al. (Eds.): ICSOB 2025, LNBIP 574, pp. 239–247, 2026.
https://doi.org/10.1007/978-3-032-14518-5_19

live telemetry to forecast failure risk, prioritize tests and fixes, detect anomalies, and optimize schedules and resources. *Generative AI* denotes language and code models that produce human-readable text and code, useful for summarizing logs and change impact, drafting release communications and runbooks, assisting code reviews and test scaffolds. This complements long-standing SPM work that frames release management as balancing stakeholder insight with computational decision support [7].

Adopting either type of AI is nontrivial. Analytical AI models depend on representative, well-labeled data and stable telemetry schemas; Generative AI systems raise questions of accuracy, provenance, and governance. Both surface explainability and accountability concerns that shape stakeholder trust and regulatory posture [1]. Integration with existing CI/CD toolchains, decision rights, and organizational cadences is itself an engineering and change-management effort [3,6].

This paper develops an integrated, evidence-based understanding of how AI supports decision-making in software release management and what limits its effective use. We investigate the problem empirically through a qualitative study of seven industry professionals from South Asian country (product managers, senior software engineers, and a director of engineering) using semi-structured interviews and thematic analysis. Across cases, automation/efficiency and predictive capability are the most frequently cited benefits, while integration complexity, transparency/black-box concerns, data quality, and human/organizational factors dominate the constraint set.

The research is driven by two research questions that emphasize decision quality and practical feasibility: *RQ1: In what concrete ways do Analytical and Generative AI improve decision quality in software release management? RQ2: What technical, organizational, and governance constraints impede successful adoption of Analytical and Generative AI in software release management?*. The scope of this early stage study is deliberately decision-focused: we analyze how teams select features and content for releases, schedule and coordinate deployments, manage risk and compliance, and determine readiness across environments. We do not attempt an exhaustive evaluation of all development methodologies or platforms. Findings are qualitative and context-dependent; organizations vary widely in size, industry, regulatory posture, and toolchains, and the technology landscape continues to evolve. Nevertheless, the patterns we report offer actionable guidance for practitioners and a research agenda for the community.

2 Background

Software release management is the structured coordination of planning, stabilizing, scheduling, deploying, and monitoring software changes so that evolving requirements are integrated safely and on time [8,9]. In plan-driven lifecycles these activities are largely sequential; in Agile/DevOps they interleave to enable frequent iterations and rapid feedback [6]. Across both settings, release management links engineering and business concerns by deciding *what* is released, *when* it is released, and *under which risk posture*, aligning code changes, operational readiness, compliance, and expectations.

Modern practice surrounds these decisions with automation. Version control coordinates parallel work; CI/CD pipelines build, test, and promote artifacts; infrastructure-as-code and containerization standardize environments; progressive delivery (canary, blue/green) limits blast radius [4–6]. These practices shorten lead times and reduce toil but also concentrate consequential choices near production: teams must pick cadence and scope, set gate thresholds, and decide when to pause, roll back, or proceed.

Decision-making remains a "wicked problem" — a pattern echoed in SPM research that calls for formalized, evidence-based processes to counter ad-hoc 'gut-feeling' choices [10]. Teams balance quality, reliability, interoperability, and security against market timing, customer commitments, and regulation [3,11]. Classical prioritization presumes stable, comparable requirements, yet dependencies, shifting stakeholder preferences, and incident learnings render the space non-stationary [11]. In practice, decisions interleave across horizons: near-term gating (pass/fail thresholds, rollbacks), mid-term scheduling and scope, and longer-term risk posture (technical debt, observability, capacity).

Recent advances in Artificial Intelligence (AI) add new instruments. We use *AI* as an umbrella and distinguish two complementary types. *Analytical AI*—predictive/diagnostic modeling over historical and live telemetry—forecasts incident risk, prioritizes tests and fixes, detects anomalies, and optimizes schedules/resources. *Generative AI*—language/code models—summarizes change impact and logs, drafts release communications and runbooks, assists code reviews and test scaffolds, and supports conversational diagnosis. Operationally, Analytical AI models integrate at quantitative gates in CI/CD, whereas Generative AI systems augment human coordination and sense-making [2].

Adoption is gated by well-documented constraints. Analytical AI depends on reliable, representative telemetry; fragmented logs, sparse labels, and schema drift degrade signal-to-noise and yield brittle models. Integration with existing pipelines and approval flows adds engineering overhead; governance demands (auditability, privacy, safety) require explainable outputs where gate decisions affect users or regulated processes [1,3]. Generative AI systems raise additional concerns around accuracy, provenance, and prompt-induced variability, making human-in-the-loop review essential for high-stakes steps. Organizational factors—skills, role clarity, change fatigue, and perceptions of "black-box" automation—shape trust and uptake as much as technical performance. These constraints motivate guardrails such as data governance and observability, explainability-by-design with evidence bundling, pilotization before scale, and native CI/CD integration.

In summary, release management decisions increasingly occur inside automated pipelines yet still require multi-objective trade-offs under uncertainty. Analytical AI can predict, prioritize, and detect at quantitative gates; generative AI can summarize, document, and assist where language and coordination dominate. What remains under-specified—both in practice and in prior work—is how these two types are combined in real release management, which decisions they reliably improve today, and which guardrails make adoption dependable. This study addresses these gaps empirically.

Table 1. Study participants

Interview participant	Experience (years)	Role
Person A	3	Product Manager
Person B	5+	Sr. Software Engineer
Person C	5+	Director of Engineering
Person D	4	Product Manager
Person E	5+	Sr. Software Engineer
Person F	5+	Sr. Software Engineer—AI
Person G	5+	Sr. Software Engineer

3 Methodology

This study *adopts* a qualitative, interpretivist multiple-expert design to explain how Analytical and Generative AI support decision-making in software release management and what constrains their adoption. We build on a data of seven semi-structured interviews and extend the analytic frame by tagging each AI reference as Analytical vs. Generative.

Sampling and Context. We used purposeful sampling to recruit practitioners who (i) decide software release scope/cadence or own gating signals, (ii) operate with Agile/DevOps and CI/CD, and (iii) have more than 3 years of experience with software product management. Seven participants (A–G) span fintech, product, and services organizations (Table 1).

Interview Protocol. Semi-structured interviews (40–45 min, video conference) followed a guide aligned with the literature review and the research questions. The interview covered: (1) current release management practices, cadences, and bottlenecks; (2) instrumentation and decision signals at each stage of the pipeline; (3) existing/planned use of AI; (4) perceived benefits and concrete examples; (5) constraints (data, integration, explainability, organizational readiness); (6) guardrails and adoption pathways (pilots, human-in-the-loop, audit trails). Probes elicited critical incidents (e.g., a recent rollback or canary failure) and asked respondents to walk through artifacts they use (dashboards, runbooks, release notes) so that claims could be anchored to specific practices.

Analysis Approach. The empirical base comprises seven interview transcripts plus researcher memos. We performed reflexive thematic analysis in six phases, implemented in NVivo and documented with memos and versioned codebooks. First-cycle coding was largely open-coding to preserve practitioner language; code units ranged from a clause to a paragraph, with each segment optionally receiving multiple tags (e.g., *Analytical AI, gating, risk forecasting*). Second-cycle coding clustered first-order codes into conceptually distinct themes and then organized them into four reporting buckets: *benefits, constraints*, and *adoption practices/guardrails.*

Table 2. Weighted benefits codes by participant (A–G) and total

	A	B	C	D	E	F	G	Total
Automation	3	1	1	1	3	3	2	**14**
Efficiency	2	2	1	2	3	3	0	**13**
Decision-making (data-driven)	0	1	1	0	2	2	1	**7**
Predictive capabilities	2	1	0	1	1	1	0	**6**
Future promise of AI	3	1	1	1	0	0	0	**6**
Bug prediction	1	1	0	0	0	0	3	**5**
Prioritization	1	0	1	1	0	0	2	**5**
Strategic focus (time reallocation)	0	2	1	0	1	0	0	**4**
Code quality	1	0	0	0	0	0	3	**4**
Accuracy	1	2	0	0	0	1	0	**4**
Time-to-market	1	0	0	0	0	0	0	**1**

4 Results and Discussion

Benefits and Promises of AI in Software Release Management. As depicted in Table 2, two themes dominate the coded benefits: *automation of repetitive work* in build–test–deploy and monitoring, and *efficiency* in throughput and cross-team coordination. Participants stressed that Analytical AI reduces manual checks by surfacing high-risk changes and noisy signals. "AI-powered monitoring tools can identify high-risk areas and reduce manual effort," noted Person A. Person B similarly emphasized that anomaly detection and test prioritization "enhance decision-making efficiency by processing large datasets." Beyond throughput, interviewees described improvements to *decision quality*: models help find the real numbers" behind go/no-go and rollback calls by combining historical defects, pipeline telemetry, and user-impact indicators. Additional but less frequent codes capture *bug prediction, prioritization* of tests/fixes by expected risk reduction, *code-quality* gains via automated checks, and modest signals on *time-to-market.* Participants also expressed cautious optimism about the *future promise* of AI in release management, anticipating tighter CI/CD integration and more adaptive post-release monitoring. These forward-looking statements often coincided with requests for stronger telemetry and clearer rationales for recommendations.

Formally addressing RQ1—how do Analytical and Generative AI improve decision quality in software release management?—improvements arise through three interacting mechanisms:

1. **Automation and shorter feedback cycles.** Analytical AI removes repetitive checks (test re-ordering, flaky-test suppression, canary comparisons) and turns diffuse telemetry into actionable signals at gates. This aligns with CI/CD practices and progressive delivery controls reported in industry.
2. **Predictive/diagnostic assistance.** Risk scoring based on historical incidents, change metadata, and runtime KPIs makes readiness and rollback decisions more evidence-based. This mechanism is consistent with work linking disciplined release management practices to improved delivery outcomes.
3. **Decision scaffolding and coordination.** Generative AI reduces cognitive and coordination overhead by drafting change-impact summaries, risk registers, runbooks, and stakeholder updates—keeping multidisciplinary actors aligned without displacing human authority.

Limitations and Challenges of AI Implementation. Despite the strong potential, participants also identified various barriers to effective AI/ML adoption summarized in Table 3. The most salient challenges were *integration complexity* and *transparency/trust.* Teams reported substantial effort to connect model outputs to existing pipelines, dashboards, and approval flows; off-the-shelf tools "rarely fit neatly" without custom integration. "Teams are hesitant to trust AI models if they don't understand how decisions are made," said Person B. Human and organizational factors—skills, role clarity, concerns about displacement, and change fatigue—moderated scope and pace of adoption. Cost (tools, skills, infrastructure) and *data quality/coverage* were also reported, though less frequently. Some interviewees warned against *over-reliance* on automation in ambiguous situations. Interviewees described pragmatic mitigations already in use: *pilots* in low-risk contexts to demonstrate value and tune interfaces; targeted improvements to *data coverage* for high-signal metrics; and maintaining *human oversight* for high-stakes gates. Transparency was articulated in two registers: (i) traceable rationales for recommendations ("why this build should wait") and (ii) *auditability* for regulated contexts. Both were repeatedly cited as prerequisites for trust.

Addressing RQ2—what technical, organizational, and governance constraints impede successful adoption of Analytical and Generative AI in software release management?—three constraint families dominate the evidence:

- **Integration and data readiness.** Connecting models to heterogeneous pipelines, metrics stores, and approval paths is nontrivial; weak telemetry and schema drift degrade model reliability.
- **Transparency and trust.** Stakeholders require traceable rationales and auditability—especially where decisions affect users or regulated processes.

Table 3. Weighted challenges codes by participant (A–G) and total

	A	B	C	D	E	F	G	Total
Integration complexity	5	0	0	5	2	0	0	**12**
Transparency (explainability/trust)	0	2	1	2	0	4	1	**10**
Human factors (skills, resistance)	3	1	1	1	1	1	1	**9**
Pilot projects (as mitigation)	1	1	0	1	1	0	0	**4**
Cost (tools, skills, infra)	0	1	1	0	1	1	0	**4**
Data quality/coverage	0	1	0	0	1	0	0	**2**
Explainable-AI (explicit demand)	0	0	0	0	1	0	0	**1**
Over-reliance on automation	0	1	0	0	0	0	0	**1**

This maps to governance expectations for explainability and post-deployment monitoring.

- **Human and organizational factors.** Skills, role clarity, and attitudes toward automation shape acceptance. Interviewees favored staged adoption, preserved human-in-the-loop control for high-impact gates, and explicit "kill switches" to contain automated actions.

5 Implications and Conclusion

This study examined AI's role in software release management by distinguishing *Analytical* from *Generative* AI capabilities and situating both within contemporary Agile/DevOps practice. Across seven practitioner interviews, a clear division of labor emerged. Analytical AI is already dependable at quantitative gates—forecasting incidents and regressions, detecting anomalies in canary and post-release monitoring, prioritizing tests and fixes, and optimizing schedules and resources—matching the most frequent benefit codes (automation, efficiency, predictive capability). Generative AI adds leverage where language and coordination dominate: summarizing change impact, drafting release notes and runbooks, assisting code reviews and test scaffolds, and accelerating incident timelines. Adoption hinges on guardrails: treat telemetry as a product; prefer explainability-by-design with evidence bundling; keep humans in the loop for high-stakes gates; pilot before scale; and integrate natively within CI/CD.

Implications for Practice. For practitioners, three priorities emerge. First, invest in "decision plumbing" before "decision models": reliable signals, consistent environments, and auditable runbooks improve outcomes even if model performance is static; this is where most early wins were reported. Second, pair every automated recommendation with an explanation pattern native to the available tools (dashboards, logs, diffs) and require explicit human acknowledgment for high-impact decisions; this responds directly to trust and accountability concerns.

Third, adopt a quarterly "binding constraint" cadence that names the most growth- or reliability-limiting bottleneck and concentrates both engineering and AI effort there; interviewees consistently described success when AI was targeted rather than diffuse.

Implications for Research. For researchers, the interview evidence suggests several testable propositions that connect AI practices to operational outcomes: (P1) greater coverage of Analytical AI signals across CI/CD and production monitoring will be associated with lower change-failure rates and faster rollback decisions, controlling for team size and baseline release frequency; (P2) use of explanation patterns that bundle underlying metrics will increase human acceptance of automated recommendations at deployment gates; (P3) staged adoption (pilot → advisory → constrained automation) will correlate with sustained use one year post-introduction; and (P4) combining Analytical AI at gates with Generative assistance for decision documentation will reduce time-to-decision in release management meetings without increasing post-release incident rates. These propositions are grounded in the weighted benefits/challenges and the lifecycle division of labor observed across cases.

Limitations. This work has the typical limitations of qualitative multiple-case designs. The sample privileges depth over breadth (seven professionals in one regional context), relies on self-report, and cannot deliver population estimates. Results should be read as analytic generalizations suitable for theory building and practice guidance, not as universal prescriptions. Future research should pair qualitative insight with quantitative metrics (e.g., change failure rate, mean time to restore, lead time for changes) to test whether teams that adopt the guardrails above realize durable improvements; it should also evaluate Generative AI interventions (release-note generation, test-suggestion prompts, ChatOps co-pilots) in controlled trials to distinguish novelty effects from sustained value.

References

1. Balasubramanian, N., Ye, Y., Xu, M.: Substituting human decision-making with machine learning: implications for organizational learning. Acad. Manag. Rev. **47**(3), 448–465 (2022). https://doi.org/10.5465/amr.2019.0470
2. Basiri, A., Hochstein, L., Jones, N., Tucker, H.: Automating chaos experiments in production. In: 2019 IEEE/ACM 41st International Conference on Software Engineering: Software Engineering in Practice (ICSE-SEIP), pp. 31–40 (2019)
3. Chang, T.C., Lin, Y., Shi, K., Meen, T.H.: Decision making of software release time at different confidence intervals with Ohba's inflection S-shape model. Symmetry **14**(3), 593 (2022)
4. Fhang, M.C.S., Swamy, R.: Best practices in release management of large projects. In: Proceedings of the 2018 7th International Conference on Software and Computer Applications, pp. 51–55. ACM, Kuantan (2018)
5. Herath, I.P., Jayawardena, S., Fadhil, A., Kodagoda, N., Arachchillage, U.S.S.: Streamlining software release process and resource management for microservice-based architecture on multi-cloud. In: 2023 25th International Multitopic Conference (INMIC), Lahore, Pakistan, pp. 1–6 (2023)

6. Karvonen, T., Behutiye, W., Oivo, M., Kuvaja, P.: Systematic literature review on the impacts of agile release engineering practices. Inf. Softw. Technol. **86**, 87–100 (2017). https://doi.org/10.1016/j.infsof.2017.01.009
7. Kittlaus, H.B., Saltan, A.: In memoriam of professor guenther ruhe: contributions to the software product management research and practice. Inf. Softw. Technol. **176**, 107548 (2024). https://doi.org/10.1016/j.infsof.2024.107548
8. Lahtela, A., Jäntti, M.: Challenges and problems in release management process: a case study. In: 2011 IEEE 2nd International Conference on Software Engineering and Service Science, pp. 10–13 (2011). iSSN: 2327-0594
9. Mohamed, S.I.: Software release management evolution - comparative analysis across agile and devopscontinuous delivery. Int. J. Adv. Eng. Res. Sci. **3**(6) (2016)
10. Saltan, A., Jansen, S., Smolander, K.: Decision-making in software product management: identifying research directions from practice. In: Proceedings of the International Workshop on Software-intensive Business (SiBW 2018), CEUR-WS, pp. 164–176 (2018)
11. Svahnberg, M., Gorschek, T., Feldt, R., Torkar, R., Saleem, S.B., Shafique, M.U.: A systematic review on strategic release planning models. Inf. Softw. Technol. **52**(3), 237–248 (2010)

Session "Digital Strategy, Enterprise Architecture, and Value Networks"

Active Personas for Synthetic User Feedback: A Design Science Study

Mario Simaremare(✉) and Henry Edison

Blekinge Institute of Technology, Karlskrona, Sweden
{mario.simaremare,henry.edison}@bth.se

Abstract. *Context*: Securing consistent user feedback is a critical yet resource-intensive challenge in new product development (NPD). Active Personas (APs), user archetypes powered by Generative AI, offer a novel approach to generate realistic user feedback on demand, enabling internal product experimentation. *Objective*: This study evaluates the effectiveness of AP in generating "user" feedback by evaluating the alignment between AP-generated feedback and actual (human) users and investigates how persona and Large Language Model (LLM) choice influence the feedback. *Method*: Adopting a Design Science Research methodology, we designed and developed AP as a novel artifact. We demonstrated and evaluated the artifact in a case of a mobile transport app, creating eight AP instances from two personas and four LLMs. The AP-generated feedback was compared against human feedback from interviews and Google Play reviews using a triangulated analysis based on Nielsen's usability heuristics. *Results*: Our findings reveal a strong alignment between AP and human feedback, with APs effectively identifying various usability and accessibility issues, confirming what the actual users also found. The persona definition significantly dictated the evaluation's criticality, and the choice of LLM further influenced the evaluative stance. *Conclusion*: APs have the potential to augment early-stage usability evaluations and are a viable option for human users for internal experimentation, providing rapid, low-cost feedback. While they supplement, not replace, direct human interaction, this work validates the transformation of personas from static artifacts into dynamic, generative agents for NPD.

Keywords: active personas · user personas · generative ai · user feedback · experimentation · new product development

1 Introduction

User feedback plays a critical role in new product development (NPD) because end users offer invaluable expertise about their lived experiences [17]. In software engineering (SE), development teams integrate user feedback into every phase of the NPD process, from idea validation and requirements engineering to design, testing, and support activities [11,30]. User feedback enables teams to identify real-world requirements, constraints, clarify assumptions, and make

G. Herzwurm et al. (Eds.): ICSOB 2025, LNBIP 574, pp. 251–266, 2026.
https://doi.org/10.1007/978-3-032-14518-5_20

strategic design decisions [27,30]. To structure user feedback, teams generate requirements engineering artifacts such as user scenarios, user stories, concept mind maps, and user personas [25]. Among these artifacts, personas vividly capture user characteristics, foster team empathy, and help the team focus design efforts on authentic user profiles [15,29]. Personas also guide participant selection in usability tests, clarify assumptions, and inspire interface and experience design decisions [8,16]. Despite its importance, securing consistent user engagement and substantive feedback at NPD stages remains challenging [16]. Relying on a small, self-selecting group restricts the diversity of viewpoints and risks overlooking critical requirements.

The persona technique has been promoted as a strong tool to understand the needs of potential users. However, this technique is not widely used in the software development industry [3]. Recently, with the emergence of Large Language Models (LLMs) and Generative AI (GenAI), an advanced AI technology capable of creating novel human-generated content [10], several attempts have been made to include personalities into conversational agents in various domains, such as mental health [1] and games [2]. Moreover, several studies have been conducted to develop personas using LLMs [12,20]. A study by Salewski et al. [28] showed that GenAI provides better feedback when it pretends to be a domain expert or persona while performing simple tasks.

To address this gap, Simaremare et al. [32] proposed the concept of Active Personas (APs), dynamic persona instances that generate realistic user feedback. Unlike traditional personas, which are static design documents [8], APs transform these descriptions into dynamic agents that can generate feedback on demand, shifting from passive design references to active evaluation participants.

APs leverage techniques like retrieval-augmented generation (RAG) and fine-tuning [14] to feed persona definitions into multi-modal LLMs. APs can simulate user feedback on demand, empowering teams to rapidly *build, measure, and learn* (BML) through internal experimentation without the logistical overhead of recruiting actual users [27]. This capability would make APs particularly well-suited for internal usability evaluations [4].

This study is built upon the AP concept [32] by answering the following research question: *How effective is Active Personas in generating "user" feedback?* We define effectiveness as the alignment between AP-generated feedback and human user feedback, measured using Nielsen's heuristics. We used Skånetrafiken[1], a transportation-related application running on the Android platform, as a case. We used four multimodal LLMs to power our APs.

This study makes contributions to research and practice. For research, our study provides an empirical evaluation of APs as a practical method for accelerating internal BML cycle. For practice, by transforming personas from static documents into dynamic, generative agents, this research offers a novel paradigm for integrating simulated user feedback into the NPD lifecycle.

[1] https://play.google.com/store/apps/details?id=se.skanetrafiken.washington.

The remainder of this paper is organized as follows. Section 2 elaborates on the study's research method, followed by the results in Sect. 3, and discussion in Sect. 4. The conclusion and future work are laid out in Sect. 5.

2 Research Methodology

We applied the six-phase process model as described in the Design Science Research (DSR) [26] methodology to answer our research question. DSR is a problem-solving paradigm focused on creating and evaluating innovative artifacts to solve real-world problems while contributing new knowledge.

Phase 1 and 2: Problem Identification and Solution Objectives

The problem motivating this research, as discussed earlier in Sect. 1, is the significant challenge development teams face in securing consistent and diverse user feedback throughout the NPD process. This issue is particularly acute for resource-constrained teams, such as software startups [25]. The primary objective was to design a tool capable of generating realistic, contextualized, and actionable user feedback on demand, thereby reducing the reliance on direct, continuous engagement with actual human users. The solution should be efficient, scalable, and capable of representing diverse user perspectives, such as those with specific needs.

Phase 3: Artifact Design and Development

Persona Definition: We adopted and adapted two personas for this study. The first, "Ingrid Henke", a data-driven persona, was adopted from a prior work by Mueller et al. [22] and adapted to emphasize the accessibility needs of a user with a vision impairment. We used the UK Government's guidelines for personas with access needs[2]. The second persona, "Claudio Eriksson", represents an average user: a young adult with moderate tech skills without accessibility needs.

Model Configuration: We developed the APs using four state-of-the-art multimodal LLMs: GPT-5, Claude 4, Gemini 2.5 Pro, and Llama 4 routed through OpenRouter[3] APIs. We used a temperature of 1.0 for each model to balance between creativity and accuracy.

Active Persona Creation: We created eight AP instances, each is a unique combination of a persona (Ingrid or Claudio) and an LLM. We instantiated each persona within its respective model by using a system prompt that applied a speaker-specific role approach [35]. In the prompt, we directed the LLM to scope its knowledge and reasoning proportionally to the persona and to respond in a speaking-like tone.

[2] https://alphagov.github.io/accessibility-personas/.
[3] https://openrouter.ai/.

Phase 4 and 5: Demonstration and Evaluation

We evaluated the effectiveness of AP in generating contextual feedback by investigating its alignment with feedback collected from human users in a specific case using a consistent evaluation framework.

Case: We selected the Skånetrafiken mobile app on the Android platform as our case. Skånetrafiken is the public transport authority for Skåne County, Sweden, managing a comprehensive network of buses, trains, and other services[4]. The app, with over 1 million downloads and a 3.1 overall rating from more than 4,000 reviews, provides functionalities for journey planning, real-time travel information, and ticket purchasing. This case was chosen due to the app's widespread use and the availability of a large body of existing user feedback. The company is committed to being fully compliant with Swedish law on the accessibility of digital public services.

Usability Evaluation: Usability refers to the extent to which a system can be used by specified users to achieve goals with effectiveness, efficiency, and satisfaction [13]. Usability can be decomposed into five dimensions: learnability, efficiency, memorability, error prevention, and satisfaction [23].

A widely used method for evaluating usability is Nielsen's heuristics evaluation framework, where a small group of usability experts assesses a user interface against a set of ten established criteria (i.e., heuristics) [23]. These heuristics include: visibility of system status (N01), match between the system and the real world (N02), user control and freedom (N03), consistency and standards (N04), error prevention (N05), recognition rather than recall (N06), flexibility and efficiency of use (N07), aesthetic and minimalist design (N08), help users recognize, diagnose, and recover from errors (N09), and help and documentation (N10). Nielsen's heuristics is a fast, inexpensive, and practical alternative to resource-intensive usability testing, with the goal of identifying and addressing usability issues early in the design process.

While Nielsen's heuristics evaluation was originally intended for usability experts, an empirical study shows that end users are capable of understanding and applying these heuristics [18], suggesting that early user involvement in internal evaluations can be highly effective. Studies by Branco et al. [5] and Matos et al. [21] are two examples of end-user involvement in usability evaluation.

The use of APs aligns with Nielsen's heuristics idea of internal experimentation, offering a method for getting simulated user feedback without needing actual user participants (i.e., external experimentation [32]). Therefore, our work investigates the viability of APs to augment or even replace human evaluators in a heuristic evaluation setting, combining the efficiency of the heuristic method with the realism of persona-driven synthetic feedback generation.

Evaluation Design: Our evaluation was based on Nielsen's heuristics for two reasons: first, it accommodates both usability experts and users as the evaluators [18], allowing us to integrate both human and AP feedback. Second, the heuristics are well-suited for evaluating static artifacts, such as the screenshots we used.

[4] https://www.skanetrafiken.se/english/.

To achieve a comprehensive and triangulated evaluation [19], we consolidated data from three sources: (human) user interviews, Google Play review analysis, and AP feedback generation. Figure 1 depicts an overview of the evaluation phase.

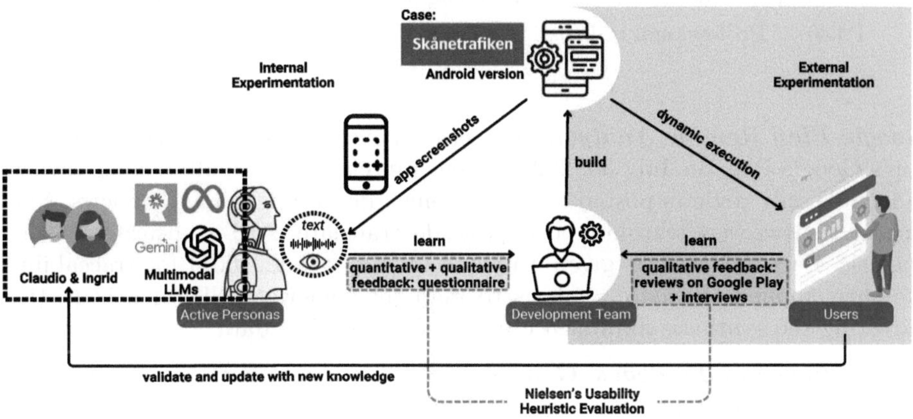

Fig. 1. Evaluation: an overview

Semi-structured Interviews: We applied online interviews [19] to gather qualitative data for in-depth evaluation. We applied a semi-structured approach, allowing us to explore the unexpected discussion [31]. We conducted four online interview sessions in August 2025, each lasting between 30 and 45 min and was recorded and transcribed. We transformed Nielsen's heuristic evaluations workbook[5] into 20 interview questions (Q01-20). Each of the heuristics was translated into two questions to capture different aspects of each heuristic. For example, the first two questions (Q01 and Q02) were aimed at collecting data related to the first Nielsen's heuristic, visibility of system status (N01).

Participants: We used convenience sampling to recruit four participants from our contacts who frequently used the app at least once a week (see Table 1). Participants were systematically selected to align with our predefined personas: P1 (vision impairment) matched Ingrid's accessibility needs; P2 and P3 (software professionals) aligned with Claudio's tech-savvy profile; and P4 represented another variant of Claudio. This purposive sampling ensured meaningful comparison between human and AP feedback.

Synthesis: We employed thematic analysis [6,9] with a deductive approach to identify patterns and insights from the interview data, using Nielsen's heuristics as our initial coding.

[5] https://www.nngroup.com/articles/ten-usability-heuristics/.

Table 1. Interview participants

ID	Age	Background	Experience	App language
P1	30–35	Master student in social science	2 years	Swedish
P2	30–35	Professional in a software company	5 years	English
P3	25–30	Master student in software engineering	1.5 years	English
P4	30–35	Professional in logistics	2 years	English

Google Play Review Analysis: We scraped over 500 textual reviews from the app's Google Play on July 30, 2025. To ensure relevance, we filtered the reviews to include only reviews posted from 2024 onwards, resulting in 46 reviews. Non-English reviews were translated using Google Translate[6] API to ensure consistent analysis. Each review was given a unique identifier (e.g., f001) for traceability. We then applied thematic analysis to map the review to Nielsen's heuristics, mirroring the synthesis approach used for the interview data.

Active Persona Feedback Generation: To generate both quantitative and qualitative synthetic feedback, we provided each of the eight AP instances with a questionnaire derived from our earlier interview protocol. This ensured direct comparability between the human and AP-generated feedback. The questionnaire consisted of 20 statements, which the AP instances evaluated on a 5-level Likert scale (1: *"strongly disagree"*, 5: *"strongly agree"*). For each statement, the AP was instructed to provide a brief rationale to support its choice.

The AP feedback was generated through a zero-shot prompting approach [7]. This method leverages the pre-trained knowledge of the LLMs without requiring any in-context examples. The prompt contains the questionnaire accompanied by nine screenshots of the app's user journey (see Table 2), and a request for a structured JSON-formatted response. The screenshots, two of which were in Swedish to evaluate language appropriateness and consistency, covered key user flows from searching for a trip to purchasing a ticket. For each AP instance, we ran ten independent evaluations, generating a total of 80 results (for eight AP instances). Each evaluation used identical inputs: the same screenshots, questionnaire, and system prompts. Nothing was changed between runs to get reliable responses. Samples of the app's screenshots are shown in Fig. 2.

Execution costs, in terms of input tokens, output tokens, and execution time, varied across persona-model combinations. Llama-based personas were the fastest (< 30s) but consumed the most input tokens ($\approx 13,000$) while generating the fewest output tokens ($\approx 1,400$). Conversely, Gemini-based personas were the most token-efficient, making efficient use of input tokens ($\approx 3,700$) while consuming a large number of output tokens ($\approx 6,000$) at a moderate time cost.

Synthesis: We mapped the qualitative feedback from the questionnaire to Nielsen's heuristic, consistent with our approach for the other two earlier sources. We then performed a comparative analysis of the feedback from all three sources.

[6] https://translate.google.com/about/.

Table 2. Description of the screenshots used in this study

No	Screenshot content	Language
1	the app's homepage, accessible through the "Search journey" tab.	English
2	the search journey screen	English
3	the journey list screen	English
4	the journey filter screen	English
5	the journey detail screen	English
6	the ticket selection screen	English
7	the ticket selection screen	Swedish
8	the ticket detail screen	English
9	the ticket detail screen	Swedish

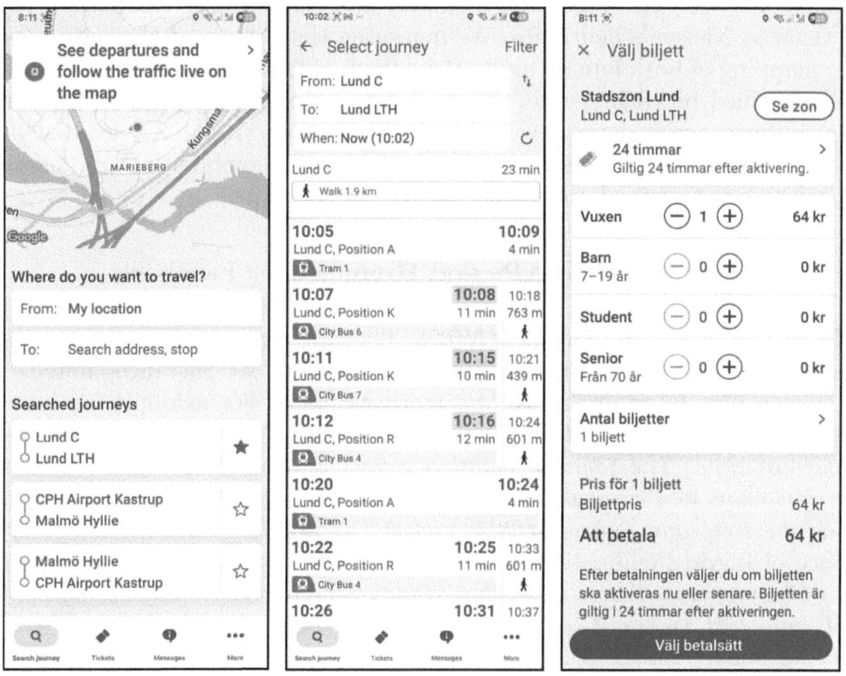

Fig. 2. Screenshots of the Skånetrafiken app

Moreover, we used descriptive statistics [34] of the ratings for each statement in the questionnaire to evaluate how the persona-model combination affects the feedback. We calculated the mean of ratings [24] given by AP instances per persona-model. We further investigated how these combinations affect the ratings per statement in the questionnaire (i.e., Q01-20). Following this, we conducted a Kruskal-Wallis test [34] to determine if the observed differences among the eight AP configurations were statistically significant. This non-parametric test is well-suited for our analysis because it is designed to compare more than two independent groups using ordinal data, such as the Likert scale ratings from our questionnaire, and does not require the data to follow a normal distribution.

Appendix: Detailed information on the used user personas (Ingrid and Claudio), the interview and questionnaire protocols, the system and evaluation prompts, the complete app's screenshots, the cost evaluation, the complete statistical analysis, reviews from Google Play, AP-generated feedback, and source code we used in this study can be found in [33].

3 Results

The effectiveness of AP in generating user feedback is measured through the alignment between AP-generated feedback and human user feedback by mapping them to Nielsen's heuristics. We measured the alignment through: (1) thematic mapping of both human and AP feedback, (2) comparing specific usability issues identified by each source, (3) analyzing rating patterns, and (4) triangulating findings across interviews, Google Play reviews, and AP feedback. We then investigate the influence of the persona-model combination on generated feedback using statistical analysis.

3.1 Alignment Between APs and Human User Feedback

Visibility of System Status (N01): The app generally communicates its system status effectively. Interview participants and AP instances noted clear information like departure times and track numbers. For example, an instance of Claudio shared, *"I can clearly see 'From: Lund C' and 'To: Lund LTH' with the current time. The journey detail screen ... shows the complete route with clear departure and arrival times, and the ticket selection screens ... clearly display the zone and journey (Q02, nielsen_4, claudio_claude)."* However, an instance of Ingrid highlighted an accessibility issue, stating, *"The journey page shows Changes and Travel time plus 'Today Monday' (s5). For my eyes, some small, pale text makes it a bit harder to read at a glance (Q02, nielsen_71, ingrid_openai)."* Google Play reviews offered a real-world counterpoint, with one user (f16) noting, *"Not showing correct departure time. When trains are delayed, the information is shown too late, and you have no chance to take an earlier train."* This feedback highlighted a potential gap between the app's static interface and the dynamic needs of a user in real-time.

Match Between the System and the Real World (N02): All interview participants found that the app's terminology reflected real-world terms. For instance, P1 stated, *"the language is consistent with its website, which is in Swedish."* Comments from AP instances aligned with the interview participants'. An instance of Claudio shared, *"It uses all the normal words I'd use when talking about taking the bus or train ... and the Swedish versions ... are exactly what* *you'd expect. There's no confusing jargon, which makes it quick to use (Q3, nielsen_17, claudio_gemini).*" An instance of Ingrid added a nuance related to icons, stating that while they are generally recognizable, "*some icons might not be immediately clear to all users, especially those with visual impairments (Q04, nielsen_65, ingrid_llama).*"

User Control and Freedom (N03): All interview participants reported sufficient freedom to navigate the app, though some preferred Android's native sliding feature over the in-app back button, as noted by P2: "*I typically navigate by sliding. I rarely use the back button.*" AP instances provided similar feedback, recognizing the app's consistent in-app back button but suggesting that some screens still require a more explicit exit button. For example, an instance of Claudio noted, "*Every screen has a consistent back arrow in the top left ... and the ticket selection screens have a clear 'X' button for closing ... This consistency makes it easy for me to know exactly how to exit any screen without getting lost ... (Q05, nielsen_7, claudio_claude).*" Similarly, an instance of Ingrid pointed out, "*the back buttons are always in the top-left corner where you'd expect them. The main menu is always at the bottom, which is good. The button for 'Filter' on screen 3 is just a small symbol and could be a bit bigger for my eyes, but it's in a normal spot, so I would find it (Q06, nielsen_58, ingrid_gemini).*" A Google Play review from a user (f030) further emphasized a navigation problem, stating, "*There is no bottom navigation bar or hamburger menu ...*"

Consistency and Standards (N04): The app maintains its consistency in styles, typography, and layouts across its screens, a finding corroborated by both human and AP feedback. The app also applies layouts similar to other transportation apps. All interview participants agreed on this point. For instance, P3 noted: "*When I look at it from the color perspective, I can really see that there is consistency, for example, in the background and foreground color. I get the same colors everywhere.*" The AP instances provided similar observations. An instance of Claudio shared, "*Typography, pill buttons, and card lists are consistent from journey search to tickets. It all feels part of one system (Q07, nielsen_32, claudio_openai).*" An instance of Ingrid added, "*Standard patterns: bottom nav, back arrow, toggles, plus/minus steppers, and card lists ... It behaves like other Swedish travel apps I use (Q08, nielsen_79, ingrid_openai).*"

Error Prevention (N05): Interview participants agreed that the app helps them avoid errors through clear layouts and confirmation dialogs. For example, P3 highlighted a helpful modal that prevents accidental ticket activation. However, participants also identified potential issues. P3 found icons confusing and noted a problem with button color: *The app has this red color here (a button) as the highlighted or selected color. But then, when you click on this, maybe you would expect that little bit of red tint to be highlighted on this as well, because this is the highlighted color to show you an active color.*" P1 found it difficult to read train names due to small text size. AP instances reported similar feedback on the potential cause of errors. An instance of Claudio warned of a possible tap error: "*On the journey detail, Monitor sits next to Select ticket and has similar weight,* *so I could tap the wrong one when rushing (Q09, nielsen_39, claudio_openai)."* An instance of Ingrid's feedback aligned with the button color issue, stating, *"The 'Select ticket' button is a small grey oval that almost blends in with the background ... these grey buttons are not very prominent and I might have to search for them (Q09, nielsen_54, ingrid_gemini)."*

Recognition Rather than Recall (N06): The app effectively leverages recognition over recall through a "recent search" feature, which was identified by most interview participants. However, P4's comment that she *"never knew that feature existed"* highlights a potential discoverability issue. The AP instances also recognized the feature's value. An instance of Ingrid noted how helpful it is for users with routines, stating, *"On the very first screen, it shows my 'Searched journeys'. I take the bus to the market every Tuesday and Saturday, the same route. Having it right there without typing is perfect. And I see a little star, so I can save it (Q11, nielsen_60, ingrid_gemini)."*

Flexibility and Efficiency of Use (N07): Both interview participants and AP instances identified features that enhance efficiency, though they did not highlight the same ones. All interview participants identified two key shortcuts: the "favorite journey" and the "buy again" ticket option. P3 illustrated the value of the latter, stating, *"When you previously purchased a ticket, you have the 'buy again' option."* In contrast, AP instances identified two shortcuts: the "favorite journey" and the "my location" feature, which helps select the nearest stop.

Aesthetic and Minimalist Design (N08): The app's design was widely seen as uncluttered, minimalist, and aesthetically pleasing by both interview participants and APs. P3 noted that while the journey information was generally sufficient, a complex journey could make the screen difficult to read due to information overload. The APs echoed this sentiment. For instance, an instance of Claudio shared, *"Most screens are clean and focused. Screenshot 2 with the destination list is well-organized, and the journey details in screenshot 5 show just what I need. However, screenshot 3 with multiple journey options feels a bit dense with all the times and details - it could benefit from slightly more spacing or clearer visual separation between options (Q15, nielsen_9, claudio_claude)."*

Help Users Recognize, Diagnose, and Recover from Errors (N09): Only one interview participant, P3, had a direct experience with an error. P3 shared that while rushing to buy a ticket, a network issue occurred, but the error message was "quite clear (P3)." In contrast, none of the AP instances recognized application errors, which was expected given that no error screens were included in the provided screenshots. For example, an instance of Claudio stated, *"No errors are shown in these screenshots, so I cannot judge. Neutral based on what I can see (Q17, nielsen_38, claudio_openai)."* However, a Google Play review from a user (f031) underscored a real-world issue with the app's error handling, noting a generic and unhelpful message: *"When I tried to register my number, I got the following error message: 'Oops, something went wrong! Contact customer service for more information'."*

Help and Documentation (N10): No interview participants reported using the in-app help or documentation features. For example, P4 shared, *"I never check the help in the app. I prefer asking friends or ChatGPT."* Similarly, the AP instances found little in-app help, tooltips, or visible guides based on the provided screenshots. An instance of Claudio noted, *"Some screens offer additional information, such as the 'Read about our tickets' option (screenshots 6 and 7). However, more visible help options or tooltips could be beneficial, especially for less familiar features (Q19, nielsen_23, claudio_llama)."*

3.2 Relationship Between Personas, LLMs, and APs Feedback

The quantitative feedback, measured on a 5-level Likert scale (1: *"strongly disagree"*, 5: *"strongly agree"*), reveals a clear interplay between the persona's definition and the LLM in shaping the final evaluation. Two distinct trends were evident. First, the persona's specific traits consistently guided the tone of the feedback. The Ingrid persona, designed with the accessibility needs of a visually impaired user, was invariably more critical than the Claudio persona. This pattern was consistent across all four LLMs, with Ingrid's agreement level (3.78 - 4.12) consistently lower than Claudio's (3.88 - 4.66).

Second, the choice of LLM acted as a distinct lens, influencing the overall level of criticality. The Llama model emerged as the most critical evaluator, producing the lowest agreement level for both personas (3.88 for Claudio and 3.78 for Ingrid). Conversely, Gemini was the most generous, yielding the highest agreement level (4.66 for Claudio and 3.99 for Ingrid). GPT and Claude performed in the median range. These results suggest that AP-generated feedback is not determined by one factor alone, but by the combination of a persona's defined perspective and the unique evaluative tendencies of the LLM.

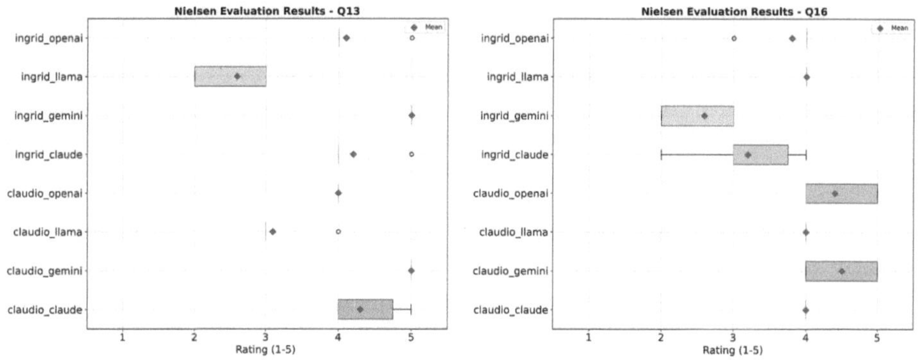

Fig. 3. Agreement levels on Q13 and Q16

A per-statement analysis provides deeper insight into these patterns. The divergence between the two personas was most pronounced in statements directly related to visual clarity and accessibility. For instance, in statements Q16 (*"Important information immediately grabs your attention"*) as depicted in Fig. 3 (the right side), Ingrid's instances gave significantly lower agreement levels, reflecting her defined visual impairment. Our analysis also highlighted specific LLM tendencies, such as Llama's consistent criticality on matters of user efficiency. For example, Q13 (*"The app visibly offers shortcuts (e.g., favorite routes) for common actions."*) as depicted in the left side of Fig. 3. Despite these variations, the AP instances reached a consensus on certain issues. For example, uniformly neutral scores for Q17 *("If visible, error messages clearly explain what went wrong,"*) as no error screens were provided. Our Kruskal-Wallis tests further confirm that the persona-model combination significantly impacts the agreement level with $pvalue < 0.05$ in all statements, except Q17.

4 Discussion

Our research question sought to understand the effectiveness of AP in generating user feedback measured through the alignment between AP-generated feedback and human user feedback. Our qualitative analysis revealed a substantial alignment, with APs successfully identifying many of the same usability issues and strengths as human participants and Google Play reviewers across Nielsen's heuristics. This suggests that APs, when properly configured, can effectively simulate a user's perspective in a heuristic evaluation context. For instance, the APs' ability to detect issues related to consistency (N04), recognition over recall (N06), and minimalist design (N08) demonstrates their capacity to process visual information and apply usability principles in a human-like manner.

The Ingrid persona, designed with a vision impairment, consistently highlighted accessibility issues such as small text and low-contrast elements. This finding shows that APs can be tailored to represent specific user needs, aligning with the core purpose of personas: to foster empathy and focus design efforts on diverse user profiles [15,29].

The APs' inability to comment on dynamic, real-world issues (e.g., incorrect train departure times) or application errors not depicted in the screenshots highlights a key limitation of our static evaluation method. Human feedback is shaped by lived experiences and interactions with a live system, a context that static images cannot fully replicate.

Our statistical analysis clearly showed that the Ingrid instances were consistently more critical than the Claudio instances, regardless of the underlying model. This demonstrates that the persona definition successfully guided the LLM's output, causing it to adopt the specified critical perspective. Furthermore, the variation in criticality among the LLMs themselves (with Llama being the most critical) suggests that factors like training data, architectural differences, and built-in safety protocols influence the model's evaluative stance. This implies that the selection of both the persona and the LLM is a critical configuration that can be tuned to achieve different evaluation goals.

Our results also indicate that all of the underlying LLMs are capable of avoiding hallucinating responses by showing their neutrality on insufficient context, for example, in Q17, where no screenshot indicating errors was given.

We recognized two limitations of the study. Firstly, the use of static screenshots prevented the APs from evaluating dynamic interactions and real-time context. Secondly, our human feedback was gathered from a small interview participant sample and reviews on Google Play.

Implications for Practice and Research

For practitioners, APs offer a practical, low-cost method for rapid internal evaluations, allowing teams to address resource-intensive issues of user involvement in early stages of NPD [25]. We also recommend practitioners not to oversimplify user experiences by relying too heavily on APs' feedback since the underlying LLMs have the potential of inherent biases accumulated from the training data. Gaps between APs' feedback and actual user feedback should be expected. We suggest continuously informing APs with new information gathered from external experimentations to make APs a better reflection of the underlying user group. However, practitioners must also consider APs' computational costs. As our findings on execution performance show, these costs are driven by factors, such as API calls, token consumption, and execution time.

For researchers, this work validates the novel GenAI application, transforming static personas into dynamic evaluation tools and opens new avenues for research into further APs' involvement in various NPD stages, such as requirement engineering and behavioral testing.

5 Conclusion

This study investigated AI-powered Active Personas (APs) to address the challenge of securing consistent user feedback in new product development. Through Design Science Research, we transformed traditional static personas into dynamic, generative agents capable of providing realistic user feedback on demand.

Our empirical evaluation confirms that APs generate high-fidelity feedback that closely aligns with human users across Nielsen's usability heuristics. A key finding is the significant influence of both persona definition and underlying LLM choice on the generated feedback.

This study validates the viability of APs in generating contextual user feedback. APs offer a practical solution for securing diverse user perspectives while maintaining focus on user empathy. Future work is to enable APs to interact with the dynamic context of applications, validate APs in other domains, and establish ethical guidelines for responsible deployment.

Acknowledgements. This work has been supported by ELLIIT, the Swedish Strategic Research Area in IT and Mobile Communications.

References

1. Ahmad, R., Siemon, D., Gnewuch, U., Robra-Bissantz, S.: The benefits and caveats of personality adaptive conversational agents in mental health care. In: Americas Conference on Information Systems (2021)
2. Barthet, M., Khalifa, A., Liapis, A., Yannakakis, G.: Generative personas that behave and experience like humans. In: International Conference on the Foundations of Digital Games (2022)
3. Billestrup, J., Stage, J., Nielsen, L., Hansen, K.S.: Persona usage in software development: advantages and obstacles. In: International Conference on Advances in Computer-Human Interactions (2014)
4. Bjarnason, E., Lang, F., Mjöberg, A.: An empirically based model of software prototyping: a mapping study and a multi-case study. Empir. Softw. Eng. **28**(5), 115 (2023)
5. Branco, A.C., et al.: Usability evaluation of a community-led innovation mobile app. In: International Conference on Computer-Human Interaction Research and Applications, pp. 81–88 (2022)
6. Braun, V., Clarke, V.: Using thematic analysis in psychology. Qual. Res. Psychol. **3**(2), 77–101 (2006)
7. Brown, T.B., et al.: Language models are few-shot learners. In: International Conference on Neural Information Processing Systems (2020)
8. Cooper, A., Saffo, P.: The Inmates Are Running the Asylum. Macmillan (1999)
9. Cruzes, D.S., Dyba, T.: Recommended steps for thematic synthesis in software engineering. In: International Symposium on Empirical Software Engineering and Measurement, pp. 275–284 (2011)
10. Ebert, C., Louridas, P.: Generative AI for software practitioners. IEEE Softw. **40**(4), 30–38 (2023)
11. Fabijan, A., Olsson, H.H., Bosch, J.: Customer feedback and data collection techniques in software R&D: a literature review. In: International Conference of Software Business, pp. 139–153 (2015)
12. Huang, Y., Kanij, T., Madugalla, A., Mahajan, S., Arora, C., Grundy, J.: Unlocking adaptive user experience with generative AI. In: International Conference on Evaluation of Novel Approaches to Software Engineering (2024)
13. ISO: ISO 9241-11 ergonomics of human-system interaction - part 11: Usability: Definitions and concepts (2019)
14. Ji, Z., et al.: Survey of hallucination in natural language generation. ACM Comput. Surv. **55**(12) (2023)
15. Karolita, D., Grundy, J.C., Kanij, T., McIntosh, J., Obie, H.O.: Lessons learned from persona usage in requirements engineering practice. In: IEEE International Requirements Engineering Conference, pp. 116–128 (2024)
16. Karolita, D., McIntosh, J., Kanij, T., Grundy, J., Obie, H.O.: Use of personas in requirements engineering: a systematic mapping study. Inf. Softw. Technol. **162**, 107264 (2023)
17. Kujala, S., Kauppinen, M., Lehtola, L., Kojo, T.: The role of user involvement in requirements quality and project success. In: IEEE International Conference on Requirements Engineering, pp. 75–84 (2005)
18. Lechner, B., Fruhling, A., Petter, S., Siy, H.: The chicken and the pig: User involvement in developing usability heuristics. In: Americas Conference on Information Systems, vol. 5, pp. 3263–3270 (2013)

19. Lethbridge, T.C., Sim, S.E., Singer, J.: Studying software engineers: data collection techniques for software field studies. Empir. Softw. Eng. **10**(3), 311–341 (2005)
20. Leão, R., Ayach, F., Lameirão, V., Fontão, A.: A prompt engineering-based process to build proto-personas during lean inception. In: Proceedings of the Brazilian Symposium on Software Engineering (2024)
21. Matos, D.P., et al.: Hansenapp: Development of a mobile application to assist primary healthcare providers to control leprosy. Tropical Med. Int. Health **27**(8), 719–726 (2022)
22. Mueller, A., Beyer, S., Kopp, G., Deisser, O.: User-centered development of a public transportation vehicle operated in a demand-responsive environment. In: Stanton, N. (ed.) Advances in Human Factors of Transportation, pp. 545–555. Springer, Cham (2020)
23. Nielsen, J.: Usability Engineering. Morgan Kaufmann Publishers Inc., San Francisco (1994)
24. Norman, G.: Likert scales, levels of measurement and the "laws" of statistics. Adv. Health Sci. Educ. **15**(5), 625–632 (2010)
25. Paternoster, N., Giardino, C., Unterkalmsteiner, M., Gorschek, T., Abrahamsson, P.: Software development in startup companies: a systematic mapping study. Inf. Softw. Technol. **56**(10), 1200–1218 (2014)
26. Peffers, K., Tuunanen, T., Rothenberger, M.A., Chatterjee, S.: A design science research methodology for information systems research. J. Manag. Inf. Syst. **24**(3), 45–77 (2007)
27. Ries, E.: Lean Startup: How Today's Entrepreneurs Use Continuous Innovation to Create Radically Successful Businesses. Crown Business (2011)
28. Salewski, L., Alaniz, S., Rio-Tirto, I., Schulz, E., Akata, Z.: In-context impersonation reveals large language models' strengths and biases. In: International Conference on Neural Information Processing Systems (2023)
29. Salminen, J., Jansen, B.J., An, J., Kwak, H., Jung, S.: Are personas done? Evaluating their usefulness in the age of digital analytics. Persona Stud. **4**(2), 47–65 (2018)
30. Sauvola, T., et al.: Towards customer-centric software development: a multiple-case study. In: Euromicro Conference on SEAA, pp. 9–17 (2015)
31. Seaman, C.B.: Qualitative methods in empirical studies of software engineering. IEEE Trans. Softw. Eng. **25**(4), 557–572 (1999)
32. Simaremare, M., Edison, H.: Accelerating new product development: a vision on active personas. In: Software Business, pp. 461–466. Springer, Cham (2025)
33. Simaremare, M., Edison, H.: Active personas for synthetic user feedback - appendix (2025). https://doi.org/10.6084/m9.figshare.29925158
34. Wohlin, C., Runeson, P., Höst, M., Ohlsson, M.C., Regnell, B., Wesslén, A.: Experiments, pp. 73–83. Springer, Heidelberg (2024)
35. Zheng, M., Pei, J., Logeswaran, L., Lee, M., Jurgens, D.: When "a helpful assistant" is not really helpful: personas in system prompts do not improve performances of large language models. In: Al-Onaizan, Y., Bansal, M., Chen, Y.N. (eds.) Findings of the Association for Computational Linguistics, pp. 15126–15154. Association for Computational Linguistics (2024)

Transitioning Towards Enterprise Architecture Management in a Software and Service Mobility Company: A Case Study

Simon Flaisch[1(✉)], Dominic Lang[2], Sedat Kilic[2], Stefan Trieflinger[1], and Jürgen Münch[1]

[1] Reutlingen University, Alteburgstraße 150, 72762 Reutlingen, Germany
Simon.Flaisch@Student.Reutlingen-University.DE
[2] ETAS GmbH, Borsigstraße 24, 70469 Stuttgart, Germany

Abstract. In the face of disruptions, increasing complexity and intensifying competitive pressure, organizations must adapt their structures and operations. In this context, Enterprise Architecture Management (EAM) is considered a promising approach to address these challenges by enabling holistic organizational overview, breaking down silos, and reducing complexity. However, the organizational implementation of EAM remains challenging, with little established methodological guidance available for context-specific realization. The research presented in this paper aims to support the organizational introduction of EAM. To this end, we present a practical evaluation approach to guide the selection of appropriate EAM implementation strategies. Through a single-case study conducted in collaboration with ETAS GmbH, this research explores a potential implementation of EAM. By conducting expert workshops and semi-structured interviews, an assessment approach and a decision-supporting "fitting matrix" were developed. The matrix evaluates twelve EAM implementation variants using seven collaboratively defined success criteria. The results indicate that a federated EAM model led by the CIO is considered the most suitable for this case.

Keywords: Enterprise Architecture Management · Enterprise Architecture Implementation Methodology (EAIM) · Business-IT Alignment · Enterprise Architecture Frameworks · Change Management

1 Introduction

Organizations across various industries face increasingly volatile economic, technological, and regulatory conditions, requiring continuous adaptation [1, 2]. This also affects the automotive sector, which is currently experiencing a period of unprecedented change driven by electromobility, the software-defined vehicle, and intensified global competition [3]. As a result, the way how companies operate and create value is fundamentally changing, yet such transformations come with significant challenges [1]. Moreover, traditional management approaches are proving inadequate to address the rising complexity and pace of change. In this context, Enterprise Architecture Management (EAM) has

G. Herzwurm et al. (Eds.): ICSOB 2025, LNBIP 574, pp. 267–273, 2026.
https://doi.org/10.1007/978-3-032-14518-5_21

become a widely recognized approach for addressing these challenges. EAM enables the development of a holistic understanding of the organization [4], promotes the breakdown of silos, and helps organizations to manage increasing complexity [5]. Moreover, authors from industry and academia emphasize that there is no one-size-fits-all approach for organizational EAM implementations, as organizational context strongly influences individual success [1, 2, 6]. Additionally, Buckl et al. [2] highlight the absence of established methodologies or practical guidance for context-specific EAM implementations. This paper addresses this gap through a single-case study in collaboration with ETAS GmbH, a company transforming from a hardware-focused to a software- and service-driven organization. To this end, we contribute a case study, in which we developed a contextual assessment approach and a corresponding "fitting matrix" to support the evaluation and selection of suitable EAM implementations.

Several prior studies have investigated the organizational implementation of EAM. For instance, Haki et al. [7] presented four EAM archetypes intended as organizational blueprints. Buckl et al. [2] proposed a design theory framework for situational EAM design. The results are rather abstract and lack elaboration on operational details such as artefacts and assessment steps. Other publication such as Schmidt and Buxmann [5] outline general principles, whereas Drews et al. [8] provide detailed insights into an agile EAM function but without providing a systematic assessment approach. Overall, the literature reveals an absence of structured evaluation approaches, which this study aims to address. A comprehensive overview of background and related work can be found in Flaisch [9]. This paper presents a condensed version of the case study, with a more comprehensive version available on Figshare[1].

2 Research Design

This research follows the case study approach from Yin [10] and adopts the research design proposed by Runeson et al. [11]. We propose the following research questions:

RQ1: *How can different organizational EAM approaches be evaluated to select the most beneficial option?* **RQ2:** *What are suitable options to establish EAM at the case company, and which is the most promising one?*

This case study examined ETAS GmbH, a subsidiary of the Bosch Group that provides embedded software, engineering solutions and services to the automotive industry. The company is currently undergoing a strategic transformation into a software and service mobility company. In this context, ETAS considers EAM a promising approach to manage its transformation. Consequently, an explorative single-case study design was chosen, as it allows to investigate real-world phenomena [11]. The primary objective was to explore the potential implementation of EAM within the case company.

To address **RQ1**, two expert workshops were conducted with two ETAS practitioners, one enterprise architect and one senior manager with experience in organizational transformation and a solid understanding of Enterprise Architecture (EA). The objective was to validate findings from a prior literature review [9] and develop an evaluation approach for different organizational EAM implementations. For **RQ2**, the developed approach

[1] Figshare Link: https://figshare.com/s/407677525a27d2011ab7.

was applied and validated in the context of ETAS through 13 semi-structured expert interviews with experts from four different companies. The expert selection encompassed architects from the case company, along with external consultants specialized in the domain of EAM. Prior, an interview guide was structured according to the fitting matrix and distributed in advance. Their responses were collected via Likert-type scales and analyzed followed Schuster and Liesen [12], providing a quantitative basis for comparing different implementations.

3 Results

Assessment Approach. In the workshops to answer **RQ1**, different EAM options were scored against success criteria that are considered essential by the experts, resulting in a scoring matrix, referred to as "fitting matrix". Overall, the approach and the associated artefact consist of three main components: ***(I) Success criteria for EAM introduction; (II) Adapted organizational EAM approaches; (III) Organizational anchoring points.***

(I) ***Success Criteria.*** In the initial phase, potential evaluation dimensions were identified based on the literature review by Flaisch [9] and discussed in the first workshop. Throughout a multi-stage process involving two expert workshops, recurring patterns and thematic overlaps across EAM challenges, best practices and success factors were synthesized and seven key success criteria were identified, that serve as the evaluation dimensions for comparing different organizational EAM options: (1) *Organizational Penetration and Effectiveness Reach of EAM,* (2) *Top Management Mandate and Governance,* (3) *Visibility and Lighthouse Character,* (4) *Suitability for EAM Work,* (5) *Ability to Function as an Architecture Guild,* (6) *Adaptability and Scalability of EAM,* (7) *Effort and Risk for Change.*

(II) ***EAM approaches.*** Based on the literature review by Flaisch [9] and practitioner workshops, three approaches were identified: ***Virtual EAM, Central Operative EAM, Governance EAM, and Supportive EAM.*** They differ in their degree of centralization, governance structures, and role of embedded architects, e.g. in the ***Virtual EAM*** model, there is no central EAM organization but architects work within a virtual community [6, 13]. In contrast, the ***Central Operative EAM*** consolidates all architects and architectural activities into a single centralized function [6, 13]. It is typically led by a Chief Enterprise Architect and follows hierarchical structures to cover all relevant domain regions [14]. The ***Governance EAM*** model combines central structure of a dedicated EAM department supervising EAM by formulating EA strategy, establishing enterprise-wide standards, while being complemented by a decentralized network of embedded architects operating within business domains [6, 13]. The ***Supportive EAM*** approach similarly integrates central and decentralized components, but with primary architectural work conducted highly autonomous within individual domains and teams, while the EAM function operates primarily in a supportive and advisory capacity [8].

(III) ***Organizational anchoring points.*** Furthermore, according to the workshop experts, selecting an appropriate organizational anchoring is essential to achieve the defined success criteria, overcome challenges, and leverage the benefits of EAM, a view supported by authors from both academia and industry [6, 15]. However, there is no universal solution, as appropriate positioning depends heavily on the organizational structure, operating model, and culture [6]. Based on these insights, organizational anchoring was included as an additional dimension to the assessment approach, considering three generic roles to avoid bias and strengthen the adaptability and reusability [16]: The ***Chief Information Officer (CIO)***, responsible for overseeing and managing all resources within an organization's IT; the ***Chief Operating Officer (COO)***, responsible for daily business operations and optimizing internal efficiency and staff coordination; and the ***Chief Executive Officer (CEO)***, who holds the highest-ranking position and is responsible for major strategic decisions, overall leadership, and supervision of the executive team.

Fitting Matrix. Figure 1 shows the final version of the "fitting matrix", which incorporates the pre-defined success criteria, four adapted EAM approaches and three potential organizational anchoring points among C-suite roles, as well as a transparent evaluation mechanism. The X-axis lists the four EAM approaches, each subdivided into three variants reflecting its anchoring under one of the three C-Suite roles and Y-axis contains the seven success criteria, which serve as the evaluation dimensions for assessing each approach, forming the evaluation logic of the matrix.

Approach Evaluation. To answer **RQ2**, the "fitting matrix" was applied using semi-structured interviews. Details can be found in the extended version of this paper. As previously outlined, the use of consistent Likert-type statements and their systematic mapping to numerical values enabled a comparable assessment across all variants [12]. Figure 1 illustrates the completed matrix for the case company, ETAS.

Success Criteria	Virtual EAM			Central Operative EAM			Governance EAM			Supportive EAM		
	CIO	COO	CEO	CIO	COO	CEO	CIO	COO	CEO	CIO	COO	CEO
Organizational penetration and effectiveness reach of EAM within organization	36	36	35	42	39	44	55	51	55	35	36	36
Top Management mandate and governance	30	31	39	48	48	59	51	48	57	34	34	36
Visibility and lighthouse character	34	37	39	48	48	50	51	52	54	34	36	39
Suitability for EAM work	45	42	42	47	46	49	56	51	51	34	36	36
Ability to function as architecture guild	40	40	37	49	49	48	53	53	49	32	33	33
Adaptability and scalability of EAM within the approach	40	39	42	49	49	50	50	49	49	31	32	32
Effort and risk for change	36	37	37	38	37	39	44	44	43	40	42	41
Summary - Final Score	261	262	271	321	316	339	360	348	358	240	249	253
Most suitable - Ranking	**9**	**8**	**7**	**5**	**6**	**4**	**1**	**3**	**2**	**12**	**11**	**10**

Fig. 1. Completed artefact "fitting matrix" for the case company

Overall, the most suitable approach for ETAS based on the evaluation is the federated "Governance EAM". However, minimal variance between C-suite roles suggests that there is no significant difference between them in the case of ETAS. Next in the ranking is the centralized "Central Operative EAM" approach, where the CEO variant trails with 339 points, relatively close to the EAM Governance variant, but still 6% lower than the top option. The decisive difference lies in the "Organizational Penetration and Effectiveness Reach of EAM" criterion which was rated lower for a central function due to the challenge of "ivory tower syndrome," consistent with prior literature [6]. While a central function may be detached from business, the federated approach fosters proximity to stakeholders through its embedded architects in relevant areas (e.g., business domains). Another interviewee insight is the preference for centralized over decentralized approaches, stating that EAM requires a clear mandate and strong authority to be implemented effectively, especially to fulfill its governance responsibilities, which is reflected in higher scores on e.g. "Top Management Mandate and Governance." Consequently, decentralized approaches are ranked last, with "virtual EAM" and "supportive EAM" receiving the lowest scores.

4 Conclusion and Outlook

This paper presents a case study conducted in collaboration with ETAS GmbH, exploring the potential implementation of Enterprise Architecture Management. Based on insights from the literature and expert workshops, a structured assessment approach and a supporting artefact, the "fitting matrix," were developed to evaluate and compare organizational EAM implementation options. Through semi-structured expert interviews, the approach was applied and validated in the context of the case company, providing a methodological foundation and decision-making support for assessing suitable organizational EAM designs. The results indicate that a federated "Governance EAM" model anchored with the CIO represents the most suitable option for ETAS. To assess the validity and reliability of the results, the framework proposed by Yin [10] was applied.

Construct validity was strengthened by communicating workshop and interview objectives in advance, clarifying terminology, and using semi-structured interviews to mitigate misunderstandings. ***Internal validity*** may be affected by the accuracy of participants' knowledge; this was addressed by selecting experienced experts and discussing differing viewpoints until consensus was reached. Internal validity was not further considered for the interviews, as no causal relationships were examined. ***External validity*** is limited due to the single-case design, restricting the generalizability of the findings. While the results may offer indicative insights for organizations in comparable contexts, they are not directly transferable without further research. ***Reliability*** may be constrained by the subjective perceptions of participants and potential company-specific bias, which was mitigated by validating selected findings with a broader expert group. As the approach has not yet been implemented or longitudinally validated, it represents a preliminary framework requiring further investigation. Additionally, the results of this paper can serve as a foundation for further academic research and practical applications. Further research should validate the preliminary approach across different organizational contexts, e.g. by introducing weighting, and quantitative studies with EAM practitioners could further substantiate and enrich the findings. Beyond validation, the identified success criteria could enrich an EAM maturity model, helping companies assess their current EAM level. Based on this study's results, ETAS has decided to establish a dedicated EAM function to systematically manage, develop and evolve the company's EA. In the long term, ETAS aims to further professionalize its EAM function, and the emerging initiative is expected to provide various benefits and may also serve as a pilot for other organizations facing similar environments and challenges.

References

1. Niemi, E., Pekkola, S.: The benefits of enterprise architecture in organizational transformation. Bus. Inf. Syst. Eng. **62**, 585–597 (2020)
2. Buckl, S., Schweda, C.M., Matthes, F.: A design theory nexus for situational enterprise architecture management. In: 2010 14th IEEE International Enterprise Distributed Object Computing Conference Workshops, pp. 3–8. IEEE (2010)
3. Gräf, H., Topuria, S.: The impact of the Covid-19 pandemic on industrial policy in Germany and the European Union - the case of the automotive industry. Eur. J. Econ. Econ. Policies **22**, 118–134 (2025)
4. Lange, M., Mendling, J., Recker, J.: Measuring the realization of benefits from enterprise architecture management. J. Enterp. Arch. **8**, 30–44 (2012)
5. Schmidt, C., Buxmann, P.: Outcomes and success factors of enterprise IT architecture management: empirical insight from the international financial services industry. Eur. J. Inf. Syst. **20**, 168–185 (2011)
6. Mittendorf, F., Thome, A., Zeeb, S., Peters, P.: Digital architecture study 2024. Capgemini Website. https://www.capgemini.com/de-de/wp-content/uploads/sites/8/2024/11/Digital-Architecture-Study-2024_vF.pdf (2024). Accessed 27 May 2025
7. Haki, M.K., Legner, C., Ahlemann, F.: Beyond EA frameworks: towards an understanding of the adoption of enterprise architecture management. In: European Conference on Information Systems (ECIS) 2012 Proceedings (2012)
8. Drews, P., Schirmer, I., Horlach, B., Tekaat, C.: Bimodal enterprise architecture management: the emergence of a new EAM function for a BizDevOps-based fast IT. In: 2017 IEEE 21st International Enterprise Distributed Object Computing Workshop (EDOCW), pp. 57–64 (2017)
9. Simon Flaisch: Relevance and realization of enterprise architecture management in a software and service mobility company: an organizational case study. Bachelor Thesis, Unpublished, https://doi.org/10.13140/RG.2.2.31410.52163 (2025)
10. Yin, R.K.: Case Study Research: Design and Methods, vol. 3. Sage (2003)
11. Runeson, P., Host, M., Rainer, A., Regnell, B.: Case Study Research in Software Engineering: Guidelines and examples. Wiley & Sons (2012)
12. Schuster, T., Liesen, A.: Einführung - Messniveaus. In: Statistik für Wirtschaftswissenschaftler. Springer Gabler Berlin, Heidelber (2017)
13. Thome, A., Feheregyhazy, M.: Enterprise architecture in an Agile World. https://www.pwc.de/de/strategie-organisation-prozesse-systeme/enterprise-architecture-in-an-agile-world.pdf (2021). Accessed 06 Feb 2025
14. Bente, S., Bombosch, U., Langade, S.: Chapter 3 - what enterprise architects do: core activities of EA. In: Collaborative Enterprise Architecture, pp. 39–104. Morgan Kaufmann (2012)
15. Radeke, F.: Toward understanding enterprise architecture management's role in strategic change: antecedents, processes, outcomes. In: 10th International Conference on Wirtschaftsinformatik Proceedings 2011 (2011)
16. Woollacott, E.: What is the C-suite? Executive roles and responsibilities. Forbes Magazine. Forbes, https://www.forbes.com/sites/emmawoollacott/article/what-is-c-suite/ (2025)

A Software-Driven Approach to Model, Simulate and Optimize Service-Oriented Value Creation

Betiel Assefaw[1(✉)], Lukas Block[1], Yannick Becerra[2], and Sibylle Hermann[1]

[1] Fraunhofer IAO, Fraunhofer Institute for Industrial Engineering IAO, Nobelstraße 12, 70569 Stuttgart, Germany
Betiel-Sabine.Assefaw@iao.fraunhofer.de

[2] FIR at RWTH, Aachen University, Campus-Boulevard 55, 52074 Aachen, Germany
Yannick.Becerra@rwth-aachen.de

Abstract. Service-oriented value creation requires coordinated decisions across partners, resources, activities, and value appropriation. To support these decisions, we develop a model-driven, software-supported approach for configuring service value networks. At its core is a metamodel derived from analytic metatheory based on literature and expert workshops. The metamodel is implemented in a modeling software tool that integrates relevant service-oriented, value creation elements and their relationships into one single data model. The approach supports comparison of partner constellations, alignment of supply and demand, and evaluation of implications across the network. It enables firms to represent their value network, assess properties, simulate value distribution and optimize feasible configurations. The metamodel and the software tool have been evaluated in mobility, construction and additive manufacturing domain. Early results indicate that it is particularly effective in the systematic identification and analysis of interdependent action areas, the design of feasible business models, and the development of implementation strategies and funding opportunities in collaboration with relevant stakeholders.

Keywords: Value Creation Network · Modeling Software · Metamodel

1 Introduction

Over the last decades, industrial value creation has shifted from product-dominated, intra-firm approaches toward service-oriented, network-centric configurations, driven by the proliferation of digital technologies, globalization, and the rising salience of intangible assets (e.g., knowledge, data and skills). Accordingly, new forms of value creation have emerged in which services, rather than products, become the nucleus of value. As a result, value creation is gradually transitioning from closed organizational structures toward complex business ecosystems and networks, where competitors, complementors, customers, and suppliers co-evolve with each other and with their environment [1–3]. Consequently, manufacturing organizations must integrate digital services into their portfolios to enhance resilience and flexibility, improve customer proximity, leverage economies of scale and maintain technological competitiveness [4]. This shift

G. Herzwurm et al. (Eds.): ICSOB 2025, LNBIP 574, pp. 274–288, 2026.
https://doi.org/10.1007/978-3-032-14518-5_22

is evident in the mobility sector, for example, where digitally orchestrated, usage-based on-demand mobility services rely on collaboration among various stakeholders (e.g., transport associations, app and service providers, and fleet operators) [5, 6]. Hence, incumbent organizations are required to strategically rethink their value creation design, transitioning from linear, product-centric models to agile, service-oriented value creation networks [7].

When conceptualizing service-oriented value creation networks, issues familiar from bilateral-relationships become more complex [8]. Therefore, the successful configuration requires addressing fundamental questions of coordinated decision-making across several dimensions: "Which partners are most appropriate?", "how should resources and tasks be allocated?", "how can quality be assured?", "what roles and responsibilities need to be defined?", "how should returns be distributed?" and, "how can value appropriation be designed to balance fairness and incentives?". This results in complex and non-linear decision-making processes that are difficult to manage adequately using conventional methods and tools (e.g., Value Chain Analysis, Stakeholder Mapping, Business Model Canvas).

We pose the following research question: How can the complex decision-making processes in the configuration of service-oriented value creation networks be supported?

Within this paper, a model-driven and software-supported approach is developed to address this issue and answer the research question.

2 Conceptual Background

The following section reviews core concepts of value and value creation, focusing on service-oriented value creation networks.

Value and value creation are fundamental concepts in economics and management, yet their interpretation varies significantly across disciplines. From an industrial perspective, value is created for the customer by the organization, embedded in goods or services, and realized at the point of exchange (value-in-exchange) [9]. In this context, value creation is commonly framed as the monetary outcome of sequential activities and quantified as the net difference between the value of total output (e.g., sales) and the value of the preliminary input (e.g., raw materials). However, this linear, primarily monetary perspective fails to capture the complex, nonlinear dynamics of value creation driven by contemporary environmental changes (e.g. globalization and digitalization). As a result, scholarship has increasingly adopted configurational perspectives that model nonlinearities and interdependencies within value creation networks.

Bassetti and Romano describe a shift from value chains to value networks, defining the latter as "a cluster of actors that collaborate to deliver the highest value to the end consumer and where each actor is responsible for the success or failure of the network." [10, p. 6]. Benger characterizes value networks as decentralized, polycentric constellations of legally autonomous actors, connected by active and latent relationships and shared information platforms. These actors are economically motivated to achieve sustainable added value through collaborative engagement [11]. Collaboration within value networks appears both vertically along supply chains or across markets, and horizontally among direct competitors. This dynamic, the coexistence of competition and cooperation, is called "coopetition" and allows organizations to align network-level objectives with firm-specific goals [12–14].

Contemporary service and management research broadens the concept of value creation beyond a goods-dominant, exchange-centric logic toward a service-dominant (S-D) logic. This logic provides a framework for societal value definition and creation, resource expansion, sustainability, and public policy [15]. Under S-D logic, organizations do not create value per se but offer value propositions. Value emerges in use through customer co-creation (value-in-use). Service value creation thus involves allocation mechanisms, core activities, and firm-customer interactions. The effectiveness of these interactions varies, potentially resulting in value co-creation or, under certain conditions, co-destruction. Thus managing this complexity requires configuring service-oriented value creation networks through orchestrated resources, defined roles, interaction patterns, and governance structures to align value-relevant processes and interactions across organizational boundaries [16–21].

3 State of the Art

Since 2004, S-D logic, introduced by Vargo and Lusch [17], has evolved into a network-oriented framework that analyzes value creation through patterns of resource integration among collaborating actors rather than through discrete outputs [22]. Its foundational premises are codified in five axioms:

> *"1. Service is the fundamental basis of exchange. 2. Value is cocreated by multiple actors, including the beneficiary. 3. All social and economic actors are resource integrators. 4. Value is always uniquely and phenomenologically determined by the beneficiary. 5. Value cocreation is coordinated through actor-generated institutions and institutional arrangements."* [23, p. 18].

Service, the core concept, is the intangible, interaction-intensive application of specialized operant resources (knowledge and skills) to operand resources (physical resources), through which parties create value for others and themselves [15, 24]. The key is a resource reorientation that distinguishes operand resources, which are acted upon, from operant resources, which act on other resources and produce effects. As operant resources drive competitive advantage, analysis shifts from output attributes to the capabilities that actors deploy and combine across network ties [17, 22]. On this basis, value is understood as emergent in use, realized in context, and is therefore inherently dynamic [25]. Therefore, for decision support, analysis should focus on interactions, role and actor configurations as well as resource combinations. The firm's contribution should be framed as a value proposition that invites participation rather than unilateral delivery [22]. Pfeiffer et. al. Operationalize this perspective by mapping roles, value propositions and resource integration across firm boundaries, and by showing that digital technology can function as an enabling operand resource and as an initiating operant resource within the same arrangement [25]. Complementary work on coopetition strengthens this network notion by demonstrating that value creation and value appropriation unfold in value networks formed by both positive and negative interdependencies. These tensions and harmonies shift where and how value is created and captured across relationships [14].

However, consistent guidelines and a widely accepted framework for research within and using S-D logic remain limited, and analyzing value and value creation networks is methodologically demanding and requires the integration of system- and subsystem-level as well as structural and process analyses [8, 21, 26].

Given this complexity, modeling helps to reduce complexity and promotes comprehension and innovation in socio-technical systems [27]. Software automates the preparation, analysis, and optimization of complex models, while metamodels define the key elements, structures, relationships, and constraints for building domain-specific models and for aligning a software tool's support with the decision problem [28].

In practice, an extensive repertoire of modeling approaches exists. OMEGA [29] and GEMINI [30] support business model and value creation modeling and analysis. Service Blueprint [31] separates frontstage customer interactions from backstage support processes. The Supply Chain Operations Reference (SCOR) model [32] provides reference processes and metrics. Business Process Modeling and Notation (BPMN) [33] formalizes standardized workflow logic. These methods offer structure but capture process and resource dynamics only to a limited extent.

Ontology-based approaches add a semantic layer for typed resources, constraints and compositions rules. The OBELIX service ontology [34], for example, supports knowledge-based configuration of service bundles and models services from value, offering, and process viewpoints. It also captures resource types but focuses on conceptual modeling rather than executable process/resource dynamics. The UFO-based Ontology of the Value Proposition [35] clarifies the distinction between value proposition and offering but leaves network dynamics unaddressed.

The Service-oriented Business Model (SoBM) Framework [25] operationalizes a service-centric, network-oriented perspective. e3value [36] addresses value allocation in multi-actor constellations and supports profitability assessment. Service Value Network (SVN) [37] enables market-based service composition from standardized modules and provides a formal model for analysis. All of these models provide economic insight but remain only partially linked to process and resource dynamics.

In digital contexts, numerous formal, partly machine-readable and machine-evaluable service-description languages exist, including Linked-USDL [38], SPARQL [39], OWL-S [40], SAWSDL, WSMO [41, 42], and BSMM [43]. OWL-S structures service descriptions for automation. Linked-USDL provides linked data vocabulary for technical, economic and legal aspects and BSMM offers a UML-profiled business service metamodel. These approaches ensure precise semantics and technical interoperability, yet they couple value appropriation with resource dynamics only weakly.

Recent research and practice show that current approaches do not meet the specific needs of service-oriented value creation networks. They offer a solid theoretical foundation, but each approach focuses on only particular perspective of service value creation. Consequently, they either overlook the multidimensional nature and interdependencies of decision-making or fail to link the different perspectives across the network. They are therefore inadequate for capturing, managing and mitigating the complexity described in Sect. 1.

We argue that value is created primarily in *use* – the integration and application of resources in a specific context – rather than in *exchange*, where value is embedded in firm outputs and reflected in price. Service systems interact through reciprocal service-exchange relationships that improve the adaptability and survivability of all systems engaged in exchange by enabling the integration of mutually beneficial resources. Accordingly, we develop a formal metamodel for service-oriented value creation and a supporting software tool [44]. This allows companies to systematically model, analyze, evaluate and optimize their value creation networks.

4 Approach

Our approach follows a model-driven and software-supported approach to mitigate the complexity of decision making in service-oriented value networks. Thus, at the core of our approach, we need to establish a metamodel, which is then integrated into a modeling software with further algorithms to depict, analyze and optimize value creation networks. To develop the metamodel, we follow established ontology engineering practices, based on the steps of Fernández et al. [45]: Acquiring and documenting knowledge, conceptualization, formalization, integration and implementation.

Acquiring and documenting knowledge: The knowledge content of our metamodel is developed via analytic metatheory development (see [46, 47]). We start with a literature review and expert knowledge to identify key concepts of service-oriented value networks among previous works. Thereby, we build up an unstructured body of knowledge based on previous scientific findings and knowledge, without own research.

Subsequently, the gathered knowledge is further structured, and a precise terminology is established (conceptualization). The precise terminology encompasses the identification of model elements for our metamodel as well as modeling mathematical relationships that connect them. Each identified meta-model element and relationship is categorized into one of three classes, with each class representing a distinct level of strength regarding the validity of the element or relationship (see also [44]):

- Axioms: Axioms represent essential and immutable findings in the gathered knowledge regarding value creation and value creation networks. As a result, they establish the foundational elements and relationships in the topology of the metamodel. Furthermore, they define constraints that must be satisfied in all models derived from the metamodel.
- Normative propositions: Normative propositions outline basic assumptions of service-oriented value creation that are commonly shared among many relevant theories. They maintain their validity unless a paradigm shift in theory occurs. Consequently, these propositions are mainly defined as relationships within the metamodel. However, they do not establish core elements or dependencies and may be subject to modification in future versions of the metamodel.
- Assumptions: Assumptions are relationships between elements that are generally regarded as true. However, for specific service-oriented value networks, their existence or specification may vary or may not apply at all. Therefore, these assumptions are not seen as hard constraints on the models derived from the metamodel, but rather as a hint towards the decision makers.

The definition of the precise terminology and subsequent metamodel for service-oriented value networks followed an iterative and a simultaneous deductive and inductive process to conceptualize the necessary body of knowledge. Firstly, the theoretical literature review in the field of service-oriented value networks (see Sect. 2 and 3) provided a deductive way to identify model elements and relationships from theory. Core elements for the metamodel were formally defined by experts by analyzing the different theories in dedicated workshops (formalization). Examples for such core elements of the metamodel are resources, activities, and actors (see Sect. 5). Subsequently, expressed relationships between the elements were identified. Finally, the experts filled the missing gaps within the metamodel from their knowledge and/or via assumptions (inductive approach). These assumptions were then again checked against a more focused literature research and further theories. The process was then started a new for a different aspect or perspective on service-oriented value networks. In total, more than 15 workshops with about 120 h in total were conducted, including four to eight experts in the field of service-oriented value creation networks.

The metamodel was then transferred into a software tool (integration and implementation). Within the software, users can model their current, planned or assumed service-oriented value network based on their knowledge, using our metamodel. Based on the relationships between the model elements from within the metamodel, the service-oriented value network can be viewed from different perspectives, it can be analyzed regarding specific properties (e.g., temporal stability), it can be simulated (e.g., with respect to value distribution) or it can be optimized (e.g., regarding service quality). The software was developed using the Eclipse Modeling Framework (EMF [48]), with the metamodel defined in XCore [49]. The software is available as an open-source release under https://gitlab.cc-asp.fraunhofer.de/sow/metamodel.

5 Metamodel and Modeling Software

The metamodel, together with its modeling environment, distinguishes itself by integrating heterogeneous perspectives on service-oriented value creation into a unified, formally specified data model. Multiple viewpoint representations can be derived from this common schema, while simultaneously, cross-view integrity constraints ensure that the model automatically maintains global consistency. Decisions, including explicit design choices and implicit assumptions, are propagated across all perspectives, rendering their implications across the system transparent and preserving coherence throughout the model. In doing so, the approach supports systematic analysis, traceable trade-offs, and consistent decision-making in the configuration and governance of service-oriented value networks.

To achieve this, the metamodel comprises the following core elements and relationships (see Fig. 1), which are assigned to different perspectives on the service-oriented value network (see Figs. 2, 3 and 4):

5.1 Metamodel Elements

Building on BPMN principles, a process represents the value creation flow and consists of activities and resources (see Fig. 2). Activities define the steps to be executed in the process and are named with verbs. Resources represent the inputs (tangible or intangible) required at each step and are deployed, modified or consumed during value creation. Branching and synchronization of the flow are modeled using AND/OR gateways (see Fig. 2).

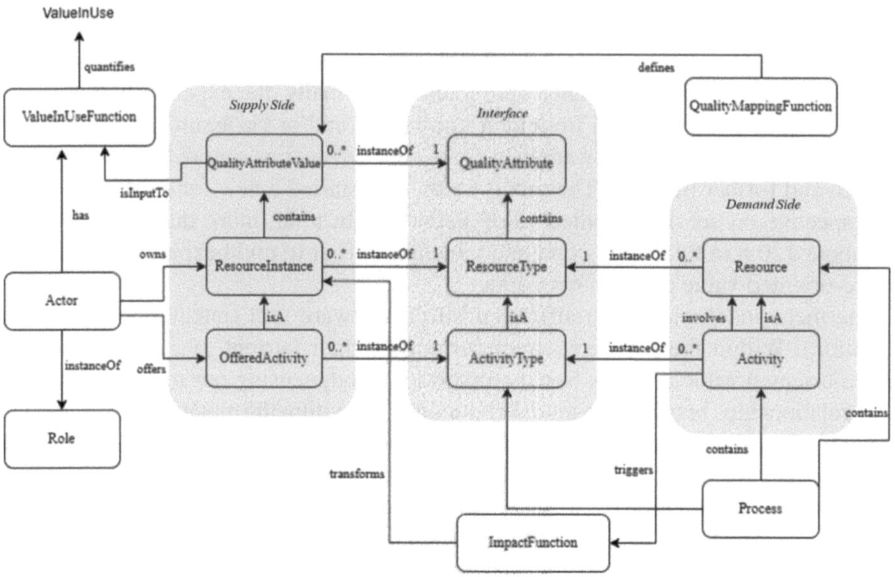

Fig. 1. Metamodel of service-oriented value creation networks—Own diagram

In the proposed model, activities are treated as resources and therefore follow the same type-instance logic as resources. Each resource is assigned to exactly one resource type. This functional classification enables an unambiguous, type-based mapping between process demands (demand side) and actor offerings (supply side). Each resource type is defined by the subset of quality attributes relevant to the value creation process.

Resource instances and offered activities constitute the supply side. They are specified by values of the corresponding quality attributes that describe their operational state in the given context.

Quality-mapping function computes the value of a specific quality attribute by deriving it from other quality attribute values, thereby making the relationship between target and inputs explicit. Overall, quality attributes delineate what matters for value creation, and their values enable execution and deployment options to be compared, selected, and evaluated.

An actor represents any person, firm, organization, or technical system within or around the network. Roles are optional classifications that restrict which kinds of activities an actor is authorized to perform and which resources it is authorized to provide or use. Actors can contribute to value creation by supplying two kinds of offerings: offered activities and resource instances.

An offered activity is an actor's commitment to perform an activity of a given type within the process. A resource instance is an actor-owned unit of a resource type that may be deployed, modified, consumed or reassigned during process. Assignments between process objects and offerings are therefore permitted only if the types match (type compatibility) and, where specified, role constraints are satisfied.

Execution effects are captured by impact functions (see Fig. 6), which specify how an activity creates, removes, reassigns or updates resources and their quality attribute values.

The actor-specific value-in-use function (see Fig. 7) measures perceived utility. It captures the benefit an actor derives from the service when acting as a beneficiary and from participation in the network when acting as a participant, based on the quality attribute values. Because the same configuration may be perceived differently, value-in-use can vary across actors and is re-evaluated whenever impact functions update the quality attribute values of resource instances.

5.2 Software Tool

The software realizes the metamodel elements within multiple complementary perspectives.

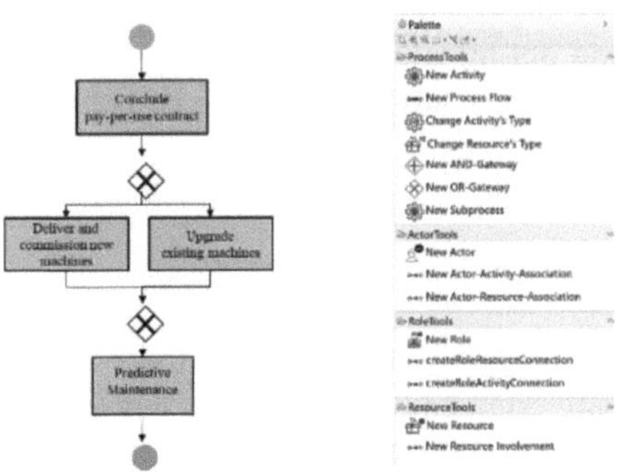

Fig. 2. Process perspective

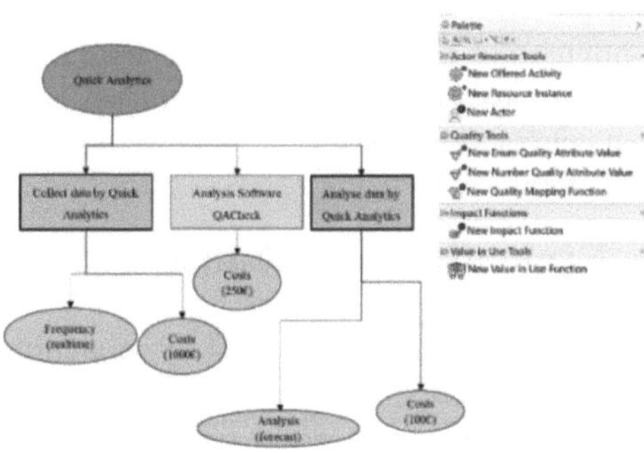

Fig. 3. Actor perspective

Consistent with established tools, the software provides a process perspective (see Fig. 2). This perspective specifies the required actions and the resources demanded by the process (demand side). It also determines the allocation of actors who can or should execute the respective activities or provide the required resources. Additionally, it defines roles that authorize activity execution and the provision or use of resources. These role specifications function as compatibility and authorization constraints for subsequent assignments and execution.

The actor perspective (see Fig. 3) instantiates the supply side by providing an inventory of the actors' capabilities, listing explicit activities, resources and the quality levels at which they can be performed or supplied.

A service-oriented value network is fully specified by (1) a defined process, (2) the necessary resources, and (3) the assignment of the actors to activities and resources.

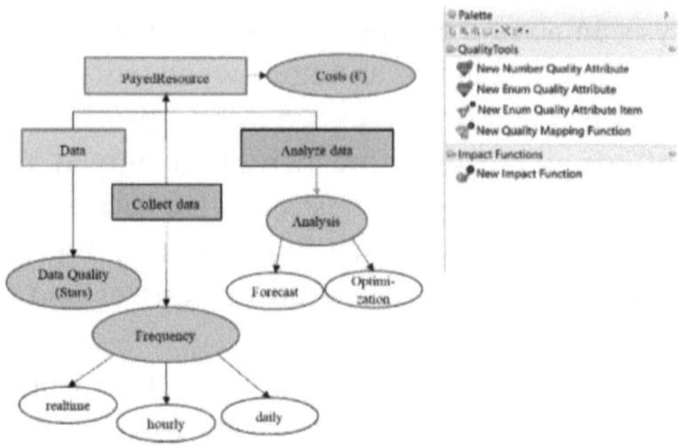

Fig. 4. Quality perspective

The service quality at network level is determined by the quality attribute values of the concrete resource and activities deployed in the process. As such, the software also incorporates a quality perspective (see Fig. 4). It specifies the relevant quality attributes, including their scales (numeric or categorical), as target or threshold levels used for evaluation.

The software represents the demand side through the process and quality perspectives, and the supply side through the actor perspective with its capability inventory. This provides a common basis for demand-supply alignment, network gap detection and configuration analysis. Integrated simulation and optimization algorithms quantify the effects of assignments and substitutions automatically, enabling results to be presented on a comparable basis.

6 Evaluation and Results

We validated the software tool by modeling and analyzing a hypothetical use case of a medium-sized spinning-machine manufacturing company considering a pay-per-use business model. We used the software tool to create a model that enables a better understanding of whether such a business model is feasible for the company and which partners need to be involved. This subscription-based approach shifts the paradigm from selling machines to delivering a value proposition based on productivity optimization and therefore maximizing machine uptime by implementing predictive maintenance. This raises several challenges, including the need to integrate new actors into the network when existing structures cannot effectively execute required resources or fail to meet the quality standards necessary to prevent machine downtime. Moreover, reconfiguring the actor network is viable only if each actor realizes greater individual value than under the previous configuration of the traditional business model. Consequently, this results in a need to find a combination of elements that enable a subscription-based business model.

The overall approach is to compare different constellations of actors performing newly defined activities or resources and to identify the scenario in which the value created for the customer and each actor is balanced at an optimal level. To this end, the model can be used to identify individual factors that contribute to value creation by simulating various epochs, allowing the modeler to iteratively adapt assumptions.

Our modelling approach uses the metamodel's elements and integrated logic to analyze how value creation is structured at each step of the process. We defined

- a value-in-use function to calculate the value for all actors,
- processes and subprocesses by making use of the activity elements,
- resources and their allocation needed to create value,
- actors that could perform activities or provide resources
- quality attributes values characterizing options, how to perform activities
- impact functions that determine how resources and subsequent activities change when an activity is performed,
- a simulation script to calculate the values created in each step and for each actor.

The value-in-use function was determined by less frequent production stops for the customer, as well as high spinning quality and low use of resources. Other actors valued high margins, data availability and customer retention.

This value creation process was mapped to a process containing four activities including an "or" decision (see Fig. 5). From "conclude pay-per-use contract", then either "upgrade machines or "deliver and commission new machines" then "predictive maintenance". The activity predictive maintenance was divided into a subprocess from collecting and analyzing data to schedule and perform maintenance.

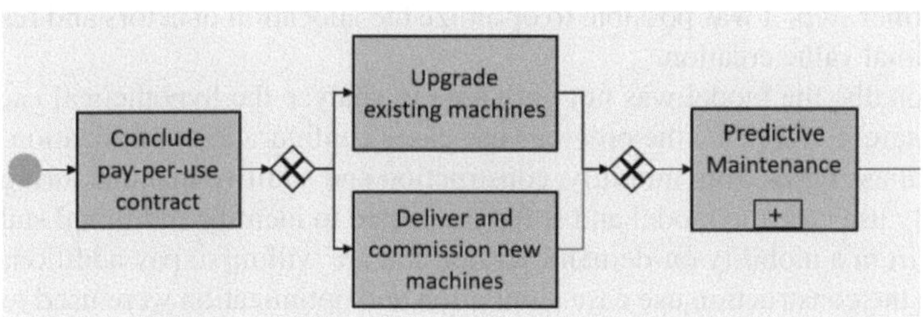

Fig. 5. Process of a pay-per-use business model

In the next step the resources "data" and "report" were defined and associated with the activities "collect data" and "analyze data". To specify the resources and activities, quality attributes like "data quality" measured in "stars" [0, 1, 2, 3, 4, 5] and "frequency" with values [realtime, hourly, daily] (see Fig. 4) allocated to the activity collect data, were defined. Actor roles like "spinning mill", "technical service provider" and "data analysis company were defined, while the role "spinning mill" was divided into two subroles "standard" and "premium customer". Each role then had specific actors like "Happy Yarns", "Müller Garne" or "Quick Analytics". For the specific actor "Quick Analytics" we defined what activities it can perform and what resources it had. In our example "Quick Analytics" could perform the activities "collect data" with the quality value "realtime" for frequency and at costs for 1000€. Lastly the functions and the simulation were scripted as described in Figs. 6, 7 and 8.

By performing the simulation, it became apparent which actors and activities contributed the most to the value creation process. This enabled us to analyze the starting question.

IF
Actor „DeeperInsights“ performs Activity „Analyze data“
THEN
Set Attribute „Analysis“ to „forecast“.
Set Attribute „Costs [€]“ + 500.
Set Attribute „Time required“ to „high“.
.
IF
Actor „QuickAnalytics“ performs Activity „Analyze data“
THEN
Set Attribute „Time required“ to „low“.
.

Fig. 6. Impact function

IF
Attribute „Analysis“ of Activity „Analyze data“ == „forecast“.
Attribute „Time required“ of Activity „Analyze data“ == „low“.
Attribute „Costs“ of Activity „Analyze data“ < 350.
THEN
Set ValueInUse to 100.

Fig. 7. Value-in-use function

Run simulation of Process „Predictive Maintenance“ for 2 epochs.

Actor „QuickAnalytics“ performs Activity „Collect data“.
Actor „QuickAnalytics“ performs Activity „Analyze data“.
Actor „QuickAnalytics“ provides Resource „Analysis Software“ through ResourceInstance „QACheck“.
Actor „Up & Running“ performs Activity „Schedule Maintenance“.
Actor „ Up & Running“ provides Resource „ Staff Planning Tool“ through ResourceInstance „Plan.AI“.
.

Fig. 8. Simulation script

In a further step, it was possible to optimize the allocation of actors and resources to obtain optimal value creation.

Additionally, the model was not only able to analyze the hypothetical use case but was also useful to replicate the previous use cases configuration optimization approach in three real use cases from mobility, construction and additive manufacturing. First, in the mobility use case the model and software helped to identify additional stakeholders that profit from a mobility on-demand service and are willing to pay additionally for it. Second, in the construction use case simulation and optimization were used to come up with optimal configurations of partners involved in a construction project, with regards to time and money saving, considering dynamic changes of the system. Third, by modelling the prosthetics ecosystem, new business models based on 3D printing technologies could be identified, that could be performed with already existing actors. In total, all use cases were defined by a complex set of questions, where the model worked as a single source of truth, and therefore was useful for discussing various perspectives regarding the system.

7 Discussion and Conclusion

The proposed metamodel and tool proved feasible and useful across one hypothetical and three industry cases as reviewed in Sect. 6. In all studies, the approach supported the end-to-end task: modeling the value creation flow as a BPMN-oriented process, representing demand through process elements (activities and resources), and supply through actors which offer activities and provide resources, deriving attributes via quality-mapping functions, propagating execution effects with impact functions, and evaluating outcomes with the actor-specific value-in-use. This combination enabled systematic comparison of alternative partner constellations and made trade-offs explicit, for example between cost, lead time, and reliability, and how these trade-offs determine value-in-use for customers, participating providers, and relevant environment actors.

The evidence, while encouraging, remains limited in scope. There are limitations that qualify the findings.

1. Modeling currently entails substantial manual effort and expert knowledge, including the selection of process-relevant attributes, the definition of quality-mapping and impact functions, the specification of actor preferences for value-in-use and the specification of role constraints. Results depend on input quality and may be sensitive to incomplete or biased input variables.
2. External validity is constrained by the small number of cases and limited sector coverage. Many organizations operate portfolios of interwoven services. Considering that, scalability and runtime behavior on very large networks have not yet been stress-tested.

Despite these limitations, the approach demonstrates practical utility. It offers a single, consistent representation that links process logic on the demand side to actor offerings on the supply side under clear assignment rules (type compatibility and roles). It renders the consequences of assignments transparent, supports what-if analysis, and helps identify missing partners, weak quality links, and promising substitutions. The explicit linkage from quality attributes and values through impact functions to value-in-use provides a clear explanatory pathway from operational assumptions to perceived value.

Future work focuses on three directions: First, we evaluate applicability to portfolios of interwoven services. Second, we reduce manual effort and expert dependence by improving the workflow and the GUI. Third, we explore AI support for the modeling process, for example assisting with attribute selection, the specification of functions as well as type- and role-consistent assignments.

Acknowledgments. The research of this paper has been carried out within the research and development project Service-oriented Value Creation (SoW). Sow is funded by the German Federal Ministry of Education and Research (BMBF) (funding no. 02K20Z000 – 02K20Z006) and implemented by Project Management Agency Karlsruhe (PTKA). The authors are responsible for the content of this publication.

References

1. Bengtsson, M., Kock, S.: "Coopetition" in business networks—To cooperate and compete simultaneously. Ind. Mark. Manage. **29**, 411–426 (2000). https://doi.org/10.1016/S0019-8501(99)00067-X
2. James, M.: The Death of Competition: Leadership and Strategy in the Age of Business Ecosystems. HarperBusiness, New York (1996)
3. Nalebuff, B.J., Brandenburger, A.M.: Co-opetition: competitive and cooperative business strategies for the digital economy. Strategy Leadersh. **25**, 28–33 (1997). https://doi.org/10.1108/eb054655
4. Oliva, R., Kallenberg, R.: Managing the transition from products to services. Int. J. Serv. Ind. Manag. **14**, 160–172 (2003). https://doi.org/10.1108/09564230310474138

5. Hensher, D.A.: The future of mobility as a service. Transp. Plan. Technol. **47**, 624–627 (2024). https://doi.org/10.1080/03081060.2024.2356619
6. Caiati, V., Rasouli, S., López, H.: Exploring the future of mobility as a service (MaaS): A co-design approach to scenario planning in European cities. J. Urban Mob. **8**, 100133 (2025). https://doi.org/10.1016/j.urbmob.2025.100133
7. Bruhn, M., Hadwich, K.: Servicetransformation. Entwicklung vom Produktanbieter zum Dienstleistungsunternehmen. Springer, Wiesbaden (2016)
8. von Stengel, R. (ed.): Gestaltung von Wertschöpfungsnetzwerken. Zugl.: Koblenz, Wiss. Hochsch. für Unternehmensführung, Diss., 1998. Gabler Edition Wissenschaft Unternehmensführung & Controlling, vol. Dt. Univ.-Verl.; Gabler, Wiesbaden (1999). https://doi.org/10.1007/978-3-322-92327-1
9. Vargo, S.L., Maglio, P.P., Akaka, M.A.: On value and value co-creation: a service systems and service logic perspective. Eur. Manag. J. **26**, 145–152 (2008). https://doi.org/10.1016/j.emj.2008.04.003
10. Bassetti, P.F., Romano, G.M.: Supply Chains and Value Networks: The Factors Driving Change and their Implications to Competition in the Industrial Sector. MIT Sloan School of Management (2003)
11. Benger, A.: Gestaltung von Wertschöpfungsnetzwerken. GITO mbH Verlag, Berlin (2007)
12. Gomes-Casseres, B.: Cooperation AND competition: how to get the best of both worlds. Strategy Leadersh. **44** (2016). https://doi.org/10.1108/SL-11-2015-0087
13. Bruhn, M., Hadwich, K.: Service coopetition—Dienstleistungen im Spannungsfeld von Wettbewerb und Kooperation. In: Bruhn, M., Hadwich, K. (eds.) Kooperative Dienstleistungen. Forum Dienstleistungsmanagement, pp. 3–34. Springer, Wiesbaden (2019). https://doi.org/10.1007/978-3-658-26389-8_1
14. Chou, H.-H., Zolkiewski, J.: Coopetition and value creation and appropriation: the role of interdependencies, tensions and harmony. Ind. Mark. Manage. **70**, 25–33 (2018). https://doi.org/10.1016/j.indmarman.2017.08.014
15. Vargo, S.L., Lusch, R.F.: Why "service"? J. Acad. Mark. Sci. **36**, 25–38 (2008). https://doi.org/10.1007/s11747-007-0068-7
16. Mustak, M., Plé, L.: A critical analysis of service ecosystems research: rethinking its premises to move forward. JSM **34**, 399–413 (2020). https://doi.org/10.1108/JSM-02-2019-0084
17. Vargo, S.L., Lusch, R.F.: Evolving to a new dominant logic for marketing. J. Mark. **68**, 1–17 (2004). https://doi.org/10.1509/jmkg.68.1.1.24036
18. Bullinger, H.-J., Ganz, W., Neuhüttler, J.: Smart services—Chancen und Herausforderungen digitalisierter Dienstleistungssysteme für Unternehmen. In: Bruhn, M., Hadwich, K. (eds.) Dienstleistungen 4.0. Forum Dienstleistungsmanagement, pp. 97–120. Springer Gabler, Wiesbaden (2017). https://doi.org/10.1007/978-3-658-17550-4_4
19. Vargo, S.L., Lusch, R.F.: Service-dominant logic. What it is, What it is not, What it might be. J. Acad. Market. Sci. **6**, 281–288 (2006)
20. Galvagno, M., Dalli, D.: Theory of value co-creation: a systematic literature review. Manag. Serv. Qual. **24**, 643–683 (2014). https://doi.org/10.1108/MSQ-09-2013-0187
21. Plé, L.: Why do we need research on value co-destruction? J. Creating Value **3**, 162–169 (2017). https://doi.org/10.1177/2394964317726451
22. Lusch, R.F., Nambisan, S.: Service innovation: a service-dominant logic perspective. MIS Quart. **39**, 155–175 (2015). https://doi.org/10.25300/MISQ/2015/39.1.07
23. Vargo, S.L., Lusch, R.F.: Institutions and axioms: an extension and update of service-dominant logic. J. Acad. Mark. Sci. **44**, 5–23 (2016). https://doi.org/10.1007/s11747-015-0456-3
24. Stauss, B., Bruhn, M.: Wertschöpfungsprozesse bei Dienstleistungen – Eine Einführung in den Sammelband. In: Bruhn, M., Stauss, B. (eds.) Wertschöpfungsprozesse bei Dienstleistungen. Forum Dienstleistungsmanagement, pp. 3–28. Gabler, Wiesbaden (2013). https://doi.org/10.1007/978-3-8349-9285-7_1

25. Pfeiffer, A., Krempels, K.-H., Jarke, M.: Service-oriented business model framework—A service-dominant logic based approach for business modeling in the digital era. In: Hammoudi, S., Smialek, M., Camp, O., Filipe, J. (eds.) Proceedings of the 19th International Conference on Enterprise Information Systems, vol. 1. April 26–29, 2017, Porto, Portugal, pp. 361–372. SCITEPRESS—Science and Technology Publications, SCITEPRESS (2017). https://doi.org/10.5220/0006255103610372
26. Ehrenthal, J.C.F., Gruen, T.W., Hofstetter, J.S.: Service Dominant-Logic als Forschungsmethode. In: Dornberger, R. (ed.) Neue Trends in Wirtschaftsinformatik und eingesetzte Technologien. Digitale Innovation und digitale Transformation, pp. 301–316. Springer, Cham (2023). https://doi.org/10.1007/978-3-031-32538-0_19
27. Walden, D.D., Roedler, G.J., Forsberg, K., Hamelin, R.D., Shortell, T.M. (eds.): Systems Engineering Handbook. A Guide for System Life Cycle Processes and Activities. Wiley, Hoboken, N.J. (2015)
28. OMG: MetaObject Facility, Object Management Group (2025). https://www.omg.org/mof/
29. Gausemeier, J., Plass, C.: Zukunftsorientierte Unternehmensgestaltung. Strategien, Geschäftsprozesse und IT-Systeme für die Produktion von morgen. Hanser, München (2014)
30. Gausemeier, J., Wieseke, J., Echterhoff, B., Isenberg, L.: Mit Industrie 4.0 zum Unternehmenserfolg - Integrative Planung von Geschäftsmodellen und Wertschöpfungssystemen (2017)
31. Shostack, G.L.: How to design a service. Eur. J. Mark. **16**, 49–63 (1982). https://doi.org/10.1108/EUM0000000004799
32. Supply Chain Operations Reference Model SCOR (2017)
33. Aagesen, G., Krogstie, J.: BPMN 2.0 for modeling business processes. In: vom Brocke, J., Rosemann, M. (eds.) Introduction, Methods, and Information Systems. International Handbook on Information Systems, pp. 219–250. Springer, Berlin (2015). https://doi.org/10.1007/978-3-642-45100-3_10
34. Akkermans, H., Baida, Z., Gordijn, J., Peiia, N., Altuna, A., Laresgoiti, I.: Value webs: using ontologies to bundle real-world services. IEEE Intell. Syst. **19**, 57–66 (2004). https://doi.org/10.1109/MIS.2004.35
35. Sales, T.P., Guarino, N., Guizzardi, G., Mylopoulos, J.: An ontological analysis of value propositions. In: Hallé, S. (ed.) 2017 IEEE 21st International Enterprise Distributed Object Computing Conference—EDOC 2017. 10–13 October 2017, Quebec City, Quebec, Canada : proceedings, pp. 184–193. IEEE, Piscataway, NJ (2017). https://doi.org/10.1109/EDOC.2017.32
36. Da Torres, I.S., Fantinato, M., Branco, G.M., Gordijn, J.: Guidelines to derive an e3value business model from a BPMN process model: an experiment on real-world scenarios. Softw. Syst. Model. **22**, 599–618 (2023). https://doi.org/10.1007/s10270-022-01074-1
37. Blau, B., Kramer, J., Conte, T.: Service value networks. In: Hofreiter, B. (ed.) 2009 IEEE Conference on Commerce and Enterprise Computing. CEC 2009 ; 20–23 July 2009, Vienna, Austria (including 4 workshops), pp. 194–201. IEEE, Piscataway, NJ (2009). https://doi.org/10.1109/CEC.2009.64
38. Pedrinaci, C., Cardoso, J., Leidig, T.: Linked USDL: A vocabulary for web-scale service trading. In: Presutti, V. (ed.) The Semantic Web: Trends and Challenges. 11th international conference, ESWC 2014, Anissaras, Crete, Greece, May 25–29, 2014 ; Proceedings. Lecture Notes in Computer Science, vol. 8465, pp. 68–82. Springer, Cham, Heidelberg (2014). https://doi.org/10.1007/978-3-319-07443-6_6
39. SPARQL 1.1 Service Description (2013). https://www.w3.org/TR/sparql11-service-description/
40. OWL-S: Semantic Markup for Web Services (2004)

41. Pedrinaci, C., Domingue, J., Sheth, A.P.: Semantic web services. In: Domingue, J. (ed.) Handbook of Semantic Web Technologies. With 96 Tables. Springer Reference, pp. 977–1035. Springer, Berlin, Heidelberg (2011). https://doi.org/10.1007/978-3-540-92913-0_22
42. Cardoso, J., Sheth, A.: Semantic e-workflow composition. J. Intell. Inf. Syst. **21**, 191–225 (2003). https://doi.org/10.1023/A:1025542915514
43. Scheithauer, G.: A Service Description Method for Service Ecosystems : Meta Models, Modeling Notations, and Model Transformations. University of Bamberg Press (2011)
44. Tombeil, A., Block, L.: Towards a metamodel for service-oriented value creation. In: Leitner, C., Neuhüttler, J., Bassano, C., Satterfield, D. (eds.) The Human Side of Service Engineering. AHFE International Conference. AHFE International (2023). https://doi.org/10.54941/ahfe1003132
45. Fernández-López, M., Gómez-Pérez, A., Juristo, N.: Methontology: From ontological art towards ontological engineering. In: AAAI Technical Report SS-97-06, vol. 33–40 (1997)
46. Encyclopedia of Sociology: Metatheory (2025). https://www.encyclopedia.com/social-sciences/encyclopedias-almanacs-transcripts-and-maps/metatheory
47. Zhao, S.: Metatheory, metamethod, meta-data-analysis: what, why, and how? Sociol. Perspect. **34**, 377–390 (1991). https://doi.org/10.2307/1389517
48. Gronback, R.C.: Eclipse Modeling Project. A Domain-Specific Language Toolkit. Safari Books Online, Upper Saddle River, N.J., Boston, Mass (2009)
49. Eclipse Foundation: Xcore—Eclipsepedia (2024). https://wiki.eclipse.org/Xcore

Startups, SaaS, and Innovation Ecosystems

The Finnish Way to SaaS Scaling: A Qualitative Study

Esa Engblom, Andrey Saltan(✉), and Sami Hyrynsalmi

LUT University, Lahti, Finland
{andrey.saltan,sami.hyrynsalmi}@lut.fi

Abstract. Scaling is a critical yet fragile phase for software startups; many fail to transition from early traction to durable growth. Existing research largely examines large, capital-rich ecosystems, leaving comparatively less known about scaling in smaller but digitally advanced economies. We report an inductive, qualitative multiple-case study of six Finnish software-as-a-service (SaaS) startups and develop an integrated model spanning three aggregate dimensions: *business*, *organizational*, and *engineering*. We show how choices across these dimensions interact to form a coherent scaling configuration suited to contexts with limited domestic demand and strong engineering talent. The paper contributes by: (i) offering a context-sensitive account of SaaS scaling in a small open economy; (ii) integrating business, organizational, and engineering choices into a unified framework, and (iii) specifying micro-level guardrails that translate operational excellence into implementable practice. We discuss implications for policymakers, investors, and founders seeking globally competitive ventures.

Keywords: Software Startups · SaaS · Scaling · Finland

1 Introduction

Software startups drive a large share of contemporary software innovation [11], increasingly through software-as-a-service (SaaS) models [15]. Operating under acute time, talent, and capital constraints, such ventures progress through distinct phases with evolving engineering and managerial goals [6]. Among these, *scaling*—a time-bounded period of rapid growth requiring coordinated changes in business model, technology architecture, and organization design—remains especially failure-prone [2,3,8,16]. Driven by the high importance of scaling, research has expanded substantially; yet most empirical knowledge still reflects practices in large, capital-rich ecosystems.

Three gaps motivate our study. First, a *context gap*: although there are well-known success cases, we know comparatively little about how SaaS ventures scale in small but digitally mature markets with strong engineering talent, such as Finland within the Nordic region [1]. Second, an *integration gap*: existing research often isolates (i) business and go-to-market (GTM) choices, (ii) organizational structures, policies, and processes, and (iii) technology and engineering

G. Herzwurm et al. (Eds.): ICSOB 2025, LNBIP 574, pp. 291–308, 2026.
https://doi.org/10.1007/978-3-032-14518-5_23

decisions, rather than explaining how choices within these pillars interact during scaling [6,7,10]. Third, a *micro-practice gap*: concrete product and architecture guardrails that preserve scalability (e.g., single-product discipline, bottleneck-first execution, instrumentation-led roadmaps) are under-specified relative to high-level prescriptions [5,12].

The aim of this paper is to build an empirical understanding of how Finnish SaaS startups approach scaling, focusing on the interplay of business, organizational, and technological choices within these dimensions. Our research is guided by one primary research question (RQ): *How do Finnish SaaS startups approach scaling?* We probe two sub-questions: (SQ1) *How do Finnish SaaS startups develop and apply internal strategies during scaling?* and (SQ2) *How do external conditions shape the scaling approaches of Finnish SaaS startups?*

We conducted a qualitative, inductive multiple-case study of six active Finnish SaaS startups. Founders and senior leaders participated in semi-structured interviews. Following the Gioia methodology [4], we developed first-order concepts, second-order themes, and aggregate dimensions to provide an auditable link from informant accounts to emergent theory.

In preview, our findings depict a coherent configuration suited to a small, digitally mature economy: early international orientation with lightweight local hubs; product-led growth (PLG) and inbound foundations augmented by partner "lighthouse" wins and staged outbound motions; lean planning with persistent experimentation; distributed, trust-based teams; and a single, unified product line with pragmatic, bottleneck-first remediation of technical debt. Product–market fit (PMF) is treated as dynamic and instrumented end-to-end, and external capital is used selectively to accelerate—rather than initiate—scaling.

This paper contributes by offering: (i) an integrated, context-sensitive model of SaaS scaling in a small open economy; (ii) micro-level guardrails that translate "operational excellence" into implementable practice; and (iii) practical insights for policymakers, investors, and founders seeking to build globally competitive software ventures.

The remainder of the paper reviews related work (Sect. 2), details the methodology (Sect. 3), presents findings (Sect. 4), discusses implications (Sect. 5), and concludes (Sect. 6).

2 Background

We organize the background around three core dimensions—*business*, *organizational*, and *engineering*. We adapt SaaS scholarship that foregrounds business and engineering concerns [14] to a scaling lens, treating scaling as an organizational process that hinges on the interplay of internal transformation, technical architecture, and evolving business models [2,3]. Because dedicated, SaaS-specific studies of scaling are scarce, we draw selectively on adjacent literatures on software startups, digital ventures, and organizational scaling to ground our empirical analysis.

2.1 SaaS Startups and Business Model

Software startups are new, growth-oriented ventures that create and market software-intensive products under acute resource and knowledge constraints [11]. They progress through distinct life-cycle phases with evolving engineering and managerial goals, moving from inception and stabilization to growth and maturity [6]. Software-as-a-service (SaaS) has become a dominant delivery and monetization model: software is operated by the provider, accessed over the internet, and monetized via recurring subscriptions, which shifts emphasis to acquisition, retention, and unit economics [15].

These conditions create characteristic tensions. Limited time, skills, and capital foster short iterations and experimentation; the associated speed–quality trade-offs can accumulate technical debt that later constrains growth [5,6]. Commercially, SaaS growth depends on compounding revenue from cohorts rather than one-off licenses, placing a premium on retention, expansion, and cost-efficient GTM (e.g., self-serve and inbound motions, with enterprise sales introduced where appropriate). Product instrumentation and data-driven decision making are central, both for improving user journeys and for managing pricing and packaging choices [15]. In small open economies (e.g., the Nordics), limited home-market scale often implies early international orientation and an emphasis on operational efficiency—themes we return to in our findings [1].

2.2 Startup Scaling

We adopt recent clarifications that distinguish *scalability* (the latent ability to grow outputs with sublinear input growth), *scaling* (the time-bounded process of rapid growth), and *scale-up* (the resulting organizational state) [2,3]. In this view, scaling is an organizational transformation that leverages digital resources so that performance grows faster than size. Timing and prerequisites are critical. Evidence suggests that premature scaling—before validating the business model through rigorous experimentation—raises failure risk; on average, ventures delay scaling several years post founding, and earlier scaling is associated with less pre-scaling experimentation and higher failure likelihood [8]. Complementary work emphasizes ongoing experimentation beyond initial market validation [16] and highlights that profitable scaling requires moving from *product–market fit* to *profit–market fit*, i.e., growing revenue while keeping marginal costs and complexity in check [12]. Process studies of digital ventures point to bundles of activities that prepare and sustain scaling—opportunity scanning, business-model refinement, operational excellence, and data capabilities [7,10]. For software startups, these logics interact with life-cycle transitions (e.g., maturing engineering and project practices) [6].

Business Aspects of SaaS Scaling. On the commercial side, ventures build repeatable go-to-market (GTM) systems while safeguarding unit economics. Research on rapid digital scaling highlights three recurring patterns: (i) systematic opportunity identification and portfolio management of growth bets; (ii) experimentation-driven refinement of value propositions, pricing, and channels; and (iii) instrumented funnels with key performance indicators (KPIs) that govern resource allocation [7,10,16]. In SaaS, self-serve or product-led acquisition with inbound motions is often supplemented by higher-touch sales in enterprise segments; in all cases, telemetry is used to move customers from activation to retention and expansion [15]. Pricing and packaging choices are governed by value parameters (e.g., seats, usage, capacity) and are commonly communicated through subscription tiers rather than purely metered billing; in practice, fixed-price tiering frequently prevails over usage-only models for budgeting simplicity and vendor operations. Strategic pricing integrates five layers—value creation, price structure (metrics, fences, controls), value communication, pricing policy, and price level—providing a governance stack for aligning price with value [13].

Sustained scaling typically requires substantial resources for market entry, customer success, and brand building, yet capital intensity and pacing vary by strategy [7,12]. Bootstrapped paths emphasize cash efficiency and controlled growth, whereas externally funded paths may prioritize speed to capture network or timing advantages; both place pressure on operational discipline and measurement. For startups in small open economies, internationalization is often not optional: companies expand beyond the domestic market early, establishing local presence where necessary to build trust while keeping core operations lean [1]. Across these choices, a recurring theme is the need to identify and remove the most binding growth constraints—commercial, operational, or architectural—through explicit goals, diagnostics, and targeted investments [12].

Organizational Aspects of SaaS Scaling. Scaling reconfigures the organization. Evidence from massive and rapid digital scaling shows investments in leadership capacity, role specialization, and lightweight structure to preserve speed as coordination demands grow [7]. Firms formalize only as necessary—clarifying goals, responsibilities, and interfaces—while protecting autonomy in small, accountable teams [12]. As founders transition into CEO roles, they face delegation, culture-building, and cross-functional alignment challenges typical of the scaling pivot [10]. A rapidly adopted pattern is to formalize these routines as Product Ops: a function that centralizes product telemetry and data management, standardizes tooling and process hygiene, serves as an operational complement to product management, and orchestrates cross-team collaboration, thereby reducing scaling friction through optimization and alignment across these four dimensions [9].

Operational excellence underwrites these changes: organizations adopt data-driven management systems with clear KPIs; integrate analytics and automation into core processes; and institutionalize fast feedback from customers and operations into roadmapping [7,10]. Experimentation persists after initial validation: companies continue controlled tests to refine segmentation, channels, and value delivery mechanisms at scale [16]. For internationally oriented SaaS startups, distributed teams combine access to talent with customer proximity but raise new coordination demands that must be counterbalanced by clear interfaces, documentation, and platform practices—topics our study surfaces empirically.

Engineering Aspects of SaaS Scaling. From an engineering standpoint, scaling usually coincides with a transition from improvisation to disciplined, instrumented delivery. Prior work on software startups identifies pre-scaling prerequisites: tight customer feedback loops and requirements discipline; more formal project management with explicit planning, metrics, and budgets; and alignment between engineering and business priorities [6]. Startups commonly accrue technical debt during early, fast cycles; unmanaged debt correlates with declining productivity and quality and can become a binding constraint during growth [5,6]. A pragmatic, ROI-aware approach to debt management—identifying major debt items, estimating impact, and sequencing remediation against growth objectives—helps preserve speed while improving resilience [6].

At scale, engineering capabilities shift toward: (i) automation of build–test–deploy through continuous integration and delivery; (ii) observability and product analytics to detect bottlenecks and inform roadmaps; and (iii) architectural and operational choices that keep a single, unified product line viable as usage and heterogeneity increase [7,10]. While many technologies (e.g., cloud-native deployment, modular architectures, data pipelines) are available, the salient principle from a scaling perspective is constraint removal: teams prioritize work that unlocks growth capacity—performance, reliability, onboarding, or extensibility—over diffuse feature expansion [12]. This engineering posture aligns with our empirical pattern of concentrating development on the highest-leverage growth bottlenecks and avoiding customer-specific forks that erode scalability.

2.3 Synthesis and Research Gaps

The literature establishes that software startups face distinctive product-centric constraints and life-cycle transitions [6]; that scaling is an organizational transformation distinct from generic growth [2,3]; that premature scaling elevates failure risk and experimentation remains vital beyond initial validation [8,16]; and that rapid digital scaling is supported by data-driven commercial processes and operational excellence [7,10,12]. However, three gaps persist that motivate our study and align with our research questions:

1. **Context gap (small open economies).** Most empirical accounts of scaling analyze ventures in large, capital-rich ecosystems. We lack fine-grained evidence on how SaaS startups in small, digitally mature markets—such as Finland within the Nordic region—configure scaling choices when domestic demand is limited and internationalization is early [1]. This gap underpins our primary research question (RQ) and our sub-question on external conditions (SQ2).
2. **Integration gap (business—organization—engineering).** Existing studies often foreground one dimension at a time (e.g., commercial playbooks, organizational design, or technology/process). We need an integrative, empirically grounded view that links GTM strategies, organizational arrangements, and engineering/architecture decisions during the scaling phase for SaaS startups [6,7,10]. This gap motivates our focus on the three aggregate dimensions.

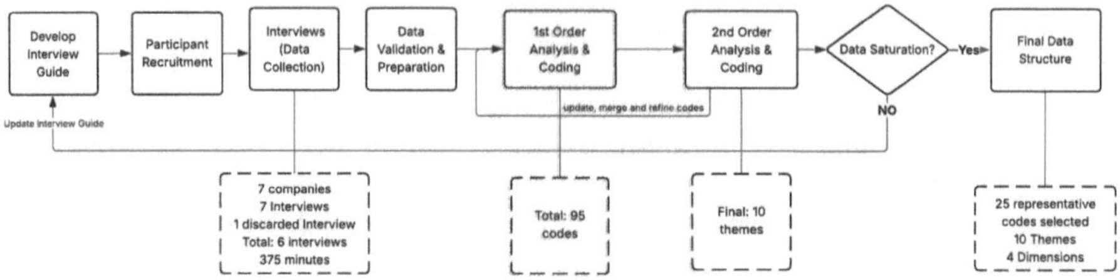

Fig. 1. Research process

3. **Micro-practice gap (product and architecture guardrails).** For SaaS specifically, the literature offers limited evidence on the concrete product and architectural guardrails that preserve scalability at growth (e.g., unified product vs. customer-specific forks; prioritizing removal of growth bottlenecks; instrumentation driving roadmaps) and on how these interact with distributed teams and early internationalization. This gap motivates our sub-question on internal strategies and practices (SQ1) [5,6,12].

In summary, SaaS scaling hinges on coordinated decisions across business, organizational, and engineering dimensions. Yet how these decisions are configured in small, digitally advanced economies remains under-documented. Our qualitative multiple-case study of Finnish SaaS startups addresses this gap.

3 Methodology

This study employs a qualitative, inductive, multiple-case design to explain *how Finnish SaaS startups approach scaling* in a small, digitally advanced economy. An interpretivist stance informs the work: founder and senior managers are treated as theory-relevant constructions of organizational reality. Consistent with the paper's framing, we analyze the interplay of business, organizational, and engineering choices. The inquiry is guided by one primary research question ***RQ: How do Finnish SaaS startups approach scaling?*** and two sub-questions:

- *SQ1: How do Finnish SaaS startups develop and apply internal strategies during scaling?*
- *SQ2: How do external conditions shape the scaling approaches of Finnish SaaS startups?*

Figure 1 depicts the end-to-end process from interview-guide development through Gioia-style coding to the three aggregate dimensions reported in the next section.

Cases, Participants, and Sampling. The unit of analysis is the company's scaling approach; the unit of observation is the founder or senior leader responsible

Table 1. Study participants

ID	Company size	Product category	Role
Int 1	501–1000	Marketing & Demand Generation Tools	Founder
Int 2	101–250	Sales Enablement & Intelligence Tools	Founder
Int 3	11–50	Customer Feedback & Engagement Tools	Founder
Int 4	251–500	Marketing & Demand Generation Tools	Founder
Int 5	11–50	Sales Enablement & Intelligence Tools	Sr. Executive
Int 6	501–1000	Developer-Oriented Software Management	Founder

for scaling and associated choices. We used purposive sampling, complemented by snowballing, to recruit knowledgeable informants who met three criteria: (1) founding member or senior executive centrally involved in scaling; (2) currently active Finnish SaaS company; and (3) company founded between 2012–2016. Seven informants were interviewed; one was excluded because the business model leaned toward consulting, yielding a final sample of six. The six interviewed companies are B2B SaaS providers, specializing in areas like marketing, sales optimization, and data or software management solutions and span headcount bands from 11–50 to 501–1000 employees. To preserve confidentiality while offering context, Table 1 reports aggregated metadata. The sampling logic seeks cross-case variation in scaling approaches while holding national context constant.

Data Collection. We conducted semi-structured interviews via Microsoft Teams. Each session lasted 45–60 min, followed a guide aligned to the three focal dimensions (business, organizational, engineering), and was audio-recorded with consent. The guide probed (i) growth triggers and readiness (e.g., PMF signals, funding), (ii) GTM evolution (e.g., PLG/inbound vs. sales-led motions), (iii) organization design (e.g., talent, structure, decision rights), (iv) engineering and architecture practices (e.g., technical-debt management, instrumentation, product-line strategy), and (v) external conditions (e.g., domestic market size, talent and capital availability, customer geographies, partner/channel ecosystems). The guide was iteratively refined as new themes surfaced. Interviews were conducted in Finnish per participant preference; participants could clarify statements at the end of each session.

Data Preparation and Use of AI. Recordings were transcribed automatically and verified line-by-line; identifiers were removed and pseudonyms assigned (e.g., *Int 3*). Finnish interviews were translated with a large-language model (LLM); translations were checked against the originals with spot back-translation of sensitive passages. An LLM assisted with (i) transcription, (ii) translation, (iii) retrieval of representative excerpts already identified by the researcher, and (iv) final grammar/spelling checks of this manuscript. Raw data remained anonymous; processing sessions were private and temporary; all outputs were human-reviewed by the author, who retains full responsibility for AI-assisted steps.

Anonymized transcripts were stored in secure cloud storage; recordings were deleted after verification. ATLAS.ti[1] was used to manage data and codes.

Analysis. We followed Gioia et al. guidelines [4] to construct an auditable link from informant accounts to emergent theoretical structure. The workflow combined immersion, coding, constant comparison, and progressive aggregation, with analytic memos throughout:

- *First-order (informant-centric) coding.* Transcripts were read line-by-line and manually coded; 95 first-order codes were initially identified across cases.
- *Second-order (researcher-centric) themes.* Through iterative clustering, comparison, and consolidation of overlapping labels, first-order codes were grouped into conceptually distinct categories. Weak or idiosyncratic categories were discarded, yielding 10 robust second-order themes.
- *Aggregate structure.* For sense-making, the 10 themes were first organized into four intermediate clusters; for reporting coherence and alignment with the paper's framing, these were synthesized into three *aggregate dimensions*—business, organizational, and engineering—which structure our findings and interpretation. To convey traceability, representative excerpts (mapped to their originating codes) are used in the data-structure display and findings narrative.

To strengthen analytic rigor within a concise design, we prepared within-case write-ups prior to cross-case comparison; used constant comparison to test emergent themes against rival explanations and negative cases; monitored codebook stabilization as an indicator of saturation (final interviews added nuance but no substantively new first-order concepts); and maintained an audit trail of code definitions, merges/splits, and memoed decisions. A light peer debrief reviewed the codebook, anonymized excerpts, and data structure for coherence and parsimony (no raw identifying data were shared). The researcher maintained reflexive memos to surface assumptions and mitigate single-coder bias.

Alignment with Research Questions and Artifacts. The final data structure directly addresses the RQ and SQs. Business-level themes (early internationalization; PLG/inbound with selective high-touch; capital strategy and unit economics discipline) and organizational themes (distributed teams; lightweight structure; role specialization; data-driven management) speak to *how internal strategies are developed and applied during scaling* (SQ1). Engineering themes (removing growth bottlenecks; instrumentation guiding roadmaps; maintaining a single unified product line to avoid customer-specific forks and manage debt) inform *how product and architecture choices enable or constrain scaling* (part of SQ1). Context and external-condition codes (domestic market size, talent and capital availability, customer geographies, partner/channel ecosystems) explain *how external factors shape scaling approaches* (SQ2).

[1] https://atlasti.com.

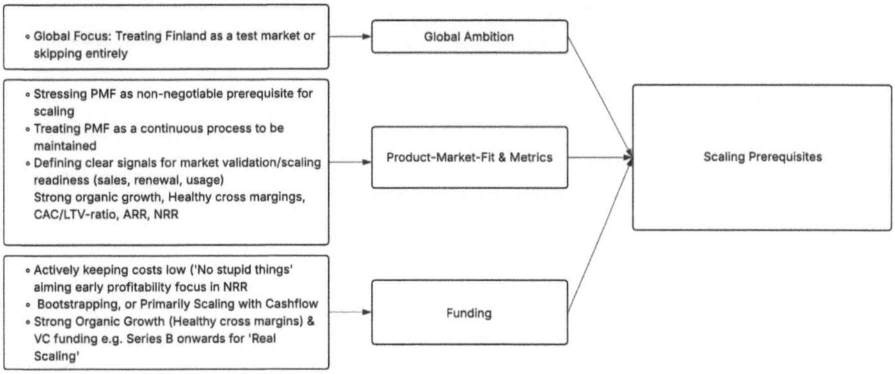

Fig. 2. Scaling prerequisites

4 Results

This section reports cross-case patterns from interviews with six Finnish SaaS startups. Mirroring the literature review, we present (i) *scaling prerequisites* and three aggregate dimensions: (ii) *business*, (iii) *organizational*, and (iv) *engineering*. We integrate short, illustrative quotations directly into the text (attributed as *Int #*) and use cautious prevalence descriptors (e.g., "most," "some") to indicate scope.

4.1 Scaling Prerequisites

Figure 2 overviews three recurring SaaS scaling prerequisites: *Global ambition*, *PMF & metrics*, and *Funding posture.*

Global Ambition. Founders commonly treated Finland as a validation ground rather than the primary market. One described moving quickly from domestic traction to a similarity market "to confirm it was global PMF" (Int 1), while another emphasized a born-global stance ("our first customer was from Mexico… Finland has always been less than 1% of our sales," Int 6). Several respondents framed market choice as data-driven, with English-first productization and minimal early localization to keep options open.

PMF & Metrics. Participants uniformly stressed that "you need product–market fit before even thinking about scaling" (Int 1) and that PMF is continuously re-validated. Decision making was explicitly metrics-driven: "find the real numbers… verify the feeling with math" (Int 3). PLG funnels were instrumented end-to-end—"Visitors → Signup → Activation → Upgrade → Retention/NRR[2]

[2] NRR, or Net Revenue Retention, is a metric used to measure how well company retain and grow revenue from existing customer base.

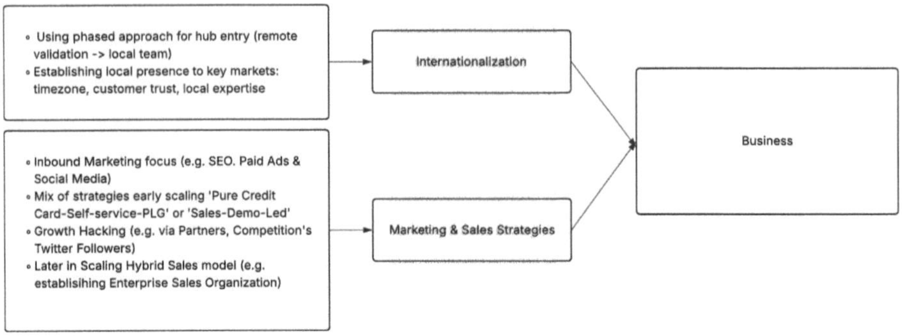

Fig. 3. Business aspects of scaling

→ LTV:CAC[3]" (Int 3)—and favorable LTV:CAC ratios were treated as investability signals (Int 3). Given finite resources, teams focused on the largest bottlenecks: "you can't solve everything at once... we focused on the biggest pains" (Int 6) (Fig. 3).

Funding Posture. A pragmatic, capital-efficient stance was salient. Some companies aimed to be "cash-flow positive" on modest external capital (e.g., "€600k to become cash-flow positive," Int 1) and "scaled purely with cash flow" (Int 2); others raised later rounds to accelerate only after strong margins and traction ("grew 3–4x a year purely organically, before raising Series B for intentional scaling," Int 6). Cost discipline—"kept costs very low... didn't do anything stupid" (Int 1)—was a common thread.

4.2 Business Aspects

Internationalization. Most cases established lightweight local hubs or subsidiaries in priority markets to build trust, manage time zones, and access customer context. One founder noted the credibility boost when "a customer called, they heard an American accent" (Int 6). Entry paths followed either adjacency (e.g., "Finland, then Sweden, then Germany... each step ensured it wasn't just a local phenomenon," Int 1) or a data-driven pull ("recruit first salespeople into regions with best self-serve traction," Int 3). Market selection combined Ideal Customer Profile (ICP) density ("Berlin, London," Int 1) with evidence from organic demand and search engine optimization (SEO) (Int 3).

Marketing and Sales Strategies. PLG and inbound formed the commercial backbone. Some operated "pure inbound" for years—"customer comes having almost decided to buy" (Int 6)—and several emphasized start-to-finish self-serve

[3] LTV:CAC ratio, or Lifetime Value to Customer Acquisition Cost ratio, is a metric that compares the total revenue a customer is expected to generate throughout their relationship with a company (LTV) to the cost of acquiring that customer (CAC).

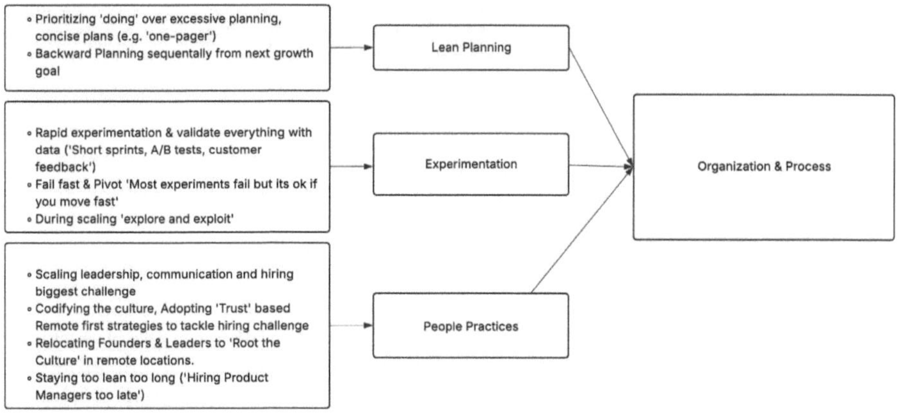

Fig. 4. Organizational aspects of scaling

("product-led… self-serve onboarding, pay… no contact needed," Int 4). Cost-efficient tactics included narrow digital targeting ("dug up followers of competitors [on Twitter]… very targeted marketing," Int 6) and partner-led lighthouse references ("helped our partner's most demanding customers… started to get intros," Int 1). Outbound was layered only when justified by Annual Contract Value (ACV)/complexity ("tested outbound during B round… not a goldmine then… later building a larger outbound machine," Int 6) (Fig. 4).

4.3 Organizational Aspects

Lean Planning. Planning was intentionally lightweight and execution-oriented. One company advanced on "one A4 page for entering Germany… go get customers, reach this point, then see what's next" (Int 1); another favored backcasting as "superior compared to the incremental approach" (Int 6). Founders highlighted decisive commits ("decide and go for it… everyone commits," Int 2) and short feedback cycles.

Experimentation. All cases described persistent, structured experimentation. Founders recalled two-week sprints where "adding onboarding steps hurt activation, [so we] quickly removed [them]" (Int 3). Several validated with prototypes—"don't bother the developer until we're 100% sure… validate with Figma, test with customers… prioritize features with most revenue potential" (Int 3)—and used frequent customer exposure ('meet 100 potential customers and see what happens… exposing software via sales was the best market research," Int 2). Teams also differentiated exploration from exploitation work—"different people for Explore vs. Exploit" (Int 1)—to avoid role conflict.

People Practices. Distributed and remote-first engineering extended talent access and supported customer proximity. One founder noted being an "early

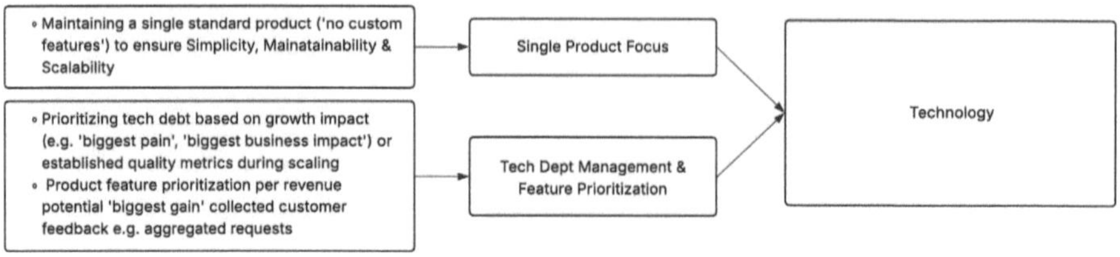

Fig. 5. Engineering aspects of scaling

adopter of remote work... first developer from Poland" (Int 4); another described norms to keep remote contributors included: "no decisions made that aren't visible to everyone... Slack, daily video calls, everything documented... the cornerstone is trust" (Int 4). Culture was seeded deliberately in new hubs—"always had someone from the company [early]... culture came via osmosis... more problems in places purely remote" (Int 6). As complexity increased, teams clarified topology (e.g., "Maintenance/DevOps plus 'Attack' [feature] team," Int 6) to balance reliability and change velocity (Fig. 5).

4.4 Engineering Aspects

Single-Product Focus. All cases protected a single, unified product line: "everyone's on the same codebase, no custom forks even for big clients... it's simpler" (Int 4). Feature pilots occurred with individual customers but were "rolled out for everyone" once validated (Int 6). English-first productization supported early global reach, with additional languages/localization added later.

Technical-Debt Management and Prioritization. Two early archetypes appeared. Some engineer-led teams over-invested pre-PMF—"spent about a year coding... de-risked future scalability issues" (Int 6)—while others accepted early debt to reach PMF fast ("incurred technical debt early, optimizing for speed," Int 1), acknowledging slowdowns ("tech debt slowed us," Int 2). Regardless of path, prioritization converged on business impact: "where are the biggest obstacles to growth right now?" (Int 1). Teams used quality proxies to guide investment (e.g., "problems per 1000 nodes... decrease via automation," Int 6) and sequenced engineering work to remove bottlenecks that constrained activation, reliability, or extensibility.

Synthesis

Across cases, a coherent configuration emerges for scaling from a small, digitally mature economy: early international orientation with lightweight hubs; PLG/inbound foundations augmented by partner referrals and staged outbound; lean planning with persistent experimentation; distributed, trust-based teams; and a single product line with pragmatic, bottleneck-first debt remediation. Variations in funding (cash-flow vs. VC-accelerated) and early build posture (engineer-heavy vs. speed-first MVP) represent pathway differences that converge on the same guardrails. Collectively, these patterns answer the RQ and show how business, organizational, and engineering decisions intertwine to produce scaling in practice.

5 Discussion

5.1 Answer to the Research Question

Finnish SaaS startups approach scaling as a context-fit operating system that tightly links GTM, organization, and architecture. Confronted with a small domestic base, teams internationalize early via lightweight, customer-facing hubs and sequence market entry by ICP density and self-serve pull; PLG/inbound functions as the default acquisition-and-learning engine, with partner "lighthouse" wins and staged outbound layered when ACV and deal complexity justify it. Execution is governed by end-to-end instrumentation (visitor → activation → retention/NRR), unit economics gates (e.g., LTV:CAC, margin), and a recurring practice of naming and removing the binding growth constraint each cycle. Organizationally, distributed, trust-based teams operate within minimalist structure, clear interfaces, and role specialization, sustaining speed through data-driven cadences and continuous experimentation. Architecturally, a single product line (one codebase, no customer-specific forks) is protected by Continuous Integration/Continuous Delivery (CI/CD) and observability, while technical debt is remediated when—and because—it becomes a growth bottleneck. Together, these mutually reinforcing choices keep coordination costs sublinear and enable durable international expansion from a small, digitally mature base.

How Internal Strategies Drive Scaling (SQ1). The cases depict a repeatable sequencing logic. Commercially, PLG/inbound creates a measurable flow from activation to expansion while preserving cash efficiency; sales-assist and enterprise motions are added selectively as ACV rises. Teams run constraint-focused cadences: each cycle surfaces the most binding obstacle (onboarding friction, reliability incidents, sales capacity) and concentrates resources there, echoing process models of digital scaling that stress opportunity scanning, operational excellence, and data-driven decision making [7,10,16]. Organizationally, lightweight planning (brief, outcome-oriented plans and backcasting) coexists with persistent experimentation and explicit separation of exploration and exploitation work, which mitigates role conflict and preserves delivery tempo. A disciplined single-product posture ties these choices together by ensuring that learning and improvements accrue to one codebase rather than fragment across forks.

How External Conditions Shape Approaches (SQ2). Operating from a small open economy modifies both pacing and posture. Limited home-market scale shifts internationalization earlier; English-tolerant customer segments reduce initial localization needs and allow English-first productization; and talent dispersion makes distributed teams a default rather than an exception. Local capital markets and a strong engineering ethos encourage capital efficiency, with external finance used predominantly to accelerate validated plays rather than to initiate them. Lightweight hubs in ICP-dense regions solve trust, responsiveness, and time-zone frictions without proliferating product variants—an organizational device that fits the combination of small domestic demand and high digital maturity [1]. Read alongside work that frames scaling as an organizational process where outputs grow faster than inputs [2,3], these boundary conditions help explain why Finnish ventures emphasize instrumentation, hub-based proximity, and architectural discipline over breadth of local build-outs.

Cross-Domain Integration: Mechanisms, Not Checklists. A central insight is that commercial, organizational, and engineering choices cohere as a mechanism rather than a set of independent practices. PLG/inbound yields high-frequency behavioral data; that telemetry powers constraint-focused governance; governance, in turn, prioritizes engineering work that unlocks growth capacity (performance, reliability, onboarding, extensibility); and single-product discipline ensures those improvements scale to all tenants. The mechanism thereby converts measurement into momentum: analytics → constraint identification → targeted investments → codebase-wide gains. This integrated view complements research streams that often analyze one pillar at a time [6,7,10] and specifies how they interact during scale-up.

Micro-level Guardrails for SaaS Scaling. Across cases, we observe a compact set of guardrails that turn general prescriptions about "operational excellence" into implementable practice:

1. **Single product line.** One codebase; no customer-specific forks; pilots are rolled to all tenants once validated.
2. **Instrumentation-first.** Uniform telemetry across the PLG funnel and product usage; KPI reviews drive resource allocation.
3. **Bottleneck-first execution.** Each cycle names a single binding constraint and concentrates cross-functional effort there.
4. **Debt as a growth variable.** Service technical debt when it blocks activation, reliability, or extensibility; make ROI explicit.
5. **Lightweight hubs.** Customer-facing presence in priority markets for trust and responsiveness without duplicating product/engineering.
6. **Minimalist structure with clear interfaces.** Small, accountable teams; explicit boundaries between explore/exploit work.
7. **Progressive localization.** English-first productization; add language/region features when validated by demand and support cost.

These guardrails are not context-free rules but design principles whose payoff depends on the small open economy conditions described above.

5.2 Positioning Within and Extending Prior Research

The configuration we document is consistent with the idea of scaling as an organizational transformation in which performance grows faster than size [2,3], but it clarifies *how* such returns are achieved in a small, digitally mature context: early internationalization through lightweight hubs, PLG/inbound as the learning-and-acquisition engine, and architecture that resists divergence. It complements process accounts of massive and rapid digital scaling by detailing the cross-domain mechanism that links measurement to investment and by showing why capital efficiency and hub discipline are locally rational choices [7,10]. Finally, it extends work on startup life-cycle transitions and technical debt [5,6] by specifying an actionable debt policy subordinated to bottleneck removal during scale-up, operationalized through CI/CD and observability.

To enable further research, we suggest the following testable propositions:

- **P1 (Internationalization efficiency).** In small open economies, early establishment of lightweight local hubs in ICP-dense markets is positively associated with NRR growth during scale-up, controlling for company age and ACV.
- **P2 (Architecture discipline).** Maintaining a single product line (no customer forks) is positively associated with release frequency and negatively associated with incident density at constant team size.
- **P3 (Instrumentation governance).** The breadth of PLG-funnel instrumentation and product-analytics use is positively associated with the speed of resolving activation/retention bottlenecks.
- **P4 (Capital efficiency).** Conditional on PMF, cash-efficient paths exhibit similar medium-term growth in ARR per FTE as capital-accelerated paths, mediated by PLG/inbound intensity.

5.3 Implications for Practice and Policy

For Founders and Operators. (1) Treat PMF as dynamic: re-validate in each new segment/market; tie roadmap changes to observed activation and retention gaps. (2) Protect architecture: resist forks; invest in CI/CD and observability; roll features to all tenants. (3) Run constraint-focused cadences: explicitly name the binding growth bottleneck each quarter and concentrate resources accordingly. (4) Exploit PLG/inbound early for capital efficiency; add sales-assist/enterprise selectively where ACV and complexity warrant. (5) Use *lightweight* hubs to build trust and proximity while preserving a centralized product/engineering core. (6) If capital is scarce, emphasize cash discipline and metric-driven hiring; if capital is abundant, avoid over-expansion that erodes architectural and organizational simplicity.

For Investors and Board Members. Evaluate scaling readiness on the integration of commercial, organizational, and architectural guardrails: evidence of

PMF *and* single-product discipline, funnel instrumentation, and a bottleneck-removal operating system. Encourage "profit–market fit" checkpoints [12] before ramping spend.

For Policymakers and Ecosystem Builders. Soft-landing support (regulatory guidance, local partner networks, and talent visas) in ICP-dense markets can substitute for expensive duplicative build-outs. Programs that strengthen analytics capability and product instrumentation may yield higher returns than generic subsidies, given their centrality to data-driven scaling.

6 Conclusion

Finnish SaaS startups approach scaling as a coordinated organizational transformation tailored to the constraints and opportunities of a small, digitally mature economy. The configuration we document—early international orientation with lightweight hubs, PLG/inbound foundations, lean planning with persistent experimentation, distributed trust-based teams, and single-product architectural discipline with bottleneck-first execution—provides a pragmatic route to the type of scaling emphasized in organizational theory [2,3]. It also reframes the role of finance: in this context, substantial external capital accelerates rather than initiates scaling, because PMF validation, unit economics discipline, and architectural guardrails do much of the heavy lifting.

The study contributes theoretically by (i) adding a context-sensitive account from a small open economy [1]; (ii) integrating commercial, organizational, and architectural domains into a coherent scaling configuration [6,7,10]; and (iii) specifying micro-level guardrails that convert general prescriptions into implementable practices for SaaS [5,12]. Practically, it offers founders and boards a compact blueprint for sequencing investments and protecting scalability while expanding globally.

This work has limitations typical of qualitative multiple-case designs. The sample privileges depth over breadth (six companies) and is situated in a single national context; translation and retrospective sense-making introduce the possibility of subtle meaning loss and recall bias despite verification steps. Future research can address these constraints by examining stalled or unsuccessful scale-ups to surface failure modes; extending to other small open economies to probe boundary conditions; linking interviews with product analytics, repository, and incident data to test propositions quantitatively; and following companies longitudinally to observe how PMF maintenance and architectural guardrails evolve across funding rounds and market entries [8].

In summary, scaling in the Finnish SaaS context is not simply rapid growth; it is disciplined growth. Ventures combine capital-efficient commercial systems, lightweight yet explicit organization, and product architectures designed to resist divergence. Working in concert, these elements help keep coordination costs sub-linear and enable sustained international expansion from a small domestic base. By articulating this configuration and the mechanisms that animate it, the study offers a context-aware contribution to the scaling literature and a practical guide for founders operating under similar boundary conditions.

References

1. Bjørndalen, A.J., Dahlström, P., Lundberg, T., Torres, A.: What's driving the Nordic countries' software export surge? McKinsey & Company (2024)
2. Bohan, S., Tippmann, E., Levie, J., Igoe, J., Bowers, B.: What is scaling? J. Bus. Ventur. **39**(1), 106355 (2024)
3. Coviello, N., Autio, E., Nambisan, S., Patzelt, H., Thomas, L.D.: Organizational scaling, scalability, and scale-up: definitional harmonization and a research agenda. J. Bus. Ventur. **39**(5), 106419 (2024)
4. Gioia, D.A., Corley, K.G., Hamilton, A.L.: Seeking qualitative rigor in inductive research: notes on the Gioia methodology. Organ. Res. Methods **16**(1), 15–31 (2013)
5. Klotins, E., et al.: Exploration of technical debt in start-ups. In: Proceedings of the 40th International Conference on Software Engineering: Software Engineering in Practice, pp. 75–84 (2018)
6. Klotins, E., et al.: A progression model of software engineering goals, challenges, and practices in start-ups. IEEE Trans. Softw. Eng. **47**(3), 498–521 (2021). https://doi.org/10.1109/TSE.2019.2900213
7. Lange, F., Tomini, N., Brinkmann, F., Kanbach, D.K., Kraus, S.: Demystifying massive and rapid business scaling - an explorative study on driving factors in digital start-ups. Technol. Forecast. Soc. Chang. **196**, 122841 (2023)
8. Lee, S.R., Kim, J.D.: When do startups scale? Large-scale evidence from job postings. Strateg. Manag. J. **45**(9), 1633–1669 (2024)
9. Moroz, B., Saltan, A., Hyrynsalmi, S.: Product ops: understanding and defining an emerging discipline. In: Proceedings of the 1st International Conference on Software Product Management (ICSPM), pp. 15–29 (2023)
10. Mula, C., Zybura, N., Hipp, T.: From digitalized start-up to scale-up: opening the black box of scaling in digitalized firms towards a scaling process framework. Technol. Forecast. Soc. Chang. **202**, 123275 (2024)
11. Nguyen-Duc, A., Kemell, K.K., Abrahamsson, P.: The entrepreneurial logic of startup software development: a study of 40 software startups. Empir. Softw. Eng. **26**(5), 91 (2021). https://doi.org/10.1007/s10664-021-09987-z
12. Rayport, J.F., Sola, D., Kupp, M.: The Overlooked Key to a Successful Scale-Up. Harvard Business Review (January-February) (2023)
13. Saltan, A., Kittlaus, H.B.: Cloud product strategy, vision, market positioning, and pricing. In: Hajizadeh, Y., et al. (eds.) Building Cloud Software Products (2025)
14. Saltan, A., Seffah, A.: Engineering and business aspects of SaaS model adoption: insights from a mapping study. In: Proceedings of the International Software-Intensive Business Workshop (IWSiB), pp. 115–127 (2018)
15. Saltan, A., Smolander, K.: Bridging the state-of-the-art and the state-of-the-practice of SaaS pricing: a multivocal literature review. Inf. Softw. Technol. **133**, 106510 (2021)
16. Sanasi, S., Ghezzi, A., Cavallo, A.: What happens after market validation? Experimentation for scaling in technology-based startups. Technol. Forecast. Soc. Chang. **196**, 122839 (2023). https://doi.org/10.1016/j.techfore.2023.122839

Democratising Work in the Software Sector: Insights on Cooperative Businesses

Joram Scholten, Chris de Nijs, Slinger Jansen, and Sergio España-Cubillo(✉)

Utrecht University, Utrecht, The Netherlands
{slinger.jansen,s.espana}@uu.nl

Abstract. To address social-environmental crises and corporate short-termism, the New Economics Foundation advocates rethinking corporate ownership and purpose. Cooperatives, being democratically managed, offer a model with potential for positive impact. Despite growing interest in platform cooperativism, software worker cooperatives remain under-explored. In this study, the first of its kind, we analyse 76 cooperative software businesses, and present insights based on interviews with members of 23 companies. Findings reveal that members are motivated by both practical benefits and ideological alignment with Social Economy values. These businesses promote workplace democracy, stakeholder engagement, and long-term value creation, though impact measurement remains a limited practice. With broader educational, institutional and governmental support, cooperatives could play a transformative role in the software sector.

Keywords: software business · workplace democracy · stakeholder engagement · social economy · ICT cooperatives · human-centered

1 Introduction

To address inequality, environmental degradation, and short-term orientation of many companies, the New Economics Foundation recommends transforming prevailing forms of ownership, control, and corporate purpose [25]. Cooperatives stand out, as their ownership structure has a profound impact on organisational priorities and performance [26]. They are governed by a set of principles last updated at the 1999 International Cooperative Alliance Assembly [19], promoting voluntary and open membership, democratic member control, member economic participation, autonomy and independence, education and training, cooperation among cooperatives, and concern for community. In many countries, worker cooperatives are regulated by law (e.g. [17]), but some businesses with other legal forms (e.g. limited liability companies) can also operate according to cooperative principles. By **cooperative software business**, we refer to an established company with decision-making autonomy and voluntary membership, created to meet the needs of its members by participating in the market

G. Herzwurm et al. (Eds.): ICSOB 2025, LNBIP 574, pp. 309–324, 2026.
https://doi.org/10.1007/978-3-032-14518-5_24

through the production of software-related goods and services. In such businesses, profit or surplus distribution and decision-making are not directly tied to capital contributions; instead, each member holds one vote. This definition, adapted from [4], accounts for situations where it is the cooperative's members who lay down the operating rules in the articles of association that enable a company to be identified as a cooperative, disregarding the specific legal entity type. We refer as **member** to an individual who (i) participates in the ownership of the company, (ii) has decision-making power, (iii) contributes labour, and (iv) shares in the risks, responsibilities, and benefits of the business.

Igalia: A well-known software worker cooperative

Igalia, founded in 2001 in Spain, is one of the most prominent worker-owned companies in the software sector. It operates as an open source consultancy specialising in web browsers, graphics, compilers, and embedded systems. All members are co-owners and participate in democratic decision-making, following a flat organisational structure. Igalia has contributed to major open source projects such as Chromium, WebKit, and Gecko, and is recognised globally for its expertise in web standards and free software. Its cooperative model enables long-term commitment to community-driven projects while ensuring equitable distribution of profits and influence among its members.

Platform cooperativism in the information and communication technologies (ICT) sector is a hot research topic, proposed as an ethical alternative to platform capitalism [31, 33]. However, cooperative businesses in the software sector have so far received limited attention. Paradoxically, they represent an entrepreneurial approach that, if scaled to a critical mass, could have a significant impact on the software sector in terms of employment opportunities, job quality, territorial rootedness, and positive social outcomes.

This paper follows with a description of the research method (see Sect. 2) and it makes the following contributions:

- We explore existing cooperative software businesses, creating a dataset where we classify them over several dimensions (Sect. 3).
- We analyse the motivations of software professionals to become part of a cooperative software business (Sect. 4).
- We investigate the extent to which these companies perform democratic management, engage other stakeholders, and measure their impact (Sect. 5).

We then discuss the results and their limitations (Sect. 6). We conclude the paper by summarising the main findings and outlining future work (Sect. 7).

2 Research Method

Creation of a Dataset of Cooperative Software Businesses. This structured repository serves both as a dataset for analysis and a sampling frame.

Table 1. List of motivations to join a cooperative business (Q-Set), each directly based on the *original* source [8], or *edited* or *added* by the expert.

Statement	Source
The worker cooperative is the most ethical form of economic enterprise one could aspire to, given the moral (either laic or religious) predispositions.	Original
The worker cooperative is consistent with anti-capitalist ideologies (including, but not necessarily relevant for the individual, socialism, communism and/or anarchism).	Original
The worker cooperative is a way to help correct the real or perceived excesses of current economic reality (e.g. the worker cooperative is the best way to achieve the changes I want to see).	Original
Establishing a worker cooperative sets an example for others to follow.	Original
The worker cooperative is one of the most rational legal entity forms available.	Edited
The worker cooperative helps with financially structuring the enterprise.	Original
The worker cooperative gives increased financial stability and debt solvency.	Original
The worker cooperative compensates worker members to incentivise productivity.	Original
The worker cooperative eases the transition to retirement for a former sole proprietor.	Original
The worker cooperative capitalises on economic benefits that this structure has been demonstrated to provide (e.g. better survival rates).	Original
The worker cooperative allows for maintaining a middle class lifestyle in an area with a high cost of living (e.g. the company pays additional dividends and higher-than-average wages).	Original
The worker cooperative gives opportunities for better pay or working conditions.	Original
The worker cooperative offers members greater involvement in many aspects of the business.	Edited
The worker cooperative provides a more flexible work-life balance.	Original
The worker cooperative fits well into the social economy.	Added
I was not aware of the existence of worker cooperatives before I joined one.	Original

We searched official directories[1] and community-maintained lists[2]. The inclusion criteria were: (1) operation within the ICT sector (NACE code J[3]), and (2a) establishment as a worker cooperative or (2b) finding evidences of their adherence to the cooperative principle of democratic governance and (when possible) shared ownership. For each company, we collected their name, website URL, contact info, legal entity type (along with the evidence for that classification decision), year of establishment, country of origin, NACE industry code[3] (with evidence), and the source through which the cooperative was found. This data was extracted from public sources (company website and documentation) or through interviews. The dataset is available in the technical report [11], and outlined in Sect. 3.

[1] The U.S. Federation of Worker Cooperatives https://www.usworker.coop/member-directory and the network Co-Tech https://www.coops.tech.

[2] https://github.com/hng/tech-coops and https://github.com/mttmyr/awesome-tech-cooperatives.

[3] A classification of economic activities https://ec.europa.eu/eurostat/web/nace.

Investigation of the Motivations to Join a Cooperative Software Business. We have applied Q Methodology, a form of factor analysis meant to unveil subjectivity [32]. It has been used in a range of software studies; e.g. exploring dynamic capabilities required by ICT entrepreneurs to face globalised challenges [5], investigating the values of software engineers [14]. We started from a list of possible motivations proposed in [8]. We then discussed it with an expert from the Dutch association of and for cooperatives[4], who validated it, corrected several statements, and proposed an additional one. The final list (referred to as Q-Set in Q Methodology) is shown in Table 1. During interviews, participants were asked to rank the motivations based on the extent to which they influenced their decision to join or stay in the company. We elicited their orderings (referred to as Q-Sorts) and the rationale. We sampled 15 out of 23 Q-Sorts following methodological advise to keep a smaller number of participants than statements [32]. For factor analysis, we used Ken-Q Analysis [3]. We first extracted 8 factors using the Centroid method. Then, for factor rotation, meant to ensure that each factor offers the most informative viewpoint, we applied Varimax since it automatically maximises the amount of variance explained by the factor, offering a mathematically sound solution [32]. Following the Kaiser-Guttman criterion, we only kept the 3 factors with an *Eigenvalue* greater than 1, meaning that they account for more variance than an individual Q-Sort [32]; namely, Factors 1, 2 and 4, having eigenvalues of 7.5, 1.16 and 1.12, respectively. Each factor reflects the viewpoint of a set of interviewees who think alike; that is, who expressed similar motivations and therefore are said to load into the factor. In Sect. 4, we provide a name to each factor and interpret the profile of people it represents.

Semi-structured Interviews with Cooperative Business Members. We conveniently sampled 23 companies from the dataset, seeking diverse legal, geographical, and sector characteristics, but also constrained by their language and availability. Interviews took place through telcos (17) and surveys (6). After introductions and informed consent, we validated the company details in our dataset. We asked them to rank the list of motivations to join the company. We then discussed their democratic management, stakeholder engagement and impact measurement practices, with prompt questions based on the *Governance*, *Membership & Community*, and *Economic and Social Performance* sections of a business model canvas adapted for cooperative enterprises [24]. Interviews were recorded, transcribed, and coded in Nvivo. The interview and qualitative analysis protocols can be found in the report [11], and the results in Sect. 5.

3 Landscape of Cooperative Software Businesses

Currently, the dataset contains data on 76 companies that were active at the time of the data collection. Most were created during the last 15 years, as shown by Fig. 1, with a notable outlier being Alpha Communication https://alpha.coop,

[4] Nationale Co-operatieve Raad https://www.cooperatie.nl.

which was founded in 1987 and is still active in 2025. Figure 2, left, shows the geographical distribution (in Sect. 6 we discuss its unevenness). All companies develop their main activity within the *Information and communication* industry sector, with Fig. 2, right, showing the distribution over sub-sectors. Most of them deliver computer programming or consultancy services, but there is a variety of other value offerings. Sofi focuses mostly on programming, self-defining as "a workers' cooperative that comprises of 10 partners, including product managers, UX/UI designers, full-stack developers, and AI professionals" https://www.sofi.coop. Igalia is "a dynamic and highly specialised open source consultancy" offering both consultancy and programming service https://www.igalia.com. We Are Open Co-op are "a not-for-profit worker co-op of strategists, innovators, and facilitators" https://weareopen.coop, focusing primarily on consultancy services. The aim of Catalyst Cooperative is "help more people bring data and analysis to the fight for clean energy and a stable climate" https://catalyst.coop. Alpha Communication specialises in animation, motion graphics, illustration, and photography. Future Club specialises in handcrafted art and traditional 2D animation for computer games https://www.futureclub.dev. And Loomio has created a widely used open source collaborative decision-making tool https://www.loomio.com.

With regard to their legal entity types (see Fig. 3, left), approximately half take forms typically attributed to Social Economy (worker cooperatives and associations) and half are incorporated under general commercial company law (private limited companies and limited liability partnerships). All showed evidence of operating like cooperatives. And in every interview, the participants further confirmed this aspect, offering insights into their governance style (see Sect. 5). Finally, cooperative software businesses tend to be small: 56.6% of the companies in the dataset are micro enterprises, 39.5% are small, and 3.9% are medium; see Fig. 3, right, for a finer-grained breakdown. Interestingly, the only two companies with over 100 members were created in the early 2000s, thus being among the oldest.

4 Reasons for Joining a Cooperative Software Business

In general, the 23 interviewees expressed motivations grounded in principles and social values. As seen in Fig. 4, most considered this type of enterprise the most ethical, believed it helps correct the excesses of capitalism, and regarded

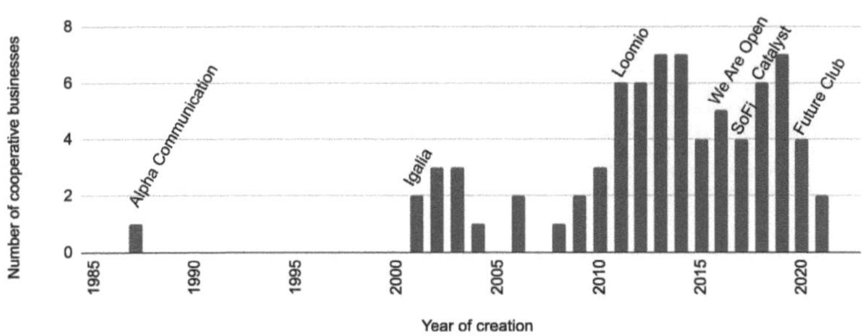

Fig. 1. Number of cooperative software businesses created over the years

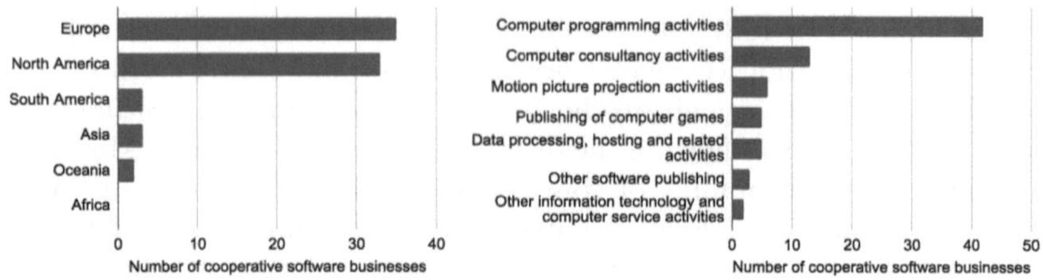

Fig. 2. Distribution of cooperative software businesses over continents (left) and industry sectors (right)

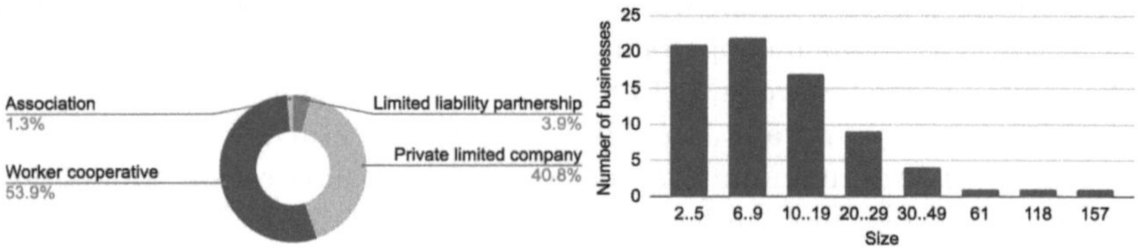

Fig. 3. Legal entity type (left) and size (right) of the businesses in the dataset

it as consistent with anti-capitalist ideologies. Practical aspects, such as worker involvement in business management, and achieving a better workâĂŞlife balance, were also highly valued. Few were unaware of the cooperative format before joining the company. Finally, very few indicated that their involvement was due to the retirement of a former owner. The Q Methodology study with 15 participants deepens the analysis of motivations. Three distinct factors emerged, each representing an archetypal member profile shared by several participants who joined and stayed in a cooperative software business for similar reasons.

Profile 1 - The ideologically-driven, community-focused member. This factor explains 50% of the total study variance and five Q-Sorts have significant

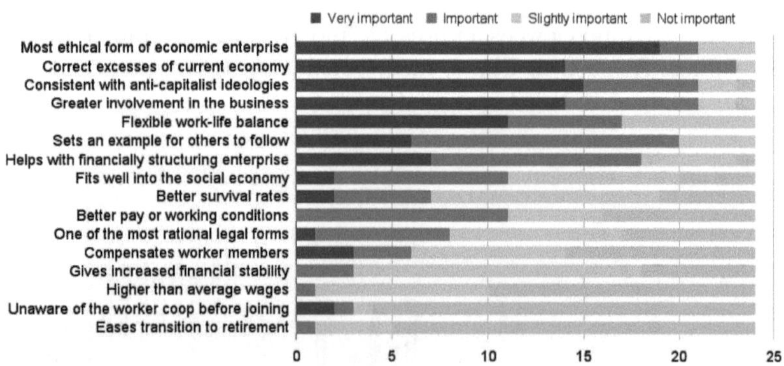

Fig. 4. Motivations to join a cooperative software business, ordered by overall importance

loadings to it (P07, P08, P10, P12, P14). Members with this profile are strongly driven by ideological and ethical considerations. They see the cooperative business as a means to achieve a broader societal good. They find it fundamentally consistent with anti-capitalist ideologies and a vital tool to help correct the real or perceived excesses of current economic reality (their two highest-ranked statements), viewing it as the most ethical form of enterprise one could aspire to (the fourth highest-ranked statement). For this group, the cooperative is not just a workplace; it is a vehicle for social-economic transformation, and they highly value greater involvement in many aspects of the business (the third highest-ranked statement), a distinguishing trait when compared to Profile 3. Their decision to join appears to be a conscious choice, as they notably rank "I was not aware of the existence of worker cooperatives before I joined one" as very low, also distinguishing them from Profile 3. Personal financial incentives for productivity or maintaining a middle class lifestyle are of significantly less concern to them. While no single statement statistically distinguished Profile 1 from all other factors at $p<0.05$, the cumulative ranking patterns clearly show the focus of this type of members on collective, ethical, and anti-capitalist principles over individual financial gain or prior lack of awareness.

Profile 2 - The autonomy-seeking, quality-focused member. Explaining 8% of the variance, two participants have significant loadings (P04, P09). Members represented by this profile are driven by personal agency and a desire for effective, rewarding work environments. They strongly prioritise greater involvement in many aspects of the business, a value shared with Profile 1, but now ranked the highest, and sharply contrasting with Profile 3. A key motivator for them is the ability of a cooperative software business to provide a more flexible work-life balance (second highest-ranked, a distinguishing statement at $p<0.05$), a factor significantly more important to them than for Profile 1. Furthermore, they uniquely value how the cooperative compensates worker members to incentivise productivity (ranked third, a distinguishing statement at $p<0.01$), indicating an appreciation for performance-driven internal structures, a stark difference from Profiles 1 and 3. Like members in Profile 1, they likely made an informed choice to join, as being "not aware of the existence of worker cooperatives before I joined one" is notably low for them (third to last), distinguishing them from Profile 3. Less critical to this profile are concerns about the company structure fitting well the Social Economy, or being a rational legal entity type.

Profile 3 - The newly aware, mission-supporting member. This factor, with a single significantly loading participant (P17), accounts for 8% of the variance. What truly sets this profile apart is their initial lack of awareness regarding cooperative businesses before joining (which is their highest-ranked and most distinguishing statement at $p<0.01$). Despite this initial unawareness, they quickly align with the broader mission of the cooperative software business, strongly endorsing its consistency with anti-capitalist ideologies (second highest-ranked statement) and viewing it as a powerful means to establish an example for others to follow (third highest-ranked statement). Their motivation appears to stem from a newfound appreciation for the societal impact and ethical stance of these companies. However, this profile places significantly less emphasis on personal financial benefits or deep operational engagement; they are less concerned with incentivising productivity or having greater involvement in many aspects of the business compared to the other profiles (low-ranked and a key distinguishing statement at $p<0.01$). Similarly, the rationality of the company's legal structure or financial stability are of low importance to them.

These profiles demonstrate the multifaceted motivations driving individuals to join and remain within cooperative software businesses. While some values like "consistency with anti-capitalist ideologies" are shared as consensus points across these groups, their distinguishing priorities reveal varied pathways and reasons for commitment. Profile 1 focuses on ethical performance and systemic change, Profile 2 values involvement and productivity, and Profile 3 is driven by a newfound appreciation for this type of company. Each are likely to play a crucial role in the function and success of the software business.

5 Approaches to Democratic and Engaging Management

Workplace democracy is commonplace across the sample, but the practices differ (see Fig. 5). The majority of interviewees (17 out of 23) engage in direct democracy. Several (4) recount indirect democratic management. The remaining (2) practice a combination of a direct and indirect democracy.

Direct Democracy. Most companies performing direct democracy follow a *consensus model* (13), where discussions involve all members and, while the voting process might differ across companies, a unanimous agreement must be reached for a proposal to be approved (e.g. as expressed by interviewee I01), or at least everyone should be able to "live with the decision" (I03). Every voice is heard, votes are equal, and a single member might theoretically exercise a veto. However, some interviewees have clarified that many decisions do not require voting, as long as no worker opposes actively, saving time during meetings. In one of the companies (I11), from Monday to Thursday they deal with operational decisions that hardly require voting. On Fridays, if someone has a strategic and impactful proposal, seconded by another worker, then the first person has two minutes to elaborate on it. They take turns sharing their views for a minute each, repeating this two or three times before voting. One proposal can take 15 or 30 min. The remaining companies (4) follow a *majority model*, where typically over half of the members should agree to approve a proposal (e.g. I08, I12). Some companies establish a threshold in their operating agreement. Some distinguish several, depending on how impactful the proposal is (the higher the impact, the

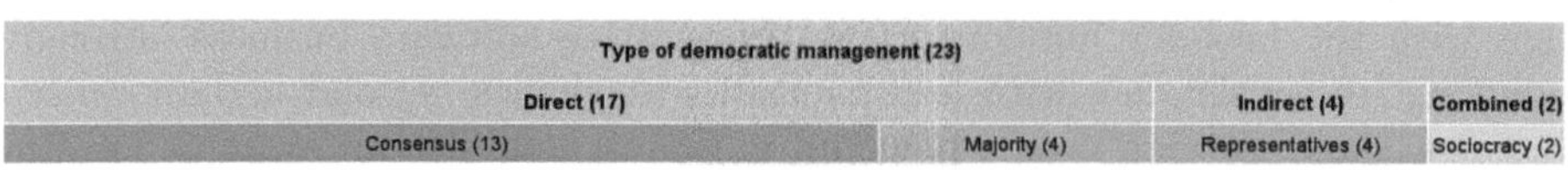

Fig. 5. Proportion of companies performing each type of democratic management

higher the threshold); e.g. accepting a new member into the cooperative might require acceptance by 75% of the current members (I16). Often, new members have a trial period between 6 and 12 months until they obtain voting rights (e.g. I16). A few companies are strictly egalitarian: "We are democratic in a very radical way. There is no hierarchy inside [our company]. We are 11 partners. We are exactly equal, irrespective of how much time they have been in the cooperative. Or how much time they have been in the labour market" (I17). Companies enacting direct democracy still delegate daily managerial tasks to an executive team, to avoid overloading other members with petty decision making.

Indirect Democracy. Enacted as a *representative democracy* (I15, S02, S03, S06). In one company (I15) a board of directors (4 out of 6 members) handles most decisions, though other members can participate. Their decision-making is a "consensus minus one" model: it takes two people to block a decision. In another (S03), a board of directors serves as a formal decision-making body, using a consensus process for proposals. Indirect models also involve governance committees with elected representatives and specific scopes (e.g. S06).

Combined Approaches. Two companies (I03, I07) combine direct and indirect democracy, implementing a *sociocracy*, which typically involves circles (I03) or organisational areas (I07) that focus on specific aspects of the business, with members having leadership opportunities within these groups. Outside these formal structures, meetings adhere to consensus-based decision-making.

Commonalities and distinctions emerge across the different models. **Hierarchy and equality.** Many companies emphasise a horizontal structure where all partners or members are equal, regardless of their tenure or experience (see claims by I17 above). **Delegation of daily tasks.** Companies employing direct democracy still delegate small, daily managerial tasks to an executive team or elected representatives. **Decision-making frequency.** The frequency of decision-making meetings varies significantly: from almost daily for operational decisions (e.g. I05), to quarterly for major strategic decisions (e.g. I12), with most companies voting some decisions weekly (e.g. I01). Some easy decisions may be handled asynchronously via Slack or Google Docs. **Voting software.** Most interviewed companies prefer to simply raise hands during meetings. "We try to avoid using any kind of voting software, because we have a pretty nice culture inside the coop, where we can work it out together" (I01). Some companies tried voting software (typically Loomio) but they stopped (mostly to save efforts; e.g. I05). A couple of companies currently use voting software: "We use Loomio for big decisions like the acquisition of a new partner or if there's some decision that's hard to roll back, but also big financial decisions like if it's about more than one salary" (I10). "Some votes take place verbally in meetings. Sometimes we process votes via Unanimous Written Consent via DocuSign" (S06). In essence, democratic management in these companies is a spectrum, often prioritising collective participation and a strong sense of shared ownership. Some companies even engage with networks promoting workplace democracy, such as Democracy at Work institute, and the Democracy Collaborative (I07).

Stakeholder Engagement. Cooperative businesses engage their stakeholders into some discussions, although only workers have voting rights. Figure 6 shows the main stakeholders mentioned by interviewees. Clients need the services or products that are provided by company; they encompass conventional companies, non-profit organisations, educational organisations, and social entrepreneurs. cooperative software businesses enjoy being in close partnerships, especially with other cooperative companies. Many take part in networks and federations of cooperative businesses, either focused on the software business (e.g. I01 mentions their company belongs to Co-Tech[5]) or cross-sectorial (e.g. I07 mentioned the U.S. Federation of Worker Cooperatives, I17's company belongs to the Spanish Network of Alternative and Solidarity Economy). They often form tightly-knit communities where some use software infrastructure developed by other cooperative businesses instead of utilising software provided by large ICT companies. A prevalent practice is the great effort made to understand stakeholder needs. This often involves proactive communication and tailored approaches. For instance, one company aims to understand their community's motivation to "avoid big tech" (I01). The cooperative ideology influences client selection, with one company refusing to work with any client who "doesn't get why we are a cooperative" (I04). Another company also scrutinises clients' business models to ensure alignment with their principles, avoiding projects that do not align with their principles (e.g. gambling) while accepting assignments related to education, healthcare, clean energy, and "software that helps the environment to be a better place" (I06). One business even charges higher rates to conventional companies so they can subsidise their work with Social Economy organisations (I17). There is a strong and consistent preference towards long-term relationships with clients and partners among many cooperatives. This is often driven by a desire for deeper collaboration and mutual trust. However, most companies engage in short-term projects as well, either to generate immediate income or as trial periods that might evolve into long-term partnerships. In a nutshell, "we love long term relationships, but I don't have a problem with short term gigs" (I15).

Decision-Making Power of Stakeholders. Most companies explicitly state that external stakeholders (e.g., clients, partners, investors) do not have direct influence or voting power over the business internal operational or strategic decisions. Decisions are reserved for the members of the cooperative business. Some companies acknowledge that client needs and feedback do influence the services and products offered, and the direction of projects. For example, a client's need for a specific back-office feature might lead a company to develop that feature for its broader framework (I17). As a notable exception, one interviewee stated that client agendas can have a "great influence" on their decision-making, even impacting major strategic choices like long-term development plans or ethical project selection (I04).

[5] Co-Tech "aims to create a better technology sector in the UK that focuses primarily on worker, customer and end-user needs rather than on generating private profit".

Impact Measurement. Finally, while most of the interviewed cooperative companies lack formal methods for measuring the impact of their business actions, there is a strong aspiration to implement them in the future. Impact is often discussed informally during internal meetings, aligning with their consensus-based democratic practices, either by discussing ethics and values but without using specific indicators (I10), discussing and deciding whether external projects align with their principles (I06), or reflecting about the impact of their projects (I11). For many, formal impact measurement is a long-term goal (e.g. I02, I04, 107, I08, I09, I14, I16, S04). The primary reasons cited for not implementing such methods are scale problems and lack of capacity (e.g. I02) or money (e.g. I08), or the difficulty to define what truly constitutes measurable impact in their context (I05). Three companies do perform formal impact measurement. Two do not measure project-specific impact, but rather relate it to their overall environmental, social and governance performance, applying the XES Social Balance method (I17) and the B Impact Assessment (S01), respectively. A notable exception is the formal measure of a company's social impact through a Social Value Policy (I03), a self-developed evaluation framework utilising a 10-point scoring system derived from client surveys and internal assessments to gauge project alignment with their mission. This rigorous approach, which is enshrined in their Articles of Association, includes a 50% project acceptability threshold and a unique self-destruction clause that triggers the transfer of company assets and the discontinuation of the software business if this standard is not consistently met over two and a half years. In the rest of the interviewed companies, impact measurement rarely directly influences strategic or managerial decisions but just appears to be informally part of discussions and feedback loops.

6 Discussion of the Results

Cooperative Software Businesses are More than Just a Legal Entity Type. We intended to focus on companies with a worker cooperative legal entity type, but soon realised that some companies that are managed according to cooperative principles are not formally registered as such. This can be due to (i) restrictive legal requirements that might discourage formalisation (e.g. minimum membership, capital obligations) [13], (ii) difficulty entering ventures or raising funding from outside investors [23], (iii) cultural and identity dynamics by which

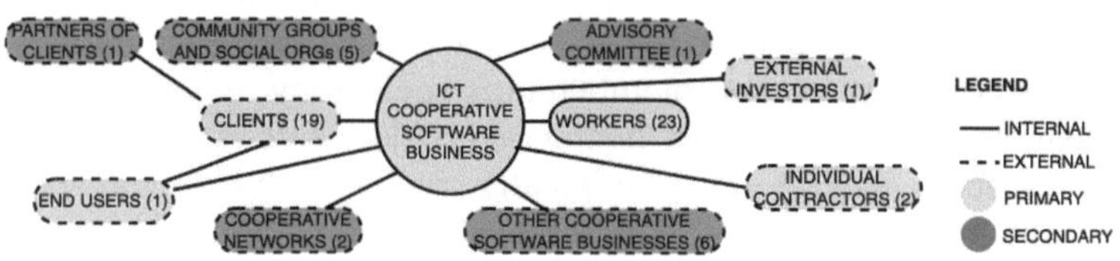

Fig. 6. Stakeholders of cooperative software businesses and the number of interviewees mentioning them

firms blend cooperative values with more conventional structures in a belief that this will bring more flexibility or avoid stigmatisation [16,28]). We refocused to consider any software business operating according to cooperative principles, what explains the diversity of legal entity types across our dataset.

While Most Cooperative Software Businesses are Small, They can Scale Up. Most companies in our dataset are micro or small, which follows the same pattern as in other sectors [22]. Worker cooperatives have barriers to growth [28]. While there are many examples of worker cooperatives overcoming such barriers (e.g. Mondragon Corporation [9]), we have not been able to find large companies within the software sector. Still, two of the companies in our dataset exceed 100 members, showing that scaling up is possible. A cooperative business should be capable of attracting members by aligning with their core motivations.

The Motivations to Join a Cooperative Software Business are Diverse. Earlier studies on technology worker cooperatives reveal a tension between idealistic adherence to cooperative principles and the practical demands of sustaining a software business [20]. And the study that inspired our initial list of motivations identified three categories of worker cooperative members, based on interviews; namely, idealists, economists and drifters. The three profiles revealed by our Q Methodology are quite consistent with those categories, revealing additional nuances in their standpoints. In particular, profiles 1 and 2 represent the tension between ideology and practicality, and the assembly and democratic nature of the interviewed companies help members navigate this tension.

Cooperative software businesses have a tendency to be driven by shared ownership and participatory culture, particularly in small organisations. Our results align with earlier, broader studies across worker cooperatives [1,27]. As cooperatives grow, direct democracy becomes less practical and representative structures can emerge to preserve member voice while enabling operational efficiency [27]. Some of the companies we interviewed, despite remaining small, do resort to representative democracy or combine direct and indirect democratic practices. Earlier studies have shown that, over time, cooperatives can experience elite emergence and hierarchical drift [6,27], develop uncontested forms of autocracy [18], or suffer member alienation and low participation when cooperatives scale up [30]. However, we have not observed these phenomena, perhaps because within the software sector cooperative businesses are rather small. In comparison to platform cooperatives, whose multi-stakeholder membership makes them prioritise sociocracy [12], within our sample of businesses with exclusively worker membership, sociocracy remains a minoritarian approach, in favour of direct democracy. Also, software businesses operating in open-source ecosystems strategically engage with external stakeholders that exert influence on requirements, feature priorities, and platform technical roadmaps, especially through strategic community engagement practices [21]. Within the cooperative businesses in our study, similar strategies are mentioned by the interviewees. However, more research is needed to better understand how these strategies take concrete shape.

While Cooperative Software Businesses Care About Their Impact, They Still Rarely Measure It. Worker cooperatives are considered integral to the Social Economy and aim to fulfil the needs of their workers and local communities [29], striving to produce positive impacts (e.g. decent employment, job satisfaction, employee well-being, income equality) [2]. Still, cooperatives typically publish annual financial statements that rarely highlight environmental, social, and governance performance [15]. They are challenged by a lack of specific reporting frameworks tailored to their unique identity and values, so many employ mainstream corporate reporting frameworks or develop in-house methods [15]. A couple of businesses we interviewed use existing methods (namely, B Impact Asses sment, REAS Social Audit/Balance, see [10]), while one has developed their own (Social Value Policy).

Limitations and Threats to Validity. In our exploratory study, we found limited available resources for collecting data on cooperative software businesses. We relied on existing online repositories but needed to curate the data, since many companies were defunct or were multi-stakeholder platform cooperatives. We do not claim that the resulting dataset is comprehensive, so we are cautious about generalisability. With 23 companies interviewed verbally or through a survey, we have been able to triangulate some findings of the dataset, increasing their validity. The interviews revealed patterns in democratic management, stakeholder engagement and impact measurement, and how these practices are interrelated. However, additional interviews would increase external validity. By excluding interviews with non-English speaking cooperatives, we limited the sample diversity, resulting on an uneven distribution in our dataset. Also, the 5 survey-based interviews allowed for less depth.

Regarding Q Methodology, we had 15 participants and 16 statements, an acceptable range for this research method. This method is designed to explore subjective viewpoints by correlating persons and not variables, with the goal not being statistical generalisation but uncovering distinct profiles of individuals [32]. As demonstrated in earlier research, Q Methodology studies can be successfully conducted with small strategic samples [14]. We asked the interviewees to sort their motivations linearly. This deviates from the typical forced quasi-normal distribution often employed in Q Methodology, but research has shown that alternative, non-forced ranking formats can still yield valid and interpretable factor structures when analysed appropriately [7].

7 Conclusion and Future Work

To the best of our knowledge, this is the first study focused on the exploration of software businesses operating like worker cooperatives, since platform cooperatives (typically consumer or multi-stakeholder cooperatives) have attracted most of the interest. This paper provides insights on the motivations of their members, their democratic management, how they engage stakeholders, and their interest in producing positive impacts. Our dataset and results can provide a foundation for future research. This could include countries where English is not a commonly spoken language, and inquire into each practice separately (workplace democracy, stakeholder engagement, impact measurement), or further investigate how these influence or require adaptation of other conventional software business practices (e.g. client acquisition and selection, portfolio management, business line development, software ecosystem management), or whether they promote or hinder ethical behaviours (e.g. management of ethics and digital rights, digital inclusion, responsible software development). All in all, this study provides early yet meaningful insights into the growing movement of cooperative software businesses. Despite their current scale and limited recognition, the values, motivations, and democratic practices explored here suggest that these enterprises hold strong potential to reshape the software sector toward more inclusive, participatory, and socially responsible models of work.

Authors' Contributions and Acknowledgements. SE conceived and led the study, secured funding through the NWO-funded SCENTISS project (KICH1.MV01.20.018), and supervised the project with SJ. SE and JS developed the methodology; JS and CdN handled validation and data curation. SE, JS, and CdN conducted the analyses, investigations, drafting, and visualisations. All authors reviewed and approved the final manuscript. We are grateful to the participants of this study, for their time and valuable insights.

References

1. Agirre, I., Reinares, P., Freundlich, F.: Does a democratic management model enhance performance through market orientation? Empirical evidence from the mondragon industrial group. Rev. Radical Political Econ. **47**(3), 345–367 (2015)
2. Albanese, M.: Are worker cooperatives green? Some reflections in terms of governance. In: The Routledge Handbook of Cooperative Economics and Management, pp. 481–488. Routledge (2024)
3. Banasick, S.: Ken-Q Analysis v2.0.1 (2023). https://doi.org/10.5281/zenodo.8310377
4. Barea, J., Monzón, J.L.: Manual for drawing up the satellite accounts of companies in the social economy: co-operatives and mutual societies. Technical report, CIRIEC and European Commission (2006)
5. Chang, C.C.: Exploring IT entrepreneurs' dynamic capabilities using Q-technique. Ind. Manag. Data Syst. **112**(8), 1201–1216 (2012)
6. Christiaens, T.: Worker co-operatives for the 21st century. Crit. Sociol. **49**(1), 157–163 (2023)
7. Danielson, S.: Q method and surveys: three ways to combine Q and R. Field Methods **21**(3), 219–237 (2009)
8. DeBalsi, B.A.: Motivating factors influencing the decision to create worker cooperative businesses. Ph.D. thesis, University of Alabama (2021)
9. Errasti, A.M., Heras, I., Bakaikoa, B., Elgoibar, P.: The internationalisation of cooperatives: the case of the Mondragon Cooperative Corporation. Ann. Public Coop. Econ. **74**(4), 553–584 (2003)

10. España, S., Ramautar, V., Martín, S., Thorsteinsdottir, G., Sinaga, Y.A., Pastor, Ó.: Why and how responsible organisations are assessing their performance: state of the practice in environmental, social and governance accounting. In: COPERMAN 2023, pp. 13–56. Springer, Cham (2023)
11. España, S., Jansen, S., Scholten, J., de Nijs, C.: Investigating cooperative software businesses: technical report and dataset. Technical report, Utrecht University (2025). https://shorturl.at/6dTz7, to be uploaded to OSF Preprints upon acceptance
12. Esposito, M.: Cooperatives and the digital commons: governance, sustainability, and shared infrastructure (2025). https://platform.coop/blog/cooperatives-and-the-digital-commons. Accessed 26 July 2025
13. Fabrizio, N.: Swiss cooperative law: Driver or obstacle to cooperative growth? In: Cooperatives in an Uncertain World, pp. 33–54. Springer, Cham (2024)
14. Ferrario, M.A., Winter, E.: Applying human values theory to software engineering practice: lessons and implications. IEEE Trans. Softw. Eng. **49**(3), 973–990 (2023)
15. Fouche, K.B., Polo-Garrido, F.: Corporate reporting by cooperatives: mapping the landscape and identifying determinants. J. Contemp. Account. Econ. **20**(3) (2024)
16. Fulton, M.E., Giannakas, K.: Corruption in agricultural processing firms: a comparison of cooperatives and investor-owned firms. Can. J. Agric. Econ. **68**(4) (2020)
17. Government of Spain: Law 27/1999, of 16 July, on cooperatives (1999). https://boe.es/buscar/act.php?id=BOE-A-1999-15681
18. Hartz, R., Tümpel, M., Hühn, M., Rybnikova, I.: Handling the organizing paradox: a multiple case study of German cooperatives. Econ. Ind. Democr. **45**(4) (2024)
19. ICA: Cooperative identity, values & principles. https://ica.coop/en/cooperatives/cooperative-identity. Accessed 10 Aug 2025
20. Ivanovski, S.: Why worker cooperatives in the tech sector? (2024). https://platform.coop/blog/why-worker-cooperatives. Accessed 26 July 2025
21. Linåker, J., Regnell, B., Damian, D.: A community strategy framework-how to obtain influence on requirements in meritocratic open source software communities? Inf. Softw. Technol. **112**, 102–114 (2019)
22. Lomuscio, M., Tortia, E.C., Cori, A.: Worker cooperatives in Italy: legislation, prevalence and recent trends. J. Particip. Employee Own **6**(2), 128–148 (2023)
23. Major, G., Preminger, J.: Overcoming the capital investment hurdle in worker-controlled firms. J. Particip. Employee Own **2**(2), 133–150 (2019)
24. Mazzarol, T., Clark, D., Reboud, S., Limnios, E.M.: Developing a conceptual framework for the co-operative and mutual enterprise business model. J. Manag. Organ. **24**(4), 551–581 (2018)
25. McCann, D., Berry, C.: Shareholder capitalism: a system in crisis. Technical report, New Economics Foundation (2017). https://neweconomics.org/2017/07/shareholder-capitalism
26. Morales Gutiérrez, A.C.: La dirección en la empresa de trabajo asociado: una revisión de estudios empíricos. CIRIEC-España **48**, 99–122 (2004)
27. Novković, S., Miner, K., McMahon, C.: Cooperative governance in context. In: Humanistic Governance in Democratic Organizations, pp. 81–117. Springer, Cham (2023)
28. Olsen, E.K.: The relative survival of worker cooperatives and barriers to their creation. In: Sharing Ownership, Profits, and Decision-Making in the 21st Century, pp. 83–107. Emerald (2013)
29. Preluca, A., Hakelius, K., Mark-Herbert, C.: Sustainability of worker co-operatives. Sustainability **14**(18), 11542 (2022)

30. Puusa, A., Saastamoinen, S.: Democratic cooperative governance: role ambiguity, pseudo-democracy and tacit acceptance? In: Humanistic Governance in Democratic Organizations, pp. 145–175. Springer, Cham (2023)
31. Sandoval, M.: Entrepreneurial activism? Platform cooperativism between subversion and co-optation. Crit. Sociol. **46**(6), 801–817 (2020)
32. Watts, S., Stenner, P.: Doing Q methodological research: theory, method & interpretation. Qual. Res. Psychol. **2** (2005))
33. Zhu, J., Marjanovic, O.: A different kind of sharing economy: a literature review of platform cooperatives. In: HICSS 2021, pp. 6392–6401 (2021)

An AI-Driven Decision Support System for Product Feature Prioritization in Software Startups

Usman Rafiq[1](✉), Trygve Amundsen[2], Frédéric Pattyn[3], Xiaofeng Wang[1], and Christoph Stöckmann[1]

[1] Free University of Bozen-Bolzano, Bolzano, Italy
{usman.rafiq,xiaofeng.wang,christoph.stoeckmann}@unibz.it
[2] Ghent, Belgium
[3] Ghent University, Ghent, Belgium
frederic.pattyn@ugent.be

Abstract. Product feature prioritization is widely recognized as a critical challenge for software startups. Fast-paced environments, extreme uncertainty, and limited resources often force these companies to make trade-offs between competing ideas. Our study investigates the potential of an AI-based decision support system for feature prioritization in the context of startups. We used a design science research methodology to design, develop, and evaluate a proof of concept (PoC) artifact for AI-based product feature prioritization. The artifact uses AI to make decisions regarding product features using criteria such as return on investment, confidence, and time-to-value. We demonstrated and evaluated this PoC artifact using semi-structured interviews with seven software entrepreneurs. We analyzed the evaluation data using thematic analysis. The evaluation results indicate that startups perceive the potential to use AI to support the prioritization process. However, adoption depends on improving transparency, explainability, interoperability, and usability in these tools. The study contributes to the literature by providing early insights into how AI-based tools for product feature prioritization are perceived by startups.

Keywords: Artificial Intelligence · Feature Prioritization · Software Product Management · Tech Firms · New Venture · Early-Stage Company

1 Introduction

Software companies strive to deliver high-quality and innovative software products. This responsibility primarily falls to product managers (PMs), who serve

T. Amundsen—Independent Researcher.

G. Herzwurm et al. (Eds.): ICSOB 2025, LNBIP 574, pp. 325–333, 2026.
https://doi.org/10.1007/978-3-032-14518-5_25

as the driving force behind product vision, development, and delivery. PMs are often referred to as 'mini-CEOs', aligning customer needs with business objectives, and working across different functions to ensure product development and success [2].

In the context of software startups, PMs face a unique set of constraints that make their responsibilities even more crucial and challenging. Unlike established companies, which benefit from stable revenue, well-defined customers, a stable product roadmap, historical data, and well-defined processes, startups often operate with limited resources, undefined requirements, and a lack of historical data [2,4]. Similarly, these companies must quickly validate ideas, implement user feedback, and strive to build a competitive product [4]. Therefore, PMs in such organizations are required to make trade-offs, often based on intuition or incomplete information, balancing short-term survival against long-term vision. Similarly, among others, one of the significant responsibilities of this role is to decide what should be implemented next in the product. This decision-making process, often referred to as requirements or product feature prioritization, is critical and is identified as one of the core responsibilities of PMs in startups [2,4]. At the same time, artificial intelligence (AI) technologies are becoming more integrated into product development workflows [3], offering new possibilities to automate or enhance decision-making. However, little is known about how AI can specifically support feature prioritization in startups, where intuition and ad-hoc processes often dominate. This study aims to address this gap by understanding how AI-based decision support systems can enhance existing feature prioritization practices. The following research question (RQ) guides this study:

RQ: How can AI-based decision support systems support feature prioritization in startups?

To address this RQ, we used a design science research method [7]. In general, we developed and evaluated a proof of concept (PoC) artifact that showcases an AI-based decision support system for requirements prioritization. It is based on the light framework discussed in [5].

2 Research Method

In this study, we used the design science research (DSR) method. DSR is a problem-solving paradigm that aims to create innovative artifacts to solve real-world problems while simultaneously contributing to theory [7]. A key part of this paradigm is to build and evaluate artifacts. Peffers et al. [6] define a six-step model to implement DSR: problem identification, objective setting for a solution, design and development, demonstration, evaluation, and finally communication.

Based on existing literature (e.g. [1] [5]), we noted that PMs in software startups struggle to prioritize features. Existing practices are ad hoc, manual, and subjective. Therefore, we identified a need and aimed to leverage AI to support this prioritization process.

The objective of our artifact (PoC) were to: (1) to support product managers in prioritizing features using a structured and transparent method, (2) to leverage AI to guide decision-making through a conversational interface (3) to base prioritization on clear criteria like ROI, confidence, and time-to-value, (4) to maintain and organize prioritization results for later review and comparison, (5) to communicate the different features visually on intuitive graphs for quick understanding.

The front end of this PoC was created using Next.JS, with additional technologies including Recharts for custom charts, Axios for API integration, and React-Bootstrap for styling and responsive design. The interface allowed users to view, compare, and interpret prioritization scores through an interactive graph and a data table.

For demonstration and evaluation, we used guided sessions with seven startup practitioners. Semi-structured interviews were conducted during these sessions. Finally, we used thematic analysis to analyze the evaluation data.

3 Findings

3.1 Overview of the Artifact

Based on the lightweight framework proposed in [5], we designed and developed the proof of concept (PoC) for AI-driven feature prioritization in software startups, which serves as our artifact. The prioritization framework used in this artifact evaluates each input, which could be a specific feature in a project or a standalone project, and then calculates a score and a sub-score from the input values. These values are time-to-market (TTM), time-to-business-value (TTBV), confidence, and return-on-investment (ROI). TTV and TTBV are initially added as days, then mapped to a score, following a mapping table. Similarly, confidence is also calculated using the ICE (impact, confidence, ease) framework for prioritization.

The architecture of the PoC consists of four key components: (1) a front-end interface for visualizing data, (2) a backend server for processing and business logic, (3) a relational database for persistent storage, and (4) a custom ChatGPT-based conversational assistant that enables user interaction.

Figure 1 illustrates the interactions between the different components of the PoC. Additional implementation details, including the user interfaces and user stories that guided the development of this PoC, are available at https://figshare.com/s/cf39a3df61ca022fe0cf.

3.2 Artifact Evaluation

To evaluate our artifact (PoC), we conducted semi-structured interviews with seven practitioners from software startups. In general, our evaluation focused on assessing usability, workflow integration, interpretability of AI-based outputs, and perceived usefulness for product prioritization decisions. Since the roles in startups are really fluid, therefore, our interviewees included not only formal

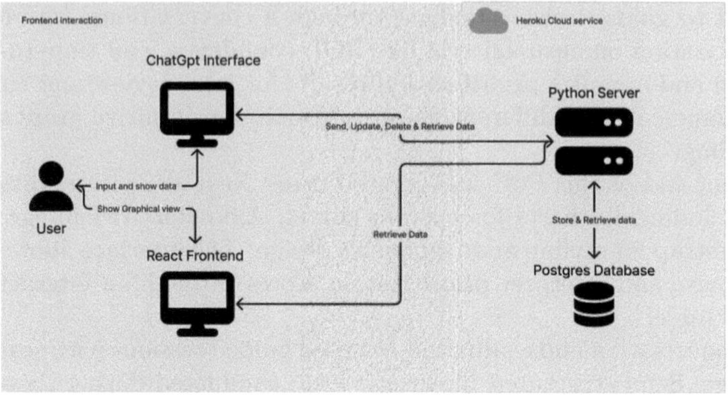

Fig. 1. Architecture of the PoC of AI-Driven Feature Prioritization Tool

software product managers but also founders, CEOs, and lead software developers, who were directly involved in product decision-making and vision. The characteristics of the interviewees and their startups are summarized in Table 1.

Table 1. Overview of Interviewees and Their Startups

ID	Interviewee Role	Startup Domain	**Employees**	Startup Stage
A	Product Manager	Digital Health	4	Growth
B	Lead Developer	Commercial Services	6	Growth
C	Founder & CEO	Healthcare	8	Growth
D	CEO & Product Manager	Food Technology	8	Growth
E	Founder & CEO	Software Solutions	7	Stabilization
F	Lead Developer	Software Development	40	Growth
G	Founder & CEO	Software Tools	1	Inception

3.3 Evaluation Results

We organized our evaluation results thematically to reflect key patterns in the data. An overview of the full thematic structure is presented in Fig. 2.

Engagement with AI

Perception of AI-Based Tools: We noticed mixed perspectives on AI-based prioritization tools and their place in startup workflows. Although most of the interviewees highlighted the clear potential for this tool, some others emphasized its

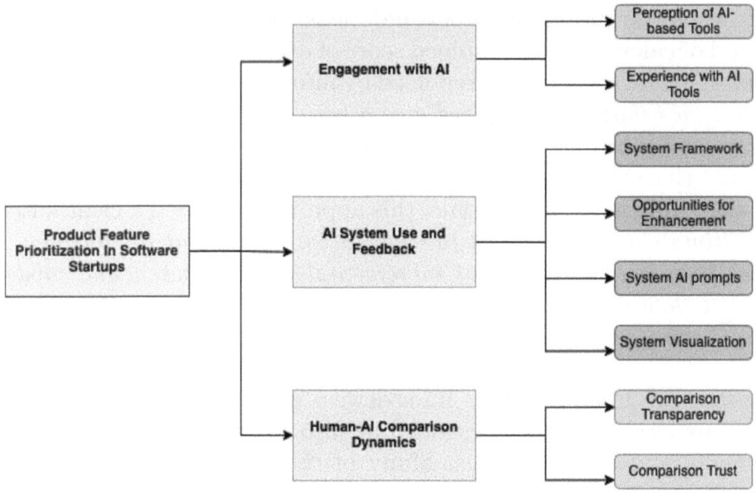

Fig. 2. PoC Artifact Evaluation Results

current limitations. In particular, interviewees mentioned a lack of context and judgment. For example, interviewee C expressed his perception in the following words: "*I think it's a great tool ... But having that extra checkpoint to understand if there are any gaps in decision-making around prioritization—I think that's definitely an add-on to the tools available for us.*"

The general perception among interviewees was that AI could serve as a useful aid, but not by any means a replacement for human decision-making. For those startups that had already implemented some AI systems into their workflow, they described the need for a human element to verify the output. This is in line with the excerpt emphasized by interviewee C. However, a few others added that trust in AI depends greatly on its transparency and how well the AI's process and reasoning were presented.

Experience with AI Tools: None of the interviewees in our data reported using any specific AI-driven tool for feature prioritization. However, interviewees from some startups reported the use of AI tools for other parts of their workflow. These included tools like ChatGPT, Gemini, or Claude to draft project outlines, summarize meeting notices, and conduct market research. For instance, interviewee A described the use of other AI tools: "*I use ChatGPT for that for any kind of research*".

AI System Use and Feedback

System Framework: The PoC was generally well-received; however, interestingly, for many startups, the metrics in this PoC were not known. An interviewee from the startup compared it to their current method of story points, saying that this approach would be more consistent and clear. Another interviewee noted that this method of calculating a combined score of each feature would help reduce the ambiguity in prioritization. It is reported by interviewee G in the following words: "*All the metrics that you described give a very good broad view of the impact of the feature, and [what] you should consider building next.*" Likewise, interviewee A supported this statement by adding that while different prioritization models may not vary drastically in outcome, this approach provided a clear and effective result: "*Ultimately it boils down to what factors you want to consider... I don't know that there's a whole lot of incremental value between one model versus another, but they all give a systematic way of evaluating what you need to do next. And I think your model works very effectively.*"

Opportunities for Enhancement: Interviewees generally responded positively to the overall experience of the system, but also expressed a few suggestions for improvements and a few dislikes. Many of these suggestions revolved around decreasing friction when inputting the values and clarification on the different metrics.

A recurring theme was the need for greater transparency in how the system actually worked and how it reached its result. As an example, interviewee A asked for: "*clarity on understanding what are those metrics like ... how those metrics are made, like what [and] how it's calculated ... can build some initial trust.*" Other interviewees proposed more technical implementations, such as having it integrated directly into GitLab or GitHub, making the workflow more seamless.

Another pointer we noticed in the data is to make the visualization reflect neglected tasks. Interviewees suggested that this could be done by increasing the size of the circle, the longer it had been in the queue. This could help teams identify forgotten tasks and adjust priorities accordingly.

System AI Prompts: Since our PoC was based on the conversational bot, in the results, we looked at how the interviewees perceived different sets of questions received from it. In general, startups' interviewees considered the prompts clear, helpful, and practical in describing their features. They also highlighted that answering these questions started a deliberate reflection process on the different values. It is reported by the interviewee G: "*It ...forces you to think about every aspect of the feature because, like, if I see the Trello tasks, I think it is OK, it takes a long time... Not that valuable... I will throw it away, but by forcing you to fill out the whole metrics, you reevaluate... Which number should I put there?*"

Likewise, beyond the specific questions on each metric, interviewees also appreciated the possibility of asking follow-up questions to the bot. This was found to be relevant when, for example, the meaning of ROI was unclear or if some examples were needed. This was especially seen as necessary if there were personnel working the tool not fully experienced with product management jargon. Similarly, some interviewees emphasized that certain prompts (RoI, Time-to-value) were difficult to answer and suggested the use of a more category-based scoring system (low-medium-high) to reduce the need for a guesstimate.

Lastly, although the questions were generally good and well-structured, some interviewees raised questions about the efficiency of the tool in terms of asking questions each time.

System Visualization: The interviewees perceived the visualization of the final results positively. For example, interviewee G explained how the visual layout supported faster and more objective decisions for their startup: "*The visualization is very helpful because now you can just focus on a very particular subset of the graph. The big dots at the top*".

The ability to compare features side by side was also appreciated in the data. Some interviewees even remarked that this could be adopted for internal communication or for yearly strategic roadmap planning. For example, in the case of interviewee E, the interviewee reflected: " *... I would expect people to want that, because you go back and forth a lot of times on the road map iteration*".

Apart from appreciations, some interviewees felt the need to have greater interaction, to change different metrics for each feature, and to see the change in position and size live. Others mentioned a need for more information on the graph, such as a tool tip or a written description of the calculation, for greater clarity. Although the visual model was valued for its clarity and simplicity, startups wanted to be able to tailor it to their workflow and systems.

Human–AI Comparison Dynamics

Comparison Trust: During the PoC demonstration, the interviewees of the startups also reflected on the trustworthiness of the system. We identified a high level of initial trust in the AI-driven system. Particularly since the AI was used to formalize a structured logic already set in the system, interviewee G explained: "*I would trust that ... just explaining the feature [with words] and then [letting the AI] come up with the metrics that you usually fill in.*"

Startups were more willing to trust it initially, in contrast to if the AI had to figure out and calculate each metric itself.

However, other interviewees voiced a bit of hesitation about the system, especially around contextual limitations. Although an interviewee thought it would make more mistakes than an average person, it would still need human oversight. It is evident from the following excerpt of the interviewee A: "*Having a certain level of experience is important, and why humans need to be part of the equation, because the model may generate something that's not accurate. But you need to be able to eyeball it...*"

Comparison Transparency: We found that while trust in the system was important, the ability to understand and explain the choices and results of the system remained equally important. Our data analysis revealed that being able to justify and explain why one feature is better than another is very important in decision-making processes. The claim was backed by the argument that in real-world product environments, decisions must be communicated, justified, and defended to stakeholders such as engineers, executives, or clients.

For instance, consider the quote of interviewee A: "*Justifying the model suggestions ... becomes kind of the lifeblood of the product managers, how to navigate the politics of moving something forward.*"

4 Discussion and Conclusions

Our findings suggest that AI-driven systems that support feature prioritization can play an important role in supporting decision-making. Startups are already leaning towards the use of AI for several reasons; however, none of them currently focus on feature prioritization. The demonstration of the PoC surfaced that the benefits of such tools are perceived by startups, but they think these are contingent. Overall, startups still do not consider this as a substitute for human decision-making for feature prioritization, and pointed out a few suggestions for improvements in this PoC. Four key improvements are discussed in our findings: (1) While startups were open to integrating AI into their workflow, they suggested connecting our tool directly to third-party applications, such as TeamHub, GitLab, or Slack, to improve integration, (2) Startups were less likely to trust the outcome if they did not know how the AI prioritized features. These results reinforce the importance of explainability in AI systems, (3) Startups appreciated the step-by-step process of talking to a bot in our PoC, as the bot helped them reflect more on the numbers and the specific feature than they otherwise would have. However, some startups with more established processes found that the conversation slowed them down and asked for another way to get input for feature prioritization, (4) Regarding the feature selection criteria, the scoring prioritization method and visual representation were described as useful and effective. This was especially the case for early-stage startups. The visualization of the graph in our PoC stood as a key strength of the system.

Based on these key takeaways, future research should investigate how improvements in integration, explainability, usability, and visualization can enhance the adoption and effectiveness of these AI-assisted feature prioritization tools in startups.

References

1. Melegati, J., Goldman, A., Kon, F., Wang, X.: A model of requirements engineering in software startups. Inf. Softw. Technol. **109**, 92–107 (2019)
2. Melegati, J., Wiese, I., Guerra, E., Chanin, R., Aldaeej, A., Mikkonen, T., Prikladnicki, R., Wang, X.: Product managers in software startups: a grounded theory. Inf. Softw. Technol. **174**, 107516 (2024)
3. Ogundipe, D.O., Babatunde, S.O., Abaku, E.A.: Ai and product management: a theoretical overview from idea to market. Int. J. Manag. Entrepre. Res. **6**(3), 950–969 (2024)
4. Pattyn, F.: The critical role of product managers and their responsibilities in software startups: a systematic literature review. Am. J. Eng. Technol. Manag. **9**(4) (2024)

5. Pattyn, F., Wang, X., Poels, G.: A requirements prioritization method: VECTR (2025)
6. Peffers, K., Tuunanen, T., Rothenberger, M.A., Chatterjee, S.: A design science research methodology for information systems research. J. Manag. Inf. Syst. **24**, 45–77 (2007)
7. vom Brocke, J., Hevner, A., Maedche, A.: Introduction to design science research. In: vom Brocke, J., Hevner, A., Maedche, A. (eds.) Design Science Research. Cases. PI, pp. 1–13. Springer, Cham (2020). https://doi.org/10.1007/978-3-030-46781-4_1

Accelerating Software-Intensive Innovation via Living Labs: Evidence from the AIAMO Project

Katharina Peine[1(✉)], Michael Ortgiese[2], Alexander Sohr[3], Lisa Schiffers[4], and Thomas Hornig[1]

[1] highQ Computerlösungen GmbH, Schwimmbadstr. 26, 79100 Freiburg, Germany
k.peine@highQ.de

[2] Deutsches Zentrum für Luft- und Raumfahrt e.V. (DLR), Institut für Verkehrsforschung, Rudower Chaussee 7, 12489 Berlin, Germany

[3] Deutsches Zentrum für Luft- Und Raumfahrt e.V. (DLR), Institut für Verkehrssystemtechnik, Technisches Transport- und Mobilitätsmanagement, Rutherfordstr. 2, 12489 Berlin, Germany

[4] ITS Germany - Bundesverband der Wirtschaft und Wissenschaft für Verkehrstechnologien Und Intelligente Mobilität e.V, Unter den Linden 10, 10117 Berlin, Germany

Abstract. In an increasingly digital world, the ability to innovate is crucial to the success of both economy and society, especially in connection with the growing use of artificial intelligence (AI). In order for such technologies to be developed and tested, open, practical environments for joint experimentation are needed. Living Labs offer a suitable framework for this. Using the example of the research project AIAMO (Artificial Intelligence And Mobility), led and coordinated by ITS Germany e.V. (ITS Germany e.V. – Federal Association of Industry and Science for Transport Technologies and Intelligent Mobility – has en working at the interface between intelligent transport systems and mobility for more than 20 years), this paper highlights how innovation processes can be established in a Living Lab to develop AI-based innovations in the mobility sector.

Keywords: Living labs · innovation · artificial intelligence · AI · AIAMO

1 Introduction and Intention of the Paper: Focus on Innovation Potential

Innovative capacity plays a central role in shaping technological and societal development, particularly in the context of ongoing digitalization and the increasing use of artificial intelligence (AI) [1]. AI refers to systems and algorithms capable of learning from data and performing tasks that require decision-making under uncertainty [2]. Building on the open innovation paradigm [3], previous studies suggest that collaborative and cross-sectoral development environments can reduce time-to-market and increase the effectiveness of innovation outcomes [4]. To this end, open, experimental environments in which new ideas can be tested together with partners from research and practice are

G. Herzwurm et al. (Eds.): ICSOB 2025, LNBIP 574, pp. 334–342, 2026.
https://doi.org/10.1007/978-3-032-14518-5_26

necessary. Software platforms (in the context of this paper, particularly in the area of mobility) are complex, especially due to the many systems and interfaces of the various partners – this effect is further amplified by the integration of AI: AI applications follow unprogrammed rules that are often inexplicable and incomprehensible [5]. This is why living labs are particularly well suited for their development, as they enable AI applications to be tested and further developed under real-world conditions, addressing socio-technical challenges such as acceptance, transparency, and targeted use. They promote participatory design, which is crucial for ensuring that the introduction of AI systems is sustainable and in line with the common good. Living Labs offer an environment that supports this kind of cooperation and collaboration between partners as well as the testbed for rapid prototyping in a real-world setting. This paper analyzes how innovation processes can be designed in a Living Lab in order to harness the potential of AI, using the research project AIAMO[1] (Artificial Intelligence And Mobility) as a case study.

2 Background: Living Labs and Artificial Intelligence – Synergies for Innovation

In recent years, Living Labs have become an effective tool for developing, testing, and implementing innovative technologies. They provide a real-world environment where researchers, companies, public institutions, and end users collaborate to design and refine solutions. As user-centered, open innovation ecosystems, Living Labs enable technologies to be developed and tested iteratively under everyday conditions, ensuring solutions are tailored to actual needs [6]. Such environments are particularly important for AI systems, as they directly address the interplay between technology, organization, and users [7].

2.1 Basic Principles and Functioning of Living Labs

Living Labs are open innovation ecosystems characterized by four key principles. Observing these solutions are more responsive to societal needs and achieve greater acceptance [8]:

- *Multi-stakeholder participation*: Integration of various interest groups (business, science, public, users) into the innovation process.
- *User centricity*: Development and validation of technologies under realistic conditions with active user involvement.
- *Iterative approach*: Continuous improvement through feedback loops, rapid prototyping, and field testing.
- *Co-creation*: Joint idea generation, development, and implementation of solutions in a collaborative process.

[1] https://www.aiamo.de/de

2.2 Artificial Intelligence as a Driver of Innovation

AI refers to software- and hardware-based systems that use algorithms to automatically solve complex tasks and learn from data. Areas of application range from speech and image recognition to optimization tasks and data-driven decision-making in the mobility, healthcare, and energy sectors [9].

AI systems enable new business models, increase efficiency, and create the basis for innovative services. At the same time, however, they require special care with regard to ethics, fairness, and data protection [10, 11]. This concerns particularly the area of mobility (subject of this paper) due to the sensitive movement data of road users, which play a major role als training input [12].

2.3 The Symbiosis: Why Living Labs Are Crucial for AI Innovation and Deployment

The integration of AI into operational systems with existing processes and infrastructures is complex and multifaceted. This is where Living Labs unfold their full innovation potential and challenges at the same time:

- *Real data and environments*: AI solutions benefit from validation through authentic data streams and usage conditions in the lab. Prototypes are tested not only under laboratory conditions, but also in real-life contexts – to the extent that this data is accessible [13].
- *User integration*: The early and continuous involvement of users makes it possible to identify and compensate for bias in AI training and to increase acceptance, while a critical mass of users is both essential for success and challenging to attain simultaneously [14].
- *Interdisciplinary collaboration*: AI projects require expertise in computer science, domain knowledge, and social science disciplines; Living Labs promote precisely this kind of collaboration. However, providing such a socio-technical environment is not straightforward [7, 15].
- *Ethics and trust*: Especially for sensitive AI applications (health, mobility), the Living Lab provides a framework for discussing and implementing ethical standards and data protection requirements in a participatory manner. User acceptance of sensitive mobility pattern data tends to be low and difficult to secure [10].
- This potential can be further expanded in the future and the described issues must be addressed. By embedding AI solutions in Living Labs, both their usability and acceptance can be significantly improved. The following section illustrates a possible approach using the case study of AIAMO.

3 Case Study: The Research Project AIAMO

AIAMO (Artificial Intelligence And Mobility) is a project funded by the BMDS in which 13 partners, led by ITS Germany e.V., are working together to develop AI-based environmental and mobility management systems that are more efficient, resource-efficient, safer, and tailored to specific needs. The AIAMO Living Lab pursues the goal of developing innovative AI applications in the mobility sector under real-world conditions and making them ready for use in real life. The AIAMO Living Lab is located at the interface between research, industry, and public actors. Here, interdisciplinary teams from AI development, mobility research, and user representatives develop solutions for real-time data integration, simulation platforms, and flexible test fields in urban areas. At regular AIAMOcamps, new developments are presented, integrated, rethought, and planned for the future. Methods such as Design Thinking and Open Innovation approaches are used to jointly define problems and develop solutions. Users are involved through feedback workshops, in which prototypes and working hypotheses are evaluated and adapted. This ensures a high degree of practical relevance and implementation potential.

In order to install AI applications in a living lab, it is necessary to set up a suitable environment that all parties have access. As an example, in this project this is achieved through the development of AIAMOnexus: As part of the project, an AI-based forecasting component was developed that uses machine learning models to analyze real-time and historical mobility data in order to identify traffic bottlenecks at an early stage. At the heart of the infrastructure is the AIAMOnexus [5, 10]. It combines the structured data access infrastructure of the integration zone with powerful AI models to provide curated, AI-optimized data for mobility management applications and handles the consolidation, processing, and quality assurance of heterogeneous data sources commonly used in traffic management, including traffic, environmental, and infrastructure data, and user information [18]. AIAMO uses AI methods for these processes, such as data cleansing, feature extraction, and merging of data from distributed information sources. The so-called AIAMOnexus can be used to connect both, external data sources (e.g. weather services, public transport systems, crowd data, digital twins) and external IT systems to the AIAMO environment. This creates an interoperable, expandable infrastructure that can integrate future requirements and new application scenarios (Fig. 1).

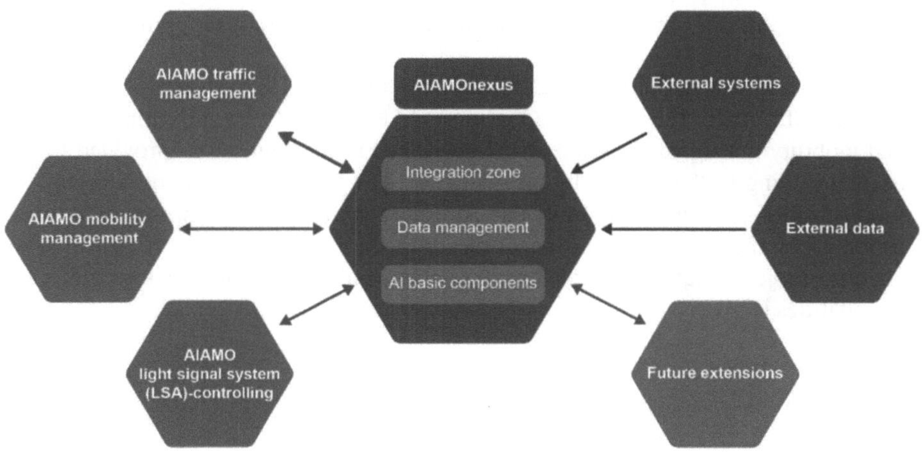

Fig. 1. AIAMO system components (ITS Germany & DLR).

In future expansion stages, the architecture will be supplemented by additional system components which, as already envisaged in the project's target vision, will also enable strategically optimized planning of the entire mobility offering at city and regional level. These include components for long-term traffic forecasts, capacity-based service planning, and dynamic incentive systems for sustainable mobility behavior.

4 AI-Based Innovation at AIAMO Living Lab

AIAMO uses AI to systematically analyze and link mobility data and develop an AI database for innovative applications, such as intelligent traffic management systems that respond dynamically to current traffic conditions, thereby preventing traffic jams and improving traffic flow. Furthermore, AI can be used to make improved traffic forecasts in order to proactively control traffic flow. The AIAMO Living Lab is initially being established in the model city of Leipzig for AI-supported traffic control. A dense environmental data measurement network with 50 stations across the city is being set up for data collection. Currently, 20 of these stations are already in operation. The primary goal is to record air pollutants such as nitrogen dioxide (NO_2) and particulate matter. This data is linked to other traffic data, such as traffic density, vehicle types, or movement patterns, and systematically analyzed with the help of AI. In combination with environmental data from other sources, this creates a "digital twin" of Leipzig, i.e., a digital model that maps traffic and the environment in real time. This twin will then help to better understand traffic patterns and propose measures for optimal traffic control by suggesting routes for road users. The environmental data measurement networks can also be used to collect data on air quality and emissions for climate-friendly mobility decisions. A mobility app will make AI-based mobility services available to road users in such a way that they can be used intuitively and encourage people to adopt sustainable transport behaviour [19]. A second AIAMO Living Lab is being set up in Landau in der Pfalz. While Leipzig is primarily responsible for environmentally sensitive traffic control in the AIAMO project, the focus in Landau i. d. Pfalz is on optimizing traffic flows with the use of AI.

For the first trial in the Living Lab, the Leipzig-based UFZ, as one of the project partners, will initially use the mytraQ editionAIAMO mobility app to improve operational mobility management based on AI-generated route suggestions provided by the AI-based routing of the DLR's digital twin [20]. The focus here is on developing and testing AI routing by linking mobility data, optimizing traffic flows, improving the organization of commuter traffic, and connecting public transportation more efficiently. What makes this project unique is that the results will be easily transferable to other cities and municipalities (Fig. 2).

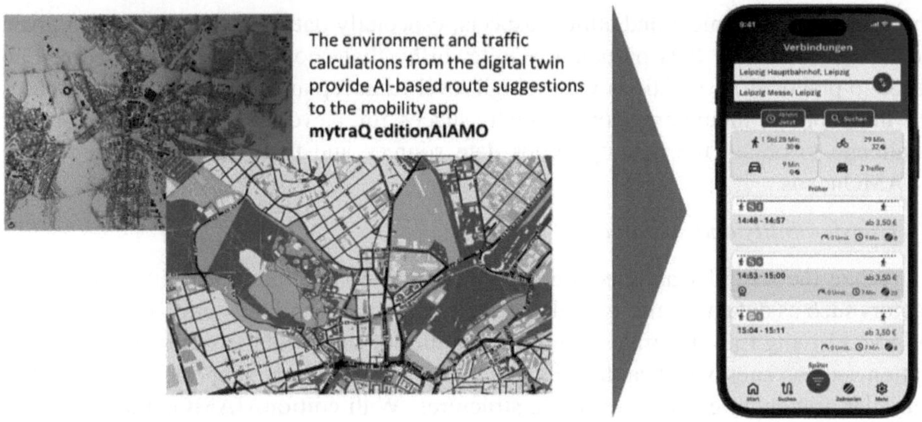

Fig. 2. mytraQ editionAIAMO: Measure-based route suggestions as an alternative for road users (highQ Computerlösungen GmbH).

5 Results, Findings, and Conclusion

The AIAMO Living Lab provides a platform for software-intensive innovation by developing and testing AI-supported systems for analyzing mobility data in order to adaptively control traffic flows and optimize individual mobility options for road users. The Living Lab enables a user-centered innovation process, as agile methods can be applied and prototypes can be evaluated with stakeholders, initially the UFZ, in iterative sprints, with improvements being integrated directly.

Key observations include:

- *Infrastructure requirements:*

The integration of AI systems necessitates a dedicated, accessible, and interoperable infrastructure. AIAMOnexus was developed in response to this need and plays a central role in data integration and (AI) application deployment.

- *Data protection and governance:*

The handling of sensitive mobility data requires a comprehensive, multi-perspective approach to data protection and ethical compliance. In AIAMO it is addressed by a multi-perspective data protection concept (especially technologies in accordance with European standards and data minimization).

- *User involvement:*

Iterative co-development with stakeholders improves the alignment of AI systems with user needs and regulatory requirements. In AIAMO the Living Lab methodology also makes it possible to integrate various interest groups into the development process, including the city of Leipzig itself. This allows the needs of end users to be identified at an early stage and technical solutions to be continuously adapted. The work at the AIAMO Living Lab shows that AI innovations are particularly successful when users are closely involved in all development phases and agile, iterative methods are used. At the same time, technical and ethical aspects, especially data protection, must be given equal consideration. It is particularly noteworthy that cooperation in the Living Lab leads to practical AI solutions with a high level of acceptance which in turn increases the likelihood of them being commercially successful. Nevertheless, it remains a major challenge to obtain the heterogeneous data sources and then integrate them via the AIAMOnexus.

- *Transferability and scalability:*

While the modular architecture supports expansion, actual scalability depends on factors such as data availability, stakeholder engagement, and institutional support. The AIAMO Living Lab illustrates the transferability of the model to other fields of innovation such as energy or health. This scalability is particularly supported by AIAMO's modular architecture and governance structures. With editionAIAMO, a development framework is available to the ITS industry that enables direct access to the optimized AI data of the AIAMOnexus, thereby ensuring close integration of data and applications. In addition, AIAMOitip bridges the gap between research and market introduction by paving the way for sustainable business models and the long-term establishment of the technologies. Another success factor is European networking: with AIAMOgoesEurope, collaboration between research, industry, and public institutions is being strengthened at the European level, supported by a governance structure in which ITS Germany provides the technical leadership and ERTICO–ITS Europe takes over political coordination. In this way, AIAMO lays the foundation for scalable, interoperable mobility solutions across Europe.

Future research should therefore focus particularly on the further development of these transfer mechanisms and their contribution to a sustainable innovation culture. Nevertheless, there are limitations: success depends on sufficient resources, interdisciplinary openness, and political support. A major challenge lies in gaining acceptance for the solution among road users, because without a sufficient number of users within the Mobility Living Lab, it will be difficult to obtain valid results. Also, a major hurdle is the provision of or access to public mobility-related data within the Living Lab, which is needed to generate AI-generated mobility measures, as data owners protect their data and large data silos still exist. For further evaluation, the inclusion of measurement results should be examined in a follow-up article. Future research should focus more on the scalability of Living Lab approaches in the context of AI and their impact on long-term innovation cultures.

References

1. Bundesministerium für Bildung und Forschung (BMBF): BMBF-Aktionsplan Künstliche Intelligenz Neue Herausforderungen chancenorientiert angehen (2023). https://www.bmftr.bund.de/SharedDocs/Downloads/DE/2023/230823-executive-summary-ki-aktionsplan.pdf?__blob=publicationFile&v=1. Accessed 29 Aug 2025
2. Copeland, B.J.: Artificial intelligence. In: Encyclopedia Britannica (2025). https://www.britannica.com/technology/artificial-intelligence. Accessed 19 Aug 2025
3. Chesbrough, H.W.: Open Innovation: The New Imperative for Creating and Profiting from Technology. Harvard Business Press (2003)

4. Rauter, R., Globocnik, D., Perl-Vorbach, E., Baumgartner, R.J.: Open innovation and its effects on economic and sustainability innovation performance. J. Innov. Knowl. **19/4/4**, 226–233, (2019)
5. Dell'Era, C., Landoni P., Gonzalez, S.J.: Investigating the innovation impacts of user-centered and participatory strategies adopted by European living labs. Int. J. Innov. Manage. **18/23/05**, 1–20 (2018)
6. Dönitz, E., Stadler, K., Zern, R.: Roadmap living labs für eine green economy 2030. Langfassung mit Roadmaps in den Konsumfeldern Wohnen, Einkaufen und Mobilität (2018)
7. Schaffers, H., Santoro, R.: The living labs concept enhancing regional innovation policies and instruments, In: 2010 IEEE International Technology Management Conference (ICE), Lugano, Switzerland, pp. 1–8 (2010)
8. Bergvall-Kåreborn, B., Ståhlbröst, A.: Living lab: an open and citizen-centric approach for innovation. Int. J. Innov. Regional Dev. **1**(4), 356–370 (2009)
9. Nikolinakos, N.T.: A European approach to excellence and trust: The 2020 white paper on artificial intelligence, In: EU Policy and Legal Framework for Artificial Intelligence, Robotics and Related Technologies—The AI Act. Law, Governance and Technology Series, vol. 23/53/, pp. 211–280, Springer (2023)
10. Bundesministerium für Bildung, Familie, Senioren, Frauen und Jugend: Gemeinsam im Wandel. Agenda für smarte Gesellschaftspolitik (2023). https://www.bmbfsfj.bund.de/resource/blob/179102/99450844ce3650c2d3f36c0e9f140952/gemeinsam-im-wandel-agenda-fuer-smarte-gesellschaftspolitik-data.pdf. Accessed 29 Aug 2025
11. Santoni de Sio, F., Mecacci, G.: Four responsibility gaps with artificial intelligence: why they matter and how to address them, Philos. Technol. **21/34/4**, 1057–1084 (2021)
12. Bharadiya, J.P.: Artificial intelligence in transportation systems, a critical review. Am. J. Comput. Eng. **2023/6/1**, 35–45 (2023)
13. Leminen, S., Westerlund, M., Nyström, A.-G.: Living Labs as open-innovation networks. Technol. Innov. Manag. Rev. **2**(9), 6–11 (2012)
14. Dutilleul, B., Birrer, F., Mensink, W.: Unpacking European living labs: analysing innovation's social dimensions. Central Eur. J. Public Policy **10**(4/1), 60–85 (2010)
15. Storr, S.: Reallabore (living labs) zur Erprobung von Anwendungen Künstlicher Intelligenz. In: Künstliche Intelligenz und Öffentliches Wirtschaftsrecht. Nomos, Baden-Baden pp. 116–135 (2022)
16. Goodfellow, I., Bengio, Y., Courville, A.: Deep Learning. MIT Press (2016)
17. Daten vernetzen, Mobilität neu denken, Straßenverkehrstechnik, auf den Seiten der Straßenverkehrstechnik (2025). https://aiamo.de/download/pdfs/Sonderdruck_AIAMO_SVT.pdf. Accessed 23 July 2025
18. FGSV: Arbeitspapier zur Gestaltung von Verkehrsmanagementstrukturen. FGSV Verlag, Köln (2009)
19. Peine, K., Hornig, T.: Social mobility als Erfolgsfaktor des Mobilitätswandels. In: Straßenverkehrstechnik, vol. 25/3/1, pp. 224–225 (2025)
20. Dalaff, C., Sohr, A.: Digitale Zwillinge ermöglichen ein umweltsensitives Verkehrsmanagement, Straßenverkehrstechnik. In: Straßenverkehrstechnik, vol. 25/6/1, pp. 396–398 (2025)

Human-Centered and Socially Responsible Software Business

Balancing Power and Participation: Ethical Contributions to Digital Strategy Development Based on a Case Study at a Public University

Isabelle Fries[1](✉), Ulrich Fries[2], and Martin Rost[2]

[1] University of the Bundeswehr Munich, Neubiberg, Germany
isabelle.fries@unibw.de
[2] University of Stuttgart, Stuttgart, Germany

Abstract. As societies undergo digital transformation, organizations face the challenge of actively shaping it. Ethical concerns need to be embedded in the process of digital strategy development itself to be effective. This paper explores not only ethics through strategy but also strategy through ethics. How is ethics perceived within a digital strategy process? In what ways can ethics contribute to the development of a more effective strategy? To address these questions, we conducted a qualitative case study at a German public university. Sixteen employees involved in IT strategy, implementation, and administration across all hierarchical levels were interviewed. While "ethics" was rarely mentioned explicitly – mostly as an individual concern – the analysis revealed that "balancing power and participation" constitutes a central tension. We argue that typical decision-making challenges, such as IT project prioritization and resource allocation, are inherently ethical. A discourse-ethical approach, with agile methods, can support such decisions in a structured, value-sensitive way. Our transdisciplinary study draws on three fields: (1) emergent strategy and Open Strategy in digitalization contexts; (2) integration of ethics into IT governance; and (3) political-philosophical theories on power and participation. The study offers practical guidance for decision-makers, developers, and staff engaged in complex implementation processes during digital transformation.

Keywords: Ethics in Digital Transformation · Digital Strategy · Open Strategy · Participatory IT Governance · Case Study

1 Introduction

Digital transformation is not only a matter of technological innovation, but also of strategic alignment and ethical responsibility. This is particularly true for public institutions such as universities, where digital strategies must balance organizational objectives with broader societal values. Legal requirements in these contexts may be more stringent and demand earlier implementation than in commercial organizations (e.g., digital accessibility; [19]). Theoretically, public sector institutions can be seen as pioneers in translating societal ideas into practice. Yet the reality is far more complex: Those responsible for

G. Herzwurm et al. (Eds.): ICSOB 2025, LNBIP 574, pp. 345–360, 2026.
https://doi.org/10.1007/978-3-032-14518-5_27

IT development and implementation are expected to "square the circle" – fulfilling legal obligations while addressing ethical aspects often perceived as softer requirements (e.g., sustainability; [33], pp. 35–36). They must do so with limited resources (both personnel and funding), and sometimes without "ethically clean" alternatives, such as in choosing software providers (initiatives exist; e.g., [9]). The political climate adds further complexity, particularly regarding trustworthy providers. Beyond GDPR compliance, which is now largely embedded in standard processes, the pursuit of digital sovereignty has become a strategic concern [38].

Our research builds on the observation that digital strategies, especially at universities, are still in their early stages, and that ethics are often treated as a secondary concern. However, an ethical perspective could lead to better strategies, for example, because a strategy that is known and supported can be more effective. We conducted a qualitative case study at a German public university, interviewing sixteen participants from IT strategy, implementation, and administration at various hierarchical levels. We examine how ethical considerations are incorporated into digital strategy development. While the term "ethics" was rarely mentioned explicitly – typically in relation to individual concerns or legal norms – the interviews revealed a recurring theme: "balancing power and participation."

We argue that decisions commonly framed technical or economic – such as IT project prioritization or resource allocation – are inherently ethical. The question of how to distribute scarce resources lies at the core of ethical theory. Ethics, in this sense, can support such decisions in a structured, value-sensitive manner.

This gives rise to three guiding research questions:

- How is ethics integrated in digital strategy development?
- What ethical implications stem from structures of power and participation?
- How can ethics contribute to digital strategy development?

By "digital strategy development," we refer to shaping processes and ensuring alignment within digital transformation. Our understanding of "ethics" focuses on procedures rather than normatively evaluating outcomes, adopting a discourse-ethical perspective centered on action and communication.

Prior to presenting the interview findings, we outline relevant theory, including H. Mintzberg's concept of emergent strategy, Open Strategy in digitalization, and approaches to integrating ethics into IT governance. Drawing on M. Foucault and J. Habermas, we link political philosophy to digital strategy development, assuming that understanding its social mechanisms can improve design and impact. Based on our findings, we propose viewing digital strategy development as a field of ethical negotiation. To support those involved, we integrate empirical insights with established theories and use agile methods to translate them into actionable recommendations.

2 Related Work

This section provides an overview of the interdisciplinary approaches that form the theoretical foundation for our study on ethical contributions to digital strategy development, with particular emphasis on the tension between power and participation.

2.1 Emergent Strategies and Open Strategy in Digitalization

An important conception of "strategy" can be attributed to A.D. Chandler [5], focusing on the pursuit of long-term goals. Strategy also includes statements about the activities and resources necessary to achieve these goals. Initially, IT provided administrative support for realizing business strategy. In the 1990s, this shifted to close coordination and alignment between business and IT strategy, with IT strategy remaining subordinate [24, 43]. According to Teubner & Stockhinger [43], digitization and digital business models have significantly transformed this interaction. They argue that the intersection of both strategies creates a digital business strategy, where digital technologies are deeply integrated into value creation.

Modern strategy research is significantly influenced by H. Mintzberg [30, 44]. One key contribution is his demonstration that intended and realized strategies often diverge. A deliberate strategy directly translates intention into realization, but in practice, only parts are realized. In addition, an emerging strategy influences the realized strategy. Strategy development thus spans a continuum between deliberate and emergent strategy [29]. Deliberate strategies are planned, emergent strategies arise from actions. "For a strategy to be perfectly emergent, there must be order – consistency in action over time – in the absence of intention" ([29], p. 258). In practice, strategies lie between these poles. Mintzberg & Waters identify eight strategy formation types. Internal stakeholder coordination and external influences can shape strategy. Planned strategies stem from senior management, entrepreneurial strategies from a leader's vision, ideological strategies from shared convictions, and consensus strategies through agreement without central control. Unconnected strategies reflect loosely linked actions [29].

Mintzberg's focus on the intentions and behavior of actors reappears in approaches like Open Strategy, which involves internal stakeholders below top management and external groups in strategy development [23, 42, 44]. This inclusion supports innovation [23]. IT tools enable broader participation [42], helping organizations leverage the skills for digital transformation [35]. However, depending on the situation, the dimension of participation can be in tension with the dimension of transparency [23]. Stadler et al. [41] show how organizations can use different practices in the three phases of the strategy development process – idea generation, strategy formulation, and strategy implementation – to extend or reduce the circle of participants. In the idea phase, new ideas can be generated with the aid of a broad circle of stakeholders without sharing sensitive organization-specific knowledge. These stakeholders can be involved, for example, through competitions or the Trend Radar tool. In the strategy formulation phase, the "what" and "how" of a strategy can be discussed in business logic contests with selected groups of employees and participants outside the organization. In the strategy implementation phase, the discussions can be facilitated by activities in the internal social networks of the organization [41]. However, the extent of participation and transparency cannot be regulated solely by upper management using a top-down approach. Indeed, the extent of both dimensions is also influenced bottom-up by the manner in which stakeholder groups participate in the strategy processes and the extent to which they independently utilize digital tools to make information transparent [35].

2.2 Integration of Ethics in IT Governance

IT governance research tends to focus less on specific ethical approaches and more on overarching societal norms to be integrated into practical applications. Ethical aspects are often treated as requirements alongside other goals. Topics like data protection, sustainability, and fairness are increasingly part of the discourse. Procedural ethical aspects of negotiating a digital strategy are rarely addressed, despite the central role of strategy development in governance.

E. Mumford's approach is well known. Through ETHICS [32], she analyzed socio-technical systems proposing a model for incorporating stakeholder interests. However, ETHICS primarily focuses on the development and implementation of information systems, not on digital strategy development. E. Ostrom's design principles represent another classic approach [36]. While she addressed governance – unsurprisingly, as a political scientist – her focus was on *Governing the Commons*. She argued that those affected by a decision should be involved in decision-making. Noteworthy is her discussion of resource scarcity. However, the transferability to strategy development is limited. IT projects within institutions cannot be compared to common goods, and the question of how to hierarchize goals when financial constraints exist was not within the scope of Ostrom's research.

Currently, L. Floridi's work is influential. He argues that "digital innovation must move to the governance of the digital" [12]. Crucial is his analysis of the "infosphere," where entities are conceived as "nodes" in a "network" (cf. [13], p. 21). Floridi wants the "information society" to include the "silent world" – such as the weak, future generations, and nature ([13], p. 30). This ties to his idea of "infraethics" ([13], p. 31): The government's task is to secure "the infrastructure of ethics." Although Floridi envisions a participatory policy, his ideas remain abstract. Where he adopts a practical stance, he seems to regard the governance level as already established, articulating principles normatively (e.g., [11]). For our research, his distinction between hard and soft ethics is important [12]: Hard ethics refers to codified rules and laws, while soft ethics encompasses what goes beyond legal requirements. Floridi does not adopt a procedural approach. By contrast, some recent approaches apply procedural justice, drawing on John Rawls' *Theory of Justice*, to the governance of IT projects [18] or examine negotiation processes in developing ethically "good" information systems [17]. F. Nascimento [33], in turn, links ethical reflection with technical practice inspired by P. Ricoeur. Such efforts remain rare. To date, the relationship between the micro level of IT project organization and the macro level of overall strategy is largely underexplored in the research literature.

There are attempts to combine both levels by means of agility. While "ethical digital strategy development" is rarely explored, "agile strategy development" is broadly discussed. One agile method to empower employees to work toward strategic goals and to measure the outcome is *Objectives and Key Results* (OKR) [6]. As supporting tool for ethics, for example, agile practices could help in the development of green and sustainability software [40]. A *Sustainability Awareness Framework*, developed in 2020 [7], was successfully implemented in scrum cycles for design and development decisions [4, 37]. Nevertheless, these approaches focus on concrete software development, not on the governance level in particular. One study explored methods of ethical public procurement of IT systems in Finland and led to a framework [26].

2.3 Key Political-Philosophical Theories on Power and Participation

In modern political philosophy, the discourse on power has been shaped notably by H. Arendt and M. Foucault. This section focuses on the latter due to his specific relevance for our study. Foucault embedded power within a socio-cultural framework, conceiving it as productive: Power enables effectiveness. It is not inherently negative (in this, he aligns with Arendt, who distinguishes power from violence; [2], pp. 35–42). Power is ubiquitous and cannot simply be eliminated ([27], p. 166). It is not possessed by certain individuals or groups but the effect of practices operating within a network of actions. Foucault was interested in the structure of power relations, as shown in *Surveiller et punir* [16]. He was not an ethicist who proposed ideals about what a just or a morally desirable balance of power and participation should look like.

For Foucault, power is inherently strategic, though not necessarily *planned*. Strategy is embedded in systems – for example, a teacher may punish a student not due to a *personal* strategy, but because the *system* defines a certain behavior as punishable. Even habitual (i.e., unconscious) behavior can be strategic, as it perpetuates certain patterns of conduct. The idea that strategy need not be planned links Foucault to Mintzberg (on Mintzberg as a conceptual extension of poststructuralism: [39]). However, Foucault saw power as distributed across decentralized networks. He spoke of "great anonymous strategies" ([14], p. 125; transl.) and envisioned a "strategy without strategists" ([1], p. 455; transl.). In *L'ordre du discours* [15], he discussed the implications of this for negotiation (with relevance for strategy development). He assumed "that in every society, the production of discourse is simultaneously controlled, selected, organized, and channeled" ([15], p. 10; transl.) and identified mechanisms that limit participation: certain statements are deemed inappropriate (prohibited or classified insane); expression presupposes specific expertise or roles (not everyone is permitted to speak); it is subject to ritual constraints (discussion spaces may serve as instruments of discursive control); and it must adhere to established conventions (e.g., the distinction between speakers and listeners).

While Foucault unmasks structural mechanisms of power within discourse, J. Habermas shapes those structures through discourse ethics. Though often contrasted, their perspectives are complementary ([22], p. 311). Habermas [21] fills the gap left by Foucault's analysis by providing normative elements. For Habermas, "strategic action" carries a negative connotation, referring to the use of power to gain advantage over others. In contrast, "communicative action" is oriented toward mutual understanding, involving rational deliberation aimed at the best argument ([21], p. 384–385). He emphasizes conditions for legitimate discourse, such as accessibility, equal participation, and truthfulness ([20], p. 161). The ideal is a discourse free from domination. Although Habermas envisions a democratic society, his focus on identifying the best reasonable solution – regardless of who proposes it – can enhance processes beyond political settings.

This returns us to "participation." Since the 1960s, various tiered models of participation have been developed to measure the degree of people's possible engagement in discourse. These models can be traced back to *A Ladder of Citizen Participation* by S.R. Arnstein [3]. Her model divides eight rungs into three categories: "Nonparticipation" (manipulation and therapy); "Tokenism" (informing, consultation, and placation); "Citizen Power" (partnership, delegated power, and citizen control). A three grade OECD framework published 2001 distinguishes information, consultation, and participation [34]. J. Morton presented a framework for tiered participation in strategy development: "Engaging Polyphony" (open informing); "Harnessing Polyphony" (collecting a wide range of voices); "Integrating Polyphony" (gathering wide feedback and incorporate ideas directly into strategy) [31]. Useful is also the *Liberating Structures* collection [28]. It contains over 33 micro structures to ensure decision finding meetings where everyone gets a voice.

3 Research Design

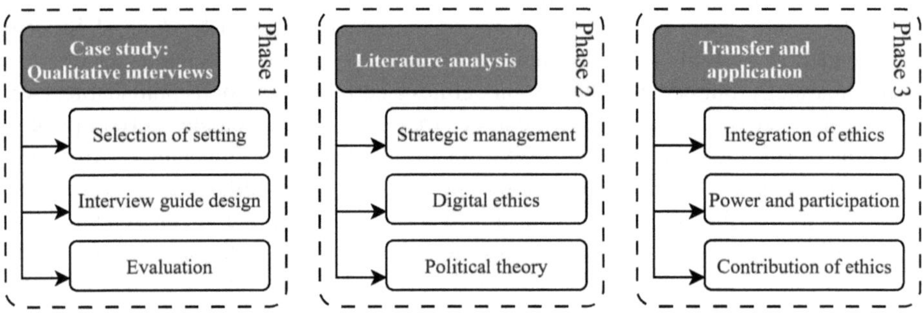

Fig. 1. Overview of the study design

We adopted an exploratory qualitative approach combining a theory-informed and data-driven analysis with an integrative, interdisciplinary review of relevant theoretical perspectives. Our research design (Fig. 1) includes a case study on digital strategy development (Phase 1), an analysis of relevant literature (Phase 2), and an application-oriented synthesis resulting in recommendations for practice (Phase 3).

In Phase 1, we conducted a case study at a German public university (> 20,000 students; > 5000 employees; technology-oriented) in 2025. The case study methodology is based on K. Eisenhardt [8]. We used a semi-structured interview guide including questions informed by the *Critical Incident Technique* [10]. Interviews addressed participants' activities, perceptions of university digital projects, related guidelines and strategies known to them, the origin and purpose of current practices, and views on how projects or strategies are or should ideally be developed. We examined understandings of "(digital) strategy," as well as internal (e.g., ethical) and external frameworks (e.g., laws, chain of command).

We conducted 16 Interviews, each lasting approximately 60 min, conducted equally by two members of our team of authors. Participants (56% female) represented various organizational areas and hierarchical levels (e.g., CIO, developer, user). Table 1 lists the interviews and participants' roles: (a) authors of strategy papers, (b) team or department managers, (c) IT developers, (d) project managers, (e) central administrative staff. The student council was invited to participate unsuccessfully.

Following transcription, we analyzed the interviews using a theory-informed and data-driven approach, combining inductive and deductive thematic coding. We identified

Table 1. Overview of interviewees; for legend see text.

Interview		1	2	3	4	5	6	7	8	9	10	11	12	13	14	15	16
Group or role	a	x	x	x			x			x		x			x		x
	b				x		x	x	x	x		x					x
	c				x	x	x										
	d	x		x		x			x				x	x		x	x
	e							x			x		x	x	x	x	

core issues and interconnections. Text segments were categorized into themes such as "Organization and IT," "Status of a central digital strategy," and "Awareness of a central digital strategy," among others. The analysis of recurring themes indicated that, in addition to responses to explicit questions (e.g., awareness of a central digital strategy or perceptions of ethics within strategic decision-making), an unanticipated theme gained particular prominence across interviews: "power and participation." The high prevalence of "power and participation" led us to adopt it as topic for further research.

In Phase 2, we conducted a corresponding literature analysis in strategic management, digital ethics, and political theory. For future recommendations, we also incorporated approaches from agility research and citizen participation. In Phase 3, we combined the empirical and theoretical parts discursively as the basis for our practical recommendations.

4 Results

Below, we provide an overview of the findings relevant to the theme presented.

Organization and IT. The case study institution has central decision-making bodies (rectorate and senate), a central administration, and centralized services such as a library and an IT service center, providing campus-wide functions, including email servers and research database hosting. Decentralized research departments largely operate their own IT infrastructure (Interview [Int.] 9). Electronic records (*E-Akten*) had not yet been implemented (Int. 15). Interviewees reported central processes with breaks in media continuity (Int. 8).

Status of a Central Digital Strategy. At the time of the case study, no central digital strategy had been adopted. However, two strategies were in advanced development (Int. 1–4, 6–7, 9). Experts at the IT service center had been working on an "IT strategy," which was intended to be derived from an overall "digital strategy" led by the CIO. Although the digital strategy was initiated later, it was completed earlier and was awaiting central approval for publication.

Awareness of a Central Digital Strategy. Employees not directly involved in drafting these documents were largely unaware of them. A quarter stated that, prior to these initiatives, the university had been "relatively lacking in strategy" in the digital – or that they themselves had been unable to discern a coherent direction (Int. 1, 4, 9–10). Half of those expressed skepticism about whether a written strategy would have any impact, given that few would be aware of it (Int. 1, 9). A similar sentiment appears in the quote: "Writing it down is easy, but implementation is what matters" (Int. 14). Some suspected that a strategy existed but that they alone were unaware of it (Int. 12), or simply assumed there might be one, without knowing for sure (Int. 13). One respondent speculated that knowledge might increase at higher levels: "Maybe my boss knows the strategy, maybe my boss's boss knows it, maybe the CIO knows it, or maybe it doesn't even exist" (Int. 5). Others had long waited for a central strategy, at times imagining it might cascade down from a state-level digital strategy (Int. 15).

Knowledge of Digital Strategy Guidelines and Action. Interviewees mentioned various guidelines relevant to their specific work (Int. 9–10, 15). They also observed strategic action on an individual level. Regarding their own actions, one respondent noted (Int. 1): "In the vacuum [...] – given the absence of a written strategy and, in some cases, a common understanding of what strategy actually means [...] – it's perfectly possible to simply set your own priorities." Regarding others, interviewees mentioned that leaders could pursue their own (sometimes self-centered) strategies without documenting them (Int. 2). Developers at the IT service center were described as free thinkers, acting relatively independently and setting priorities in digitalization they deemed useful (Int. 4). Some explained that they actively sought information to gain guidance by attending meetings or reading committee reports (Int. 8, 13) – "not only to find out where the journey is headed, but also to help shape it" (Int. 13).

Challenges in Digital Alignment. Most interviewees identified scarcity of funding in the public sector as a major challenge to digital alignment (Int. 4–7, 10–13, 15–16). Nearly half mentioned a lack of qualified personnel (Int. 1–3, 7, 10–11, 15). Two respondents noted the challenge of not starting from scratch, but of dealing with diverse software used across the organization (Int. 11–12). A few addressed geopolitical challenges, particularly in relation to Microsoft 365 and cloud solutions (Int. 3, 7–8, 14). Internal university politics were cited more frequently. These will be taken up under the points "Power" and "Participation."

Knowledge of Legal Frameworks. The majority thought (Int. 2): "Laws are there to be obeyed." All participants were familiar with the GDPR as "the guideline that we have to adhere to" (Int. 4), which aligns with (Int. 5): "I think that anything that is clearly defined and regulated is easy to understand and easy to adhere to." Laws related to digital invoicing (Int. 2, 11, 15), energy efficiency (Int. 2–3,10), the Online Access Act in German public administration (Int. 11, 16), and e-government (Int. 7) were mentioned. All participants were aware of a law on digital accessibility, though it was only occasionally raised unprompted (Int. 6–7, 9). One person noted (Int. 3): "I think that's the area where the least happens when you don't pay attention to it, even though you really should."

Awareness of Ethical Issues Within Digital Alignment. The question of how ethical aspects shape digital strategy development initially led to deliberation. One person said ethics played no role here (Int. 14). Some mentioned sustainability (Int. 2–4, 6, 13), while others viewed sustainable digitalization as greenwashing (Int. 11). One interviewee said they look for certificates when purchasing software, such as regarding accessibility (Int. 2). When digitalization is seen as work facilitation, an ethical element can be indirectly perceived: Automation of standard processes gives people time for creative tasks (Int. 1, 7–8, 10, 12).

Individual and Corporate Ethics. Ethics was seen less as a part of strategy development and more as an individual attitude: "Individuals bring their own personal values to the table" (Int. 3). One interviewee thought of ethics as something for people who are interested in it – with specific spaces for this within the university (Int. 8). Another person mentioned (Int. 4): "Ethical issues are always secondary at first [...]. But it's actually extremely important. In my line of work, I do think about ethics." "Intrinsic motivation" (Int. 12) and the Golden Rule (Int. 5) were cited as a guide for one's actions. In terms of values, reliability was noted, both regarding partners (software provider, supply chain; Int. 1, 3, 7, 15) and in terms of having a consistent strategy (Int. 11). Transparency was also emphasized (Int. 6–7, 9, 12, 15). Equal opportunities were implicitly mentioned regarding access and usability (Int. 3). Several stated they had chosen to work in the public sector to promote the common good (Int. 5–6, 10). The use of Microsoft 365 was explicitly identified as a value conflict (Int. 7–8).

Institutionalized and Personalized Ethics. Ethical issues seemed to receive particular attention when they were "institutionalized" or "personalized:" when structures involve the works council in decisions, attention is paid to employee welfare (Int. 8, 12); when a family office representative is present in committees, regulations on work-life balance, such as remote work, are promoted (Int. 13); involving the data protection authority ensures compliance with the GDPR (Int. 4, 8, 12). However, such positions were also seen as "obstacles" (Int. 8, 12).

Power. Resource scarcity was described as a source of power struggle (Int. 11, 14). Influence was exerted through funds, behavior, and relationships (Int. 1, 3, 6, 11, 16), and the implementation power of IT personnel (Int. 3, 4, 6, 7, 9). Arbitrary decisions by leaders were seen as disruptive (Int. 1–2, 10–11). Unclear responsibilities were identified as challenging (Int. 1, 7–9, 11–12). Conversely, certain department heads received positive feedback for fostering employees' work autonomy (Int. 5). The organization's size was noted to facilitate unregulated projects (Int. 6, 7, 10–11), while committees were expected to strategically prioritize or reject IT projects (Int. 2–3, 9, 14), though requiring legitimization from the rectorate (Int. 3, 11, 15). Those outside of IT had to personally advocate for their projects (Int. 12–13). The decision-making authority of those in power was considered legitimate (Int. 3, 14), whereas lack of decisions was seen as problematic (Int. 15, 16).

Participation. Three people did not comment on participation (Int. 11, 14, 16), one even stated that workshops would "beat the strategy to death" (Int. 14). All other 13 interviews emphasized the demand for broad information sharing. The most extensive forms of participation requested included: experts should be involved in the writing process (Int. 4, 9, 13); the results should be open for discussion (Int. 3, 7, 15); participation processes on a broad basis, for example, with interested parties or those affected (Int. 1–2, 6, 8); unrestricted moderated participation processes (Int. 5, 10, 13).

Agile Approaches. Five people mentioned or described OKR or other agile approaches as suitable participation strategy frameworks (Int. 1, 4, 7, 13–14). Sufficient time, but not excessive, should be allowed for the processes and discussions (Int. 1, 5, 13, 15). Some explicitly stated that the results of discussion processes should also be taken into account, regardless of the role of the author (Int. 1, 5, 7, 9). The results for the strategy from a participation process should be selected by a responsible manager (e.g., CIO, chancellor) within a durable decision (Int. 5, 9–11, 14, 16). A strategy created only by one person or an isolated management group was rated as worst-case scenario (Int. 5–6, 8–10, 15).

5 Discussion

In this chapter, we will discuss the research background in relation to the interview findings, following the research questions introduced at the beginning.

5.1 Integration of Ethics in Digital Strategy Development

If one focuses solely on the interview question regarding the role of ethics in the strategy development process, it may seem that ethics plays a marginal role at best. This is likely due to associations the term "ethics" triggered. Some linked ethics to values (e.g., reliability, transparency), while others thought of guiding principles (e.g., the Golden Rule). Most were unaware that by adhering to laws they were also following ethical principles. This aligns with Floridi's distinction between hard and soft ethics [12]. It also highlights that for ethics to have a greater impact, it needs to become a legally enforceable, essential standard. At the same time, ethical values at the individual level repeatedly played a role. It is noteworthy that, for some participants, the very context of public service was associated with an intrinsic motivation to promote the common good. This conviction is reflected, for example, in a developer's attention to ethically relevant certifications when selecting providers.

Interviews revealed a deliberative and an emergent understanding of strategy – an ambidextrous approach familiar in poststructuralism and strategic management. Notions that strategy implementation involves power resonate with both Foucault and Habermas, reflected in participants' attitudes: for some, power was not inherently negative, but structurally embedded; for others, it linked to a desire for greater participation. Habermas' discourse ethics aligns with the desire to be heard in appropriate formats. Foucault's analysis, in turn, holds true: participation is constrained by conditions (e.g., expertise, rank). Some interviewees perceived "strategy" as a matter of leadership, differing in whether they endorsed this view or criticized a lack of participation. Certain developers wished to have their practical concerns embedded at a strategic level but felt overlooked. Conversely, some administrative staff (users) placed trust in their supervisors' strategic decisions.

Overall, ethics in strategy development is not fully captured when reduced to identifying objectives as strategic goals. In this case, ethics is also about processes. This makes a discursive approach suitable, in line with recent advancements in digital ethics as mentioned earlier. The reference to a contemporary study on John Rawls' *Theory of Justice* in software development fits well with the integration of political theory in strategy development. Building on that study, the observation of "personalized" ethics suggests a practical extension: consulting sustainability and accessibility experts during decision-making to integrate these issues into standard processes.

5.2 Ethical Implications of Power and Participation Structures

Interviews revealed that the strategy development process involves a struggle for resources, making prioritization necessary. A personal strategy in this context may involve emphasizing own priorities, such as increasing presence in meetings. The interviews confirmed manifestations of power through expertise (e.g., IT developers) and positional authority (e.g., decision-making bodies with restricted access). Some interviewees emphasized the need for greater access to information to better perform their work. There also appeared to be a lack of transparency regarding the criteria used to prioritize and select specific IT projects. In the absence of clearly communicated guidelines, project selection sometimes seemed influenced by informal factors. Some individuals used the lack of clear directives to pursue their own agendas.

These insights indicate that Foucault's analysis of power structures resonates with the participants' experiences. Foucault frames power as a structural phenomenon. The various dimensions, inspired by Foucault and Habermas identified through the interviews, are shown below. Figure 2 provides a structured, concise overview; detailed explanations of each dimension are beyond this scope.

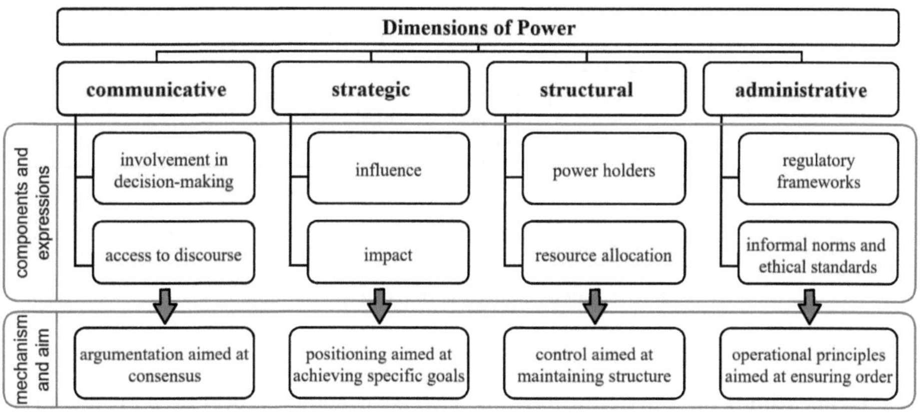

Fig. 2. Dimensions of power

Where Foucault's descriptive analysis ends, the focus shifts to participatory models (Habermas; agile frameworks). From an ethical view, it is desirable to safeguard the interests of all stakeholders, to implement fair and transparent decision-making procedures, and to ensure that employees have reliable structures to support their work.

5.3 Ethical Contributions to Digital Strategy Development

It should be clear by now that the foundation for ethics' contribution to digital strategy development – regardless of the promotion of values for orientation – lies in a procedural and discourse-ethical approach. This approach aligns with advancements in strategic management (though motivations may differ), which emphasizes leveraging innovative potential through participation, as well as digital ethics, where all stakeholders should be involved. By also addressing the relationship between "power and participation," the interdisciplinary research presented here converges.

The following goes beyond transdisciplinary synergies, offering a practical application. We recognize that participatory approaches require top management's willingness and are constrained by it. Although digital transformation affects all employees and students as users, management authorization and support remain essential prerequisites for translating discourse-ethical elements into practical formats.

Both developers and administrative staff demanded involvement. Their desire for participation aligns with the tiered model (information, consultation, participation; [34]), as well as with Morton's stakeholder involvement methods in strategy dialogues [31]: Engaging, Harnessing, and Integrating Polyphony. The Open Strategy approach [23] suggests methods, supported by IT tools, to continuously involve stakeholders in all phases of strategy development. In the following, we propose applying the participation levels in reverse order to the strategy development phases (Fig. 3). The aim is to ensure participation and value implementation while taking into account the organization's resources. In doing so, we also move toward realizing the ideal of discourse free from domination in the Habermasian sense.

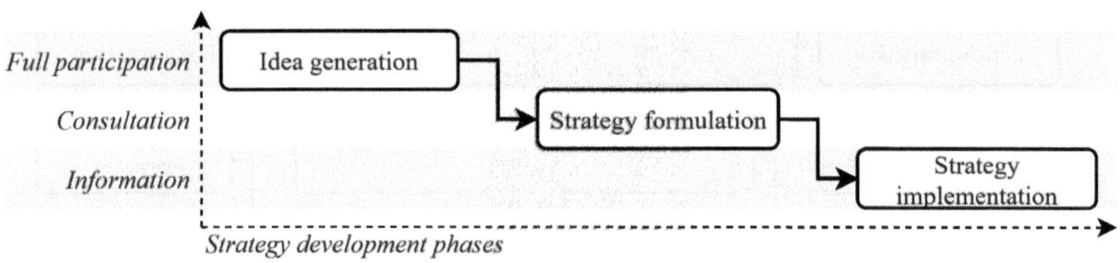

Fig. 3. Strategy phases with participation tiers

Idea Generation/Full Participation. An exclusive author group or representatives appointed solely by the management do not secure broad support for the strategy. For ethical value elicitation and idea generation, integration of all stakeholders is essential. We propose two practical formats: (a) A competition among all stakeholders to submit suggestions and needs related to digital transformation, with ethical in mind. Competitions attract attention; the "prize" could be the opportunity to represent the topic in the strategy committee. This reflects Habermas's idea of a contest of the best argument.

(b) Face-to-face workshops with all stakeholders using democratic discourse methods such as *Liberating Structures*. This requires time and skilled facilitation. Internal (social) media campaigns with comment functions should accompany both formats.

Strategy Formulation/Consultation. Consultation is a sufficient form of participation during the formulation phase, as the topics have already been collected. Interview findings indicated no desire for endless discourse. Regarding "institutionalized ethics," topic representatives (selected via open application or stakeholder election) participate to ensure the impact of their ideas and transparency in the further process. At this phase, categories and transparent guidelines for the realization and prioritization of IT projects can be established.

Strategy Implementation/Information. To avoid a paper strategy, outcome monitoring is essential. Adopters of the *Sustainability Awareness Framework* [4, 7, 37] suggest cyclical checkpoints for verification. Scrum works best for linear projects and is less effective for complex, multi-threaded, or asynchronous workflows. As some interviewees mentioned, OKR would be useful. The objectives of cycles should derive from the digital strategy, to ensure participation is met. From Scrum, the practice of presenting products or interim results in a review could be adopted. An "ethics review," involving topic representatives, could be institutionalized – published via livestream or made available through recordings for a broad reach.

Perhaps, in the business sector there will be less focus on ethics and more on profit-oriented promotion for a methodological practice as described above. Certainly, ethicists would criticize such purely profit-oriented reasoning and the instrumentalization of ethics (possibly citing Foucault and Habermas). The interplay between power, participation, and profit remains a further challenge for digital transformation.

6 Conclusion and Outlook

This study explored digital strategy development from an ethical perspective, guided by three questions: how ethics is integrated, what implications arise from power and participation structures, and how ethics can contribute to strategy development. To address these questions, we conducted a qualitative case study at a German public university and reviewed interdisciplinary research. We propose framing digital strategy development as a field of ethical negotiation. Drawing on empirical insights, interdisciplinary theory, and agile methods, we offer practical guidance to support decision-makers, developers, and administrative staff in balancing power and participation. We suggest a participatory, deliberative format to negotiate interests and the fair allocation of scarce resources in a strategic manner likely to achieve broad acceptance, rather than attempting to remedy resource scarcity itself.

Nonetheless, there are limitations. Results from one public institution may not generalize to all public organizations or the private sector. While we assume "balancing power and participation" is fundamental in negotiation processes, future comparative studies could verify this. We also consider resource scarcity to be a fundamental challenge that extends beyond public institutions to the private sector. A comparative study could assess whether individuals' commitment to public-service–oriented values influences their commitment to ethically shaping strategy. As this paper presents initial findings, some aspects remain exploratory. Further research can deepen specific points, such as focusing more on deliberative and emergent elements or on the proposed dimensions of power. Future research could also reflect the extent to which conceptions of leadership affect not only strategy development processes but also the ethical framing of strategic decisions. Lastly, our practical recommendations invite future implementation and evaluation.

Acknowledgments and Concluding Remarks. This research was conducted by researchers from two projects: (1) LIONS – funded by dtec.bw, which we gratefully acknowledge. Dtec.bw is funded by the European Union – NextGenerationEU. (2) Agility Lab – a project at the University of Stuttgart – funded by the DFG, whose support we gratefully acknowledge. We would also like to thank all interview participants, the case study university, and Karolina Laksa and Michelle Muhr for support with the transcription of the interviews.

Contributions can be attributed to the coauthors as described below:

– Isabelle Fries contributed expertise in philosophy, ethics, and political theory. She was responsible for the overall structure and conclusions of the paper and participated in the writing of nearly all sections.

– Ulrich Fries contributed expertise in IT project management and change management. He authored the sections on agility and participation within 2.2 and 2.3, parts of 3 and 4, as well as 5.3, for which he also developed the conceptual content. In addition, he was responsible for the design of all figures.

– Martin Rost contributed expertise in management and strategy research. He was responsible for the interview guide, 2.1, and provided additions to other sections.

AI tools (DeepL, ChatGPT) assisted with translation and linguistic correction. All suggestions were critically reviewed and adapted to ensure accuracy and quality.

References

1. Aggeri, F.: Les régimes de gouvernementalité dans le domaine de l'environnement. In: Hatchuel, A., et al. (eds.) Gouvernement, organisation et gestion: l'héritage de Michel Foucault, pp. 431–464. Presses de l'Université Laval, Quebéc (2005)
2. Arendt, H.: On Violence. Harcourt, Brace & World, New York (1970)
3. Arnstein, S.R.: A ladder of citizen participation. J. Am. Inst. Planners **35**(4), 216–224 (1969)
4. Bambazek, P., et al.: Application of the sustainability awareness framework in agile software development. In: 2023 IEEE 31st International Requirements Engineering Conference (RE), pp. 264–274 (2023)
5. Chandler, A.D.: Strategy and Structure: Chapters in the History of the American Industrial Enterprise. MIT Press, Cambridge, Massachusetts (1962)
6. Doerr, J.: Measure What Matters: How Google, Bono, and the Gates Foundation Rock the World with OKRs. Portfolio, New York (2018)
7. Duboc, L., et al.: Requirements engineering for sustainability: an awareness framework for designing software systems for a better tomorrow. Requir. Eng. **25**(4), 469–492 (2020)
8. Eisenhardt, K.: Building theories from case study research. AMR **14**(4), 532–550 (1989)
9. Ethical: Ethical Alternatives for Tech Stuff. https://ethical.net. Last accessed 08 Aug 2025
10. Flanagan, J.C.: The critical incident technique. Psychol. Bull. **51**(4), 327–358 (1954)
11. Floridi, L., Cowls, J.: A unified framework of five principles for AI in society. In: Floridi, L. (ed.) Ethics, Governance, and Policies in Artificial Intelligence. Springer, Cham (2021)
12. Floridi, L.: Soft ethics, the governance of the digital and the General Data Protection Regulation. Phil. Trans. R. Soc. **A376**, 20180081 (2018)

13. Floridi, L.: The green and the blue: a new political ontology for a mature information society. In: Floridi, L., Noller, J. (eds.) The Green and the Blue: Digital Politics in Philosophical Discussion, pp. 9–51. Karl Alber, Baden-Baden (2022)
14. Foucault, M.: Histoire de la sexualité I. La volonté de savoir. Gallimard, Paris (1976)
15. Foucault, M.: L'ordre du discours. Gallimard, Paris (1971)
16. Foucault, M.: Surveiller et punir. Naissance de la prison. Gallimard, Paris (1975)
17. Fries, I., et al.: On the way to the best information system of the future–reflections on scenarios in favor of good technology development. In: Papatheocharous, E., et al. (eds.) Software Business. ICSOB 2024, pp. 68–82. Springer, Cham (2025)
18. Fries, I., Greiner, M.: Technology-enabled fairness? Reflections on fairness within blockchain-based supply chain consortia. In: EURAM 2023 Proceedings (2023)
19. GOV.UK: Understanding Accessibility Requirements for Public Sector Bodies. https://www.gov.uk/guidance/accessibility-requirements-for-public-sector-websites-and-apps. Last accessed 08 Aug 2025
20. Habermas, J.: Erläuterungen zur Diskursethik. Suhrkamp, Frankfurt a. M. (1991)
21. Habermas, J.: Theorie des Kommunikativen Handelns, vol. 1: Handlungsrationalität und gesellschaftliche Rationalisierung. Suhrkamp, Frankfurt a. M. (1981)
22. Haus, M.: Grundlagen der Politischen Theorie. Springer VS, Wiesbaden (2023)
23. Hautz, J., et al.: Open strategy: dimensions, dilemmas, dynamic. LRP **50**(3), 298–309 (2017)
24. Henderson, J.C., Venkatraman, N.: Strategic alignment: leveraging information technology for transforming organizations. IBM Syst. J. **32**(1), 472–484 (1993)
25. Koski, A., et al.: The ethical landscape in public procurement of ICT systems. In: Papatheocharous, E., et al. (eds.) Software Business. ICSOB 2024, pp. 35–43. Springer, Cham (2025)
26. Ladwig, B.: Moderne politische Theorie: Fünfzehn Vorlesungen zur Einführung, 3rd edn. Wochenschau, Frankfurt a. M. (2022)
27. Lipmanowicz, H., McCandless, M.: The Surprising Power of Liberating Structures: Simple Rules to Unleash a Culture of Innovation. Liberating Structures Press, Seattle (2013)
28. Mintzberg, H., Waters, J.A.: Of strategies, deliberate and emergent. Strateg. Manag. J. **6**(3), 257–272 (1985)
29. Mintzberg, H.: Four forms that fit most organizations. Calif. Manag. Rev. **66**(2), 30–43 (2023)
30. Morton, J.: Strategy making as polyphony: how managers leverage multiple voices in pursuing agility. Calif. Manage. Rev. **65**(4), 22–42 (2023)
31. Mumford, E.: Designing Human Systems for New Technology: The ETHICS Method. Manchester Business School, Manchester (1983)
32. Nascimento, F.: Digital Poetics: A Ricoeurian Approach to Digital Technologies. Bloomsbury, New York (2025)
33. OECD: Citizens as Partners. Information, Consultation and Public Participation in Policy-Making. OECD, Paris (2001)
34. Ortner, T., et al.: Open strategy and digital transformation: a framework and future research agenda. Int. J. Manag. Rev. **27**(3), 324–345 (2024)
35. Ostrom, E.: Governing the Commons. Cambridge University Press, Cambridge (1990)
36. Oyedeji, S., et al.: Integrating sustainability into scrum agile software development: an action research approach. In: Papatheocharous, E., et al. (eds.) Software Business. ICSOB 2024, pp. 236–250. Springer, Cham (2025)
37. Pohle, J., et al.: Unthinking digital sovereignty: a critical reflection on origins, objectives, and practices. Policy Internet **16**(4), 666–671 (2025)
38. Rasche, A.: The Paradoxical Foundation of Strategic Management. Physika, Heidelberg (2008)
39. Rashid, N., Ullah Khan, S.: Agile practices for global software development vendors in the development of green and sustainable software. J. Softw. Evol. Proc. **30**(10), e1964 (2018)

40. Stadler, C., et al.: A user's guide to open strategy. Harv. Bus. Rev. **11**(02) (2021)
41. Tavakoli, A., et al.: Open strategy: literature review, re-analysis of cases and conceptualisation as a practice. J. Strateg. Inf. Syst. **26**(3), 163–184 (2017)
42. Teubner, A.R., Stockhinger, J.: Literature review: understanding information systems strategy in the digital age. J. Strateg. Inf. Sys. **29**(4), 1–28 (2020)
43. Whittington, R.: The practice turn in organization research: towards a disciplined transdisciplinarity. Account. Organ. Soc. **36**(3), 183–186 (2011)

Practical Adoption of Green Coding: A Comparative Study Across Organizations in Finland and Globally

Ichchha Moktan[1], Muhammad Asif Khan[1], Shola Oyedeji[1(✉)], Mikko Puonti[2], Mikhail Ola Adisa[1], and Jari Porras[1]

[1] LUT University, Lappeenranta, Finland
{Asif.khan,Shola.oyedeji,Mikhail.adisa,Jari.porras}@lut.fi
[2] Solita, Helsinki, Finland
Puonti@iki.fi

Abstract. As the environmental impact of digital technologies gains increasing attention, green coding has emerged as a critical aspect of green software engineering. This study investigates the practical adoption of green coding practices in organizations in Finland and globally to understand how they approach green coding in their software-development workflow. This study adopts a qualitative research methodology, combining a systematic literature review and semi-structured interviews. Key findings indicate that while organizations adhere to academic-recommended coding practices such as caching, lazy loading, asynchronous processing, microservices, and content/UI optimization, industry prioritization often depends on business needs, with less emphasis on energy-efficient programming languages or priority in green coding, especially in organizations outside the EU. Interestingly, in larger organizations, such as banks, green coding initiatives are mostly driven from the bottom up and led by software engineers. This reflects a positive change. However, innovative academic proposals, such as large language model (LLM)-based assistants for recommending green libraries, remain prototypes without industrial adoption. While LLM-based assistants show potential in recommending greener libraries, their current energy demand raises questions about net sustainability. Future research should evaluate their carbon trade-offs to ensure these tools contribute positively to sustainability goals. This study underscores the need for closer collaboration between academia and industry to promote the practical adoption of effective tools, along with standardized guidelines and sustainability-oriented education, to enable the wider adoption of green coding practices.

Keywords: green coding · energy efficiency · green software engineering · sustainability · Finland

G. Herzwurm et al. (Eds.): ICSOB 2025, LNBIP 574, pp. 361–378, 2026.
https://doi.org/10.1007/978-3-032-14518-5_28

1 Introduction

Green information and communication technology (ICT) is becoming increasingly popular, especially in the European Union (EU). The ICT sector currently accounts for approximately 2–7% of global greenhouse gas emissions and is projected to reach 14% by 2040 [1]. Many countries, including Finland, have pledged to become carbon neutral by 2050, as decided at the UN Climate Change Conference in Glasgow (COP26). Finland has set an even more ambitious target, aiming to achieve carbon neutrality by 2035, creating a challenging climate goal for the ICT industry [2]. Within the broader ICT industry, the software sector plays a crucial role, given its rapid growth and the increasing use of digital services in daily life. Organizations like the Green Software Foundation[1] are enhancing software sustainability in the EU by establishing standards, offering training, and collaborating with technology companies to minimize emissions associated with software usage. Similarly, in Finland, TIEKE[2] is leading efforts such as the Green ICT Ecosystem, which brings together academia, businesses, and government to promote the development of energy-efficient software.

Green coding, a subset of green software, is gaining popularity among software practitioners. Research has also shown its potential to reduce energy consumption and enhance energy efficiency through various approaches, techniques, and strategies [3]. For example, one study demonstrated that the selection of an appropriate algorithm for data collection can reduce energy consumption by 38% [4]. Similarly, another study demonstrated that energy consumption can be reduced by up to 67% through various energy-efficient architectural design strategies [5]. Although there is a growing awareness and desire among professionals to adopt green coding practices, they lack practical examples to guide them in integrating green coding into their daily workflows [6–9]. Therefore, this study aims to fill this gap by providing practical insights and real-world examples through exploring industry practices, perceptions, and experiences. Furthermore, this study offers a comparative perspective by examining how these strategies are implemented in various regions. This study focuses on the following three key research questions (RQ):

- RQ1: What green coding practices are proposed in academic literature (state-of-the-art)?
- RQ2: What are the green coding practices adopted in organizations in Finland and globally (state of practice)?
- RQ3: How do green coding practices vary across organizations in Finland, other EU countries, and non-EU regions?

This study contributes by (i) mapping academics vs. industrial practices, (ii) identifying adoption gaps, and (iii) providing recommendations for bridging these gaps.

[1] https://greensoftware.foundation/.
[2] https://tieke.fi/en/green_ict_ecosystem.

The remainder of this paper is organized as follows: Sect. 2 outlines the background and related work. Section 3 details the study's design. Section 4 presents the results and analyses. Section 5 discusses the findings and implications. Section 6 presents the conclusions and future work.

2 Background and Related Work

2.1 Green Coding: Concept, Importance, and Impact

Green coding refers to writing and optimizing code to reduce energy use and environmental impact through efficient algorithms, minimal data transfer, and removal of redundant processes [10]. Growing regulatory and stakeholder pressures further encourage the adoption of sustainable software practices [11]. Academic and industrial discussions increasingly emphasize the role of software efficiency in mitigating the carbon footprint of digital systems, linking performance optimization with environmental responsibility [12].

Numerous green coding strategies have been proposed in academia; however, their practical adoption remains limited [8]. This study examines how organizations translate sustainability goals into coding practices by comparing current advancements with practices observed in Finland and globally.

2.2 Related Work

Melo et al. [13] conducted a qualitative study involving 21 Brazilian software professionals to investigate how sustainability is understood and practiced in real-world settings. Their findings revealed growing awareness among developers but also showed that practical implementation is limited due to limited expertise and insufficient dissemination of sustainable practices within teams. This concern is echoed by Karita et al. [6], who conducted a state-of-practice survey that revealed that developers often recognize sustainability as a quality attribute. The current literature also reveals a gap between the state-of-the-art and practice. Junger et al. [14], in their review of existing research on green software development, point out that while academic discourse increasingly explores the potential and principles of green coding, there is a notable lack of empirical studies that examine how these principles are translated into actual development workflows, tools, or organizational practices. Other researchers have examined the organizational and systemic factors influencing the adoption of green software. For example, Pathiranage and Madrika [15] explored the adoption of Green Information Systems (Green IS) in global IT organizations, finding that while these practices have the potential to improve environmental outcomes, many organizations lack the strategic commitment to adopt them. Similarly, Lohikoski [16] identified barriers such as the absence of formal policies, unclear incentives, and low organizational support through interviews with ICT professionals, even in cases where developers were personally committed to sustainable software development.

3 Study Design

This study was designed to study both the state of the art and state of practice through a systematic literature review and semi-structured interviews to gain a comprehensive understanding of the green coding practices mentioned in academia and their practical adoption in the industry across Finland and globally. The overview of the study structure is detailed in Fig. 1 with three interconnected phases:

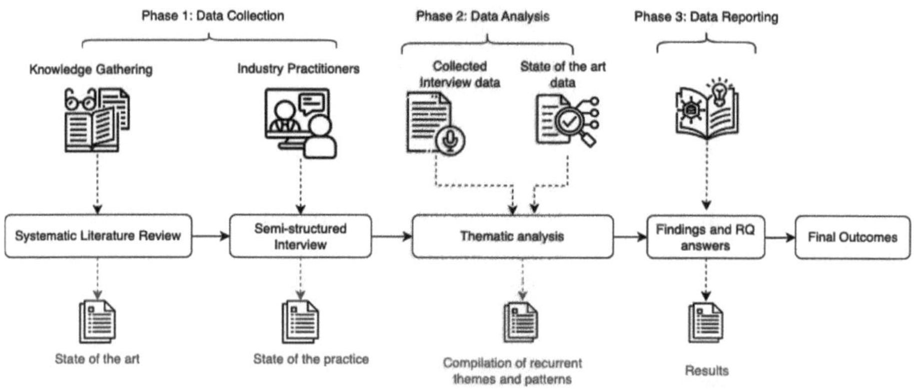

Fig. 1. Overview of the research design.

3.1 Systematic Literature Review

The Systematic Literature Review followed a structured protocol to ensure consistency and reliability of the results. This protocol includes database searches, inclusion and exclusion criteria, and an important categorization of the selected studies into different themes. The search covered publications from 2015–2025. Four different databases, IEEE Xplore, ACM, Web of Science, and Scopus, were utilized according to their reputation for publishing a substantial number of articles related to the field of study and covering the most relevant publications. The overall data collection process for the SLR is shown in Fig. 2. The following search string was used to search for primary studies:

"Green coding" OR "green software" OR "sustainable software" OR "energy-efficient software" OR "software sustainability") AND ("adoption" OR "implementation" OR "practice" OR "use" OR "integration") AND ("software industry" OR "software companies" OR "software development"

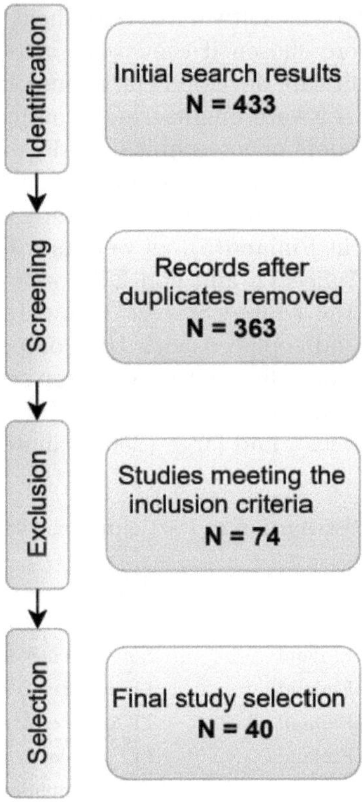

Fig. 2. Overview of the literature review process

3.2 Semi-structured Interviews

To gain qualitative insights into the real-world adoption and perception of green coding practices among software professionals, 15 semi-structured interviews with software professionals from organizations in Finland (5) and outside Finland (10) were conducted.

A. Interview Design: The interviews were designed to be flexible, guided by a structured framework that ensured consistency among participants while allowing for elaboration based on individual experiences and contexts. Each interview session lasted approximately 45–60 min and was conducted using Microsoft Teams. Participants were asked to provide their consent for the recording of the meeting. To capture how organizations approach green coding adoption with different regulations, the sample included five organizations, each from Finland, other EU countries, including the UK, and non-EU countries.

B. Participant recruitment: Potential organizations were identified by reviewing publicly available materials, such as company sustainability reports, corporate blogs, and official websites, to identify those that explicitly referenced green coding or energy-efficient software development practices, particularly in the EU. Organizations were chosen if they were involved in software development or had an internal software development team. Eligible participants needed a solid understanding of software engineering practices, regardless of whether they were hands-on developers or in technical leadership roles (e.g., developers, architects, and tech leads). In total, 15 organizations participated in the study, with one representative from each organization interviewed. The participating organizations were based in Finland(5), as well as other EU countries, such as the Netherlands(3) and France(1), and non-EU countries, including the United Kingdom(1), Canada(1), the United States(1), and India(3). The organization names were anonymized and replaced with the company A-N placeholders, as shown in Table 1 before proceeding with data analysis, to protect confidentiality. The size of each company is classified as small (fewer than 50 employees), medium (50 to 249 employees), and large (250 or more employees).

Table 1. Distribution of Participating Organizations

S.N.	Organization Name	Country	Type	Size
1	Company A	France	Financial Institution	Large
2	Company B	Finland	Software Development	Medium
3	Company C	Finland	IT Services & Consulting	Small
4	Company D	Finland	IT Services & Consulting	Small
5	Company E	Finland	IT Services & Consulting	Large
6	Company F	Finland	Telecommunications	Medium
7	Company G	Netherlands	Software Development	Large
8	Company H	Netherlands	Financial Institution	Large
9	Company I	India	Software Development	Large
10	Company J	India	IT Services & Consulting	Large
11	Company K	Canada	Software Development	Small
12	Company L	USA	Financial Institution	Large
13	Company M	India	Software Development	Large
14	Company N	UK	Software Development	Small
15	Company O	Netherlands	Financial Institution	Large

3.3 Data Analysis

Thematic analysis was used to identify key patterns in both the academic and industry sectors. It followed Braun and Clarke's six-phase framework [17], which started with the extraction of interview recordings as text-based transcriptions. The transcripts were thoroughly examined and relevant data segments related to the research questions were highlighted. The codes started to emerge from the data rather than having a prepared set of codes; therefore, an inductive coding (bottom-up) approach was employed. Each relevant segment/sentence was assigned a code that reflected its core idea with the help NVivo. Thus, a codebook was iteratively developed to track and organize all the codes across the transcripts. Once all data were coded, similar codes were further grouped into broader categories, which formed the basis of preliminary themes. Based on this, potential themes such as architecture & design patterns, code-level optimization, etc., have started to emerge. Each preliminary theme was critically reviewed, and themes that were too broad, overlapped, or weakly supported were refined, combined or removed. After the review and refinement process, each theme was given a descriptive name to ensure that it communicated the core idea effectively. Sub-themes were also created wherever necessary to reflect a better description of the software development experiences and practices on green coding in software-development projects.

4 Results and Analysis

4.1 State of Art: Systematic Literature Review Findings

The literature highlights a wide spectrum of practices, ranging from code-level optimizations to architectural and infrastructure-level practices, as detailed in the Table 2 below and explained in the subsequent subsections.

A. Code-Level Optimization: Research emphasizes the need to optimize the source code to improve energy efficiency. The choice of programming language plays an important role, with native languages such as C and Rust offering higher efficiency [1,18,19] and virtual machine languages such as C# along with the use of green compilers [18,20,21]. Database-specific strategies, such as indexing, caching, and compression, help reduce data storage energy consumption [21], whereas algorithmic optimizations, such as dynamic programming and memoization, reduce computational energy demands [23]. Refactoring codebases further contributes to significant savings over time [19,24].

B. Content and UI Design: Studies have highlighted UI/UX strategies to reduce energy consumption, including minimizing unnecessary graphics and animations, adopting energy-efficient designs such as dark mode and adaptive streaming, and using compressed image formats (WebP, SVG) [21,23]. Techniques such as lazy loading, asynchronous content loading, push notifications over polling to minimize background activity, implementing race-to-idle patterns, using dynamic retry delays and batch operations, and favoring WiFi connections over mobile data improve both energy efficiency and user experience [21,23,26].

C. Architecture and Design Patterns: Sustainable software architecture patterns, such as modular architectures, microservices, edge computing, and caching, promote reusability and flexibility while reducing energy consumption [19] [21]. Genetic Improvement (GI) methods further optimize architectures over time, integrating AI-based optimization for enhanced efficiency [27].

D. Cloud and Infrastructure: Green DevOps practices, such as putting idle servers to sleep, disabling unused ETL pipelines, and demand shaping, help

Table 2. State of the Art in Green Coding: Strategies, Focus Areas, and Emerging Trends

Category	Focus Areas	Green Coding Strategies
Code-Level Optimization	Programming Language Choices	Use of native languages (C, Rust) [1,18,19]; energy-efficient VM languages [18]; green compilers and optimized native code [20,21]
	Database and Data Storage Optimization	Efficient databases (SQL vs. NoSQL) [22]; indexing, caching, and compression [21]; efficient data structures [19]
	Algorithm-wise Optimization	Dynamic programming, memoization, and merge sort [23]; refactoring energy smells [3]
	Code-Specific Optimization	Code refactoring and optimization [19,24]; reduce algorithmic complexity; select energy-efficient algorithms [20,25]
Content & UI Design	UI/UX	Avoid unnecessary graphics or animations [21,23]; energy-efficient interfaces (dark mode, adaptive streaming, and compressed images) [21,23]; lazy/asynchronous loading [21,26]
	Content-specific	Use of compressed and responsive images [23]; adaptive video streaming [21]; efficient formats (WebP, SVG) [21]
	Device/User-Aware Operations	Push notifications instead of polling; race-to-idle mechanisms [23]; dynamic retry delays and batch operations [23]; prefer WiFi over mobile data [23]
Architecture & Design Patterns	Green Software Design Patterns	Edge computing, caching, modularization [19,21]
	Sustainable Software Architecture	Genetic Improvement (GI) methods [27]; modular and microservice architectures [19]; agile, reusable, and flexible design [24,28]
Cloud and Infrastructure	Green DevOps Practices	Green continuous testing [29]; sleep modes, and disabling unused ETL processes [30,31]; demand shaping and workload scheduling [19]
	Virtualization and Cloud Optimization	VM scaling and consolidation [20]; energy-aware infrastructure [19]; choosing green cloud providers [1]
Emerging Technologies & Trends	Advanced Technologies	AI, IoT, Blockchain integration for optimization [32]; multi-objective optimization (e.g., GEMMA for GUIs) [33]
	Tool Proposals	SPELL, GreenAdvisor, PEEK [19,34]; LLMs recommending green libraries [35]; auto-generated energy reports [36]

reduce energy usage [29,30]. Virtualization strategies, such as VM scaling and consolidation, minimize over-provisioning [20], whereas choosing green-certified cloud providers and energy-aware libraries enables developers to reduce the carbon footprint of hosted applications [1,19].

E. Emerging Technologies and Trends: Emerging technologies such as IoT, AI, and blockchain have been studied for both their energy impacts and mitigation potential [32]. Green coding tools (e.g., SPELL, GreenAdvisor, and PEEK) have been proposed to help developers monitor and improve the energy profile of their software [19,34]. LLMs are being explored as intelligent assistants that recommend greener library alternatives during development [35].

Although various effective strategies have been documented, the literature highlights a fragmented landscape, lacking standardized and consolidated guidelines for practitioners. This highlights the need for standard and centralized guidelines, such as the Web Content Accessibility Guidelines (WCAG)[3] to support developers in the easy adoption of green coding practices. Furthermore, innovative tools and techniques, such as LLM-based assistants for recommend-

[3] https://www.w3.org/TR/WCAG21/.

Table 3. State of Practice: Green Coding Strategies and Focus Areas Across Organizations (bold = mentioned by all organizations [A–N]).

Theme	Category	Practices Mentioned [Organizations]
Code-Level Optimization	Clean Coding Principles	Naming conventions and modular functions [O, F]; SOLID principles [I, L]; efficient data structures (e.g., dictionaries over lists) [G, L]
	Code Efficiency	Time/space complexity considerations [O, A, L] efficient constructs (e.g., `StringBuilder` over concatenation) [A]; code reviews for quality, consistency, and security [A, F, K, L, N]
	Data Handling	**DB optimizations (indexing, query tuning, selective fetching) [A–N]**; database engine optimization; regular cleaning and maintenance [A]
	Network Load	**Lean API design, minimized payloads, batching [A–N]**; avoid redundant API calls [H, N]
Architecture & Design	Design Patterns	**Caching, lazy loading, memoization [A–N]**
	Architecture	microservices and modular design [I, L, M] event-driven architecture [A, D]
	Concurrency	Multithreading and concurrent programming [A, J, L]
Frontend & UI	Asset Optimization	Minify and compress assets [B, H, K]; use WebP; compress media such as videos/animations [C, H]
	UI Design	Streamlined UI and short user journeys [B, C]; accessibility standards [B, L]; dark mode [H]; lazy loading [B, K]
DevOps	CI/CD Pipelines	Parallel jobs to reduce the build time [C]; scheduled builds and automated testing [I, E]
Cloud & Infrastructure	Resource Management	Automated shutdowns [O, A, E, F, H, L]; right-sizing and demand-based usage [A, D, I, K, E, H]
	Scaling/Scheduling	Serverless deployments and autoscaling [C, D, G, H, J]; Energy-aware scheduling carbon-aware datacenters [H, M, N]
	Cleanup	Delete unused resources and avoid cloud waste [D, A, F]
Tooling & Monitoring	Carbon Estimators	`CO2.js`, CodeCarbon, Cloud Carbon Footprint → estimate emissions from code, cloud, or web workloads [A, C, O]
	Website Assessment	EcoIndex, Ecograder, Google Lighthouse, WebsiteCarbon, ElectricityMaps → website environmental and performance assessments [A, B, C, H, K]
	Monitoring Dashboards	Kepler (K8s), Azure/AWS dashboards, and custom BI tools → monitor infrastructure energy and resource usage [A, D–L, H]
	Others	DailyClean, SlimFaaS → lightweight Kubernetes automation [A]; Firefox Profiler, Playwright → resource profiling and test automation [A, B]

ing green libraries and tools such as SPELL for energy leak detection in code, show promise, but they remain conceptual or underutilized in real-world development environments. This gap between academic proposals and industrial adoption underscores the importance of applied research focused on integrating these tools into real-world industrial practices. Future research should therefore focus on bridging this gap by emphasizing usability, empirical evaluation, and integration within industry-standard practices.

4.2 State of Practice: Interview Findings

Six dominant themes emerged from the analysis that are related to green coding practices and perceptions, as shown in Table 2. The industry findings, as detailed in Table 3, show a key focus on clean coding principles, modular design, SQL query optimization, API/payload reduction, and caching as common practices.

A. Code-Level Optimization: Most participants emphasized efficient, clean, and optimized code as a key green coding strategy for achieving green coding. Common practices include applying clean coding principles, such as clear naming conventions, modular functions, selecting appropriate data structures (e.g., dictionaries over lists), optimizing algorithms for time and space complexity, and reducing redundant application programming interface (API) calls. Batch processing, SQL query optimization, and regular database maintenance were also highlighted to improve performance and reduce resource utilization. Code reviews are also used to check for inefficient patterns, such as redundant loops or non-performant data structures.

B. Architecture and Design Patterns: Organizations employ architectural choices and design patterns to optimize processing, reduce unnecessary data handling and improve resource utilization. One participant shared: *"We use event-driven architecture to respond only when an event occurs rather than continuously processing."* Other approaches include caching and memoization to reduce redundant processing, lazy loading to defer data or resource loading until necessary, and asynchronous or concurrent programming to maximize CPU efficiency. Modularization and microservice architecture are also used, one participant shared, *"We make everything modular to ensure that each service can be scaled or updated independently."* A minimalism mindset is also embraced, a participant shared *"We try to fetch as little data as possible, only what is wise and necessary."*

C. Tooling and monitoring: Organizations use different tools to monitor, measure, and improve the efficiency of their codes, software, and infrastructure. Google Lighthouse was commonly used for web performance and environmental impact assessment, and traditional code analysis tools such as SonarQube, but with integrated 'green' rulesets or performance criteria to catch memory leaks or flag inefficient code. One participant shared *"Lighthouse provides a good baseline."* Another shared, *"We use tools like Daily- Clean to automatically shut down unused Kubernetes pods, and SlimFaaS to run only minimal functions when needed."* Some organizations are also developing in-house tools. One participant shared, *"We are building a CI/CD pipeline monitoring tool so that the developers can see whether the current deployment process is taking less or more energy."* Infrastructure-level dashboards, such as AWS CloudWatch and Azure CO_2 monitoring, are also used to monitor and reduce idle resource usage.

D. Cloud and Infrastructure Efficiency: Most organizations employ strategies to optimize cloud resources, including resource right-sizing, automated scheduling and shutdown of idle resources, dynamic scaling, and serverless architecture. One participant stated, *"For every name space in production, we check if we are over-sizing or under-sizing to maintain the right resource level."* Another participant stated, *"Our lambda-based services only run when needed."* Energy-aware scheduling, which schedules workloads when energy is green, is also practiced.

E. Content and Design: Organizations optimize their digital content and design to improve performance, user experience, sustainability, and accessibility by minimizing file sizes and network bandwidth using media compression and optimized images. They also streamline user journeys by eliminating unnecessary elements to reduce both cognitive and computational efficiency and improve overall efficiency. For example, one participant shared: *"We design the UI to minimize the number of steps users take to complete tasks."* Dynamic content loading techniques, such as lazy loading, are utilized to enhance efficiency, along with accessible design practices to ensure inclusivity and sustainability. Another participant shared, *"We use dynamic input so that only the required components are loaded per page."*

F. DevOps practices: Four participants emphasized DevOps strategies to enhance the efficiency and sustainability of software development pipelines. Key practices include optimizing CI/CD processes, strategically deploying to avoid unnecessary builds and tests, and optimizing the size of deployment packages to reduce resource consumption during builds. For example, one participant shared: *"We managed to cut 30% of processor time used in the CI/CD build step by parallel execution of tasks."*
Interestingly, organizational culture emerged as a key enabler in some organizations in Finland and the EU. Awareness campaigns, internal guidelines, and educational initiatives are being implemented to promote sustainable thinking among developers, helping to embed green coding into long-term practice. To accelerate deliberate adoption, organizations can integrate green coding criteria into existing code review processes, as code reviews are commonly used in software development workflows.

5 Discussion

5.1 Bridging the State of Art and State of Practice

There is a clear convergence across various evidence sources regarding effective, high-leverage practices. The literature review and interviews highlighted recurring strategies such as database and query optimization, caching and memoization, minimizing API payloads, implementing lazy and asynchronous loading, utilizing modularization and microservices, and adopting auto-scaling and serverless architectures [19,21,23]. These techniques are appealing because they provide measurable performance improvements while reducing resource consumption and can be easily integrated into existing workflows. Similar to the findings of Wyoski [3] and Ahmed [20], this study confirms that awareness of energy-efficient coding is growing, yet adoption often follows performance or cost drivers rather than clear sustainability goals.

The Literature highlights the importance of programming language and compiler selection, as well as the potential of tools such as SPELL [34], GreenAdvisor [18], and LLM-based assistants. However, according to Luhikowski [16] and Pathiranage [15], our interviews show that these research tools are underutilized because of limited industrial integration and unclear incentives. It shows that the difference between theory and practice is not due to a lack of awareness but due to the absence of workflow-embedded tools and standards.

Adoption occurs where integration costs are low and benefits are visible. Common practices such as query tuning, cache design, and auto-scaling are often implemented. [19,21]. In contrast, high-friction recommendations, such as language shifts or prototype tools, tend to be more time-consuming. These findings strengthen the earlier work of Junger et al. [14], which notes that although the concepts of green coding are well articulated academically, there is little evidence for empirical adoption. This study contributes by providing such an empirical basis in multiple areas and organizational contexts.

5.2 Regional Patterns in Adoption

The common ground of practices is evident across regions, although the importance varies with policy and cultural contexts. Finnish organizations, formed by strong sustainability goals and the CSRD frameworks [11], focus on code performance, event-driven design, and CI/CD optimization. Other EU organizations have more frequently experimented with carbon estimation tools and highlighted memoization, object pooling, concurrency, caching, and lazy loading [19,21]. While non-EU organizations generally regard sustainability as a secondary outcome of engineering best practices, they rely on cloud-native provider tools and, in some instances, adjust deployment frequency as a strategic lever. These regional differences align with the findings of Pathiranage [15], who showed that regulatory pressure strongly drives sustainability integration, consistent with the influence of frameworks such as the CSRD [11] and the motivation patterns illustrated in Fig. 3 (3a and 3b). Our findings align with Lohikoski [16], who noted that organizational structures and incentives shape sustainability adoption.

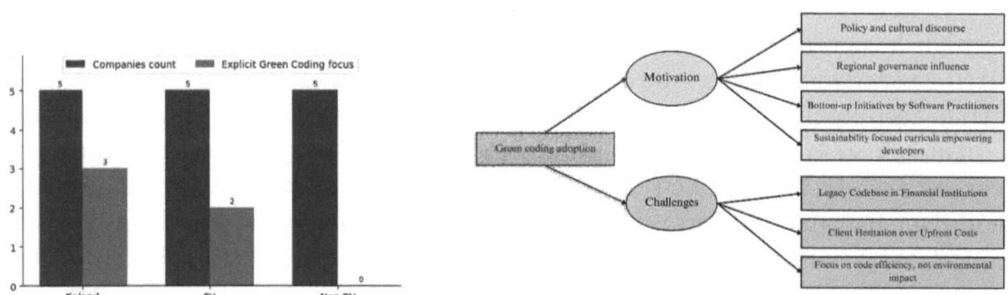

(a) Variation in green coding focus

(b) Motivations and challenges in green coding adoption

Fig. 3. Green coding practices

5.3 Organizational Dynamics: Bottom Up vs. Top Down

Interviews indicate that adoption typically occurs from the bottom up, particularly in large sectors, such as finance. Developers and technical leads incorporate sustainability checks into code reviews, promote right-sizing and idle shutdowns, and suggest energy-aware scheduling, even without formal mandates. This finding echoes Melo et al. [13], who observed that sustainability practices are often initiated by developers rather than management. Similarly, Lohikoski [16] identified the lack of organizational incentives and policies as a key barrier, a pattern consistent with our observations across several firms. Our proposed Capability-Constraint-Context (3C) model, mentioned below, builds on these earlier insights by providing a structured lens that connects individual initiative, organizational limitations, and environmental context. The 3C framing extends prior qualitative frameworks, such as those by Pathiranage [15], by clarifying how team-level capabilities interact with constraints and contextual drivers to shape practical adoption and also aligns with the Technology–Organization–Environment (TOE) framework [37], in which capability reflects technological readiness, constraint parallels organizational inertia, and context mirrors environmental drivers. The 3C framework aligns with sociotechnical priorities and capability-based perspectives in sustainability research, linking the actions of developers at the micro-level with larger organizational structures and policy environments. For instance, a team's ability to incorporate energy-efficient CI/CD checks (Capability) relies on the tools they have access to and the priorities set by management (Constraints). Additionally, broader policy instruments, such as the CSRD, help define an enabling environment (context).

- ► **Capability (Team-Level)**: → When both know-how and workflow fit are strong (e.g., through PR templates and IDE/CI checks), low-friction practices can spread quickly.
- ► **Constraint (Organization-Level)**: → Legacy systems, compliance requirements, and the availability of skills limit the feasibility of implementing more profound interventions (e.g., language migration and advanced architectural optimization) [5,16].
- ► **Context (Policy/Market)**: → In the EU, policy pressure promotes the adoption of measurement and review-embedded criteria, while non-EU contexts tend to focus more on provider efficiencies and portfolio strategies [11].

5.4 Practical Implications and Opportunities

The results highlight practical implications for key stakeholder groups and propose a clear framework for moving research into practice in academia and industry.

- **Academia (Translate Research into Workflow-integrated Tools):** Prioritize translation-based research by integrating results into workflow-native tools such as IDE plugins, pull request (PR) bots, and CI/CD processes that provide actionable insights (e.g., query selection checking, cache

hit rate regression, and carbon estimation) [34,35]. Evidence from interviews confirms that workflow integration is an important factor in adopting indigenous delivery.
- **Industry (Embed Green Coding Standards in Code Review Templates:** Institutionalize effective practices by incorporating green standards into the evaluation and development workflow. Enhance code review templates and static analysis to address database integrity, caching efficiency, and payload budgets. Use performance dashboards such as *Lighthouse* and *Cloud Provider Matrix*, and integrate CO_2 estimators into CI pipelines to enable lightweight governance and continuous monitoring of sustainability goals [29].
- **Policymakers and Professionals (Develop Standardized Checklists):** The systematic literature review (SLR) highlights the need for standardized practices similar to the Web Content Accessibility Guidelines (WCAG) [4]. Establishing a clear, checklist-style standard aligned with the Corporate Sustainability Reporting Directive (CSRD) would reduce compliance efforts, streamline procurement processes, and enable the definition of measurable key performance indicators (KPIs) [11].
- **Education (Integrate Sustainability into Core Computing/Software Engineering Curricula:** Integrate sustainability-focused content into software engineering/computing curricula and corporate training programs [8,14, 25,38], as developers often play a central role in driving sustainable change. This approach prepares future practitioners to apply evidence-based practical methods to develop green and energy-efficient software systems.

5.5 Challenges and Future Directions

The absence of standardized guidance remains a major barrier. Practitioners currently lack a unified framework or benchmark for green coding [8]. Legacy systems and modernization pose challenges, as technical debt and migration costs in sectors such as finance restrict the possibility of adopting new languages or toolchains, as well as implementing advanced optimization methods [5,16]. In the short term, organizations should focus on incremental improvements, such as query tuning, cache design, payload reduction, auto-scaling, and idle shutdowns, which our data indicate are both practical and effective [19]. The lack of standardized guidance remains a major challenge. Practitioners do not have a collective reference point [8]. Creating guidelines for green coding similar to WCAG with explicit criteria, illustrative examples, and default benchmarks is a highly beneficial, low-risk measure, as noted in the SLR synthesis [4]. Many promising green coding tools are still in the prototype phase and have not yet been integrated into real workflows [34,35]. To address this issue, future efforts should focus on conducting industrial trials of research tools embedded within IDEs and CI/CD pipelines, evaluating usability, the effort required for integration, and the trade-offs between performance and emissions [34]. Additionally, it is important to conduct quasi-experiments on legacy modernization to compare incremental refactoring against disruptive migration in terms of energy consumption, cost, and reliability [5]. Furthermore, the collaborative development of standards and incentives, such as procurement criteria and reporting requirements, that align sustainability with business objectives is essential [11]. Organizations are more likely to adopt low-friction, high-return practices that seamlessly fit into existing workflows, whereas deeper or experimental interventions necessitate stronger integration, a clearer ROI, and supportive policies. This study provides a comprehensive context-sensitive perspective on how research and practice align **(RQ1–RQ2)**, how regional and organizational factors influence adoption **(RQ3)**, and what is necessary to transform promising ideas into industry-ready solutions.

5.6 Threats to Validity

The research methodology has some limitations, as the small sample size and region-specific focus may limit the generalizability of the findings to broader populations in a regional context. Likewise, Green coding can have varying definitions and interpretations depending on the organizational context, geography, and technical scope. Therefore, the potential threat lies in how the participants in the interviews understood and interpreted the term green coding. However, to mitigate this, a clear working definition of green coding was shown on the slides at the beginning of each interview, and participants were asked to describe it based on their technical scope within their organization.

6 Conclusion and Future Work

This study investigated the adoption of green coding practices in Finnish and global organizations through interviews with software professionals. The literature highlights a range of practices, including code-level optimization, sustainable architecture, content and UI design, and DevOps, as well as emerging tools, many of which remain conceptual or lack validation in industrial contexts. The findings indicate that while efficient coding is common globally, the explicit focus on green coding is mainly evident in European organizations, influenced by stricter corporate policies and regulations. Outside the EU, sustainability is generally an incidental outcome of prioritizing code quality and clean coding. To promote broader adoption, standardized, checklist-based guidance could provide practical and centralized directions for implementing green coding across organizations. Academia also plays a crucial role in embedding sustainability-focused education into computer science and software engineering programs. Bottom-up initiatives, especially in large organizations, demonstrate how software engineers can exemplify their voices to lead grassroots efforts, highlighting the importance of cultivating a sustainability mindset among future professionals.

References

1. Mehra, R., Sharma, V.S., Kaulgud, V., Podder, S., Burden, A.P.: Towards a green quotient for software projects. In: Proceedings of the 44th International Conference on Software Engineering: Software Engineering in Practice, pp. 295–296 (2022)
2. Ojala, T., Mettälä, M., Heinonen, M., Oksanen, P.: The ICT sector, climate and the environment: interim report of the working group preparing a climate and environmental strategy for the ICT sector in Finland (2020)
3. Wysocki, W.: Why don't software companies care about software energy efficiency? A survey of software industry developers. Procedia Comput. Sci. **246**, 5054–5063 (2024)
4. Hasan, S., King, Z., Hafiz, M., Sayagh, M., Adams, B., Hindle, A.: Energy profiles of Java collections classes. In: Proceedings of the 38th International Conference on Software Engineering, pp. 225–236 (2016)
5. Jagroep, E.A., van der Werf, J.M.E.M., Spauwen, R., Blom, L., van Vliet, R., Brinkkemper, S.: An energy consumption perspective on software architecture. In: Weyns, D., Mirandola, R., Crnkovic, I. (eds.) ECSA 2015. LNCS, vol. 9278, pp. 239–247. Springer, Cham (2015). https://doi.org/10.1007/978-3-319-23727-5_19
6. Karita, L., Mourão, B.C., Martins, L.A., Soares, L.R., Machado, I.: Software industry awareness on sustainable software engineering: a Brazilian perspective. J. Softw. Eng. Res. Dev. **9**, 2–1 (2021)
7. Gross, J., Ouhbi, S.: Clearing the path for software sustainability. arXiv preprint arXiv:2405.15637 (2024)
8. Oyedeji, S., et al.: Green coding: state of practice. In: 2025 11th International Conference on ICT for Sustainability (ICT4S), pp. 91–99. IEEE (2025)
9. Oyedeji, S., Naqvi, B., Adisa, M.O., Abdulkareem, M., Penzenstadler, B., Seffah, A.: The interplay between usability, sustainability and green aspects: a design case study from a developing country (2019)
10. Mahmudova, S.: Green coding in programming and practices. J. Eng. Technol. (JET) **15**(2) (2024)
11. Abur, V.: The dimension of green coding in software quality control processes. In: 2024 9th International Conference on Computer Science and Engineering (UBMK), pp. 1–6. IEEE (2024)
12. Naumann, S., Dick, M., Kern, E., Johann, T.: The greensoft model: a reference model for green and sustainable software and its engineering. Sustain. Comput. Inform. Syst. **1**(4), 294–304 (2011)
13. Melo, R., Vilela, J., Silva, C., Peixoto, M., Araújo, J.: The Brazilian practices for handling sustainability in software engineering: a replicated survey. In: Proceedings of the XXIII Brazilian Symposium on Software Quality, pp. 298–308 (2024)
14. Junger, D., et al.: Potentials of green coding-findings and recommendations for industry, education and science (2023)
15. Pathiranage, R., Madrika, H.: Green information systems practices adoption in global it organisations: exploring challenges, practices and strategies (2024)
16. Lohikoski, A.: of thesis green software development-challenges and implementation AP (2024)
17. Braun, V., Clarke, V.: Thematic Analysis. American Psychological Association (2012)
18. Camargo-Henríquez, I., Martínez-Rojas, A., Castillo-Sánchez, G.: Energy optimization in software: a comparative analysis of programming languages and code-execution strategies. In: 2024 9th International Engineering, Sciences and Technology Conference (IESTEC), pp. 507–511. IEEE (2024)

19. Majuntke, V., Obermaier, F.: Towards sustainable software (2023)
20. Ahmad, R.: Software sustainability practices and awareness amongst software practitioners in Malaysia: an exploratory study. In: 2022 2nd International Conference on Electronic and Electrical Engineering and Intelligent System (ICE3IS), pp. 192–197. IEEE (2022)
21. Bhadane, S., Unde, V., Pathan, A., Kadam, A., Shinde, G.R., Mahalle, P.N.: Sustainable programming: a new paradigm shift towards sustainable development. In: 2024 IEEE Pune Section International Conference (PuneCon), pp. 1–6. IEEE (2024)
22. Lella, H.S., Chattaraj, R., Chimalakonda, S., Kurra, M.: Towards comprehending energy consumption of database management systems-a tool and empirical study. In: Proceedings of the 28th International Conference on Evaluation and Assessment in Software Engineering, pp. 272–281 (2024)
23. Rani, P., Zellweger, J., Kousadianos, V., Cruz, L., Kehrer, T., Bacchelli, A.: Energy patterns for web: an exploratory study. In: Proceedings of the 46th International Conference on Software Engineering: Software Engineering in Society, pp. 12–22 (2024)
24. Ahmad Ibrahim, S.R., Yahaya, J., Sallehudin, H.: Green software process factors: a qualitative study. Sustainability **14**(18), 11180 (2022)
25. Oğuz, K.: Achieving sustainable software systems by reducing bloat and by promoting green practices in software engineering education. In: 2024 Third International Conference on Sustainable Mobility Applications, Renewables and Technology (SMART), pp. 1–5. IEEE (2024)
26. Wysocki, W., Miciuła, I., Plecka, P.: Methods of improving software energy efficiency: a systematic literature review and the current state of applied methods in practice. Electronics **14**(7), 1331 (2025)
27. Di Pompeo, D., Tucci, M.: Harnessing genetic improvement for sustainable software architectures. In: 2024 IEEE 21st International Conference on Software Architecture Companion (ICSA-C), pp. 248–249. IEEE (2024)
28. Taherikhonakdar, Z., Fazlollahtabar, H.: Integrated delphi-interpretive structural modeling for sustainable green software development. Int. J. Ind. Eng. **35**(2), 1–26 (2024)
29. Nayak, K., Route, S., Sundararajan, M., Jain, A., et al.: Sustainable continuous testing in devops pipeline. In: 2024 1st International Conference on Communications and Computer Science (InCCCS), pp. 1–6. IEEE (2024)
30. Letrache, K., El Beggar, O., Ramdani, M.: Green data warehouse design and exploitation. In: Proceedings of the 12th International Conference on Intelligent Systems: Theories and Applications, pp. 1–6 (2018)
31. Procaccianti, G., Fernández, H., Lago, P.: Empirical evaluation of two best practices for energy-efficient software development. J. Syst. Softw. **117**, 185–198 (2016)
32. Atadoga, A., Umoga, U.J., Lottu, O.A., Sodiy, E.: Tools, techniques, and trends in sustainable software engineering: a critical review of current practices and future directions. World J. Adv. Eng. Technol. Sci. **11**(1), 231–239 (2024)
33. Linares-Vásquez, M., Bavota, G., Bernal-Cárdenas, C., Penta, M.D., Oliveto, R., Poshyvanyk, D.: Multi-objective optimization of energy consumption of guis in android apps. ACM Trans. Softw. Eng. Methodol. (TOSEM) **27**(3), 1–47 (2018)
34. Pereira, R., Carção, T., Couto, M., Cunha, J., Fernandes, J.P., Saraiva, J.: Helping programmers improve the energy efficiency of source code. In: 2017 IEEE/ACM 39th International Conference on Software Engineering Companion (ICSE-C), pp. 238–240. IEEE (2017)

35. Gupta, S., Gupta, A.: Advancing carbon-efficient software development: a sustainable path forward. In: Proceedings of the 26th International Conference on Distributed Computing and Networking, pp. 325–330 (2025)
36. Ournani, Z., Rouvoy, R., Rust, P., Penhoat, J.: On reducing the energy consumption of software: from hurdles to requirements. In: Proceedings of the 14th ACM/IEEE International Symposium on Empirical Software Engineering and Measurement (ESEM), pp. 1–12 (2020)
37. Tornatzky, L., Fleischer, M.: The process of technology innovation, lexington, ma (1990)
38. Moreira, A., et al.: A roadmap for integrating sustainability into software engineering education. ACM Trans. Softw. Eng. Methodol. **34**(5), 1–27 (2025)

Playing Against Creative Burnout in Sprint Retrospectives: A Design Science Research Study

Phuong Thao Nguyen[1(✉)], Stephen Huynh Chung[1], Toke Witt Rasmussen[2], and John Stouby Persson[1]

[1] Department of Computer Science, Aalborg University, Aalborg, Denmark
{ptn,john}@cs.aau.dk, stephenhuynh@live.dk
[2] Saphe, Aalborg, Denmark
tokewittrasmussen@gmail.com

Abstract. Creative burnout, characterized by stagnation, exhaustion, and rigid routines, can hinder creativity and well-being in software development teams. Although widely acknowledged in practice, creative burnout remains underexplored in academic research on software development. This study investigates how playful interaction design can help mitigate creative burnout in Sprint Retrospectives. Using a Design Science Research approach, we developed and evaluated 'Scrumstinct', a design artifact for introducing playfulness into retrospective practices, tested in workshops with eight teams across diverse industries. Based on qualitative analyses of pre- and post-session interviews and video observations, we propose six design principles for integrating playfulness to address team-level creative burnout. Our findings show that playful retrospectives can reframe problems, foster openness, and reduce emotional fatigue. We argue that playfulness in agile practices holds the potential to reshape team culture and support sustainable creativity in software development.

Keywords: Scrum · Design Science Research · Playfulness · Software Development Teams · Creative Burnout

1 Introduction

Burnout is a well-documented challenge across many professions [16], but creative burnout remains underexplored in academic research [13]. In practice, it is described as a state of mental and emotional fatigue that limits creative engagements [10]. This phenomenon is especially relevant in software development, which relies heavily on creativity in tasks such as requirement engineering, architecture, design, and programming [18]. Nevertheless, the barriers to creativity and their effect on team well-being have received limited scholarly attention

G. Herzwurm et al. (Eds.): ICSOB 2025, LNBIP 574, pp. 379–393, 2026.
https://doi.org/10.1007/978-3-032-14518-5_29

[1,11,25]. Creative burnout in software development teams (SDTs) often manifests as an inability to explore new ideas, falling back on conventional solutions, and overall rigidity in workflows [11,25]. These symptoms not only reduce individual motivation but also hinder team-level adaptability and creativity, reinforcing stagnation [2,26]. Thus, addressing such issues is essential for fostering SDTs sustainable creativity and everyday well-being.
One promising approach is to introduce playfulness into SDTs existing practices. Research on playfulness shows it can stimulate creativity [4], support emotional relief [22], and enhance team interaction [21]. In the widely used agile framework Scrum [12], Sprint Retrospectives provide a natural setting for introducing playful interaction design. These recurring sessions are intended for reflection and process improvement [24], but often become repetitive, lack engagement, or fail to surface deeper team concerns [8,15,23]. Although retrospective activities such as Sailboat or Mad/Sad/Glad [23] are widely used, the potential of playfulness as a strategic intervention against creative burnout remains largely unexplored.

In this study, we investigate how playful interaction design can mitigate creative burnout in SDTs by applying the Design Science Research method [20], developing and evaluating 'Scrumstinct', a design artifact for introducing playfulness into retrospectives. It was evaluated with eight SDTs across different industries. Based on qualitative analyses of pre- and post-session interviews and video observations, we propose six design principles for incorporating playfulness in retrospectives to address team-level creative burnout.

2 Related Research

2.1 Creative Burnout

Although there is no unified understanding of the psychological structure or definition of creative burnout [13], it is widely described in opinion articles, blog posts, and videos. Descriptions include creative stagnation, overwhelm by creative work, or a lack of creative thinking. Simultaneously, it is explained as mental and physical fatigue, reflecting the exhaustion dimension of burnout [16]. Related terms include creative exhaustion [10], encompassing the experience of being creatively stuck; innovation fatigue, characterized by a lack of mental capacity to create [5]; and creativity clogs, hindering the flow of creative ideas [25]. While often examined at the individual level, these struggles also occur collectively as creativity, and by extension creative burnout, takes shape in the shared ongoing activity of working together. As such, a team's creative burnout can hamper collective work engagement and well-being [2,26].

Struggling with creativity in SDTs manifests as limited idea flow, reliance on familiar approaches, and repetition [11,25]. When a team becomes monotonous in its task execution [25], it rejects exploration and reinforces a status quo of expected ways of working that limit creative contributions [19]. Considering these insights, we define creative burnout of a team as *the tendency to avoid creative pursuits, characterized by mental and emotional exhaustion and an inhibited capacity to produce new ideas.* In the context of this study, creative burnout in SDTs is described through three dimensions: *stagnation*, a decline in creative exploration of alternatives, *exhaustion*, by mental weariness, and *rigidity*, in maintaining a monotonous task execution.

2.2 Playfulness

To address creative burnout characterized by stagnation, exhaustion, and rigidity, SDTs can pursue playfulness to reconnect with their creativity and well-being. Playfulness has been defined as the tendency to *frame (or reframe) a situation in such a way as to provide oneself (and possibly others) with amusement, humor, and/or entertainment* [3]. Individuals having this predisposition were described as funny, humorous, spontaneous, or unexpected, among others [3]. This definition has been expanded to include playfulness as a coping strategy for tense situations [22], and a contributor to well-being [4,27]. Moreover, it has a social dimension, as highly playful individuals often seek opportunities for playful interaction [22]. It was further found to cultivate relationships and express creativity [21]. This frames playfulness as both an instrument for alleviation and a social phenomenon within human interaction. Playfulness has further been viewed as the dispositional tendency to engage in play for amusement [14,27], highlighting its autotelic and intrinsic nature.

Drawing on these definitions, we understand playfulness as a quality of an activity that is: *fun*, based on descriptors of humor and frivolity, *exciting*, referring to spontaneity and unpredictability, as playfulness can emerge unexpectedly in social interactions, and *desirable*, covering the autotelic dimension of playfulness where playful situations are sought out for the enjoyment of the activity itself.

2.3 Playfulness in the Scrum Framework

A promising context for exploring playfulness in software development is the Scrum framework. Notable for its introspective nature, the Sprint Retrospective in particular presents an opportunity for teams to address challenges, such as creative burnout [24]. Activity-based retrospectives have demonstrated equal engagement, improved communication, increased team morale, and new perspectives [8,17]. Studies also show that they increase creativity and overall effectiveness in counteracting monotony and inefficiency [23]. Additionally, gamified retrospectives can promote collaborative learning and process improvements [15]. At the same time, these alternatives do not necessarily equate to effective retrospectives and must balance engagement with purpose [17], and may only be suitable as a supplemental activity [15]. These studies highlight the potential of playful activities in Sprint Retrospectives, such as enhanced collaboration, creativity, and participation.

However, it is important to distinguish playfulness from gamification of retrospectives. While both promote engagement and share elements of fun [8,15,17], they differ in motivation. Gamification is driven by external incentives, which may be experienced as superficial by reducing well-being to measurable outcomes, thereby failing to address the core issue [7]. Playfulness, in contrast, is intrinsically motivated and reflects openness and curiosity [3]. It shapes how we approach work and relationships [21,22], which allows for exploration and connection without external pressure. Building on this research, we shift the focus toward fostering playful spaces, where teams can discuss work challenges openly, encourage acknowledgment, and deepen understanding to enhance team well-being. In particular, this study explores the integration of playful interaction design in Sprint Retrospectives and how it can be utilized in the context of mitigating team-level creative burnout.

3 Research Approach

To investigate how playful interaction design can mitigate creative burnout, we applied Design Science Research [20] with a pragmatist aim of constructive knowledge that is useful in action [9]. This approach enabled us to investigate the effect of playfulness by embodying it in a design artifact, developed over six iterative phases. Our process is illustrated in Fig. 1.

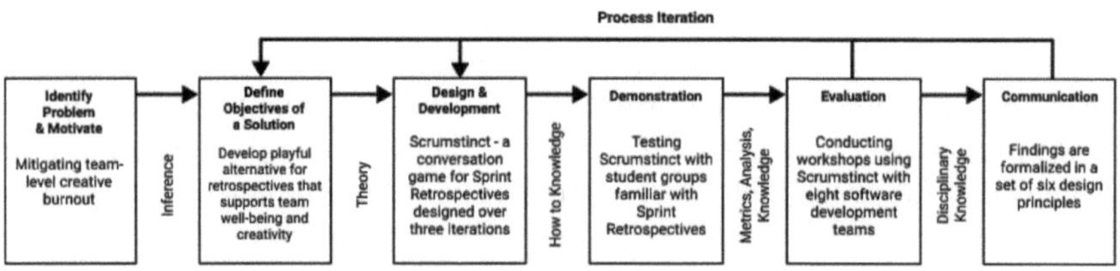

Fig. 1. Our process according to the Design Science Research model

Building on related research in Sect. 2, we integrated playfulness into Sprint Retrospectives through the development of the design artifact 'Scrumstinct', created over three iterations and demonstrated to student groups to validate and refine the artifact. We then evaluated Scrumstinct by conducting workshops with eight professional SDTs, formalizing insights into a set of DPs that inform how to design for playful retrospectives targeted towards improving team well-being. The participating teams were recruited through mail, career fairs, and in-person inquiries. The teams ranged from 3 to 12 members, 4 months to 4 years of team tenure, 0 to 20 held retrospectives, and members were between 24 to 65 years old. Each team, presented in Table 1, is assigned pseudonyms based on their area of expertise in the industry.

We conducted a 90–120 minute workshop with each team, which was audio- and video-recorded. The procedure included a study introduction, a preliminary focus group interview, playing Scrumstinct, and a debriefing focus group interview. Grounded in our conceptualization of playfulness as *fun*, *exciting*, and *desirable*, and creative burnout as a *stagnation*, *exhaustion*, and *rigidity*, these dimensions guided our evaluation. This enabled us to qualitatively assess how playfulness mitigated creative burnout through team experiences before and after playing Scrumstinct.

Table 1. Overview of participating teams and their characteristics

Team	Team size	Team Tenure (years)	Retrospectives held (avg.)	Age range	Additional notes
BarrelCo	4	3.5	1	26 - 32	Bi-weekly retrospectives. Recent team addition 1 month ago.
Tramark	3	2.5	2	28 - 30	Bi-monthly retrospectives. Recent team addition 7 months ago.
FrontPress	6	3	10	24 - 60	Bi-weekly retrospectives. Recent team addition 5 months ago.
UtilyTech	6	2	0	38 - 63	The team has just started to work according to the Scrum framework. Recent team addition 4 months ago.
EduCloud	3	3	20	32 - 38	Retrospectives every 3 weeks. Sometimes skipped due to the absence of team members.
CodeBank	5	1.5	20	31 - 50	Team had 3-5 years of collaborative experience from another company, but have been a team at CodeBank for 1.5 years, having bi-weekly retrospectives.
PayCraft	7	4	2	27 - 51	Bi-weekly retrospectives. Recent team addition 1 month ago.
SocialTech	12	3.5	7	28 - 65	Team had 3-4 years of collaborative experience, averaged to 3.5. Has bi-annual 'team days' allocated for discussing work processes, similar to a retrospective.

The data were analyzed through the six dimensions in two phases: 1) collective coding of pre-interviews to capture team opinions, and 2) thematic analysis to systematically interpret and cluster recurring patterns [6]. The codes were synthesized into themes representing the teams' overall experiences, determining their baseline levels of playfulness and creative burnout. The same process was applied to post-interviews, supplemented by video reviews of the tonality of their statements, non-verbal cues, and team interactions, which produced themes that reflected Scrumstinct's impact.

4 Findings

This study led to the development of Scrumstinct, a design artifact that facilitates a playful approach to Sprint Retrospectives, see Fig. 2, aimed to enable reflections on sprint events through creative interpretations of artifacts. An overview of the teams playing Scrumstinct is shown in Fig. 3. This section presents the findings of conducting workshops with SDTs using Scrumstinct, organized around the themes that emerged from the thematic analysis, leading to a set of DPs. The overview of the results can be viewed in the Tables 2 and 3, which sum up the change induced by Scrumstinct. In the following sections, participants are given aliases with the same initials as their team's pseudonym.

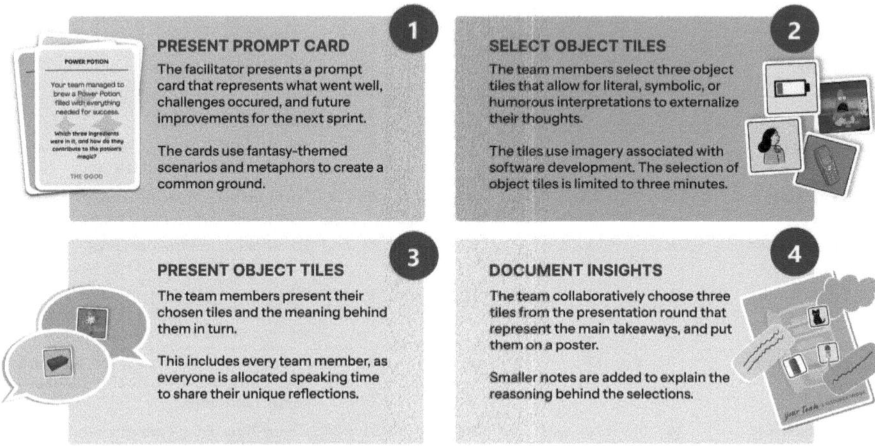

Fig. 2. The four phases in Scrumstinct

Fig. 3. The teams playing Scrumstinct during the workshop

4.1 Playfulness: Experiencing Fun

6 out of 8 teams reported an increase in the *fun* dimension. Previously characterized as boring, PayCraft's retrospective took on an uninhibited yet positive tone, evident in playful banter, and at BarrelCo where they mocked each other's

Table 2. Effects of Scrumstinct on the three dimensions of playfulness

Team	Fun	Exciting	Desirable
BarrelCo	Serious → Lighthearted	Predictable → Surprising	Unenthusiastic → Keen
Tramark	Bland	Lackluster	Unenthusiastic ← Keen
FrontPress	Efficient → Entertaining	Straightforward→ Anticipatory	Dutiful → Enthusiastic
UtilyTech	Serious → Interesting	Lackluster	Unenthusiastic
EduCloud	Bland	Anticipatory	Indifferent
CodeBank	Serious → Entertaining	Unpredictable → Anticipatory	Enthusiastic → Engaging
PayCraft	Boring → Uninhibited	Predictable → Surprising	For the outcome → Keen
SocialTech	Casual → Entertaining	Predictable → Unexpected	Indifferent → Engaging

Table Description: A positive effect is illustrated by (→). A negative effect is illustrated by (←). No effect is a standalone word.

tile choices. These interactions illustrate how Scrumstinct created a light atmosphere, bringing fun into the retrospective. In particular, humor was used to convey concerns, as observed at CodeBank: *"Lastly, in situations like these, we must accept that it can be a bit of a circus [points to the tile of a clown]."* Instead of labeling their process as poorly managed, the metaphor of a circus softly delivered the message, easing reception. Humor thus enabled them to raise critique while staying positive.

Teams that reported no change did not experience this, exemplified at Tramark in Tim's unbothered response to the time running out, underscoring the team's disinterest in the activity. EduCloud also showcased lackluster and disinterested responses to the concerns raised, creating a somber atmosphere. These exchanges suggest that playful artifacts can create a joking, lighthearted, and relaxed atmosphere, allowing the teams to discuss the topics in a distanced yet constructive manner, leading to DP1: **Playful artifacts prompt humorous interpretations of serious concerns in the Scrum team.**

4.2 Playfulness: Feeling Excited

5 out of 8 teams reported an increase in the *excitement* dimension. BarrelCo and SocialTech linked this to the surprising format. As BarrelCo noted: *"I have to think about it instead, and express it in a different way [...] What was the reason behind them?"*, highlighting how Scrumstinct unexpectedly encouraged thoughtful reflection. Similarly, FrontPress highlighted the element of anticipation during the tile presentation rounds:

> *"I thought it was fun to see which tiles the others chose. Sometimes, it's 'Yep, I knew you'd pick that one', and sometimes 'Why on earth did you pick that?' I was really looking forward to finding out why. I found that very entertaining."*

These interpretations introduced ambiguity, which made team members interested in understanding each other's perspectives. Excitement also emerged around the topics from the interpretations, as stated by PayCraft: *"I think Palmer's hamster wheel over there, it surprised me a bit that you felt like that"*, challenging existing assumptions and encouraging team members to think beyond the obvious. Contrary, UtilyTech showed no shift in excitement: *"Well, we know each other really well, we're colleagues. So I wouldn't say I'm surprised by it"*, demonstrating that outcomes are predictable when recurring topics emerge. However, EduCloud, who did not report a change, remarked that even though the topics themselves might be predictable, the use of visual artifacts obscured their understanding, resulting in an element of surprise. These findings suggest that when outcomes are unpredictable, teams tend to become more curious and excited, leading to the creation of DP2: **Playful activities with unpredictable outcomes afford excitement about the Sprint Retrospective.**

4.3 Playfulness: Desire to Play

5 out of 8 teams experienced an increase in the *desirable* dimension. From describing their retrospectives with indifference, the teams displayed high levels of engagement when playing Scrumstinct, evident at SocialTech during the tile selection phase:

> Susan: [is already standing up, scanning the tiles]
> Seth, Samuel, Sarah: [stand and lean over the table to inspect the tiles]
> Simon, Silas, Shawn: [stand up to get a better look at the tiles]
> Shawn: [points at a tile across the table, while talking to Silas]

PayCraft, FrontPress, and CodeBank also walked around in search of tiles. Active engagement was further reflected in sustained involvement after they had picked tiles, such as reevaluating choices or helping others select theirs. These interactions, including eye contact and active listening, signaled strong engagement. Other teams displayed playful competitiveness, such as PayCraft, where Peter leaped over the table to grab a tile, reflecting playful engagement by layering lighthearted competition onto the activity. In contrast, the three teams reporting no change exhibited signs of disinterest, such as EduCloud shifting their attention elsewhere, or UtilyTech checking their phones, indicating a lack of desire to engage. Teams that enjoyed the activity also emphasized the importance of doing it in moderation, as reflected by CodeBank: *"If we did this every time we did Scrum Retrospectives, I think we would burn out at some point."*. Despite this notion, Scrumstinct's playful qualities drew the majority of the teams in through in-the-moment engagement and away from the sentiment of having to endure a retrospective, leading to DP3: **Playful activities that invite voluntary engagement make a Sprint Retrospective desirable.**

4.4 Creative Burnout: Experiencing Stagnation

5 out of 8 teams reported a reduction in the *stagnation* dimension of creative burnout. Before playing Scrumstinct, teams often defaulted to the same approach, indicating signs of being creatively stagnant. Yet, the teams demonstrated

the ability to engage creatively with the tiles to form meaningful reflections and discussions, as seen in UtilyTech:

> Ulrich: *"I like the one-way sign [tile], that we have a collective goal and everyone's focus is in the same direction."*
> Ulysses: *"I don't like that one, because if you drive down a one-way street, how do you go back if you've gone too far?"*

These interpretations reframed process challenges and showcased creative thinking. Similar reflections emerged across the teams, highlighting Scrumstinct's ability to prompt new ways of thinking, as PayCraft noted: *"I'm especially thinking about how doing it [retrospectives] in a different way might lead to different thoughts, than if we did it the same way we usually do."* The playful artifacts also fostered creativity by encouraging teams to challenge conventional thought patterns, as BarrelCo initially stated: *"I try to think out of the box, but my mind is very square"*, to later acknowledging: *"I think it has sparked a lot of thoughts."*

On the other hand, the artifacts became a hindrance for Tramark, who had difficulties interpreting them creatively or applying them literally, which impeded their retrospective, as they felt limited by having to relate to the artifacts. Creative interpretation of artifacts thus supported divergent thinking for most teams, stimulating associative and metaphorical reasoning to reframe challenges from new perspectives, informing DP4: **Playful artifacts that prompt reframing of a team's problems and solutions counter stagnation in the Sprint Retrospective.**

4.5 Creative Burnout: Feeling Exhausted

5 out of 8 teams reported a reduction in the *exhaustion* dimension. From describing their retrospectives as tiring, the teams commonly experienced moments of openness. At BarrelCo, Scrumstinct opened up for a conversation about fear of judgment:

> *"Sometimes I catch myself, when I send a PR [pull request], I'm scared that it's not good enough [...] I've started to close my Outlook when the comments roll in, so I don't get caught in it. I feel like it's becoming a negative thing for me that I have to put something out there to be judged. I have to remember that it's never anything personal, but it's only because we wanna improve together."*

Despite the topics being emotionally heavy, the playful activity created a light, supportive setting, as they ended with acknowledgment and offers to help, as seen at CodeBank: *"I feel like things are moving incredibly fast for you [. . .] I wonder whether it might suddenly become too much, whether you would collapse, or if we could help."* Scrumstinct thereby enabled the teams to open up and receive support, which provided mental relief and resolved unaddressed tensions. Subsequently, Scrumstinct became an outlet for expressing frustrations, exemplified at FrontPress, where they admitted feeling close to burnt out due to unclear

Table 3. Effects of Scrumstinct on the three dimensions of creative burnout

Team	Stagnation	Exhaustion	Ridigity
BarrelCo	Repetitive → Thought-evoking	Tiring → Relieved	Habitual → Eye-opening
Tramark	Hindered ← Sufficient	Neutral	Habitual → Option aware
FrontPress	Incurious → Inspiring	Bottled-up → Relieved	Habitual → Eye-opening
UtilyTech	Stuck	Draining → Cathartic	Conventional → Open-minded
EduCloud	Supports divergent thinking	Rebooting	Experimental
CodeBank	Dabbling → Inspiring	Unresolved → Resolved	Conventional → Open-minded
PayCraft	Unsuccessful → Inspiring	Tiring → Outlet	Habitual → Open-minded
SocialTech	Repetitive → Thought-evoking	Draining	Habitual → Open-minded

Table Description: A positive effect is illustrated by (→). A negative effect is illustrated by (←). No effect is a standalone word.

task directions. UtilyTech also aired frustrations regarding their work culture of back-to-back unproductive meetings, which provided relief in itself by releasing bottled-up emotions. Conversely, the three teams that reported no change kept a surface-level tone. Their reflections suggest they did not need emotional relief, indicating that team exhaustion was not a part of their current experience. These unguarded moments highlight how the playful activity served as an entry point to openness, releasing frustrations, and easing emotional tensions that drive exhaustion. Thus, playfulness enabled the teams to provide social support for one another, forming DP5: **Playful activities relieve mental exhaustion during the Sprint Retrospective.**

4.6 Creative Burnout: Experiencing Rigidity

7 out of 8 teams reported a reduction in the *rigidity* dimension. FrontPress pointed to a lack of facilitation: *"The fact that we don't have a Scrum Master as such to facilitate these things, and that it's up to us to handle it ourselves, also makes it a bit easier to fall back into the familiar format"*, illustrating how rigidity often stems from habit or limited support. The teams that experienced the most impact reported the experience as eye-opening, showing high levels of reflection upon their retrospectives afterwards, as articulated by FrontPress:

> *"[...] It's actually quite interesting, this idea that it should be more fun. It's never really something we've talked about, is it? How can we make things more fun? [...] In our everyday work life, all the fun happens outside the regular meetings."*

While fun was often compartmentalized from work, they acknowledged that integrating playful activities could enhance the quality of their retrospectives. It further helped the teams reflect on their usual approaches to retrospectives, with many acknowledging they had become stuck in routine. EduCloud reported no substantial change, as they had already experimented with various retrospective formats and did not experience a greater positive effect. The teams' experiences of engaging with Scrumstinct thereby contributed to reflections on their rigid approaches, encouraging them to reconsider how playfulness might disrupt the inertia of routine, leading to DP6: **Playful activities that deviate from routine practices challenge rigidity in the Sprint Retrospective.**

5 Discussion

This design science research study shows how integrating playful interaction design into Sprint Retrospectives can help mitigate creative burnout. Previous research on retrospective activities emphasizes process improvement, efficacy, and engagement [8,15,17,23], but overlooks teams' playfulness. Our contribution comprises six DPs that guide the creation of playful activities for mitigating team-level creative burnout. Scrumstinct represents a concrete manifestation of the DPs, demonstrating how playfulness can be integrated into software development practice. In the following, we discuss how the three DPs for designing playfulness and the three DPs for using it to alleviate creative burnout relate to existing research.

5.1 Designing for Playfulness

Playfulness can emerge in SDTs' engagement with Scrumstinct across three dimensions: *fun, excitement*, and *desire*, as viewed in Table 4.

Table 4. Design principles for playfulness

No.	Design Principle	Scrumstinct Implementation	Related Research
DP1	Playful artifacts prompt humorous interpretations of serious concerns in the Scrum team.	Humorous imagery in object tiles for surfacing team concerns in a Sprint Retrospective.	Playful reframing of situations and managing tension [3,22].
DP2	Playful activities with unpredictable outcomes afford excitement about the Sprint Retrospective.	Turn-based presentations of interpretations using ambiguous imagery.	Spontaneity, unexpectedness, and the social dimension of playfulness [3,22].
DP3	Playful activities that invite voluntary engagement make a Sprint Retrospective desirable.	Structural limitations that introduce light competition.	Balancing playfulness, competition, and purpose [15,17] and the autotelic nature of playfulness [14,27].

Using humorous artifacts to ease discussions of serious concerns (DP1), we demonstrate that humor can be deliberately integrated as a meaningful workplace practice. Consistent with research defining playfulness as the ability to reframe situations for entertainment [3], our findings extend this view, demonstrating that reframing through humor also facilitates constructive dialogue, alleviating potential tensions in workplace settings [22]. Designing for *fun* may thereby involve artifacts that legitimize and invite humor to address serious concerns that affect well-being [22].

Playfulness moreover affords *excitement* through anticipation (DP2), evident in the team interactions during Scrumstinct. This corroborates spontaneity and unexpectedness as key qualities of playfulness [3]. Although design cannot guarantee specific interactions to unfold, playful frameworks can support anticipation, for instance, through information disclosure in tile presentation rounds and ambiguous artifacts. Designing for playfulness thus extends beyond concrete artifacts to overarching structures that balance structure with openness, allowing playful surprises to emerge [22].

Our findings also revealed how teams extended their participation beyond the given instructions for Scrumstinct (DP3), demonstrating high levels of desirability. We propose two avenues for designing for *desire*: (1) by grounding playfulness in meaningful work to create a "sense of stakes", motivating the team's active participation [17], and (2) by incorporating playfulness into how work is approached, such as layering light, playful competition onto existing work practices, motivating the team's participation because the work itself is intrinsically enjoyable [15]. Thus, we demonstrate that routine tasks can elicit desire through the way work is performed, rather than from their underlying purpose [14,27].

5.2 Playfulness Against Creative Burnout

To explore the implications of playfulness, we examined its relationship to creative burnout approached through its three dimensions: *stagnation, exhaustion*, and *rigidity*, as presented in Table 5.

Table 5. Design principles for mitigating creative burnout with playfulness

No.	Design Principle	Scrumstinct Implementation	Related Research
DP4	Playful artifacts that prompt reframing of a team's problems and solutions counter stagnation in the Sprint Retrospective.	Inspiring imagery on object tiles for reframing work-related problems and solutions.	Playfulness to induce new perspectives [8,23], creativity [21], and problem-solving [25].
DP5	Playful activities relieve mental exhaustion during the Sprint Retrospective.	Humorous design artifacts and turn-based structure allow a sense of lightness and a feeling of being heard.	Playfulness for increasing well-being [4,22,27] and cultivating relationships [21].
DP6	Playful activities that deviate from routine practices challenge rigidity in the Sprint Retrospective.	Metaphorical prompts, ambiguous tiles, and turn-based structure that position well-being as a key outcome.	Challenging monotony [19, 23] and alternative retrospective practices [8,15, 17].

In addition to prompting humor, playful artifacts encouraged creativity and new perspectives regarding *stagnation* (DP4), corroborating prior research [8,21, 25]. As stagnation often involves low ideation [5,11,25], playfulness mitigated it by enabling creative ways of engaging with problems, such as encouraging new perspectives or restructuring conventional thinking [23].

In the dimension of *exhaustion*, the playful activity provided mental relief (DP5). Playfulness recharged mental resources by creating a safe context for sharing challenges and concerns. It further enabled social support, extending its role beyond tension alleviation [22]. Teams became action-oriented by sharing their mental resources and collectively addressing problems to manage the issues that drain SDTs, affirming playfulness as a means to cultivate team relationships and improve overall team well-being [4,21,27].

Playfulness also challenged routine approaches, regarding *rigidity* (DP6). While routine is not inherently problematic, it can be when habitual work patterns lead to stagnation and exhaustion. On the contrary, playfulness introduced novelty and variation, providing relief from routine [23]. Yet, some teams were still hesitant about playful activities, reflecting an ingrained culture that favors familiar practices and discourages deviation from established approaches [19]. For instance, the Scrum framework itself focuses on prescribed outcomes, emphasizing productivity, efficiency, and process improvements [24]. While these outcomes are relevant and key to a functioning SDT, softer effects, such as engagement, creativity, and social support [8,15,17], are equally important and crucial for addressing creative burnout. We thus argue that promoting outcomes, exemplified by Scrumstinct, can enhance well-being in SDTs, and that further efforts guided by the proposed DPs may help demonstrate its value and support adoption in SDTs.

5.3 Limitations and Future Research

It is important to acknowledge the limitations of our study. Each team participated in a single retrospective, limiting the ability to observe changes over time. Although it provided a brief inspection of how playful interaction design may reduce creative burnout, it does not capture the potential long-term effects of sustained implementation. A longitudinal study, involving repeated retrospectives with the same teams, could uncover richer insights. In particular, how the ongoing integration of playfulness might shape team culture and engagement, alleviate tension, and possibly mitigate creative burnout. Future researchers could provide a more nuanced understanding of these dynamics. Another prospect is to broaden the conceptualization of playfulness and creative burnout beyond the dimensions in this study. As our current lenses only capture parts of two complex constructs, widening the scope could surface novel nuances and yield comprehensive insights on the effects of introducing playful interaction design against creative burnout in SDTs.

6 Conclusion

This paper examines how playful interaction design can mitigate creative burnout in software development teams. Following the Design Science Research methodology, we iteratively developed and evaluated 'Scrumstinct', a design artifact for Sprint Retrospectives. Workshops with eight software development teams demonstrated how playfulness, understood as *fun, excitement* and *desire*, fostered social support, emergence of new perspectives, and a sense of mental relief. This alleviated creative burnout, understood as *stagnation, exhaustion*, and *rigidity*, in a majority of the eight teams in our study. Our contributions to the existing research on well-being in software development are: (1) three design principles on how to introduce playfulness in Sprint Retrospectives, (2) three design principles on how playfulness can mitigate creative burnout, and (3) Scrumstinct as a concrete embodiment of these six design principles.

References

1. Amin, A., et al.: The impact of personality traits and knowledge collection behavior on programmer creativity. Inf. Softw. Technol. **128**, 106405 (2020)
2. Bakker, A.B., Emmerik, H., Euwema, M.C.: Crossover of burnout and engagement in work teams. Work Occupations **33**(4), 464–489 (2006)
3. Barnett, L.: The nature of playfulness in young adults. Personality Individ. Differ. **43**(4), 949–958 (2007)
4. Bateson, P., Martin, P.: Play, Playfulness, Creativity and Innovation. Cambridge University Press, New York (2013)
5. Chung, G.H., Choi, J.N., Du, J.: Tired of innovations? Learned helplessness and fatigue in the context of continuous streams of innovation implementation. J. Organ. Behav. **38**(7), 1130–1148 (2017)
6. Clarke, V., Braun, V.: Thematic analysis. J. Posit. Psychol. **12**(3), 297–298 (2017)
7. Dah, J., Hussin, N., Zaini, M.K., Isaac Helda, L., Senanu Ametefe, D., Adozuka Aliu, A.: Gamification is not working: why? Games Cult. **20**(7), 934–957 (2025)
8. Derby, E., Larsen, D., Schwaber, K.: Agile retrospectives - making good teams great. Pragmatic Programmers, Raleigh, NC (2006)
9. Goldkuhl, G.: Pragmatism vs interpretivism in qualitative information systems research. Eur. J. Inf. Syst. **21**(2), 135–146 (2012)
10. Gray, C.M., McKilligan, S., Daly, S.R., Seifert, C.M., Gonzalez, R.: Using creative exhaustion to foster idea generation. Int. J. Technol. Des. Educ. **29**(1), 177–195 (2019)
11. Groeneveld, W., Luyten, L., Vennekens, J., Aerts, K.: Exploring the role of creativity in software engineering. In: 43rd International Conference on Software Engineering, pp. 1–9 (2021)
12. Hron, M., Obwegeser, N.: Why and how is scrum being adapted in practice: a systematic review. J. Syst. Softw. **183**(111110) (2022)
13. Kryshtanovych, M., Akimova, L., Akimov, O., Parkhomenko-Kutsevil, O., Omarov, A.: Features of creative burnout among educational workers in public administration system. Creativity Stud. **15**(1), 116–129 (2022)
14. Lieberman, J.N.: Playfulness: Its Relationship to Imagination and Creativity. Academic Press Inc., New York (1977)
15. Marshburn, D.G., Sieck, J.: Don't break the build: developing a scrum retrospective games. In: 52nd Hawaii International Conference on System Sciences (2019)
16. Maslach, C., Leiter, M.: Chapter 43 - burnout. In: Fink, G. (ed.) Stress: Concepts, Cognition, Emotion, and Behavior, pp. 351–357. Academic Press, San Diego (2016)

17. Matthies, C., Dobrigkeit, F.: Towards empirically validated remedies for scrum retrospective headaches. In: Proceedings of the 53rd Hawaii International Conference on System Sciences (2020)
18. Mohanani, R., Ram, P., Lasisi, A., Ralph, P., Turhan, B.: Perceptions of creativity in software engineering research and practice. In: 43rd Euromicro Conference on Software Engineering and Advanced Applications, pp. 210–217 (2017)
19. Monteiro, C.V., da Silva, F.Q., Capretz, L.F.: The innovative behaviour of software engineers: findings from a pilot case study. In: Proceedings of the 10th ACM/IEEE International Symposium on Empirical Software Engineering and Measurement, pp. 1–10 (2016)
20. Peffers, K., Tuunanen, T., Rothenberger, M.A., Chatterjee, S.: A design science research methodology for information systems research. J. Manag. Inf. Syst. **24**(3), 45–77 (2007)
21. Proyer, R.T.: Perceived functions of playfulness in adults: does it mobilize you at work, rest, and when being with others? Eur. Rev. Appl. Psychol. **64**(5), 241–250 (2014)
22. Proyer, R.T.: A new structural model for the study of adult playfulness: assessment and exploration of an understudied individual differences variable. Personality Individ. Differ. **108**, 113–122 (2017)
23. Przybyłek, A., Kotecka, D.: Making agile retrospectives more awesome. In: 2017 Federated Conference on Computer Science and Information Systems (FedCSIS), pp. 1211–1216. IEEE (2017)
24. Schwaber, K., Sutherland, J.: The scrum guide (2020). https://scrumguides.org/docs/scrumguide/v2020/2020-Scrum-Guide-US.pdf
25. Tobeña, A.C., Barceló, M.M., Pichaco, A.M., Calafat, A.L.M.: Creativity clogs: identifying and addressing barriers to innovation. IEEE Softw. **42**(3), 75–81 (2025)
26. Urien, B., Rico, R., Demerouti, E., Bakker, A.B.: An emergence model of team burnout. Revista de Psicología del Trabajo y de las Organizaciones **37**(3), 175–186 (2021)
27. Van Vleet, M., Feeney, B.C.: Play behavior and playfulness in adulthood. Soc. Pers. Psychol. Compass **9**(11), 630–643 (2015)

Understanding Consumer Behavior and Sustainability Perception for Digital Technology Products and Services: Addressing End-Users' Unmet Sustainability Concerns

L. Abdullai[1(✉)], M. O. Adisa[1], M. S. Haque[1], S. A. Miller[2], S. Oyedeji[1], R. Anupindi[2], and J. Porras[1]

[1] LUT University, Yliopistonkatu 34, 53850 Lappeenranta, Finland
larry.abdullai@lut.fi

[2] University of Michigan, 500 S State St, Ann Arbor, MI 48109.17, USA

Abstract. In today's digital economy, sustainability concerns for digital products and services have become critical for governments, businesses, academic institutions, and the general public. The complex phenomena of digital transformation and environmental stewardship pull stakeholders to sustainability in different directions. Although there are extensive studies on technology and sustainability, much of the research has focused either on digital technologies themselves or on the companies behind them. Through a global survey of 490 technology end-users, this study investigates the sustainability perception and behavior of digital technology end-users, including their unmet expectations. The study thus provides key insight into the end users' sustainability perspectives and unmet sustainability needs. The results showed that product durability, transparency, legitimacy, ethical concerns, right to repair, water and energy consumption, and pollution were the most pressing unmet end-user needs. Our findings indicate that technology and software businesses need to engage with their end users and bridge the communication gap about their efforts towards sustainable digital transformation. The study contributes to the theory of consumption value and offers practitioners insights to take actions that promote end-users' sustainable consumption.

Keywords: Consumer behaviour · end-user sustainability perception · unmet sustainability concerns · sustainable production and consumption

1 Introduction

In the digital age, rapid innovations in the information and communication technology (ICT) industry remain crucial for strengthening the global digital economy, securing future survival and supporting business growth and survival [1–3]. ICT products and services are considered necessary for achieving sustainable development [4]. However, the growth of software and hardware innovations, including large-language models and data centers, raises sustainability concerns such as pollution, water use, biodiversity loss,

G. Herzwurm et al. (Eds.): ICSOB 2025, LNBIP 574, pp. 394–410, 2026.
https://doi.org/10.1007/978-3-032-14518-5_30

and carbon emissions, among others. Most scholars in diverse disciplines, including software engineering and information systems, acknowledge the importance of addressing digital sustainability [5–7] as an ethical and existential calling of our time [8]. Digital sustainability concerns the "design, development, configuration, deployment, and decommissioning of digital resources and artifacts toward improving the environment, and economic welfare" [9]. Thus, the use of ICT products and services to satisfy consumer needs without jeopardising the needs of future generations [10]. These sustainability concerns can be economic, social, environmental, technical or individual [11].

There has been increasing recognition that many sustainability challenges, such as climate change, biodiversity loss, carbon emissions, and e-waste, result from human activities [12]. This acknowledgment requires a rethink of how products and services, including digital technologies, are produced and consumed. Following the famous sustainable development definition in a post-Brundtland world "Our Common Future" [13], achieving digital sustainability therefore becomes the responsibility of everyone [9], including consumers.

While scholars have investigated the sustainability efforts of leading technology companies [14], research from an end-user sustainability perspective remains scarce. We address this gap through a global survey of technology end-users' sustainability perception, consumption behaviour, and unmet sustainability needs. Thus, the study aims to deepen understanding of end-users' digital technology consumption behavior and sustainability concerns by exploring the following research questions: RQ1: What does the sustainability of digital products and services mean to end-users? RQ2: How do end-users perceive the current technology firms' sustainability claims? RQ3: What are the current unmet sustainability needs of digital technology consumers?

The study builds on the theory of consumer behavior (TCB), the theory of consumption value (TCV) and the theory of importance-performance analysis (IPA) to deepen our understanding of end-users' unmet sustainability concerns. In this study, we identified that sustainability issues such as product durability, transparency and legitimacy about company sustainability practices, ethical issues concerning social impacts, right to repair, water and energy consumption as well as pollution were among the most pressing end-users' unmet sustainability concerns.

The remainder of the paper is organized as follows. In Sect. 2, we develop the theoretical background. Sect. 3 describes the methodology. Next, we present the results, followed by the discussion. The last section concludes with the paper and provides directions for future studies.

2 Background and Related Work

Public sustainability expectations of ICT and software businesses emphasize transparency, credibility, and responsibility. However, diagnostic approaches, such as Importance–Performance Analysis, reveal persistent gaps between what sustainability concerns end-users regard as important and their perception about technology companies' efforts towards addressing sustainability challenges, highlighting the need for more transparency and close collaboration with broader ICT ecosystem actors.

2.1 Consumer Behaviour

Scholars have studied consumer behaviour towards technological innovations [15] and have proposed different models and frameworks such as the widely used technology acceptance model (TAM) [16, 17] and diffusion of innovations [18]. Information and communication technologies such as mobile phones and laptops are not only useful for most people, providing essential services such as connecting people across the globe, online shopping, learning, working or even entertainment [19], but also a crucial tool for policymakers and non-governmental organizations to develop innovative solutions and stimulate socioeconomic growth for the vulnerable and society at large [20]. With billions of technology consumers worldwide, the cell phone is positioned as crucial to the future of digital media [21]. While studies show that young adults are making sustainable consumption decisions driven by health awareness, lifestyle choices [22], the situation seems different with technology. According to World Bank data, in some countries, the number of mobile phone subscriptions exceeds the population [23]. This means there are more people with access to mobile phones worldwide than safe sanitation [20, 24]. It is projected that in 2026, global ICT spending will reach about $6.08 trillion, a 9.8 percent increase from $5.54 trillion in 2025 [25]. These projected expenditures include data center systems, hardware devices, software, IT and communication services, with software expenditure experiencing the most significant growth of 15.2 percent from 2025. According to [25], the trend is driven by consumer spending on mobile phones and the availability of AI devices. Although consumer behaviour is influenced by numerous factors from personal and psychological, to social, economic and cultural [26, 27], as spending on ICTs increases, so do other unintended consequences. For instance, in 2022, global e-waste generated totaled 62 million tons, equivalent to 1.55 million trucks, and is forecast to reach 82 million tons by 2030 [20, 24].

2.2 Theory of Consumption Value

The rapid digital and emerging technology innovations as well as penetration of e-commerce in rural areas is driving consumption [28]. Similarly, people's purchasing power continues to increase as a result of global economic development leading to increased unsustainable consumption and waste in the apparel industry [29], food [30] and electrical and electronic products [31]. Scholars posit that consumption decisions are complex phenomena influenced by personal, psychological, and social factors [32]. The theory of consumption value developed by [33], builds on three principles: (1) multiple consumption values drive consumption behavior, (2) each consumption value affects every consumption decision differently, and (3) each of the consumption values function autonomously. The theory identifies functional, social, emotional, epistemic and conditional values as the five values that influence consumer behavior. They defined the functional values as the perceived satisfaction a consumer gets from patronising a product or service to solve direct or immediate need. Social values are the perceived benefit or satisfaction derived from an alternative's relationship with one or more specific social groups. With digital products, end-users may choose a specific technology brand or possess multiple technologies to gain symbolic social prestige rather than its functionality [26, 34]. The emotional value refers to the perceived emotional feelings derived from patronising a specific product or service. For consumption of digital technologies, the emotional feeling might mean the feeling of belonging to a particular ecosystem. For example, studies found that incidental emotions can shape whether consumers rely more on peripheral or central cues, depending on how well the emotional tone matches the message content [35]. Epistemic value refers to the perceived benefit gained from an alternative's capacity to invite curiosity or satisfy a desire for knowledge. Finally, conditional value refers to the perceived satisfaction a consumer derives from an alternative product in each situation or a set of circumstances confronted by the consumer [33].

2.3 Importance-Performance Analysis Theory

The success of every business lies in understanding its customers' pain points and the features of its product or service that make them satisfied [36]. The pain points or sustainability concerns of end-users are what they consider to be direct or indirect value, ranging from economic and individual concerns (e.g., price, health) to social, environmental, and technical concerns (e.g., relations, pollution, functionality) [11]. In services and product marketing, Importance–Performance Analysis (IPA) is a well-known diagnostic technique for locating where firms under-deliver on what users value [37, 38]. In a traditional IPA, consumers provide the average value of importance and performance of different service attributes, which is then calculated in a four-quadrant coordinate system to ascertain their satisfaction [36]. However, in this study, we do not estimate an IPA outcome model, instead, we report user-stated importance, perceived firm efforts, and expressed barriers to sustainable digital consumption, and we synthesize unmet needs from thematic and descriptive evidence. We position IPA as a follow-on approach for attribute-level gap quantification and outcome modeling in future research. Applying the IPA concept to digital sustainability is a helpful exercise due to sustainability concerns regarding greenwashing, transparency, product durability, limited right to repair, and social and environmental concerns, which map directly onto known antecedents of trust and satisfaction [39–42]. The capacity to act on sustainability information is not uniform. Differences in access, skills, and usage, the "beyond access" layers of the digital divide, can shape whether disclosure and design cues translate into sustainable behaviour.

Following ongoing discussions, the link between values, digital sustainability, and consumer behavior depends on several factors, including conflicting goals and individual differences in self-regulation [43]. As such, adopting consumer-centered sustainability concerns into ICTs and software requires integrating consumers into digital processes, such as retailing and specifically purchasing and consuming products and services [44]. Digital technologies are unique and distinct from many other consumables due to their ability to acquire data, process and transmit data, their updating capability while still with the end-user, their reinforcement learning feature, such as an AI-powered device, and the power to provide and enable value or satisfaction to multiple people from a single device [45].

3 Methodology

This study employed a qualitative survey approach [46] to explore end-users' sustainability behavior and concerns to digital technologies. We identify these sustainability concerns descriptively and thematically, focusing on issues such as end users' perception, behaviour, and unmet sustainability expectations. While Importance–Performance Analysis offers a structured way to quantify attribute-level gaps and link them to outcomes such as trust and satisfaction, we position this as a direction for future research. Two reasons informed us of our methodological choice. First, we wanted to examine digital technology consumers from different parts of the world with diverse educational and socio-economic backgrounds, not just end users from one particular geography. Second, end-user unmet sustainability concerns and expectations have not yet been studied in the software engineering context, making exploratory qualitative study more appropriate and positioning our study as a foundation for future work. The study established methodological rigor and robustness by designing relevant research questions to address the phenomenon under investigation, pilot testing the questionnaire for clarity, selecting an appropriate sampling strategy thoughtfully, using multiple data collection strategies and adopting a systematic data analysis process for reliability [47–49]. In the subsequent paragraphs, we detail the questionnaire design, sampling process, data collection strategy, and data analysis techniques.

3.1 Questionnaire Design

The survey instrument was developed based on a comprehensive review of prior literature on technology consumer behavior and motivation, sustainable consumption, and development. Open-ended questions were constructed to elicit nuanced insights into consumers' current sustainability practices regarding ICT product and service patronage, their sustainability perceptions, and expectations of technology companies. Some constructs, for instance, perceived ICT companies' sustainability efforts, were measured using a 10-point Likert scale (ranging from 1, "very poor," to 10, "excellent"). The questionnaire also included a 4-point Likert scale to measure the level of importance that end users assign to how technology is produced in terms of sustainability. The survey questionnaire was divided into three parts. The first part collects demographic and socioeconomic data, including nationality, gender, field of study, level of education, profession, and frequency of technology use. The second part focused on end-users' sustainability perceptions and technology use. The third part focused on the sustainability concerns and expectations that end-users have concerning the ICT and software business. The researcher adopted a reflexivity strategy to reflect on the analysis and discuss among themselves to resolve any differences.

3.2 Sampling

Our research employed multiple sampling strategies, including convenience, snowball, and purposive sampling [50]. First, the researchers randomly recruited study participants through their social and professional networks who possess the relevant information to address the phenomenon. Next, the researchers relied on snowballing from the initial set of respondents or to recruit more respondents. These two sampling strategies resulted in 190 responses. To mitigate the tendency of bias from the data, the researchers employed the service of Prolific, a data collection platform that helps researchers to recruit online participants for conducting surveys or experiments [51]. Prolific was used to collect an additional 300 responses, bringing the total to 490. Table 1 provides characteristics of the study participants. The respondents consist of 252 men and 232 women, with 6 identified as non-binary. Also, the respondents were distributed across the globe, providing representativeness of the sample and generalizability of the findings.

Table 1. Characteristics of study participants.

Variables	Components	Frequency
Gender	Male	252 (51.4%)
	Female	232 (47.3%)
	Non-binary	6 (1.2%)
Education	Graduate level	215 (43.9%)
	Bachelor's degree	189 (38.6%)
	Some college courses	43 (8.8%)
	High school courses	28 (5.7%)
	Associate degree	15 (3.1%)
Time spent interacting with technology	10+ h	217 (44.3%)
	6–9 h	147 (30%)
	3–6 h	88 (18%)
	1–3 h	38 (7.8%)
Geographical distribution	North America	202 (41.2%)
	Africa	188 (38.4%)
	Asia	45 (9.2%)
	Europe	43 (8.8%)
	South America	3 (0.6%)
	Unclear category	9 (1.8%)

3.3 Data Collection

The surveys were administered online from February to June 2025 using Google Forms, a free and convenient platform [52]. The survey was first pilot tested with three participants, which led to a few minor streamlining of the questionnaire. Purposive sampling based on demographic characteristics was not used to mitigate researcher bias, ensure representativeness, or increase generalizability [53]. Particularly, we focus on the following open-ended and closed questions: (i) What does ICT sustainability mean to you as an end user? (ii) How are you currently contributing to sustainability through mindful and responsible tech usage? (iii) How would you rate the current sustainability efforts by tech and software businesses? (iv) How important is it to you that ICT products and services are developed with sustainability in mind?

3.4 Data Analysis

A two-step data analysis strategy was adopted to maximize the breadth and depth of insights. Following recent scholars [54], we used a reflexive thematic analysis (RTA) [55], an approach used for identifying, analysing, and reporting patterns or themes. We first familiarized ourselves with the data and manually coded them. The authors employed a thematic coding technique [56] and the Gioia method [57] to thematically organize and interpret the qualitative data as shown in Fig. 1.

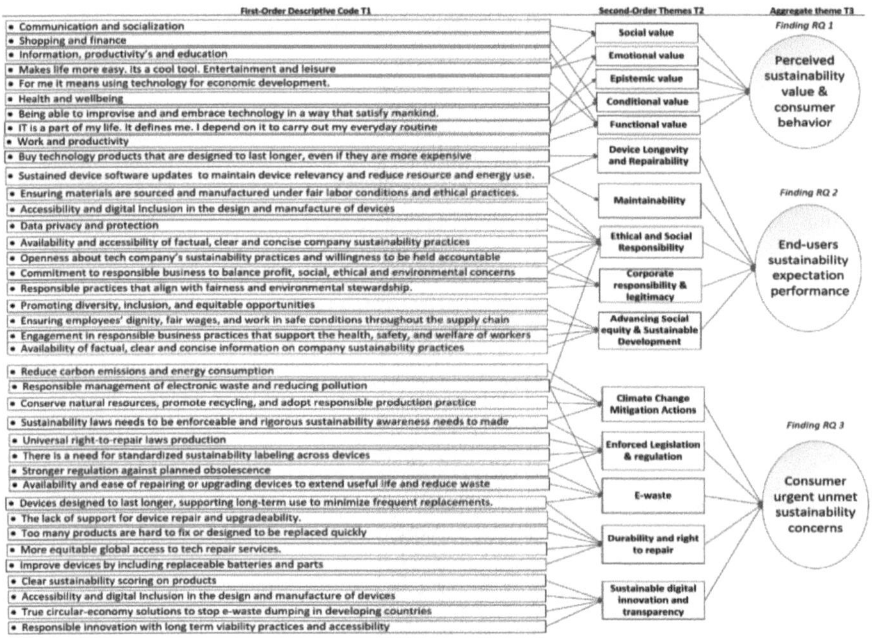

Fig. 1. Thematic analysis.

The analysis started with familiarization with the data. Next, the authors identified relevant information from the response to generate initial descriptive codes. Open coding was performed to capture meaningful segments related to the research objectives with assigned descriptive labels [58]. Subsequently, the open codes were grouped into broader categories to organize the data into more coherent, manageable themes that aligned with the study objectives and the phenomenon under investigation. For instance, first-order descriptive codes related to "long-lasting device" and "ease of repair" were grouped under the theme "device longevity and repairability". Constant comparisons were made to ensure consistency and accuracy. Finally, the emerging themes are aggregated to form overarching concepts. Next, following recent studies [59], the data were further analyzed using the Ailyze software, an emerging AI tool for qualitative research analysis. This allowed for triangulation of findings and identification of patterns that may not have been immediately realized through our manual coding [54]. Results from both analytic approaches were compared and synthesized to inform the interpretation and discussion of consumer perception and behaviour regarding sustainability.

4 Findings

As consumers' sustainability behaviour and practices are influenced by a combination of social, economic, psychological and political factors, we first present the contextual analyses of the participants, followed by the findings relevant to the research questions. The educational level of respondents skewed high, with 215 participants (43.9% of the total) holding a graduate degree or higher. Bachelor's degree holders accounted for 38.6% while other education levels included some college (8.8%), high school graduates or equivalent (5.7%), and associate degrees (3.1%). Overall, regardless of level of education, all respondents use technology for at least 1–3 h daily. Specifically, more than 4 in 5 respondents report using one form of technology or the other for more than 3 h a day, with almost half stating they use digital devices for more than 10 h a day. The results show that software and digital technologies are being adopted in most fields, including education, health, entertainment, mobility, commerce, and communication. For instance, technology was primarily used for educational and learning purposes (86.5%), entertainment and leisure (85.7%), and work-related tasks (77.8%). Other significant uses included health and well-being (57.1%), communication and socializing (48.4%), shopping and finance (46.1%), and travel or navigation (43.7%).

4.1 RQ1: What Does the Sustainability of Digital Products and Services Mean to End-Users?

Sustainability means different things to different end-users, ranging from social, economic, environmental, functional, technical, and personal reasons. For instance, majority (65.7%) said they choose durable, high-quality products even if expensive, and 46.5% preferred to repair devices before replacing them. This could be economically, socially or environmentally motivated. Few participants reported buying from sustainability-focused companies (28%), recycling or donating electronics (10.4%), enabling power-saving modes (8.6%), or managing digital waste like unnecessary emails or closing unused opened tabs. Sustainability awareness among technology end-users is still developing and means different things to different people. For some, it means "using it for interacting with friends and family," while for others, it means "using technology in ways that are environmentally responsible, socially ethical, and economically sensible over the long term". For a few others, they "...do not care about the relation between sustainability and tech use".

Another interesting consumer behavioral choice and sustainability practice concerns energy efficiency and waste prevention. For example, some respondents mentioned performing simple but important sustainability actions such as "shutting down laptops overnight, unplugging devices when not in use, using battery efficiency modes," which reveal practical steps taken to reduce energy consumption. The acknowledgement that energy efficiency spans from "my phone charger to the data centers running the internet and AI" shows the depth and awareness of the energy implications of modern technology for consumers. Consumers also associated energy efficiency with product longevity, as one user noted the importance of "minimizing the environmental and social impact of the technology I use while maximizing its efficiency and longevity," suggesting the link between energy use, waste reduction, and extending device lifespan. These simple yet effective consumer behavioral choices collectively help reduce the negative impacts of digital technologies on the planet.

Finally, the idea of rewarding or punishing companies' ICT and software businesses for their engagement or otherwise in sustainability practices forms another critical aspect of respondents' sentiments. A respondent remarked that sustainability means "choosing companies that are eco-conscious and responsible," which highlights the demand for sustainable IT products and services and the role of consumer preference in driving sustainable production. Similarly, for another respondent, sustainability means "choosing energy efficient products, buying from ethical companies etc.," demonstrating how users incorporate values of corporate responsibility into their consumption decisions.

4.2 RQ2: Consumer Expectations Relating to ICT and Software Business?

Public scrutiny of organizations continues to increase. Of the 490 respondents, almost half (46.5%), said that it is very important to them that ICT and software businesses are conducted with sustainability as an integral component, while 37.3% rated it as extremely important. Only 1.4% believed it was not at all important, signaling strong overall concern about the social and environmental impacts of technology. When asked to rate the performance of technology companies' sustainability claims on a 1–10 scale, with 1 being the worst and 10 being excellent, most respondents rated ICT and software businesses at 6, as shown in Fig. 2.

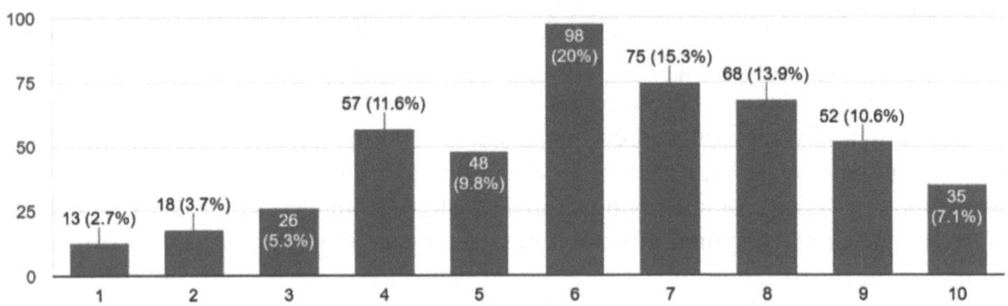

Fig. 2. End-users' perceived sustainability performance of ICT companies.

Most respondents' ratings clustered between 6 and 8, indicating moderate satisfaction but room for improvement as captured in the following quote "While many IT companies have made visible progress in addressing sustainability, such as committing to carbon neutrality, using recycled materials in devices, or investing in renewable energy, there's still a long way to go". As depicted in Fig. 2, consumers express mixed sentiments regarding the perceived sustainability of ICT and software businesses. End-users perceive tech businesses to be engaging in greenwashing, as mentioned by some consumers in the following quote: "The majority of tech companies pretend to care about sustainability, but in actuality, only care about money". Consumers expect more transparency and genuine commitment to taking concrete actions towards addressing sustainability challenges, as expressed by some consumers in the following quote "many companies talk about sustainability, but very few follow through with transparent and measurable actions. Most still produce electronics that are hard to repair, use rare materials, and generate huge amounts of e-waste". Others expect energy "efficient code that doesn't demand excessive processing power or storage, reducing the need for constant hardware upgrades,". Similarly, consumers think tech companies "...want us to buy products every year, yearly release of products", and that they need "technological devices that can be updated and not needing to be replaced every year,". Thus, the need for digital technologies to be "durable, repairable devices," indicating longevity and reparability as key to reducing e-waste and conserving scarce resources. Furthermore, consumer expectations from technology companies concern social and ethical responsibility. For instance, they highlight social justice concerns, noting, "It's important that the informal sector, who are mostly involved in producing resources used for these IT products, are paid fairly and involved in sustainability discourse to ensure social justice". The social dimension includes "ethical AI development, fair labor practices in supply chains, and digital inclusion." This underscores the need for ICT and software businesses to ensure fair labor practices and protect vulnerable workers, often overlooked in the mining and manufacturing of digital devices throughout the supply chain.

4.3 RQ3: Consumer Unmet Sustainability Concerns

Unmet digital sustainability concerns refer to the gap between end-users' current assessments of ICT and software businesses' sustainability efforts and the future digital environment they would like to see. These concerns include addressing climate change, responsible resource and energy use, and fostering sustainable development. Addressing these gaps requires coordinated action across various sectors and stakeholders, as the end-users themselves acknowledge they are part of the solution. In their efforts to advance sustainability, end-users cited barriers such as the cost of purchasing high-quality technology, mentioned by 73.3% of respondents. It is worth noting that buying quality, expensive technology might not be for sustainability reasons, but to meet any of the five consumer values supported by the TCV. Other challenges included concerns about planned obsolescence (30.4%), limited availability of sustainable technologies (16.5%), lack of clear sustainability information and awareness (11.6%), and lack of transparency regarding tech businesses' actual sustainability efforts (10.8%). Thus, consumers require transparent and credible information about the origins of components in digital devices, energy consumption, supply chain management, and corporate sustainability practices to make decisions aligned with their values.

5 Discussion

Technology sustainability is a complex and evolving paradigm that integrates environmental stewardship, ethical considerations, and user engagement to foster a responsible digital ecosystem. Our survey highlights that sustainability is highly valued by end-users, with over four in five rating it is very or extremely important. Yet, perceived firm performance was only moderate. This gap reflects prior research showing that while eco-labels and CSR claims shape consumer attitudes, they only influence behavior when firms are seen as credible and transparent [26, 60].

Transparency and legitimacy emerged as another key unmet sustainability concern that serves as a barrier for user awareness and sustainable consumption, echoing findings that vague communication and greenwashing erode consumer trust by increasing consumer confusion and perceived risk [41, 61]. Several respondents emphasized the importance of ethical sourcing, with one associating sustainability with "the mines in Congo and Bolivia," underscoring the need for firms to demonstrate responsible supply chains. We argued that without such openness, users are constrained in their ability to make informed and sustainable choices. The transparency requirement promotes user autonomy and responsibility, encouraging behaviors that reduce environmental destruction and promote social equity.

Our findings also emphasize durability and repairability as central to sustainable digital consumption. More than 65% of respondents reported choosing durable devices, and nearly half preferred repair over replacement. This resonates with [40], who stress the significance of lifetime extension for ICT sustainability. At the same time, relatively few respondents reported consistent recycling, donating, or using energy-saving features. This pattern supports prior observations of an intention–action gap in sustainable behavior, cautioning against the assumption that awareness automatically translates into practice [62, 63]. Sustainable digital consumption thus lies in understanding the ramifications of end users' technology habits and in a proactive effort to align them with sustainability principles.

Cost was cited as the most pressing barrier (73%), far surpassing information gaps or lack of transparency. While earlier work placed strong emphasis on information provision and eco-feedback mechanisms, our evidence suggests that affordability is a binding constraint that cannot be overlooked. This finding broadens the discourse on sustainable consumption by shifting attention from informational interventions to economic accessibility. Many consumers are willing to reward or punish ICT and software businesses by patronizing or boycotting their products. These sentiments highlight a broader systemic impact of sustainable digital consumption and a willingness to align personal use with organizations that prioritize sustainability, thereby fostering a more responsible digital ecosystem. Our respondents highlighted expectations that extend beyond environmental impact to include software efficiency, updated policies to avoid premature obsolescence, and privacy protection. These perspectives expand the scope of sustainability in ICT by placing software engineering and data stewardship alongside hardware design. This shift reflects a growing recognition that digital sustainability encompasses not only material practices but also ethical and social dimensions of technology use [39].

The study shows that consumers have expectations about which sustainability concerns they perceive as valuable. However, their perceptions and realities often do not match, resulting in dissatisfaction and unmet needs. Based on our study, we conceptualize the importance of consumer sustainability and company performance outcomes as shown in Fig. 3.

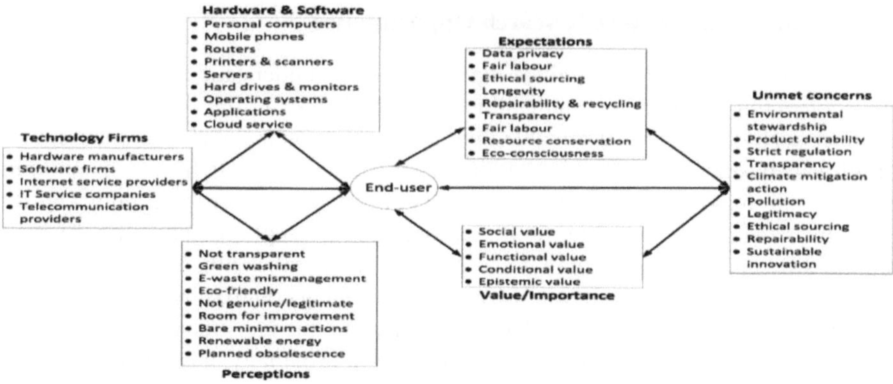

Fig. 3. Digital technology sustainability value-expectation outcome model.

5.1 Theoretical and Managerial Implications

One of the key characteristics of the sustainable transformation of current ICT and software businesses is continuous innovation, agility, data-driven decision-making, connectivity, extensive use of energy and water, and a deep focus on customer experience. ICT and software businesses are under pressure to advance sustainability, yet our findings show that end-users have mixed perceptions of technology and software firms' sustainability performance. Theoretically, this study highlights the persistent gap between consumer expectations and organizational delivery, reinforcing prior work on the depth of the intention–action gap while extending it by showing that energy efficiency, resource utilization, and environmental stewardship are now central attributes of digital sustainability. It also broadens the concept of sustainability in ICT by incorporating software-level practices, such as green coding as well as social factors, such as accessibility and fairness. The study also contributes to the theories of consumption value (TCV) and importance-performance analysis (IPA) by proposing a digital technology sustainability value-expectation model.

For practitioners, our findings highlight that end-users are not passive recipients of sustainability messaging, but rather relatively active evaluators of firm practices. To strengthen trust and satisfaction, ICT and software businesses should provide verifiable disclosures that demonstrate transparency and legitimacy, since opacity and greenwashing quickly undermine credibility. They also need to prioritize product longevity and repairability, which users rated as more influential than downstream practices like recycling. At the same time, affordability emerged as the most pressing barrier, suggesting that sustainable transformation requires business models that make greener digital choices financially accessible. We call on an ecosystem approach towards advancing digital sustainability and promoting sustainable production and consumption in the ICT sector.

5.2 Limitations and Future Research Opportunities

To the best of our knowledge, this is the first study to understand end-users' sustainability perception and unmet sustainability concerns. While it offers timely insights into consumer behavior toward sustainable digital consumption and expectations from ICT and software businesses, several limitations also point toward future research opportunities. First, the study relied on thematic analysis of survey responses to capture end-user perspectives. Although valuable, future research could adopt a comparative design to examine differences between the Global North and Global South. Such analysis may uncover important nuances in how affluent and developing contexts interpret sustainable technology consumption, and the extent to which economic constraints shape consumer behavior. Second, our focus was limited to end-users, one of many stakeholders in the ICT ecosystem. Sustainability transitions require collective engagement; therefore, future studies should include multi-stakeholder perspectives, integrating insights from firms, policymakers, civil society, and other actors to generate a more systemic understanding. Third, the sample was skewed toward educated participants, as all respondents had at least a high school qualification. Education level and professional background may have influenced the findings, potentially limiting their generalizability. Future research should examine more diverse populations to better understand how socioeconomic background influences sustainable consumption behaviors and motivations. Furthermore, the study relies on self-reported perceptions and behaviors, which may be subject to bias. Consumer perception of sustainability impacts or performance may not necessarily reflect the actual impact. Future research could combine multiple data sources to gain a deeper understanding of perceived and actual end-user contributions to digital sustainability. Finally, there seems to be a dichotomy between the actual sustainability activities of ICT and software business and end-users' perception and awareness of these activities. Future research could combine studies involving both tech companies and end-users to bridge the information gap and build trust and satisfaction.

References

1. Chaudhry, I.S., Ali, S., Bhatti, S.H., Anser, M.K., Khan, A.I., Nazar, R.: Dynamic common correlated effects of technological innovations and institutional performance on environmental quality: evidence from East-Asia and Pacific countries. Environ Sci Policy **124**, 313–323 (2021). https://doi.org/10.1016/j.envsci.2021.07.007
2. Khanna, R., Sharma, C.: Do technological investments promote manufacturing productivity? A firm-level analysis for India. Econ. Model. **105**, 105672 (2021). https://doi.org/10.1016/j.econmod.2021.105672
3. Zhu, Z.-Y., Xie, H.-M., Chen, L.: ICT industry innovation: knowledge structure and research agenda. Technol. Forecast. Soc. Change **189**, 122361 (2023). https://doi.org/10.1016/j.techfore.2023.122361
4. Jayaprakash, P., Radhakrishna Pillai, R.: The role of ICT for sustainable development: a cross-country analysis. Eur. J. Dev. Res. **34**(1), 225–247 (2022). https://doi.org/10.1057/s41287-021-00369-1
5. Ahmad, N., Youjin, L., Žiković, S., Belyaeva, Z.: The effects of technological innovation on sustainable development and environmental degradation: evidence from China. Technol. Soc. **72**, 102184 (2023). https://doi.org/10.1016/j.techsoc.2022.102184

6. Penzenstadler, B., et al.: Software engineering for sustainability: find the leverage points! IEEE Softw. **35**(4), 22–33 (2018). https://doi.org/10.1109/MS.2018.110154908
7. Sarkis, J., Koo, C., Watson, R.T.: Green information systems & technologies—this generation and beyond: Introduction to the special issue. Inf. Syst. Front. **15**(5), 695–704 (2013). https://doi.org/10.1007/s10796-013-9454-5
8. Kotlarsky, J., Oshri, I., Sekulic, N.: Digital sustainability in information systems research: conceptual foundations and future directions. J. Assoc. Inf. Syst. **24**, 936–952 (2023). https://doi.org/10.17705/1jais.00825
9. Lock, I., Seele, P.: Theorizing stakeholders of sustainability in the digital age. Sustain. Sci. **12**(2), 235–245 (2017). https://doi.org/10.1007/s11625-016-0404-2
10. Workshop on 'Consumption in a Sustainable World,'. IISDO, Oslo (1998) [Online]. Available: https://enb.iisd.org/events/workshop-consumption-sustainable-world/summary-report-2-4-june-1998. Accessed 27 Oct 2025
11. Duboc, L., et al.: Do we really know what we are building? Raising awareness of potential sustainability effects of software systems in requirements engineering. In: 2019 IEEE 27th International Requirements Engineering Conference (RE), pp. 6–16 (2019). https://doi.org/10.1109/RE.2019.00013
12. Nguyen, N., Johnson, L.W.: Consumer behaviour and environmental sustainability. J. Consum. Behav. **19**(6), 539–541 (2020). https://doi.org/10.1002/cb.1892
13. Sneddon, C., Howarth, R.B., Norgaard, R.B.: Sustainable development in a post-Brundtland world. Ecol. Econ. **57**(2), 253–268 (2006). https://doi.org/10.1016/j.ecolecon.2005.04.013
14. Jones, P., Wynn, M.: The leading digital technology companies and their approach to sustainable development. Sustainability **13**(12), 6612 (2021). https://doi.org/10.3390/su13126612
15. Vieira, K., Pinto, G., Yutaka, J.: Consumer behavior towards technological innovations: a systematic review. J. Inf. Syst. Technol. Manag. **19** (2022). https://doi.org/10.4301/S1807-1775202219004
16. Davies, F.D., Venkatesh, V.: Measuring user acceptance of emerging information technologies: an assessment of possible method biases. In: Proceedings of the Twenty-Eighth Annual Hawaii International Conference on System Sciences, vol. 4, pp. 729–736 (1995). https://doi.org/10.1109/HICSS.1995.375675
17. Lee, Y., Kozar, K.A., Larsen, K.R.T.: The technology acceptance model: past, present, and future. Commun. Assoc. Inf. Syst. **12** (2003). https://doi.org/10.17705/1CAIS.01250
18. Rogers, E.M., Singhal, A., Quinlan, M.M.: Diffusion of innovations. In: An Integrated Approach to Communication Theory and Research. Routledge (2008)
19. Wei, R.: From luxury to utility: a longitudinal analysis of cell phone laggards. J. Mass Commun. Q. **78**(4), 702–719 (2001). https://doi.org/10.1177/107769900107800406
20. GSMA: The Mobile Economy 2025 (2025)
21. Goggin, G.: Global Mobile Media. Routledge, London (2010). https://doi.org/10.4324/9780203842805
22. Agustina, T., Susanti, E., Rana, J.: Sustainable consumption in Indonesia: health awareness, lifestyle, and trust among Gen Z and Millennials. Environ. Econ. **15**, 82–96 (2024). https://doi.org/10.21511/ee.15(1).2024.07
23. World Bank Group: Mobile cellular subscriptions. Mobile cellular subscription (per 100 people) [Online]. Available: https://data.worldbank.org. Accessed: Oct. 27, 2025
24. CSSUM: Information Technology Factsheet. Center for Sustainable Systems, University of Michigan, Factsheet Pub. No. CSS09-07 (2025) [Online]. Available: https://css.umich.edu/publications/factsheets/built-environment/information-technology-factsheet. Accessed 27 Oct 2025

25. Gartner: Gartner Forecasts Worldwide IT Spending to Grow 9.8% in 2026, Exceeding $6 Trillion For the First Time [Online]. Available: https://www.gartner.com/en/newsroom/press-releases/2025-10-22-gartner-forecasts-worldwide-it-spending-to-grow-9-point-8-percent-in-2026-exceeding-6-trillion-dollars-for-the-first-time. Accessed 27 Oct 2025
26. Bhattacharjee, A., Berger, J., Menon, G.: When identity marketing backfires: consumer agency in identity expression. J. Consum. Res. **41**(2), 294–309 (2014)
27. Ramya, N., Ali, S.M.: Factors affecting consumer buying behavior. Int. J. Appl. Res. **2**(10), 76–80 (2016)
28. Liu, Y., Zhou, M., Li, Q.: How penetration of e-commerce in rural areas drives consumption in China. China Agric. Econ. Rev. **17**(2), 339–357 (2024). https://doi.org/10.1108/CAER-01-2024-0016
29. Wu, Y., Lee, Y.-S.: A study on the impact of the consumption value of sustainable fashion products on purchase intention based on the theory of planned behavior. Sustainability **17**(10), 4278 (2025). https://doi.org/10.3390/su17104278
30. Sarker, A., Ahmmed, R., Ahsan, S.M., Rana, J., Ghosh, M.K., Nandi, R.: A comprehensive review of food waste valorization for the sustainable management of global food waste. Sustain. Food Technol. **2**(1), 48–69 (2024). https://doi.org/10.1039/D3FB00156C
31. Shahabuddin, M., et al.: A review of the recent development, challenges, and opportunities of electronic waste (e-waste). Int. J. Environ. Sci. Technol. **20**(4), 4513–4520 (2023). https://doi.org/10.1007/s13762-022-04274-w
32. Mullen, B., Johnson, C.: The Psychology of Consumer Behavior. Psychology Press, New York (2013). https://doi.org/10.4324/9780203782002
33. Sheth, J.N., Newman, B.I., Gross, B.L.: Why we buy what we buy: a theory of consumption values. J. Bus. Res. **22**(2), 159–170 (1991). https://doi.org/10.1016/0148-2963(91)90050-8
34. Jin, S.-A.A., Phua, J.: Following celebrities' tweets about brands: the impact of Twitter-based electronic word-of-mouth on consumers' source credibility perception, buying intention, and social identification with celebrities. J. Advert. **43**(2), 181–195 (2014). https://doi.org/10.1080/00913367.2013.827606
35. Laran, J.: The influence of information processing goal pursuit on postdecision affect and behavioral intentions. J. Pers. Soc. Psychol. **98**(1), 16–28 (2010). https://doi.org/10.1037/a0017422
36. Ormanovic, S., Ćirić, A., Talović, M., Alić, H., Jelešković, E., Čaušević, D.: Importance-performance analysis: different approaches. Acta Kinesiol. **11**, 58–66 (2017)
37. Bose, A., et al.: Evaluation of urban sustainability through perceived importance, performance, satisfaction and loyalty: an integrated IPA–SEM-based modelling approach. Sustainability **15**(12), 9788 (2023). https://doi.org/10.3390/su15129788
38. Martilla, J.A., James, J.C.: Importance-performance analysis. J. Mark. **41**(1), 77–79 (1977). https://doi.org/10.2307/1250495
39. Acquisti, A., Brandimarte, L., Loewenstein, G.: Privacy and human behavior in the age of information. Science **347**(6221), 509–514 (2015). https://doi.org/10.1126/science.aaa1465
40. Ardente, F., Mathieux, F.: Environmental assessment of the durability of energy-using products: method and application. J. Clean. Prod. **74**, 62–73 (2014). https://doi.org/10.1016/j.jclepro.2014.03.049
41. Delmas, M.A., Burbano, V.C.: The drivers of Greenwashing. Calif. Manage. Rev. **54**(1), 64–87 (2011). https://doi.org/10.1525/cmr.2011.54.1.64
42. Horne, R.E.: Limits to labels: the role of eco-labels in the assessment of product sustainability and routes to sustainable consumption. Int. J. Consum. Stud. **33**(2), 175 (2009). https://doi.org/10.1111/J.1470-6431.2009.00752.X
43. Armitage, C.J., Conner, M.: Efficacy of the theory of planned behaviour: a meta-analytic review. Br. J. Soc. Psychol. **40**(4), 471–499 (2010)

44. Prasad, D.S., Pradhan, R.P., Gaurav, K., Sabat, A.K.: Critical success factors of sustainable supply chain management and organizational performance: an exploratory study. Transp. Res. Procedia **48**, 327–344 (2020). https://doi.org/10.1016/j.trpro.2020.08.027
45. Li, H., Li, Q., Xu, Z., Ye, X.: Digital technologies. J. Digit. Econ. **3**, 240–248 (2024). https://doi.org/10.1016/j.jdec.2025.02.001
46. Melegati, J., Conboy, K., Graziotin, D.: Qualitative surveys in software engineering research: definition, critical review, and guidelines. IEEE Trans. Softw. Eng. **50**(12), 3172–3187 (2024). https://doi.org/10.1109/TSE.2024.3474173
47. Jansen, H.: The logic of qualitative survey research and its position in the field of social research methods. Forum Qual. Sozialforschung Forum Qual. Soc. Res. **11**(2) (2010). https://doi.org/10.17169/fqs-11.2.1450
48. Ju, T.L., Chen, Y.-Y., Sun, S.-Y., Wu, C.-Y.: Rigor in MIS survey research: in search of ideal survey methodological attributes. J. Comput. Inf. Syst. 47(2). Accessed 27 Oct 2025 [Online]
49. Ziniel, S., McDaniel, C., Beck: Bringing scientific rigor to survey design in health care research. Hosp. Pediatr. **9**(10), 743–748 (2019). https://doi.org/10.1542/hpeds.2019-0101
50. Emerson, R.W.: Convenience sampling, random sampling, and snowball sampling: how does sampling affect the validity of research? J. Vis. Impair. Blind. **109**(2), 164–168 (2015). https://doi.org/10.1177/0145482X1510900215
51. Palan, S., Schitter, C.: Prolific.ac—a subject pool for online experiments. J. Behav. Exp. Finance **17**, 22–27 (2018). https://doi.org/10.1016/j.jbef.2017.12.004
52. Torrentira, M.C., Torrentira, M.J.R.: Online data collection as adaptation in conducting quantitative and qualitative research during the COVID-19 pandemic. Eur. J. Educ. Stud. **7**(11) (2020)
53. Weyant, E.: In: Creswell, J.W., David Creswell, J. (eds.) Research Design: Qualitative, Quantitative, and Mixed Methods Approaches, 5th edn, pp. 304. SAGE, Los Angeles, CA (2018). ISBN: 978-1506386706. J. Electron. Resour. Med. Libr. **19**(1–2), 54–55 (2022). https://doi.org/10.1080/15424065.2022.2046231
54. Cahusac de Caux, B., Pretorius, L.: Learning together through collaborative writing: the power of peer feedback and discussion in doctoral writing groups. Stud. Educ. Eval. **83**, 101379 (2024). https://doi.org/10.1016/j.stueduc.2024.101379
55. Braun, V., Clarke, V.: Thematic Analysis: A Practical Guide, pp. 1–100 (2022)
56. Wuetherick, B.: Review: 'Basics of qualitative research: techniques and procedures for developing grounded theory 3e' (Corbin and Strauss). Can. J. Univ. Contin. Educ. **36** (2010). https://doi.org/10.21225/D5G01T
57. Gioia, D.A., Corley, K.G., Hamilton, A.L.: Seeking qualitative rigor in inductive research: notes on the Gioia methodology. Organ. Res. Methods **16**(1), 15–31 (2013). https://doi.org/10.1177/1094428112452151
58. Corbin, J., Strauss, A.: Basics of Qualitative Research: Techniques and Procedures for Developing Grounded Theory. SAGE Publications (2014)
59. Lufungulo, E.S., Jia, J., Mwila, K.: Exploring factors of open educational resources (OER) in Zambian community schools: a qualitative study. Soc. Sci. Humanit. Open **11**, 101465 (2025). https://doi.org/10.1016/j.ssaho.2025.101465
60. Thøgersen, J.: Psychological determinants of paying attention to eco-labels in purchase decisions: model development and multinational validation. J. Consum. Policy **23**(3), 285–313 (2000). https://doi.org/10.1023/A:1007122319675
61. Chen, Y.-S., Chang, C.-H.: Greenwash and green trust: the mediation effects of green consumer confusion and green perceived risk. J. Bus. Ethics **114**(3), 489–500 (2013)
62. Blevis, E.: Sustainable interaction design: invention & disposal, renewal & reuse. In: Proceedings of the SIGCHI Conference on Human Factors in Computing Systems, pp. 503–512. ACM, San Jose, California, USA (2007). https://doi.org/10.1145/1240624.1240705

63. Froehlich, J., Findlater, L., Landay, J.: The design of eco-feedback technology. In: Proceedings of the SIGCHI Conference on Human Factors in Computing Systems, pp. 1999–2008. ACM, Atlanta Georgia, USA (2010). https://doi.org/10.1145/1753326.1753629

Author Index

G. Herzwurm et al. (Eds.): ICSOB 2025, LNBIP 574, pp. 411–412, 2026.
https://doi.org/10.1007/978-3-032-14518-5

MIX
Papier aus verantwortungsvollen Quellen
Paper from responsible sources
FSC® C105338

If you have any concerns about our products,
you can contact us on
ProductSafety@springernature.com

In case Publisher is established outside the EU,
the EU authorized representative is:
Springer Nature Customer Service Center GmbH
Europaplatz 3, 69115 Heidelberg, Germany

Printed by Libri Plureos GmbH
in Hamburg, Germany